The New United Nations

The third edition of this successful text highlights new international trends toward global governance, nation-building, and human development, while also assessing the extraordinary challenges confronting the United Nations at this critical moment in international affairs, not least being the ubiquity of conflict in Africa, the Middle East, and Europe, and the global threats of disease, climate change, and the retreat from multilateralism by the great powers. A comprehensive guide to the world body's institutions, procedures, policies, specialized agencies, historic personalities, initiatives, and involvement in world affairs, *The New United Nations* is organized thematically, blending both topical and chronological explanations, making reference to current scholarly terms and theories.

New to this edition:

- Fully updated chapters and a new Introduction, including discussion of the Paris Climate Change Agreement, the world's response to COVID-19, and the revival of ultranationalism and great-power rivalry.
- New sections on the theory and practice of neoliberalism and populism, the UN's use of the "Responsibility to Protect" in the Middle East, the Arab Spring, and multifaceted roles in the developing world, especially in Africa.
- Updated analysis of twenty-first-century challenges to collective security, including in Syria and, particularly, in Ukraine.
- Unique special section on the student Model United Nations experience.
- Coverage of the UN's efforts to implement the Sustainable Development Goals.
- eResources with supportive materials and documents.

John Allphin Moore, Jr. is a Professor Emeritus of History at California State Polytechnic University at Pomona, USA.

Jerry Pubantz is a Professor of Political Science at the University of North Carolina at Greensboro, USA.

Praise for *The New United Nations*, Third Edition

The authors' writing style is clear and easy to read even for students who are not IR or political science majors. I applaud the authors' recognition of the new role of regional international organizations. The authors' strategy to provide a narrative that grabs students' interest and curiosity in the introduction will engage students to learn more about the dynamism of the UN in the context of twenty-first century peace and security issues, such as terrorism, cyber security, and the seeming intractable poverty, ethnic, gender and development problems in the developing countries.... The book has the potential to serve colleges and universities nation-wide in the United States, and internationally.

Sunday P. Obazuaye, *Cerritos College*

Accurate and meticulously researched. A well-written, up to-date treatment of the United Nations not only as an intergovernmental institution but also as the embodiment of the rule of law among and within states. Written in plain, easy-to-understand language, the authors aptly describe and fairly assess the strengths and weaknesses of the United Nations as well as the ways it has adapted and continues to evolve in order to meet the monumental challenges that it faces today.

Nikolaos Zahariadis, *Rhodes College*

The third edition of *The New United Nations* is a very comprehensive, yet readable, introduction to what the UN is and what it could yet be. The writing is crisp, transporting the reader from global conferences of diplomats into the locales where much of the work of the United Nations is performed. Even though it's intended to be a textbook, it reads in parts like an action thriller. Professors Moore and Pubantz empower readers to understand so they are better prepared to act as informed (global) citizens.

Michael Eaton, *National Model United Nations*

The New United Nations

International Organization in the
Twenty-First Century

Third Edition

**John Allphin Moore, Jr. and
Jerry Pubantz**

Routledge
Taylor & Francis Group

NEW YORK AND LONDON

Cover image: Getty/Tetra Images

Third edition published 2023
by Routledge
605 Third Avenue, New York, NY 10158

and by Routledge
4 Park Square, Milton Park, Abingdon, Oxon, OX14 4RN

Routledge is an imprint of the Taylor & Francis Group, an informa business

First Edition published by Pearson Education, Inc. 2006
Second Edition published by Routledge 2017

Library of Congress Cataloging-in-Publication Data
Names: Moore, John Allphin, 1940– author. | Pubantz, Jerry, 1947– author.
Title: The new United Nations: international organization in the twenty-first century /
John Allphin Moore, Jr., Jerry Pubantz.
Description: Third edition. | New York: Routledge, 2023. | Includes bibliographical
references and index.
Identifiers: LCCN 2022023063 (print) | LCCN 2022023064 (ebook) |
ISBN 9781032250991 (hardback) | ISBN 9781032250960 (paperback) |
ISBN 9781003281535 (ebook)
Subjects: LCSH: United Nations. | International relations.
Classification: LCC JZ5005 .M66 2023 (print) | LCC JZ5005 (ebook) |
DDC 341.23—dc23/eng/20220623
LC record available at https://lccn.loc.gov/2022023063
LC ebook record available at https://lccn.loc.gov/2022023064

ISBN: 978-1-032-25099-1 (hbk)
ISBN: 978-1-032-25096-0 (pbk)
ISBN: 978-1-003-28153-5 (ebk)

DOI: 10.4324/9781003281535

Typeset in Times New Roman
by codeMantra

Visit the Support Material: www.routledge.com/9781032250960/

Dedicated to the thousands of UN System personnel who have fought COVID-19 relentlessly around the world while continuing to address humanitarian crises from Central Africa to South Asia to Central Europe

Brief Contents

Contents

Figures and Photos

Figures

Photos

Preface

Over the last two decades, while international events and issues have arisen and changed, the United Nations has addressed unremitting international pressures with a flexibility in ideas and policies that suggests not only an enduring world body but one that remains capable of reinventing itself. With that evidence in hand, now a decade and a half since we published the first edition of our UN text, we remain confident that the moniker "New United Nations" is valid.

In this third edition, we describe and assess an institution that has had to adapt to real-world, and frequently novel, challenges. The UN's many institutions, at least most of them, have evolved, and if the patter of the twenty-first-century's third decade has meant anything, it has foretold unavoidable future evolution as well. Since the publication of the first edition of this text, the member states have crafted new doctrines, such as the Responsibility to Protect, launched, first, the Millennium Development Goals, then the Sustainable Development Goals, pursued holistic democracy in failing states, sought to empower women both in their own nations and internationally, tried to make the new Human Rights Council truly effective, and queried how the world could address Ebola, terrorism, the Arab Spring, sectarian turbulence, civil war, nuclear proliferation, climate change, COVID-19, and ominous Great Power tensions with an effective United Nations.

While the world's media tends to point, understandably, to the traditional UN—usually the Security Council—and then only when large geopolitical issues are at the forefront, day-to-day UN behavior, maturing over the past three decades, has signaled an expansion of the UN's role in international affairs, and even in the internal affairs of some countries, all this irrespective of the Charter's injunction against interference in sovereign states. We attempt to chronicle both the seen and the unseen United Nations in this volume. In all cases, our hope is to capture the world body as not only the sum of its parts, the instrument of its member states, and a venue for diplomacy, but also as an actor in its own right in the emergent global governance network.

The thesis and ideas found in this text are the outcome of more than a quarter of a century of research collaboration that we commenced just as the United Nations was celebrating its fiftieth birthday. We extend our thanks for the intellectual challenges and helpful guidance over these years provided by colleagues at myriad conferences and professional engagements whose reflections on our theories and propositions have honed our conception of what we think the UN's importance is to current times. Important influences on our work have come from Peter Ashby, Simon Duke, Taina Järvinen, Elvira Osipova, Warren Kimball, Blanche Wiesen Cook, Scott Kaufman, Dave Benjamin, Errol Clauss, Cindy Combs, Kenneth J. Grieb, Douglas Becker, Donna Schlagheck, Thomas Weiler, Karen Vogel, Sunday Obazuaye, Charlene Martin, Mel Boynton, Amanda Podany, Mahmood Ibrahim, Zuoyue Wang, Georgia Mickey, Shelton Williams, Owen Lancer, and Michael Eaton.

We began our joint interest in the subject as young faculty advisers accompanying our students to the National Model UN annual conference in New York, the *Ur* simulation of the United Nations. Given the significance we judge Model UN to be to the international education of undergraduates, we include in Chapter 7 a discussion of the simulation experience and provide guidance to this generation of "Model UNers." During the more than three decades we pursued this activity, we learned from our students and refined our understanding from contact with talented fellow advisers. The *New United Nations* has benefited from their insights and help. We are particularly in debt to the Model UN advisers and other teachers of the UN who supplied trenchant critiques serving as Routledge's external reviewers for this third edition: Sunday P. Obazuaye, Marc Scarcelli, Nikolaos Zahariadis, and Mark McQuinn.

We have been privileged to have been in the very able hands of Routledge's Senior Editor for Politics, Jennifer Knerr, who has been an excellent and most amicable guide for us in completing three recent works. Unhappily for us, she will now move into retirement. Jennifer's adept assistant, Jacqueline Dorsey, has become an indispensable point person for our efforts, and has piloted this book expertly through to publication. We savor our professional engagement with Jennifer and Jacqueline, and we know this book is better for their involvement. We are also indebted to copy editor Sumeet Kumar for the refinement of the text.

URLs for web sites in this text were accessed between fall 2021 and spring 2022.

As always, we tender our deep appreciation to our spouses—Linda and Gloria—who have had their own active careers but are somehow able to tolerate, even appreciate, their conjugal scribblers.

Fortunate as we are with the encouragement and assistance we have received, we remain fully apprised that any errors of omission or commission in the current text rest firmly on our shoulders.

John Allphin Moore, Jr.
Claremont, California
Jerry Pubantz
Clemmons, North Carolina
June 2022

Introduction

The UN System

LE BOURGET, FRANCE

Le Bourget, France, is probably best-known for its namesake hundred-year-old airport. But from November 30 to December 12, 2015, this northeastern suburb of Paris gained a new recognition as the epicenter of global climate politics. Representatives of most of the world's governments and major environmental nongovernmental organizations gathered for final negotiation and signing of the **Paris Agreement** on climate change. Longtime French politician and former prime minister Laurent Fabius—in 2015 the country's foreign minister—presided over the closing session. On the conference's final day, when Fabius asked if there were any objections to the proposed pact, there were none from the 195 participating countries. He declared the 2015 Paris Agreement approved unanimously. The treaty called for "holding the increase in the global average temperature to well below 2°C above pre-industrial levels and pursuing efforts to limit the temperature increase to 1.5°C above pre-industrial levels."[1] It required national governments to "prepare, communicate and maintain successive nationally determined contributions that [they intended] to achieve" (Art. 4.2). The accord addressed myriad climate change issues such as mitigation policy, reporting, monitoring, and international review of national progress, carbon trading, and technology transfer. While critics noted accurately that the agreement established no mandatory enforcement measures, advocates argued that requiring signatories to establish national carbon-reduction targets and report their progress on a regular basis (a pledge and review system) would create a significantly effective "blame and shame" process in the international community.[2]

By any measure, the achievement of the Paris Agreement was a success story of UN diplomacy. For a quarter century, the United Nations had provided the architecture and theoretical framework for addressing climate change and global warming. The conference at Le Bourget was the twenty-first yearly session of the Conference of the Parties (COP-21) to the **United Nations Framework Convention on Climate Change** (UNFCCC) and the 11th session of the Meeting of the Parties (CMP-11) to the 1997 **Kyoto Protocol**. The UNFCCC was the foundational document to the process culminating in Paris. Attendees at the UN's 1992 "Earth Summit" in Rio de Janeiro agreed to some basic approaches, norms, and expectations in the effort to address the human causes of global warming. Each year following, the Parties to the Framework Convention met to find consensus on "protocols" that would meet the Convention's objective to stabilize greenhouse gases (GHGs) "at a level that would prevent dangerous anthropogenic interference with the climate system."

DOI: 10.4324/9781003281535-1

The most important was the Kyoto Protocol. It set specific GHG emission targets for industrialized states to meet by 2012. The goal was to lower overall emissions of carbon dioxide, nitrous oxide, methane, hydrofluorocarbons, perfluorocarbons, and sulfur hexafluoride 5 percent below 1990 levels. While it eventually attained sufficient signatories, Kyoto never had the support of the United States and China, the world's two largest GHG emitters, making the agreement ineffective. The frustration of twenty years of unsuccessful negotiations led many to believe no global agreement could be reached, or, if reached, could not be effective in slowing global warming. The Paris Agreement dissipated some of those concerns. Key to its achievement as a replacement for Kyoto was a 2014 U.S.-China summit where the two countries reached bilateral agreement on setting emission targets. The commitment of U.S. President Barack Obama and China's President Xi Jinping provided the momentum to clear the final hurdles to a successful global treaty. Once the Paris negotiators had voted their approval on December 12, the Paris Agreement was scheduled to become legally binding once ratified by at least fifty-five countries that together represented at least 55 percent of global greenhouse emissions. That was achieved in November 2016.

BRIEF OVERVIEW OF THE UNITED NATIONS

Most people are aware of the United Nations and understand that it plays an important role in world affairs. In their mind's eye, the United Nations is in New York City (and its headquarters surely is), but few would see Le Bourget, France, as one of the UN's "places" or the conference that occurred there as a product of two decades of UN work. The United Nations is too often marginalized in discussions of world affairs beyond conflicts that rise to the top of newspaper headlines and internet webpages. Part of this disregard undoubtedly is due to certain misconceptions about the organization. From a certain perspective, the United Nations is a simply understood body yet at other times a mystery. We will provide much useful detail about the United Nations, including events like those in France in 2015 and its history and functioning in the pages that follow. Here, however, we offer a brief overview of bare facts, laying out the basics for our study.

The United Nations is an *intergovernmental organization* (IGO), in fact the largest intergovernmental organization in history, currently counting within its membership 193 nations and two observer states. Although it can also be classified as an *international* organization, "intergovernmental" lends a clarifying precision to the definition since the members of the UN's principal organs are nation-states. Nation-states make decisions in the UN System, as demonstrated by the Paris Agreement; policies tend to be initiated by decisions of member states.

The *intergovernmental* United Nations is a "confederation," not a unitary or federally organized government like China or the United States, for example. That is, it is made up of sovereign members. Unlike a conventional nation-state, it has no overarching authority over its realm (the world!) as does, for example, China and the United States over their territories. It is, then, essentially what its members make of it. It acts most effectively by means of diplomatic agreement. As former Secretary-General Dag Hammarskjöld (1906–1961) once explained: "The United Nations is not…a superstate, able to act outside the framework of decisions by its member governments. It is an instrument for negotiation…[it] can serve, but not substitute itself for the efforts of its member governments."[3] Thus, it acts effectively only by means of consensus, not by strict majority vote. Moreover, it cannot fulfill utopian notions of world peace and order because, as former Israeli representative Abba Eban said, it is an "international organization…a mechanism, not a policy or principle."[4]

With the preceding information in mind, we should note that the organization of the United Nations, which, at the time of its founding, was something of a mystery to Russia's then-leader Joseph Stalin (1878–1953), rings familiar to citizens of the Western world or individuals conversant with presidential or Westminster-parliamentary systems of government. For example, the United Nations has legislative (the General Assembly), executive (the Secretariat combined with the Security Council), and judicial (the International Court of Justice (ICJ)) institutions. The UN Charter with its 19 chapters and 111 articles serves as a constitutional foundation authorizing and limiting the actions of the organization's bodies and establishing its procedures. It is also worth noting that the Charter's Preamble begins with the words "We the People," envisioning a higher order *compact* among the peoples of the world, not simply a treaty among the governments that signed and ratified it at the end of World War II. Ambassador Eban's view notwithstanding, the Charter does declare basic liberal values as universal and at the core of the organization's purpose.

Fifty nations adopted the UN Charter at a large international conference (much like a constitutional convention) in San Francisco on June 25, 1945. With sufficient member states' ratifications, the UN officially began operations on October 24, 1945.The UN, as a successor to the failed League of Nations, was formed to prevent conflict such as the world had recently undergone in World War II, and to promote peace, human rights, the international rule of law, and prosperity worldwide.

The main headquarters of the UN is in New York City. The world body has six principal organs, five of them located in New York: the General Assembly, where all member

Photo I.1 United Nations headquarters in New York City. On the left is the General Assembly building and to the right is the Secretariat building.

Source: UN Photo. Reproduced by permission of the United Nations.

nations are represented equally; the Security Council, with 15 members, including five permanent members; the **Economic and Social Council** (ECOSOC), with 54 members; the Trusteeship Council, which is no longer operative; and the UN Secretariat, the adminis-trative unit, headed by a Secretary-General. The sixth organ is the International Court of Justice in The Hague, Netherlands. There are other important sites in the world with UN organs, some of which we visit in this introduction.

Beyond its six principal organs, there exists a broader UN *System* that includes many *specialized agencies, related agencies, funds, forums,* and *programmes.* Some of these are well known, such as the World Health Organization (WHO), the World Bank, the International Monetary Fund (IMF), World Food Programme (WFP), International Civil Aviation Organization (ICAO), and UN Children's Fund (UNICEF). The UN Environ-ment Programme (UNEP) and World Meteorological Organization (WMO) were major sponsors of the lengthy negotiation process that brought the Paris Agreement to frui-tion, showing the merits of institutionalized multilateral cooperation in responding to global challenges. They operate in a political environment that includes both state and non-state actors. Importantly, there are "nongovernmental organizations" (NGOs) that have gained *consultative* status with ECOSOC under the UN Charter. There are many of these, and they include organizations such as the International Chamber of Commerce, the International Center for Research on Women, Amnesty International, Doctors With-out Borders, Feed the Children, and many more. They lobby and advocate for UN action, observe at UN agencies and meetings, and sometimes perform consulting roles. Other times, they are non-voting constituents at UN-convened world conferences.

The United Nations is a "universal" organization and is thus different from, for example, NATO (North Atlantic Treaty Organization) or the EU (European Union), which have dis-tinct, not universal, memberships. As an aspect of its current universality, it is important to keep in mind that the United Nations is not alone on a pinnacle above all other institutions that connect the world. Rather, it is a consolidating axis for those organizations that link sovereign states into ever-widening and more closely knit international networks.

The intricate international order purposely crafted following World War II has proved durable and mature. At Vienna in 1993, human rights were proclaimed and accepted by most nations as "universal." By the twenty-first century, the General Agreement on Tariffs and Trade (GATT) had become the World Trade Organization (WTO); the World Bank and the IMF had extended their activities; and regional groupings such as the North American Free Trade Association (NAFTA), the Association of Southeast Asian Nations (ASEAN), the Asian Pacific Economic Cooperation organization (APEC), the African Union (AU), and the EU were working in close coordination with the United Nations. And the United Nations, unlike any comparable multistate organization in history, has remained opera-tive for an unprecedented three-quarters of a century, expanding its membership to vir-tual universality. As this expansion has continued, the organization has found itself at the forefront in some of the most significant international developments, fighting to preserve the planet's environment through collective action being only one of its many initiatives.

The United Nations, it may be said, is more than the sum of its parts. As former U.S. Deputy Assistant Secretary of State for International Organizations Suzanne Nossel has noted, it "remains the closest thing to a system of global governance that the world has ever known."[5] It may be found around the world, in action in the most challenging of places. This feature of worldwide involvement is in part due to the UN's steady evolution while facing unexpected, sometimes abrupt, trials. Much of the remainder of this intro-duction will acquaint you with the expanded role of the UN around the world. And this geographic tour, then, along with the above brief definition, should prepare you for what is to follow.

NEW YORK CITY

In late September, each year representatives of the UN's 193 member states gather in the General Assembly Hall for the opening of the latest annual session of the United Nations. The opening week of the session is marked by **General Debate**, during which time national presidents, foreign ministers, and ambassadors address the world community on what they see as the most pressing challenges faced by the international system. Usually, they call upon the UN to address current global problems and crises through collective security and cooperative efforts.

On September 25, 2018, U.S. President Donald J. Trump stepped to the rostrum with a different message, one that heaped more criticism than praise on the world body. In his most memorable line, he said, "We reject the ideology of globalism, and we embrace the doctrine of patriotism." He argued that "responsible nations must defend against threats to sovereignty not just from global governance, but also from new forms of coercion and

Photo I.2 President Donald J. Trump addresses the 72nd Session of the United Nations General Assembly (Official White House Photo by D. Myles Cullen).

Source: Executive Office of the President of the United States via Wiki Commons.

domination."[6] His case was based on an appeal to the rising phenomenon of cultural nationalism, evident at the time in many countries and movements. He juxtaposed the mental construct that representatives in the Hall were emissaries "of a distinct culture, a rich history, and a people bound together by ties of memory, tradition, and the values that make our homelands like nowhere else on Earth" against what he saw as "old dogmas, discredited ideologies, and so-called experts who have been proven wrong over the years, time and time again."[7] Presumably, the old dogmas included the foundational principles that underlie the United Nations, for he went on to threaten a major cut in the U.S. contribution to the UN peacekeeping budget, to condemn the work of the UN Human Rights Council from which he had already withdrawn the United States, to say that the work of the International Criminal Court (ICC) had no legitimacy, and to assert, "We will never surrender America's sovereignty to an unelected, unaccountable, global bureaucracy."[8]

In the immediate post-Cold War era at the turn of the millennium, optimism existed that the United Nations could unite the world's efforts in the creation of a new world order that lived up to the promise placed in the UN by its founders. One challenge to that expectation was the emergence of a backlash to globalization and global governance in their many forms, part of that backlash being a revival of ultranationalism, tribalism, and sectarian hatreds. President Trump's nationalist, anti-globalist views were not unique. They were held by several proto-authoritarian leaders at the time and by sovereigntist political movements that rejected the perceived imposition of global norms and the institution that authored those norms. By the third decade of the new millennium, the UN faced a challenge from authoritarian and right-wing nationalism that could limit its impact on world affairs.

Despite all the media attention given to Trump's and the other leaders' high-profile speeches each year, in that same marble and steel building, governments use the occasion to lobby for UN action on a number of other issues important to their national interests. They also consult with their colleagues in their respective UN missions scattered across the city. Over the ensuing year, they combine **parliamentary diplomacy**—democratic legislative procedures, committees, and political persuasion, while representatives of sovereign governments pass resolutions, usually by large majorities, in support of their interests—with old-fashioned intergovernmental negotiation. The member delegations seek to commit the United Nations on not only matters of peace and war, but also human rights, economic development, humanitarian assistance, peacekeeping, environmental issues, social well-being, and gender equality.

In order to address these issues—issues that were not central to UN consideration sixty years ago—the United Nations has developed a comprehensive bureaucratic and policy-making structure, much of it out of the view of world attention. Other principal organs created by the Charter operate in the same political environment of UN headquarters as the General Assembly and Security Council, and may have even more impact on a day-to-day basis on the world's population. The ECOSOC, charged with carrying out the Charter's instruction "to promote social progress and better standards of living in larger freedom,"[9] coordinates and recommends funding for the work of dozens of UN commissions, standing committees, programs, special funds, specialized agencies, and regional bodies. In Chapter 4, you will read about the extensive work and responsibilities of the fifty-four nations on ECOSOC. Its agenda each year includes reports from commissions that range in subject matter from the status of women, indigenous peoples, children, and political prisoners to the vast economic and social needs of poverty-stricken parts of the globe.

Looming over the UN Plaza in New York is the 544-foot-tall office building that houses the UN **Secretariat**, headed by the **Secretary-General**. The Secretary-General is the chief administrative officer for the organization, responsible for managing more than 37,000 employees scattered around the globe. Only about 5,000 of the staff work in New York City.[10] These civil servants provide administrative support for all UN activities in New York and around the world. Divided into departments for every aspect of international policy making at the UN, the secretariat's personnel are often the human face of the United Nations to those who are the recipients of its activities. They are the professional bureaucrats who are charged with carrying out the decisions made by the member nations. But they also help crystallize the agenda, the hopes, and the initiatives of the world organization.

From the New York Headquarters building, the **Department of Peace Operations** oversees more than 125,000 peacekeepers around the world, operating in as many as sixteen separate dangerous missions.[11] On a much smaller scale, also among the headquarters staff are units such as the **Office of the High Representative for Least Developed, Landlocked, and Small Island Nations** (OHRLLS) working to mobilize the international community's resources to assist particularly vulnerable, smaller countries, as they confront rising oceans due to global warming, severe economic development issues, and humanitarian crises. What these two very different types of operations demonstrate is that the work of the United Nations has expanded to areas of concern well beyond those contemplated in the 1940s. With this expansion, so too has the organization grown, in terms of both its institutional structure and what is demanded of it. Today, the institution is expected to respond as well to ethnic and religious violence, HIV/AIDS, pandemics, childhood diseases, disintegrating nations, demands for democracy, human rights violations, climate change, and sundry other "people problems." You will find in Chapters 7 and 8 discussions of UN policy making on these issues.

As an evolving institution, the United Nations is an expanding organization with offices beyond the UN Plaza in New York, reaching into many cities of the world—the most important being Geneva, Switzerland; Nairobi, Kenya; Vienna, Austria; Rome, Italy; The Hague, Netherlands; Paris, France; and Washington, DC, in the United States. In addition, significant UN operations can be found in Addis Ababa, Ethiopia; Bangkok, Thailand; Tokyo, Japan; Santiago, Chile; Beirut, Lebanon; and all of the major cities in countries where a peacekeeping presence exists. During any given week, the United Nations is active on every continent, with much of its work having an impact on both international and domestic affairs around the globe.

For many UN agencies and bodies other than the organization's principal organs, New York provides the hub for their activities as well. Even as the world gathers in the Assembly Hall or urgently convenes in the Security Council, critical work is being done by these agencies. In New York, for example, if you walk a couple of blocks west on 42nd Street from the UN headquarters on First Avenue, you will pass near the offices of the **UN Population Fund** (UNFPA). A subsidiary organ of the General Assembly, UNFPA receives voluntary contributions from UN member states amounting to more than $900 million annually. Since its founding in 1969, the agency has worked to make available family planning education, restored health care systems in war-torn countries, safe motherhood practices, gender equality, and the resources necessary for women to make their own fertility choices. The Population Fund shares an executive board with the **United Nations Development Programme** (UNDP), also located in New York. UNDP is the largest and most comprehensive economic assistance organization in the world. With more than 130 offices in all geographic areas, UNDP has struck partnerships with other development agencies, environmental organizations, the World Bank, governments, and **nongovernmental organizations**. It serves as the coordinator for nearly all UN initiatives in the developing world. The **United Nations Children's Fund** (UNICEF) also has its headquarters in New York, and has worked from there since its creation in 1946. So too the chief executives of the key agencies in the UN System fly regularly to New York to orchestrate plans for coordinated UN activities worldwide. Still, most UN initiatives take place beyond the borders of New York and the United States, and define a large portion of all ongoing global diplomatic affairs.

GENEVA, SWITZERLAND

Sitting in front of a blue backdrop with the emblem of the World Health Organization (WHO) reprinted on it several times, Dr. Tedros Adhanom Gebreyesus, WHO's Director-General, met the world's press on March 11, 2020, via all the virtual means available to the organization—Zoom, Twitter, Facebook, and its own YouTube channel. He was there to give an update on the spread of COVID-19 as he had done many times over the previous two months. This time, however, he declared it a global pandemic, having at that point registered 118,000 known cases in 114 countries and taken 4,291 lives.[12] It was the first time the organization had declared a pandemic caused by a coronavirus. Reported to WHO in December 2019, by the People's Republic of China as an unusual number of atypical pneumonia cases in the city of Wuhan, public health officials worldwide only learned of COVID's capability to spread human-to-human at the turn of the new year. WHO, which had managed the international response to recent health emergencies—Avian flu, Ebola, SARS, the Middle East Respiratory Syndrome (MERS)—issued its first guidance on the mysterious new infection on January 10, 2020. In the two weeks leading up to Tedros's March briefing, cases outside China increased 13-fold.

By spring 2020, WHO and its leader faced intense criticism from many quarters for not acting sooner and more aggressively, with greater transparency to gather information from the Chinese government on the origins of the disease and to aid countries in the poorer parts of the world deal with the pandemic. But Dr. Tedros noted the "alarming levels of inaction" by national governments to work collectively to meet the challenge. In particular, he was worried about the provision of lifesaving treatments for poorer countries incapable of meeting the overwhelming medical demand imposed by the disease. Instead, a number of major developed states turned to national strategies and moved rapidly to create vaccines for their own populations. Russia, the United States, Great Britain, and China all produced effective vaccines by the beginning of 2021. In some cases, their governments contributed to COVAX, the vaccine distribution system developed by WHO, the UN Children's Fund, and a few other international organizations. But more often, these states practiced "vaccine diplomacy," using the valuable product to expand influence in key areas of the world. The response to COVID-19 proved far more nationalist than global, pointing to an emergent challenge in the twenty-first century to collective IGO solutions.

At the founding UN San Francisco Conference, there were proposals to create a world health body. The WHO was established at a 1947 conference of 61 nations, bringing together the work of the International Office of Public Hygiene founded in 1907 and the earlier League of Nations health organization. Dr. Tedros, a former Ethiopian health minister and foreign minister, was elected by the 70th World Health Assembly to a five-year term as the Director-General in 2017.

WHO's headquarters is on the Avenue Appia 20 in Geneva, Switzerland, across the street from **UNAIDS**, the UN's program to combat HIV/AIDS, down the street from the **International Organization for Migration** (IOM), and a block away from the U.S. Mission to the UN's Geneva headquarters. WHO offices form a small part of the large international community that operates in Geneva, including other UN specialized agencies and non-UN intergovernmental organizations that have taken up residence in the city. Technical UN sessions are almost always in progress—each with long-term consequences for millions of people around the globe.

The work of the UN in Geneva is coordinated by the **United Nations Office at Geneva** (UNOG) located in the Palais des Nations. It oversees more than three hundred international conferences and 6,500 half-day meetings annually. More conferences are convened each year in Geneva than in New York. The city is often the first choice of parties seeking a venue for conflict-resolution negotiations, given its long pre-UN history as the seat of diplomatic activity and its presence in hospitable, neutral Switzerland.

Many of these groups hold their meetings in the Palais Wilson, a former grand hotel for the wealthy and famous on the shore of Lake Geneva dating from 1875. It was occupied in 1920 by the secretariat of the League of Nations, the ill-fated predecessor to the United Nations. Today, it holds the offices of the **UN High Commissioner for Human Rights** (UNHCHR). The presence of the UNHCHR, one of the UN's newest creations, in the halls and offices of this magnificent *grande dame* on the Rue des Pâquis, has brought new attention to the role of the Geneva headquarters.

The Palais des Nations on the Avenue de la Paix is an extraordinarily spacious facility first opened in 1936 to house the League permanently. When the League was dissolved in 1946, the United Nations took over the Palais with its large Assembly Hall, added new wings to the building, and used it for conference and negotiation purposes.

More than 170 governments maintain permanent missions in Geneva accredited to UNOG, as do several intergovernmental organizations, including the EU, the African Union, and the Arab League. At least 3,900 NGO representatives are accredited to the Geneva headquarters. Approximately nine thousand employees work for components of the UN System in Geneva, more than 4,300 of them for UNOG directly.[13] Large staffs also serve the United Nations Conference on Trade and Development (UNCTAD— discussed in Chapter 8) and the Economic Commission for Europe. The oldest and most famous specialized agency in Geneva is the **International Labour Organization** (ILO), founded at the time of the League's initiation. Attracted by the presence of the United Nations in Geneva, more than thirty thousand diplomats, international civil servants, and

Photo I.3 Palais des Nations, UN Headquarters in Geneva, Switzerland.
Source: UN/DPI Photo/P. Klee. Reproduced by permission of the United Nations.

NGO representatives work in the city, making it the "most active center for multilateral diplomacy in the world."[14]

The Palais des Nations biennially hosts the Economic and Social Council, and every year it serves as the venue for meetings of the Human Rights Council, both for its regular meetings and for special sessions. On rare occasions, the UN General Assembly has met here in special session. The United Nations staff also provides administrative services for the autonomous **Conference on Disarmament**, the world's principal multilateral negotiating forum for disarmament issues. Additionally, the ILO and the WHO convene their annual plenary assemblies in the facility.

The active use of Geneva for disparate negotiations symbolizes the emerging "new" United Nations, an institution increasingly decentralized, but centered on basic human needs, in addition to the diplomacy of nation-states. This activity gives new life to this old seat of international organization.

NAIROBI, KENYA

If Geneva, Switzerland, is a reflection of the old European roots of international organization, then the UN headquarters in Nairobi, Kenya, represents the new directions in which global governance is taking us. Due in part to the growing universality of the world body produced by the national liberation movement of the mid-twentieth century that added new states to the globe's map, the UN General Assembly and Secretariat over the past fifty years have given increased attention to states of the South.[15] These countries have serious development challenges, grievances with the old colonial powers, and different value priorities than those states that originally created the UN.

The UN Gigiri Compound, with nature trails in over twenty-seven acres that let the visitor wander past indigenous African trees, spot Egyptian geese, green pigeons, marsh mongooses, and olive baboons, and view a seasonal swamp, seems even farther than its 7,360 miles as the crow flies from the UN Headquarters in New York City. As one of the four UN "headquarters" worldwide, Nairobi feels like a place that none of the world body's founders could have contemplated as a center of the organization's activities. Yet, the Nairobi office services many of the four dozen or more UN Funds, programs, and agencies operating in Kenya. The city is recognized as the capital of the UN global environmental effort, and it provides facilities for the work of many international organizations—private and public—that are addressing the overwhelming human challenges confronting the people of Africa.

The **UN Office in Nairobi** (UNON) was officially created in 1996, but UN operations here date from the 1970s' efforts to solve emerging issues then presented by environmental degradation and Third World development. In 1972, the United Nations convened the world conference on the human environment in Stockholm, Sweden. The attending governments recommended establishing an agency to address the problems associated with environmental conservation. Developing nations attending the Stockholm meeting, however, worried that efforts to create environmentally friendly global policy would limit what national governments could do to stimulate industrial growth and development. The General Assembly's placement of the **United Nations Environment Programme** (UNEP) headquarters in Kenya sent a signal that the organization's mandate was not antithetical to the developing world's interests.

An executive director administers UNEP and oversees its work in many nations. The 1997 Nairobi Declaration, which launched an era of activism for UNEP, set a global agenda that included developing international environmental law aimed at sustainable development, monitoring state compliance with environmental agreements and principles, and serving as a link between the scientific community and policy makers. UNEP played a critical leadership role in bringing about the Paris Agreement described at the beginning of this Introduction.

UNEP officials focus much of their work on organizing the international bargaining process and promoting new ideas for international environmental cooperation. It has become an important negotiator in the world's efforts to move toward pollution control, protection of the ozone layer, regulation of transboundary shipments of hazardous wastes, and the protection of biodiversity.

UNEP provides the secretariat for several international environmental conventions, including the Convention on Biological Diversity, the Convention on International Trade in Endangered Species of Wild Fauna and Flora, and the Convention on the Conservation of Migratory Species of Wild Animals. It also provides secretariats for conventions on climate change, desertification, and regional seas. Its success can be credited in significant part to the development of scientific and technical expertise that it employs in a number of successful monitoring and information-sharing programs. UNEP also has carved out areas of special expertise, including early efforts to protect the world's oceans through a number of regional seas agreements. Nine were signed in the 1970s, beginning with an agreement among countries bordering the Mediterranean. This was followed in the 1980s with six more agreements, together covering many of the regional seas of the world.

In addition to UNEP, **UN-HABITAT** (UN Human Settlements Programme) has its headquarters in Nairobi. It is the UN agency dedicated to the promotion of socially and environmentally sustainable cities and towns, with the goal of providing adequate shelter for everyone. UN-HABITAT is the central agency for implementing the Habitat Agenda, derived from a Declaration and Global Plan of Action adopted at the UN Conference on Human Settlements held in Istanbul, Turkey, in June 1996, and by the Sustainable Development Goals established by the United Nations in 2015. Its work is directed by a Governing Council that meets every two years in Nairobi.

Under its 2020–2023 strategic plan, UN-HABITAT sees itself as a "thought leader" in developing both ideas and projects that advance "sustainable urbanization" and closes the inequality gap between urban and rural communities.[16] Its work is all the more important considering the UN prediction that by 2025 over 60 percent of the world's people will live in urban areas, posing enormous strains for prospective social services, housing, and health facilities. As the diplomatic activity surrounding UNEP and UN-HABITAT demonstrate, Nairobi reflects the broadened mandate of the United Nations.

VIENNA, AUSTRIA

The Viennese refer to it as "UNO-City." Its official name is the Vienna International Centre, located on the Danube River not far from downtown. It serves as the newest of the UN's four headquarters and is home to several UN bodies and treaty organizations, the most important being the International Atomic Energy Agency (IAEA). In recent years, it has been at the center of the debate over Iran's nuclear program, citing Tehran several times for not living up to its obligations under the Nuclear Nonproliferation Treaty (NPT). It was the findings and reports of the IAEA that led to sanctions against Iran and then negotiations between Iran and the P5+1 (five permanent members of the UN Security Council—the United States, Great Britain, Russia, China, France—and Germany). After months of negotiation elsewhere, the parties finally reached a deal in Vienna in July 2015. The Joint Comprehensive Plan of Action (JCPOA) prohibited Iran's nuclear development for at least ten years, barred it from obtaining conventional weapons for five years and ballistic missiles for eight, imposed international monitoring of the flow in and out of the country of materials needed for nuclear production, and provided for "snap-back" sanctions should Iran not live up to terms of the agreement. Iran agreed to subject itself to the Additional Protocol of the IAEA that allows the agency to inspect military facilities. In return, once the IAEA certified that Iran was living up to the terms of the agreement, international sanctions against the country would be lifted.

To much fanfare—and regret from critics of the nuclear agreement—the U.S. secretary of state and the Iranian foreign minister were on hand in Vienna on January 16, 2016, as the IAEA reported that Iran had met its obligations under the agreement and, thus, UN-imposed sanctions could be lifted. The United States later, under the Trump administration, withdrew from the JCPOA. Nonetheless, the events in Vienna reinforced the importance of the **International Atomic Energy Agency** to slowing the proliferation of nuclear weapons. Under the signed comprehensive plan, the IAEA was assigned the key role in monitoring the implementation of its terms.

The IAEA's founding statute commits the agency "to accelerate and enlarge the contribution of atomic energy to peace, health and prosperity throughout the world." To that end, the agency, an independent intergovernmental organization under UN aegis, maintains a safeguard program first developed to implement the verification provisions of the 1968 Non-Proliferation Treaty. More than 1,300 nuclear facilities are under IAEA safeguards. IAEA members have employed the system to enforce the compliance terms of international treaties, including nuclear-weapons-free zone agreements in Africa, Latin America, and the South Pacific. Following the 1991 Gulf War, IAEA safeguard inspectors

Photo I.4 Security Council unanimously adopts resolution 2231, July 20, 2015, following the historic agreement in Vienna between the P5+1 and Iran on a Joint Comprehensive Plan of Action (JCPOA) regarding Iran's nuclear program.

Source: UN Photo. Reproduced by permission of the United Nations.

enforced nuclear provisions of the armistice agreement imposed on Iraq. Forced out of Iraq in 1998, the inspectors returned in 2002 at the direction of the Security Council to verify whether Saddam Hussein's regime still had a nuclear program. The international concern about weapons of mass destruction, their possible use by terrorist groups or aggressive states, and the proliferation of nuclear materials and technology since the end of the Cold War, has elevated the agency's visibility. The regular budget has risen to more than $690 million annually.

In addition to IAEA, the Vienna International Centre is headquarters for the UN's Industrial Development Organization (UNIDO), the preparatory commission for the Comprehensive Nuclear Test Ban Treaty Organization (CTBTO), the United Nations Commission for International Trade Law (UNCITRAL), and the United Nations Office on Drugs and Crime (UNODC). The last of these encourages international efforts to stop the production and trafficking of narcotic drugs. Much of its effort is undertaken in cooperation with nongovernmental organizations. UNIDO assists with the development of industry in developing countries and states with economies in transition. It is also one of four implementing agencies of the **Montreal Protocol**, which phases out the use of ozone-depleting substances in industrial production. UNCITRAL's mission is to harmonize national trade laws, to draft model laws and conventions on international trade law, and to encourage conformity among states to common standards, leading to one worldwide commercial law. With accelerated globalization, the commission reflects an effort by the United Nations to play a more active role in reducing or removing obstacles to the free flow of international trade.

THE HAGUE, NETHERLANDS

In contrast to the political swirl that surrounds the UN activities in Vienna, Nairobi, Geneva, and New York—where delegates and NGO representatives seek support for resolutions, reports, and individual agenda items—there is a sedate decorum to the serious UN work conducted in The Hague. Here, the only principal organ of the United Nations located outside of New York City, the **International Court of Justice** (ICJ), can be found. Its fifteen judges continue a long tradition of applying international law to cases brought by sovereign states. It is the successor to the Permanent Court of International Justice (PCIJ), the judicial arm of the League of Nations. Chapter 4 will introduce you to the work of the Court and its importance. The seat of the Court, like that of the PCIJ, is at the Peace Palace, a gift of American entrepreneur Andrew Carnegie.

As is tradition, each of the permanent members of the Security Council has an individual on the Court, although they serve as independent jurists. They are joined by ten other judges elected by the UN General Assembly and Security Council to nine-year terms. No two sitting judges may come from the same country. There is a concerted effort to represent all of the regional blocs in the United Nations. In 2021, there were three African, two Latin American, three Asian, four Western European, one middle Eastern, and one Eastern European judge, and one vacancy due to the death of Judge James Richard Crawford from Australia. The Court's docket is made up of disputes between states and requests for advisory opinions by either states or international organizations. Since the turn of the century, the Court has heard nearly seventy cases and issued four advisory opinions.

The Hague's long tradition of hosting international legal conferences and adjudicatory bodies makes it the logical venue for other UN-related tribunals. In 1993, the UN Security Council authorized the establishment of the International Criminal Tribunal for the Former Yugoslavia (ICTY) to prosecute alleged war criminals in the aftermath of the

Balkan civil wars of the 1990s. These bloody conflicts, encompassing Serbia-Montenegro, Croatia, Kosovo, Bosnia, and Slovenia, produced some of the worst human atrocities Europe had witnessed since World War II. The world community responded to the tragic events in the former Yugoslavia with peacekeeping operations in the area, but also with trials at the ICTY of war criminals charged with genocide and crimes against humanity.

Among the most sensational of its trials was that of Slobodan Milosevic, Yugoslavia's former head of state. Charged with crimes against humanity, war crimes, and genocide, Milosevic challenged the authority of the international community to try him, the former leader of a sovereign state. Two hundred ninety-five witnesses testified and five thousand exhibits were presented. The trial went on with no resolution imminent. Milosevic died of a heart attack before the trial could be concluded.

The ICTY was the first war crimes court instituted by the UN and the first international war crimes tribunal since the Nuremberg and Tokyo tribunals. The Security Council established it in accordance with Chapter VII of the UN Charter. During its lifespan (1993–2017), the tribunal indicted more than one hundred seventy individuals and convicted nearly one hundred. Its proceedings validated the UN's commitment to normative principles of international law, reviving an interest in judicial instruments that can be used to deal with those who violate the laws of humanity.

The Hague is also the site of the International Criminal Court (ICC). While not part of the UN System, the ICC has an agreement with the world organization that allows the Security Council to refer cases to its jurisdiction. Unlike the ICJ, which only hears cases between states, the ICC tries individuals charged with genocide, war crimes, crimes against humanity and the crime of aggression.

MONTREAL, CANADA

The United Nations responds to countless other human challenges through a broad range of specialized agencies, programs, funds, and research and training institutes, in addition to using the formal organs created by its Charter. Each **specialized agency** is an intergovernmental organization with a contractual relationship to the United Nations. Some of these bodies were established well before the founding of the United Nations, others came about at the behest of the world organization. Chapters 3 and 4 provide extensive information on these agencies. An additional dozen "programmes" report to both the General Assembly and ECOSOC. Finally, five research and training organizations are part of the UN System.

In Montreal, the **International Civil Aviation Organization** (ICAO) serves as the primary agency for cataloguing standardized rules and practices in the aviation industry worldwide. Created by the Chicago Convention of December 1944, the ICAO became a UN specialized agency in 1947. It is a good example of an IGO within the UN System that addresses an important functional task, in this case necessary for safe and effective travel and communication. Through negotiation among its nearly universal membership, the agency adopts standards that are then put into practice by its member states. Areas of standardization include the operation of aircraft, personnel licensing, air traffic services, navigation rules, aeronautical communications, search and rescue, accident investigation, airworthiness, and the transport of dangerous goods. ICAO is also involved in the development of satellite-based navigation systems, regional planning, the facilitation of passenger movement through national terminals of entry and egress, and the development of international air law.

One of the services provided by ICAO is the facilitation of negotiations among specific states over contentious aviation issues. For example, on the eve of the 58th General

Assembly session, ICAO announced that it had brought about a "historic" agreement between Greece and Turkey.[17] In the short term, the agreement facilitated air traffic services in the route network over the Aegean Sea during the 2004 Olympic Games in Greece. More importantly, it marked another step in improving relations between two states that regularly have had tense relations over territorial claims in the area. Another example came in October 2021, when ICAO convened a High-level forum to develop a consensus, supported by the commitments of member states, to enable the safe and efficient recovery of the aviation industry from the effects of the COVID-19 crisis.

ROME, ITALY

If Montreal is the world's capital for international aviation policy, then Rome is the food policy capital. Two UN specialized agencies—the **Food and Agriculture Organization** (FAO) and the UN's **World Food Programme** (WFP)—have their headquarters here and work closely together to feed the starving and malnourished around the globe. Their work became exceedingly critical to the developing world during the COVID-19 pandemic. The founding date of FAO—October 16, 1945—is now observed as World Food Day. FAO has operated from Rome since 1951. The WFP was added in 1961, reporting to both FAO and ECOSOC. Also in the city is the International Fund for Agricultural Development (IFAD). It commenced operations as an international financing institution in 1977. In 1996, FAO hosted the World Food Summit in Rome, where 186 nations approved a set of commitments intended to achieve universal food security and halve hunger by 2015. Following the Summit, there was a concerted effort to coordinate the work of the three agencies. This effort received reinforcement from the UN's Millennium Development Goals (MDGs) announced in 2000, which committed the entire UN System to meeting the Food Summit's target on hunger, and from the MDGs' replacement with the Sustainable Development Goals of 2015.

More than 11,000 staff work for FAO, a third of them in Rome with the rest assigned to field operations in more than 130 countries. The organization provides help to developing nations through assistance programs; it collects, analyzes, and disseminates information about nutrition, food production, agricultural issues, and forestry and fisheries matters; and it acts as a clearinghouse for farmers, scientists, and governments on food and agriculture issues. It encourages nations to seek its advice on strategies for rural development, food security, and poverty reduction, particularly in rural areas.

The WFP—the 2020 Nobel Peace Prize Laureate—is the largest international food aid provider in the world, feeding more than 115 million people in 84 countries. With an annual budget in excess of $5 billion, supporting a staff of more than fourteen thousand, WFP distributes more than 3.4 million tons of food annually. The organization is funded and receives food supplies from donor nations on a voluntary basis. In 2021, more than one hundred nations supported WFP's projects. The United States was the largest donor ($3.6 billion), Germany was second in donations ($1.1 billion), followed by the United Kingdom ($562 million).

The WFP uses its food to meet emergency needs, support economic and social development, provide logistical support for the delivery of food, and to achieve the Sustainable Development Goal of ending hunger in the world by 2030. Its services include food distribution to people in emergency circumstances—natural or human-made—to poor people in developing countries, to communities where the food assistance will help with economic development projects, and to refugees in civil conflicts.

The changing nature of world politics has seriously affected UN food efforts. In 1990, two-thirds of all UN food aid went for development projects, attempting to make individuals self-reliant. By the end of the decade, 80 percent of food distributed went for the humanitarian relief of people in crisis, and that trend has only accelerated over succeeding decades. For example, the WFP fed several hundred thousand refugees who were displaced by civil war in Syria, and at the same time fed eighty million people in seventy-four other countries. It directed much of the relief aid to vulnerable populations, such as women and children, and provided food to ex-combatant soldiers. In order to get food efficiently to those who need it, WFP maintains working agreements with several international nongovernmental organizations, including Catholic Relief Services, Save the Children, CARE, World Vision International, and Food for the Hungry.

The International Fund for Agricultural Development (IFAD) works with the World Bank, regional development banks, and UN agencies to co-finance projects in poor countries. These countries use the funds for rural agricultural projects and repay the loans, usually over forty years. From the time it began work in 1977 through 2015, IFAD financed over 970 projects in 122 countries and territories. The cost of these projects was about $24 billion in grants and loans.

KABUL, AFGHANISTAN; NORTH KIVU PROVINCE, DEMOCRATIC REPUBLIC OF THE CONGO; TIGRAY, ETHIOPIA

We close this tour of the many places where the UN works by briefly introducing you to three peacekeeping/nation-building and/or political operations where the UN is trying to repair broken states and protect vulnerable populations; it is doing so at a great cost to peacekeepers' lives.

Let's look first at Kabul, Afghanistan. Following the horrific terrorist attacks in the United States on September 11, 2001, America and its allies, with UN endorsement, intervened in Afghanistan, driving the al-Qaeda leadership that had orchestrated the attacks underground and its allied Taliban government from power. After the overthrow of Taliban rule, the UN and other major actors convened the Bonn Conference, which effectively mandated nation-building in the country to establish a stable and democratic Afghan government with constitutional safeguards. In addition to security forces commanded by the United States and by NATO, the Security Council established the United Nations Assistance Mission in Afghanistan (UNAMA) with its headquarters in Kabul. Allied military forces remained in Afghanistan for twenty years, only to be removed quickly in September 2021 as the result of an agreement struck earlier between the United States and the Taliban insurgency.

The two-decade multilateral effort to build a stable, democratic Afghanistan ended in failure. The departure of security forces led to the collapse of the government and return of a Taliban regime, raising global concerns for human rights, the role of women in Afghan society, and humanitarian assistance in Afghanistan. The United Nations soon made clear that it would stay in the country. The Security Council extended UNAMA's mandate until March 2022.[18] The Council's resolution took cognizance of "recent political, security, and social developments," and called for an "inclusive and representative government," noting the "importance of the full, equal and meaningful participation of women." It asserted "the critical importance of a continued presence of UNAMA and other (UN) Agencies, Funds, and programmes."[19] There was a general sense that the chaotic collapse of the previous government and the weak economy would require international assistance to the Afghan people for the foreseeable future.

From its inception in 2002, one of the major tasks of UNAMA was to coordinate the efforts of nearly one thousand international nongovernmental organizations operating in the country. The massive Afghan need for assistance left much of the construction of social service infrastructure (schools, clinics, housing) and basic services (food, shelter, medicine) to the international community.

From Kabul, UNAMA-coordinated UN operations that include the involvement of many of the organizations we have already highlighted in this introduction, such as UNDP, UN-HABITAT, UNEP, UNIDO, WFP, and FAO. Remember, these agencies have their own agendas and operate from disparate headquarters around the world. Through these components of the UN System, UNAMA attempted to provide humanitarian relief, reconstruction, disarmament, conflict resolution, social services, food aid, and fair elections. The return of the Taliban to power disrupted all of these efforts and imposed uncertainty on whether the UN Mission could continue much longer. The 2021 Security Council resolution requested that the Secretary-General prepare a report on the future viability of the UN presence in Afghanistan.

While events in Afghanistan often dominated the news headlines, over the last two decades persistent conflict was consistently centered in central and eastern Africa, where the continent experienced the collapse of national governments' authority and the rise of rebel and terrorist movements, with the concomitant effects of mass migration, violations of human rights, civilian deaths, and devastated economies. A good example is the Democratic Republic of Congo.

UN involvement in Congolese turmoil dates from the country's independence in 1960 and the ensuing civil war. But the contemporary conflict in the Democratic Republic of the Congo (DRC) was triggered by the 1994 Rwandan genocide, when refugees and their political movements poured over the DRC's eastern border. Their presence destabilized the political rule of longtime dictator Mobuto Sese Seko and led to his downfall amid what came to be called Africa's "First World War." Rwanda, Uganda, Burundi, Eritrea, and Angola all sent military forces into the country in the late 1990s. The DRC also faced new ethnic conflict as the country seemed to fall apart. The UN Security Council responded with the creation of a peacekeeping mission known as MONUC. The peacekeepers found themselves on the defensive, particularly in the northeast part of the country. The city of Bunia in the Ituri District and towns in North Kivu had become centers of rebel activity. As many as fifty thousand civilians may have lost their lives during the fighting. It was also the site of ethnic massacres. In Bunia, foreigners and UN forces were regularly attacked. MONUC used both infantry and helicopter gunships to strike enemy positions.

In 2010, the Security Council replaced MONUC with the United Nations Organization Stabilization Mission in the Democratic Republic of the Congo (MONUSCO). In a departure from past peacekeeping operations, the Council decided in 2013 to establish an "intervention brigade"[20] as part of MONUSCO, consisting of three infantry battalions, one artillery and one special force and reconnaissance company to operate under direct command of the UN force commander, with the responsibility of neutralizing armed groups and contributing to civilian security in the eastern section of the country. While the council specifically said the intervention brigade should not be seen as a precedent, the creation of a war-fighting unit allied with the central government converted MONUSCO into a peace enforcement or "intrusive" peacekeeping operation. By taking sides, the peacekeepers became targets for the major rebel groups. In North Kivu, where an estimated 100,000 people had been displaced, UN and government forces were ambushed on December 7, 2017, and 14 peacekeepers were killed. By the beginning of the 2020s, MONUSCO had incurred more than 200 fatalities and was costing the United Nations more than $1 billion annually with no promise of future peace and stability in the DRC.

At the same time that the UN was in a long-term commitment in the Congo, it faced a new humanitarian and human rights crisis in Tigray Province, Ethiopia. Civil war against the central government broke out in November 2020, when Ethiopia's president, Abiy Ahmed, attempted to consolidate political parties under his control, directly challenging Ethiopia's ethnic federalism. In succeeding months, atrocities were charged against both sides, but Tigrayan refugees laid the blame on the central government that was pursuing, in their view, ethnic cleansing of the region.

The Ethiopian government cut off Tigray from the rest of the world, severing telecommunications, including cellphones, and stopped electricity transmission to the province. The government blocked UN humanitarian assistance and any aid to Tigray from outside its borders. By August 2021, more than two million people had been displaced, famine put at risk at least 400,000 people, and UN Secretary-General António Guterres reported refugee camps and hospitals had been destroyed.[21] During the first ten months of the conflict the Security Council met eight times on the crisis but could find no consensus on a strategy to restore peace or to aid those traumatized by the war. The UN and specialized agencies, however, continued pressing Ahmed's government for access to the region.

The "success" or "failure" of the United Nations in the new century turns not only on how debates turn out in New York on the potential for nation-building, but also on the "facts on the ground" in Ethiopia, Afghanistan, the Democratic Republic of the Congo, and other conflict zones where more than ninety thousand UN peacekeepers and civilian employees are challenging old principles of state sovereignty and trying to create or maintain viable and peaceful communities. We will discuss thoroughly UN peacekeeping efforts in Chapter 6. In these out-of-the-way "places" of the United Nations, it is not at all clear that the organization has the ability to turn events decisively toward peace and stability.

THE NEW UNITED NATIONS

The United Nations is an intergovernmental organization that is more far-reaching than a review of its Charter would suggest, and more comprehensive than its founders contemplated. It has persisted for over three-quarters of a century in an ever-changing environment through a process of evolution. This has contributed to its longevity. The political will did not exist to make its predecessor, the League of Nations, responsive to the difficult circumstances it faced after World War I and we witnessed its demise in the accumulating war clouds of the 1930s. A formalistic "reading" of the UN Charter equally would not authorize many of the UN activities—peacekeeping, protecting civilians from their own governments, human rights interventions—that we expect of the world organization today. The history of the UN's formation and Charter development, and its unique evolution, regularly recreating itself as a "new" United Nations, will be outlined in the next three chapters.

Today, as Figure I.1 on the next page demonstrates, the United Nations is a collective of specialized agencies, institutional structures, forums, programs, and funds scattered around the world that increasingly addresses global and domestic issues that formerly were not considered central to the maintenance of international peace and security.

Former Secretary-General Kofi Annan described a "new" United Nations in his Millennium Summit Report in September 2000, titled *We The Peoples*. At this extraordinary gathering of world leaders, nongovernmental organizations, and private individuals in New York City, the Secretary-General noted the diplomatic origins and purposes of the United Nations that made it a "forum for sharing information, conducting negotiations, elaborating norms and voicing expectations, coordinating the behavior of states and other

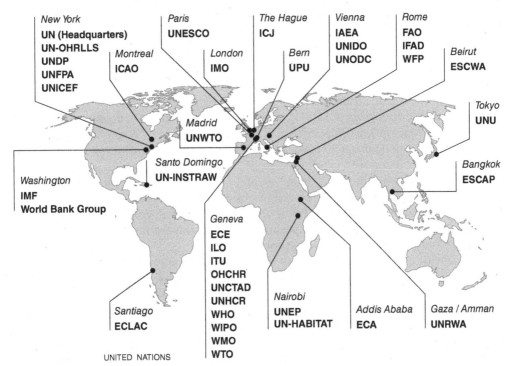

Figure I.1 Principal offices of the United Nations. Department of Field Support, Cartographic Section. Map No. 4218(E) Rev. 1, March 2008. Reproduced by permission of the United Nations.

actors, and pursuing common plans of action." But he also described it as something much more than a universal IGO committed to collective security. Noting that the Charter was written in the name of "We the Peoples," he called for a new emphasis on the rights of the person in both domestic and international lives. He envisioned a United Nations that acknowledged state sovereignty, but that would never let that principle stand in the way of defending individual rights or providing critical international humanitarian assistance.

What Annan was describing is an institution in the throes of change. In at least five ways, an evolutionary process is occurring, changing the character and mission of the United Nations. First, the UN agenda includes a new interest in thematic diplomacy, by which is meant a consideration of human problems that confront humankind on a global level, and require for their solution the involvement of not only national governments but also the cooperation of international and subnational organizations. **Functionalism**, the belief that peace and security between nations may best be achieved through the "spill-over" effect of expanding cooperation among peoples and through international organizations on nonpolitical problems that confront the world community, has a rich two-century history of advocates and organizational experiments. But the impetus to the UN's creation was the "high" politics of diplomatic relations on the questions of war and peace between states, with functional concerns such as economic development and human welfare relegated to the periphery of its work. Annan's promotion of thematic diplomacy moved functional world politics to center stage. Today, the United Nations is pursuing many areas of thematic diplomacy, including a sustainable environment, women's rights and empowerment, the control of HIV/AIDS and other communicable diseases like Ebola and COVID-19, disarmament, sustainable development, globalization, human rights, nation-building, poverty eradication (especially in Africa), population, democratization, international law, human settlements, migration, climate change, and the information revolution.

Each thematic policy area originated as a focus of UN attention at a particular point in the history of the organization. Concern for the environment, for example, can be dated, as we noted in our discussion of UNEP, from the 1972 Stockholm Conference. Each developed through the adoption of declarations, conventions, and UN resolutions. In the field of human rights, the Universal Declaration of Human Rights laid out the principles to which the world community committed itself. They were subsequently codified in two international covenants in 1966. In the areas of sustainable development and nation-building, UN efforts created evolving definitions and international standards of behavior for nation-states and their leaders. In all of these areas, world conferences, preparatory meetings, implementing programs, special funds, and intense multilateral negotiations were used to address perceived human problems.

Second, while the United Nations is an organization made up of sovereign states, increasingly non-state actors play a role in its deliberations, in the formation of UN global policy, and in the success or failure of established UN programs. The growth in thematic diplomacy has accelerated this trend. Two groups of non-state participants can be easily identified. The first is nongovernmental organizations. These are associational members of international civil society. In effect, they are global interest groups or domestic groups that have an international agenda. Welcomed in a peripheral way by the UN Charter to "consultative status" with ECOSOC, the NGO community now dominates much of the work of UN world conferences, formulates a global agenda that the world organization generally addresses, and serves as the most serious critic of UN programs. Since the early 1990s, UN Secretaries-General have courted the participation and goodwill of NGOs, hoping through them to mold public opinion and to implement UN initiatives more effectively than could be done solely through member governments. The second group of non-state actors is the private for-profit sector of the global economy. Once viewed as the enemy of UN social, economic, human rights, and social policy, global corporations are now recruited as helpful financial supporters for UN activities. Beginning with Secretary-General Annan's "Global Compact" initiative in 1999, more than one thousand companies have voluntarily associated themselves with the work of the United Nations.

Third, the United Nations increasingly seeks to impose the rule of law on individuals within countries as much as it does among its member states. This trend is controversial, since it is in obvious conflict with the Charter's admonition in Article 2 that "Nothing contained in the present Charter shall authorize the United Nations to intervene in matters that are essentially within the domestic jurisdiction of any state." In domestic democratic society, nothing is more central to its functioning than the rule of law. In the broader international community of states, the proclamation and enforcement of law have been extremely difficult, given the sovereign nature of nation-states. International law allows for the voluntary adjudication of controversies among states, but it does not reach to individuals nor carry the force of imposable sanctions. In the past, only in rare cases has the world community sought to apply legal standards and penalties to individuals who have been found to have violated standards of universal legal decency. The Nuremberg tribunals stand as an isolated example of that natural law tradition in the twentieth century.

The 1990s, however, witnessed a revival of this international legal trend with the establishment under the UN auspices of the international criminal tribunals for the Former Yugoslavia and Rwanda to try "war criminals." The experience of the Yugoslav and Rwandan ad hoc tribunals laid the basis for the ICC as provided in the 1998 Rome Statute. The ICC is intended as a permanent judicial body with a universal jurisdiction over the crimes outlined in its founding document.

Intervention in the form of intrusive peacekeeping, a post-Cold War evolution of an earlier relatively neutral monitoring process, also reflects the new concern for individual rights over state sovereignty. Decried by some, and imposed with varying degrees of effectiveness, "nation-building" and the defense of minorities clearly mark a move away from the letter of the UN Charter, but may be a proper reinterpretation of its spirit in the context of the twenty-first century.

Fourth, the United Nations appears to be moving away from being solely an IGO of sovereign states primarily concerned to keep the immediate peace among its members to becoming a member itself of international civil society. In 1997, Kofi Annan released his long-awaited reform program for the United Nations, titled *Renewing the United Nations*. In it, he described the United Nations as the central institution of that society, itself a product of irreversible globalization. He defined civil society as

[that] sphere in which social movements organize themselves around objectives, constituencies and thematic interests. These movements include specific groups such as women, youth and indigenous people. Other actors have also taken on an increasingly important role in shaping national and international agendas. They include local authorities, mass media, business and industry, professional associations, religious and cultural organizations and the intellectual and research communities.

Annan contended that international civil society was the product not only of globalization but also of "the quest for a more democratic, transparent, accountable and enabling governance." He also warned that there was an "uncivil society" made up of terrorists, drug traffickers, those engaged in organizing prostitution and trafficking in women and children, and others who have taken unjust advantage of globalization. Only new multilateral partnerships between the United Nations and subnational levels of government and non-state actors could provide a basis for the UN success in countering these challenges. The United Nations System increasingly has sought these kinds of cooperative ties, enlarging its role beyond its traditional character as a forum for interstate negotiation and decision-making.

Fifth, the United Nations has made an ideological choice, opting for democratization, externally in new and troubled nation-states, internally in terms of its own reforms (which we will discuss in Chapter 3), and substantively in terms of the issues that have moved to the head of its agenda. The United Nations was founded as an intergovernmental organization for the maintenance of peace and security. To be sure, there were other concerns. These desires were reflected in Charter provisions for a trusteeship system, economic and social functions, decolonization, and human rights, and in specialized agencies to address the many functional issues shared by humans in all settings. This was the first international organization that recognized the rights of women in its originating document.

These features of international attentiveness anticipated what we have labeled the "Other UN." These concerns were primarily enshrined in the Universal Declaration of Human Rights, not in the UN Charter. The former document was crafted in the late 1940s by the Commission on Human Rights, chaired by Eleanor Roosevelt. Mrs. Roosevelt placed her faith in world public opinion, and its ability ultimately to win the day and move governments and the United Nations to secure these rights for all individuals. If the primary United Nations was Franklin Roosevelt's, the "Other UN" was Eleanor's. And, increasingly, the United Nations of the post-Cold War era is also Eleanor's UN. The "rebirth" of the United Nations has been characterized by its rapid "democratization," with the concomitant diminution of state sovereignty's claim on the institution's life. People's rights, people's participation, the application of the rule of law all take up far more UN time, attention, and resources than was the case during its first forty-five years of existence.

In late 1999, demonstrators gathered in the streets of Seattle, Washington, to protest the third ministerial meeting of the WTO, successor to the Bretton Woods institution, GATT (The General Agreement on Tariffs and Trade). Among other charges, the activist alliance criticized the WTO for its undemocratic nature. Like other post-World War II institutions, it was seen as unaccountable to the populations it affected, particularly in the developing world. Accused of being in the hands of corporate giants and government bureaucrats, WTO meetings were subjected to violent protests not only in Seattle, but also in Washington, DC; Prague, the Czech Republic; and Genoa, Italy.

It is probably not without significance that the United Nations so far has avoided the popular fate of the Bretton Woods institutions. It has been able to do so in part because of a timely democratization that has provided for greater participation, accountability, and transparency. It has also changed its agenda, making the "Other UN" central to its work, implicitly recognizing that the maintenance of international peace and security depends in due course on fulfilling human needs.

The UN's past ability to "renew" itself is no promise of future relevance or success. New challenges regularly present themselves, and by the third decade of the twenty-first century some of those challenges seemed particularly daunting for IGOs seeking to overcome them. Rising ultranationalism and sovereigntist sentiment, global threats such as a rapidly warming climate and pandemics, great power rivalry, increased frequency and magnitude of natural disasters, migration of peoples not seen since the end of World War II, a volatile global economy, and economic inequality both within and between countries seem out of the range of solution by the UN and other international organizations without further reform, increased financing, and firmer political will of their most powerful members.

During the opening of the 76th UN General Assembly in 2021, Secretary-General Guterres expressed both the pessimism that pervaded international politics at the time and the danger to the peace of the world for lack of collective action on these challenges. He declared,[22]

> I am here to sound the alarm: The world must wake up. We are on the edge of an abyss — and moving in the wrong direction. Our world has never been more threatened or more divided. We face the greatest cascade of crises in our lifetimes…Solidarity is missing in action — just when we need it most.

The way out of the divisions he saw in world affairs was through multilateral cooperation. He opined, "The best way to advance the interests of one's own citizens is by advancing the interests of our common future. Interdependence is the logic of the twenty-first century. And it is the lodestar of the United Nations."[23] Whether the UN can refashion itself yet again to meet these new adversities will determine the future not only of the UN but also of our world.

Photo I.5 United Nations Secretary-General António Guterres.
Source: Marisol Grandon/UK Department for International Development via Creative Commons
Attribution 2.0 license.

SUMMARY

Far beyond the drama of global politics conducted for all to see in UN facilities in New York City, the United Nations, located in its many "homes" around the world, has forged a web of agencies, programs, and initiatives that more and more address human needs, in the belief that these concerns underlay much of the conflict in the world today. The UN System of the twenty-first century exceeds the envisioned breadth of the organization as conceived by its founders in 1945. Its aims extend beyond the traditional interest in inter-state diplomacy to include the "sovereignty" of the individual, with all of its implications for global UN efforts. Thus, we postulate a "new" United Nations, with new opportunities, as well as new limitations, and difficult if novel challenges. Challenged in some quarters as irrelevant, a leftover from the last era of international politics, the United Nations nonetheless remains the only truly universal international organization in today's world.

The United Nations is more than speeches, resolutions, and negotiations at world headquarters. It is also soldiers in blue helmets, aid workers in developing countries, civilian administrators in post-civil war states, police, doctors, engineers, volunteers, demining experts, agronomists, and a wide variety of professions and services. The "United Nations System" is found in many more places than the photogenic buildings on the east side of Manhattan. In other offices in New York, and in special cities around the globe, the UN operations are underway on every continent. While other international organizations, alliances, and even states of the Cold War era have vanished or have had to remake themselves wholly, the United Nations shows both the wear of changing times and the durability that makes it as potentially relevant today as when Franklin Roosevelt, Joseph Stalin, and Winston Churchill first agreed to replace the far more mortal League of Nations. With all of its warts and weaknesses, the United Nations simply is part of our expected international reality, and the epitome of international organization in the twenty-first century.

In the following pages, we offer a thesis and a structure meant to help the student grasp the full range and meaning of the United Nations. We present the history and functioning of the institution by looking at both the "old" United Nations—that is, the organization as its founders envisaged it in the 1940s and as the public often views it today—and, markedly, the "new" United Nations, by which we mean what it has become in the almost eight decades of its evolution.

At times, you may find yourself in a state of bewilderment—as one would while studying U.S. government and politics—trying to absorb a battery of information. We have tried to assist you in several ways. We have organized each chapter with sections and subsections around clear themes. We have highlighted certain words or phrases in each chapter and then listed them at the end of the chapter to encourage you to focus on and distinguish specific institutions and ideas. Cross-references to other chapters covering similar topical material appear throughout the text. A brief and select bibliography of books, articles, documents, and web sites at the end of each chapter provides access to further information about the topics. Finally, the inclusion of graphics should clarify textual comment.

KEY TERMS

Conference on Disarmament (10)
Department of Peace Operations (7)
Economic and Social Council (4)
Food and Agriculture Organization (15)
Functionalism (19)
General Debate (5)
International Court of Justice (13)
Intergovernmental organization (2)
International Atomic Energy
    Agency (12)
International Civil Aviation
    Organization (14)
International Labour Organization (9)
International Organization for
    Migration (8)
Kyoto Protocol (1)
Montreal Protocol (13)
Office of the High Representative for Least
    Developed, Landlocked, and Small
    Island Nations (7)

Paris Agreement (1)
Parliamentary Diplomacy (6)
Secretariat (6)
Secretary-General (6)
Specialized agency (14)
United Nations Environment
    Programme (10)
United Nations Framework Convention
    on Climate Change (1)
UN-HABITAT (11)
UNAIDS (8)
United Nations Children's Fund (7)
United Nations Development
    Programme (7)
United Nations High Commissioner for
    Human Rights (9)
United Nations Office in Geneva (8)
United Nations Office in Nairobi (10)
United Nations Population Fund (7)
World Food Programme (15)

DISCUSSION QUESTIONS

How effective has the United Nations been in mobilizing the world to address human-made global warming?

What are the most serious challenges to the United Nations in terms of its effectiveness in world affairs?

Should the United Nations intervene in nations' internal affairs to protect human rights?

RESOURCES FOR FURTHER RESEARCH

Relevant Web Sites

United Nations Department of Peace Operations (peacekeeping.un.org/en)
United Nations Homepage (www.un.org)
United Nations Office at Geneva (ungeneva.org/en)
United Nations Office at Nairobi (www.unon.org)
United Nations Office at Vienna (www.unov.org)
Locator for the UN System bodies (https://www.un.org/en/about-us/un-system)

Books, Articles, and Documents

Basic Facts about the United Nations. New York: UN Department of Public Information, published periodically.

The Europa Directory of International Organizations, 2021. 23rd Edition. London: Routledge, 2021.

Moore, John Allphin, Jr., and Jerry Pubantz. *Encyclopedia of the United Nations.* 2nd Edition. New York: Facts on File, 2008.

Report of the Secretary-General on the Work of the Organization. New York: United Nations, published annually.

United Nations Handbook. Wellington, NZ: Ministry of Foreign Affairs and Trade, published annually.

Notes

1 Paris Agreement, Article 2, 1(a) at unfccc.int/sites/default/files/english_paris_agreement.pdf.
2 Radoslav S. Dimitrov, "The Paris Agreement on Climate Change: Behind Closed Doors," *Global Environmental Politics* 16, no. 3 (August 2016): 7.
3 Dag Hammarskjöld, "The Promise of the UN," *New York Times Magazine* (September 15, 1957), 21.
4 Aba Eban, "The U.N. Idea Revisited," *Foreign Affairs* (September/October, 1995), 40.
5 Suzanne Nossel, "The World Still Needs the UN: Building Global Governance from Scratch Is a Fool's Errand," March 18, 2021, at www.foreignaffairs.com/articles/world/2021-03-18/world-still-needs-un?utm_medium=newsletters&utm_source=fatoday&utm_campaign=Al%20Qaeda%20Versus%20ISIS&utm_content=20210914&utm_term=FA%20Today%20-%20112017.
6 "Remarks by President Trump to the 73rd Session of the United Nations General Assembly," September 25, 2018, at <www.whitehouse.gov/briefings-statements/remarks-president-trump-73rd-session-united-nations-general-assembly-new-york-ny/>.
7 Ibid.
8 Ibid.
9 UN Charter, Preamble.
10 United Nations. Department of Management, November 2011.
11 As of March 15, 2015.
12 https://www.youtube.com/watch?v=Btlzrwl9Lcw, March 11, 2020.
13 www.unog.ch/80256EDD006AC19C/(httpPages)/BE8ACD4E8CD424F2C-1257CE60042D970?OpenDocument
14 Geneva Eco'Diagnostic, *International Geneva Yearbook, 2000–2001* (Geneva: United Nations, 2000), 74.
15 The "South" is a common parlance reference to the poor and developing states that are largely located in the Southern Hemisphere. It is a term used in counterpoise to the "North," a category including the major industrialized developed states found mostly in the Northern Hemisphere.
16 *A Better Quality of Life for All in an Urbanizing World.* Strategic Plan, 2020–2023. Nairobi: UN-Habitat, 2020, 3.
17 "Historic agreement on the Air Traffic Services route network in the Aegean Sea," ICAO press release, September 15, 2003.

18 S/Res/2596, September 17, 2021.
19 Ibid.
20 S/Res/2098 (2013), March 28, 2013.
21 United Nations, "Catastrophe 'unfolding before our eyes' in Ethiopia's Tigray region – UN chief," August 26, 2021, at https://news.un.org/en/story/2021/08/1098582.
22 United Nations, "Secretary-General's address to the 76th Session of the UN General Assembly," September 21, 2021, at https://www.un.org/sg/en/node/259283.
23 Ibid.

Chapter 1

Ways of Thinking about the United Nations and International Organizations

As we see in the Introduction, the United Nations, having commemorated its seventy-fifth birthday in 2020, remains a fully engaged international organization (IO), plying its trade globally. That remarkable fact alone makes the organization unique in world history. No other multinational political arrangement has ever lasted so long. Still, however extraordinary, the truth of endurance does not necessarily bring equally extraordinary commendation. This text is intended neither as a glorification of the United Nations, nor as a reproof of its ineffectiveness or its potential menace. Rather, we describe what the United Nations is and what it does. This is not a simple task. Students who have examined their own national government often find themselves faced with a baffling array of institutions, bureaucracies, personalities, and long-term practices that make full understanding difficult. The United Nations presents a similar, daunting challenge.

INTERNATIONAL ORGANIZATIONS

The study of the United Nations falls conveniently within the larger academic field of international organization (IO). Scholars who study international organizations come from a variety of academic fields, including political science, history, economics, geography, sociology, law, philosophy, and international relations. As we point out in the Introduction, the study of *intergovernmental organizations* is also included in the field of IO. The extensive UN System (described in Chapter 4) is the quintessential **international organization** of modern times.

International organizations differ in many respects from other common social combinations, such as a family, a religion, or a nation. Individuals' allegiance to a family, a religion, or a nation tends to be much firmer than their commitment to a more distant, multiethnic, and multinational organization like the United Nations. Thus, people are less inclined to forgive or overlook flaws in the United Nations than in the other groupings to which they belong. As individuals, we are close to our family, faithful to our religion, and

DOI: 10.4324/9781003281535-2

patriotic to our country. Our connection to the United Nations is, understandably, more tenuous, particularly since *other*—less familiar—religions, nations, and cultures are also represented there. You should keep in mind this personal remoteness and the extraordinary diversity of the United Nations as you study it.

THEORIES OF INTERNATIONAL RELATIONS

International relations is a field of academic study often considered part of the discipline of political science, although some people would insist that it is also a field of public policy or even of history. Academicians in this field investigate and analyze the relationships among nation-states within what is frequently called the *international system*. Thus, they are interested in international organizations like the United Nations. However, how someone understands the role, importance, and possible merits of an international organization in the current global system may depend on the theoretical framework he or she adopts concerning international relations in general. Many such frameworks exist—some with academic and scholarly credentials, others arising from political or social movements. While you should become aware of those that are most familiar, we are not suggesting that you adopt a single or definitive schema for understanding contemporary international relations. In the following pages, although we mention certain theoretical perspectives when doing so is appropriate, the main aim of this text is to explain the United Nations straightforwardly rather than theoretically. Still, theoretical approaches to international relations permeate its study.

Scholars often think of international relations as being either *positive* or *normative*. In this context, the word *positive* refers to how things actually are, rather than how they should be. *Positivism* comes from a system of thought associated with the nineteenth-century sociologist Auguste Comte that recognized only positive facts and observable phenomena. In contrast, *normative* refers to how things ought to be, at least in someone's eyes. It gives prominence to standards or *norms*, which could originate from more metaphysical (beyond observable facts) prescriptions of proper behavior. These two perspectives have produced two familiar viewpoints on international relations: realism and idealism. Other viewpoints include neoconservatism (sometimes inadequately tied to realism and other times to idealism), neoliberalism (a spin-off of "liberalism," which, in turn, is often associated with idealism), functionalism, and deviations from the conventional realist/idealist formulations, such as Marxism (and a variety of neo-Marxist spin-offs, for example, dependency theory and feminism), critical theory, constructivism, and postmodernism. We also add a newer term for analysis, arriving from an older era: "populism," which, in recent times, has come to describe a hyper-nationalist, even ethnocentric, behavior toward international affairs.

Realism and Neoconservatism

Realism is a strategy discernible from the early modern period of Western history that we associate with thinkers from Niccolò Machiavelli and Thomas Hobbes through recent scholars like Hans Morgenthau, Kenneth Waltz, and John Mearsheimer. Realists—whether followers of Mearsheimer's robust "offensive realism"[1] or Waltz's "defensive" or "structural realism"[2]—suppose that we can and should look at world affairs as they really are and not as we might wish them to be. The realist faults idealism for its eagerness to spread its bold and forward-thinking ideology, sometimes via military action, and too often in the face of resistance. Among the historic idealist excesses cited by realists is the

French Revolution, which, following on the laudable "Declaration of the Rights of Man and the Citizen," descended into a puritanical zealotry that resulted in general European war and in the murderous policy of Terror at home. These were hardly "liberal" feats.

Realists contend that the principal players in the international arena are nation-states, usually with quite different cultural traditions, each acting in its rational self-interest within an environment of international anarchy. No sovereign authority exists above nations that can control their relations; states must develop their interactions with other states on their own.[3] Realists usually do not encourage the use of international politics to try to force upon other nations and cultures specific patterns of good behavior. We have to live with what we have as we strive to maintain our security (Waltz) or seek to expand our advantages against potential rivals (Mearsheimer). International or multinational organizations like the United Nations may be useful but are not of primary consequence. A struggle for power is ongoing in world politics, and in pursuing the national interest above all, policy makers use various tools, including diplomacy, economic power, and, ultimately, military force to try to attain their aims. A country's relative level of power, including economic and military power, determines its relations with other states. Realists emphasize national interest, power, security, and the centrality of the nation-state. In the quest for security, nations try to build up resources.

"Balance of power" realists often recommend that a nation join at times with other nations who share specific security concerns in countering a potentially dangerous rival. As we say above, realists do not encourage the use of international politics to try to force upon other nations and cultures specific patterns of "good" behavior. Nor do realists believe that it is possible to change (or improve) human nature, which is constant and can be both good and evil.

***

A variant of realism, ***neoconservatism***, by conventional accounting, originated in the 1960s, when former hawkish liberals in the United States began to react to the "new left" and to the Vietnam War protests. Thus, it is a theoretical approach nurtured distinctly by certain American thinkers and policy makers. It may be called an ideology characterized by an emphasis on unrestrained capitalism and on a robust, militarized, interventionist foreign policy to promote American national interests *and American conceptions of democracy*. Thus, there is a counterintuitive "idealist" ingredient in the creed.

Neoconservatism reached a peak of influence in the United States during the George W. Bush administration following the 9/11 attacks and declined in favor and influence as American military involvement in Afghanistan and Iraq lingered into the second decade of the twenty-first century. Intellectual and journalistic leadership for the movement came from a number of individuals, including the editor of *The Weekly Standard*, William Kristol, syndicated columnist Max Boot, and author Robert Kagan.[4] Within the Bush administration were a number of policy makers often depicted as neoconservatives; Vice President Dick Cheney was perhaps the most conspicuous of these. By 2003, American neoconservative policy stressed unilateralism instead of cooperative diplomacy, announced the legitimacy of "preemptive" or "preventive" war, and was observably more pugnacious than policies of the recent past. It regarded the United Nations as ineffective and useless.

Calling neoconservatism a variant of realism, as we have done above, may well be ill-advised. The prominent realist John Mearsheimer, in his 2018 book *The Great Delusion*, excoriates the imperialist, interventionist policies promoted by neoconservatives. Yet, Mearsheimer, in a firm realist tradition, finds the chief culprits for such a policy to be progressive liberals. We can go all the way back to Woodrow Wilson, he suggests, to find the origins of our distress. And, for realists like Mearsheimer, as well as for the neoconservatives he would declaim, the United Nations seems to have little value in our modern world.[5]

Idealism, Liberalism, and Neoliberalism

The so-called "balance of power" competitive system accepted by realists was seen by many early advocates of ***idealism*** as a cause of the breakdown of international order leading to World War I. These liberal internationalists—like Woodrow Wilson—envisaged replacing the system with a more rules-based and morally inspired international structure such as the League of Nations.

The idealism which fueled the movement for the League had philosophic roots. The term is associated with Plato, who taught that all properties and objects that people could imagine have independent, "ideal" existence. Plato spoke of "higher truths" than what humans can know in the material world. The eighteenth-century Prussian philosopher Immanuel Kant (1724–1804) elaborated the modern conception of idealism, placing politics at the service of morality. He postulated what was called a *transcendent idealism* beyond concrete reality, and he believed that by rigorous mental effort people could come

Photo 1.1 Immanuel Kant.
Source: Creative Commons via Wiki Commons {{PD-US-expired}}.

to understand it and profit by the understanding. Kant encouraged all republics (which he supposed were growing in number) to unite into a federation of peaceable nations. He was convinced that republics would not war against one another. He assumed that growing interdependence, in terms of both world trade and international communication, would eventually ensure the growth of republicanism, homogeneity, and peace. He hoped that standards of appropriate political behavior on the international stage could be measured by the world's public in terms of what rightly ought to be done, rather than by national leaders, who often act in secret according to their primary standards—power and self-interest. U.S. president Woodrow Wilson reformulated Kant's hopes. Wilson's principles were sometimes referred to as *liberal internationalism.*

Steadfast followers of idealism can be found in the academy today, and among some policy makers. A body of scholarship devoted to the so-called democratic peace thesis has emerged to try to prove that the number of democracies expanded during the late twentieth century, that democracies will not war against one another, and that international regimes of law and cooperation can be developed and then studied as examples of human progress. Such liberalism covers a wide range of views and activities, from Wilsonian idealism, as reflected in the Fourteen Points of 1918 and the League of Nations Covenant (explained in Chapter 2), through the contemporary so-called neoliberal theories (defined below), such as the advocacy of transparent and equitable trade and finance rules for the world community, and the democratic peace thesis just mentioned.

For liberal idealists, nation-states are only one set of actors in international affairs, and even they can cooperate by means of transnational institutions like the United Nations. In so doing, they can demonstrate that the world's peoples are able to rise above base interests and military aggression. Believing in higher, "idealistic" goals for humans beyond mere existence and security, idealists insist on the independent and significant role that multilateral organizations can play. Unlike realists, they tend to emphasize the goodness of human nature. Nonetheless, in some instances, idealists may justify military action to force reform on recalcitrant nation-states, such as in Bosnia in the late 1990s or in Syria in the 2010s. Realists tend to resist military action for idealistic goals. (Also keep in mind that policy makers sometimes seem to be idealists, and, at other times, realists.)

The so-called "liberal international order"—an *idealist* quest sometimes disparaged as a delusional fiction that is neither liberal, international, nor orderly—originates in the equally elusive word *liberalism*.[6] Liberalism derives, understandably, from the word "liberty." Thus, its core conviction is the sanctity of individual rights, refined in our day to encompass "civil rights" and "human rights." It thus emphasizes the autonomous individual rather than dependency on a hierarchical system with a dominating king, family, ideology, or religion. Liberalism's modern origins, by traditional understanding, emerged during the Enlightenment in the Western world.[7] Its other principal features include equality (of people, cultures, and nations), consent to govern (thus self-government, or democracy), secularism (and tolerance), and conventional freedoms—freedom of the press, freedom of religion, etc. Liberalism generally promotes cosmopolitanism, honors science, and hints at human progress. Liberalism favors market economics over command economics; it has been historically contiguous to capitalism. Thus, it is entrepreneurial and market-driven—it can be unsettling.

It also, at least in modern form, is *international.* Liberals sense that liberal principles should extend to the whole world, and, as a consequence, the world will be more cooperative and more stable, there will be fewer chances of great-power conflict, and the world should realize economic growth and the gradual diminution of poverty, disease, and inequalities. Accordingly, the "**liberal international order**" promotes diplomacy and cooperative multilateral institutions designed to support liberal principles. By the post–World War

II period, the United Nations and subsequent multilateral groupings became the bedrock of that hope.

The term *neoliberalism* is often used as a pejorative by critics of the post-World War II economic and financial settlement, which has led to what is often called "globalization." The initiation of UN-related institutions, such as the World Bank, the International Monetary Fund, and the General Agreement on Tariffs and Trade, brought neoliberalism into sharp focus. The UN's founders believed that the world required not only political integration but also economic integration.

By the turn of the century, the term neoliberalism had become a fashionable disparagement of efforts to integrate further the world's economy—including initiatives such as the North American Free Trade Agreement (NAFTA), the World Trade Organization (WTO), and proposed free trade regimes between the Americas and Asia and between the Americas and Europe.

Neoliberalism, or "new" liberalism, as would be expected, derives from traditional liberal internationalism that, as seen above, mirrors some features of *idealism*. Liberal internationalism emphasizes democracy, equality (of classes, races, ethnicities, religions, and genders), human rights, progressive immigration policies, and resolving disputes via international law and international organizations, such as the United Nations. Liberal internationalism also stresses the benefits of rules-based market capitalism, open world trade, the cross-border liquidity of finance, and the fluid movement of goods, people, and money internationally. This economic feature of idealistic liberalism is the one most often associated with neoliberalism.

Advocates of neoliberalism emphasize the benefits to the world's people from economic integration and lubricated trade and investment. Neoliberals see these economic and financial reforms as complementary to all other liberal objectives. Opponents of neoliberalism believe that its benefits, dependent on capitalist practices, go primarily to large banks and to the wealthy living in first world countries. They also believe that "globalization" is damaging labor rights, native traditions, and the environment. By the late twentieth century, criticism arose over reform recipes that the UN's Washington, DC-based International Monetary Fund and World Bank, often in conjunction with the U.S. Department of the Treasury, pressed on financially strapped developing countries. Prompting economic stabilization and the encouragement of market-based economic practices, these prescriptions (dubbed "the Washington Consensus") seemed to the recipient countries to mandate unacceptable austerity.[8] The European Union found itself under similar criticism as it tried to address the mid-2010s crises of financially failing member states such as Greece. An additional important recrimination has to do with the climate change vexation. Neoliberal capitalism stresses endless growth and the quest for individual gain within a rational and beneficial market. Yet, insist detractors, the pursuit of gain and the workings of an unregulated market bode ill for the climate, as the waste products from accelerating capitalism spew into the atmosphere.[9] Of course, defenders of the international order, including some purported "neoliberals," insist that the proper way to address climate change is via international agreements such as the Paris Climate Accord of 2015. In lock-step tandem, advocates have consistently argued that international agreements are the best way to address labor rights as well as environmental concerns while at the same time bolstering economic growth worldwide.

Functionalism—in harmony with some features of liberal idealism and neoliberalism—sees integration developing logically as states recognize the value of cooperative governance, first in economic matters such as trade, eventually in more political spheres. Although some doubters may resist integration (as they have even within Europe, most specifically exemplified by Brexit), functionalists believe that they are unable to obstruct the momentum for integration as the benefits become obvious and the very process develops anchored habitual activities. That is, integration develops its own internal dynamic; it *functions* in ways that forward further integration. The hypothetical result is the gradual erosion of nation-state sovereignty and the growing use of scientists, experts, and trained bureaucrats in developing common policies. Functionalism thus attempts to describe regional integration such as in the European Union, anticipates possible global convergence, and brings to high pitch the hopes of liberal internationalists.[10]

Critical Theory

There are, as well, theoretical approaches to international relations that diverge from the more conventional ones suggested in the section above. Known as **critical theory**, these perspectives have influenced attitudes about international relations and about the United Nations.

Marxism derives from the historical studies and political and economic theories of Karl Marx (1818–1883), nineteenth-century philosopher and "father" of modern "scientific" socialism, or communism. Some scholars have refined Marx's notions and posited an approach to international relations shrewdly different from the more traditional realist and idealist attitudes. A number of terms characterize Marxist theory. Among the terms of interest to us are *economic determinism, class struggle, revolution,* and *historical materialism.* Although Marxism as a political program became a worry for much of the Western world during the twentieth century, you should bear in mind how students of history, politics, and international affairs have tried to use its insights for analytical purposes. Marx stressed that economics—not ideas or ideals or spiritual, religious, or cultural values—chiefly influence the course of history. This "economic determinism" produced an inevitable historical process of class conflict between the oppressor and the oppressed. People, institutions, and forces in a society that control the means of production and the distribution of goods (the landed aristocracy in the Middle Ages, corporation capitalists in the modern world) not only represent the wealthiest members of society and its upper classes, but also determine the sources of information, the education, indeed the broad culture of a society (including its values), and dominate its social and political life to their own advantage.

Marxism differs from realism and idealism in asserting that class divisions are more important determinants in history than are national interests or ideals. Classes are determined by economic relationships; higher classes are those that dominate the economy. However, the prospect of a lower class gaining the upper hand by taking advantage of innovative economic changes always exists. Inevitably, a revolutionary "leap" to a new stage of history occurs. Thus, the *bourgeoisie* (middle-class, profit-minded entrepreneurs living in cities) gained control of the new capitalist system of banks, money, and commerce, and by the nineteenth century replaced aristocratic landowners as the prevailing political and cultural force in the Western world. From the Marxist perspective, the world is dominated by this bourgeois class, intent upon maintaining its ascendancy worldwide; and it uses *the state* to maintain its power. The dominant class is not necessarily crude, vicious, or overtly imperialistic. Through foreign aid, international loans, grants, investment, trade agreements, cultural exchange programs, and participation in international organizations, the bourgeoisie attempts to draw into its orbit those outside who might represent a threat to its supremacy. The late U.S. historian William Appleman Williams described this kind of policy as an "informal empire."[11]

For Marxists, international organizations like the United Nations can best be studied if you consider them as the settings in which an economic struggle takes place between the fortunate class and those representing an immediate challenge (such as the "Second World" of the Soviet region during the Cold War) or those (such as the less fortunate in the "Third World") beneath it. In an era of globalization, the worldwide capitalist class uses international organizations, financial institutions, and competitive markets to maintain its dominance.

***

A variant of Marxism, ***dependency theory***, became attractive to the developing world during the 1970s, although its popularity has diminished since then. Proponents of dependency theory maintain that the inadequate level of economic development in poor countries is caused chiefly by their asymmetrical dependence on the more dominant highly developed countries. Some dependency theorists believe that less affluent countries (most in the Southern Hemisphere) will remain poor because the developed countries will continue to use multinational corporations to siphon off whatever surpluses the impoverished countries produce. One damaging result is that no profit is left for the poor countries to use for reinvestment.

As a rule, the countries ill affected by the current world economic order are former colonies of wealthier Northern Hemisphere nations. Even as these countries became independent, they remained poor. Some dependency theorists believe that poorer nations should discontinue economic ties with wealthier nations, protect their surplus production, and pursue more nationalist and protectionist—even socialist—policies to break the cycle of underdevelopment. Other theorists, dismissing the neoliberal theories of economic growth through international markets, criticize capitalism as a system that perpetuates inequality. They find particularly noxious international institutions such as the WTO and the International Monetary Fund, which, they charge, only benefit the rich. Thus, only a radical reform of the world economic system, including a fundamental redistribution of income and resources from the Northern Hemisphere to the Southern and the introduction of a world progressive tax system on foreign exchange transactions will rectify inequalities and end poverty. Many dependency theorists favor complete elimination of Third World debt and the full funding, by means of grants (not loans), of large development projects. According to dependency theorists, the United Nations, and its related international organizations, can best be examined as the institutions most capable of forwarding a restructuring of world economic relations. Once the states of the "South" gained a majority in the UN General Assembly in the 1970s, they passed resolutions demanding equitable distribution of global resources, a demand largely ignored by the "North" until the turn of the century.

The international relations approach of ***feminism*** is couched in an emphasis on "gender." The terms *gender* and *sex* are not identical. Rather, gender roles are "socially constructed," not a product of biological sex differences. Thus, at your college all department secretaries could be women, not because only women are genetically capable of being secretaries, but because the role of secretary has been "genderized" or "socially constructed" by U.S. culture so that only women perform the role.

Whatever differences exist among feminists (and there are many), all agree that gender is significant in world affairs and the fact that, for the most part, only men have composed the main theories about international relations—whether realist, idealist, or Marxist—has made a difference. For feminists, this fact means that a large segment of the academy is ignored at the peril of thorough exploration from as many perspectives as possible. Some feminists might argue that if the writing of international relations theory and the formulating and crafting of international diplomacy were infused with women's perspectives, less violence would exist in the world. Of course, such an argument in itself posits a "genderized" notion of international affairs.

Moreover, mostly men have been in control of nation-state governments and state-to-state interactions. Even women may ignore the possible role of their sex when thinking about international relations, acceding to the common assumption that women necessarily find themselves in a "separate sphere" of domestic life, engaging in activities wholly separate from the large issues of world politics. Again, this disregard underscores the genderized notion that men, but not women, are competitive, rational, and power-seeking. Particularly obvious to feminists is the male-oriented "realist" doctrines of an aggressive world of competitive nations in a state of international anarchy. Within this anarchic "jungle" international organizations like the United Nations traditionally have served male-oriented expectations by emphasizing diplomatic and military purposes and the adjustment of relations among states. A feminist sees the value of these organizations in serving broader communal interests and agendas.

***

Critical theorists reject realism and idealism. They likewise deny the reasonableness of positivism, finding that humans simply cannot find abstract "objective" truths. For critical theorists, any premise, theory, or idea has a purpose and is designed for or useful to someone or some group. That is, a relationship exists between a person's knowledge and his or her actual practice or, that is, between the knower and the known. Thus, separating fact from value is difficult, or impossible. Knowledge, then, is not impartial and obtained by objective study but is, rather, "constitutive" (i.e., a product and result) of existing values and interests. The comparable *"constructivist" theory* emphasizes that norms and culture, which produce (or "construct") a group's "identity" as a people or nation, play important roles in international affairs (although any one group must share the world stage with other "constructed" identities, and relations among different cultures, institutions, and norms can affect the way nations interact).

We as individuals can easily sense the force of these contentions because we all likely have preliminary views springing from our distinctive culture (American, Christian, liberal, conservative) that guide our interpretation of any international event, irrespective of what might be the independent facts of the event. According to critical theorists and constructivists, for us to study international relations adequately, we must concede the predispositions of diplomatic actors, critique positivism's insistence on traditional objective problem solving, and emphasize new forms of international harmony that recognize plural perspectives and possibilities for cooperation among them. In this approach, international organizations (like the UN) are "conveners" of diverse actors, are perceived differently by each participant, and have a changing value and importance depending on how international affairs are generally constructed at any given time. In the post-Cold War era, with its advances in global communications, some constructivists believe that the United Nations can be used by the multitude of actors to push forward the global discourse on issues and norms related to women's empowerment, human rights, and economic inequality, among other topics.

Postmodernism (sometimes called *poststructuralism*) first became fashionable in language studies. It has begun to make an impression on other humanities and on the social sciences, although its impact on international relations theory remains limited. Postmodernist theory is linked with a number of twentieth-century French philosophers, including Michel Foucault (1926–1984) and Jacques Derrida (1930–2004). The term "postmodernism" can be understood by noting that the term *modernism* is associated with the Enlightenment, a period in Western history that emphasized science, empiricism, rationality, secularism, objective truth, and individualism. "Post" modernism (that is, "after" modernism) finds the Enlightenment a wholly inadequate guide to understanding the world. It critiques objectivity, rationality, and the individual. In this sense, it is related to critical theory, constructivism, and feminism, which were discussed previously.

Postmodernists make use of literary theory to dispute the possibility of an objective reality in world affairs. They jettison the "dominant discourses" in the field of international relations—realism, idealism, and Marxism—which are based on Enlightenment notions of objective reality, but are, in fact, according to postmodernists, simply reflections of a Western (and white male) culture that has sought to dominate the rest of the world. By insisting that the *words* of modernity (*liberty, freedom, rights, equality, written law, impartiality, individualism, economic entrepreneurship*, and so forth) are universally applicable, Western theorists of these schools of thought are simply exerting their command over other, equally valid opinions of reality (including communitarian, uncommon, ancient Asian, ancient African, and pre-modern notions of social order). Postmodernists urge a new and radical politics in place of these imposed Western ideas, to give voice to groups and nations that have been marginalized by authoritarian discourses. Postmodernists insist that international organizations must be open to these groups and their issues.

In rejecting the Enlightenment, postmodernists emphasize relativism rather than certainty, nihilism rather than optimism, and historical circumstance rather than the independent individual. They seek to "deconstruct" texts—such as treaties, constitutions, or charters (like that of the United Nations)—in order to find the real source of hierarchical power hidden behind the (only apparently benign) words that Western thinkers have put in the texts. In this way, postmodernism gives some sustenance to critical theory, feminism, and dependency theory and, at best, allows postmodernists to see the UN and other international organizations as venues for the discursive development of progressive ideas in the global system.

Populism

In the 2016 U.S. presidential campaign, an outlier appeared in the debate over U.S. foreign policy, the liberal international order, and even the worth of the United Nations. When presidential candidate Donald Trump called for a retreat to "Make America Great *Again*" (italics added), he seemed to advocate, among other things, a withdrawal from the internationalist practices so characteristic of U.S. policy since 1945. The novel prescriptions Trump announced were quickly labeled "populist." They were compared to right-wing, nativist programs that had emerged recently in Europe,[12] which had experienced a steadily rising clamor against establishment elites, against the unusual acceleration of incoming migration caused by the impact of the Syrian civil war and destabilization in Africa, and against the malfeasance that had caused the 2008 economic turndown.[13] The new posture, discernibly revealing sentiments similar to neoliberalism's critics, harkened back to a pre-World War II isolationist tendency in the United States as well as to an "on our own" bearing among many nations, while at the same time calling to mind a powerful populist tradition in U.S. political history.[14] Like the populist movement of the 1890s, the new program garnered considerable support from non-urban, rural, and working-class Americans unhappy with the pace and direction of cultural change and what they sensed as inequitable economic and financial transformation. It is no accident that populist sentiments tended to rest in rural areas where educational attainment was the lowest and hardship from the effects of economic globalization the harshest.

Issues that underscored the fresh dissatisfaction were immigration (particularly from Latin America and from Islamic countries), multilateral trade agreements (a concern shared with the left side of the Democratic Party), government-mandated policies on environmental reform and racial and social justice that objectors saw as coming from an insensitive and treacherous "deep-state," and anything apparently associated with the indistinct specter of "globalization."

Nationalist movements elsewhere in the world shared these sentiments. As but just a few examples, a populist movement in Great Britain succeeded in removing that country from the European Union and promised a go-it-alone posture. Hungary and Poland fell under the sway of populist and nativist politics; India, under charismatic Prime Minister Narendra Modi, seemed to abandon its secular traditions in favor of an emotionally charged and ominous Hindu-nationalism. Brazilian President Jair Bolsonaro, appealing to the street, criticized "secularism" and rolled back protections for indigenous groups in the Amazon rainforest, while condoning deforestation.

As had been the case with historic populist movements, legitimate grievances sometimes devolved into troubling politics. Opposition to immigration heightened racial and religious animosities, anti-globalization fostered nativism, neo-nationalism, and too often an uncomfortable resurgence of anti-Semitism. In the United States, suspicion of open and free trade encouraged economic protectionism and trade wars. Overseas, Euroskepticism resulted in the confusion of Brexit and the ascendance of nationalist, right-leaning governments in eastern Europe.

In the middle of the summer 2018, the populist prime minister of Hungary, Victor Orbán, delivered a dramatic speech, encouraging the Western world to follow him in establishing what he called separate national "illiberal democracies" that would be pro-traditional family, anti-multiculturalism, anti-immigration, anti-religious diversity, and anti-European integration. In a central section of the long speech, he accentuated his theme by praising his friend Donald Trump for making good on his promises to bring an end to "the multilateral world order—the world order based on multilateral agreements."[15]

Unlike other of the "theories" we have highlighted in the pages above, **populism** seems to have arisen from popular grievance rather than from studious discourse. It has appeal for both the political left and political right, and it reflects a common historical pattern of resistance to hierarchy as well as to cosmopolitanism. While populism emphasizes "the people," who the people are remains vague. They are typically juxtaposed against "the elite," "the establishment," and "the media." Populism flourishes in democratic societies; a populist movement is often led by a charismatic and dominant personality who appeals to ethnocentric or nativist passions. In its present form, populism represents a serious challenge to the UN's global aspirations. It is certainly as significant—perhaps more so—as other ways of thinking about the UN and international affairs.

***

Many more perspectives than those just mentioned have been adopted by various groups, but these give you a taste of how scholars tie theoretical frameworks to studies of international relations or how politicians craft popular themes dealing with complex international affairs. We restate that this text does not require you to look at the United Nations through the eyes of any particular hypothesis. We prefer that you hold in abeyance speculative assumptions and instead concentrate initially on examining the United Nations with a clear eye and an inquiring, almost Socratic, demeanor.

KEY TERMS

Critical Theory (33)
"constructivist" theory (35)
Dependency Theory (34)
Feminism (34)
Functionalism (32)
Idealism (30)
International Organization (27)

Liberal International Order (31)
Marxism (33)
Neoconservatism (29)
Neoliberalism (32)
Postmodernism (35)
Populism (37)
Realism (28)

DISCUSSION QUESTIONS

What are the key differences between "Critical Theories" of international relations and the more conventional theories of realism and idealism?

Compare and contrast the approach to international relations (and to the UN) of Marxism and constructivism.

What is your general impression of the United Nations and how international affairs work? What does your answer to this question suggest to you about your own implicit theoretical approach to world politics?

RESOURCES FOR FURTHER RESEARCH

Relevant Web Sites

International Relations, Principal Theories: scholar.princeton.edu/sites/default/files/slaughter/files/722_intlrelprincipaltheories_slaughter_20110509zg.pdf

The IR Theory Homepage: www.irtheory.com

Books, Articles, and Documents

Benhabib, Seyla. "Feminism and Postmodernism." *Feminist Contentions: A Philosophical Exchange.* New York: Routledge, 1995, 17–34.

Ikenberry, G. John. *A World Safe for Democracy: Liberal Internationalism and the Crises of Global Order.* New Haven, CT: Yale University Press, 2020.

Judis, John B. *The Populist Explosion: How the Great Recession Transformed American and European Politics.* New York: Columbia Global Reports, 2016.

Kant, Immanuel. *Perpetual Peace.* Lewis White Beck, ed. New York: Liberal Arts Press, 1957.

Kubálková, Vendulka, Nicholas Onuf, and Paul Kowert, eds. *International Relations in a Constructed World.* London: M.E. Sharpe, 1998.

McCormick, John. *The European Union: Politics and Policies.* Boulder, CO: Westview Press, 2008.

Mearsheimer, John. *The Tragedy of Great Power Politics.* New York: W.W. Norton and Company, 2014.

Onuf, Nicholas. *World of Our Making: Rules and Rule in Social Theory and International Relations.* Columbia: University of South Carolina Press, 1989.

Pubantz, Jerry, and John Allphin Moore, Jr. *Is There a Global Right to Democracy: A Philosophical Analysis of Peacekeeping and Nationbuilding.* Lewiston: Edwin Mellon, 2012, Chapter 2.

Sarup, Madan. *Post-Structuralism and Postmodernism.* Athens: The University of Georgia Press, 1989.

Stelzer, Irwin, ed. *The Neocon Reader.* New York: Grove Atlantic, 2005.

Taylor, Astra. "Time's Up For Capitalism. But What Comes Next?" *The Nation,* May 6, 2019, at <www.thenation.com/article/democracy-environment-astra-taylor/>.

Waltz, Kenneth. *Theory of International Relations.* Boston: McGraw-Hill, 1979.

Williams, William Appleman. *The Tragedy of American Diplomacy.* New York: Delta Publishing, 1962.

Notes

1 John Mearsheimer, *The Tragedy of Great Power Politics* (New York: W.W. Norton and Company, 2001), 35. Mearsheimer published an updated edition in 2014.

2 Kenneth Waltz, *Theory of International Relations* (Boston: McGraw-Hill, 1979).

3 In an intriguing variation from the realist presumption, the late Samuel P. Huntington, in *The Clash of Civilizations* (New York: Simon & Schuster, 1996), postulated a globe separated among antagonistic "civilizations" rather than hostile nations. Thus, for example, Europe and the United States share much in common—religion, the Enlightenment, and ideas of liberal politics—and are not then in the nation-to-nation competition with one another implied by traditional realist thought; instead, they are challenged by other quite different, likely adversarial, "civilizations."

4 See Irwin Stelzer, ed., *The Neocon Reader* (New York: Grove Atlantic, 2005). The anthology contains essays by neoconservatives Max Boot, William Kristol, Robert Kagan, and others.

5 John J. Mearsheimer, *The Great Delusion: Liberal Dreams and International Realities* (New Haven, CT: Yale University Press, 2018). For further elaboration of Mearsheimer's influential thinking, see his latest edition of *The Tragedy of Great Power Politics* (New York: W.W. Norton and Company, 2014).

6 In the Fall of 2018, the UK-based *Economist* was celebrating its 175th birthday. Considering itself a major promoter over the years of "liberalism," it published a series of thoughtful essays explaining, and defending, the term as it had metamorphosed over that history. See "A Manifesto for renewing Liberalism," September 13, 2018, at: <www.economist.com/leaders/2018/09/13/a-manifesto-for-renewing-liberalism>.

7 For a sweeping account, see Jerry Pubantz and John Allphin Moore, Jr., "The Moderns," in *Is There a Global Right to Democracy?* (Lewiston, NY: The Edwin Mellon Press, 2012), 87–95.

8 The author and biographer Jonathan Alter has pointed to an unmerited leftist criticism of American neoliberals, who, Alter says, "may have gone overboard on financial deregulation in the 1990s but have staunchly opposed Republican austerity measures." Johnathan Alter, "'The Populist Explosion' Dissects the History of the Anti-Elite Worldview," *New York Times*, October 7, 2016, at <www.nytimes.com/2016/10/09/books/review/populist-explosion-john-b-judis.html>.

9 See Astra Taylor "Time's Up For Capitalism. But What Comes Next?" *The Nation*, May 6, 2019, at <www.thenation.com/article/democracy-environment-astra-taylor/>.

10 See John McCormick, *The European Union: Politics and Policies* (Boulder, CO: Westview Press, 2008).

11 Williams' influential argument was developed in his classic study *The Tragedy of American Diplomacy*, originally published in 1959 and revised and updated thereafter.

12 John B. Judis, *The Populist Explosion: How the Great Recession Transformed American and European Politics* (New York: Columbia Global Reports, 2016).

13 See James Kirchick, "The Rise of Populism in Europe," *Great Decisions 2019* (New York: Foreign Policy Association, 2019), 51–58, and the full discussion in Judis, *The Populist Explosion*.

14 John D. Hicks' classic study, *The Populist Revolt: A History of the Farmers' Alliance and the People's Party* (Minneapolis: University of Minnesota Press, 1931) detailed, usually sympathetically, the early populist movement.

15 Prime Minister Viktor Orbán's speech at the 29th Bálványos Summer Open University and Student Camp, July 28, 2018, found at <www.kormany.hu/en/the-prime-minister/the-prime-minister-s-speeches/prime-minister-viktor-orban-s-speech-at-the-29th-balvanyos-summer-open-university-and-student-camp>.

Chapter 2

Origins and History of the United Nations

To understand the evolution of an organization, a person must first know its origins and early history. In this chapter, we cover the various attempts at establishing world peace and unity before the United Nations was formed. Then, we cover its beginnings, the setbacks it has faced, and the more recent challenge to one of its basic tenets: the principle of collective security.

OVERVIEW OF EARLY HISTORICAL EFFORTS TO ESTABLISH INTERNATIONAL ORGANIZATION

In their historical semblance, certain events foretold the founding of the United Nations. Among these events were the Peace Conference of Westphalia in 1648, which addressed the reorganization of Europe after the ruinous Thirty Years' War; the Vienna Conference of 1814–1815, which ended the Napoleonic Wars; and the Paris Peace Conference, where diplomats attempted to craft a peaceful international system following World War I. At Westphalia, the sovereign secular state became the prime actor in international affairs. The gathered emissaries hoped for peace among these states based on "the just equilibrium of power." At Vienna, for the first time, the architects of the new order sought to maintain the peace through succeeding regular meetings of the so-called great powers. A little more than a century later, at Paris in 1919, the world's leaders established the League of Nations, the immediate predecessor to the United Nations. Other historical examples of efforts to fashion fixed diplomatic relations and ongoing political international organizations exist, but they, like the three peace conferences just referenced, mostly failed. Whether in their failure they left sufficient lessons for the UN's founders that would result in an enduring international order remains patently uncertain. Nevertheless, the UN's existence for close to eight decades suggests that something must have been learned.

INTERNATIONAL RELATIONS BEFORE THE TWENTIETH CENTURY

The so-called Enlightenment period of the eighteenth century brought modern rationality to learning while imposing on international affairs fresh notions that would eventually motivate world leaders and show the way, much later, to the United Nations. Eighteenth-century developments in politics, economics, international law, science,

DOI: 10.4324/9781003281535-3

and conceptions of individual rights led to what some people have called *modern liberal democratic nationalism.*[1] In turn, influenced by liberals in the American and French revolutionary traditions and by Prussian philosopher Immanuel Kant, thinkers envisioned a peaceful world that would be characterized by democracy, economic interdependence, and international law and institutions.[2] Such notions may strike the twenty-first-century reader as commonplace examples of what the current age calls *globalization* and of normal contemporary international politics. However, nearly two centuries, bloody conflicts, and agonizing efforts would be necessary to effect a world organization that conformed to the prescriptions of enlightened notions of diplomacy.

Long before the eighteenth century, formal relations between and among nations, empires, and peoples characterized human activity.[3] The diffusion and ultimate availability of texts and treaties dealing with such relations suggest a pattern in world history of cross-cultural intercourse among political elites the world over that designed what might be called international relations. Basic principles and precedents emerged as different communities sought to impose order on their mutual relations and to resolve disagreements without resorting to force—unless those principles or their interests might allow or require such measures.

For most of history, public order was maintained by hierarchical imperial administrations whose dominance was punctuated by sporadic uprisings and dissolution that too often resulted in violence.[4] For example, the great periods of Chinese history are considered the times when powerful consolidating empires brought pervasive peace, some prosperity, Confucian (or later, Maoist) standards of conduct, artistic grandeur, and systematic rule to a society that nonetheless intermittently plunged into chaotic and disruptive civil strife. The Roman Empire is the prototypical administrative unit of the Western legacy. Rome brought stability, peace (the *Pax Romana*), law, infrastructure, a common language, and eventually Christianity to the known Western world. Byzantium was the imperial reflection of Rome in much of eastern Europe, and it lasted longer and left an impressive legacy of Slavic orthodox culture that was neither nationalist nor liberal in character. The Ottoman Empire imposed a flexible bureaucracy on a wide swath of land with an extremely diverse population. Likewise, great Russian empires, whether Romanov or Bolshevik, brought to heel the squabbling medley of ethnic groups covering their large landmass. As a rule, when the imperial power was challenged, the consequence was unwelcome disruption and sometimes anarchy. Empire, whether imposed willingly and brutally, or reluctantly and benignly, seemed the common solution to international disorder. In fact, as late as the turn into the twentieth century, international diplomacy was something characteristically conducted among empires (the Romanovs in Eurasia, the Manchus in China, the Ottomans in the Middle East, the Hapsburgs in south-central Europe, the Hohenzollerns in Germany and east-central Europe, and the British and French worldwide).

What might be termed the *post-empire* era of political organization is more familiar to the modern world. The idea of *national sovereignty* provided nation-states the ultimate authority over populations within discernible boundaries. The nation-state, considered to have originated in Europe in the fifteenth and sixteenth centuries, heralded what some scholars have called *international anarchy.* Because no commanding sovereign authority rested above the nation, international order depended on the good faith of its individual sovereign members. In the West, this phenomenon led to the development of modern international relations and international law. Scholars and practitioners such as Hugo Grotius (1583–1645) and Emmerich de Vattel (1714–1767) sought to codify rules of international behavior based on the understanding that each sovereign state would determine whether to abide by them. This "state of nature" in international matters presupposed an underlying possibility of conflict.

An initial response to this problem was the **balance of power theory**, which suggested that if any one nation were to gain overwhelming power so as to represent a danger to other nations, the latter would unite to restrain—that is, balance—the powerful entity. In addition to introducing the balance of power theory, early European theorists proffered notions of what might now be called *international human rights law*. The earliest approaches to this issue came from alarm about the treatment of native populations in the new Spanish colonies of the sixteenth century, and then of civilians during the brutal religious wars, particularly the Thirty Years' War (1618–1648). Grotius and Vattel, and their readers in Europe and the United States, sought to codify into an embryonic international law accepted practices against what society currently calls *war crimes*.

By means of the Peace of Westphalia, which ended the Thirty Years' War, sovereignty became the criterion for authority in any political entity. For example, sovereign rulers were authorized to determine the religion within their state to prevent internal wars between competing religions, which had too often drawn in outside forces. Under the Westphalian settlement, Europe came to be characterized by sovereign nation-states theoretically abiding by an international law, including the rules of war, but, first and foremost, defending their national power and interests. Following World War I, new nation-states appeared in Central Europe. After World War II, India and Pakistan became independent of Great Britain, while various states emerged out of the former Ottoman Empire and the mandates administered there by Great Britain and France between the wars. From 1945 to 1970, many new states in the "developing world" gained independence. The nation-state had become the accepted mode of political organization.

THE CONCERT OF EUROPE

Meanwhile, the American and French Revolutions had brought to world politics the idea of universal principles applicable at all times and to all peoples. The idea that all human beings were, by nature, equal inspired but also disturbed existing politics. The French Revolution culminated in a long world war and the Age of Napoleon. The victorious allies who finally defeated the French general met at Vienna during 1814–1815 and restructured Europe and its diplomatic practices in an attempt to bring order to the continent and prevent another descent into violence. The Congress of Vienna crafted an arrangement—dubbed the **Concert of Europe**—to build a peaceful Europe. Diplomats settled on a new and transformed balance of power, complemented by territorial compromise among all the former belligerents, monarchical legitimacy and restoration, and an agreement to meet in the future to consult on actions to take to meet disruptive crises (which signaled the so-called congress system of European affairs).[5] Often considered a conservative settlement, the Vienna program was followed by a reasonably tranquil nineteenth century that experienced a creative expansion of international organizations. Early river commissions, such as the Central Rhine Commission (1815) and the European Danube Commission (1856), were examples. The International Red Cross was in place by the middle of the century, and the International Telegraphic Union (1865) and the Universal Postal Union (1874) paved the way for numerous future international agencies dealing with issues as diverse as narcotics, agriculture, health, weights and measures, railroads, time zones, and tariffs. The Paris Convention for the Protection of Industrial Property (1883) and the Berne Convention for the Protection of Literary and Artistic Works (1886) brought issues of protecting patents and copyrights into the larger realm of international law. In 1899 and 1907, The Hague Conferences marked a culminating phase in the arbitration movement, establishing the Permanent Court of Arbitration and expanding rules governing arbitral procedures.

THE LEAGUE OF NATIONS AND WORLD WAR II

Despite such progress, crises challenged both the arrangements of the Concert of Europe and international cooperation up to the plunge into the Great War of 1914–1918. When that disastrous war ended, a new participant—the United States—encroached on the club of the more traditional great powers to attempt a solution to the disorder that had caused the war.

The League of Nations

U.S. president Woodrow Wilson joined other leaders at the Paris Peace Conference. He brought with him positions he had articulated earlier in his liberal "Fourteen Points" speech, including an outline for a new worldwide organization—a **League of Nations**—committed to collective security and the elimination of war. The precursor to the United Nations, the League would be the first world organization intended to maintain peace and security, foster international cooperation, and develop international law on an ongoing basis.

The League's initiation had resulted from the unparalleled bloodshed and carnage of World War I, which convinced many leaders of the necessity of a world organization to avert another such conflict. Immanuel Kant had envisioned a global federation of republics, and the nineteenth century had witnessed the growth of numerous international cooperative ventures. The war solidified opinion among an active group of diplomats, including South African Jan Smuts, Great Britain's Lord Robert Cecil, and Frenchman Léon Bourgeois, who all advocated a society of nations. As early as 1914, President Wilson had spoken with his closest adviser, Colonel Edward House, about the merits of forming a world association to avoid the kind of war just under way. The president may also have been influenced by the British writer Norman Angell, with whom he spoke before publicly articulating his ideas on a League. In 1917, the American Institute of International Law issued a recommendation in Havana, Cuba, calling for a world organization that dovetailed agreeably with Wilson's proposal.

At the Paris Peace Conference in 1919, Wilson insisted on including the Covenant of the new League in the text of the Treaty of Versailles. The U.S. president headed a special committee at the conference that shaped the Covenant of the League and made it an "integral part of the General Peace Treaty." The Covenant, coming into force on January 10, 1920, included twenty-six articles, provided for an assembly composed of all members, a council to include permanent members from the great powers (at first the United Kingdom, France, Italy, and Japan, which were later joined by Germany and the Soviet Union), and a secretariat. Both the assembly and the council required unanimity on any decision. The Covenant called for disarmament, territorial integrity, and political independence of nation-states; establishment of the Permanent Court of International Justice; a mandate system (whereby existing colonial administrators would prepare colonial areas for independence) that foreshadowed the end of colonialism; international cooperation in humanitarian affairs; and provisions for amending the Covenant. The most controversial provision of the Covenant, highlighted in Article 10, called for collective security to ensure nations League protection against aggression.[6]

The council's inaugural session took place in Paris in January 1920, but Geneva became the permanent home of the new League, which met at first in the Hôtel National (before construction of the Palais des Nations, which opened in 1936). By a two-thirds vote of the assembly, membership could be extended to any state, dominion, or even self-governing colony. The war's victors were the original members: of the thirty-two winning Allies,

Photo 2.1 U.S. President Woodrow Wilson.
Source: Harris & Ewing Collection, Library of Congress Prints and Photographs Division.

twenty-nine joined the League initially. The largest victor not to join was the United States, because the Senate refused to ratify the Treaty of Versailles. In 1920, membership stood at forty-two states. The Soviet Union—isolated from world affairs during the Bolshevik Revolution—and several neutral nations did not become members in 1920. Germany, unhappy with the peace treaty, did not enter the League until 1926. Russia joined in 1934, just as the strains on the organization were becoming unbearable. The greatest number of members, achieved in 1937, was fifty-eight; by 1943, only ten remained. The offices of the League's secretariat were in a building along Lake Geneva that in 1924 was renamed the Palais Wilson, following the death of the former U.S. president. Sir Eric Drummond, the first and longest-serving Secretary-General, assembled a genuinely international secretariat, and early on the League realized some successes. The League settled a Finnish–Swedish dispute over the Åland Islands in the Gulf of Bothnia (1920–1921), guaranteed the security of Albania (1921), aided Austria's economic reconstruction after the war, guided the peaceful division of Upper Silesia between Germany and Poland (1922), and helped prevent hostilities between Greece and Bulgaria in the Balkans (1925). The League also extended help to refugees, worked to suppress the white slave trade and to restrain the traffic in opium, and published surveys and data on a number of pressing international issues, such as world health, labor conditions, and economics.

Nevertheless, intractable problems confronted the organization. For instance, without the United States as a member, the League lacked one of the influential players in world affairs. In addition, the problem of including the Soviet Union in international diplomacy was not resolved until late in the League's history. The nonparticipation of important nations, along with unwieldy rules of procedure, such as requiring unanimity in both the council and the League assembly, made effective enforcement impractical. Meanwhile, the worldwide depression that engulfed most countries by the 1930s made dealing with nations that were looking out for their own interests even more difficult. Then, as the dismantling of world order ensued, the League seemed destined to sit aside as aggressions proceeded. The League could do nothing as the French occupied the Ruhr Valley in 1923, the Japanese invaded Manchuria in 1931 (when the League accepted the U.S. policy— called the *Stimson Doctrine*—of simply not recognizing the occupation), the Japanese withdrew from League membership (1933), and Bolivia and Paraguay fought the Chaco War (1932–1935). In 1935, Italy invaded Ethiopia, and in the end all the League could do in response to the impassioned appeal from Ethiopia's leader, Haile Selassie, was to call for voluntary economic sanctions against Italy. Despite the seemingly automatic imposition of sanctions according to Article 16, many powerful nations, including the United States, ignored the League's request. Collective security was essentially dead as an effective instrument against the bellicose dictators of the time.

In 1935, the League completed a fifteen-year administration of the Saar Territory (in Germany) with a plebiscite, but Germany had already left the League (1933). Adolf Hitler's remilitarization of the Rhineland and repudiation of the Treaty of Versailles augured an ominous future for the organization. The Spanish Civil War (1936–1939); the Japanese invasion of China (1937); the appeasement of Hitler at Munich, which allowed the dismemberment of Czechoslovakia (1938); and German demands on Danzig, Poland—which a League commissioner in the city could not resist—culminated in the outbreak of World War II. The League's inconsequence became obvious when in 1939 the council—for the only time in the League's history—expelled a nation, the Soviet Union, for its attack on Finland following the German–Soviet Pact of August 23, 1939, by which the two totalitarian regimes agreed to divide Eastern Europe. At the moment of the agreement, war became inevitable. This novel experiment in world cooperation virtually ceased to function with the outbreak of World War II, and in 1946 it officially dissolved itself. Several affiliated organizations and powerful ideas of international cooperation, however, did survive the crisis of World War II, and merged with the new United Nations after the conflict.

Woodrow Wilson and the Elemental Weaknesses of the League

The completed Versailles peace agreement had contained several compromises that troubled President Wilson's most resolute supporters. Almost no one seemed happy with the final national boundaries bequeathed by Versailles; many critics believed that the final settlement had actually frustrated Wilson's bedrock principle of ethnic and national autonomy. Opponents in the United States complained that the president had made too many compromises in Paris and feared that he had overcommitted the country to international collective security. In September 1919, campaigning for Senate approval of the League, the president collapsed with a stroke in Colorado. His resulting illness removed the most ardent supporter of the League from the nationwide debate.[7] Meanwhile, resistance to his plans mounted and partisan bickering between U.S. political parties made compromise in the Senate improbable. The Republicans had won a narrow majority in Senate elections in 1918, which elevated the Democratic president's most commanding opponent, Henry Cabot Lodge, to both majority leader and chairman of the crucial

Senate Foreign Relations Committee. Combined, these troubles made the Senate's refusal to ratify the peace agreement inevitable and thus prevented U.S. entrance into the new League of Nations.

The Versailles settlement may have been doomed to failure irrespective of the U.S. snub. Diplomats at Paris had before them a dangerously disintegrating world. Most of the major organizing empires of the previous century were gone. The Manchu dynasty in China had collapsed in 1911, replaced by a weak republican government, and a disruptive civil war followed. In Russia, a revolution ended the Romanovs' rule in March 1917, and by the end of the year, the Bolsheviks found themselves in control of a truncated state, because the former empire had lost considerable territory to the Germans months before the war concluded. By war's end, the Hohenzollerns in Germany and the Hapsburg rulers of the Austro-Hungarian Empire were likewise gone, as was the Ottoman Empire, now completely dissolved. Within the resulting vacuums in the center of Europe, in the Middle East, and elsewhere were a variety of religions and myriad ethnic entities that demanded sovereign independence along religious and ethnic lines. Wilson's contrapuntal principles of self-determination and internationalism, inherent in the treaty, were now put forward as the post-war formula to fill the vacuum and to promote communal peace. Nonetheless, the end of imperial rule left unsettled cleavages in many parts of the world. In one respect, world leaders have been trying since 1918 to restore order out of the chaos left by World War I.

Despite the U.S. rebuff, the League came into being and introduced innovative organizational advances in the development of international organizations, including three new permanent organs—a plenary assembly with equal representation from all member states, a council with permanent and nonpermanent members, and a secretariat. Although earlier international conferences had made some use of secretariats, the League secretariat, providing centralized administration, expert advice, and day-to-day coordination, embodied a novel concept of a permanent international civil service. Outside the Covenant framework, but related to the League, were the Permanent Court of International Justice (the so-called World Court) and the International Labour Organization (ILO). Despite the ultimate failure of the League, its organizational structure and various activities provided a basis for its UN progeny.

Although the League, then, was a model for the later United Nations, five important discernible differences can be seen between the defunct League and the current organization. First, the League had been ensconced in the full Treaty of Versailles; thus, to reject the League, the U.S. Senate had to reject the entire peace agreement. Conversely, the United Nations was purposely separated from the terms of peace that ended World War II; U.S. president Franklin Roosevelt, informed by Wilson's lack of success, determined on a separate process of ratification in the United States. Second, the League Covenant had been a traditional agreement among governments, who were called in the Covenant "The High Contracting Parties." In contrast, the preamble of the UN Charter begins, "We the *Peoples* of the United Nations." Third, the League required unanimous votes in both the assembly and the council, but decision-making in the United Nations is more flexible. Fourth, parties to a dispute before the League were prohibited from voting because of the obvious conflict of interest. In the United Nations, in a concession to the realities of power politics, member states have no such limitations. This freedom, coupled with the veto, means that a permanent member of the Security Council can block UN action. Fifth, in 1945 the United States, never a member of the League or the Permanent Court of International Justice, eagerly entered the United Nations and decided to play a major role in all post-World War II international organizations.

U.S. AND ALLIED VISIONS OF THE POST-WORLD WAR II PERIOD

The challenges confronting the UN founders were not those that the world community would face in the twenty-first century, but they were no less momentous:

- Western leaders needed to assuage Russian suspicions of any Western-bred organization to which Moscow would be asked to commit.
- The United States was obliged to convince its people and the rest of the world that it would not again retreat from leadership in this post-war period.
- Great Britain required encouragement to complete the Wilsonian dream of dismantling worldwide empires, the largest of which was administered from London.
- The defeated nations needed to be reconstructed and fused into the new global framework.
- Urgent rebuilding and rehabilitation of a war-devastated world awaited action.
- Displaced persons and roaming refugees required immediate attention.
- The impaired world economy demanded restitution and rational orderliness.
- The globe awaited a general, broad, and forceful commitment to the fundamental human rights so long promised by enlightened liberals and so clearly desecrated in the war years.

Whatever criticisms can be mounted against the early United Nations, it—and its associated organs—met and resolved every one of these challenges within a few short years following the most destructive war in history. However, this accomplishment was not easy.

By the end of the 1930s, the League had become effectively inoperative. Seeds for a new organization were planted in the Atlantic Charter of August 1941, issued by U.S. president Franklin Roosevelt and British prime minister Winston Churchill. The document obliquely referred to a future international organization for "general security." On January 1, 1942, with the United States now in the war, twenty-six nations joined in a *Declaration by United Nations* (a term coined by Roosevelt), reaffirming the principles of the Atlantic Charter and committing themselves to defeating the Axis powers. At a meeting in Moscow in October 1943, the foreign ministers of the United States, Russia, Great Britain, and China signed the Moscow Declaration on General Security, explicitly recognizing "the necessity of establishing at the earliest practicable date a general international organization." Planning for the new body was centered in the U.S. State Department, where Secretary of State Cordell Hull organized a special committee of advisers to draft a proposal as the governing document of the new organization. The committee's draft charter became the outline eventually massaged into the final Charter of the United Nations (or UN Charter). Talks in August and September 1944, at Dumbarton Oaks, an estate in Washington, DC, furthered planning. At the crucial Yalta Conference, held in the Russian Crimea in February 1945, Roosevelt, Churchill, and Joseph Stalin hammered out the final compromises that became the basis for the San Francisco Conference on International Organization. In June 1945, at the conference, attendees witnessed the signing of the completed Charter. With sufficient ratifications, the United Nations came into being at 4:50 p.m. on October 24, 1945. The history that preceded this event was intricate, interesting, and involved the participation of three of the most compelling figures of the twentieth century—**Franklin Roosevelt**, **Winston Churchill**, and **Joseph Stalin**. These three men are often considered the most critical figures in initiating the United Nations. The birth of the organization is best told by following the intertwining biographies of these political giants.

Franklin D. Roosevelt (1882–1945)

Franklin Delano Roosevelt, the thirty-second president of the United States, was elected to the office four times (1933–1945). No one before or since has accomplished such a feat (and, with the Twenty-Second Amendment to the U.S. Constitution, it will never happen again). Born into a family of wealth and connection in Hyde Park, New York, Roosevelt was the fifth cousin of President Theodore Roosevelt, from whose enthusiasm for public service "FDR" developed a motivation to pursue politics and elective office. During his attendance at Harvard University, he met, and then became engaged to, President Roosevelt's niece, Eleanor Roosevelt. They were married in 1905. President Wilson appointed FDR assistant secretary of the Navy in 1913. During World War I, he was a strong advocate of military preparedness and of Wilson's internationalism. Running for vice president with the Democratic nominee James M. Cox in 1920, Roosevelt campaigned for ratification of the Treaty of Versailles, which would have brought the United States into the League of Nations. After the Democrats lost to Warren G. Harding, he returned to New York and a promising political future.

FDR's political fortunes received a severe blow in August 1921, when he contracted polio. Nonetheless, with the support of his wife, Eleanor, he kept his name before the public and in 1928 New York elected him its governor. In 1932, he soundly defeated Republican incumbent—and former Wilson adviser—Herbert Hoover for the presidency, promising a "New Deal" to address the Great Depression. As president, Roosevelt faced not only the worst economic downturn in U.S. history, but also the rising threat of European dictatorships, an expanding Japanese empire, and then World War II.

We can accurately say that Roosevelt became the "architect" of the United Nations. Out of the ruins of World War II, he and his advisers—principally his first secretary of state, Cordell Hull; Russian-American Leo Pasvolsky (a devoted internationalist in the State Department); diplomat Sumner Welles; and FDR's last secretary of state, Edward Stettinius—crafted a new world organization that they hoped would avoid all the League's weaknesses. The president convinced Winston Churchill and Joseph Stalin to accept U.S. plans for a post-war organization as the primary vehicle for maintaining peace and security. However, FDR's central role emerged only gradually as the war progressed.

When Churchill broached the idea of a post-war organization during the Atlantic Conference, off Newfoundland in 1941, before the U.S. entrance into the war. The cautious president would concede only to "the establishment of a wider and permanent system of general security,"[8] believing that former president Wilson's League had been too dependent on world public opinion and had not been adequately sensitive to the realities of power. Three weeks after the Japanese attack on Pearl Harbor, Roosevelt and Churchill drafted the Declaration by United Nations, presenting the Allies' war aims. Roosevelt decided that a signing ceremony would be held first for the representatives of the United States, the USSR, the United Kingdom, and China. The following day representatives of twenty-two "lesser" powers that were committed to defeating Germany in the war affixed their signatures. The president personally decided on the order of signatories, listing them on the basis of power differentials.

In 1942, Roosevelt assured Sumner Welles that when "the moment became ripe," he would push for a new world organization. His conception of it at the time was illustrated in his "Four Policemen" proposal, which emphasized the use of military power by the "Big Four" of the wartime Grand Alliance, who, he was convinced, needed to cooperate to ensure post-war peace. During 1943, Roosevelt shared his views of a great-power-dominated association of nations with Churchill (who at the time preferred the idea of regional security arrangements), and, at the Teheran Conference, with Stalin. In FDR's early view, the Soviet Union, Great Britain, China, and the United States would have regional responsibilities for maintaining peace and would act together to enforce world stability, even forcibly carrying out the disarmament of smaller powers. Public reaction to his proposal was lukewarm. Moreover, practical problems with the concept were evident: it did not provide a place in the scheme for France, it did not envision how Great Britain and the USSR would disentangle their conflicting national interests in Europe, and it did not provide much enticement for smaller states to become part of the new organization.

While the president continued to proselytize for the Four Policemen as peacekeepers, his secretary of state, Cordell Hull, was moving in another direction. As early as July 1942, Hull mentioned to the president a growing sense in the State Department of the need for a post-war agency that could enforce the rule of law and the pacific settlement of international disputes. A planning group proposed a "United Nations Authority" with a security commission consisting of the four great powers, thus incorporating Roosevelt's idea into a more general universal organization. The secretary set up a technical committee to draft plans for such an international organization. This committee, largely under Leo Pasvolsky's leadership, worked until the end of the war to develop the ideas that would ultimately be the basis for the Dumbarton Oaks proposals (detailed below) and for the UN Charter.

In March 1943, Hull's committee forwarded a draft constitution to Roosevelt. The projected charter created a general conference, a secretariat, agencies for technical services, and, most important, an executive committee consisting of the Four Policemen and a council made up of the four powers plus seven other representatives of regional organizations. In a series of meetings, Roosevelt informally gave his blessing to the effort to obtain British and Soviet assent to a new international organization, at least "in principle," along the lines of the draft charter.

As the Allies took the military offensive in 1943, concerns about maintaining cooperation among the great powers after the war were of growing importance to the president. Cordell Hull traveled to the Moscow Conference of Foreign Ministers in October. He hoped to convince Great Britain, Russia, and China that cooperation in a global organization would serve their interests after the war. The secretary made the necessary concessions to achieve the Joint Four-Nation Declaration, which supported the U.S. initiative. Following the conference, the Roosevelt administration found domestic public sentiment overwhelmingly supportive of a new institutional structure designed to maintain the peace. Even many Republicans, including the party's standard-bearer in 1940, Wendell Willkie, criticized Roosevelt only for not moving fast enough to put an organization in place by the end of hostilities.

After the Moscow Conference, the president became much more directly involved in the planning for the new organization and in the negotiation of its details. By the time the Teheran Conference convened in November 1943, Roosevelt's thinking about postwar arrangements had evolved to the point of combining Wilsonian organizational solutions with a hoped-for long-lasting friendship among the great powers. At Teheran, FDR outlined his proposal for a worldwide assembly with an executive committee and a four-nation enforcement body. The president assured a perplexed, likely concerned Stalin that the new organization would not be able to impose its will on its members. Stalin and his emissaries would revisit this commitment during ensuing negotiations whenever proposals materialized that seemed to give the body some control over the great powers. In particular, Stalin would insist on an absolute veto for the Soviet Union. Stalin, in effect, demanded a fundamental revision of the earlier League of Nations voting procedure, which had not allowed states to vote on disputes in which they were involved.

Following his return from the meeting with Soviet and British leaders, Roosevelt approved the Plan for the Establishment of an International Organization for the Maintenance of International Peace and Security. According to the plan, not only would the new organization be responsible for international peace, it would have additional agencies for economic and social activities. It would also have trusteeship responsibilities, taking over the mandate system from the League of Nations and revising it to encourage decolonization. The U.S. government would now push for full self-determination. The future United Nations, through its Trusteeship Council (an explicit Charter-authorized entity endorsed by the wartime leaders at their Yalta meeting in February 1945 and finally approved at the San Francisco founding conference the following April), would provide the mechanism. Included in the president's plan for the United Nations, in addition to the Trusteeship Council, was a Security Council, a General Assembly, a Secretariat of international civil servants, and an International Court of Justice to replace the League's Permanent Court of International Justice. (A detailed description of each of these UN organs is provided in Chapter 4.)

The most serious Charter issue Roosevelt had to resolve in the final months of the war was the question of voting; from his perspective, the issue was how to protect the traditional sovereignty of the nation-states that would be members of the world organization, yet not allow the United Nations to fall victim to the requirement of unanimity among the members that had so hampered the League. The administration addressed this issue in many settings, but not until the 1944 Dumbarton Oaks Conference and the **Yalta Conference** in February 1945 did Roosevelt bring the matter to conclusion.

As the president prepared to travel to Yalta for his summit with Stalin and Churchill, his administration proposed a compromise on the voting procedure in the Security Council by limiting the requirement that a party to a dispute abstain from voting only on the questions of discussing the issue and recommending methods of pacific settlement. The unanimity rule for permanent members would still apply to decisions about enforcement when a breach of the peace had been determined. In essence, so that all the great powers would participate in the United Nations, Roosevelt conceded the political necessity of the veto in instances of forceful action by the world body. At the Yalta meeting, Stalin agreed to accept the U.S. formulation on voting in the Security Council.

The president spent the last two months of his life making plans for his address to the UN Conference on International Organization, which was scheduled for April 25; preparing the delegates to the conference; and fending off objections to the agreements made at Yalta. The administration made a concerted effort to sell the American people on the view that the United Nations marked a wholly new form of peaceful international relations in the history of world politics. According to *New York Times* correspondent Anne O'Hare McCormick, Roosevelt saw the United Nations as the crowning achievement of his political career, and in late March he opined to the reporter that when the war was over, he might consider resigning the presidency to become the UN's first Secretary-General.[9] Many issues remained to be debated and settled at the San Francisco Conference. As late as April 9, Roosevelt told the State Department that on his return from Warm Springs, Georgia, the two weeks before the conference convened would be sufficient time to make final decisions about the trusteeship of non-self-governing territories under the United Nations and other outstanding issues. Three days later, the architect of the United Nations was dead. A testament to his achievement was that his successor, Harry S. Truman, within minutes of being sworn in as president of the United States, made his first presidential decision—to proceed with the San Francisco Conference to organize the United Nations.

Winston Churchill (1874–1965)

Winston Churchill served as British prime minister from 1940 to 1945 and again from 1951 to 1955. He had first gained the attention of the British public as a reporter covering foreign events. His capture and imprisonment by the Boers of South Africa while he was reporting the British-Boer conflict raised his visibility sufficiently to win him election to Parliament in 1900 as a Conservative. He switched to the Liberal Party during World War I and served in several capacities in the government. Shortly after World War II broke out, he replaced Neville Chamberlain as the prime minister. As the leader of one of the "Big Three" wartime Allies—the United States, the United Kingdom, and the Soviet Union—he played a central role in crafting the United Nations. Churchill developed what he perceived to be a "special relationship" with President Roosevelt, both before and during the U.S. involvement in World War II. America's "nonbelligerent" relationship with war-beleaguered Great Britain reached a peak with the Atlantic Conference, when the two men met in August 1941 aboard the naval vessel *Prince of Wales* in Placentia Bay near the harbor of Argentia, Newfoundland. There, Churchill and Roosevelt discussed strategic issues and announced war aims and a joint vision of the post-war world. The most famous product of the meeting was the eight-point concluding statement called the *Atlantic Charter*, which contained a hazy reference to a post-war "system of general security," as discussed earlier.

When the United States entered the war in December 1941, Churchill journeyed to Washington, DC to coordinate Anglo-American strategy more formally. At U.S. secretary of state Cordell Hull's suggestion, the two leaders signed the Declaration by United Nations. The declaration created a wartime alliance against the Axis powers but failed to announce a post-war international organization as many people had hoped. Neither Churchill nor Roosevelt was yet committed to such a proposition. The two leaders instead concentrated on winning the war in the desperate year of reverses, 1942.

When the tide of war turned more favorable for the Allies in late 1942 and early 1943, Churchill began to think of regional councils to stabilize the post-war world (and to protect the British Empire). Roosevelt, however, devised his concept of the Four Policemen to win the war and ensure the peace. Neither vision reflected the idealism of Woodrow Wilson's League of Nations.

The year 1943 was not only the turning point for the Allies' fortunes of war, but was also the embryonic phase of the United Nations. In March, Churchill delivered an important radio address and at the same time sent an aide-mémoire to Washington, DC, each outlining his vision of the post-war world. Dismissive of China and suspicious of the Soviet Union, the prime minister expressed the hope that the United States, Great Britain, and the USSR would create some sort of vague umbrella organization after victory, with the focus on a Council of Europe and a Council of Asia to ensure regional stability. Churchill's initiative compelled Roosevelt to begin focusing his attention on post-war issues, and by the time of the Quadrant Conference in Quebec in August, the president's advisers had devised a counterproposal to present to the British that combined elements of FDR's Four Policemen with Churchill's regional approach.

Stalin, however, was uninterested in any schemes that went beyond the wartime coalition against Germany. Churchill brilliantly suggested that the best approach to the Soviet leader was to present post-war plans as merely a continuation of wartime collaboration and to do so while the war was still ongoing. During 1944, both Churchill and Stalin (each in his own way a realist) began to realize that Franklin Roosevelt's United Nations, dominated by the Four Policemen, reflected the realism of Theodore Roosevelt rather than the idealism of Woodrow Wilson. Nevertheless, the Yalta Conference in February 1945 revealed a surprising divergence of opinion between the Anglo-American allies. Churchill agreed with Stalin that the Big Four should be granted an absolute veto power over the discussion of disputes presented to the Security Council. U.S. Secretary of State Edward Stettinius and British Foreign Secretary Anthony Eden spent the first evening of the Yalta Conference attempting to change Churchill's mind. The prime minister finally accepted Eden's view that the small nations would refuse to participate in such an arrangement of raw power. At their last meeting, Churchill, Roosevelt, and Stalin announced that all nations that had signed the Declaration by United Nations would be invited to a conference at San Francisco on April 12, 1945, to create a new world organization.

Still troubling Churchill, however, was American insistence on a role for the United Nations in the self-determination of colonial peoples. Ever an advocate of the civilizing role that Britain had played in the reaches of its empire, Churchill was concerned about the threat to British national interest if the United Nations promoted decolonization. As early as 1943, Roosevelt approved a State Department draft adding an "agency for trusteeship responsibilities" to the contemplated UN Charter. British objections postponed final acceptance of the UN's Trusteeship Council until the UN Conference on International Organization in 1945. In the final negotiations, Churchill's government accepted a UN commitment to "self-government," but not "independence," of colonial peoples. During the remainder of his time in office, he rebuffed efforts by U.S. presidents Truman and Eisenhower to soften his position on this issue.

Joseph Stalin (1879–1953)

In documents revealing early talks about the new emerging international organization, Stalin sometimes appeared to be mystified.[10] In part, this mystification can be attributed to his quite different political and social background, as well as to his isolated personality and brutal style of rule.

Born to a peasant family in Gori, Georgia, Iosif Vissarionovich Dzhugashvili came to be known by his revolutionary pseudonym *Joseph Stalin*. Unlike Roosevelt and Churchill, he came from humble origins to lead one of the Big Three—the Communist Soviet Union—through World War II, establishing his country as one of the two superpowers at the conclusion of the war.

Attracted to Karl Marx's writings, Stalin joined the nascent Russian workers' movement at the turn of the century, and in 1903 he joined Vladimir Lenin's Bolshevik faction of the Russian Social Democratic Workers Party. He ascended to membership in the party's Central Committee and after the overthrow of the tsar in March 1917 he joined Lenin, Leon Trotsky, and a small group of Bolsheviks who ousted the provisional government in November (by the Western calendar at the time).

Stalin had not spent much time outside Russia before the revolution. He was parochial; he had no special oratorical skills or political following. His talents for organization, however, would serve him well, allowing him to defeat his rivals for power following Lenin's death in 1924. Two years earlier, he had been appointed the general secretary of the Central Committee, using the post to fill key bureaucratic positions with supporters and with others opposed to Trotsky, Stalin's chief competitor for leadership. Despite Lenin's admonition in his final testament that the Georgian could not be trusted to work well with other party leaders and should be removed as general secretary, Stalin managed to win the intraparty struggle for power and emerged as the uncontested leader of both the party and the state by 1929.

In the name of "socialism in one country," Stalin carried out the massive industrialization of the Soviet Union, the collectivization of agriculture, and the imposition of totalitarianism. Using the terror of the police state, he imposed centralized economic planning through "Five-Year Plans" that eliminated the vestiges of capitalism. Much of the hardship Stalin imposed—including the 1930s purges that wiped out Bolshevik revolutionary veterans, the high command of the Red Army, and millions of peasants as "enemies of the people"—was rationalized as the requirement of a socialist state facing inevitable future war with the imperialist capitalist states. The Soviet leader, now turned ardent Russian nationalist, saw the world divided into antagonistic ideological "camps," with the defense of the USSR dependent on the rapid development of the country and its military, the surreptitious encouragement of Communist parties in capitalist states, and the pursuit of a geopolitical, rather than a revolutionary, foreign policy.

The rise of Adolf Hitler in Germany in 1933 threatened Soviet security directly and led Stalin to ease his antipathy toward the capitalist countries. He sought and achieved U.S. recognition of the Soviet state. The USSR also joined the League of Nations. As the Nazi regime progressively violated the provisions of the Treaty of Versailles and moved against governments in Central and Eastern Europe, Stalin became convinced that Great Britain and France intended to goad Germany into a war with the Soviet Union. Particularly following the Western powers' appeasement of Hitler's demands on Czechoslovakia in 1938 (at the Munich Conference), Stalin concluded that an imperialist conspiracy was under way to destroy the socialist state through German aggression. Announcing that the Soviet Union would not be the country to "pull the chestnuts out of the fire" for Europe, Stalin secretly negotiated a nonaggression pact with the Third Reich.

Stalin was a powerbroker and realist. When Germany reneged on its agreement and invaded the Soviet Union in June 1941, the Soviet leader quickly forged an alliance with Great Britain, and after December 8, with the United States—not to create a new post-war global order as Churchill and Roosevelt had intimated in their 1941 Atlantic Charter, but to crush Germany and secure the future defense of the USSR through Soviet dominance of the region. The Soviet leader declined to attend early Allied summits, and his government played no role in initial planning for a post-war international organization. Only in the fall of 1943, following the August Quadrant Conference between Churchill and Roosevelt in Quebec, did Stalin receive from his allies a formal proposal for such an entity.

Knowing Stalin's incentive to join a post-war body would be the highest while the war was still under way, the allies presented the idea of general international organization at the Moscow Conference of Foreign Ministers in late October 1943. Only after U.S. Secretary of State Cordell Hull and his British counterpart agreed to open a second front from the West was Stalin ready to consider the proposal. Throughout the negotiations in Moscow and later, the Soviet Union focused on the implications of such a body for Soviet geopolitical concerns.

Stalin had his first opportunity to discuss the proposed organization with Roosevelt at the Teheran Conference, which was held November 27–December 1, 1943. The president described how the United States, the Soviet Union, the United Kingdom, and China would have sole authority to enforce the peace and prevent aggression. He also outlined the likely organs that would be part of the organization, including an executive council. Stalin, apprehensive that the council might limit Soviet actions, asked FDR whether the proposed body would be able to make decisions binding on the great powers. The president said it would not. The Soviet leader and his representatives would revisit this commitment by FDR many times during the next two years. By the end of the Moscow and Teheran meetings, however, Stalin indicated his willingness to support a post-war organization.

At the Dumbarton Oaks Conference in 1944, Stalin's representatives, led by Ambassador Andrei Gromyko, accepted nearly all the U.S. proposals for the expected Charter. Only on the matter of the veto in the Security Council did the Soviet delegation raise objections. As we noted before, the United States opposed the use of the veto by a permanent member to bar the council from hearing a dispute in which the member was involved. Yet, Stalin always saw this veto power as an essential protection for Soviet freedom of action. The matter would remain unresolved until the Yalta Conference five months later. At Yalta, a new matter, which Gromyko had raised at Dumbarton Oaks, would also have to be resolved. Faced with an organization that would have an overwhelmingly pro-American membership, Stalin sought to gain in effect sixteen votes for the Soviet Union by admitting each of the USSR's union republics to the world body as discrete members. The other participants (the United States, the United Kingdom, and China) found this proposal completely unacceptable. Roosevelt and Stalin would, nevertheless, also settle this issue at Yalta.

When the final summit among Churchill, Roosevelt, and Stalin convened at Yalta in February 1945, the most important concerns for Stalin were the political and military arrangements in post-war Eastern Europe and the disposition of defeated Germany. Instead of seeing collective security embodied in the United Nations as the formula for peace in the future, Stalin sought to protect his foreign policy options from any UN limitations. Only when matters concerning the future government of Poland and the occupation of Germany were resolved was he ready to make accommodations on the membership of the world body and the extent of the veto power. He reached a compromise with Roosevelt on the number of Soviet republics to be admitted—Byelorussia and Ukraine would be original members in addition to the USSR. He then conceded the position on when the veto could be used, agreeing that a permanent member could not block discussion of a dispute in which it was involved.

The Soviet Union served as a sponsor of the 1945 UN Conference on International Organization in San Francisco. Yet, it sought significant changes in the Charter on matters supposedly resolved earlier. Stalin's delegation once again challenged the veto limitations but eventually accepted the earlier-agreed-upon formula.

THREE WARTIME CONFERENCES

We next take a look at three specific, late wartime conferences, treating them in a chronological order. Two were important in crafting the United Nations (and were discussed briefly in the foregoing paragraphs), and the third introduced the post-war financial and trade regime we have today, albeit much evolved by circumstance and the formal decisions of the major financial powers.

Dumbarton Oaks Conference (August 21–October 7, 1944)

In 1944, two stages of diplomatic conversations took place in the elegant music room at **Dumbarton Oaks**, a nineteenth-century mansion in a bucolic wooded area of Georgetown in Washington, DC. (The mansion name derives from the Rock of Dumbarton in Scotland.) Representatives from the United States, the Soviet Union, and Great Britain met during the first stage and then Chinese envoys joined those from the United States and the United Kingdom. Negotiations at this conference clarified earlier wartime discussions on a new international organization and thus represented a key step on the way to establishing the United Nations.[11]

The conference gave rise to the Dumbarton Oaks Proposals for the Establishment of a General International Organization. These proposals were in the form of twelve "chapters" and were important for four reasons. First, the proposals spelled out a structure for the evolving international organization. Chapter IV listed the General Assembly, the Security Council, the International Court of Justice, and the Secretariat as the principal organs of the United Nations; Chapter IX called for the formation of the Economic and Social Council (ECOSOC), the functions of which would include the promotion of respect for human rights and fundamental freedoms. Second, the proposals assigned different responsibilities to each organ. Chapter VI gave the proposed Security Council responsibility for international peace and security, while Chapter V designated the General Assembly as the organ to be more involved in economic and social spheres and to supervise the overall operations of the organization. Third, Chapter III made membership open to "all peace-loving nations," which underscored what would become the principle of universal membership in a single organization—an idea that transcended the notion of dominant regional power arrangements like those broached earlier in wartime meetings. Fourth, the proposals articulated the idea that the permanent members of the Security Council—China, the United Kingdom, the United States, the USSR, and France (which was to become a permanent member "in due course," according to the language of the Dumbarton Oaks proposals)—should be able to veto any substantive (non-procedural) matters before the body.[12]

The Dumbarton Oaks proposals, like the UN Charter, did not use the term *veto*. Rather, Chapter VI noted that an affirmative vote of the council would require the "concurring votes of the permanent members." A negative vote by any of the permanent members would then mean the failure of a proposed resolution. Although this idea contains the meat of the veto as it is known today, the Dumbarton Oaks Conference did not bring finality to the issue of the veto. At the Yalta Conference, Roosevelt, Churchill, and Stalin took up the matter again, and it arose a final time in San Francisco in the spring. Ultimately, the permanent members did receive veto power in the UN Charter. Signifying the transitional nature of the Dumbarton Oaks proposals, the conferees appended a "Note" at the end of the chapters, explaining, "In addition to the question of voting procedure in the Security Council referred to in Chapter VI, several other questions are still under consideration." Thus, while the Dumbarton Oaks Conference represented a significant step, more work remained.

Yalta Conference (February 4–11, 1945)

Yalta, on the Crimea, was the site of the final meeting of the legendary Big Three personalities. There, at the Livadia Palace (built in 1911 as a summer residence for Tsar Nicholas II) overlooking the Black Sea harbor, the Allies resolved crucial post-war-era questions. These issues included arrangements for the occupation of Germany, for political settlements in East Asia and in liberated Eastern Europe, and for the organization and procedures of the United Nations. The three heads of government met daily, often with only translators present, and planned the final stages of the war while addressing a range of post-war policies. Despite important steps regarding the United Nations had been taken before the meeting at Yalta, various stumbling blocks still required resolution. In fact, Stalin had yet to consent fully to Soviet membership in the new organization.

At Yalta, the three leaders refined their understanding about the UN's structure and membership and set the date of the San Francisco organizing conference. The leaders agreed that the United Nations would include an International Court of Justice (as provided at Dumbarton Oaks) and determined, for the first time, to create a separate trusteeship system to succeed the League of Nations' mandate system.

The Big Three also agreed on a definition of "peace-loving" and therefore on which nations would join the United Nations as original members. Stalin had insisted that only nations currently at war with the Axis be admitted as founding members. Roosevelt, responding to the concerns of Latin American nations, secured the Soviet leader's agreement that nations not yet in the war could, by entering no later than March 1, be defined as "peace-loving" and thus become members. This agreement allowed Argentina and Chile to enter the new organization and set the stage for a united Latin American bloc in the United Nations.

An awkward disagreement about the voting power of the Big Three was also resolved at Yalta. The USSR had persistently sought votes for each of its Soviet republics, contending that the nations of the British Empire gave the United Kingdom control of multiple votes. Roosevelt sympathized with Stalin's concerns but insisted that to secure U.S. congressional agreement to this arrangement, he would need votes for each of the forty-eight U.S. states. Stalin backed down but insisted that in view of the huge wartime destruction in Ukraine and Byelorussia, those two states must become members. Roosevelt conceded this much, since with the inclusion of a substantial and assumed pro-U.S. Latin American contingent, plus the anticipated Western European support for the United States, Washington would appear to have an effective voting majority in the organization. In addition, Stalin finally acceded to some restrictions on the veto power in the Security Council. Retreating from his previous insistence on an absolute veto over all issues, he agreed that the veto would not apply to procedural matters and could not be invoked by a state that was a party to a dispute in order to prevent the Security Council from discussing the matter.

Roosevelt's apparent concessions on the use of the veto and on membership appear minor in retrospect. At that moment, he needed Soviet help for the continuing war in Asia. Roosevelt achieved Stalin's promise to enter the war against the Japanese and to recognize the pro-U.S. government of Chiang Kai-shek in China. Moreover, the United States conceivably benefited even more in terms of membership in the new organization by the decision at Yalta to allow all nations at war with Germany by March 1, 1945, to be original members. This decision resulted in the membership of several Latin American countries friendly to the United States. A pro-U.S. China and France joined the Soviet Union, the United States, and Great Britain as permanent members on the Security Council. However, probably most important, when Russia entered the U.S.-sponsored United Nations, it agreed to join an international organization that had the clear mark of an American enterprise, presided over by Roosevelt. Sitting in the well of the House of Representatives, Roosevelt reported to the legislators upon his return:

> [Yalta] ought to spell the end of the system of unilateral action, the exclusive alliances, the spheres of influence, the balances of power, and all the other expedients that have been tried for centuries—and have always failed. We propose to substitute for all these, a universal organization in which all peace-loving Nations will finally have a chance to join.[13]

Bretton Woods Conference (July 1–22, 1944)

In addition to addressing issues of peace and security, Allied leaders determined to forge international cooperation in financial and economic realms, believing that trade barriers, monetary manipulations, and practices of economic nationalism had been factors dragging the interwar world into dangerous clashes. As in the case of UN negotiations, Americans took a leadership role in these financial negotiations.

Photo 2.2 British Prime Minister Winston Churchill, U.S. President Franklin Roosevelt, and USSR Marshal Joseph Stalin (seated from left to right) meet at the Yalta Conference.

Source: The National Archives via Wiki Commons.

The UN Monetary and Financial Conference convened in **Bretton Woods**, New Hampshire, in summer 1944. The conference members drafted agreements establishing three institutions meant to create a post-war global free trade system: the International Monetary Fund (IMF), the International Bank for Reconstruction and Development (IBRD)—better known as the World Bank—and the General Agreement on Tariffs and Trade (GATT). The last of these was supposed to be an "interim" agreement until an International Trade Organization (ITO)—which would provide a more ambitious regulatory framework for world trade—could be established. GATT, however, remained in place until January 1, 1995, when it was superseded by the World Trade Organization (WTO).

Sponsored by the United States, the Bretton Woods Conference and its ensuing agreements attempted to create a new international monetary and trade regime that was stable and predictable. Negotiators structured the IMF to limit the fluctuation of foreign currency exchange rates while using the World Bank to pump needed capital investment into war-drained nations. The U.S. planners hoped to avoid the economic nationalism of the interwar years by gradually removing protectionist barriers to free trade. Through "rounds" of negotiation, GATT members eliminated tariffs, quotas, and other impediments to international commerce. The success of the measures initiated at Bretton Woods depended, however, on the willingness of the United States—whose economy in 1944 accounted for more than half of the world domestic product—to fund these institutions and to maintain monetary policies conducive to global economic growth.

One point worth noting is that the Bretton Woods meeting was held during the latter stages of World War II while negotiations on a draft charter for the United Nations proceeded. The Roosevelt administration saw these courses of action as complementary. At Bretton Woods, delegates undertook the launching of a post-war international framework that would avoid the instability that had followed World War I. Soon after the Bretton Woods institutions came into being, Washington pegged the dollar to gold at $35 an ounce, enacted large foreign aid programs to pump liquidity into the international economic system, and made the largest subscription of funds of any IBRD member to the assets of the World Bank.

The IMF and the IBRD both came into operating existence on December 27, 1945, when twenty-nine nations signed the IMF's Articles of Agreement that had been proposed at Bretton Woods, and twenty-one signed the IBRD's Articles of Agreement. By the end of the year, the World Bank had thirty members. GATT began operations when twenty-three countries signed the GATT treaty on April 10, 1947. Although independent institutions, these three Bretton Woods-initiated entities were considered part of the UN System.

UN CONFERENCE ON INTERNATIONAL ORGANIZATION (APRIL 25–JUNE 25, 1945)

You can find a considerable amount of literature on the Treaty of Westphalia, which concluded the Thirty Years' War in 1648; the Congress of Vienna, which brought an end to the Napoleonic imperial period in 1814–1815; or the Treaty of Versailles negotiations following World War I. Oddly, little information can be found on the conference that brought the United Nations to definitive birth, and, for at least a moment in mid-1945, engaged the world's attention. (Stephen Schlesinger's comprehensive study of the San Francisco conference is one of the exceptions. A full citation can be found at the end of this chapter.)

About 5,000 people descended on San Francisco for this historic meeting. Some 850 delegates from 50 countries, 2,600 members of the media, 1,000 public servants of the nascent UN Secretariat, 300 security personnel, 120 translators, 37 foreign ministers, and 5 prime ministers, plus an untold number of local citizens, attended.[14] The conference also witnessed cameo appearances by a number of the famous or near-famous, including a rookie journalist named John Kennedy, filmmaker Orson Welles, and future television host and historian Alistair Cooke. Yet, transcending the media hoopla at the gathering were the heroes (many were bipartisan Americans, reflecting the leadership role that the United States played in the whole enterprise). Russian-born Leo Pasvolsky's diligence in the State Department and at the conference was vital; Republican John Foster Dulles worked with Pasvolsky to resolve the most contentious challenges brought by, among others, smaller nations, as well as the Soviet Union. A central figure was the U.S. delegation chair and secretary of state Edward Stettinius, whose steady diplomacy, constant attention to untested President Truman, and sensitivity to others' views proved indispensable at a conference that without him may have collapsed.

The Charter's basics, formulated in the U.S. State Department, had undergone diplomatic refinement during wartime meetings. However, San Francisco represented a decisive moment when the entire UN enterprise could have miscarried over touchy issues such as the great-power veto, the seating of Argentina, the situation in Poland, and more. Energetic diplomacy was crucial to ensure success.

The official sponsors—the United States, the United Kingdom, the USSR, and China—convened the formally titled **United Nations Conference on International Organization (UNCIO)** in the recently refurbished San Francisco Opera House. The conference invited as participants the "peace-loving nations" that had declared war on the Axis powers by March 1, 1945. The purpose of UNCIO was to consider the proposals drafted at Dumbarton Oaks the previous fall. The meeting concluded its work on June 26, when fifty "original members" signed the Charter. Poland, not in attendance because of the ongoing dispute between the Soviet Union and the Western powers over the makeup of its government, signed the document later as the fifty-first member.

Although the Big Three had already agreed on important decisions about the workings of the new United Nations, the participation of many other nations, with their own interests, made the San Francisco Conference a complex exercise in multilateral diplomacy. The great powers were often required to make meaningful alterations in the proposed Charter to achieve the necessary votes for passage of its provisions. At the opening session, even the question of who could participate in the deliberations did not escape intense debate. Latin American nations (twenty-one of the participating fifty states) pressed for inclusion of Argentina in the conference, which both the United States and the Soviet Union opposed because of the Argentine government's friendly relations with the Axis powers during the war. The proposal to seat Argentina led to an angry counter request from Soviet Foreign Minister Vyacheslav I. Molotov that the Russian-backed Lublin government in Poland also be invited to participate, even though that government was not recognized by any Western state. He also reopened the matter of Byelorussia's and Ukraine's participation. Both were to be admitted to the United Nations under the terms of the Yalta agreement, but Washington had invited neither to San Francisco. After five days of argument, Byelorussia, Ukraine, and Argentina were admitted to the conference; Poland was not.

Plenary sessions of UNCIO were chaired on a rotating basis by the heads of the sponsoring countries' delegations—Stettinius (United States), Molotov (USSR), Foreign

---

IMPORTANT MOMENTS IN THE FOUNDING OF THE UNITED NATIONS

August 14, 1941   U.S. president Franklin Delano Roosevelt and Winston Churchill, the British prime minister, issue the Atlantic Charter.

January 1, 1942   Twenty-six nations issue the Declaration by United Nations.

October 30, 1943   The Moscow Conference of Foreign Ministers meets, and China, the USSR, the United States, and the United Kingdom agree on the need for a post-war international organization.

July 1–22, 1944   The UN Monetary and Financial Conference convenes at Bretton Woods, New Hampshire.

August 21–October 7, 1944   The Dumbarton Oaks Conference convenes the United States, Great Britain, the USSR, and China agree on the structure of the new United Nations.

February 4–11, 1945   The Yalta Conference convenes. The Big Three agree on the voting formula for the Security Council.

April 9–20, 1945   Jurists from forty-four nations meet to draft the Statute of the International Court of Justice.

April 25–June 25, 1945   The San Francisco Conference convenes. Fifty nations sign the UN Charter on June 26.

October 24, 1945   The UN Charter enters into force.

Secretary Anthony Eden (United Kingdom), and Premier T. V. Soong (China). Stettinius opened the conference as its temporary chairman, then chaired the Steering and Executive Committees, the most important bodies in the conference structure. The Steering Committee, comprising four sponsoring nations, decided important issues of policy and procedure. On April 27, it decided that the Dumbarton Oaks proposals and the supplementary decisions made at the Yalta Conference would serve as the agenda for the meeting. It also decided that decisions in all the working bodies dealing with the Charter draft must be made by a two-thirds majority. In so doing, the Steering Committee set aside the traditional rule of unanimity that had applied in diplomacy among sovereign states and had been the guiding principle during the drafting of the Covenant of the League of Nations. The Executive Committee, made up of the United States, the United Kingdom, the USSR, China, and ten additional states, made recommendations to the Steering Committee on critical and controversial topics. These structural and voting arrangements created a system of "parliamentary diplomacy" that gave smaller states a substantive role in the decision process at San Francisco.

The final drafting of the Charter was the responsibility of the Co-ordination Committee, chaired by Leo Pasvolsky. Recommended language for the Charter flowed into the Co-ordination Committee from four conference commissions and twelve technical

Photo 2.3 5 Soviet Foreign Minister Molotov (*wearing eyeglasses with no temples*), U.S. Secretary of State Stettinius (*center, holding pencil*), and British Foreign Secretary Eden (*sitting to Stettinius's left*) conferring in the San Francisco Opera House, where the UN Conference on International Organization was meeting on May 1, 1945.

Source: UN/DPI Photo/Rosenberg. Reproduced by permission from the United Nations.

committees. These bodies proposed dozens of amendments to the Dumbarton Oaks draft. Among their contributions was to elevate the Economic and Social Council and the Trusteeship Council to the status of principal organs of the United Nations, both of which would thus become coequal in the Charter with the General Assembly, Security Council, Secretariat, and International Court of Justice.

The success of the conference turned on the resolution of several touchy issues. The most serious were matters related to the enforcement organ of the United Nations—the Security Council. An evolution of President Roosevelt's Four Policemen concept, the proposed Security Council was made up of five permanent members and six nonpermanent members and was authorized to impose mandatory enforcement measures against an aggressor. Several proposals were put forward at San Francisco to ensure that the nonpermanent seats were filled by states from certain regions of the world, or by states capable of contributing to international peace and security. Middle powers particularly emphasized this last point. Canada sponsored a proposal to hold seats on the council only for states with the means to carry out enforcement responsibilities. India recommended that only states representing a significant proportion of the world's population be elected to the council. From the outset, Latin American representatives sought a greater role for Western Hemispheric states, including guaranteed representation on the Security Council. El Salvador recommended the addition of five more members to the council. Although the proposal gained support from small states in other regions, Brazil determined instead to seek a permanent seat on the Security Council for one Latin American country.

The sponsoring powers marshalled the votes to defeat all these proposals, successfully arguing that any attempt to alter the council's proposed composition would upset arduously worked out settlements and delay the establishment of the United Nations. They made known that any major change in the composition, powers, or responsibilities of the council would mean the end of great-power support for the organization. After intense negotiations among the four powers, the Steering Committee proposed language for the qualifications for election to the council that mollified some of the delegations. According to the draft, nonpermanent members would be elected by the General Assembly

> [with] due regard being specially paid, in the first instance to the contribution of Members of the United Nations to the maintenance of international peace and security and to the other purposes of the Organization, and also to equitable geographical distribution.[15]

Separate from the matter of council membership was the ongoing debate about the veto retained by the permanent members. Early in the conference, the Soviet delegation resurrected Stalin's persistent demand for an absolute veto on *all* matters (procedural and substantive) before the council, contrary to his commitment at Yalta that procedural matters could be decided by an affirmative vote of seven council members and that the veto would not be allowed. He had also accepted the U.S. position that when permanent members were parties to a dispute, they could not veto a discussion of the dispute. To convince Stalin of America's resolve on this issue, President Truman sent a special envoy (former FDR confidant Harry Hopkins) to Moscow to explain that the Charter would not pass the U.S. Senate on the terms proposed by the Soviet Union. Stalin backed down and directed his delegation to accept the Yalta formula.[16]

The veto issue highlighted one general concern of smaller states at the conference: that the predominance of the great powers' control over peace and security issues would denigrate their role within the organization, diminish the competence of the General Assembly, and demote other purposes dear to weaker powers. For Latin American states in particular, one concern was that the use of the veto could limit the region's ability to deal with hemispheric threats. A long history of cooperation in the Pan-American Union led hemispheric leaders to seek a major role for regional organizations on security matters, and greater autonomy from Security Council intervention. The U.S. delegation, however, feared that public support and U.S. Senate approval would be lost if the Security Council was not given absolute authority to address all threats to the peace. Facing an impasse, the United States orchestrated a compromise that recognized the authority of "regional arrangements" to manage local or regional affairs, provided their activities were "consistent with the Purposes and Principles of the United Nations" (Chapter VIII, Article 52). In addition, under Article 51 states were permitted to undertake "collective self-defense" until the Security Council had taken sufficient steps to restore peace. The new wording in the Charter, however, limited this grant of autonomy by asserting the right of the council to investigate and take action on any threat to the peace. It also allowed any state to bring any dispute directly to the council.

Also in response to small-state concerns, the competence of the General Assembly was expanded during the San Francisco negotiations. It was given control of the UN budget. The conference as well agreed that the assembly could discuss any issue, including security concerns and threats to the peace, at least until the Security Council was "seized" with the issue. Furthermore, the Secretary-General, elected by the General Assembly, would be able to bring any matter that he or she believed threatened international peace and security to the council's attention (Article 99).

States from Latin America, Africa, and Asia envisioned an institution of universal membership with extensive activities in the economic, cultural, and human rights domains, acting beyond the initial security concerns of the great powers. In particular, they pressed for a UN role in the achievement of "independence" for existing colonial possessions. President Truman was likewise deeply concerned about the projected duties of the United Nations in the newly liberated territories of the enemy states and in the old colonial empires of the European powers. On this matter, he found Churchill adamant in opposing any structure that might endanger the British Empire. So, too, the French delegation opposed Charter provisions that might limit France's policies in Indochina and Africa. During the Yalta meeting, the Americans had devised a formulation that was acceptable to the British by limiting the jurisdiction of the UN's trusteeship system to territories still held under the League's mandate system, territories detached from the enemy states during World War II, and "territories voluntarily placed under the system by states responsible for their administration." This solution, however, had the unintended consequence of raising concerns by Syria and other former mandate regions that were independent states in the spring of 1945. The formulation could be interpreted to allow renewed administration by outside powers. Article 78 was added to the Charter to exclude this possibility by prohibiting the application of the trusteeship system to territories that had become UN members.

The more serious trusteeship challenge came from the states at San Francisco that wanted a Charter commitment to full independence and decolonization. Led by Carlos Romulo of the Philippine delegation, small states urged much stronger commitments in policy and structure on the question of ending imperial control. In the lengthy negotiations that ensued, the British and the French made clear that no reference to "independence" would be allowed in the Charter. Nevertheless, the sponsoring powers did accept a commitment to "self-government" and took the unusual step of allowing the placement of the Declaration Regarding Non-Self-Governing Territories into the Charter text (Chapter XI). The declaration called on administering states "to assist [these territories] in the progressive development of their free political institutions."

Even the United States, which generally supported a trusteeship system dedicated to ending colonial control, sought and obtained a limitation of the Trusteeship Council's authority with regard to "strategic" trust territories. As the U.S. armed forces liberated important Pacific islands from Japanese control toward the end of the war, the military expressed concern with plans to have the United Nations take these holdings into the trusteeship system. Shortly before his death, President Roosevelt approved dividing designated trusteeship areas into "strategic" and "nonstrategic" territories and limiting the role of the Trusteeship Council in the former areas. This step was accomplished in Articles 82 and 83, which allowed administering states to declare specific areas as "strategic" territories, then made those areas subject to the Security Council, where the United States had the veto.

Shortly before convening in San Francisco, Latin American governments met with a U.S. delegation in Mexico City. There they endorsed an enlarged role for the United Nations in social, economic, and human rights cooperation. At the San Francisco Conference, they were joined by other states on the Economic and Social Co-operation Committee in passing broadened objectives for the United Nations in these areas. The committee recommended that the new organization promote "universal respect for, and observance of, human rights and fundamental freedoms for all without distinction as to race, sex, language or religion." The U.S. planners had earlier pushed for Charter provisions on human rights, but other participants at Dumbarton Oaks had rebuffed these efforts. At San Francisco, many proposals were made to incorporate the "protection" of human rights into the Charter obligations of the organization.

Much discussion, diligently covered by the media, centered on establishing in the Charter a Commission on Human Rights. Time constraints made drafting a Bill of Human Rights for Charter inclusion impossible. However, a desire to meet public expectations for action in this area after the horrors of the Holocaust, and strong endorsement from a majority of the delegations, persuaded the sponsoring powers to agree to Article 68, authorizing ECOSOC to set up commissions "in economic and social fields and for the promotion of human rights." Thus, a consequence of the deliberations was that ECOSOC, in February 1946, established the Commission on Human Rights, which proceeded, under Eleanor Roosevelt's leadership, to draft the Universal Declaration of Human Rights.

On June 25, two months to the day after the conference opened, the delegates to UNCIO adopted the Charter. The minutes of the session recorded, "At this point, the delegates and the entire audience rose and cheered." The following day, President Truman addressed the closing session and congratulated the delegates on fulfilling their roles as, what he described two months earlier, "architects of a better world ... a new world in which the eternal dignity of man is respected."

ELEANOR'S UN: BEYOND INTERNATIONAL PEACE AND SECURITY

As we just pointed out, smaller nations attending the San Francisco Conference, along with the United States, pressed for Charter commitments on decolonization, economic and social issues, and human rights. As a result of a serendipitous decision by the U.S. government, which was seeking to build public support for the United Nations, several unofficial "consultants" and other observers were invited to the San Francisco meeting and allowed to sit in on working sessions. These groups included representatives from the Council on Foreign Relations, the National Association for the Advancement of Colored People, the Catholic Welfare Conference, the National Education Association, the Congress of Industrial Organizations, and many more. Under the influence of these numerous organizations, the U.S. delegation acceded to Charter language regarding education, human rights, and the formal recognition of the consultative role of nongovernmental organizations (NGOs) at the United Nations. Article 71 led to the enduring collaboration between NGOs and the United Nations.[17] References to "education" and "human rights" appear early in the Charter (Article 13, paragraph 1b), and these words are sprinkled throughout the document. In addition, provisions empowering ECOSOC to make use of "specialized agencies" (Articles 57, 62, 64, and 67) augured a future of activities in the large province of economic, social, educational, and human rights policy.

This expanded thrust for the new organization was closely associated in its formative years with the work of Eleanor Roosevelt, the former first lady of the United States. Mrs. Roosevelt lived a long and fruitful life (1884–1962). Considered one of the most influential presidential spouses in U.S. history, she outlived her husband, Franklin Delano Roosevelt, by seventeen years, and during that time she served spiritedly in a number of important public service posts. In 1962, President John F. Kennedy appointed her to the first U.S. Commission on the Status of Women, and both presidents Truman and Kennedy made her a U.S. ambassador to the United Nations.

First appointed to a UN post by President Truman, Mrs. Roosevelt served from 1945 to 1953 and treasured her service at the United Nations, believing that forceful labors by dedicated and talented people from throughout the world were needed to launch this new organization that her late husband had envisaged. She once said of the United Nations that it was "a bridge upon which we can meet and talk."[18] Her prestige and personal qualities were key factors in developing the Universal Declaration of Human Rights. As she served, first as a U.S. representative on the General Assembly Third Committee and then as chair of the Commission on Human Rights, she became friends with, and was considered a leader by, some of the most significant thinkers and diplomats of the postwar period.

In early 1946, the newly formed ECOSOC asked her to serve on a "nuclear" commission that was to make recommendations regarding a permanent commission on human rights. This small committee convened at Hunter College in New York City that spring, where its first act was to elect Mrs. Roosevelt as its chair. The most important recommendation forwarded by this small committee was that the proposed Human Rights Commission write a bill of human rights. From the establishment of the commission in June 1946 until December 10, 1948, when the General Assembly approved the Universal Declaration of Human Rights, Mrs. Roosevelt was consumed with guiding the intricate negotiations and seeking broad public support for a UN role in nonsecurity issues. She convinced a reluctant U.S. State Department to accede to the inclusion in the declaration of social and economic rights along with more traditional political and civil rights. With skilled diplomacy, she encouraged and cajoled powerful individuals from different philosophical and political backgrounds to come together and agree on the final composition of the document.

Her success warrants even more approbation when considering the environment in which she worked. Representatives from the Western nations; from the Soviet bloc; from Latin America; from the developing world; and from Christian, Islamic, Hindu, Buddhist, Confucianist, and secular traditions all converged to discuss a "universal" statement on rights. This discussion took place as the world plunged into new and difficult divisions caused by the onset of the Cold War, serious divisions in South Asia as India and Pakistan gained independence, and the intractable dispute initiated with the partition of Palestine. Moreover, Mrs. Roosevelt had to guide the document through a drafting committee and the full commission, where serious disagreement occurred over the type of document to recommend to the General Assembly. Several small states wanted a binding covenant with methods of implementation. Others, particularly the great powers, wanted a nonbinding, vague declaration. The Soviet Union wanted no document at all.

Mrs. Roosevelt endorsed a process that divided the commission into three working groups. She chaired the First Working Group, which proceeded to draft a declaration with the persuasive "moral value" of past momentous proclamations, such as the U.S. Declaration of Independence and the French Declaration of the Rights of Man and Citizen. The other working groups focused on drafting binding covenants and implementation procedures. Having crafted the Universal Declaration of Human Rights through this procedure, Roosevelt then shepherded it through the debate in the Third Committee of the General Assembly (where each of the thirty articles was thrashed out in detail) and before the General Assembly. In the end, the declaration passed without a negative vote. The final tally was forty-eight in favor, eight abstentions (Saudi Arabia and seven nations from the Soviet bloc), and none opposed. The president of the General Assembly, Herbert Evatt, closed the session with a tribute to Eleanor Roosevelt:

> It is particularly fitting that there should be present on this occasion the person who, with the assistance of many others, has played a leading role in the work, a person who has raised to greater heights even so great a name—Mrs. Roosevelt, the representative of the United States of America.[19]

The economic, social, and humanitarian tasks assigned by the Charter to the fledgling United Nations were perceived in the late 1940s as peripheral matters to the organization's central role in keeping the peace. However, as Cold War politics increasingly paralyzed the world body, deadlocking the Security Council, and as UN membership grew during the next two decades to include states from the developing world, the United Nations found itself more often addressing the problems of human existence and social development that were of deep concern to Mrs. Roosevelt and her colleagues. With the close of the Cold War in the late 1980s, the agenda of **Eleanor's UN** moved center stage, even within the Security Council and the global security strategies of the great powers. States recognized that the extraordinary human problems facing large portions of the world's population raised the real specter of global instability and regional war. In a number of ways, Eleanor's UN—in terms of both issues and UN policy making—became the bedrock of the "new" United Nations we describe in this text.

Specialized Agencies and Eleanor's UN

Since 1945, the extensive activities of UN-related specialized agencies and nongovernmental organizations (NGOs) have furthered the more sprawling view of UN responsibilities suggested by Eleanor Roosevelt's diplomatic career. Article 57 of the UN Charter describes specialized agencies as separately chartered, independent organizations "having wide international responsibilities ... in economic, cultural, educational, health and related fields." Each deals with a particular issue or problem that the international community has identified as requiring action or regulation. Some specialized agencies, such as the Universal Postal Union, date from the nineteenth century; others were established by the League of Nations and later adopted by the United Nations. Most have been created since 1945, often urged into existence by the United Nations or by conferences it sponsored. Articles 63 and 64 of the Charter authorize ECOSOC to coordinate their work. By 2021, seventeen specialized agencies were in operation. Their activities spanned a wide swath of topical areas, from international finance (the World Bank Group and the IMF) to the kinds of issues (education, development, and human rights) that attracted the attention of Mrs. Roosevelt and others of her perspective at the commencement of the United Nations. Since the end of World War II, these UN-related agencies have carried forward mandates exterior to the more traditional concerns of maintaining peace and security. (Specialized agencies are covered in detail in Chapter 4.)

Nongovernmental Organizations, Civil Society, and Eleanor's UN

Also advancing an agenda outside traditional international diplomacy have been the NGOs provided for in the UN System in Article 71 of the Charter. An NGO is any non-profit, voluntary citizens' group. It may be organized on a local, a national, or an inter-national level. Most are organized with specific issues in mind, such as human rights, environmental improvement, educational reform, women's or children's rights, labor con-ditions, health concerns, and more. Some of the best known are Amnesty International, Human Rights Watch, and the World Wildlife Fund. Other examples of NGOs are the World Young Women's Christian Association (with interest in children's and women's rights), the Institute of World Affairs (dedicated to conflict resolution), the Franklin and Eleanor Roosevelt Institute (promoting education), the National Collegiate Conference Association (which holds the largest collegiate simulation of the United Nations—the National Model United Nations—at the New York headquarters), and the International Campaign to Ban Landmines. A full discussion of the role of NGOs in contemporary UN affairs can be found in Chapter 7.

According to Article 71 of the UN Charter, NGOs may attain consultative status with the Economic and Social Council. ECOSOC Resolution 31, passed in 1996, granted an expanded role to qualifying NGOs, allowing them to serve as technical experts, advis-ers, and consultants to governments and to the Secretariat. Qualifying NGOs are often invited to attend UN conferences, General Assembly special sessions, and other interna-tional meetings. The statistics on NGOs granted consultative status are telling: 41 in 1948; 377 in 1968; 1,200 in 1997; 2,200 in 2003; and 4,360 in 2014. By summer 2021, more than 5,500 NGOs had obtained consultative status, and, in a clear reflection of the "new" UN direction represented by these organizations, about 400 were accredited to an important subsidiary body of ECOSOC—the Commission on Sustainable Development. Some UN agencies actually require NGO consultation in their deliberations. The Joint UN Pro-gramme on HIV/AIDS (UNAIDS) was the first UN body to welcome NGO representa-tives to full membership on its coordinating board.

Although Article 71 links NGOs to only the Economic and Social Council, other prin-cipal UN organs, and most specialized agencies, have followed the pattern ECOSOC established and have created consultative status for relevant private groups. Among the agencies to have done so are the International Labour Organization (ILO), the UN Conference on Trade and Development (UNCTAD), the World Intellectual Property Organization (WIPO), the International Telecommunication Union (ITU), the World Health Organization (WHO), the Food and Agriculture Organization (FAO), and the International Maritime Organization (IMO).

Millennium Development Goals and Eleanor's UN

We should not leave the topic of Eleanor's UN without a look at the outcome of the Millennium Summit held at UN headquarters in New York in the fall of 2000. This meet-ing, which attracted the most prominent world leaders, concluded with the unanimous adoption of a list of goals that the representatives intended to be met by 2015. While the eight goals were general in tone, they represented a statement of "new," or "Eleanor," UN ambitions:

- Eradicate extreme poverty and hunger.
- chieve universal primary education.
- Promote global equality and empower women.
- Reduce child malnutrition.
- Improve maternal health.
- Combat HIV/AIDS, malaria, and other diseases.
- Ensure environmental sustainability.
- Develop a global partnership for development.

These eight goals, accepted by all members of the United Nations in 2000, expanded considerably on the defined goals that the UN's founders anticipated for the organization they created at the end of the most destructive war in history. By the turn of the twenty-first century, the United Nations certainly continued to be burdened with pursuing the aims of the "old," or original, United Nations, but it had also taken on the much more expansive aspirations Eleanor Roosevelt had articulated.

In 2015, the date targeted for attainment of the Millennium Development Goals (MDGs), the United Nations issued a report on the goals' progress.[20] *The Millennium Development Goals Report 2015* acknowledged that shortfalls remained in realizing all of the 2000 goals' particulars. However, the MDGs had, according to the report, "produced the most successful anti-poverty movement in history," and served as a stimulus for a new sustainable development agenda that was adopted later in 2015. Secretary-General Ban Ki-moon said that "Following profound and consistent gains, we now know that extreme poverty can be eradicated within one more generation ... [particularly if] governments, business and civil society can work together to achieve transformational breakthroughs."

Specifically, as the report noted, extreme poverty had declined by more than half, falling from 1.9 billion in 1990 to 836 million in 2015. More girls were in school, and women had gained considerable ground in parliamentary representation in nearly 90 percent of the 174 countries with data. The rate of child deaths before the fifth birthday had declined by more than half, and the maternity mortality ratio had gone down 45 percent worldwide, with most of the progress recorded since 2000. At the same time, targeted investments in combating diseases such as HIV/AIDS and malaria and in improving sanitation—meeting MDG aspirations—had brought unprecedented positive results. Still, the report pointed out, progress had been uneven, inequalities persisted in parts of the world, and civil conflict remained the chief impediment to more substantial progress.

The year of the MDGs report—2015—witnessed the UN launching an even more ambitious project: on September 25 of that year, the General Assembly adopted Resolution 70/1, inaugurating the "2030 Agenda for Sustainable Development." The UN intended that seventeen new, even more expansive, goals now supplement the MDGs. The UN's 2020 Report for the Sustainable Development Goals (SDGs) noted that progress had been made in improving maternal and child health, expanding access to electricity, and increasing women's representation in government. Yet, the COVID-19 pandemic had caused unexpected disruption to SDG progress, and the world's poorest and most vulnerable were affected the most.[21] Among the seventeen SDG goals, number thirteen, "Climate Action," seemed to be among the most pressing by 2122. The SDGs will be discussed thoroughly in Chapter 8 (as will the preceding MDGs). Suffice it to say at this point that Eleanor's UN is at the forefront of global practice and strategy.

THE COLD WAR

Unfortunately, the hopes of both the UN's originators and its innovators of the mid-1940s received an early and unwelcome setback at the end of the decade, as, concurrent with the debut of the United Nations, the world descended into something called a **Cold War** that would hamper the anticipated functioning of the new organization. This term refers to the U.S.-USSR rivalry following World War II that lasted until about 1991. The two "superpowers," as they became known, engaged in a global competition with political, military, economic, ideological, and diplomatic dimensions that persisted as a "cold" confrontation, always with the potential to turn into a "hot," or shooting, war. Each side attracted allies, and the contest came to be seen as a struggle between the "West" (the United States and its allies) and the "East" (the Soviet Union and its allies). Other nations, declining to join either side, began calling themselves "non-aligned." Because the Cold War shaped the global environment into a sharply divided "bipolar" arrangement, it significantly influenced the function and development of the United Nations. It differed sharply from earlier great-power conflicts in its intense ideological struggle, with single-party Communism on the one side and democracy and capitalism on the other, and further manifested itself in a conventional arms race as well as massive stockpiling of weapons of mass destruction (WMDs; nuclear, biological, and chemical) by both sides. The rivalry was also waged within the United Nations.

Because of the existence of the veto, the success of the organization seemed to depend in the beginning on continuing the wartime cooperation among the permanent Security Council members. However, this apparent necessity evaporated as the United States disputed Soviet plans to impose a *cordon sanitaire*, or buffer zone, in Eastern Europe to defend against any future attack from Western European nations. Washington, instead, favored open, multiparty states and market economies in the center of Europe. Stalin, paranoid that U.S. insistence would result in anti-Soviet regimes at his border, reimposed iron-fisted control at home, subverted the provisional coalition governments in Eastern Europe, supported Communist movements in Greece and Turkey (though he later relented), hesitated in removing Soviet troops from Iran and Austria (but, under Western pressure, eventually did), raided Russia's occupation zone in East Germany for industrial resources and personnel, and declined participation in the Marshall Plan. U.S.-Soviet cooperation turned to rivalry and hostile suspicion.

The United States declared its plan to "contain" Communism until the Soviet dictatorship would be forced to collapse or change, a policy recommended by diplomat George Kennan and initiated by President Truman. Containment became the main aim of both the Truman Doctrine (1947) and the rebuilding of former World War II foes by means of the Marshall Plan (1947), and it found expression in military alliances, such as the North Atlantic Treaty Organization (NATO), initiated in 1949. The United States blocked the admission of pro-Soviet applicants to the United Nations, such as Albania, Bulgaria, Hungary, and Romania, and maintained that the Republic of China, seated in Taiwan—not the Communist regime in Beijing—was the "legitimate" representative of the Chinese people at the United Nations. Meanwhile, the USSR objected to the admission of pro-Western countries such as Austria, Italy, Ireland, and Japan. This deadlock was broken only in 1955, when several nation-states from each rival bloc were admitted to the organization. However, mainland China was not admitted until sixteen years later.

The Cold War competition affected the working of the Security Council most intensely, beginning with its first session in 1946, which was called to address the failure of the USSR to remove its troops from Iran. During World War II, both Great Britain and the Soviet Union had stationed troops in Iran to guard against a Nazi seizure of oil resources located there; British troops had withdrawn from the country, complying with an agreement with Stalin who, nonetheless, then refused to pull out Red Army forces occupying northern Iran. The Security Council struggled to find a viable role in mediating the conflict consistent with its charge in the Charter to "maintain international peace and security, and to that end: to take effective collective measures for the prevention and removal of threats to the peace" (Article 1). However, since the Cold War had divided the UN members into competitive "East" and "West" camps, authentic collective action on Iran became impossible. In the end, only the threat of U.S. military action convinced Stalin to withdraw his forces. Because of the ideological divide and the superpower veto in later years, the Security Council was constrained from taking up serious matters such as the French, and then the U.S., intrusions in Vietnam (1947–1974) and the Soviet dispatch of troops and tanks to Hungary (1956) and Czechoslovakia (1968) to suppress anti-Communist movements. Nor did the Soviets or Americans participate with significant troop deployments to UN peacekeeping operations.

Korea

Stalin used the veto regularly to block Western initiatives. Going even further, when Mao Zedong's revolutionary forces secured power in China in 1949, Stalin ordered a boycott of the Security Council to protest rejection of the Communist regime's taking the seat held by the Nationalist Chinese government. Shortly thereafter, Stalin gave his approval to a North Korean invasion of South Korea, which triggered a UN decision to use force to repel the attack. In June 1950, the Soviet leader found himself, by means of a surrogate, at war with the United Nations. When the Soviet delegate returned to the Security Council to block any further UN actions in Korea, the United States circumvented the council by pushing through the General Assembly the Uniting for Peace Resolution, which allowed the assembly to make recommendations on the restoration of peace and security when the council was deadlocked by the veto. (See Chapter 5 for a complete discussion of the resolution.) Stalin's government protested the maneuver as an unconstitutional revision of the Charter.

   Korea was a prime early indication of the impact of the Cold War on the United Nations. When Japan surrendered in 1945, which ended World War II, both U.S. and Soviet military forces occupied parts of the formerly Japanese-dominated Korean peninsula. By agreement, the United States established a post-war occupation zone in the south, and the USSR controlled the north. The General Assembly had first considered the question of Korea at its session in 1947, with unsuccessful efforts to reestablish a unified country through elections. By 1948, two competing countries came into being, divided at the thirty-eighth parallel. The assembly called for the withdrawal of all foreign troops and established the UN Temporary Commission on Korea (UNTCOK). When, in June 1950, North Korean troops invaded the south, the Security Council, with staunch U.S. encouragement, recommended that member states furnish assistance to repel the attack. The UN Command in Korea (UNC) carried the UN flag, although it was not a UN peacekeeping operation under the Secretary-General, but, in fact, a unified force under U.S. command. The Soviet Union declared the council's action illegal because it was adopted without the presence of two permanent members (the USSR and China). Moscow refused to provide any assessed funding for the operation, and, by all accounts, supported the North Koreans during the conflict. The UN military operations became, in the eyes of the Russians, U.S. warfare against an ally, and a demonstration of the unwelcome control of the organization by their Cold War enemy. Troops from the People's Republic of China (PRC) also entered the war as allies of the North Koreans, and Americans (under a UN flag) found themselves in direct combat with these Chinese forces. Thus, the Korean War came to be seen as a "hot" war within the larger context of the global Cold War. Fighting ended with an armistice in 1953, but the country remained—into the twenty-first century, long after the end of the Cold War—the last divided country dating from the end of World War II.

Nuclear Weapons

One of Stalin's great concerns was the U.S. nuclear monopoly, maintained directly after the war. He had ordered the secret and rapid development of a Soviet atomic capability, but until a Soviet arsenal could be advanced, the USSR was at a disadvantage in the Cold War contest. At the United Nations, Stalin used disarmament talks to criticize U.S. nuclear intentions and policies and to call for large cuts in the U.S. stockpiles. When the United States put forward the Baruch Plan in the UN Atomic Energy Commission in June 1946, calling for the creation of an International Atomic Development Authority (IADA) that would own and manage all aspects of atomic energy "potentially dangerous to world security," the Soviets rejected it as a clumsy move made to maintain the U.S. monopoly. The commission suspended its meetings on July 29, 1947, because of the deadlock between the United States and the Soviet Union. No further serious U.S.-Soviet disarmament discussions would occur until after Stalin's death. Then, when the UN disarmament negotiations revived in the 1950s and 1960s—as described in Chapter 5—the most serious arms control issues were discussed bilaterally between the superpowers, which left secondary disarmament efforts to the multilateral UN machinery.

Persisting Tensions

Events from 1945 to 1953 in the United Nations reinforced Stalin's theory of international politics. He berated the institution and its first Secretary-General, **Trygve Lie**, as tools of U.S. anti-Soviet policy. He responded largely by closing off the Soviet world behind what Winston Churchill in 1947 called an *Iron Curtain*. Within the Eastern European bloc, the USSR sustained Stalinist regimes, and in the Soviet Union the effort to root out bourgeois and capitalist influences was renewed. A cult of personality, which had begun during the terror of the 1930s, returned with new enthusiasm. In 1955, to counter NATO, Stalin's successor, Nikita Khrushchev, engineered an alliance—the Warsaw Pact—with the satellite states.

Stalin died on March 5, 1953. Despite initial hopes for a thaw as Dwight Eisenhower and Nikita Khrushchev assumed control of their respective governments, Cold War tensions persisted. During the early days of President Eisenhower's administration, Secretary-General Trygve Lie, under pressure from Washington, allowed the Federal Bureau of Investigation (FBI) to fingerprint and question all the U.S. employees of the United Nations. McCarthy-era suspicions that Communist sympathizers had infiltrated the UN headquarters led to the investigation. The practice continued until November 1953, when the new Secretary-General, **Dag Hammarskjöld**, ordered the FBI to end it. The U.S. government then established the International Organizations Employees Loyalty Board to investigate all the U.S. employees at the United Nations. Among those scrutinized was the highly respected Ralph Bunche, a senior member of the Secretariat.

Despite these political attacks on the institution, the United States took several Cold War disputes to the United Nations during the Eisenhower presidency, or used the institution as a setting for propagandistic debates with the USSR. The Middle East Crisis of 1956 and the diplomatic promotion of Eisenhower's Open Skies Proposal for limiting weapons development were cases in point. (You can find extensive coverage of these events in Chapter 5.) Then, in 1960, U.S. spy planes (a U-2 surveillance craft piloted by Francis Gary Powers and an RB-47 lost over the Arctic) were shot down over Soviet territory, which sent the Cold War into a deep freeze. Each side proceeded to use the United Nations for bombastic speeches about the perfidy of its opponent. Soviet leader Khrushchev appeared at that year's General Assembly session, where he banged his shoe on a desk to protest Western treachery, while in the Security Council, U.S. Ambassador Henry Cabot Lodge, Jr. accused the Russians of planting secret microphones in the U.S. embassy in Moscow. Television viewers were entranced. Non-aligned nations decried the inability of the United Nations to meet their needs or temper the contest between Moscow and Washington.

The Congo crisis of the early 1960s further underscored the challenge of the Cold War to the United Nations. When the Congo became independent from Belgium in 1960, a complicated civil war broke out, in which one side was supported by the Soviet Union, one side was supported by Washington, and a third side was trying to secede. In the confusion, Secretary-General Dag Hammarskjöld tried to insert a UN presence to bring the disorder to an end. Believing Hammarskjöld to be carrying out the wishes of the United States and its Cold War partners in the West, the Soviet Union demanded a reorganization of the Office of Secretary-General that would involve replacing the single secretary with a **troika**—a three-person executive with equal representation from the Western bloc, the Eastern bloc, and the neutral countries in the United Nations. The Soviets, along with the French, also refused to donate their assessment for the Congo operation, claiming it to be illegal because the Security Council had not approved it. Their refusal to pay contributed to a serious financial crisis for the United Nations that would plague the organization for the rest of the century.

Deflecting the Soviet challenge, Hammarskjöld persisted in his efforts, in the event dying in a plane crash in a remote part of Northern Rhodesia (now Zambia). The Congo dissolution persisted into the middle of the decade, after which the country was kept together but was left with an unsatisfactory dictatorship. The center of Africa continued to be a place where Cold War differences disrupted any UN attempts at resolution. The UN efforts in the Congo and elsewhere raised serious questions about the efficacy of UN peacekeeping, particularly in the era of Cold War tension. Meanwhile, the Soviet troika proposal languished as U Thant of Burma succeeded the deceased Hammarskjöld as the Secretary-General. In the wake of the Congolese fiasco, the Secretariat and the organization as a whole confronted new criticisms from its powerful member states.

Perhaps the most dangerous encounter between the superpower rivals occurred during the Cuban Missile Crisis in 1962. In October of that year, U.S. intelligence discovered that the Soviet Union was placing in Cuba intermediate-range missiles capable of carrying nuclear weapons. The Kennedy administration challenged the Soviets to remove the missiles under a clear threat of military action against Cuba and, of necessity, against the Soviet Union. Adlai Stevenson, the U.S. ambassador to the United Nations, argued with vigor the U.S. position in the Security Council and worked in private with Secretary-General U Thant in an effort to craft a liaison role for the Secretary-General in ending the crisis. Soviet leader Khrushchev also suggested using the Secretary-General as intermediary. The U.S. administration, imposing a naval quarantine on Cuba, hoped to incorporate the United Nations into its efforts to avoid war while ensuring the removal of the missiles. Meanwhile, urgent secret negotiations transpired in New York and in Washington to defuse the crisis. However, the final resolution resulted from direct U.S.-Soviet negotiations, with almost no UN participation. By the end of October, the Russians agreed to remove the weapons, and the United States, in response, was poised to dismantle its nuclear weapons in Turkey. The incident seemed to have a deep impact on the rival leaders in the Cold War—President Kennedy and Soviet leader Khrushchev—who, in mid-1963, agreed to sign a nuclear test ban treaty.

Following the Cuban Missile Crisis, relations between the Cold War adversaries never reached such dire peril again, but within the United Nations the competition continued to have an effect. Each side was interested in using the United Nations to criticize the other in its foreign adventures—the United States in Vietnam, the Soviets in Afghanistan. The United Nations had virtually no impact on the U.S. involvement in Southeast Asia, but the United States and its allies were able to gain resolutions in the General Assembly criticizing the Russian involvement in Afghanistan.

In 1971, the United States witnessed an embarrassing reversal of its Cold War China policy when, by an overwhelming vote in the General Assembly, the government in Beijing replaced the Republic of China in the organization, becoming an official permanent Security Council member. At first, the United States had used its overwhelming support in the General Assembly to keep the seat for the government in Taiwan. Then, as the majority in the assembly shifted during the 1960s, Washington used the tactic of making any motion to replace Taiwan with a delegation from the PRC an "Important Question." Under the Charter, Important Questions require a two-thirds majority to pass in the assembly. This strategy worked until 1971, when supporters of the PRC surmounted the two-thirds threshold, and the assembly not only seated Mao Zedong's government, but also humiliated the United States by removing Taiwan from the world body.

The international events that appeared on the front pages of major newspapers during the 1970s and 1980s rarely referenced the United Nations. In Vietnam, Afghanistan, Central America, and the Middle East, the Cold War competitors frequently acted outside the framework of the world organization. On a few occasions, however, the United Nations was called into a major crisis. In 1967, the Security Council found itself sufficiently unified, despite the Cold War, to pass Resolution 242, which became the legal basis of a future settlement of the Israeli-Palestinian standoff. Again, in 1973, the Security Council supplemented the earlier action with Resolution 338, reaffirming the essential principles of Resolution 242. (These Middle Eastern events are covered fully in Chapter 5.)

Waning of the Cold War

The 1980s witnessed the depths of U.S. Cold War animosity toward the United Nations, followed by the first glimmer of a new respect for, and even co-option of, the world body. President Ronald Reagan withdrew the United States from the UN Educational, Scientific and Cultural Organization, which the administration accused of being too politicized. The U.S. withdrawal was a part of a general conservative attack on the United Nations. In 1985, the government also unilaterally cut its assessment payments to the world body from 25 percent of the UN's total budget to 20 percent, which made the United States one of the largest debtors to the United Nations by the end of the decade. The White House demanded significant UN reform before it would support repayment of its debt. (A full explanation of the UN reform movement and the U.S. role in it can be found in Chapter 3.) At the same time that it was harshly criticizing the UN's performance, it was also moving haltingly toward using the UN mechanisms in new ways. The rise of Mikhail Gorbachev to power in the Soviet Union in 1985, and the Kremlin's rapid fashioning of a new, less antagonistic foreign policy, opened the door to possible cooperation with Russia, under the UN auspices, to address global conflicts. The most dramatic example was the collaboration of the United States and the Soviet Union to end the bloody seven-year Iran-Iraq

War. For the first time in history, the superpowers jointly sponsored a UN resolution on the Middle East. On July 20, 1987, the Security Council unanimously passed Resolution 598, calling for a cease-fire in the war and threatening unspecified measures against either belligerent that did not accept the resolution.

At the United Nations in December 1988, Soviet leader Gorbachev made an important gesture toward ending the Cold War. After a genial meeting on Governor's Island in New York with outgoing President Reagan, the Soviet president addressed the full General Assembly, insisting that it was now "high time to make use of the opportunities provided by this universal organization."[22] By the time of the Iraqi invasion of Kuwait in 1990 and the Gulf War in 1991, Gorbachev's anticipation of an effective United Nations seemed prescient as Moscow and Washington cooperated within the Security Council in ways that would have astonished earlier diplomats in both countries. Evidence of the end of the Cold War was visible early in 1991, before the demise of the Soviet Union that year, when the Russian delegation did not veto a British/U.S. resolution before the Security Council authorizing the use of "any means necessary" (Resolution 678) against Iraq to restore the sovereignty of Kuwait. The action was all the more important because Iraq had previously been a Soviet ally.

With the demolition of the Berlin Wall in 1989 and then the dissolution of the Soviet Union in late 1991, the Cold War was over. The impact rippled through the international system and within the United Nations. In 1991, the USSR's and Yugoslavia's dissolution into several new independent nations contributed to swelling UN membership. Joining the United Nations between 1991 and 1993 were Macedonia, the Czech Republic, Croatia, Slovakia, Bosnia and Herzegovina, Slovenia, Georgia, Estonia, Armenia, Azerbaijan, Latvia, Lithuania, Moldova, and the former central Asian Soviet republics of Tajikistan, Kazakhstan, Turkmenistan, Kyrgyzstan, and Uzbekistan. The Russians also joined a UN-sponsored multilateral peacekeeping operation in Bosnia in 1995 and helped end the NATO bombing of Yugoslavia in 1999 by convincing the government led by Slobodan Milosevic to withdraw its forces from Kosovo.

With the end of the Cold War, peacekeeping and peacemaking became central concerns of the United Nations, as demand for UN intervention in conflicts continued to rise. The September 2000 summit of 150 heads of state at the UN headquarters in New York (the Millennium Summit) affirmed the importance of peacekeeping operations, then no longer blocked by issues of superpower proxies and rivalry. The importance of arms control and weapons proliferation also moved to the forefront of the UN's agenda with the Comprehensive Nuclear-Test-Ban Treaty (CTBT) signed by the United States and Russian governments in 1996, and the extension of the Treaty on the Non-Proliferation of Nuclear Weapons (Nuclear Non-Proliferation Treaty, or NPT) in 1995.

THE POST-COLD WAR UNITED NATIONS

The end of the Cold War seemed to presage the rebirth of the founders' United Nations. Even as the Soviet Union suffered from the ills that would eventually destroy it, the Gorbachev government joined the United States in opposing the first real threat to international peace and security in the post-Cold War era—Saddam Hussein's invasion of Kuwait in August 1990. Acting with alacrity never characteristic of the League of Nations, the Security Council unanimously passed tough resolutions condemning the invasion, demanding the withdrawal of Iraqi forces and the reestablishment of the sovereignty of Kuwait, and, by the close of the year, authorizing a coalition of forces under the U.S. command to expel the invaders from Kuwait. In January 1991, an extraordinarily large coalition, including many Arab and European states, launched the first UN-authorized military action since the Korean War, driving Iraq out and restoring Kuwait's government and sovereignty. Iraq's Hussein accepted all UN conditions, including recognition of an independent Kuwait and near-mandate post-war impositions by the world community, as the price for ending the war before coalition forces marched on Baghdad.

Following the termination of military hostilities in Iraq in 1991, the Security Council, under Chapter VII authority, imposed internal controls on many aspects of Iraqi life and politics. It affirmed Iraq's liability under international law "for any direct loss, damage, ... or injury to foreign governments, nationals and corporations, as a result of Iraq's unlawful invasion and occupation of Kuwait." The Security Council created a compensation fund to pay claims by victims of Iraqi aggression, its assets coming from 30 percent of Iraqi oil export revenues. In addition, the council created the UN Special Commission on Iraq (UNSCOM) to verify Iraqi compliance with all UN resolutions and to carry out no-notice inspections inside Iraq for the purpose of finding and destroying all WMDs. UNSCOM was also charged with establishing a permanent system of monitoring and verification to ensure that Iraq could not rebuild nuclear, biological, or chemical weapon capabilities. UNSCOM conducted its work under continuing challenge and obstruction from the Baghdad government until Iraq ended all cooperation with the UN agency in 1998. During UNSCOM's seven years of operation, its demands on the regime were often buttressed with air reprisals, largely carried out by U.S. and British warplanes.

The rapid crumpling of Iraqi resistance to the UN-sanctioned coalition assault in 1991 sparked secessionist efforts by Shia and Kurds in southern and northern Iraq, respectively. President Hussein responded with air attacks against both groups. Iraqi army attacks against rebels in the northern part of the country produced more than two hundred thousand Kurdish refugees who fled toward the Turkish border, and five hundred thousand crossed into Iran. On April 5, the Security Council called on "the Secretary-General to use all the resources at his disposal ... to address urgently the critical needs of the refugees." The United States, with the assistance of Turkey, Great Britain, and France, established "no-fly" zones in both the north and the south. The four powers launched Operation Provide Comfort, creating a massive humanitarian airdrop operation and protective "enclaves" for Kurds inside Iraq. Shortly thereafter, the United Nations took control of the camps, imposing a near protectorate over large parts of the country, with military backup from coalition forces.

We should mention that during President Bill Clinton's days in the White House (1993–2001), the United States used what it called *assertive multilateralism*.[23] The administration sought to contain Iraq's development of WMDs, to defend minority communities, to encourage the collapse of the regime, and to limit Saddam's influence in the region through UN mechanisms. To give credence to the UN resolutions and to back demands by UNSCOM inspectors, Washington regularly carried out air strikes against Iraqi military and radar installations. A critical moment came in 1998, however, when President Clinton ordered four days of bombing in retaliation for Iraqi unwillingness to allow inspectors into requested sites. The United Nations withdrew the inspectors for the duration, citing safety considerations. Baghdad then announced that it would not allow the return of UNSCOM, calling it an espionage vehicle for the United States. While both Washington and the United Nations condemned the Iraqi decision, no forceful means were used to reinsert the inspection teams. At the time, President Clinton faced impeachment proceedings that politically undercut any contemplated military action to enforce the UN resolutions.

Unrecognized then, the 1998 events set in motion a slow erosion of U.S.-UN unanimity on Iraq. UNSCOM was soon replaced by the UN Monitoring, Verification and Inspection

Commission (UNMOVIC),[24] an agency thought more acceptable in its personnel and leadership to Baghdad. The Swedish diplomat, Dr. Hans Blix, was appointed the executive secretary; only one of UNMOVIC's sixteen commissioners was an American.[25] The Clinton administration, while it supported UNMOVIC and encouraged an expansion of programs to use Iraqi oil sale proceeds for humanitarian assistance, increasingly operated without reference to the UN Security Council to keep the Iraqi regime "in its box." In part, the U.S. reticence was in response to growing criticism from UN members that the effort to isolate Saddam and penalize his government was imposing unacceptable pain on the Iraqi population. Having failed to topple Saddam Hussein, U.S. policy was criticized by many UN members as at least ineffective if not counterproductive.

Age of Terrorism

The crisis of September 11, 2001 molded the Iraq policy of the George W. Bush administration and affected its bumpy relationship with the United Nations. The unconscionable terrorist attacks on the World Trade Center and the Pentagon required a forceful and calculated response. They also elicited considerable worldwide empathy. On September 12, 2001, the Security Council unanimously adopted Resolution 1368, denouncing the assault. Council members departed from tradition and stood during the resolution's adoption. In the text of the resolution, the council held that any act of international **terrorism** was a threat to international peace and security. Specifically, the resolution instructed the council to remain "seized" with the matter, meaning that, in a subtle shift from past policy, the council now viewed combating terrorism as a primary responsibility under the UN Charter. The General Assembly, convening the following day—September 13—also condemned the attack. On September 28, the Security Council passed Resolution 1373, calling on all states to "prevent and suppress the financing of terrorist acts." Council members invoked Chapter VII of the Charter, which made the provisions of the resolution mandatory on all member states. The council decided that all states should criminalize the provision or collection of funds for such acts. It called on states to freeze the assets of suspected terrorist groups and prohibit their nationals or organizations from making funds and financial assets available to potential terrorists. The resolution instructed states to deny safe haven to individuals or groups who financed, planned, supported, or committed terrorist acts. Finally, the council urged that states afford one another the greatest measure of assistance for criminal investigations and prosecution of terrorist groups.[26]

Washington received wide-ranging multilateral support to remove the Taliban from power in Afghanistan, curtail Al-Qaeda activities there, and seek the reconstruction of the country. Liberated from Taliban rule in early 2002 through a cooperative effort, Afghanistan faced deep problems of political instability and economic despair. Regional warlords remained and the drug trade persisted. In outlying areas, the Taliban rematerialized as a threat to the government in Kabul. Still, with international encouragement, the Afghans, in a traditional *loya jirga*, or grand council, had, by early 2004, agreed to a constitution and to democratic elections. Abiding by a post-Taliban blueprint negotiated at an international conference in Bonn, Germany, in 2001, warlords began to turn in heavy weapons to the central government. There was a visible UN presence in the country. The UN special representative Lakhdar Brahimi, along with the UN High Commissioner for Refugees and a variety of staff personnel, plied their trade with uncommon dedication. Hampered by a lack of money, the slow inflow of promised funds, and the diversion of attention to Iraq, the UN contingent worked to distribute an international aid disbursement, to increase security, to develop infrastructure, and to strengthen the Afghan government.

In August 2003, NATO took command of the International Security Assistance Force (the first time NATO had acted outside Europe). In October 2004, elections were held with international observers in attendance. That is, from late 2001, a multilateral approach was used to try to solve the Afghan crisis. Meantime, the international community, dedicated to creating a democratic and stable regime, encouraged President Hamid Karzai's government to appoint competent, reform-oriented personalities to administrative positions and to tackle corruption. There was also a strong push for the protection of women's rights and the elevation of the rule of law. By the 2010s, a vast array of nongovernmental and international humanitarian organizations, most associated with the United Nations, had descended on Afghanistan to aid in encouraging "civil society" and nation-building.[27] In a messy and protracted presidential election in 2014, Ashraf Ghani bested Abdullah Abdullah. International pressure encouraged Afghans to accept the election results. Ghani became the president and Abdullah took on an important, rather contrived, position in the government called the Chief Executive Officer. The election would be the first time in Afghanistan's history that power was democratically transferred.

Yet, Afghanistan continued to be plagued by a tenacious insurgency, domestic corruption, inadequate governance, disputed elections, and poverty. Although tentative plans for the U.S. military withdrawal from the country were in place by 2014, both U.S. and NATO allied troops, in diminished number, remained in the country until the precipitous U.S. withdrawal in August 2021. The departure of U.S. and NATO forces was the outcome of direct American-Taliban negotiations—without participation by the Afghan government—leading to the Doha Agreement in February 2020. The agreement called for the withdrawal of all foreign forces from the country by May 1, 2021. In return, the Taliban pledged to deny a reemergence of Al-Qaeda in the country and to engage with the Afghan government in cease-fire talks. When Joe Biden entered the presidency, there were about 2,500 U.S. military personnel still in Afghanistan. The president, in partial compliance with the Doha Agreement, announced that he would not pull forces out by May 1, but delay until September 11. Later in the summer the president settled on an August 31 departure date, by which time remaining U.S. troops were withdrawn. Other NATO forces also left. By then, the Afghan government had collapsed and the Taliban had established control over most of the country.

With foreign forces gone and the Taliban in charge, severe problems faced the country and worried neighbors. In addition to persistent poverty, hunger, unemployment, and deteriorating health—for which, at the moment, there seemed no financial aid (more than 40 percent of Afghanistan's GDP came from international assistance in 2020)—there was also, oddly, a menacing *terrorist* insurgency *against* the Taliban, in the form of the so-called Islamic State Khorasan, or ISIS-K.[28] Diplomatically isolated, the Taliban, and the country, confronted a humanitarian, governance, and diplomatic crisis.

Into this breach came, immediately, the United Nations. On September 17, 2021, the Security Council unanimously renewed the mandate for the UN Assistance Mission in Afghanistan (UNAMA) to March 2022, which had been operating in the country since 2002. The Council requested the Secretary-General to prepare a written report by the end of January, detailing "strategic and operational recommendations for UNAMA's mandate in light of recent political, security, and social developments," and authorized UNAMA to continue to coordinate humanitarian assistance and ensure access and security to UN staff to allow for the delivery of assistance. In a follow-up resolution (S/RES/2596 (2021)), the Council stressed the importance of establishing an inclusive government and protecting and preserving human rights and international law.

After the Taliban takeover, a number of UN agencies and humanitarian NGOs remained in Afghanistan, providing food assistance to more than 3.8 million people. The humanitarian community launched the Afghanistan Flash Appeal, calling for $606 million to be raised for relief efforts. Among the UN personnel who remained in the country were a UN Resident Humanitarian Coordinator, a Deputy Representative for UNHCR (High Commissioner for Refugees), a Country Representative for the World Health Organization, a Country Director for the World Food Programme, a Representative of UNICEF (UN Children's Fund), a Resident Representative for UNDP (UN Development Programme), and a Representative for the UN's Food and Agriculture Organization.

In mid-September, Secretary-General António Guterres sent the Under-Secretary-General for Humanitarian Affairs and Emergency Relief (Martin Griffiths) to Kabul to meet with the Taliban leadership. There, he emphasized, among other matters, the critical role of women in the delivery of aid, and the imperative of ensuring the safety, well-being, and rights of all civilians, especially women, girls, and minorities. About the same time, the Secretary-General assured a High-Level Ministerial Meeting on the Humanitarian Situation in Afghanistan that the United Nations family—and the humanitarian system at large—would continue to assist the people of Afghanistan. He also urged support for the recently announced Flash Appeal.[29]

Of course, terrorism had not been isolated to Afghanistan. Al-Qaeda affiliates, while probably weakened, had emerged in many parts of the world. They had been joined by other local jihadist organizations, like Boko Haram in Nigeria and, perhaps most significantly, the regional group ISIS (the Islamic State, sometimes called ISIL, for Islamic State of Iraq and the Levant). Following the 2004 bombing of four commuter trains in Madrid by an Al-Qaeda affiliate which killed more than two hundred people, the Security Council passed Resolution 1540 under the authority of the Charter's Chapter VII making its obligations mandatory on all states. The resolution required all states to "refrain from providing any form of support to non-State actors that attempt to develop, acquire, manufacture, possess, transport, transfer or use nuclear, chemical or biological weapons and their means of delivery," and to "adopt and enforce appropriate effective laws which prohibit any non-State actor to manufacture, acquire, possess, develop, transport, transfer or use nuclear, chemical or biological and their means of delivery." Reinforcing the UN commitment to combat terrorism, the General Assembly at the 2005 World Summit called for a comprehensive global strategy against terrorist organizations.

There are sometimes differences of opinion regarding what constitutes a terrorist action. China, for just one example, at times charges Uyghurs living in Xinjian Province in the far northwest of the country as harboring terrorists. Most of the world rejects that and similar allegations, seeing Uyghurs as the afflicted/repressed not the afflicting/repressing parties in Xinjian. However, there has developed since the September 11, 2001 attacks something of a definitional consensus on straightforward features of terrorism, and the United Nations—particularly via the Security Council—has recognized and acted on this consensus. For example, Al-Qaeda and ISIS (and their various spin-offs) represent, by common consent, terrorists. Thus, by Resolution 2560 of December 29, 2020, the Security Council, "*Expressing* its gravest concern about the presence, ideology, and actions of ISIL and Al-Qaida, and the growing presence of their affiliates around the world," reaffirmed "the need to combat by all means [consistent with International Law]... threats to international peace and security caused by terrorist acts, stressing in this regard the important role the United Nations plays in leading and coordinating this effort."[30]

The Decline of Security Council Unanimity

Despite the ongoing challenge of Afghanistan, attention in Washington, perhaps unfortunately, shifted to Iraq in late 2002. Afghanistan slipped from the front pages of U.S. newspapers as the Bush administration announced, with a noticeable combativeness, that nations were "either with us or against us," that some unwelcome nations made up an "axis of evil," and that one of them at least—Iraq—needed to be struck immediately, preemptively, even unilaterally if the other Security Council members refused to accede to the U.S. demands for military action. This posture merged with Washington's rejection of the laboriously negotiated Kyoto Protocol, its "unsigning" of the International Criminal Court agreement, and its withdrawal from the 1972 Anti-Ballistic Missile Treaty.

President Bush seemed determined to attack, even without UN approval. During much of 2002 and into early 2003, disagreements within the Security Council on the reasonableness of war with Iraq became public. Washington began warning of the certain "irrelevancy" of the United Nations should the Security Council fail to accede to war, although, in fact, the United Nations had proved fairly vibrant in addressing various serious problems like Iraqi aggression. In resolutions following the invasion of Kuwait in 1990, the Security Council had imposed on Iraq the most debilitating control regime imaginable. Arms inspectors roamed the country; "no-fly" zones in the north and south, legitimized at the behest of the United States, removed large portions of the land from Baghdad's political control; and, with Resolution 1441, pressed on Iraq in November 2002 by unanimous vote of the Security Council, arms inspectors with even more robust authority returned.

Still the crisis simmered into the late winter of 2003. At the Security Council meeting of February 14, 2003—after UNMOVIC executive secretary Hans Blix and IAEA director general Mohamed El Baradei issued their largely negative reports on Iraqi compliance with Security Council Resolution 1441, which had required immediate and complete WMD disarmament—each Security Council member responded, on live television, with careful, studied remarks. As the drama unfolded, one fact became clear: a majority of the council, most of the world's population, and even the plurality of the American people—at least according to virtually all the public opinion polls at the time—favored military action against Iraq only with full UN consent.[31] This outcome resulted despite the efforts of a popular U.S. president during the previous ten months to paint Iraq as a member of the "axis of evil." Bush had also, in June 2002, asserted a new foreign policy of preemption, coupling fundamental U.S. security concerns with the need for "regime change" in Baghdad.

We must note, however, that the inability to generate broad public and coalition support for a preemptive attack on Iraq had led the president back to the rostrum of the UN General Assembly in September 2002, where he announced a subtle change in U.S. Iraqi policy. Asserting that preventing the United Nations from going the way of the League of Nations was essential, he argued that the United States would seek to fulfill UN resolutions dating to the 1991 Gulf War that demanded Baghdad divest itself of all WMDs.

To see President Bush, no apparent friend of the United Nations during his first eighteen months in office, stand before the General Assembly and make his case for authorization to act in Iraq and to call the world to honor and enforce previous UN resolutions was an extraordinary assent to legitimizing the UN's role in Middle East affairs. Whatever his administration's short-term purposes or self-interested motivations, the appeal by the United States, the world's preeminent power, for the UN enforcement of past Security Council resolutions encouraged the emergent global acceptance of the United Nations in Middle Eastern disputes. It also placed constraints even on the United States—that is, on actions that Washington would otherwise not sense—constraints taking the form of time limits, definition of goals in Iraq, continuing consultation with both allies and other Security Council members, and rising world antipathy for perceived violations of UN mandates. Having begun down this road, President Bush was forced into lengthy negotiations on the terms of Resolution 1441, delays brought on by the renewed inspection process, and effective restraint led by France and Germany. By the spring of 2003, the United States even faced the distasteful prospect of initiating military action against Iraq in the face of formal rejection of its proposed authorizing resolution.

Nonetheless, that is exactly what happened in March 2003, as the United States, with a "coalition of the willing," invaded Iraq. Although the United States seemed to "win" the 2003 war in Iraq, post-war challenges proved more intractable than originally thought. No WMDs were found. David Kay, who resigned in late January 2004 as the head of the U.S. Iraq Survey Group trying to find weapons, declared before the Senate Armed Services Committee that no chemical, biological, or nuclear weapons existed in Iraq and no evidence that Baghdad had transferred any such weapons to Al-Qaeda or any other terrorist group had been found.[32] As disquieting to public opinion, the U.S. military and civilian administration of Iraq had not gone as hoped. By summer 2005, more than seventeen hundred Americans had been killed in the country since the U.S. invasion had begun. More than 80 percent of these deaths had occurred after President Bush announced the end of combat on May 1, 2003 (compared with many fewer American deaths in Afghanistan during a longer period of involvement). The usefulness of unilateral "preemption" outside UN sanction was at the least open to debate.

Evidence showed that the State Department had mounted an effort to move the U.S. policy back to multinational cooperation (and at least to convince the U.S. public that it was succeeding). In an article published early in 2004, Secretary of State Colin Powell denied that the second Bush administration favored a unilateral, assertive foreign policy or that it had turned its back on the collaborative tradition dating from the UN's origins. The secretary stressed that Washington had continued to follow "a strategy of partnership," cooperation with other nations, and diplomatic regard for the United Nations.[33] Moreover, by early 2004, the U.S. Iraqi policy had appeared to shift abruptly, as officials announced the U.S. intention to transfer sovereignty to an interim Iraqi government—a government selected by Secretary-General Annan's Special Representative Lahkdar Brahimi. To contain the certain confusion and possible instability that might result, Washington was now even making "urgent appeal[s]" to the United Nations to take an active role in restoring order in that country.[34] On June 1, 2004, Brahimi and President Bush acceded to decisions by Iraqi Governing Council members to appoint immediately their own selections for a new government, with authority to manage Iraqi affairs until scheduled elections the following January. The new leaders urged the UN Security Council to recognize the full sovereignty of Iraq and the government's complete control over the country's affairs and resources. President Bush accepted these recommendations and worked closely with other major powers on the Security Council to fashion multilateral reconstruction of Iraq. On January 30, 2005, Iraq held an election, and after long deliberation a government was formed by the end of April.

This instance would not be the first time in the post-World War II period that a U.S. administration, initially reversing the foreign policy of its immediate predecessor, reverted to continuity. That seemed to be the aim of Powell's State Department. However, the question lingered as to whether preference for going it alone, so forcefully articulated during President Bush's first term, or going together with others would win out in Washington. This issue had been one of the great questions of international politics in the twentieth century. When it faced U.S. policy makers in 1945, the trajectory of U.S. diplomacy at that time seemed fixed. However, by January 2005, Powell was gone from the State Department, replaced by former national security adviser Condoleezza Rice. Then, in March, the president announced his nomination of undersecretary of state for arms control John Bolton—a tough proponent of unilateralism and preemption, and a harsh critic—to become the U.S. ambassador to the United Nations, which indicated that the United States would likely persist in its adversarial posture toward the organization.

President Bush's doctrine of unilateral preemption, if maintained, challenged the 1945 commitment to collective security embodied in the UN Charter. By acting without UN authorization, or early UN ratification after the fact, when no imminent threat to U.S. national security seemed to exist, the Bush administration circumvented the bedrock principles on which the United Nations was founded. Other major powers on the Security Council noted the grave precedent set by U.S. action and sought ways to constrain Washington's unilateral foreign policy. Even Secretary-General Kofi Annan expressed concern about the viability of the "old" UN formulations for maintaining international peace and security in a "new" age with both new and novel threats and a hyperpower finding itself unsafe and unable to ensure its security through current UN mechanisms.

The topic of a U.S. policy of unilateralism or multilateralism, a crucial topic for the United Nations, emerged in the 2008 U.S. presidential election. The new president, Barack Obama, indicated that he would revert to the more traditional stance of multilateralism, a promising signal for the United Nations. But President Obama's intentions and the flow of events did not always move the pendulum toward a renewed global commitment to collective security.

Sparked by the so-called Arab Spring, in February 2011, a civil uprising broke out in Libya against longtime strongman Muammar Gaddafi. The center of the uprising was in the town of Benghazi that soon came under threat from Gaddafi's security forces. Faced with the likelihood of a civilian massacre, the UN Security Council authorized a no-fly zone and the use of "all necessary measures" to protect the Benghazi populace. The United States and several of its European allies cited the resolution as they launched aerial bombardments on Gaddafi's forces, in effect aiding the rebel cause. The regime was toppled and a transitional government put in place in October. In the view of the Russian government, the overthrow in Libya was a unilateral misuse of UN authority by the United States and the West. It would subsequently veto all similar resolutions related to the expanding civil war in Syria, a Russian ally. The inability to act collectively allowed the Syrian conflict to spin out of control.

Instead of a new era of collective security, a "cold peace" came to dominate great-power relations globally and at the UN. The emerging adversarial relationship between Russia and the United States reached a new plateau in 2014 when a popular revolution in Kyiv, Ukraine, brought down the Russian-leaning elected President Viktor Yanukovych. The country's eastern regions, the ex-president's base of support, now demanded secession from the new interim government in the capital. Segments of the ethnically dominant Russian population in the east and in Crimea demanded reunion with Russia, severed since the collapse of the Soviet Union.

In late February 2014, on orders from Russia's president, Vladimir Putin, his country's forces surreptitiously moved into Crimea to support secession efforts. A referendum followed, unauthorized by Ukraine and unrecognized internationally. Nonetheless, on March 16, voters voted to join the Russian Federation, and two days later the Kremlin annexed the peninsula. Protests in the UN Security Council and efforts to pass resolutions of condemnation were all blocked by the Russian veto. So too as the civil war in the eastern provinces continued, Russia blocked meaningful UN action. The United States and the European Union turned to the collective imposition of economic sanctions against Russia as the price for Russian involvement in Ukraine.

One of the more tragic events in the Ukrainian civil conflict was the downing of a Malaysian passenger plane on July 17, 2014. Two hundred ninety-eight passengers and crew lost their lives to an apparent shoot-down by Russian-backed rebels. The Security Council at the time unanimously condemned the act. But, in July 2015, Russia vetoed a measure that would have established an international tribunal to prosecute persons responsible for the downing. The era of council unity that extended from the late 1980s to 2003 had largely come to an end. That unity came under even more stress in the winter and spring of 2022, when Russian troops invaded all of Ukraine. Shortly before the invasion, Russian Leader Vladimir Putin and Chinese President Xi Jinping signed a joint statement in which they called for a "transformation of the global governance architecture" and a "redistribution of power in the world."[35] In the Security Council and the General Assembly, emergency meetings to address the war in Ukraine revealed an ominous further splintering of the Security Council's great powers.

Strains within the Security Council were but a partial cause of the difficult relationship between the United States and the United Nations that seemed to come to full light during the Trump administration. In his address to the General Assembly of September 2019, President Trump, who had campaigned for an "America First" foreign policy, announced that "The future does not belong to globalists." By ending participation in international trade agreements, in the UN-inspired Paris Climate Agreement, the Iran Nuclear Agreement, in arms control measures, and in UN organizations such as UNESCO, UNRWA, the Human Rights Council, and the WHO, the President made stark an accelerated disengagement with the world. By the time Joe Biden reached the White House, the UN-U.S. relationship could be characterized as fragile, and the United Nations as precariously marginalized as major powers seemed to be going their own way.

SUMMARY

The United Nations originated out of a lush history of attempts to bring peace, stability, and regularity to international relations. Most immediately, its founders sought to craft an organization that would avoid the pitfalls of the predecessor League of Nations. At a number of wartime meetings, the leaders of the major Allied governments—Franklin Roosevelt, Winston Churchill, and Joseph Stalin—eventually agreed on the outline of the United Nations. The organizing conference at San Francisco in mid-1945 brought the organization to fruition, and early on, led by Eleanor Roosevelt, the United Nations came to be as interested in social, humanitarian, and human rights issues as it was with international peace and security. However, the simultaneous onset of the Cold War hindered the new organization's ability to fulfil its hoped-for promise. Only in the post-Cold War era did such promise seem possible. Nevertheless, as is too often true in human affairs, multiple troubling challenges arose even in the post-Cold War period. Three of the most significant and divisive were the crisis over Iraq, the concomitant assertion by the UN's most important power—the United States—of a foreign policy doctrine inherently challenging to the principle of collective security, a principle ascribed to by the world community in the 1940s largely at the urging of the United States, and Russia's muscular military action on its periphery.

KEY TERMS

Balance of Power Theory (42)
Bretton Woods (57)
Cold War (68)
Concert of Europe (42)
Dag Hammarskjöld (70)
Dumbarton Oaks (54)
Eleanor's UN (65)
Franklin Roosevelt (48)
Joseph Stalin (52)

League of Nations (43)
Terrorism (75)
Troika (71)
Trygve Lie (70)
United Nations Conference on
    International Organization
    (UNCIO) (58)
Winston Churchill (1) (51)
Yalta Conference (65)

DISCUSSION QUESTIONS

Compare and contrast the League of Nations and the United Nations.

Discuss why the United Nations Conference on International Organization, meeting in San Francisco in 1945, has not had the historical coverage of other important post-war conferences, such as those in Vienna (1814–1815) and in Versailles (1918–1919).

How does "Eleanor's UN" differ from more traditional views of the United Nations?

RESOURCES FOR FURTHER RESEARCH

Relevant Web Sites

The Avalon Project at Yale Law School: Twentieth-Century Documents (avalon.law.yale.edu/subject_menus/20th.asp)

Cold War International History Project (www.wilsoncenter.org/program/cold-war-international-history-project)

Foreign Relations of the United State (history.state.gov/historicaldocuments)

NGO-ECOSOC information (www.un.org/ecosoc/en/ngo)

UN Millennium Development Goals Information (www.un.org/millenniumgoals/)

UN Sustainable Development Goals Information (sdgs.un.org/goals)

Books, Articles, and Documents

Cook, Blanche Wiesen. *Eleanor Roosevelt*. New York: Penguin, 2000.

Divine, Robert. *Second Chance: The Triumph of Internationalism in America during World War II*. New York: Atheneum, 1967.

Gaddis, John Lewis. *We Now Know: Rethinking Cold War History*. Oxford: Clarendon, 1998.

Glendon, Mary Ann. *A World Made New: Eleanor Roosevelt and the Universal Declaration of Human Rights*. New York: Random House, 2001.

Hoopes, Townsend, and Douglas Brinkley. *FDR and the Creation of the U.N.* New Haven, CT: Yale University Press, 1997.

Kimball, Warren. *Forged in War: Roosevelt, Churchill, and the Second World War*. New York: Morrow, 1997.

Krasno, Jean. "A Step along an Evolutionary Path: The Founding of the United Nations." *Global Dialogue* 12, no. 2 (Spring 2000): 9–18.

McCants, William. *The ISIS Apocalypse: The History Strategy, and Doomsday Vision of the Islamic State*. New York: St Martins Press, 2015.

Mingst, Karen, and Margaret Karns. *The United Nations in the Post–Cold War Era: Dilemmas in World Politics*. Boulder, CO: Westview, 2007.

Moore, John Allphin, Jr., and Jerry Pubantz. *American Presidents and the United Nations: Internationalism in the Balance*. New York; Routledge, 2022.

Northedge, Frederick Samuel. *The League of Nations: Its Life and Times, 1920–1946*. New York: Holmes & Meier, 1986.

Russell, Ruth B. *A History of the United Nations' Charter: The Role of the United States, 1940–1945*. Washington, D.C.: Brookings Institution, 1958.

Schlesinger, Stephen C. *Act of Creation: The Founding of the United Nations*. Boulder, CO: Westview, 2003.

U.S. Department of State. *Postwar Foreign Policy Preparation, 1939–1945*. Washington, D.C.: U.S. Government Printing Office, 1949.

Notes

1 Jack C. Plano and Robert E. Riggs, *Forging World Order* (New York: Macmillan, 1967), 7.

2 Bruce Russett and John R. O'Neal, *Triangulating Peace: Democracy, Interdependence, and International Organizations* (New York: Norton, 2001), 10, 29, 35.

3 See Raymond Cohen and Raymond Westbrook, eds., *Amarna Diplomacy: The Beginnings of International Relations* (Baltimore, MD: Johns Hopkins, 2000); and James B. Pritchard, ed., *Ancient Near Eastern Texts Relating to the Old Testament* (Princeton, NJ: Princeton University Press, 1969), 199–206, 529–541.

4 Here and elsewhere in the early pages of this chapter, liberal use has been made of Chapter 1 of John Allphin Moore, Jr., and Jerry Pubantz, *To Create a New World? American Presidents and the United Nations* (New York: Peter Lang, 1999), and, by the same authors, the Introduction to *Encyclopedia of the United Nations*, 2nd Edition (New York: Facts on File, 2008).

5 Paul W. Schroeder, *The Transformation of European Politics, 1763–1848* (Oxford: Clarendon, 1994); and Margaret Olwen MacMillan, *Paris 1919: Six Months That Changed the World* (New York: Random House, 2002).

6 John Milton Cooper, *Breaking the Heart of the World: Woodrow Wilson and the Fight for the League of Nations* (New York: Cambridge University Press, 2001).

7 In an interview in 2020, at the height of the COVID-19 pandemic, John Barry, author of *The Great Influenza: The Epic Story of the Deadliest Plague in History* (New York: Penguin Books, 2004), suggested that Wilson's health problems may have been complicated by infection during the flu pandemic of 1918-1919. See Steve Coll, "Woodrow Wilson's Case of the Flu and How Pandemics Change History," *The New Yorker*, April 16, 2020, at <www.newyorker.com/news/daily-comment/woodrow-wilsons-case-of-the-flu-and-how-pandemics-change-history>.

8 Warren F. Kimball, ed., *Churchill and Roosevelt: The Complete Correspondence* (Princeton, NJ: Princeton University Press, 1984), 1: 227–228.

9 Anne O'Hare McCormick, "His 'Unfinished Business' and Ours," *New York Times Magazine*, April 22, 1945, 43–44.

10 See U.S. Department of State, *Foreign Relations of the United States: Diplomatic Papers: The Conferences at Cairo and Teheran, 1943* (Washington, D.C.: U.S. Government Printing Office, 1961), 530–532.

11 Robert Hildebrand, *Dumbarton Oaks: The Origins of the United Nations and the Search for Postwar Security* (Chapel Hill: University of North Carolina Press, 1990).

12 France had no representation at Dumbarton Oaks or at Yalta. Moreover, it was not considered one of Roosevelt's original Four Policemen, and it was occupied by Germany during the war. However, as the war drew to an end, both Churchill and Roosevelt (persuaded by planners in the Department of State), despite personal uneasiness with Charles DeGaulle, determined that a strong France was needed as a pro-West ally in a stable post-war world. By the time the Yalta agreement was written, Section 1.4 had elevated France (or the "Free" France of DeGaulle) to coequal status with the United States, the USSR, and China. Thus, France, though dismissed as a second-rate power by Stalin, gained an occupation zone in Germany and a permanent seat on the Security Council. Secretary of State Stettinius, in a long advisory memorandum on all post-war plans, explained the matter to Truman less than one day after FDR's death: the French, he said, must be treated on the basis of "potential power and influence." Kimball, *Churchill and Roosevelt*, 3:633.

13 Franklin D. Roosevelt, "Address to Congress on the Yalta Conference, March 1, 1945," in *Public Papers of the Presidents of the United States: Franklin D. Roosevelt, 1933–1945* (Washington, D.C.: Office of the Federal Register, National Archives and Records Administration), http://www.presidency.ucsb.edu/ws/.

14 Stephen C. Schlesinger, *Act of Creation: The Founding of the United Nations* (Boulder, CO: Westview, 2003), 121. Schlesinger's well-received book and Ruth Russell's classic *A History of the United Nations' Charter: The Role of the United States, 1940–1945* (Washington, D.C.: Brookings Institution, 1958) are two of the few detailed renditions of the San Francisco Conference available to students.

15 United Nations, "Article 23," in *Charter of the United Nations* (New York: United Nations, 1945), http://www.un.org/aboutun/charter/index.html.

16 Schlesinger, *Act of Creation*, Ch. 13.

17 Ibid., 122–124; and Dorothy Robbins, *Experiment in Democracy: The Story of U.S. Citizen Organizations in Forging the Charter of the United Nations* (New York: Parkside, 1971).

18 Mary Ann Glendon, *A World Made New: Eleanor Roosevelt and the Universal Declaration of Human Rights* (New York: Random House, 2001), xix.

19 Ibid., 170.

20 The full report can be found at <www.un.org/millenniumgoals/2015_MDG_Report/pdf/MDG%202015%20rev%20(July%20l).pdf>. The accompanying press release, with Secretary-General Ban Ki-moon's remarks, is at <www.un.org/millenniumgoals/2015_MDG_Report/pdf/MDG%202015%20PR%20Global.pdf>.

21 The 2020 report is at: <www.un.org/sustainabledevelopment/progress-report>.

22 Mikhail Gorbachev, *Memoirs* (New York: Doubleday, 1995), 442.

23 Madeleine Albright, President Clinton's first permanent representative to the United Nations and later secretary of state, coined this term to describe the overall approach of the new administration in 1993.

24 UN Security Council, *Resolution 1284 (1999)*, S/RES/1284, December 17, 1999, http://www.un.org/Depts/unscom/Keyresolutions/sres99–1284.htm.

25 A full description of the work of UNMOVIC can be found at <www.un.org/depts/unmovic>.

26 For relevant SC Resolutions on the September 11, 2001 tragedy, see <iilj.org/wp-content/uploads/2016/08/Afghanistan-SC-Resolution-1368-2001.pdf>.

27 See David F. Mitchel, "NGO Presence and Activity in Afghanistan, 2000–2014," *Stability: International Journal of Security and Development* 6, no. 1 (2017), at https://doi.org/10.5334/sta.497/.

28 Victor J. Blue, Thomas Gibbons-Neff, and Christina Goldbaum, "ISIS Poses a Growing Threat to New Taliban Government in Afghanistan," *New York Times*, November 3, 2021, at <www.nytimes.com/2021/11/03/world/asia/isis-afghanistan-taliban.html>.

29 UNAMA reports of these developments can be found at <unama.unmissions.org/un-security-council-renews-unama's-mandate>, <unama.unmissions.org/un-and-humanitarian-partners-scale-life-saving-response-crisis-afghanistan-and-call-all-donors>, and <unama.unmissions.org/united-nations-secretary-general-antónio-guterres-remarks-high-level-ministerial-meeting>.

30 <www.securitycouncilreport.org/atf/cf/%7B65BFCF9B-6D27-4E9C-8CD3-CF6E4F-F96FF9%7D/s_res_2560.pdf>.

31 At the height of the war in Iraq, U.S. public opinion gravitated toward considerable support for the U.S. unilateral military action. However, 50 percent of Americans believed that the United Nations should lead reconstruction efforts, whereas 29 percent believed that the United States alone should be responsible. See the opinion poll results in Ronald Brownstein, "Support Grows for Military Actions," *Los Angeles Times*, April 5, 2003.

32 Bob Drogin, "Iraq Weapons Data Flawed, Congress Told," *Los Angeles Times*, January 29, 2004, A1.

33 Colin L. Powell, "A Strategy of Partnerships," *Foreign Affairs* 83, no. 1 (2004): 22–34.

34 Steven R. Weisan and John H. Cushman, Jr., "U.S. Joins Iraq to Seek U.N. Role in Interim Rule," *New York Times*, January 16, 2004; and Edward Wong, "U.N. Aide Backs Cleric on Elections; Offers No Timetable," *New York Times*, February 12, 2004.

35 Joint Statement of the Russian Federation and the People's Republic of China, February 4, 2022, at <en.kremlin.ru/supplement/5770>.

Chapter 3

The Evolving UN Charter

CONTENTS OF THE CHARTER

The Charter of the United Nations (UN Charter) is the "constitution" of the organization. Member states agree to abide by its principles and procedures, which are laid out in a preamble and nineteen chapters containing 111 articles. The Charter was signed on June 26, 1945, at the San Francisco organizing conference and, sufficiently ratified, came into force on October 24, 1945. (The full Charter can be found in Resource 1.)

Chapter I of the Charter outlines the UN's purposes and principles, including the maintenance of international peace and security, respect for equal rights and self-determination, the encouragement of rights and freedoms, and the principle of sovereign equality of all member states. Chapter I establishes a collective security system among the UN members, requiring them to "settle their international disputes by peaceful means." Some observers have questioned whether the United Nations can live up to the purposes announced in Chapter I without fundamental reform, and others have voiced reservations about the relevancy of a collective security paradigm in an age of terrorism, civil wars, and great power rivalries.

Chapter II deals with UN membership, the main qualification for which is to be a "peace-loving" state. The vagueness of this criterion has allowed the United Nations to become a "universal" international organization made up of states with significantly different political, cultural, and ideological systems. Admission into the United Nations requires a Security Council (SC) recommendation, followed by General Assembly (GA) approval by a two-thirds majority. Chapter II also allows for suspension of the membership of a state against which the United Nations has taken enforcement measures. Under the direst circumstances, the General Assembly may expel a state upon Security Council recommendation. Some critics have argued that the UN's universality has made the organization unwieldy and ineffective. Proposals have been put forward to establish weighted voting, to limit participation by "ministates" in UN bodies, and even to bar states from serving in UN organs to which they can contribute little.

Chapter III lists the five principal organs and explicitly mandates no restriction on "the eligibility of men and women to participate" in them. Chapters IV and V spell out provisions for the General Assembly and the Security Council, including voting procedures for both bodies and the jurisdiction and actions each can take. GA membership is based on the principle of sovereign equality: each country, whatever its size, wealth, or power, has one vote. While a majority vote effects most actions, the GA also decides "Important Questions," which require a two-thirds vote of the members present and voting (Article 18). In the fifteen-member Security Council, nine votes are required to pass a procedural matter; "all other matters" require not only nine affirmative votes, but also concurrence

DOI: 10.4324/9781003281535-4

of the five permanent members (the veto provision in Article 27). Probably no clause of the UN Charter has been criticized more than the grant of the veto power to these five states. Many amendments have been proposed to limit or revise this privilege.

Chapters VI and VII are the core of the historical development of UN peacekeeping policies and outline the collective security measures that the United Nations may use to restore peace. Chapter VI describes the procedures for dealing with the pacific settlement of disputes and threats to the peace. It lists the traditional international diplomacy methods that the parties should use to resolve their differences: negotiation, mediation, conciliation, arbitration, and judicial decisions. Chapter VII emphasizes the role of the Security Council under international law to "determine the existence of any threat to the peace, breach of the peace, or act of aggression" and to "decide what measures shall be taken" to halt the threat or punish the aggressor. In enabling the Security Council to take coercive measures to achieve these tasks, Chapter VII installs the United Nations as the international guarantor of peace and security.

Chapters VIII and IX define and sanction regional organizations to keep the peace and encourage economic and social cooperation. These organizations have become increasingly important in the UN's effort to address civil conflicts during the last two decades. We will discuss their important emerging role in Chapter 5. Article 57 encourages specialized agencies to develop a relationship with the United Nations in order to expedite the mandate of Article 55 to raise living standards, resolve economic and social problems, and enhance human rights. These chapters are followed by the related Chapter X, which defines and sets the parameters for Economic and Social Council (ECOSOC) action.

Chapters XI and XII deal with non-self-governing territories (typically colonies). The first of these two chapters is a declaration of the UN's intent to promote decolonization and the progressive development of "free political institutions." Chapter XIII establishes the Trusteeship Council and defines its membership (the states administering trust territories, the remaining permanent members of the Security Council that do not administer any territories in the system, and sufficient member states elected by the General Assembly to ensure an equal number of administering and non-administering governments on the council). The Trusteeship Council is now defunct because decolonization and self-determination ended the great colonial empires of the past five centuries. The council suspended operation on November 1, 1994, with the independence of Palau, the last remaining UN trust territory.

Suggestions abound for the transformation of the Trusteeship Council into a purposeful UN organ that could address some of the new challenges faced by the world community. UN Secretary-General Kofi Annan recommended the elimination of the council, but that would require a revision of the UN Charter, which, despite his encouragement, had not been accomplished as of 2022. Chapter XIV provides for the International Court of Justice (ICJ), the judicial arm of the United Nations. By stipulation of Article 92, the ICJ replaced the Permanent Court of International Justice, became an integral part of the United Nations, and gained its own statute, which was annexed to the UN Charter.

Chapter XV creates the Secretariat, headed by a Secretary-General appointed by the General Assembly upon Security Council recommendation. In addition to being the chief administrative officer of the United Nations, the Secretary-General plays an important political role. Article 99 allows him or her to bring to the Security Council's attention any matter that he or she believes threatens peace and security. The Secretariat is designed to be the administrative arm of the United Nations. Its members are "international officials responsible only to the Organization" (Article 100).

The "miscellaneous provisions" of Chapter XVI call for all treaties and international agreements to be registered with the Secretariat, establish the priority of the Charter over other international agreements, and extend to the United Nations (within all member states) privileges and immunities necessary to carry out its purposes. Chapter XVII, titled "Transitional Security Arrangements," sorts out specific matters that concluded World War II, and Chapter XVIII explicates the difficult method for amending the Charter (discussed in the next section), while the concluding Chapter XIX describes the timeline and process of Charter ratification.

As we review the Charter, we find comparing it to the earlier Covenant of the League of Nations useful. Such comparison draws attention to certain new, or elaborated, principles of international law introduced by the later document. For example, the League's Covenant essentially suggested a voluntary commitment not to resort to force, whereas the Charter, in Article 2, paragraph 4, confirms the non-resort-to-war concept as an established principle: "All Members shall refrain in their international relations from the threat or use of force against the territorial integrity or political independence of any state, or in any other manner inconsistent with the Purposes of the United Nations." The preamble of the League's Covenant speaks of the dealings of "organized peoples with one another," as though "disorganized" or, perhaps, "less civilized" peoples existed in the world. The Charter disavows such distinctions with provisions devoted to decolonization (especially Chapters XI–XIII) and to the equal sovereignty of states (Article 2), and by its encouragement of universal membership (Chapter II).[1] Of equal significance is the principle of obligatory registration of treaties at a single, universally visible place and with a single institution—the United Nations—as provided in Article 102. This article also directs the Secretariat to accumulate and publicize all registered treaties.

AMENDMENTS TO THE CHARTER

Article 108, in Chapter XVIII, provides the method for **amending the Charter**, but as of 2022 it has been used on only five occasions. For an amendment to be added, it must be adopted by a vote of two-thirds of the GA members and then ratified according to the respective constitutional processes of two-thirds of the member states, including all the permanent Security Council members. Amendments to the Charter include alterations to Articles 23 and 27. The General Assembly adopted these amendments on December 17, 1963, and they came into force on August 31, 1965. The amendment to Article 23 enlarged the Security Council membership from eleven to fifteen, and changes in Article 27 altered voting requirements in that body—increasing the number of affirmative votes needed to pass all resolutions from seven to nine. The veto for the five permanent members remained. Article 61 was amended twice, first in 1965 to enlarge ECOSOC membership from eighteen to twenty-seven members, and then again in 1973 to fifty-four states. The General Assembly amended Article 109 on December 20, 1965, and the amendment came into force on June 12, 1968. The change in Article 109 increased the number of SC votes necessary to call a general conference to review the Charter from seven to nine. The two-thirds vote required of the General Assembly remained.

These Charter amendments resulted from the dramatic growth in UN membership in the 1950s and 1960s. Most of the new member states—products of the national liberation movements in Africa and Asia—clamored for representation, particularly in the UN bodies where their security and economic development interests could be most affected. The great powers were willing to accept the enlargement of these organs so long as no amendment diminished the permanent members' ultimate check on SC actions or subjected them to mandatory resolutions in ECOSOC.

There have been a few changes to the structure and practice of the UN effected without formal amendments. The requirement in Article 27 that all non-procedural decisions of the Security Council be made with concurring votes of the permanent members—the veto—has, in practice, been interpreted to mean that abstentions by a permanent member represent a silent concurring vote. Also, following the dissolution of the Soviet Union in 1991, Russia assumed the USSR's permanent status on the Security Council; and the Beijing government in China became an SC permanent member in 1971, replacing Taiwan. Otherwise, by 2021, the Charter remained as it was in 1945 with the caveat that, as we will detail in the remainder of this chapter, a number of reinterpretations and reforms have been instituted so that the organization can more readily meet fresh demands.

Such minimal change in the fundamental document does not mean that serious proposals for Charter amendments have not surfaced repeatedly since 1945. Even at San Francisco, major proposed revisions were put forward that the "Big Three" rejected in the end. They argued that the Charter was a carefully negotiated document whose formula could not be adjusted without the loss of major-power participation. Charter amending has always been a delicate balancing act among three phenomena: (1) the democratic legislative process inherent in parliamentary diplomacy; (2) the sovereign equality of each member state, which gives that state an equal vote with every other member, as well as the equal right to ignore many UN decisions; and (3) the reality of power inequality among the UN's members, which allows the permanent members to "outvote" all other states in many circumstances. At one time or another, nearly every chapter of the Charter has been recommended for revision and subjected to the pressures of these three countervailing forces.

Informal Modifications of the Charter

Although the Charter has seldom been amended, the United Nations has evolved appreciably since 1945. This disparity is logically possible only because the interpretation of the UN's "constitution" has allowed informal "amendments" of the originally intended blueprint. Two of the Charter's accentuated themes have sometimes seemed at cross-purposes and have led to many informal adjustments of the Charter. First is the principle of the independence and sovereignty of equal member states (Article 2) and the concomitant principle of noninterference in the domestic or internal affairs of states, as explicated in Article 2, paragraph 7:

> Nothing contained in the present Charter shall authorize the United Nations to intervene in matters which are essentially within the domestic jurisdiction of any state or shall require the Members to submit such matters to settlement under the present Charter.

Second is the promotion of universal respect for human rights and fundamental freedoms, as found in Article 1, paragraph 3; in Article 13, paragraph 1; and in Article 55, section c—which, in succession, promote and encourage "respect for human rights," advocate "assisting in the realization of human rights," and call on the United Nations to promote "universal respect for, and observance of, human rights." On the one hand, sovereignty and noninterference appear to denote the right of a nation-state to enforce its own version of human rights. Yet, on the other hand, the Universal Declaration of Human Rights and several Charter provisions seem to proclaim rights as universal rather than culturally or nationally determined. In 1999, Secretary-General Kofi Annan maintained that such human rights could not be abridged in the name of state sovereignty. By the early twenty-first century, the proposition that sovereignty and the principle of noninterference deny any other nation, group of nations, or the United Nations, the right—even less the duty—to interfere in a state's domestic affairs came under increased challenge as the world community found itself dealing with human tragedies in collapsing and dysfunctional states in the former Yugoslavia, Indonesia, and areas of Africa and the Middle East. The Security Council, for example, authorized direct humanitarian intervention in Somalia, Rwanda, and East Timor, not always at the clear invitation of any central government. Moreover, the Brahimi Report—prepared by a special committee on peacekeeping operations (chaired by Lakhdar Brahimi) and available for international consideration at the Millennium Summit of 2000—underscored Annan's view. Its authors recommended strengthening UN peacekeeping and encouraged a more robust and offensive posture in dangerous and out-of-control situations in disintegrating states.[2]

One of the most provocative steps taken by the United Nations in the defense of human rights against a population's own government was its development of a "responsibility to protect" principle (R2P), first as an obligation of the state itself and then of the international community when the state violates its citizens' rights egregiously. The 2005 World Summit affirmed that "every sovereign government has a 'responsibility to protect' its citizens and those within its jurisdiction from genocide, mass killing, and massive and sustained human rights violations." When states fail their responsibilities, as expressed by former Secretary-General Annan, personal sovereignty supersedes state sovereignty, and the world community must act. Although there are critics of R2P—who fear renewed neo-colonial interventions and who continue to privilege state sovereignty—the General Assembly endorsed the principle in 2009 and again in May 2021, with Resolution A/75/277, confirmed its support of "The responsibility to protect and the prevention of genocide, war crimes, ethnic cleansing and crimes against humanity." The resolution was adopted with 115 states voting in favor, 28 abstaining and 15 voting against.[3] (For fuller details of R2P, see Chapter 5.) Responsibility to Protect remains a debatable proposition because of (1) its evident dismissal of state sovereignty and (2) its sparse record of successes. However, about four score passed and proposed Security Council resolutions have invoked R2P, specifically in crises such as those in Central African Republic, Côte d'Ivoire, Democratic Republic of the Congo (DRC), Liberia, Libya, Mali, Somalia, South Sudan, Syria, and Yemen, as well as in thematic resolutions seeking to prevent genocide and armed conflict. The principle has also been cited in several GA and Human Rights Council resolutions.[4]

Chapter VI½ Provisions

Peacekeeping operations are not explicitly mentioned in the Charter. Through the decades, Charter responsibilities given to the General Assembly, and particularly to the Security Council and the Secretary-General, have been interpreted as providing legal bases for UN peacekeeping. Because Chapter VI calls for the pacific settlement of disputes and Chapter VII authorizes the Security Council to decide what actions must be taken to effect a peaceful resolution to conflict, diplomats and scholars have, by fusing these two UN responsibilities, invoked the term *Chapter VI½* to describe the guiding principles for peacekeeping operations. Chapter VI½ does not actually exist. Thus, individuals who cite it implicitly recognize the informal amendment of the Charter to meet changing demands. By the early twenty-first century, UN "Blue Helmets" (i.e., UN peacekeepers) found themselves in various parts of the world helping to "nation build," acting as a trip wire between contending factions, monitoring elections, and providing daily assistance. We discuss peacekeeping operations and Chapter VI½ fully in Chapter 6.

The Charter's original authors may not have foreseen these recent developments. For the most part, as discussed in Chapter 2, the founders saw the new United Nations as an association of sovereign nations set up to prevent war and to deal with international security issues. Still, the preamble indicates that the Charter is an agreement not among "governments" or "states," but among the "peoples" of the world, a notion that caused considerable debate in San Francisco in 1945. Less deliberation was directed to the remaining paragraphs of the preamble, which deal with saving the future world from the "scourge of war," emphasize human rights and the legitimacy of treaties and international law, and promote social progress and better standards of living. Thus, intimations that the United Nations might expand its functions beyond those constrained by the Charter's concession to traditional state sovereignty were present from the start.

THE COLD WAR, EXPANDING MEMBERSHIP, AND THE CHARTER

As described in Chapter 2, the onset of the Cold War affected the UN's workings in ways the institution's founders did not always foresee. For example, the United Nations was often used as an instrument of Cold War rivalry rather than as a tool to resolve international problems. The Congo Crisis of the early 1960s and the Cuban Missile Crisis of 1962 (discussed in Chapter 2) are illustrative. Both superpowers used the United Nations as a forum to promote their views rather than as a negotiating agency. Likewise, arms limitation talks were substantive only when the two main nuclear powers conducted them, which meant that the United Nations was rarely the initiating organization for issues of arms limitation or disarmament.

Perhaps the most obvious impact of the Cold War was on the Security Council, which had been expected to deal with all major international security matters. However, the council waned as an active institution. It held 130 meetings during the late 1940s, but by 1949 only five. Between 1945 and 1975, the Soviet Union used its veto power 114 times, begetting frequent deadlock in the council.[5] One consequence was to elevate the activities of the General Assembly. An early example was the Uniting for Peace Resolution, passed by the GA on November 3, 1950 (see Chapter 5 for further information). Through the resolution, the assembly granted itself SC-like authority to convene in an emergency session and discuss a threat to the peace, a breach of the peace, or an act of aggression, and to make recommendations for collective measures whenever "the Security Council, because of lack of unanimity of the permanent members, fails to exercise its primary responsibility for the maintenance of international peace and security." This authority allowed the GA to circumvent the Soviet veto in the Security Council and to recommend the use of UN forces in the Korean War. The provision was used sparingly, and usually ineffectively, during the Cold War—first regarding conflict in Korea in the early 1950s, then in the Suez Crisis and the Soviet intervention in Hungary, both in 1956, and then with reference to Moscow's invasion of Afghanistan in 1980.

Membership

The Cold War also influenced—and was influenced by—the changing **membership** in the United Nations. Beginning with 51 member states in 1945, the United Nations grew to 193 nations by 2022. This growth was the product of Cold War politics, decolonization, and the desire for universality, and it transformed the operations and relationships of the principal organs of the institution from those contemplated by the founding states. It also significantly affected internal UN politics and the agenda of the world body.

New members are admitted by GA vote, on the recommendation of the Security Council. As the Cold War deepened, the USSR and the United States both vetoed the admission of members associated with the other bloc. Only nine states of thirty-one applicants became members between 1946 and 1955. A large pro-American majority in the original UN membership allowed the United States to muster the needed votes in the Security Council to block Eastern European candidates that Washington saw as satellite Communist regimes. Moscow, in turn, used its veto forty-seven times prior to 1955 to prevent states friendly to the United States from being admitted. The deadlock was resolved in December 1955 with what was known as a "package deal," which admitted sixteen nations from both the Soviet and Western camps and thus kept the voting balance little changed.

Separate from Cold War politics, rapid decolonization in the 1950s and 1960s placed pressure on the organization for enlargement. Membership grew from 76 at the end of 1955 to 110 in 1962. Almost all the new members came from the developing world. With their admission, virtually all membership requirements, other than statehood, were set aside. Many of the new members were geographically small and poor, and each often represented only a minute portion of the world's population. By the turn of the century, more than thirty members had populations of less than one million people. Among the smallest, Tuvalu, admitted in 2000, had a population of ten thousand, and Nauru, admitted in 1999, had eleven thousand. These states' ability to fulfill Charter obligations was suspect. The General Assembly, however, was willing to accept their applications if they maintained friendly relations with other states and fulfilled other international obligations that they had made. After 1955, only a few "partitioned" states were initially barred from membership—East and West Germany, North and South Korea, and North and South Vietnam. A unified Vietnam gained membership in 1977; the two Germanies joined in 1973 and became the one state of a unified Germany in 1990, at the end of the Cold War. By 2022, the only divided country left from the post–World War II period was Korea, whose two halves each gained UN membership in 1991.

The growth in membership, coupled with the principle of sovereign equality that awarded an equal vote to each member, produced a new majority in the General Assembly capable of passing sweeping resolutions but without the power or resources to fulfill new UN commitments. This majority also could, and did, shift the agenda of the world body from peace and security interests among the great powers to economic development concerns. The enlarged size of the world body also led to the formation of caucus groups, the expansion of membership in UN bodies like the Economic and Social Council, and the proliferation of programs and funds for activities promoted by the new states.

North-South Relations and the United Nations

The growth in membership, particularly from formerly colonized areas, highlighted socioeconomic differences within the United Nations. Diplomats and scholars referred to these differences as those between the "North" and the "South." The designations North and South to indicate economic and political differences are comparable to the terms *First World* and *Third World*. Typically, nations north of the equator are considered those that historically were in the forefront of economic and political modernization and benefited most by the Industrial Revolution. Also, colonial powers usually came from the Northern Hemisphere. Conversely, the so-called Third World nations and peoples are often located south of the equator, are economically underdeveloped, and are often the countries and areas colonized prior to the last half of the twentieth century. Within the United Nations, observers and participants use the terms *developed* and *less developed* or *least developed* to denote differences between nations of the North and nations of the South, although the labels *First World* and *Third World* continue to be widely used by the general public. (The designations *North* and *South* have not always been precisely accurate in describing the complete configuration of the world's countries. Some developing countries are found north of the equator, and some developed nations in the south—Australia and New Zealand, for example.) During the Cold War, the Soviet Union and its allies in the Soviet bloc were sometimes placed in yet another category, then called the *Second World.* Many of these states are now alluded to (as was China until recently) as *economies in transition.*

Within the United Nations, the idea of different interests and aims between the North and the South came to have procedural meaning. Particularly in the GA and ECOSOC, caucus groups formed to promote common interests and highlight common concerns for the so-called South. For instance, the *Group of 77* was originally organized as a caucus bloc of Third World nations at the 1964 UN Conference on Trade and Development. The Group of 77 held its first ministerial meeting in 1977; as of 2022, it counted 134 member countries, most from the Southern Hemisphere.

Several of the countries of the South were also non-aligned during the Cold War, joining neither Western alliances of northern states nor Soviet-inspired alliances, such as the Warsaw Pact. These countries, becoming the majority from the 1960s onward, often acted together as the largest bloc in UN organs, frequently frustrating the more powerful nations of the North who had initiated the United Nations in the 1940s and who found forming their own caucus group—the West European and Other States bloc (or Western bloc)—necessary.

During the 1970s, and with less vigor in later years, the countries of the South attempted in the United Nations to create international measures to provide for a significant transfer of economic resources from the North to the South. The Group of 77 proposed the **New International Economic Order (NIEO)** at the 1974 special session of the General Assembly, seeking a drastic revision of global trading rules and processes to replace the Bretton Woods system described in Chapter 2. The Group of 77 sought more favorable terms of trade for primary commodities and urged a revaluation of trade that would have constituted a global redistribution of wealth. The proposal was based on the *theory of dependency*, which charged that industrialized nations had rigged the rules of international trade to keep developing nations permanently impoverished and "dependent" on developed nations for goods, support, and markets for their under-priced exports. Specifically, the Group of 77, in cooperation with the UN Conference on Trade and Development, advocated commodity agreements, the transfer of technology to the developing world, a generalized system of preferences on tariffs for poorer countries, the establishment of producer cartels to negotiate with importing countries, and increased financial aid from the developed North to the South. By the mid-1980s, however, because withholding production had little effect on most commodity prices and the key to development was foreign direct investment, developing nations modified their objectives and adopted more pragmatic goals. The most radical ideas—the development of an entirely new trading system and a global redistribution of wealth—were abandoned and replaced with calls for debt reduction, debt forgiveness, grants, and foreign direct investment.

National Liberation and the United Nations

Contributing to the North-South division in the United Nations was the phenomenon of "national liberation." **National liberation** refers to the efforts of a people—sometimes an ethnic group, sometimes a self-defined "nation"—to free itself from colonial control or from any kind of oppressive rule. Wars of national liberation, then, are a means of seeking independence from outside or repressive regimes. The American and French Revolutions have often been considered the first successful "national liberation movements" of modern history, in that the first event liberated thirteen colonies from an external, imperial overlord and the French upheaval freed a "people" from an internal, authoritarian monarchy. In the post-World War II period, national liberation struggles became common in world politics and succeeded in establishing the independence of several former colonial possessions in Africa and in Asia. Examples spanned the second half of the twentieth century and included ancient civilizations such as India (gaining independence from the United Kingdom in 1947); former French colony Vietnam, where national liberation guerrillas fought first the French and then the Americans; and many other polities that became new states and were usually located in the geographic South. In the 1950s and 1960s, newly liberated nations joined the United Nations, becoming the majority of the UN's membership. As a rule, the new states became members of the Group of 77 as well.

The Palestine Liberation Organization (PLO), founded in 1964 and led by Yasser Arafat from 1967 into the twenty-first century, represented several characteristics of national liberation movements. It sought to resist the intrusion of the state of Israel into territories it believed belonged to the Palestinian people. In effect, the PLO defined an Arab population as "Palestinian" by virtue of its existing in the geographic area of Palestine, it organized a political infrastructure and a military arm for guerrilla resistance, and it led a diplomatic effort to convince the world of the legitimate national aspirations of the Palestinians. It signed international agreements and succeeded in receiving considerable support in the United Nations—particularly from nations recently successful in their own national liberation efforts—achieving observer status in the General Assembly in 1974. In November 2012, the GA (via Resolution 67/19) upgraded Palestine to a "non-member observer state" in the United Nations, making Palestine's status equate with that of the Holy See.

The Non-Aligned Movement and the United Nations

With the expanding membership during the Cold War, the **Non-Aligned Movement** became the most significant caucus group in the UN System. It was initiated at a summit conference in Belgrade, Yugoslavia, in 1961 so that newly independent former colonies could resist Cold War pressures to affiliate with either of the two superpowers. Its summits continue to be held every three years, and foreign ministers meet in the interim. These non-aligned states have been held together informally and have included most of the Group of 77 countries. The United Nations became the main site of their diplomacy, their contact with other nations, and their involvement in global affairs. The movement transcended continental regional blocs, and the number and diversity of its member nations—in size, economies, governments, and ideologies—required it to adopt broad policies and concentrate on global issues. While seeking to balance itself between the East and West blocs, it also opposed colonialism and apartheid, supported the Palestinian cause, and called for development assistance, all of which underscored important shifts in the UN's emphases during the Cold War. Because of the overlap in policy preference and the similarity of membership in the Group of 77 and the Non-Aligned Movement, the distinction between the two became blurred. As of 2022, the Non-Aligned Movement represented 120 member states and eighteen observer countries. Although critics often contended that no longer did anyone exist to be non-aligned with, given the end of the Cold War, the movement maintained momentum into the twenty-first century. By emphasizing global rather than bilateral negotiations, the Non-Aligned Movement continued its efforts to enhance the UN's role in international affairs.

EVOLUTION OF INTERNATIONAL LAW

We discuss the International Court of Justice in Chapter 4 (also see Resource 4 on the Routledge eResources webpage for the Statute of the ICJ). At this point, we need note only that the court—and the progression of international law[6] that is part of the court's history—like the Cold War, the emergence of formerly colonized countries, and the specific amendments of the Charter, has rendered the UN's environment different, and in some respects more expansive, from what it was in 1945.

The Statute of the ICJ, by containing the modern definition of *international law* (Article 38), codified world legal standards in the post-World War II era. Study of the United Nations (especially what we term the "new United Nations") requires at this stage of our text a recounting of the evolution of international law so that you can grasp the central connection between international law and the United Nations.

The rules and norms regulating activities between and among nation-states—often called *the law of nations*—were, according to tradition, termed *international law* by the English philosopher Jeremy Bentham (1748–1832). Bentham's term became preferred by the middle of the twentieth century, although it was often expanded to *public international law* to contrast it with *private international law* (also called the *conflict of laws*), which involves regulating private matters affected by more than one legal jurisdiction. By the beginning of the twenty-first century, in part because of quickening developments in the international community, and particularly because of activities within the UN System, the province of international law expanded, in some instances including areas of jurisdiction once thought to be outside its realm. For example, the late twentieth century witnessed a development in the field of international economic law that is a mix of public and private. The expansion can also be seen in the war crimes tribunals at the turn of the century in which individuals were accused of violating human rights, even within their own country. Nonetheless, the new applicability of international law has not resulted in any comparable supranational means of enforcement. While law within nations is enforced by means of what might be called the *police function* of the state, no such mechanism exists in an international community composed of sovereign nations.

Article 38 of the Statute of the ICJ names the sources of international law as international conventions, international custom, general principles of law recognized by civilized nations, judicial decisions, and teachings of the most qualified publicists on the topic. Of these, ratified international conventions and treaties carry the most weight. Some legal experts also consider arbitration awards as precedents for developing law in the international arena. International law is usually considered part of national or municipal law. For example, Article 6, paragraph 2 of the U.S. Constitution declares the following:

> All treaties made, or which shall be made, under the authority of the United States, shall be the supreme law of the land; and the Judges in every State shall be bound thereby, anything in the Constitution or laws of any State to the contrary notwithstanding.

Sometimes, we (the current generation) think we have originated all the most progressive human procedures. However, the development of formal relations between and among nations, empires, and peoples has been a human activity since the millennia before the Common Era. In fact, scholars have seen a pattern in world history of cross-cultural intercourse among political elites the world over that has led to what might be called *international affairs* or even *international law*. Basic principles and precedents emerged as different political communities sought to impose order on their mutual relations and to resolve disagreements without resorting to force, except as those principles might allow or require it.

The modern concept of **international law** emerged at the end of the Middle Ages in European history. Typically, international law regulated diplomatic practices (i.e., protection of diplomatic personnel, rules of seniority among ambassadors to a specific country, and related diplomatic matters), maritime intercourse, restrictions on weapons, and the commencement and conduct of war among princely states. In 1625, the Dutch jurist **Hugo Grotius** (1583–1645) published his *De jure belli ac pacis* (*Concerning the Law of War and Peace*), the first comprehensive text of international rules. His views were frequently studied and on occasion applied in international interactions. One point worth noting is that Grotius and many early publicists on international law—including Dutchman Cornelius van Bynkershoek (1673–1743), German philosopher Christian von Wolff (1679–1754), Swiss jurist Emmerich de Vattel (1714–1767), and German Georg Friedrich von Martens (1756–1821)—highlighted the sovereignty and legal equality of states, principles later placed in the UN Charter (Article 2, paragraph 1). The concept of the sovereign state was enshrined in the 1648 Treaty of Westphalia, which prohibited interference by outside powers in a state's internal affairs. In the Westphalian system, states took on obligations in the international community only by their voluntary commitments, which were made largely through treaties. By the late eighteenth century, the use of treaty agreements had advanced the course of international law.

Grotius developed many of his concepts of modern international law from an empirical study of what nations actually did in his time. However, the Dutch scholar also asserted that international law was a reflection of the law of nature based on reason. This assertion divorced his view from earlier theological conceptions of higher law. Accordingly, Grotius's 1625 work invigorated an already existing "naturalist" school of international law. In the works of Francisco Vitoria (1480–1546), Father Suarez (1548–1617), and Samuel Pufendorf (1632–1694), these naturalists argued that international law should codify not simply what states do, but rather what states *should* do to conform to the principles of justice. The natural law tradition these scholars espoused remained a secondary thread of international law until the 1940s, when the horror of the Nazi era produced a new interest in using international law to defend human rights, protect values even if states had not officially agreed to them in treaties, and punish states for "crimes against humanity." In this spirit, the preamble of the UN Charter "reaffirm[ed] faith in fundamental human rights, in the dignity and worth of the human person, [and] in the equal rights of men and women."

The period of the Napoleonic Wars in the early nineteenth century witnessed a disregard for the law of nations. The Congress of Vienna (1814–1815), which concluded these wars, sought the restoration of traditional rules of diplomacy and introduced newer and more standardized legal principles, such as respect for the freedom of navigation on international waterways and more precise classification for and protection of diplomatic personnel. What had been "customary" international law—accepted practice—was clarified in legally binding international agreements. These changes in thought marked the beginning of the long era of "legal positivism." The Declaration of Paris (1856) following the Crimean War represented the first major attempt to codify the rules of maritime warfare and served as the accepted rule of law on the high seas until it became infeasible with the introduction of submarines in World War I. As the century proceeded, multilateral agreements were negotiated that established international rules for weights and measures, trademarks, copyrights, patents, and other matters for which legal uniformity was desirable. New technologies resulted in international conferences that established the International Telegraph Union (at Paris in 1865) and the Universal Postal Union (at Berne, Switzerland, in 1874). In the post-World War II period, these early unions became UN specialized agencies: the International Telecommunications Union and the Universal Postal Union.

Meanwhile, arbitration became fashionable as a means of settling disputes. With the Jay Treaty of 1794, the United States and Great Britain initiated the practice of setting up mixed commissions to settle disagreements unyielding to normal diplomacy. The post-U.S. Civil War *Alabama claims* arbitration in 1872 between the United Kingdom and the United States marked a decisive phase in the arbitration movement that culminated with the establishment of the Permanent Court of Arbitration at The Hague Conference of 1899. Subsequently, The Hague Conference of 1907 expanded rules governing arbitral procedures. Both Hague Conferences also issued a number of declarations and conventions dealing with the laws of war, including those banning aerial bombardment, submarine mines, and poison gas. In the meantime, Pan-American Congresses in the Western Hemisphere established several continent-wide diplomatic practices. The onset of World War I brought this progress to a halt. Many provisions of international law were violated, and new problems arose (e.g., submarine warfare and the use of chemical weapons) for which existing standards of international behavior were inadequate.

The creation of the League of Nations and the Permanent Court of International Justice following the war were attempts to create multinational institutions that could subject disputes among nations to the rule of law. The League represented the first attempt in history to maintain a permanent organization committed to developing and codifying international law. League conferences brought forth more than one hundred twenty international understandings covering a range of subjects. Although many of these understandings fell short of full ratification, they became a model for the future United Nations, and some—such as those dealing with the control of narcotics, traffic in persons, economic statistics, and slavery—remained in force through UN amendments or further treaty action. Moreover, the UN Secretary-General's office became responsible for the depository of extant League documents.

The rise of Fascism and Nazism in Europe and of militarism in Japan and then the collapse of international order in the 1930s brought discredit to the effectiveness of international law and international agreements and destroyed the League of Nations. The advent of World War II tainted international law with the darkest of hues.

Yet, phoenix-like, out of the war rose the United Nations and the new International Court of Justice. In fact, during the post-World War II period, international law underwent considerable maturation. Although this momentum clearly did not and could not promise a world utopia, the crafting of such an international framework represented an extraordinary human achievement, and, from 1945 onward, the United Nations was at the heart of these developments.

Since the end of World War II, differing opinions have been expressed about exactly what international law is and how it is to be executed. One straightforward view is that all nations should obey international law, just as individuals should obey domestic (or municipal) law. Yet, some lofty thinkers—Samuel Pufendorf and Thomas Hobbes in the seventeenth century, John Austin in the nineteenth, and Henry Kissinger in the twentieth—have challenged even the notion of an international "law," because no legitimate enforcer exists. Sociologists have emphasized the behavior of states rather than overarching principle and thus have argued that international law cannot shape international politics but merely adjust to it. Marxists have regarded international law as only an instrument of class oppression; Chinese scholars, whether or not followers of Mao Zedong, have described international law as a set of platitudes that have historically been ruinous to non-Western cultures. Many citizens of Third World nations have believed themselves victimized by Euro-centered notions of international law. Feminists have argued that "the rules of international law privilege men," that women are "marginalized," and that international law is "a thoroughly gendered system,"[7] and postmodernists—emphasizing relativism, difference, and the problematic nature of language itself—have questioned any "universalist" assumption of a fundamental international law deriving from a narrow, elitist political tradition in the Western First World. Naturally, a common commitment to a single conception of legal principles is less likely when the core interests of one nation diverge from those of other nations. Yet, in practice, international law is widely recognized, and most nations have participated in its evolution. The penalties for failing to comply, although less severe than in national cases, and often unenforceable, are economic sanctions, the constraint of public opinion, intervention by third states, international condemnation (e.g., by means of UN resolutions), and, as a last resort, war.

The wider reach of international law in the early twenty-first century is due in no small part to the activities of UN-related organizations. The International Court of Justice, which replaced the Permanent Court of International Justice after World War II and is popularly known as the *World Court*, has made modest but significant contributions to the development of international law. The ICJ has done so through judgments and advisory opinions that have affected maritime law, questions of diplomatic immunity, the legitimacy of mandates under the League of Nations, the competence of the United Nations, the jurisdiction of UN principal organs, and other matters. By virtue of Article 13, paragraph 1, of the Charter, the General Assembly acquired the obligation to initiate studies and make recommendations for "encouraging the progressive development of international law and its codification." In 1947, the assembly gave this Charter function to the International Law Commission, an auxiliary, autonomous organ of the assembly, which began the slow process of codification. The GA Sixth Committee works closely with the International Law Commission; it reviews the work of the UN Commission on International Trade Law (UNCITRAL), negotiates relevant treaties and agreements to submit to the General Assembly Plenary (the Sixth Committee spent thirty years in intricate negotiations to determine an internationally acceptable definition of *aggression*), and deals with reports from all UN bodies on legal matters. UNCITRAL, created by the GA in 1966, develops conventions, rules, and legal guides to harmonize international trade law. The UN Office of Legal Affairs, initiated in 1946, serves the Secretariat and provides legal advice to the Secretary-General. The World Intellectual Property Organization (WIPO), established in 1970, promotes the protection of intellectual property worldwide, and the International Maritime Organization (IMO), begun in 1959, is the only UN agency solely involved with issues of shipping safety and environmentally sound oceans. The UN's efforts to internationalize outer space and bring it into the realm of recognized international law resulted in the 1966 Outer Space Treaty and the 1979 Agreement Governing Activities of States on the Moon and Other Celestial Bodies (the so-called Moon Agreement). The Committee on the Peaceful Uses of Outer Space, set up by the General Assembly in 1959 to review and encourage international cooperation, has adopted several additional treaties and conventions to regulate outer space, and in 1974 the committee set up the Office for Outer Space Affairs, which maintains a registry of space objects.

Other important areas of developing international law that are less directly connected with the United Nations derived from various arms agreements (beginning with the Limited Test Ban Treaty of 1963), from the internationalization of Antarctica (1959), and from a number of agreements regarding international economic and financial relations. The General Agreement on Tariffs and Trade (GATT), a negotiating regime initiated in 1948 to encourage lowering trade barriers around the world, became the World Trade Organization (WTO) in 1995. GATT/WTO, along with related organizations (the International Monetary Fund and the World Bank) founded at the Bretton Woods Conference (the UN Monetary and Financial Conference) in 1944, sought to bring harmony and common rules

Photo 3.1 The International Court of Justice (ICJ) in session in The Hague, The Netherlands.
Source: UN/DPI Photo/A. Brizzi. Reproduced by permission of the United Nations.

to world trade and finance. The Bretton Woods institutions and the WTO's trade decisions became controversial in the late 1990s. These controversies are covered in Chapter 4.

One of the most comprehensive agreements affecting the development of international law was the UN Convention on the Law of the Sea (UNCLOS), which established a framework to deal with questions of sovereignty, jurisdiction, use, and national rights and obligations in ocean areas. The convention was opened for signature in 1982, entered into force in 1994, and served as the basis over the next two decades for important legal decisions by both the ICJ and the Permanent Court of Arbitration.

In addition, the United Nations has been involved in the growth of international environmental law. Usually, the United Nations Environment Programme administers the many treaties brokered by the United Nations, including agreements on desertification, biological diversity, movement of hazardous wastes, protection of the ozone layer, and control of acid rain. The Kyoto Protocol, negotiated at a UN conference in 1997, set standards for states to use to curtail greenhouse emissions and thus combat global warming. Climate change concerns intensified, and in 2015, the Paris Climate Agreement, covered in the Introduction and elsewhere in this text, replaced the Kyoto Protocol. The new regime included, at the time, support from China and the United States, the world's major greenhouse polluters.

Undoubtedly, the most celebrated UN contribution to the creation of new international law is in the broad area of human rights. The contemporary development of international law as an expression of a higher law that governs all human activity found its first modern expression in the international war crimes trials following World War II at Nuremberg and for Japanese enemies in Tokyo. Nothing like the trials had happened before and nothing like them took place again until the late twentieth century. Captured German and Japanese leaders were not charged with violating any particular treaty commitment, or even with violating their own domestic laws. Rather, they were tried, convicted, and punished for crimes against humanity. Following the trials, with time, an abundance of international agreements and rules developed that seemed to proscribe the atrocities classified as human rights violations. In 1946, the General Assembly affirmed "the principles of international law recognized by the Charter of the Nuremberg Tribunal and the judgment of the Tribunal." At the same time, the assembly declared, "Genocide is a crime under international law," and in 1948 the GA approved the Genocide Convention (Convention on the Prevention and Punishment of the Crime of Genocide).

In 1946, ECOSOC established the UN Commission on Human Rights, chaired by Eleanor Roosevelt. This commission was given a mandate to compose a Universal Declaration of Human Rights. Working with a group of celebrated international legal minds from various cultures, Mrs. Roosevelt discovered that conceptualizing rights and fleshing out international law were multicultural, even multicivilizational, endeavors. Peng-chung Chang, a Chinese philosopher, brought an Asian and Confucianist perspective to the commission's discussions; Charles Habib Malik, a view from the Arab Middle East; Hernán Santa Cruz, from Chile, a Latin American political left perspective; and Hansa Mehta, an Indian outlook and an insistence that women's equality be clearly articulated. René Cassin, a French Jew, had a unique outlook, colored by the most recent, and appalling, example of human rights violations. When in late 1948 the General Assembly passed the Universal Declaration without a dissenting vote, no longer could anyone assert without challenge the notion that rights and the practice of international law were strictly Western conceits. René Cassin noted a significant, if subtle, breakthrough in his 1968 acceptance speech upon receiving the Nobel Peace Prize: after the Universal Declaration, nations still retained jurisdiction over their citizens, he said, but it would "no longer be exclusive."[8] From the seventeenth century to 1948, absolute state sovereignty had been the underpinning of international law. With the ascension of the primacy of rights, international law entered a new, uncertain phase. Combined with the declaration, the International Covenant on Economic, Social and Cultural Rights, and the International Covenant on Civil and Political Rights—both opened for signature in 1966 and both brought into force in 1976—made up the *International Bill of Human Rights.*

The UN organs passed other conventions and declarations announcing an assortment of human rights. Among these new rights were those of the child, indigenous people, women, refugees, stateless persons, migrant workers, and the disabled. The United Nations also defined rights to development, employment, and family life. In the summer of 1993, more than one hundred seventy nations met in Vienna and adopted a sweeping declaration affirming the principle that "all human rights are universal" and that "it is the duty of states, regardless of their political, economic and cultural systems, to promote and protect all human rights and fundamental freedoms." Add to this the establishment of UN-related war crimes tribunals (for Rwanda, the former Yugoslavia, Cambodia, and Sierra Leone), which at the turn of the century were prosecuting individuals for crimes against humanity *in their own countries,* plus the adoption in Rome in 1998 of a statute establishing an International Criminal Court to try individuals for genocide, crimes against humanity, war crimes, and aggression, and the implication Cassin discerned comes into fuller relief. (In Chapter 7, we will discuss these developments fully.)

As the third millennium began, international law was on a trajectory far beyond anything imaginable at its start.

FINANCIAL CRISIS AND THE IMPETUS FOR REFORM

The expansion of international law and human rights (as well as the UN's response to the demands of its new members in the developing world) reflects the institution's continuing evolution. From the moment of the UN's initiation, many governments have noted flaws in its structure and procedures and have recommended changes to make the organization more effective in the face of new challenges. Acceptance of the Charter by several original members was predicated on their ability either under the amendment process or through normal diplomatic interchange within the United Nations to pursue future alterations in a decidedly imperfect organization. The membership growth in the United Nations and the strains of the Cold War only aggravated the weaknesses in the Charter, compelling the major powers, the Secretary-General, and the GA to make both formal and informal changes in how the United Nations operated. During the first twenty-five years, these changes included the expansion of membership of both the Security Council and ECOSOC. Such changes also included informal "amendments," like the Uniting for Peace Resolution and the elaboration of peacekeeping. Out of this last innovation—peacekeeping—a financial crisis emerged during the 1950s and 1960s that dramatically worsened during the ensuing thirty years and contributed to the most sweeping UN reforms in its history.

Responding to the British, French, and Israeli 1956 invasion of the Suez Canal, the General Assembly created the UN Emergency Force (UNEF)—the UN's first peace-keeping operation. The assembly, on the recommendation of Secretary-General Dag Hammarskjöld, determined that UNEF's costs were "expenses of the Organization" as defined by the UN Charter. Therefore, all members were required to pay their assessed share of the expenses. The Soviet Union, Eastern European states, and Arab governments balked at paying for the operation. They argued that these costs should be charged to the "aggressors."

The financial situation was aggravated further in the early 1960s by the huge expenditures required to deploy a UN force in the Congo. The General Assembly endorsed Hammarskjöld's initiative to put a UN operation into the midst of the Congolese civil war and use the force to protect and extend the authority of the central government. At its height, the UN effort cost more than the entire remaining budget of the world body. Making matters worse, the Soviet Union and France refused to pay for the operation. These states asserted that since the Security Council had not authorized the operation under Chapter VII of the Charter, the United Nations could not mandate assessments for it. Even a 1962 advisory opinion by the ICJ upholding the GA's position could not move the delinquent governments to meet their financial obligations to the organization.

Unable to raise the requisite funds through the normal budgeting process, the United Nations turned to unorthodox financing methods. The General Assembly authorized the sale of $169 million in bonds, effectively borrowing against future assessment income. The United Nations also postponed payment to countries that contributed troops and matériel to the Congolese and subsequent peacekeeping operations, in effect making these governments pay the UN costs out of their national treasuries. In 1965, the assembly established a special account for sought-after voluntary contributions as a cushion against future unexpected expenses. In other words, the United Nations went hat in hand to its largest contributors, particularly the United States, to try to keep the organization financially solvent.

These measures were not popular with many governments that opposed the UN actions on policy grounds. The USSR, which saw the Congolese operation and Hammarsk-jöld's actions as little more than an extension of U.S. Cold War foreign policy, refused to participate in any of these financing schemes. Other countries prorated their contributions or targeted their payments to avoid paying for the UN activities with which they disagreed. These tactics became a common practice and by the end of the century, nearly one-third of the UN membership had not paid its assessments in full for the regular budget, amounting to $244.2 million.

Article 19 of the UN Charter states the following:

> A Member of the United Nations which is in arrears in the payment of its financial contributions to the Organization shall have no vote in the General Assembly if the amount of its arrears equals or exceeds the amount of the contributions due from it for the preceding two full years.

As the UN's deficit mounted during the Congo operation, the United States attempted to force the payment issue by threatening to invoke Article 19 against the Soviet Union. When the USSR said it would withdraw from the United Nations if it lost its vote in the General Assembly, the United States relented. In announcing his government's decision in 1965 to drop the matter, the U.S. permanent representative Arthur Goldberg said:

> If any member can insist on making an exception to the principle of collective financial responsibility with respect to certain activities of the United Nations, ... the United States reserves the same option to make exceptions if, in our view, strong and compelling reasons exist to do so.[9]

Known as the **Goldberg Reservation**, this statement appeared at the time to be just an expression of disgust and an admission of defeat, for the alternative to achieving full payment by all states in the United Nations was increased contributions by the United States. By the end of Lyndon Johnson's term as president of the United States, the U.S. government was paying nearly one-third of all UN bills. However, following the 1980 election of President Ronald Reagan, Washington willingly exercised the Goldberg Reservation, which produced an extraordinary financial crisis.

THE CONTINUING BUDGET CRISIS

The United Nations is a membership organization in which each member state pays a certain percentage of the budget. From the beginning, the General Assembly, which approves the scale of assessment triennially, has based the amount each nation is expected to contribute on its "capacity to pay." Therefore, the rich developed states pay a much larger percentage of the budget than developing countries do, although the desperate circumstances of the poorest countries often means that even the minimal contribution demanded of these states amounts to a high per capita payment and is often beyond the means of the government. Nearly all the nations that have lost their votes in the GA at one time or another under Article 19 were among the poorest states with the lowest-percentage assessments. For example, in January 2015, thirteen nations, including Kyrgyzstan, the Former Yugoslav Republic of Macedonia, Vanuatu, Tonga, Rwanda, Grenada, Liberia, Marshall Islands, Comoros, Guinea-Bissau, Sao Tome and Principe, Somalia, and Yemen, fell far behind in their payments. Some of these states had been on the list for many years—Comoros, for example, since 2002. These nonpayments occurred even though in some cases the assessment was as little as $4,800.[10] However, in the end, the General Assembly allowed all except Yemen to continue voting in the Chamber.

To the extent that a country's share of world income determined the "capacity to pay," the United States would have had to pay 50 percent of UN expenses during the organization's early years. This situation would have been politically untenable for Americans; thus, the "ceiling" set for any contributor was 40 percent of the budget. By the early 1970s, the United States was paying approximately one-third of UN expenses but demanding that this amount be reduced. In 1973, the ceiling was set at 25 percent, at U.S. request, which remained the American assessment until radical revisions in the budgeting and assessment process occurred at the close of the century.

The growing unwillingness of the United States to pay its share of the budget as a result of consternation with UN policies or with specific UN agencies, coupled with the nonpayment of dues by other states, left the United Nations in a perennial funds shortfall. This deficit was particularly true in its peacekeeping budget, which along with the "regular" budget and the international criminal tribunals budget compose the organization's expenses for which members have an obligation to pay. Even in the aftermath of the terrorist attacks of September 11, 2001, the United States moved slowly to make up its payments to these various budgets, owing in November of that year $265 million to the regular budget, $800 million to peacekeeping, and $14.6 million to the tribunals account.[11] The United States was not alone in its selective payments. Half the debt owed was held by members other than the United States. Between 1993 and 2021, the shortfall between actual payments and assessed contributions from all countries ranged between $200 million and $860 million annually for the regular budget, and up to $3.3 billion for peacekeeping.

Washington has been particularly concerned about funds going to specialized agencies with which it disagrees. On occasion, it has even threatened funding to other groups if they cooperate with those agencies. In March 2002, the Bush administration withheld $34 million from the UN Population Fund (UNFPA) and additional funding in 2003 because the White House believed UNFPA's policies promoted abortion: a claim the agency denied. Then, in 2004, the United States pressured the UN Children's Fund (UNICEF) and the World Health Organization (WHO) to limit cooperation with UNFPA or have their financing cut. The succeeding administrations of presidents Barack Obama and Donald Trump pursued the same strategy. When the United Nations Educational, Scientific and Cultural Organization (UNESCO) membership voted to admit Palestine as a full member in 2011, the United States pulled its dues payment of $60 million, effectively crippling UNESCO's ongoing programs, and then in October 2017, it completely withdrew from the organization. In July 2020, amidst a global pandemic, the Trump administration announced that the United States would also withdraw from the World Health Organization, a step it could not formally take until the succeeding July. The election of Joe Biden to the White House granted a reprieve to both agencies, given the new administration opposed both moves.

International organizations are the creatures of the states that establish and maintain them. Thus, they cannot move far beyond their financiers' agendas. During the first decades of the new millennium, the UN System remained financially captive to its members' political and ideological goals, particularly those of the United States.

Scale of Assessment and the Budget Process

The proposed UN budget for 2021 (only the second time that the organization allocated funds for a one-year cycle) was $3.2 billion, with another $6.7 billion allocated for peacekeeping operations. That may seem a large amount. But, by comparison, consider that the total budget for the U.S. State Department, the Agency for International Development, and other U.S. international programs was approximately $40 billion in the same year. The U.S. Department of Defense's budget for the equivalent period was more than $700 billion. Given the breadth of UN activities, the organization's budget is quite small.

The criterion of "capacity to pay" is subject to interpretation, debate, and political controversy. The GA's Fifth Committee, supported by the Committee on Contributions and by the Advisory Committee on Administrative and Budgetary Questions (ACABQ), determines both the UN budget and the assessment each country contributes toward the budget.

The **scale of assessment** used to calculate the percentage of the budget each member state is to pay uses "ceilings" and "floors" above and below which no nation's dues may be set. These ceilings and floors were set in recognition that factors other than simply the capacity to pay are part of the triennial allocation of budget shares. The minimum assessment was initially .04 percent. It was lowered progressively to .001 percent in 1997. This downward shift has resulted from recognition of the economic challenges confronting the least developed and low-income states. The consequence is that the major industrialized nations pay the preponderance of the UN budget, particularly its peacekeeping budget. In December 2000, the U.S. contribution was lowered from 25 percent to 22 percent of the regular budget and from 31 percent to 27 percent of the peacekeeping budget, which effectively set the ceiling for the largest contributor. As of 2021, after the United States, Japan paid 8.56 percent of the UN budget; Germany, 6 percent; France, 5.6 percent; Russia, 3 percent; and Great Britain paid 5.8 percent.[12]

On the basis of each country's share of world income, a nation's contribution to the UN budget is "discounted" to account for the poverty level in the country. Thus, although two states may have the same share of world income, one will pay far less as a result of a per capita income that is considerably less than that of the other member state. A "scheme of limits" also arbitrarily prevents a state's assessment from rising or falling precipitously when its share of world income dramatically changes. This scheme sometimes benefits states that experience significant economic improvement, but it can also injure the same states when economic conditions worsen. The oil-producing nations of the Middle East argued for this system when recognition of their increasing share of world revenues from oil sales would have driven their share of UN assessments higher, but then they found themselves with excessive payments when oil prices plummeted.

The upshot of these artificial restraints on the capacity to pay has been a financially strapped United Nations and many nations unhappy with the amounts they are required to pay for UN operations. Not only the United States, but also Japan and other large contributors have complained about their assessments. In 2004, Japan announced that it intended to cut its voluntary contribution to a number of UN agencies, including the UN Development Programme (UNDP), the UN Population Fund, and the UN Children's Fund.[13] A year earlier, Japan threatened to cut its contribution to UN peacekeeping and UN regular operations by as much as 25 percent.[14] These cuts would have a dramatic impact on the United Nations, because Japan's contribution amounted to more than that of Germany, France, Russia, and Great Britain combined.

Japanese objection to its UN dues level was driven in part by the United States' ability to cut its contribution while Japan's rose. The U.S. diminution to 22 percent in 2000, coupled with a 19.5 percent assessment for Japan, irked Japanese lawmakers at a time when Japan's economy accounted for 14.4 percent of the world's gross domestic product (compared with the United States' 30.3 percent share). Japan was also unhappy that, despite long-standing commitments from major powers, it had not been able to secure a permanent seat on the Security Council. Under pressure from Tokyo, the UN gradually lowered the Japanese contribution over several budget years to its current rate.

The Japanese recalcitrance to pay its assessed dues demonstrated the financial frailty of the United Nations, dependent at all times on the economic largesse of its most important members. The financial crisis that set in during the 1960s lingered into the new millennium, which limited the UN's ability to fulfill its commitments. In 2004, for example, Secretary-General Kofi Annan worried aloud whether the UN's international tribunals would be able to even continue their work.[15] In fact, they had to borrow money from the peacekeeping budget to stay afloat. From 2018 onward, Secretary-General António Guterres regularly warned that the United Nations faced "the worst cash crisis in a decade." He had to shift funds from one account to another to pay operating expenses and feared that a point was coming when the UN could not cover payroll or buy supplies.[16] The world body also had to turn to outside donors—countries that were willing to make additional voluntary contributions, such as Canada, or private contributors, such as media mogul Ted Turner and Microsoft's Bill Gates—for funds to cover shortfalls or to pay for planned humanitarian programs. Guterres recommended several budgetary reforms detailed later in this chapter.

The irony of the situation was that, given that in the 1960s the United States had led the effort to force the Soviet Union and others to pay their ascribed UN dues, the U.S. debt owed to the United Nations was the factor that most severely weakened the United Nations. By the close of the millennium, the United States, always the UN's largest creditor, had become its biggest debtor, and by 2020 it owed the organization slightly less than one billion dollars. The United States' unwillingness to pay generated questions about the survivability of the world organization.

U.S. Nonpayment of UN Dues and the Demand for Reforms: Is the United Nations Worth It?

The UN's creation was part of the idealist and multilateralist traditions. American advocates of realism, beginning with President Truman's secretary of state, Dean Acheson, have criticized the organization for seeking to achieve ends it cannot bring about in a geopolitical world. *Unilateral* idealists such as presidents Ronald Reagan and George W. Bush have complained that the multilateral nature of the UN has limited U.S. action and made the body unworkable. These schools of thought, however, were in the minority and limited in their impact on the U.S. policy toward the United Nations until the early 1970s. Americans' disappointment with the United Nations emerged with the anti-U.S. tilt of the UN General Assembly in that era. The assembly's seating of the People's Republic of China (1971) and simultaneous removal of Taiwan (a U.S. ally), plus its shift to a decidedly pro-Palestinian posture in the Arab-Israeli standoff, undermined public support for the world organization. U.S. politicians asked aloud whether continuing to pay so many of the UN's bills made sense, since the new developing-world majority was using the platform of UN bodies to denounce Washington's policies and support friends of the Soviet Union. The Nixon administration (1969–1974), given its geopolitical outlook on world affairs, did little to dampen public hostility toward the organization.

The 1981 arrival of Ronald Reagan in the White House meant an even harsher approach to financial support of the United Nations. In the body politic, Reagan's conservative wing of the Republican Party had been the strongest critic of the United Nations. Under Reagan, this philosophy translated into the administration's refusal to pay its assessments.

During Reagan's first term, the Heritage Foundation, a Washington-based conservative think tank, published an anthology titled *A World Without a U.N.*[17] Its authors urged the president to rethink U.S. membership in the United Nations. They made the radical argument that U.S. interests could best be served by leaving the world body. The author of the book's foreword was Charles M. Lichenstein, a former alternate U.S. representative to the United Nations, who, after sitting through a UN committee meeting in September 1983 at which several Third World delegates berated the U.S. policy, advised the assembled diplomats to "seriously consider removing themselves and this organization from the soil of the United States." He continued, "We will put no impediment in your way and we will be at dockside bidding you a fond farewell as you set off into the sunset."[18] Other Reagan appointees joined the anti-UN campaign. Secretary of State Alexander Haig called the world body "with its vociferous anticolonialist coalition of Third World and Marxist members ... ineffective."[19] Even the U.S. permanent representative Jeane Kirkpatrick took an adversarial approach at the United Nations. Among the many speeches she gave as the UN ambassador were those with the titles "Standing Alone" and "The Problem of the United Nations."[20] The president himself evaluated the United Nations as an institution that had diverged from the values and ideals that originally motivated its founders and was now "too often fraught with strife, division, and conflict."[21] However, his critics cited the president's UN policy as one of the sources of this strife and division.

Disillusioned with the "politicized" character of the UN Educational, Scientific and Cultural Organization, the administration withdrew its membership and canceled funding for the specialized agency. In 1985, twenty years after U.S. ambassador Goldberg suggested that the United States would exercise its right to halt payments to the United Nations if it believed its interests required the action, President Reagan signed congressional legislation unilaterally reducing the U.S. contribution to the UN regular budget from 25 percent to 20 percent and limiting its payments for peacekeeping operations until institutional reforms were made. The *Goldberg Reservation* was reinforced with the *Kassebaum Amendment* (named for Kansas senator Nancy Kassebaum), which cut U.S. payments to the UN organs until their staffs were reduced significantly and until these organs made revisions to their charters to allow weighted representation based on the size of the members' financial contributions. These actions led to a growing U.S. debt owed to the United Nations that by 2000 left the United States on the verge of losing its vote in the GA. Only a last-minute compromise between Washington and the United Nations led to a payment of U.S. arrearages in 2001. The U.S. payment was made possible by the most extensive reform program in the UN history.

UN REFORM

The departure of the United States and its funds from UNESCO produced a change in leadership at the agency and the introduction of a reformed system for staff appointments and promotions. The agency shifted resources to field operations more compatible with U.S. interests. Many delegations decried UNESCO's reaction as an inappropriate concession to the world's most important power. However, by 1993 the new Clinton administration was willing to tell Secretary-General Boutros Boutros-Ghali that "in principle" the United States would soon be willing to return to the agency. The lesson was not lost on Boutros-Ghali. The UNESCO episode was a harbinger of future change in the organization. U.S. financing was so critical to UN survival that reforms demanded by Washington had to be accommodated in New York.

Efforts by Pérez de Cuéllar and Boutros-Ghali to Accommodate U.S. Demands for Reform

Responding to pressure from the U.S. government has been a recurring necessity for the United Nations and its Secretaries-General.[22] The mounting demands from Washington in the 1980s for changes in UN operations and policy led successive UN leaders to look for some accommodation that would ease U.S. complaints and lead to U.S. payment of its arrearages.

Nothing in the UN Charter allows a national government to conduct an internal review of UN management. Yet, Secretary-General Javier Pérez de Cuéllar opened the records of the UN's Joint Inspection Unit (JIU), the auditing and evaluation arm of the General Assembly, to a full review by the U.S. General Accounting Office (GAO). Seeking to identify waste in UN agencies and operations, the GAO cited poor record keeping and little value to the reports the JIU had developed. The agency recommended to Congress that the UN office make significant reforms before new U.S. funds were sent to the organization.

To assuage the U.S. criticism, Pérez de Cuéllar's successor, Boutros Boutros-Ghali, launched a highly visible management review. In 1992, he appointed a former U.S. attorney general, Richard Thornburgh, as the new under-secretary-general (USG) for administration and management. Thornburgh was given a free hand to review the full UN administration and to make recommendations for dramatic reform. After a year's study, he issued a stinging indictment of the Secretariat. In the **Thornburgh Report**, the former attorney general noted a high percentage of "deadwood" in the UN bureaucracy and called for a cut in staff.[23] Thornburgh proposed the creation of an inspector general's office that would root out fraud, waste, and abuse. Thornburgh also asked the Ford Foundation to fund its own study on UN administrative reform. The foundation appointed Paul Volcker, former chairman of the U.S. Federal Reserve System, and Shiguro Ogata, former deputy governor of the Japan Development Bank, to head the project. The final **Volcker-Ogata Report** focused primarily on UN financial operations. It called for a unified peacekeeping budget to be charged against the national defense budgets of the member states and for more efficient use of UN resources.

The United States said that it would not support any UN budget increases until these recommendations and other significant administrative reforms were undertaken. After 1994, the Clinton administration's hard line was surpassed by the conservative Republican Congress, which also wanted to limit the UN peacekeeping operations and U.S. participation in them. Senator Jesse Helms called the United Nations a "power-hungry and dysfunctional organization" and demanded a 50 percent cut in its staff.[24]

Boutros-Ghali responded by freezing the UN budget and embracing the idea of an inspector general. His support led to the 1994 creation of the Office of Internal Oversight Services (OIOS), headed by a director with a five-year term and considerable independence from the Secretary-General. The office was mandated to conduct internal audits and to search out mismanagement. OIOS claimed in 2004 to have identified waste and fraud totaling $290 million and to have made more than five thousand recommendations to improve organizational efficiency and effectiveness.[25] OIOS established a sophisticated internal audit system and turned to investigating high-charged controversies such as sexual abuse claims and other corrupt practices against UN personnel in peacekeeping operations. In 2020–2021, it had more than 890 of its recommendations accepted, saving the organization $3.5 million.[26]

By appeasing the United States, the Secretary-General hoped his reforms would allow the United Nations to take an expanded role in post-Cold War security efforts. It seemed to pay off in that following the Gulf War of 1991 both presidents George H. W. Bush and Bill Clinton called for a wider UN role in keeping world peace, particularly through the expansion of its peacekeeping functions. They, along with other world leaders, directed Boutros-Ghali to recommend ways to strengthen the United Nations and make it more efficient in "preventive diplomacy" and peacekeeping. In June 1992, he published his report, Entitled *An Agenda for Peace*, that outlined the most ambitious UN program for peacekeeping in the organization's history. Boutros-Ghali recommended, among other things, that military forces be placed at the UN's disposal for rapid action in times of crisis.

Photo 3.2 Boutros Boutros-Ghali, Sixth Secretary-General of the United Nations.
Source: UN Photo/Milton Grant. Reproduced by permission of the United Nations.

On the heels of his recommendations, the Secretary-General attempted to mobilize the United States and the rest of the world community to deal with the collapse of order in the east African nation of Somalia. At his initiative, Security Council Resolution 751 (April 1992) created UNOSOM I (UN Operation in Somalia I), a small, unarmed peacekeeping force for Somalia. In November, faced with warlord threats to the peacekeepers, he sought U.S. military assistance to restore order and to deliver food supplies to the starving population. The Americans soon became enmeshed in a nasty civil conflict between rival warlords. In October 1993, eighteen U.S. soldiers were trapped in a firefight and killed. Lurid photographs and videos of one of them being dragged through the streets of Mogadishu appeared in the world press. U.S. support for more vigorous UN peacekeeping efforts waned, troops were home within the year, and criticism mounted that the United Nations was incapable of ordering the internal affairs of any country.

For Rwandans, the shifting mood was particularly perilous because a brutal, genocidal civil conflict had broken out between the rival Tutsi and Hutu tribes. Although the United States had originally supported the UN Assistance Mission for Rwanda (UNAMIR), the outbreak of massacres in April 1994 caused it to propose cutting the number of peacekeepers in the region for fear of their safety. Even more important, in May, Clinton issued Presidential Decision Directive 25 (PDD-25), which severely limited U.S. involvement in UN peacekeeping operations and ended U.S. support for expanded UN missions. The administration set eighteen preconditions that would have to be met before the United States would support a peacekeeping operation. U.S. endorsement would hinge on, among other measuring sticks, whether the UN operation advanced U.S. interests, whether all parties consented to UN intervention, whether the proposed operation had "well-defined" goals, and whether the U.S. Congress and the American people supported the operation.[27]

PDD-25 urged extensive reform of the peacekeeping process. It proposed a unified peacekeeping budget—in line with the Volcker-Ogata recommendations—funded by a single, annual peacekeeping assessment overseen by professional budget experts. It set as policy the goal of reducing the U.S. contribution to the peacekeeping budget from 31 percent to 25 percent. The directive called for an overhaul of the Department of Peace-keeping Operations (DPKO) as well.

The 1994 off-year congressional elections in the United States brought the Secretary-General and his ideas about an invigorated United Nations into direct conflict with a new legislative Republican majority made up of senators and members of Congress who saw the United Nations as inefficient, inept, yet bent on gaining too much power at the expense of U.S. sovereignty. Conservatives even pointed to nongovernmental organizations with the UN consultative status that held values different from theirs. In one telling case, the U.S. Senate voted to withhold millions of dollars in payments to the United Nations if the organization continued to recognize the International Lesbian and Gay Alliance. In the Senate, the Congress's most severe UN critic, Senator Jesse Helms of North Carolina, became the chairman of the Foreign Relations Committee. In this position, he could block all U.S. funding earmarked for the United Nations. He made clear that only the most dramatic reform would lead to U.S. payments of its arrearages.

The Secretary-General and Senator Helms then engaged in a public argument in the pages of the respected journal *Foreign Affairs*. In the spring of 1996, Boutros-Ghali penned a defense of his ideas about an active Secretary-General at the head of a more vigorous, reformed United Nations committed to expanded peacekeeping and nation-building. Five months later, in the same journal, Helms used blunt language to lambaste the United Nations and excoriate its leader. He accused Boutros-Ghali of resisting reform that "gets down to the fundamentals" and of protecting unqualified and unneeded UN bureaucrats. The senator charged the Secretary-General with wasting U.S. funds on unnecessary world conferences and ineffective peacekeeping missions. Helms said the U.S. Congress would not pay its debt to the United Nations unless Boutros-Ghali was replaced with a reformer acceptable in Washington, DC.

Although Boutros-Ghali had disavowed a second term when he entered office in 1992, a number of nations, including some of America's closest allies, strongly supported his ree-lection in 1997, and the Secretary-General, having changed his mind, made a spirited campaign to save his job. However, the political climate in Washington, DC clearly made his continuance impossible. Boutros-Ghali had become the lightning rod in the United States for displeasure at all that seemed wrong with the United Nations. Despite unprecedented diplomatic pressure on Washington from some of its major allies to reverse its position,

---

The time has come for the United States to deliver an ultimatum: Either the United Nations reforms, quickly and dramatically, or the United States will end its participation ...

I am convinced that without the threat of American withdrawal, nothing will change....

The United Nations has neither reformed nor died. The time has come for it to do one or the other.

—Senator Jesse Helms,

- "Saving the U.N.: A Challenge to the Next Secretary-General," *Foreign Affairs* 75, no. 5 (1996): 2–7.

the United States held to its decision to veto Boutros-Ghali's renomination in the Security Council. Having entered office at a high point of optimism within the United Nations, Boutros Boutros-Ghali, the victim of a spate of uncontrollable in-state collapses, a continuing decline in UN financing, and U.S. antipathy, left office after one tumultuous term.

Kofi Annan and the Reform "Revolution"

Four factors drove the UN reform process at the end of the millennium:

*   U.S. government demands for serious institutional changes.
*   A long-term financial crisis brought on by many members' nonpayment of their UN assessments, including the unwillingness of the United States to deal with its financial indebtedness to the organization.
*   The expansion of UN obligations, particularly for peacekeeping—the UN Administrative and Budgetary Committee approved $2.8 billion for peacekeeping in 2004–2005, with an expectation that the cost could rise by 60 percent in the following year—including engaging in nation-building, battling terrorism, and providing humanitarian assistance (within a decade the cost would be nearly $8 billion).
*   The election of an activist Secretary-General who made reform the hallmark of his tenure in office.

With the reelection of Boutros-Ghali blocked, the Security Council nominated and the General Assembly chose Kofi Annan of Ghana as the seventh Secretary-General. He was clearly Washington's choice, and was immediately welcomed to the White House in January 1997. Annan promised the president and the U.S. Congress a serious reform program. On July 16, he delivered on his commitment, issuing *Renewing the United Nations*, the most sweeping set of administrative and financial reform proposals made in the institution's history. During the next six years and into Annan's successor's term, reform would come in three broad areas: administrative, programmatic, and structural.

Administrative Reform

During his first month in office, Kofi Annan eliminated one thousand UN staff positions that were unfilled at the time. He also moved to consolidate more than two dozen departments, funds, and programs into four thematic groupings. A trusted aide of Annan's chaired the executive committee for each group and was later added to a "cabinet" for the Secretary-General, known as the *Senior Management Group (SMG)*. The thematic groups ensured coordination and lessened duplication among Secretariat offices, specialized agencies, and UN bodies that answered to the General Assembly. The largest was the Development Group, chaired by the head of the UN Development Programme, which brought together representatives of the five regional economic commissions, the UN Conference on Trade and Development, the UN Population Fund, the Food and Agriculture Organization, and nine other organizations.

These coordination and streamlining measures sent a signal to Washington that Annan was earnest about administrative reform and they were pretext to the extensive proposals in *Renewing the United Nations*. The GA approved the SMG in December 1997 as a strategic planning body to assist the Secretary-General. Annan also created four executive secretariat committees at the senior level to coordinate UN policies. These were replaced in 2017 by a single executive committee under Secretary-General Guterres. Annan's most dramatic and lasting administrative proposal was the appointment of a

Photo 3.3 Secretary-General Kofi Annan and Nane Annan, arriving in Zagreb for their official visit to Croatia.
Source: UN Photo/Sergey Bermeniev. Reproduced by permission of the United Nations.

deputy Secretary-General who would manage the Secretariat when the Secretary-General was away from headquarters, would spearhead the reform movement within the organization, and would promote coherence in the efforts of the entire UN System. The General Assembly approved this post at the end of 1997, and Annan appointed Louise Fréchette of Canada, who became the highest-ranking woman in UN history.

Annan's reforms consolidated twelve Secretariat entities into five, cut UN personnel 25 percent below 1987 levels, reduced administrative costs by 33 percent, set up a development account in which cost-cutting savings could be held for development programs in poor countries, and decentralized "decision-making at the country level while [consolidating] the United Nations presence under 'one [UN] flag.'"[28] This last change reflected Annan's effort to enhance the role and authority of the UN resident coordinator in each country where the organization had programs, and to bring together all in-country UN agencies into one "UN House." Two decades later, António Guterres would officially make the Resident Coordinator the top administrator in each country where the UN worked.

The approved reforms addressed the near-bankruptcy of the United Nations by shifting the organization to a "results-based budgeting" system, enhancing accountability requirements for all UN subdivisions and specialized agencies, calling for the creation of a revolving credit fund of one billion dollars, and establishing "sunset provisions" to guarantee that bodies no longer needed would be disbanded.[29] They were sufficient to jar the U.S. Congress and the president into promises of final payment of the UN arrearages. Even Senator Helms noted the substantive changes being made in New York and urged U.S. funding.

On April 26, 2002, the Secretary-General appointed M. Patricia Durrant, Jamaica's permanent representative, the UN's first ombudsman. Her job was to provide impartial and independent service to staff members with employment-related problems. Completely independent of any UN organ or official, the **ombudsman** operates under strict confidentiality, hearing complaints from any staff member about work conditions, and advises the parties as well as the organization of conflict resolution options within the organization. The ombudsman cannot be dismissed, except by the Secretary-General; serves a five-year nonrenewable term; and cannot be appointed to any other UN System post after service in the ombudsman's office.

Annan's appointment of Durrant as the first ombudsman reflected another major "reform" of the UN administration: the concerted effort to bring talented women into the Secretariat and other important UN offices. Notoriously male dominated, the United Nations attempted a sea change in its personnel structure, work environment, and policy orientation that reflected the importance of women to its work and vision. In addition to appointing Durrant, the Secretary-General made several other highly visible female appointments; important among them were Louise Fréchette as deputy Secretary-General; Mary Robinson, former president of Ireland, as UN High Commissioner for Human Rights; Catherine Bertini, former director of the World Food Programme, as the under-secretary-general for management; and Carolyn McAskie as Annan's special representative to war-torn Burundi. This last appointment was particularly noteworthy because only one other woman had ever headed a UN peacekeeping mission: Margaret Joan Anstee of the United Kingdom, whom Secretary-General Boutros-Ghali appointed in 1987 to direct the operation in Angola.

Although women have found a voice and recognition in the work of the United Nations, the Louise Fréchettes and Eleanor Roosevelts have been in a distinct minority. Most female employees have served in gender-traditional and junior-level positions. Studies of the bureaucracy, professional ranks, and specialized agency staffs demonstrated at the end of the twentieth century that women were significantly underrepresented. In pursuit of gender parity, which the GA set as a goal to be achieved by 2000, the Secretary-General reported in 2001 that women accounted for only 33.5 percent of the professional and higher-level staff of the UN System as a whole.[30] The percentages were slightly better in the Secretariat (40.2 percent as of July 2001). At the time, only one UN agency—the UN Population Fund—had a majority of women (50.4 percent) on its staff. To address the imbalance, the Secretary-General focused attention on the aspects of the workplace that might deter women from serving, including improving sexual harassment policies and gender-neutral promotion criteria. Many of these changes were encouraged by the organized activities of UN female workers, NGO lobbying, and diplomatic pressure from government delegations.

In some UN employment categories, significant progress was made over the ensuing fifteen years, with women coming to constitute a majority in lower professional ranks. But at the highest levels of the UN, women made up only 41.8 percent of the total in 2014. Fifteen years after Secretary-General Annan's Senior Management Group included women in only a quarter of the posts, Ban Ki-moon's SMG had eight women in the thirty-eight-member cabinet, and António Guterres improved to thirty-one women among the SMG's forty-four members. As part of the reform agenda to improve the position of women in UN administration, in 2010 the General Assembly created UN Women. The new body focuses on gender equality and women's empowerment around the world, but among its goals is to promote women's roles in the UN structure.

Secretary-General Ban Ki-moon continued the reform effort, setting up a special panel to make recommendations on effective ways to bring the UN Secretariat into the twenty-first century. The panel proposed *The Change Plan*, which was meant to lessen the sense of rigid hierarchy and to create a "collaborative working culture" in the Secretariat.

The panel urged making the UN more "user-friendly" by working closely with partners outside the bureaucracy and moving UN offices closer to their beneficiaries around the world. Most importantly, it encouraged the Secretariat to enter the digital age, eliminating much of the paperwork of the organization. Ban's successor, Secretary-General Guterres, achieved a landmark GA resolution in May 2018 (A/RES/72/279), agreed to by all 193 member states, authorizing him to move forward on many of the previously proposed reform items.

Beyond the demands of the world body's most powerful member states, administrative reform at the United Nations was being driven in 2021 by many additional factors. Not only was the United States not paying its bills, so too the majority of states were behind on their contributions. Yet, the UN faced upfront costs presented by emergent conflicts to which it needed to respond, unexpected crises like the COVID-19 pandemic, and a global environment with actors who no longer turned first to the UN for solutions to overwhelming problems. The Secretary-General argued that only by making the United Nations "more nimble, effective, transparent, accountable, efficient, pragmatic and decentralized," could the organization better support its expected activities.

Programmatic Reform

Administrative reform can make the United Nations more efficient and, therefore, more effective. However, the legitimacy and usefulness of the United Nations in the eyes of its most important members in the post-Cold War era turn more on the efficacy of its programs and the perceived relevance of its institutional structures. Is the organization still relevant? A creation of the 1940s, premised on collective security, the United Nations can make a meaningful contribution to peace and security in the twenty-first century only if, first, the major states of the world take it seriously and, second, its actions seem to respond effectively to the challenges of the new era.

Most of the programmatic reforms have come in the wake of the Millennium Summit of 2000. They can be grouped into three categories: peacekeeping, development and democratization, and UN relations with international civil society.

In *Renewing the United Nations*, Secretary-General Annan gave special attention to peacekeeping and the work of the Department of Peacekeeping Operations (DPKO). He had headed that department from 1993 to 1995, when the United Nations experienced some of its worst failures in nation-building and peacemaking. After apparent peacekeeping successes in Angola (1988), Namibia (1989), and Cambodia (1992), confidence was heightened that the United Nations could intervene in disintegrating states and not only restore peace but also effectively encourage nation-building. In this atmosphere of optimism, Boutros-Ghali had issued *An Agenda for Peace*, calling for more, not less, UN activism in conflict zones. In Somalia (1993), however, not only UN efforts to deal with the region's warlords, but also the inability of U.S. forces under UN mandate to restore national peace led to recrimination against Boutros-Ghali and demands from Washington that DPKO be overhauled. When ethnic tensions then rose dramatically in Rwanda (1994), SC members, particularly the United States, cautioned against UN intervention, and the genocide of nearly eight hundred thousand Tutsis ensued; even more Rwandans (Tutsi and Hutu) fled the country into makeshift refugee camps in the Congo and other surrounding states. After Somalia and Rwanda, many people questioned whether UN peacekeeping efforts were sufficient for the challenges of the time.

In his 1997 report, Annan called for significant changes in how DPKO managed operations. He also picked up on Boutros-Ghali's earlier recommendation and proposed that the United Nations strengthen its capacity for nation-building. To give coherence and executive leadership to peacekeeping operations, Annan appointed his own special representative to take charge of each mission. The General Assembly responded positively to Annan's proposals and increased DPKO's staff by 50 percent. Then, in March 2000, as we noted previously, the Secretary-General appointed the former Algerian foreign minister, Lahkdar Brahimi, to chair an expert panel on peacekeeping operations, with a view to making sweeping reform recommendations. In the weeks leading to the 2000 Millennium Summit, the panel issued a final document calling for a complete overhaul of the UN's peacekeeping function. (See Chapter 6 for a full discussion of the report.)

The Millennium Summit at world headquarters in New York City in September was a watershed moment in the evolution of the United Nations. Kofi Annan used the occasion to resurrect an old idea about the UN Charter and about the organization it created. In his address to the gathering, and in his accompanying report, he reminded the world that the Charter opens with the words "We the *Peoples,*" not "We the *States.*" Annan acknowledged that the United Nations was a forum for coordinating the interests and behavior of states, but he asserted that it was something more than this:

> Even though the United Nations is an organization of states, the Charter is written in the name of "we the peoples." It reaffirms the dignity and worth of the human person, respect for human rights and the equal rights of men and women, and a commitment to social progress ... in freedom from want and fear alike. Ultimately, then, the United Nations exists for, and must serve, the needs and hopes of people everywhere.... No shift in the way we think or act can be more critical than this: we must put people at the centre of everything we do.[31]

The Secretary-General called for a new understanding of the Charter's charge to "maintain international peace and security."

By the conclusion of the summit, Annan had convinced the assembled nations, often with divergent views about issues like development and human rights, to approve a declaration of the world's hopes for the twenty-first century. They agreed on six "fundamental values" essential to international relations: freedom, equality, solidarity, tolerance, respect for nature, and a sense of shared responsibility. These values were those of a new era in international politics, potentially inherent in the UN Charter but never at the heart of the day-to-day diplomacy within the international organization. The declaration set specific goals, including the following: to halve by 2015 the number of people living on less than one dollar a day, living in hunger, or having no access to clean water; to ensure by 2015 that all children complete primary school and that no gender inequality exists in education; to reduce maternal mortality by three-fourths and the deaths of children younger than five years old by two-thirds; to stop the spread of HIV/AIDS, malaria, and other infectious diseases; to achieve significant improvement in the lives of at least one hundred million slum dwellers; to promote gender equality and the empowerment of women; to encourage the pharmaceutical industry to make essential drugs more widely available; and to provide the benefits of new technologies to all the world's peoples.

These goals were a combination of both development and democratization targets. As world conflicts shifted from Cold War causes to religious, ethnic, and economic origins in the developing world, Annan saw an opportunity to shift the focus of UN activity. Through the nexus of peacekeeping and nation-building, the United Nations could address the overwhelming internal problems of states at risk, could raise the standard of living for millions of people, and could promote international stability by ending human rights abuses within countries. He wrote, "A new understanding of the concept of security is evolving. Once synonymous with the defense of territory from external attack, the requirements of security today have come to embrace the protection of communities and individuals from internal violence." He argued for the United Nations to defend "personal sovereignty." Upholding the new era of peacekeeping, humanitarian intervention, and nation-building, he made this case: "Surely no legal principle—not even [state] sovereignty—can ever shield crimes against humanity." The United Nations has a "moral duty" to intervene on behalf of the individual.[32]

A concerted effort was made to promote democracy in each new peacekeeping operation. The United Nations sought to introduce democratic practices, most particularly regular elections and popular participation. This new approach was used in El Salvador, Mozambique, Cambodia, Guatemala, and Angola.[33] No longer was simply restoring peace between contending forces sufficient. The UN also needed to provide a transitional administration, overseeing the entire political process. According to Kofi Annan:

> Inevitably that means political institutions. At the center of virtually every civil war is the issue of the state and its power—who controls it, and how it is used. No armed conflict can be resolved without responding to those questions. Nowadays the answers almost always have to be democratic ones.[34]

Implied in a UN commitment to protect personal sovereignty and to promote democratic nation-building in failed states is an assertion of the right of the international community to intervene in the domestic affairs of acknowledged sovereign states. The UN Charter specifically cites the "sovereign equality of all Members" and promises no interference "within the domestic jurisdiction of any state" (Article 2, sections 1 and 7). But the Charter also leaves open a slender window by insisting that the provisions just cited "shall not prejudice the application of Enforcement Measures under Chapter VII" (Article 2, section 7). Horrific recent examples have underscored the growing demand for international intervention in state matters. The violence of the civil wars in the Former Yugoslavia (1990s); genocide in Rwanda (1994); violence in Timor-Leste (1999), bloodbath in Darfur (2006–2007), anarchic civil strife in the Central African Republic (2014), and serious human rights violations in the Congo, Myanmar, Syria, and elsewhere have all contributed to the UN's growing willingness to intervene and attempt to create viable democratic states.

The complexity, costs, and goals of peacekeeping operations steadily expanded during the first twenty years of the new millennium. Recognizing the administrative weight of the demands on peacekeeping operations, António Guterres pushed through a major structural change, replacing the Department of Peacekeeping Operations with a new, more broadly mandated Department of Peace Operations (DPO), supported by a new Department of Operational Support.

Responsibility to Protect and the Promotion of Democracy

As noted earlier in this chapter and discussed at length in Chapter 5, a doctrine emerged in 2005, sanctified by the UN's World Summit, to justify active intervention on behalf of personal sovereignty. Known as the Responsibility to Protect, R2P is one of the most ambitious and intrusive conceptual inventions of modern diplomacy. R2P insinuates that external actors (preferably with UN approval) may be required to intervene in the internal affairs of a dysfunctional state that is unable or unwilling to protect its own inhabitants from serious harm.

R2P, a new and novel notion in international relations and international law, marks an extension of evolving moral sensibilities deriving from heightened interest in an individual's human rights, even balanced against the rights of a state. Implicit in the maintenance of individual rights is a presumption of popular sovereignty, best expressed in the modern era through limited democratic government. Secretary-General Ban Ki-moon became a major advocate of advancing democracy and personal sovereignty through nation-building in post-conflict states. In 2009, he published a *Guidance Note on Democracy*, in which he espoused "holistic democracy."[35] The document laid out a blueprint on the purposes, substance, and procedures for the implementation of democratization in failed, transitioning, weak, or non-democratic states.

Ban Ki-moon acknowledged "the internationally agreed normative content" of democracy that had come about through "intense debate" among all stakeholders—local, national, and international. He noted the universal norms and standards that informed even the most local of democratic practices. While maintaining that the United Nations "has never sought to export or promote any particular national or regional model of democracy," the Secretary-General noted that the organization "has long advocated a concept of democracy that is holistic,"[36] and is concretely defined largely by the provisions of the Universal Declaration of Human Rights, which he argued has been given "legal effect in many subsequent UN treaties and instruments." In the new millennium, the United Nations has given democratization the broadest operational definition of any actor in the international system.

The UN's state-building initiatives include the protection of opposition factions, the political mobilization of often-marginalized groups such as women and indigenous peoples, and the restoration or creation of judicial institutions to ensure the rule of law and the defense of individual liberties. These activities necessarily involve UN subsidiary bodies and agencies. By 2009, democratic governance in all of its components had become the largest area of UNDP investment, accounting for 37 percent of the agency's budget. In 2015, the UN Development Programme spent $772 million on 723 democratic governance projects in countries around the world.[37] The United Nations has also turned to partnerships with civil society on the international, national, and subnational levels. It works not only with the governments that are its members but also with the non-state actors that are so much a part of contemporary global affairs. Kofi Annan defined *civil society* as follows:

> [The] sphere in which social movements organize themselves around objectives, constituencies and thematic interests. These movements include specific groups such as women, youth and indigenous people. Other actors have also taken on an increasingly important role in shaping national and international agendas. They include local authorities, mass media, business and industry, professional associations, religious and cultural organizations and the intellectual and research communities.[38]

Early efforts by the Secretary-General to engage civil society included the creation of the *Global Compact*, which invited corporations to establish formal relationships with the United Nations. He also encouraged NGO participation in world conferences and the work of UN agencies, and the cultivation of influential individuals in different countries. By 2021, nearly 15,000 companies in 162 countries had joined the Global Compact.

In February 2003, the Secretary-General appointed a panel of eminent persons, headed by Fernando Henrique Cardoso, the former president of Brazil, to look at UN–civil society relations and to make recommendations on how such relations might be deepened. The panel issued the **Cardoso Report**.[39] It acknowledged that components of civil society had been among the prime innovators and motivators in global relations. The 1992 Earth Summit was a watershed as thousands of private citizens and groups gathered in Rio de Janeiro to publicize a global agenda for environmental protection. From that moment forward, excluding the private sector from the UN deliberations became not only impossible, but also counterproductive. The authors of the report encouraged the involvement of a wide range of civil society actors in UN affairs. Panel members called for a "paradigm shift" in the work of the United Nations, with reforms based on four principles:

- The United Nations should become an "outward-looking organization," serving as the "convener" of multiple constituencies, facilitating rather than "doing." It should put global issues rather than the institution at the center of its work.
- The United Nations should include more, not fewer, actors in its deliberations, creating permanent partnerships whenever possible. The United Nations must recognize that "global civil society now wields real power in the name of citizens."
- The United Nations must attempt to connect the global with the local, recognizing that in the process of globalization, the nation-state cannot always be the mediator between the citizen and the world. The United Nations will implement its programs effectively only if it has a working relationship with the subnational actors present in local communities.
- The United Nations should accept an explicit role in strengthening global governance. It needs to go beyond its intergovernmental nature and become an actor itself in civil society.
- Cardoso and his colleagues urged the Security Council to engage civil society entities in its work. The authors of the report recommended an experimental series of "Security Council seminars" to discuss emerging issues.

Structural Reform

It would be the American decision in March 2003 to employ preventive war against Iraq without Security Council authorization that created an existential crisis for the world organization. Secretary-General Annan recognized sooner than many the danger President Bush's approach represented for the United Nations and the principle of collective security. Leading up to the American invasion, acrimonious debate pitted the United States against France, Germany, and Russia over the necessity for a resolution formally authorizing enforcement action before the United States moved to militarily topple Saddam Hussein. Annan opined, "We seem no longer to agree on what the main threats are, or how to deal with them."

Annan believed the American unilateral decision required the United Nations to find a viable formula to preserve collective security while accommodating a great power's desire to defend itself from what it perceived to be an overwhelming threat. At the opening session of the General Assembly in September 2003, he expressed his fear to the gathered national representatives that the United Nations had reached "a fork in the road." It had to make reforms to sustain its purpose in a world in which states might now act with impunity. The principle of preventive war coupled with unilateral action by great powers could lead to a world of rationalized aggression, the disease the UN was created to cure.

The Secretary-General appointed the High-level Panel on Threats, Challenges and Change. In his charge to the committee, Annan asserted that the U.S. invasion of Iraq without Security Council approval had "shaken the foundations of collective security, and undermined confidence in the possibility of collective responses to our common problems." He charged the Panel to make recommendations on structural reforms that would ensure the effectiveness and relevance of the United Nations in the new era. The group issued its recommendations in December 2004. Entitled *A More Secure World: Our Shared Responsibility*, the report called for "a new security consensus" that would allow for a broader definition of collective security than currently understood in the UN Charter.

On the basis of the panel's recommendations and previous reform documents, Annan put forward structural reform proposals. Entitled *In Larger Freedom*, the Secretary-General's 2005 report called for an expansion of the Security Council to twenty-four members, either by adding six new permanent seats (none with the veto)[40] and three two-year-term nonpermanent seats divided among the major regional groups, or by adding no new permanent seats but creating a new category of eight 4-year renewable-term seats and one new two-year nonpermanent, nonrenewable seat. The Secretary-General warned, however, that simply increasing the size of the council would be insufficient. Any changes would also need to enhance the SC's ability to take prompt and realistic action. This reform issue quickly became bogged down in squabbles over whom the new members should be.

At various times in the past, the United States, Great Britain, and France had all indicated that they would support the addition of Germany and Japan as permanent members to the council (without the veto).[41] In 2010, U.S. president Barack Obama endorsed the addition of India as a permanent member. However, council expansion raised both membership expectations among important regional powers—including, in addition to India, Brazil, Nigeria, Argentina, and Egypt—and countervailing opposition to their permanent appointment. China, in particular, indicated that it was in no hurry to expand the Security Council.

When the Secretary-General appointed the High-level Panel, he charged it with finding some way to allow the United Nations to take preventive action, rather than simply responding to already committed acts that violated international peace and security. Otherwise, the organization could become irrelevant to the decision-making processes of states that felt threatened by potential dangers. Critical for a more effective Security Council, in Annan's view, was the determination to use force before genocide or massive violations of human rights occurred in conflict situations. However, the panel could find consensus only in a restatement of "just law theory" and a set of procedural standards for the council when it was deciding whether to use force. That decision should turn on the seriousness of the threat, the belief that the proposed action addressed the threat, the proportionality of the proposed action, the recognition that force should be used only as a last resort, and a calculation that the benefits of using force outweighed the costs of inaction. None of these changed normal practice or moved the institution toward its own preemptive policy.

In addition to altering the makeup of the Security Council, the Secretary-General recommended eliminating not only the Military Staff Committee (see Chapter 4 for a description of this body), which never functioned as intended, but also, and more important, one of the principal organs of the United Nations: the Trusteeship Council. When the former trust territory of Palau gained its independence in 1994, the trusteeship system accomplished its founders' goal of ending five hundred years of colonial rule and thus rendered the council's continued existence pointless.

Annan also advised the creation of two new bodies and a revitalization of the Secretariat, ECOSOC, and the General Assembly. To address the growing challenges of peacekeeping and nation-building, he urged the creation of a **Peacebuilding Commission** (PBC). He called the nonexistence of an agency to "help states with the transition from war to peace" a "gaping hole" in the UN structure.[42] This commission would focus on creating new national institutions, ensure necessary reconstruction financing, enhance coordination among international agencies, and review progress on post-conflict recovery. The commission would comprise members from the Security Council and ECOSOC, from major troop-contributing states, and from states that contributed significantly to a proposed standing fund for peacebuilding. Annan also recommended a dramatic replacement of the existing Commission on Human Rights with a new, smaller **Human Rights Council**, possibly as one of the principal organs of the United Nations. He argued that the current body had lost legitimacy, given its rotating membership, which often included states accused of human rights abuses, and therefore needed to be replaced with a council having "a status, authority, and capability" commensurate with its importance.[43] He urged that the new council be elected at large by a two-thirds vote in the General Assembly.

CHRONOLOGY OF UN REFORM

December 1985 General Assembly creates the *Group of 18* to consider and make recommendations on the reform of UN administrative and financial operations.

August 1986 The Group of 18 makes seventy-one recommendations on UN reform to the Secretary-General.

March 1993 The *Thornburgh Report* calls for the creation of an office of inspector general and other reforms.

July 1994 General Assembly creates the *Office of Internal Oversight Services.*

January 1997 Secretary-General Annan creates *thematic executive committees* to coordinate policy in four broad areas.

March 1997 Secretary-General Annan merges three departments into one *Department of Economic and Social Affairs.* He also announces his intention to cut administrative costs from 38 percent to 25 percent of the UN budget.

July 1997 Secretary-General Annan issues *Renewing the United Nations: A Programme for Reform.*

December 1997 The General Assembly approves the first set of reform measures that Secretary-General Annan put forward.

March 1998 The post of *deputy secretary-general* is created and charged with overseeing reform.

January 1999 Kofi Annan proposes a *Global Compact* with corporations.

August 2000 Reform recommendations of the Panel on UN Peace Operations (*Brahimi Report*) are published.

September 2000 The *Millennium Declaration* is adopted.

December 2000 The General Assembly endorses *results-based budgeting.* It also lowers the "ceiling" in the scale of assessment to no more than 25 percent for any member.

July 2002 The *UN ombudsman* is appointed.

November 2003 The Secretary-General appoints the *High-level Panel* to make recommendations on UN reforms to address world security challenges.

June 2004 The *Cardoso Report* recommends more active involvement of global civil society in the UN affairs.

December 2004 The *High-level Panel* makes its recommendations on UN reforms to address security challenges in the world, calling for a broader interpretation of collective security and enlargement of the Security Council.

March 2005 In his report *In Larger Freedom*, the Secretary-General proposes enlargement of the Security Council, creation of a Peacebuilding Commission, replacement of the Commission on Human Rights with a smaller Human Rights Council elected by two-thirds vote of the General Assembly, and major Charter revisions.

October 2005 World Summit endorses many of Secretary-General Annan's reform proposals: establishes the Peacebuilding Commission and Human Rights Council. Endorses "Responsibility to Protect" principle.

November 2006 High-Level Panel on UN System-Wide Coherence in the Areas of Development, Humanitarian Assistance and the Environment recommends that the UN System should "Deliver as One" at the country level, with one leader, one program, one budget and, where appropriate, one office.

December 2008 The *Prodi Report* calls for closer cooperation between the UN and regional organizations, particularly the African Union, in peacekeeping efforts.

July 2009 Department of Peacekeeping Operations publishes *New Horizons* calling for interoperability between UN and regional peacekeeping operations.

September 2009 General Assembly creates *UN Women*, pulling together four existing agencies in order to promote gender equality internally and internationally.

December 2011 UN Panel proposes *The Change Plan* meant to create a "collaborative working culture" in the Secretariat, move UN offices closer to their beneficiaries around the world, remove underperforming staff, and bring the UN bureaucracy into a paperless and digital environment.

June 2015 Two Advisory Groups of Experts issue *The Challenge of Sustaining Peace* and *Comprehensive Review of Peacekeeping Operations*, respectively. The first report was in preparation for a complete review of the PBC and its integration with other UN post-conflict efforts. The *Comprehensive Review* called for a thorough reform of the UN peacekeeping architecture and operation.

January 2019 The Department of Peacekeeping Operations becomes the Department of Peace Operations (DPO), supported by a new Department of Operational Support.

Secretary-General Annan's initiatives were part of a long history of efforts to improve the work of the major UN bodies, particularly that of the Security Council. The peculiar combination of sovereign equality, democratic voting procedures, and recognized great-power predominance in the council through the possession of the veto by the permanent members often resulted in frustration over the inability to exercise UN authority in times of international crisis. The end of the Cold War renewed the hope that the council might be able to act as it was intended by the founding nations, and, in fact, for several years in the 1990s unanimity among the permanent members led to the regular exercise of Chapter VII enforcement measures in any number of hot spots. However, the changes in U.S. foreign policy following the terrorist attacks of September 11, 2001, and the preemptive, and largely unilateral, decision by Washington to go to war to drive the Iraqi regime from power undercut the council's consensus. They also led the Secretary-General and major powers such as France, Germany, and the United Kingdom to look for revisions in the Charter that would restore the effectiveness of the council and the world body as a whole.

Some observers, believing the veto has constrained the SC's effectiveness and accorded too much influence to just a few superpowers, have proposed adding to the council new, veto-laden permanent members. Other people have recommended abolishing the privilege altogether or refining the use of the restraint by means of a "weighted" veto, by allowing only two or three members collectively to veto any given proposal. Still other individuals would amend the Charter to establish a requirement that a veto-wielding nation publicly explain the action. However, apart from the Uniting for Peace Resolution of 1950, which momentarily finessed the Soviet Union's veto authority during the Korean crisis, nothing has been done to curtail its use. Following the Iraq war, the veto and the threat of the veto became mainstays of great power politics at the United Nations. Russia blocked UN action following its support of separatists in Georgia (2008), in Ukraine after its annexation of Crimea (2014), in Syria during that country's civil war, and even prevented declarations that the COVID-19 pandemic and climate change were threats to international peace and security. The United States regularly blocked SC action in the Palestinian-Israeli conflict and the lifting of sanctions against Iran. The possibility that any current member would support amending the Charter to limit its own participation, cut its veto powers, or extend the veto to others seemed slim.

Only Annan's proposed Peacebuilding Commission found broad support. It was created, along with a Peacebuilding Fund, by the General Assembly and the Security Council in December 2005 with a mandate to recommend integrated strategies for post-conflict peacebuilding and recovery, to improve the coordination of all relevant actors within and outside the United Nations, and to help ensure predictable financing for peace operations.

Despite the broad expectations of member states that the new commission would strengthen the UN's impact on post-conflict states, in its early years it failed to find a central function in the search for international peace and security. Consequently, Secretary-General Ban Ki-moon's primary reform focus was on integrating the PBC into the broader UN peace operations architecture. Two reviews in 2010 and 2015 respectively sought the integration of the Peacebuilding Commission into the decision-making process of the Security Council and its inclusion in the implementation of peace in post-conflict states. The reviews additionally recommended close coordination with the World Bank and other actors to find common strategies that would lead to a multiplier effect, as well as PBC strategies that would bring "coherence" among the UN agencies and between intergovernmental organizations in the advancement of sustainable peace.[44]

Annan's proposed Human Rights Council was not as popular with the UN membership as the Peacebuilding Commission. There was initial opposition from states and regions that feared a "moral imperialism" by major Western powers. Nonetheless, the forty-seven-member body came into being in March 2006, but has continued to be a venue of contention, particularly for the United States, which withdrew from it in 2018 during the Trump administration, only to return after Joe Biden was elected to the White House.

Scandal and the United Nations

The legitimacy of an institution, and the authority and power that flow from its legitimacy, depends significantly on its public image. Internal reforms mean little if the organization is perceived as corrupt, abusive of its power, contributing to the problems it is supposed to ameliorate, or ineffective. Scandal can destroy an organization or be an impetus for reform. Given that large organizations, including corporations, governments, and international organizations, are likely to have some level of mismanagement, fraud, or scandal, an entity's ability to survive and maintain its legitimacy depends on how it responds to internal miscreant behavior. The United Nations, the largest international organization in history, is not immune to these forces.

Since 2004, scandals large and small have plagued the United Nations. The most significant early outrage was the charge that its oil-for-food program, which it operated under SC authorization to provide humanitarian supplies (food, medicines, etc.) to the Iraqi population living under the dictatorial rule of Saddam Hussein and paid for with Iraqi oil revenues, had been fleeced for billions of dollars in kickback payments to Iraqi officials, in excessive payments to outside vendors, and in laundered funds to UN officials.

Driven in part by the extensive reporting of influential *New York Times* columnist William Safire, the U.S. Congress launched several committee investigations. Safire called the oil-for-food program a scam and a "great cash cow"[45] that milked $10 billion into the pockets of contractors, traders, banks, and the UN inspectors, including Kofi Annan's son, Kojo Annan, who worked for Cotecna, one of the contracting companies. The Secretary-General sought to demonstrate that the United Nations took the charges seriously and would find the truth and punish anyone involved in wrongdoing. Annan appointed Paul Volcker, mentioned previously in this chapter, to head an independent investigation. The Volcker panel found that Kojo Annan had concealed his continuing relationship with Cotecna, in which he received more than $150,000 following his departure from the company. He was also accused of lying to the committee and failing to cooperate with the investigation. The panel revealed that documents had been destroyed, and it criticized an unacceptably limited investigation by the Secretariat. Volcker faulted the Secretary-General for lax governance and for not questioning his son's activities more carefully, but he said the panel found no evidence of wrongdoing or cover-up by the Secretary-General.[46]

For the long-term reputation of the UN, a far more serious set of charges emerged in 2004. Three young staff members published *Emergency Sex and Other Desperate Measures: A True Story from Hell on Earth*, detailing their demoralizing and even sordid experiences in UN operations in crisis areas around the world.[47] The book left the impression that many individuals serving in the UN missions were unqualified and psychologically unfit for their positions. The publication described excessive alcohol use and sex parties among the UN workers and underscored unremitting despair for some workers who saw the UN efforts to assist people as ineffective, and even, in some cases, immoral.

Emergency Sex appeared on bookshelves just as the Security Council learned about internal studies of UN staff in peacekeeping missions that found serious misconduct toward local populations and poor internal policing by the United Nations. The most serious seemed to be in the Democratic Republic of the Congo (DRC), where peacekeepers were reported to have traded food for sex with local women, to have had regular liaisons with prostitutes, and to have been involved in sexual exploitation of women and girls. The Secretary-General announced a "zero tolerance" policy for such practices not only in the Congo but in any UN peacekeeping operation, a position reinforced by each of his successors. The Security Council reaffirmed this policy in its reauthorization of the DRC operation,[48] calling on troop-contributing countries to prosecute offenses involving their personnel.

Secretaries-General Ban Ki-moon and António Guterres understood that they would have to press for truly qualitative changes in how the UN operated in peacekeeping settings, particularly as reports of abuses accumulated. In 2006 and 2007, more than four hundred cases of sexual exploitation of both women and children by UN personnel were reported.[49] During the period, the UN suspended eight hundred peacekeepers in Côte d'Ivoire on allegations of sex with minors, and sent home one hundred Sri Lankan personnel from Haiti because of accusations of sexual abuse against underage girls and solicitation of prostitution.[50]

Even in hybrid peacekeeping operations, sexual misconduct has been prevalent. French troops acting under UN mandate in the Central African Republic were accused in 2014 of abusing children, mostly boys nine to fifteen years old. Adding to the scandal was the revelation that UN authorities knew about the activity for nearly a year and took no action, deferring to the French government. One of the UN officials was Flavia Pansieri, deputy high commissioner for human rights. She was forced to resign. The Secretary-General appointed an independent panel headed by a former Canadian supreme court justice to investigate the affair and recommend action. Based on the findings of that report, on March 11, 2016, the Security Council, by a 14–0 vote (Egypt abstaining), passed Resolution 2272, the first resolution specifically aimed at the problem. The resolution authorized the Secretary-General to repatriate full military or police units "where there is credible evidence of widespread or systemic sexual exploitation and abuse." The resolution represented a new UN policy and struck a stern note.

Other than possible referral of abusers to their national governments for criminal prosecution or to the International Criminal Court, better training of peacekeepers and careful monitoring of personnel during operations are essential. Guterres launched the A4P program (**Action for Peacekeeping Initiative**) to provide well-structured, well-equipped, well-trained forces. As part of A4P, the Secretary-General appointed a system-wide Victims' Rights Advocate to work with governments and civil society to ensure that victims had a clear way to report allegations.[51] He also established the Voluntary Compact on Preventing Sexual Exploitation and Abuse, which, as of May 2021, had been signed by 103 member states.[52]

There are limited tools available to the UN to end this egregious behavior. Peacekeepers generally have immunity from local law enforcement, yet are not directly subject to the United Nations. The UN cannot impose its own disciplinary procedures on most peacekeepers. Troops are national contingents sent by their nation's armed forces, and, therefore, are only subject to their own nation's laws, which likely cannot be enforced outside their home jurisdiction. With the huge expansion of peace operations in the twenty-first century, the problem of misconduct could remain a serious challenge to the effectiveness of the world body.

Beyond the obvious misconduct of peacekeepers, they, and the UN generally, can be perceived sometimes as ineffective, or even contributing to the problem they were assigned to solve. The UN operations in Haiti following a devastating earthquake in 2010 serve as an example. The UN peacekeepers introduced cholera into the country through fecal matter released as sewage into a river. More than 10,000 Haitians died and hundreds of thousands were made ill. The United Nations accepted "moral," but not legal responsibility, so as to avoid likely millions of dollars in forced compensation. The organization did set up a trust fund to help victims directly affected and to provide material assistance. Since then, the UN has also seemed helpless to stop human rights violations in Myănmar or solve the resulting refugee crisis, end the civil war in Syria, or slow the steady rise in great power tensions around the world. All of these vexations have the effect of undermining the legitimacy and authority of the only universal and longest-lasting collective security association in the world.

SUMMARY

The UN Charter provides a constitutional framework for the United Nations. Like any written foundational document, it lays out an organizational and functional arrangement that met its authors' needs but has required amendment and reinterpretation as times and conditions have changed. Although the Charter has been amended formally only five times in the UN's history, the majority of changes in the United Nations have resulted from informal revisions in UN practice. Most importantly, the growth in UN membership, Cold War pressures, financial woes, the U.S. discontent with the United Nations, and peacekeeping and new-era demands on the organization have forced concerted reform in the world body. The reform process has been closely associated with the secretary-generalship of Kofi Annan, who tried to refocus the organization on the challenges of human rights protection, development, democratization, and emerging international civil society. In this process, questions about the UN's relevance and structural change became paramount. The need to amend in fundamental ways how the United Nations operates seemed obvious to one and all. Annan's successors, Ban Ki-moon and António Guterres, focused on administrative and programmatic reforms, streamlining the delivery of services worldwide and addressing inefficiencies and failures in UN operations. Real structural change seemed too difficult to achieve in the new century, despite the stated desire by nearly all stakeholders to do so, leaving the world organization with a worrisome and uncertain future.

KEY TERMS

Action for Peacekeeping (A4P) Initiative (122)
Amending the Charter (87)
Article 19 (101)
Cardoso Report (115)
Goldberg Reservation (101)
Hugo Grotius (95)
Human Rights Council (118)
In Larger Freedom (117)
International Law (95)

Membership (90)
National Liberation (92)
New International Economic Order (92)
Non-Aligned Movement (93)
Ombudsman (111)
Peacebuilding Commission (117)
Renewing the United Nations (109)
Scale of Assessment (103)
Thornburgh Report (106)
Volcker-Ogata Report (106)

DISCUSSION QUESTIONS

Compare and contrast the UN Charter with the fundamental document of your home country (such as the U.S. Constitution).

What was the impact of the Cold War on the evolution of the UN Charter?

How has International Law evolved since the founding of the United Nations?

Can you think of a way to reform the membership and voting powers on the Security Council that would be politically acceptable to the permanent members?

RESOURCES FOR FURTHER RESEARCH

Relevant Web Sites

See Resource 4 on the Routledge eResources page for the Statute of the International Court of Justice: www.routledge.com/9781138185807
Global Policy Forum (www.globalpolicy.org)
International Law-Related Web Sites: (ejil.org/links/index.php)
International Law Site of the United Nations (www.un.org/en/global-issues/international-law-and-justice)
UN Foundation (www.unfoundation.org)

UN Office of Internal Oversight Services (oios.un.org/)
UN Reform Website (reform.un.org)
UN Wire Website (www.smartbrief.com/un_wire/index.jsp)

Books, Articles, and Documents

Annan, Kofi. "'In Larger Freedom': Decision Time at the UN." *Foreign Affairs* 84, no. 3 (2005): 63–74.

Ban Ki-moon. *Guidance Note of the Secretary-General on Democracy.* New York: United Nations, 2009, found at Roland Rich, Special Report, muse.jhu.edu/article/379589/pdf.

Beck, Robert J., Anthony Clark Arend, and Robert D. Vander Lugt, eds. *International Rules: Approaches from International Law and International Relations.* New York: Oxford University Press, 1996.

Beigbeder, Yves. *The Internal Management of the United Nations Organizations.* New York: St. Martin's Press, 1997.

Change Management Team. *The Change Plan.* New York: United Nations, 2011.

Drifte, Reinhard. *Japan's Quest for a Permanent Security Council Seat: A Matter of Pride or Justice?* New York: St. Martin's Press, 2000.

Fassbender, Bodo. *UN Security Council Reform and Right of Veto.* The Hague, The Netherlands: Kluwer Law International, 1998.

Fasulo, Linda. *An Insider's Guide to the UN.* 4th Edition. New Haven, CT: Yale University Press, 2021.

Gregg, Robert W. *About Face? The United States and the United Nations.* Boulder, CO: Lynne Reinner, 1993.

High-level Panel on Threats, Challenges and Changes. *A More Secure World: Our Shared Responsibility.* UN Document A/59/565. New York: United Nations, December 2, 2004.

Jackson, Richard L. *The Non-Aligned, the UN, and the Superpowers.* New York: Praeger, 1983.

Moore, John Allphin, Jr., and Jerry Pubantz. *American Presidents and the United Nations: Internationalism in the Balance.* New York: Routledge, 2022.

Murphy, Craig. *The Emergence of the NIEO Ideology.* Boulder, CO: Westview, 1984.

Panel of Eminent Persons on the United Nations—Civil Society Relations. *We the Peoples: Civil Society, the United Nations and Global Governance.* UN Document A/58/817. New York: United Nations, June 21, 2004.

Renewing the United Nations: A Programme for Reform. UN Document A/51/950. New York: United Nations, July 16, 1997.

Simma, Bruno, ed. *The Charter of the United Nations: A Commentary.* New York: Oxford University Press, 1994.

Singh, Nagendra. "The UN and the Development of International Law." In *United Nations, Divided World: The UN's Roles in International Relations*, 2nd Edition, edited by Adam Roberts and Benedict Kingsbury, 384–419. Oxford, UK: Clarendon, 1993.

Thakur, Ramesh. *The United Nations, Peace and Security: From Collective Security to the Responsibility to Protect.* Cambridge: Cambridge University Press, 2006.

Weiss, Thomas G. *The Responsibility to Protect.* E-International Relations, 2011. Found at www.e-ir.info/wp-content/uploads/R2P.pdf.

Notes

1 See Nagendra Singh, "The UN and the Development of International Law," in *United Nations, Divided World: The UN's Roles in International Relations*, 2nd Edition, eds. Adam Roberts and Benedict Kingsbury, 384–419 (Oxford: Clarendon, 1993).

2 The full report can be found at <peacekeeping.un.org/en/report-of-panel-united-nations-peace-operations-brahimi-report-a55305>.

3 <www.globalr2p.org/resources/2021-unga-r2p-resolution/>.

4 <www.globalr2p.org/what-is-r2p/>.

5 Karen A. Mingst and Margaret P. Karns, *The United Nations in the Post–Cold War Era* (Boulder, CO: Westview, 1995), 23, 42.

6 What follows is based in large part on the entry for the term *international law* in John Allphin Moore, Jr., and Jerry Pubantz, *Encyclopedia of the United Nations*, 2nd Edition, Vol. I (New York: Facts on File, 2008), 237–242.

7 Robert J. Beck, Anthony Clark Arend, and Robert D. Vander Lugt, "Feminist Voices," in *International Rules: Approaches from International Law and International Relations*, eds. Robert J. Beck, Anthony Clark Arend, and Robert D. Vander Lugt, 253–255 (New York: Oxford University Press, 1996).

8 Quoted in Mary Ann Glendon, *A World Made New: Eleanor Roosevelt and the Universal Declaration of Human Rights* (New York: Random House, 2001), 114.

9 Thomas Franck, *Nation against Nation* (New York: Oxford University Press, 1985), 85–86.

10 Ban Ki-moon, Letter dated 12 January 2015 from the secretary-general to the President of the General Assembly. A/69/722.

11 For extensive information on the UN financial crisis, see the Website for the Global Policy Forum: at <www.globalpolicy.org/en>.

12 In Focus Report, Congressional Research Service, October 26, 2021, at <crsreports.congress.gov/product/pdf/IF/IF10597>.

13 Thalif Deen (Reuters), "Squeezed Japan Threatens Cuts to UN Agencies," January 7, 2004, at www.globalpolicy.org/finance/docs/2004/0107japan.htm.

14 David Pilling, "Japan May Cut Its United Nations Contribution," *Financial Times*, January 16, 2003.

15 Mark Turner, "UN Warns of Funds Shortfall for Tribunals," *New York Times*, November 21, 2003. Also see UN General Assembly, "UN financial status 'good, but only in parts,' under-secretary-general for management tells Budget Committee," press release, GA/AB/3614, May 4, 2004.

16 António Guterres, Remarks to the General Assembly 5th Committee, June 4, 2019, at <www.un.org/sg/en/content/sg/speeches/2019-06-04/remarks-the-fifth-committee>.

17 Burton Yale Pines, ed., *A World without a U.N.: What Would Happen if the U.N. Shut Down?* (Washington, D.C.: Heritage Foundation, 1984).

18 Ibid., ix.

19 Alexander M. Haig, Jr., *Caveat: Realism, Reagan, and Foreign Policy* (New York: Macmillan, 1984), 270.

20 Jeane J. Kirkpatrick, *The Reagan Phenomenon—and Other Speeches on Foreign Policy* (Washington, D.C.: American Enterprise Institute, 1983), 79–91, 92–98.

21 Office of the Federal Register, National Archives and Records Administration, *Public Papers of the Presidents of the United States* (Washington, D.C.: U.S. Government Printing Office, 1981), 905–906; (1982), 2:1154.

22 Not only on budgetary matters has the UN bent to U.S. demands. For example, Trygve Lie, the organization's first Secretary-General, in the midst of Senator Joseph McCarthy's campaign to root out Communists in American life, allowed the U.S. Federal Bureau of Investigation (FBI) to investigate Secretariat members for possible ties to the Communist Party, even allowing an FBI office to be opened in the UN headquarters.

23 House Committee on Foreign Affairs, Management and Mismanagement at the United Nations: Hearing before the Subcommittee on International Security, International Organizations and Human Rights, 103rd Cong., 1st session, March 5, 1993.

24 Jesse Helms, "Saving the U.N.: A Challenge to the Next Secretary-General," *Foreign Affairs* 75, no. 5 (1996): 2–7.

25 UN Office of Internal Oversight Services, *Achievements*, June 18, 2004, at <www.un.org/Depts/oios/achievements.htm>.

26 <oios.un.org/>.

27 "Key Elements of the Clinton Administration's Policy on Reforming Multilateral Peace Operations," [U.S. Administration, Presidential Decision Directive 25, May 3, 1994], in *Documents on Reform of the United Nations*, eds. Paul Taylor, Sam Daws, and Ute Adamczick-Gerteis, 125–126 (Brookfield, VT: Dartmouth, 1996).

28 Kofi Annan, *Renewing the United Nations: A Programme for Reform, UN Document A/51/950* (New York: United Nations, July 16, 1997).

29 The sunset provisions may have been a response to President Clinton's announcement, just weeks before, that the United States intended to withdraw from the UN Industrial Development Organization because UNIDO no longer served a useful purpose in the view of the United States.

30 Kofi Annan, *Improvement of the Status of Women in the United Nations System*, UN document A/56/472 (New York: United Nations, October 15, 2001).
31 Kofi A. Annan, *We the Peoples: The Role of the United Nations in the 21st Century* (New York: United Nations, 2000), 6–7.
32 Ibid., 48.
33 For a discussion of UN activities in these states, see Gregory H. Fox, "International Law and Entitlement to Democracy after War," *Global Governance* 9, no. 2 (2003): 183–187.
34 Kofi A. Annan, "Democracy as an International Issue," *Global Governance* 8, no. 2 (2002): 137.
35 Ban Ki-moon, *Guidance Note of the Secretary-General on Democracy* (New York: United Nations, 2009), found at Roland Rich, Special Report, at <muse.jhu.edu/article/379589/pdf>.
36 Reiterating the definition given by the late Sergio Vieiro De Mello, former UN High Commissioner for Human Rights, in April 2003, Ban described that holistic concept as "encompassing the procedural and the substantive; formal institutions and informal processes; majorities and minorities; men and women; governments and civil society; the political and the economic, at the national and local levels."
37 <open.undp.org/#2015>.
38 Annan, *Renewing the United Nations*.
39 Panel of Eminent Persons on United Nations–Civil Society Relations, *We the Peoples: Civil Society, the United Nations and Global Governance*, UN document A/58/817 (New York: United Nations, June 21, 2004).
40 The permanent seats would be distributed in the following way: two seats for Africa, two seats for Asia and the Pacific, one seat for Europe, and one seat for the Americas. See Kofi Annan, *In Larger Freedom: Towards Development, Security and Human Rights for All*, UN document A/59/2005 (New York: United Nations, March 21, 2005), 43.
41 See, for example, Robin Gedye, "Britain Seeks Radical Security Council Shake-Up," *Telegraph* (London), June 20, 2003. In late August 2003, French foreign minister Dominique de Villepin added his voice to the voices of other people publicly recommending the expansion of SC membership. See Tom Heneghan (Reuters), "France Urges International Force, Quick Vote in Iraq," August 28, 2003.
42 Kofi Annan, "'In Larger Freedom': Decision Time at the UN," *Foreign Affairs* 84, no. 3 (2005): 31.
43 United Nations, "Secretary-General Outlines Major Proposals to Reform UN Human Rights Machinery, in Address to Geneva Human Rights Commission," press release, SG/SM/9808, HR/CN/1108, April 7, 2005.
44 Report of the Advisory Group of Experts, *The Challenge of Sustaining Peace*, June 29, 2015, at <reliefweb.int/report/world/challenge-sustaining-peace-report-advisory-group-experts-2015-review-united-nations>.
45 William Safire, "The Great Cash Cow," *New York Times*, June 23, 2004.
46 Independent Inquiry Committee into the United Nations Oil-for-Food Programme, *Second Interim Report: The 1998 Procurement of the Humanitarian Goods Inspection Contract, Other Conduct of United Nations Officials* (New York: Independent Inquiry Committee into the United Nations Oil-for-Food Programme, March 29, 2005).
47 Kenneth Cain, Heidi Postlewait, and Andrew Thomson, *Emergency Sex and Other Desperate Measures: A True Story from Hell on Earth* (New York: Miramax, 2004).
48 UN Security Council, *Resolution 1592 (2005)*, S/RES/1592, March 30, 2005, at <unscr.com/en/resolutions/1592>.
49 Muna Ndulo, "The United Nations Responses to the Sexual Abuse and Exploitation of Women and Girls by Peacekeepers during Peacekeeping Missions," *Berkeley Journal of International Law* 27, no. 1 (2009): 142.
50 Ibid., 143.
51 Secretary-General's remarks to Security Council High-Level Debate on Collective Action to Improve UN Peacekeeping Operations, March 28, 2018, at <www.un.org/sg/en/content/sg/statement/2018-03-28/secretary-generals-remarks-security-council-high-level-debate>.
52 Voluntary Compact, at <www.un.org/preventing-sexual-exploitation-and-abuse/content/voluntary-compact>.

Chapter 4

Evolving Institutions

COORDINATION OF THE UN SYSTEM

Because the United Nations (UN) is the umbrella organization for 193 member states and several nongovernmental organizations, it can be said to be more than the sum of its parts. Although considering the United Nations in exactly this way is appropriate, remembering that it is also a collection of distinct institutions is important. Thus, while the UN's clichéd image in the public's mind is often unidimensional and reflects its early history, the evolving functions of its various parts suggest the protean nature of the organization and underscore the emergence of a "new" United Nations.

The **UN System** includes the full array of UN organizations, functions, programmes and funds, specialized agencies, and international bodies related to the United Nations. It is sometimes called the *UN family of organizations.* Some groups in the system act independently, but, as a rule, intrasystem communication is directed from the various wings to the six principal organs of the United Nations. Of these six organs, four—General Assembly, Security Council, Economic and Social Council, and Secretariat—provide guidance and a communications network for all of these entities.

The Secretary-General manages this sprawling system by means of the **Chief Executives Board (CEB) for Coordination**—the successor to the Administrative Committee on Coordination (ACC), which was initiated in 1946. The CEB comprises the executive heads of UN bodies and agencies (for example, Specialized Agencies, Funds and Programmes, and Related Organizations; all described below). While it had only four member organizations when it originated in the 1940s, almost eight decades later, thirty agency leaders meet twice a year under the Secretary-General's chairmanship. UN Office for Projects Services (UNOPS), established in 2016, is the latest member to join the CEB. In the new millennium, the CEB has an increasingly important, yet complicated task: to mobilize the UN System coherently to address new and difficult world issues.[1] Also, as explained in Chapter 3, the Senior Management Group (SMG), established by the General Assembly in 1997 as part of Secretary-General Kofi Annan's reform measures, serves as a cabinet for the Secretary-General. It is composed of some senior officials in the Secretariat and in the Funds and Programmes at the Under-Secretary-General and assistant Secretary-General rank. The objective of the SMG is to ensure timely coherence and direction in the UN's overall work. In 2022, there were forty-four members of the SMG.[2]

DOI: 10.4324/9781003281535-5

PRINCIPAL ORGANS

General Assembly

The General Assembly (GA) is the first of the main organs described in the UN Charter (Chapter IV). Articles 9 through 22 explain its composition, functions, powers, and procedures. Acting as the "legislative" branch of the United Nations, the GA meets in formal session every fall at the UN headquarters in New York City. Some UN members think of the assembly as the most important of the six principal organs, given that it is the one forum in which all member states are represented and in which each member, no matter its size or population, has an equal vote. Smaller nations and former colonies particularly value these principles and thus consider the assembly the hub of the United Nations.

The GA's importance as a meeting place has grown through the years with the expansion of UN membership. Beginning with fifty-one nations at the end of World War II, the General Assembly comprised 193 members as of 2022. As we described in Chapter 2, this increase was a result of the end of colonialism in the 1950s and 1960s, which brought many non-aligned and developing countries into the organization. The end of the Cold War also led to the addition of new states from Eastern Europe and the former Soviet Union. The admission of all internationally recognized states—with the single exception of the Vatican—made the United Nations by the turn of the century the first international organization in history to achieve virtually universal membership. Each member state may have five representatives and five alternates in the assembly. These representatives serve on the GA committees (explained below) as well as in the assembly plenary.

Because currently two of the other principal organs—the Economic and Social Council and the Secretariat—plus the Human Rights Council (HRC) and the Peacebuilding Commission (PBC), report to the GA, it plays a role in most of the main UN activities. No specific requirement mandates that the Security Council (SC) and the International Court of Justice (ICJ) report their decisions to the GA for review, although Article 24 of the UN Charter commands the Security Council to submit "annual, and when necessary, special reports" to the GA for the latter's "consideration."

The General Assembly deals with a range of international topics. Like other legislative bodies, it employs a system of standing (i.e., permanent) committees, each addressing a particular subject area. Within these standing committees, delegates debate, review, and vote on issues, then, frequently, pass resolutions that are presented to the GA plenary for consideration.

The six **main committees** are as follows: the **GA First Committee**—the Disarmament and International Security Committee—deals with disarmament issues, considered early in UN history to be such an important concern that it was consigned to a specific committee. The First Committee is now charged with addressing the broader category of "disarmament and international security." The other main committees are the **GA Second Committee** (the Economic and Financial Committee—or ECOFIN); the **GA Third Committee** (the Social, Humanitarian and Cultural Committee—SOCHUM); the **GA Fourth Committee** (originally the Trusteeship Committee), which in the late 1990s, with decolonization completed, was merged with an earlier Special Political Committee to become the Special Political and Decolonization Committee; the **GA Fifth Committee** (the Administrative and Budgetary Committee); and the **GA Sixth Committee** (the Legal Committee). Every member state is represented on each committee, which reflects the sovereign equality of all members in the assembly.

Characteristic of a legislative branch of government, the GA has also established several special committees and working groups to deal with distinct questions, or to fulfill

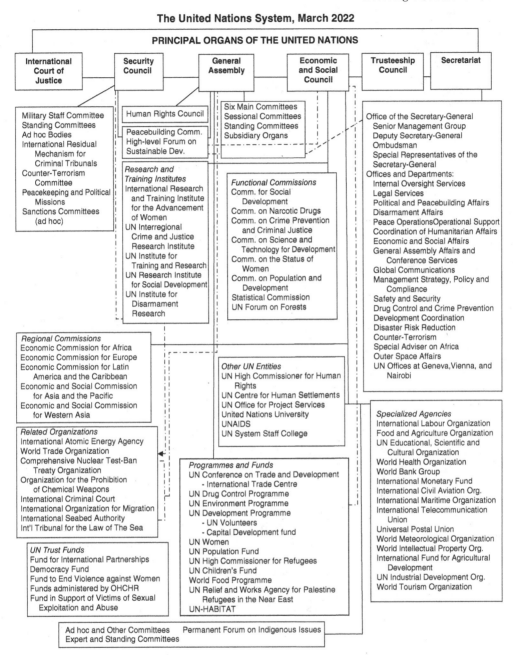

The United Nations System, March 2022

PRINCIPAL ORGANS OF THE UNITED NATIONS

International Court of Justice | Security Council | General Assembly | Economic and Social Council | Trusteeship Council | Secretariat

Military Staff Committee
Standing Committees
Ad hoc Bodies
International Residual
   Mechanism for
   Criminal Tribunals
Counter-Terrorism
   Committee
Peacekeeping and Political
   Missions
Sanctions Committees
   (ad hoc)

Human Rights Council

Peacebuilding Comm.
High-level Forum on
Sustainable Dev.

*Research and
Training Institutes*
International Research
   and Training Institute
   for the Advancement
   of Women
UN Interregional
   Crime and Justice
   Research Institute
UN Institute for
   Training and Research
UN Research Institute
   for Social Development
UN Institute for
   Disarmament
   Research

Six Main Committees
Sessional Committees
Standing Committees
Subsidiary Organs

Functional Commissions
Comm. for Social
   Development
Comm. on Narcotic Drugs
Comm. on Crime Prevention
   and Criminal Justice
Comm. on Science and
   Technology for Development
Comm. on the Status of
   Women
Comm. on Population and
   Development
Statistical Commission
UN Forum on Forests

Office of the Secretary-General
   Senior Management Group
   Deputy Secretary-General
   Ombudsman
   Special Representatives of the
      Secretary-General
Offices and Departments:
   Internal Oversight Services
   Legal Services
   Political and Peacebuilding Affairs
   Disarmament Affairs
   Peace OperationsOperational Support
   Coordination of Humanitarian Affairs
   Economic and Social Affairs
   General Assembly Affairs and
      Conference Services
   Global Communications
   Management Strategy, Policy and
      Compliance
   Safety and Security
   Drug Control and Crime Prevention
   Development Coordination
   Disaster Risk Reduction
   Counter-Terrorism
   Special Adviser on Africa
   Outer Space Affairs
   UN Offices at Geneva,Vienna, and
      Nairobi

Regional Commissions
Economic Commission for Africa
Economic Commission for Europe
Economic Commission for Latin
   America and the Caribbean
Economic and Social Commission
   for Asia and the Pacific
Economic and Social Commission
   for Western Asia

Other UN Entities
UN High Commissioner for Human
   Rights
UN Centre for Human Settlements
UN Office for Project Services
United Nations University
UNAIDS
UN System Staff College

Related Organizations
International Atomic Energy Agency
World Trade Organization
Comprehensive Nuclear Test-Ban
   Treaty Organization
Organization for the Prohibition
   of Chemical Weapons
International Criminal Court
International Organization for Migration
International Seabed Authority
Int'l Tribunal for the Law of The Sea

Specialized Agencies
International Labour Organization
Food and Agriculture Organization
UN Educational, Scientific and
   Cultural Organization
World Health Organization
World Bank Group
International Monetary Fund
International Civil Aviation Org.
International Maritime Organization
International Telecommunication
   Union
Universal Postal Union
World Meteorological Organization
World Intellectual Property Org.
International Fund for Agricultural
   Development
UN Industrial Development Org.
World Tourism Organization

Programmes and Funds
UN Conference on Trade and Development
   - International Trade Centre
UN Drug Control Programme
UN Environment Programme
UN Development Programme
   - UN Volunteers
   - Capital Development fund
UN Women
UN Population Fund
UN High Commissioner for Refugees
UN Children's Fund
World Food Programme
UN Relief and Works Agency for Palestine
   Refugees in the Near East
UN-HABITAT

UN Trust Funds
Fund for International Partnerships
Democracy Fund
Fund to End Violence against Women
Funds administered by OHCHR
Fund in Support of Victims of Sexual
   Exploitation and Abuse

Ad hoc and Other Committees   Permanent Forum on Indigenous Issues
Expert and Standing Committees

Figure 4.1 The United Nations System, March 2022.

procedural and administrative tasks. Among the most important of these are the **General Committee**, the Credentials Committee, the Advisory Committee on Administrative and Budgetary Questions (with the unwieldy acronym ACABQ), and the Committee on Contributions, which, in sequential order, prepare the agenda, certify members' delegations, advise the assembly on budget issues, and establish each member's dues contribution.

Photo 4.1 General Assembly Hall at UN headquarters in New York City.
Source: UN Photo/Marie Gandois. Reproduced by permission of the United Nations.

The GA may also call **special sessions** to deal with particular issues. Article 20 of the Charter authorizes the assembly to convene them "as occasion may require." Often the Security Council, by means of a resolution, starts the process by requesting that it call a session. Since the 1970s, nations from the developing world, with little diplomatic sway but a majority status in the GA, have used special sessions as a way of arousing public attention to issues related to development, women, children, human settlements, HIV/AIDS, apartheid, the Coronavirus pandemic, and other topics. At the same time, special sessions have been called to address more traditional concerns, such as disarmament.

The annual meeting of the GA usually convenes on the second or third Tuesday each September and concludes by mid-December. This period of early fall into winter includes the most intense portion of the session, when the assembly considers the majority of agenda items. Less frequent meetings may resume in January and continue through April to deal with additional or lingering matters. The September session begins with opening statements by each nation during two weeks of General Debate. These statements are member nations' formal policy declarations about current international affairs and they articulate a nation's official stance on questions before the United Nations. Because these opening statements are usually the most comprehensive and widely broadcast of a nation's foreign policy position, each nation often sends its president, prime minister, or minister of foreign affairs to deliver the address.

The GA's agenda comprises subjects proposed by any member state as well as continuing items contained in previously adopted assembly resolutions. Although member states thus determine the agenda, the Secretary-General may also recommend items for consideration.

CHRONOLOGY OF GENERAL ASSEMBLY SPECIAL SESSIONS

1947	Palestine
1948	Palestine
1961	Tunisia
1963	The Financial Situation of the United Nations
1967	South West Africa (Namibia)
1974	Raw Materials and Development
1975	Development and International Economic Cooperation
1978	(April) Financing the UN Interim Force in Lebanon
	(April–May) Namibia
	(May–July) Disarmament
1980	New International Economic Order
1982	Disarmament
1986	(May–June) Africa
	(September) Namibia
1988	Disarmament
1989	Apartheid
1990	(February) Drug Abuse
	(April) International Economic Cooperation
1997	Earth Summit +5
1998	World Drug Problem
1999	(June–July) Population and Development
	(September) Small Island Developing States
2000	(June) Women 2000: Gender Equality, Development and Peace for the Twenty-First Century
	(June) Social Development
2001	(June) Implementation of the Outcome of the United Nations Conference on Human Settlements (HABITAT II)
	(June) Problem of Human Immunodeficiency Virus/Acquired Immunodeficiency Syndrome (HIV/AIDS) in All Its Aspects
2002	World Summit for Children
2005	Commemoration of the Sixtieth Anniversary of the Liberation of the Nazi Concentration Camps
2014	Follow-up to the Programme of Action of the International Conference on Population and Development
2016	The World Drug Problem
2020	Coronavirus Disease
2021	Challenges and measures to prevent and combat corruption and strengthen international cooperation

Continuing items can come directly to the assembly without going through a committee, but most successful resolutions appear first in the appropriate committees, where they are meticulously discussed and then passed before being sent to the full assembly for a final vote. Because the standing committees also have a plenary membership, resolutions sent to the General Assembly are usually ensured passage, most of the time by consensus without a vote. However, the volume of agenda items—many of them repeated each year—and the many draft resolutions, for which the outcome is known in advance of the vote, have burdened the assembly with a heavy work load. Reformers have argued that the GA's authority would be strengthened if it concentrated on fewer and more critical issues.

The leadership and committee structure of the General Assembly can seem as bewildering as it would for any legislative branch. Those of you who have examined the U.S. Congress, or a parliamentary system such as that in Great Britain, each with its elaborate leadership and committee arrangements, may appreciate the GA's equally complex structure. A key difference, which adds to the complexity, is that, while in a national legislature the majority party assumes dominant positions and individuals could be in power for a long time, the GA has sought to establish leadership positions according to annual rotation and regional equity. The assembly elects its president—that is, its presiding officer—approximately equivalent to the speaker of the U.S. House of Representatives. The presidency, however, is more honorific than supervisory. It is accorded generally to a respected diplomat from a middle-range or smaller nation; no representative from a permanent member of the Security Council has ever been elected.

In addition to electing the president, the GA elects twenty-one vice presidents at least three months in advance of the start of the new session in September. The assembly chooses the president on a rotating basis from five geographic groups—Africa, Asia, Eastern Europe, Latin America and the Caribbean, and Western European and Other States (which includes Canada, Australia, New Zealand, the United States, and Israel)—and the vice presidents proportionally, also according to geographic areas. Five of the vice presidencies are always allotted to the five permanent members of the Security Council. The GA president, the vice presidents, and the elected chairs of each of the six standing committees make up the General Committee, one of the GA's so-called procedural committees. The General Committee acts as a steering committee and, as noted previously, sets the agenda for the assembly.

Although the assembly has passed some famous (perhaps infamous) resolutions by majority vote, as a rule, the General Assembly tries to act by consensus rather than by majority. The practical reason for this preferred modus operandi is that, although a majority vote can ensure passage of a resolution, and it is all that is required by Article 18, paragraph 3 of the UN Charter, the General Assembly is made up of individual sovereign nations and it does not have police authority or any legitimate overweening power to impose its will on its members. GA resolutions are not binding but rather rely on the readiness of member states to implement them, much as would be required in a *confederation*. Consequently, resolutions passed by a majority vote are futile unless all member states—especially the most powerful—are willing to abide by their terms. The overwhelming majority of GA resolutions, particularly since the end of the Cold War, have been adopted by consent, usually without necessitating even a formal recorded vote. At the same time, the use of abstentions—more common than negative votes—has increased. Nations usually vote negatively only when their national interests or perceived national security is endangered. There have been few exceptions to the general rule of consensus. For example, in 1971 a majority of the GA voted to accept the People's Republic of China in the UN seat formerly held by the Republic of China on Taiwan. The vote overrode strong opposition by the United States and several of its allies.

The Charter further provides that GA decisions on "important questions shall be made by a two-thirds majority of the members present and voting."[3] Article 18 of the Charter identifies **"Important Questions"** as those involving international peace and security, the choice of nonpermanent SC members and ECOSOC members, trusteeship, admission of new members, suspension of membership rights and privileges, expulsion of a member, and the budget. However, this Charter requirement has had a modest impact because resolutions have rarely been adopted with less than a two-thirds majority.

Because the GA uses parliamentary procedures and passes resolutions by large majorities or consensus, it is a hybrid, combining characteristics of a parliament and a global diplomatic conference. For sensible reasons, the GA functions as a negotiating body rather than as a typical legislative body. Yet, delegates lobby participating nations to gain their votes and to ensure the broadest support for any resolution. To this end, legislative factions known as **caucus groups** have emerged in the assembly in hopes of guaranteeing sufficient votes for favored resolutions.

Caucus groups are organized by geographic proximity, national identification with internationally recognized political or economic issues, or shared interests. In the United Nations, these voting blocs perform the function provided by political parties in a legislative body. They are formed, both formally and informally, according to a number of commonalities, which vary with any particular issue. The most influential caucus groups in the General Assembly are, first, the Non-Aligned Movement, a cluster of states organized during the Cold War that was not associated with either superpower and subsequently played a critical role in negotiations on trade issues, and second, the Group of 77. The latter caucus grew out of UN negotiations on North-South issues in the setting of the 1964 UN Conference on Trade and Development (UNCTAD). Other caucus groups parallel the recognized geographic blocs in the world body. In practice, these groups are also the points at which diplomatic negotiations begin on any given issue. Each group, agreeing on a common position, presents it to the body at large. Such groups are particularly important to small and midsize nations, which have difficulty exerting influence individually and, hence, are more likely to agree on a common position representing the entire group.

Some subgroups form within geographic groups (such as the Nordic Group). Other subgroups span geographic regions (such as the Middle Eastern Group). Specific groupings often emerge on a given issue, including the Group of 7 on economic matters, the Nuclear Powers Group on disarmament matters, the Organization of Petroleum Exporting Countries (OPEC), the Least Developed Countries, the Small Island Developing States, and many other special-issue groups formed by nations that share a particular concern with and usually a similar viewpoint on a given issue. While all nations are members of an officially recognized geographic group, most nations are also members of several caucuses, which at times overlap and vary with each issue under consideration.

The size of the General Assembly, its many voting blocs, its use of parliamentary methods among sovereign and equal members, and the visible role of small, even weak, states in the assembly contribute to a recurring impression of GA dysfunction and ineffectiveness. Because each state has one vote in the assembly, nations with small populations and limited power can and have collectively steered GA business. The great powers and rich nations often criticize the resolutions passed in this atmosphere; consequently, such resolutions have a little chance of implementation. Through the cumbersome process of attempting to achieve consensus, often the resulting resolutions are overly long, broad in their assertions, and, as a result of the diplomatic language needed to obtain opposing states' support, open to differing interpretations. Assembly and standing committee negotiations customarily carry on until provisions of various initial proposals are adjusted to reach wide compromise on a single resolution for each agenda topic. Only when full agreement is reached or when a few holdouts remain is an item usually brought to a plenary vote. A resolution that cannot command overwhelming majority support may be withdrawn.

Beyond its legislative responsibilities, the GA has other duties. In addition to electing nonpermanent SC members and Economic and Social Council members, the assembly, on the recommendation of the Security Council, selects the Secretary-General and the judges of the International Court of Justice. The GA can propose, by a two-thirds vote, amendments to the Charter, which then must be ratified by the governments of two-thirds of the member states, including all five permanent members. According to Article 109 of the Charter, the GA can also set a place and time for a general conference in which Charter amendments can be proposed, although such a conference has never happened. While the Security Council is authorized to deal with questions affecting international peace and security, the General Assembly may also consider such questions and make recommendations to the Security Council. Under the 1950 Uniting for Peace Resolution (explained in

Chapter 2), the GA authorized itself to make recommendations in cases when a veto has prevented the Security Council from taking action.

Finally, you should note that the GA is a unique gathering place for, in effect, all the governments of the world. As such, it provides a constructive social environment for contact among markedly different nations—large and small, rich and poor, powerful and powerless. As a result, in the delegate lounge and the halls near the General Assembly Hall at the UN building, you can find representatives from friendly or antagonistic nations—some who even refuse to recognize one another—engaging in informal, behind-the-scenes diplomacy. The GA has evolved to become, in fact, the world's first "town hall" meeting place.

Security Council

When issues of war and peace reach the United Nations, they are taken before the Security Council. For many of the world's people, and for the world's media, the council becomes the focus of UN news in such cases. The reason is that the council, according to Article 39 of the UN Charter, carries the organization's responsibility "to maintain or restore international peace and security." At the council, the great powers, including those who originally founded the organization, play out international power politics, as they have done since the end of World War II.

Council Organization

The Security Council comprises fifteen members. Ten are nonpermanent members; the remaining five have permanent membership, accompanied by the right of veto. The United States, the United Kingdom, France, the Russian Federation (formerly the USSR), and the

Photo 4.2 Security Council members adopting the Brahimi Report, November 13, 2000 (Resolution 1327).

Source: UN Photo/Eskinder Debebe. Reproduced by permission of the United Nations.

People's Republic of China are the five permanent members (the so-called **P5**). The GA elects the nonpermanent members for two-year terms. In 1965, an amendment to Article 23 of the Charter enlarged the number of nonpermanent members from the original six to ten. Currently, the assembly elects nonpermanent members according to an equitable geographic distribution: five from Africa and Asia (including the Middle East), two each from Latin America and the Caribbean and Western European and Other States and one from Eastern Europe. Five new members are elected each year to serve overlapping terms, and no nonpermanent member can be reelected for a second continuous term.

In 1946, abiding by Article 30, which grants the Security Council authority to establish its own rules, it adopted "Provisional Rules of Procedure," which have been amended several times. We should note, however, that Article 27 specifies the SC voting procedure. Each council member has one vote. Article 27 requires nine votes for a proposal to pass (raised from seven with the enlargement of the council in 1965) and distinguishes between "procedural" and "substantive" matters. All of the P5 must support (or abstain) for a substantive resolution to pass. This provision is often referred to as the principle of *great-power unanimity* or, more commonly, the *veto power* (the word *veto* does not appear in the Charter). A proposal may fail because of the mere threat of a veto. By long practice, determination as to whether an issue is procedural or substantive is itself considered a substantive question, which thus gives the permanent members in effect a **double veto** on all matters before the council. Each of the five permanent members has at one time or another exercised the veto. A permanent member may also abstain, thus officially not supporting a decision but not blocking it.

Theoretically, the Security Council is in a continuous session at the UN headquarters in New York City, although it has occasionally met elsewhere. For instance, the council held its inaugural meeting on September 17, 1946, in London. Other meetings have been held in Addis Ababa, Ethiopia, in 1972, and in Panama City, Panama, the following year. In September 2003, to encourage a preliminary discussion of a U.S.-requested resolution regarding Iraq, Secretary-General Annan summoned the foreign ministers of just the P5 to an unusual gathering in Geneva while the regular SC remained at the UN headquarters. In November 2004, the council met in Nairobi, Kenya, to highlight its concern about the deteriorating situation in Sudan's Darfur region. SC members are expected to have representatives in New York continuously. At important times, heads of state may also attend meetings, as was the case in January 1992, when thirteen heads of state or government and two ministers of foreign affairs met at a summit meeting of the council, and again in September 2000, when heads of state represented SC member countries during the special session of the Millennium Summit. The SC presidency rotates monthly, following an alphabetical order for the English names of each country.

The SC presidency is a demanding and politically sensitive position. Although a representative of a specific country, and in office for only a month at a time, an SC president is expected to seek consensus among council members and to speak for the council. Thus, "presidential statements" carry the imprimatur of the full council, not the views of a specific country. For example, following the attacks of September 11, 2001, and the bombing of UN headquarters in Baghdad on August 19, 2003, SC presidential statements transcended parochial positions. Of notable interest was President Fayssal Mekdad's statement responding to the Baghdad bombing. Syria had abstained in a 14–0 vote to authorize the UN mission that had been attacked. Yet, President Mekdad, the representative from Syria on the council, declared:

> The United Nations mission in Iraq has been established by the Security Council to help the Iraqi people to achieve their objectives. The United Nations is in Iraq on a mission of peace, and for the reconstruction of the country and to support the Iraqi people.[4]

Presidential statements, like resolutions, are hammered out in private, and the council's president guides these negotiating sessions and is principally responsible for drafting SC documents. Unlike most other UN organs, the Security Council is small and can work efficiently as a committee of the whole, where members find negotiating directly and candidly with one another expedient. In this environment, the president makes suggestions, arbitrates among the various members, and strives to find compromise so that a proposal, preferably with unanimous backing, can be composed and made public.

In the UN's early years, and during certain crisis moments, SC gatherings could be seen on television. Although the organization's founders may have expected sessions to be conducted openly (and some of the most legendary—such as the 1962 meeting on the Cuban Missile Crisis and the 2003 session regarding imminent war in Iraq—have been), when a member so requests, the council will convene in private. In fact, private meetings (sometimes called *consultations*) have become a common practice. In some instances, actual debate among SC representatives occurs in meeting rooms adjacent to the Security Council chamber and only official voting (and often careful explication of a country's vote) is conducted within the chamber. Articles 31 and 32 of the Charter provide that nonmembers who are affected by a council decision may be invited to participate in the discussion. Such was the case in the televised sessions in late winter 2003, when the Iraqi ambassador to the United Nations sat with the council and issued an oral defense of his country during the deliberations on how best to compel Baghdad to comply with Security Council resolutions.

The Charter's Article 47 provided for a Military Staff Committee, made up of the P5 chiefs of staff. The founders envisioned the committee somewhat as a "joint chiefs of staff," which would take responsibility for carrying out council decisions on the use of armed forces. However, because of the onset of the Cold War and the consequent divisions among the permanent members regarding any number of international issues, the Military Staff Committee never materialized as the imagined potent tool of the Security Council and has become, instead, like an archaic Latin phrase, a neglected contrivance, perhaps curious only to academic ruminators. In 2005, Secretary-General Annan proposed its abolition. The *spirit* of Article 47, however, rests in the policies, either by preference or by constitutional mandate, of some nations—India and Norway, for example—to commit armed forces outside their countries only with SC authorization.[5]

The Security Council can create ad hoc committees as needed. These committees are composed of all council members and meet in a closed session. Examples include the Governing Council of the UN Compensation Commission established in 1991, and the Counter-Terrorism Committee created after the terrorist attacks of September 11, 2001. Additionally, the council has set up more than a dozen sanctions committees to manage SC-approved sanctions regimes. In some cases, "smart sanctions" have targeted specific individuals and government entities, hoping to avoid imposing general hardship on a country's population. We will discuss targeted sanctions in detail in the next chapter, but in summary, they usually involve the freezing of assets and blocking the financial transactions of political elites or entities whose behavior the council wishes to change.

The Security Council was also responsible for the operation of two international war crimes tribunals, which concluded their work by the middle of the new millennium's second decade—the International Criminal Tribunal for the Former Yugoslavia (ICTY), meeting at The Hague and established by SC Resolution 808 in 1993, and the International Criminal Tribunal for Rwanda (ICTR), convened at Arusha, Tanzania, and deriving from SC Resolution 955 in 1994.

Council Powers

Alone among the UN organs, the Security Council has the authority to execute its mandates and to require all members to abide by its directives (Article 25) when it imposes enforcement measures against a state. Unlike GA resolutions, those passed by the council are legally binding under international law. This authority makes the SC's power greater than that belonging to any other UN organ or, for that matter, any international body in history.

When the council determines that a threat to international peace and security exists, it will act under Charter provisions in either Chapter VI or Chapter VII. A lengthy history and description of the council's use of these two Charter sections can be found in Chapter 5. For the current discussion, you need note only that under Chapter VI, titled "Pacific Settlement of Disputes," the council can recommend that the parties in a dispute use traditional diplomatic methods. These methods include mediation, conciliation, arbitration, and submission of the dispute to judicial determination. The council is expected initially to recommend diplomacy if a complaint about a threat to the peace is placed before it. Increasingly, the SC has asked the Secretary-General to appoint special representatives or to use "good offices" to resolve the dispute. Ultimately, the Security Council (provided all permanent members agree, abstain, or fail to vote) can determine to take military action against an aggressor. As of 2021, the council had endorsed war on only two occasions: in 1950 to defend South Korea against North Korea, and in 1991 to remove invading Iraq from Kuwait.

Often, council action is not as clear as it was in the cases of North Korea and Iraq. This has opened the door for coalitions of states to undertake military action, claiming UN authorization. When a US-led invasion of Iraq occurred in 2003, the administration of President George W. Bush claimed that it was only carrying out previous SC resolutions that the government in Baghdad had ignored for more than a decade. The United States argued that Resolution 1441, passed by the council the previous fall, allowed for military action, a claim strongly rejected by other members of the council. In the spring of 2011, a multi-state military intervention in Libya was launched to implement UN Security Council Resolution 1973, which had called for a no-fly zone in the country, a cease-fire, and an end to attacks against civilians. Following the death of Muammar Gaddafi in October 2011, the military incursion into Libya ended. The legitimacy of using the Security Council Resolution as a basis for conducting war was questioned by Russia, one of the P5.

Chapters VI and VII are powerful weapons in the hands of the Security Council. However, during the Cold War, members came to recognize the need in some cases for more forceful tools than those stipulated in Chapter VI; yet, they found superpower differences standing in the way of using Chapter VII enforcement measures. In these circumstances, the council frequently authorized "peacekeeping" operations, which scholars have placed under a non-Charter rubric of **Chapter VI½ provisions**. The Security Council found that peacekeeping actions—not explicitly anticipated by the UN's founders—are an evolving mission for the United Nations and a traversal between the instruction in Chapter VI to settle disputes peacefully and the concern in Chapter VII about potential breaches of the peace. Moreover, the term *Chapter VI½* recommends itself as a way of defining SC actions to seek resolution to conflicts *within* states as well as *between* states.[6] As discussed in Chapter 6, the council also sends, or authorizes specific countries to send, peacekeeping (or even what might be called *peacemaking*)[7] forces into troubled areas.

Issues of peace and security understandably consume much of the SC's time and attract more public attention than other issues the United Nations addresses. At the same time, the Security Council has some other duties that are of consequence. For example, it recommends to the GA the candidate for the post of Secretary-General as well as new members to be admitted to the United Nations. The council's Committee on Admission of New Members evaluates applicant countries and then reports to the full body, which forwards its recommendation to the General Assembly. The council recommends to the GA terms of admission for non-UN states who want to join the Statute of the International Court of Justice (Article 93), and jointly with the GA, elects judges to the court.[8] Other SC duties described in the Charter include recommending suspension or expulsion of a member (Articles 5 and 6), investigating international disputes that may lead to conflict, recommending methods for adjudicating disputes, devising strategies to control armaments, determining whether a threat to the peace exists and proposing methods to defuse the threat, and directing the UN members to place economic and trade sanctions against aggressor nations.

The Call for SC Reform

Since the 1960s, several proposals have been made to reform certain aspects of the Security Council. First, a number of critics have suggested finding ways to restrain the use of the veto. The Soviet Union and its successor, the Russian Federation, have used the veto more than any other P5 member. The second largest number have come from the United States, often deflecting resolutions aimed at Israel.

Given the nature of the United Nations, the likelihood is practically nonexistent that the most powerful members of the council would ever accede to limiting their power of veto. Even when the use of the veto was in decline, states still could threaten its use, which forced other members to withdraw contemplated draft proposals from council consideration. For example, in 2003, France's asserted willingness to veto the U.S. proposals seeking UN authorization for its actions in Iraq convinced the United States to act outside UN approval when it invaded Iraq. From a certain perspective, as the scholar John Stoessinger has argued, the veto—by ensuring the great powers of their ultimate sovereignty (which thus attracts them to abjuring unilateral action and persevering with negotiations in the council) and by causing the Security Council to move from the idea of majority rule to the more realistic principle of diplomacy and consensus among sovereign entities—has actually strengthened the United Nations.[9] Still, others see the veto as a sign of hapless deadlock.

A second reform issue—SC membership—is more problematic. One recurring complaint is that the council is too small and, on the whole, unrepresentative. You should recall that UN membership grew from 51 in 1945 to 113 members at the time of the 1965 enlargement of the council, and to 193 half a century later. Yet, no new council seats have been added since the increase in 1965. At the same time, the P5—representing logical power configurations at the end of World War II—includes no African, Middle Eastern, or South American state, while three European countries are represented. Germany and Japan, the defeated nations of World War II, are now seen as equally influential, economically and politically, with some other P5 members. Thus, as we discussed in Chapter 3, advocacy for expanding SC membership, including granting permanent status to countries from overlooked geographic areas, is mounting. At the same time, the prospect of expanding membership raises issues of efficiency and effectiveness and leaves some doubters worried that future council consensus will be even more difficult to achieve.

The call for internal reform is only one feature of the disquiet routinely directed at the Security Council. Critics often complain that the UN, and particularly the SC, is ineffective and symptomatic of an irrelevant organization headed to the same antiquarian dust heap of history inhabited by the ineffective League of Nations. Although this characterization may seem excessively harsh, no one can deny that the council's historical record has been checkered. At times the council has passed resolutions it knew had no chance of being implemented, and sometimes its resolutions have seemed out of touch with international realities. For instance, the so-called safe areas the council set up in Bosnia in the mid-1990s (during the horrendous civil wars in the former Yugoslavia) were anything but "safe" for the Muslim populations who sought protection in them. The council also turned its gaze from the barbarous internal genocide that ravaged Rwanda in 1994. Then, on August 19, 2003, the council, refusing heavy security for a political mission it had sent to Iraq, suffered one of its most mortifying and heartbreaking moments when a bomb exploded at the UN compound in Baghdad and killed twenty-two dedicated international public servants, including Sergio Vieira de Mello, the UN High Commissioner for Human Rights (UNHCHR) and the Secretary-General's special representative to war-damaged Iraq. The UN mission had been authorized by a unanimous (14–0; Syria abstaining) council resolution (Resolution 1483). The bomb attack undercut the UN effort to provide much-needed humanitarian relief in Iraq, and by the end of September, nearly all UN personnel were withdrawn from the country. And, as the Syrian civil war escalated in the years after the so-called "Arab Spring" of 2011, the SC seemed to observers to be frozen in attempting any containment of the violence. China and Russia vetoed attempts to impose sanctions on the Syrian government of Bashar al-Assad. Yet, at roughly the same time, the council unanimously passed resolutions establishing a UN Supervision Mission in Syria—ended in 2012—creating a framework for elimination of chemical weapons in the country, and calling for access for humanitarian aid. Evidence suggests that the council's actions did not deter the Syrian government from keeping some chemical weapons and using them as late as 2017.

We must remark that, in each of these instances, the Security Council was no more or less than the determinations of its member states. That is, whatever disappointments we can document, they are not so much failures of an abstract and autonomous apparatus as they are the collective failure of all its members. Moreover, the apparent failures, circuitously, draw attention to the evolving, and extremely difficult work of the SC. Intended as the commanding instrument of the United Nations—to be led by the most powerful members of the organization—the council was designed not only to combat traditional state aggressors such as those believed to have caused World War II, but also to check other states from accumulating the most dangerous weapons—tasks it has pursued with alacrity and by and large in harmony. Its dedication to these causes was demonstrated in the war against the aggressor Iraq in 1991 and through the resolutions regarding Iraqi disarmament, as well as in the Iran nuclear agreement, negotiated with Iran by the P5+1 in 2015, and in its continuing sanctions on North Korea for its pursuit of nuclear weapons.

However, by the conclusion of the second decade of the century, the council found itself, in the bargain, dealing with novel new crises, such as unraveling dysfunctional states, disconcerting ethnic and religious conflict, brutal civil wars, enduring boundary clashes, aspiring and potentially radicalizing nationalist movements, the specter of fanatical terrorism, climate change, and a global health pandemic, all of which was much more than could be anticipated in 1945. There was also a growing adversarial relationship among several of the permanent members that undercut optimism for future cooperation on these problems, forcing the council to experiment with diplomatic mechanisms that could get around the veto.

Particularly between the United States and Russia, and China and the United States, new discord—beyond Syria and the Middle East—emerged to complicate cooperation in the Security Council. In 2014, Russia annexed Crimea from Ukraine and tensions accelerated as Moscow feared an eastward expansion of NATO to Ukraine and the United States feared a Russian military incursion into the country. China began to exert its long-desired (and expected) great-power capacity by intruding militarily into the South China Sea, cracking down on Hong Kong democrats, accelerating unification pressure on wayward and resistant Taiwan, and, in the view of the West, grievously violating human rights of the Uyghur people in Xinjiang Province. (For more on a rising China's impact on the UN, see the discussion at the end of this chapter.)

One good sign, however, was the determination of council members to find methods outside the glare of formal council votes, where vetoes would have to be cast, to make progress on some of the hardest issues in the new millennium. One of these is the use of presidential statements, which we have already described in this chapter. Council members do not cast official votes on these documents, but they are not issued without unanimous agreement among the members. Another method, emergent in the twenty-first century, is the use of "contact groups." We will have more to say about these entities later in the chapter, but you will recall the use of the P5+1 contact group (CG) to negotiate the nuclear deal with Iran. That particular group contained all of the veto-wielding members of the council. If, at any point in the negotiations, the permanent members had to address the thorny issues of the contemplated agreement in formal votes in the council chamber, it is very likely that the unanimity of the group would have broken. Working together outside of the UN headquarters' limelight allowed a consensus position to emerge that Iran in the end would accept.

On balance, the Security Council since the end of the Cold War has taken on an active and productive engagement with world affairs. Sergio Vieira de Mello's biography discloses in vivid profile the SC's changing and expanding role. Prior to his highly visible service as the UN's High Commissioner for Human Rights, this distinguished international diplomat had, under council direction, dealt with the riskiest situations in the nastiest trouble spots around the globe. He was best known as the head of the UN Transitional Administration in East Timor (UNTAET), which had adroitly guided East Timor to democratic elections and full independence after that tiny country's bloody separation from Indonesia. Success in East Timor, fittingly, was considered a major triumph for both the United Nations and the Security Council. Other council-authorized operations included the missions in Bosnia, Kosovo, Afghanistan, and Liberia. By council direction, each of these missions was to be the lead institution in stabilizing traumatized post-war societies.

Election-monitoring operations have perhaps been even more significant. During the 1990s, the UN monitors—in groups established by SC resolutions—guided elections in Cambodia and in various Central American countries. As of the early days of the new millennium, these nations, previously beset by outside interference and gory civil conflict, were living in relative peace. In each of these mandates (and more), the SC usually found itself in unanimous accord. In fact, what deserves emphasis is that the council, especially since the end of the Cold War, has performed for the most part with harmony and purpose. At the same time, its resolutions have addressed the ever-tougher issues facing the "new" United Nations while taking on the force of legitimacy in world affairs like no unilateral national decision could. By way of recent example, consider that in December 2021—as tensions among the United States, Russia, and China radiated from news headlines—the Security Council unanimously extended the mandate for the UN Stabilization Mission in troubled Democratic Republic of Congo (Resolution 2612) and unanimously authorized a vigorous UN humanitarian relief project in beleaguered Afghanistan (Resolution 2615).[10]

So, although prospects for achieving sweeping reform of the SC's structural and compositional inadequacies may languish for the moment, the council remains the main global organization that brings legitimacy to world affairs. It is, understandably, the focus of attention when we think of the United Nations.

Economic and Social Council

A great deal of UN activity occurs outside the more visible realms of peace and war and great-power rivalries. When you consider the beneficial works of the United Nations and the many emergent issues that have become the province of the "new" United Nations, you more often than not should think of the Economic and Social Council, or ECOSOC. One of the six principal organs of the United Nations, ECOSOC is charged by Chapter X, Articles 62–66, to supervise activities in the economic and social sphere (by far, the largest percentage of the UN's budget funds ECOSOC-related activities). ECOSOC is the UN organ most associated with the worthy but elusive goals of raising standards of living; advancing full and useful employment; promoting economic and social progress; identifying and solving economic, social, and health problems; encouraging cultural and educational cooperation; and strengthening respect for human rights and fundamental freedoms.

The UN Charter has been amended twice to enlarge the size of ECOSOC. These two amendments represent 40 percent of the five Charter amendments that have been ratified, which reflects the importance many nations accord ECOSOC. When colonialism ended and UN membership grew, so did ECOSOC membership. The increased membership fulfilled the wishes of newly independent countries to be represented in this organ, which had responsibilities they deemed so indispensable. In 1965, membership rose from eighteen to twenty-seven, and in 1971 to fifty-four. Nations represented on ECOSOC serve three-year terms; one-third are elected annually by the GA to overlapping terms, following a formula ensuring equitable geographic distribution (fourteen are allocated to African states, eleven to Asian states, six to Eastern European states, ten to Latin American and Caribbean states, and thirteen to Western European and Other States). Each member can have only one representative on ECOSOC, but unlike the proscription on nonpermanent SC members, retiring members of ECOSOC are eligible for immediate reelection. Each member country has one vote, and all decisions are made by a majority of members present and voting.

The Bureau of the Economic and Social Council, the executive arm of ECOSOC, is elected at the beginning of each annual session. The bureau, comprising a president and four vice presidents, is responsible for proposing the agenda, drawing up a program of work, and organizing annual sessions in cooperation with the UN Secretariat. ECOSOC parcels out work to three standing committees: the Committee for Programme and Coordination, the Committee on Non-Governmental Organizations, and the Committee on Negotiations with Intergovernmental Agencies, as well as to five regional commissions and eight functional commissions.

According to Article 62, ECOSOC's responsibilities are wide ranging. The council may "make or initiate studies and reports with respect to international economic, social, cultural, educational, health, and related matters." ECOSOC is expected to make recommendations to the General Assembly, to UN member nations, or to specialized agencies. It can prepare draft conventions that deal with its designated areas of competence, which may then be submitted to the GA, or even call international conferences to deal with topics falling within its orbit. ECOSOC regularly requests reports from specialized agencies and UN member states that explain how its recommendations are being carried out. In fact, ECOSOC's singular ability to exert influence in the international community rests for the most part in its monitoring and publicizing compliance. That is, ECOSOC's main exercise is to focus world attention on economic and social challenges. Deciding how best to address the issues thus raised then becomes the responsibility of the GA or individual member states. The council often offers requesting nations assistance in composing legislation to meet ECOSOC benchmarks. ECOSOC's aims may also be met in a summit conference or, more potently, in a treaty.

Other council responsibilities include:

- Coordinating the activities of independent specialized agencies (in 2022, fifteen of these agencies were under ECOSOC purview; an explanation of *specialized agencies* appears below).
- Accrediting the many nongovernmental organizations that over time have played a growing role in ECOSOC deliberations and specialized agencies' activities.
- Receiving reports from UN funds and programmes.
- Establishing regional and functional commissions to deal with specific issues of concern to the council.

In terms of this last council responsibility, the five regional economic commissions—for Africa, Europe, Latin America and the Caribbean, Asia and the Pacific, and Western Asia—encourage cooperation and coordination among governments in geographically proximate areas and help finance development projects in their respective regions. In contrast, **ECOSOC functional commissions** deal with specific topics of global merit. ECOSOC established six of them in 1946: the Commission on Human Rights (one of the better known, replaced in 2006 by the Human Rights Council), the Commission for Social Development, the Commission on the Status of Women, the Statistical Commission, the Commission on Population (renamed in 1994 the "Commission on Population and Development"), and the Commission on Narcotic Drugs. The remaining commissions, established in later years, reflected ECOSOC's escalating concentration on issues affecting developing countries. In 1992, the council created commissions on Crime Prevention and Criminal Justice, and Science and Technology for Development; in 1993, on Sustainable Development, which was disbanded in 2013 and replaced with the High-level Political Forum on Sustainable Development, a joint subsidiary body of ECOSOC and the GA. The United Nations Forum on Forests became an ECOSOC commission in 2000.

Each of these commissions is the principal UN agency in its field. They draft treaties, compose suitable rules, and monitor the fulfillment of previous agreements. In addition, the council and its commissions publish useful informational guides and model legislation in relevant fields. ECOSOC and its commissions advertise and bolster existing agreements and encourage voluntary adherence to international standards of behavior within the council's province.

Each July, ECOSOC convenes a month-long substantive session known as the *High-Level Segment*. These meetings alternate between the headquarters in New York City and that in Geneva and attract major government figures from the member states and the chiefs of international agencies. These sessions concentrate on a selected theme of global significance. For example, in the summer of 2015 in New York, the session addressed the expected transition by the world community from the Millennium Development Goals approved in 2000 to a newly agreed set of "Sustainable Development Goals" (SDGs).

ECOSOC's role in the UN System is less explicit than that of the other main organs. Given the expansive nature of ECOSOC's mandate, different member states often voice dissimilar views about what ECOSOC should be doing. The opening declaration of the UN Charter includes the aspiration "to promote social progress and better standards of life." Developing nations often view this injunction as important as the traditional aims of preserving peace, enhancing human rights, and developing international law, which are also catalogued in the preamble. ECOSOC's dealing with the issue of economic and social development has pleased impoverished countries.[11] Conversely, industrialized First World nations often regard development as secondary to the maintenance of international peace and security and see expanded trade and emergent globalization as the keys to lifting poorer nations into the economic mainstream. Nevertheless, the so-called Third World countries use the word *development* to articulate what they believe to be the central purpose of the United Nations; poorer nations have, at times, suggested that helping them with economic and social development constitutes a necessary precondition for the ultimate maintenance of international peace and security. So, when some nations talk about reforming the United Nations, they are hoping to strengthen ECOSOC rather than address the various complaints richer members voice. The debate about ECOSOC seems to mirror the debate over an "old" and a "new" United Nations, both of which, in fact, subsist.

ECONOMIC AND SOCIAL COUNCIL: ITS NETWORK OF COMMISSIONS, COMMITTEES, BODIES, FUNDS, PROGRAMMES, AND EXPERTS

Functional Commissions

Statistical Commission
Commission on Population and Development
Commission for Social Development
Commission on the Status of Women
Commission on Narcotic Drugs
Commission on Crime Prevention and Criminal Justice
Commission on Science and Technology for Development
Forum on Forests (UNFF)

Regional Commissions

Economic Commission for Europe (ECE)
Economic Commission for Africa (ECA)
Economic Commission for Latin America and the Caribbean (ECLAC)
Economic and Social Commission for Asia and the Pacific (ESCAP)
Economic and Social Commission for Western Asia (ESCWA)

Standing Committees

Committee for Programme and Coordination
Committee on Non-Governmental Organizations
Committee on Negotiations with Intergovernmental Agencies

Funds and Programmes That Send Reports to ECOSOC

UN Children's Fund (UNICEF)
UN Development Programme (UNDP)
UN Environment Programme (UNEP)
Office of the UN High Commissioner for Refugees (UNHCR)
UN Population Fund (UNFPA)
UN Relief and Works Agency for Palestine Refugees in the Near East (UNRWA)
UN Office on Drugs and Crime (UNODC)
World Food Programme (WFP)
UN Human Settlements Programme (UN-HABITAT)
UN Entity for Gender Equality and the Empowerment of Women (UN-Women)

Trusteeship Council

Of the six major UN organs, the Trusteeship Council most dramatically demonstrates the UN's evolution and, arguably, its success. The Trusteeship Council is actually defunct, having accomplished the goals given it by the Charter in Chapter XIII: overseeing the territories placed under the UN's Trusteeship System and ensuring the advancement of these territories from colonial status to self-government. It suspended its operations on November 1, 1994, following the independence of Palau (October 1, 1994), the last remaining UN trust territory. All eleven trust territories identified at the end of World War II had become self-governing, independent states or had merged with neighboring independent nations. Secretary-General Kofi Annan suggested—in his 1997 reform proposal, *Renewing the United Nations*—that the council be converted into a forum on global environmental issues and protection of common areas such as the oceans, the atmosphere, and outer space. Then, in 2005, the Secretary-General advocated terminating the council. However, as noted in Chapter 3, the council continued to exist as of 2022, only on paper.

Secretariat

The **Secretariat** is the international civil service staff that administers the day-to-day operations of the United Nations. Provided for in Chapter XV, Articles 97–101, of the Charter, the Secretariat works at UN headquarters in New York City and around the world, serves other principal organs of the United Nations, and administers the programs and policies determined by these organs. The Secretariat's job is comparable, on the international stage, to the job carried out by a sovereign nation's bureaucracy. Besides performing other functions, these international civil servants administer SC-authorized peacekeeping operations; handle refugee problems; mediate international disputes; survey economic and social trends; prepare studies on human rights, economic development, and sustainable development; and undertake anything else commanded by any UN organ. The Secretariat provides information to the general public about the United Nations, organizes international conferences, monitors the implementation of UN directives, interprets speeches and translates documents into the UN's official languages, and more. Although its main headquarters is in New York, the Secretariat maintains an important presence in Geneva, Vienna, and Nairobi, as well as where related UN agencies are headquartered in yet other cities.

The head of the Secretariat is the Secretary-General. The General Assembly, on recommendation of the Security Council, appoints the Secretary-General for a five-year term, and the occupant can be reelected.[12] Because the five permanent members of the SC retain a veto, a nominee could receive fourteen votes yet be unsuccessful. All five permanent members must accede to any nomination. Tanzania's foreign minister, Salim Ahmed Salim, was a challenging candidate to Kurt Waldheim in 1981 and would have become the first sub-Saharan African to serve in the post. However, the new Reagan administration in Washington, resistant to the recent tilt in the United Nations toward what it perceived as the developing world's radicalism, supported Waldheim, as did, interestingly, the Soviet Union, which ended Salim's candidacy.

The Secretariat consists of an assortment of offices and agencies, each headed by an Under-Secretary-General, an assistant Secretary-General, or a senior official, all reporting to the Secretary-General. There are a bewildering number of these units, some serving internal administrative purposes (e.g., the Executive Office of the Secretary-General and the Office of Internal Oversight Services), while others address critical world concerns, such as the Office for Disarmament Affairs and the Department of Peace Operations. The

Senior Management Group serves as a central policy-planning body to ensure strategic coherence to Secretariat activities and shares an administrative role with the Chief Executives Board for Coordination, both discussed earlier in this chapter. In addition, the UN ombudsman, although largely independent of outside control, reports to and can be removed only by the Secretary-General.

There were about 37,000 people from over 140 countries working for the Secretariat in 2022 (compared to about three million U.S. federal government civilian employees). These workers are international civil servants and are not answerable to specific nations but to the United Nations alone. Secretariat employees take an oath not to seek or receive instructions from any government or outside authority. According to the Charter, member states must respect the exclusive international character and responsibilities of Secretariat personnel and not seek to influence their activities in an improper way.

Although the public rarely hears about the day-to-day workers in the Secretariat—more likely aware of the current Secretary-General or perhaps a highly visible appointee—these international public servants, working unassumingly within the Secretariat's many offices, in related agencies, and for the Secretary-General's special representatives dealing with distinct issues, are the most palpable UN presence in much of the world. The twenty-two individuals killed in the bombing of the UN mission in Baghdad in 2003 were representative. An example was Nadia Younes. Born in Egypt, Ms. Younes earned a bachelor of arts degree at Cairo University and a master's degree in international relations from New York University. She began her UN career at the age of 24 in the Office of General Services. Later she moved to the Department of Public Affairs, and then for a number of years was UN Chief of Protocol. From 1999 to early 2001, she was in charge of information and communication for the UN Mission in Kosovo. She then became executive director for external relations at the World Health Organization. At the time of her death, she was the chief of staff for Special Representative Vieira de Mello. She had served the Secretariat for a third of a century.[13]

Despite its impartial and international character, the Secretariat has at times been the target of suspicion and criticism by member governments. At the height of the Cold War, both the United States and the Soviet Union accused the Secretariat of serving as a tool for the other side. During the 1980s and 1990s, the most serious charges were that the Secretariat was too large, inefficient, and wasteful. Consequently, Kofi Annan, presented his reform and reorganization plans in 1997, consolidating and regrouping some twenty-four agencies into five divisions and creating a new position—Deputy Secretary-General (DSG)—to preside over the streamlined bureaucracy.

The Secretary-General has extensive latitude over the arrangement, programs, and reform of the Secretariat. As the "chief operating officer" of the organization's administration, the Secretary-General can consolidate, expand, and alter the duties of departments and agencies within the bureaucracy, and must respond to new challenges and opportunities when they arise.

The United Nations is an international organization of sovereign nations that serves as a forum for interstate diplomacy and collective action. However, in the new millennium, the organization has expanded its involvement with the private sector and with non-governmental organizations. Secretary-General Annan launched a "Global Compact" between the United Nations and multinational corporations, administratively housed in the Executive Office of the Secretary-General, to protect human rights, international labor standards, and the global environment. Decreases in donor-state funding made this partnership a necessity. The UN's focus on private actors in the international arena also reflected recognition by the organization's leadership that international civil society could have an impact on the success or failure of UN initiatives.

In 2022, the Global Compact had over 12,000 signatories from 160 countries. Its board members came from the world's most powerful business, labor, and finance spheres. In December 2021, the GA reaffirmed support for the Compact's private-sector engagement in combatting COVID-19 and in advancing the Sustainable Development Goals (a major concern of Microsoft founder Bill Gates).[14]

On March 2, 1998, Louise Fréchette became the UN's first Deputy Secretary General. (In 2022, it was Amina J. Mohammed of Nigeria.) The duties of the DSG are to act for the Secretary-General at the UN headquarters when the SG is absent, to enhance coherence and cooperation among the UN bodies, to provide leadership in the UN economic and social activities, to represent the SG at conferences and official functions, and to "undertake such assignments as may be determined by the secretary-general." The DSG serves only during the term of the Secretary-General who appoints him or her. As the first occupant of the office, Fréchette defined, by her actions and assigned duties, the initial parameters of the position. Fréchette served on the Senior Management Group and other Secretariat committees. As the first DSG, she gave the post a public legitimacy that made the DSG more than just another senior member of the UN Secretariat.

International Court of Justice

The ICJ is the UN's principal judicial organ. It was established in 1945 in the Charter (Chapter XIV) as the successor to the Permanent Court of International Justice (PCIJ). While the court functions as the UN's legal arm, it is an independent institution. Its governing document—the Statute of the International Court of Justice—accentuates this independence, however, the statute is a part of, and usually appended to, any published copy of the UN Charter. It is based on the 1922 Statute of the Permanent Court of International Justice and details the organization, procedures, and jurisdiction of the court. The ICJ, like the predecessor PCIJ, is often called the *World Court.*

The outbreak of world war in 1939 ended the work of the PCIJ, which met for the last time on December 4, 1939. In 1942, U.S. secretary of state Cordell Hull and the foreign minister of the United Kingdom, Anthony Eden, declared their support for a post-war reestablishment of an international court. In early 1943, the United Kingdom invited a number of experts to London to discuss the subject. Forming the Inter-Allied Committee, under the chairmanship of Sir William Malkin, the group held nineteen meetings and published a report on February 10, 1944. Later that year, at the Dumbarton Oaks Conference, the four attending powers agreed on including an international court of justice in the emerging structure of the United Nations. In April 1945, a meeting of jurists from forty-four nations convened in Washington, DC, and composed a draft statute for the new court, which was then submitted to the UN's organizing conference in San Francisco. To retain a sensible continuity with evolving international law, the authors of the UN Charter made clear in Article 92 that the ICJ statute was based on that of the PCIJ. The old court convened in October 1945 to dissolve itself and transfer its archives to the new court. The sixth and last president of the PCIJ, Judge J. Gustavo Guerrero, became the first elected president of the new ICJ.

The ICJ is the only principal organ of the United Nations not based in New York City. The seat of the court is at the Peace Palace in The Hague, the Netherlands. Its first session took place April 18, 1946. Since then, the ICJ has been considered in continuous session. The court determines its own rules of procedure, elects its own president and vice president, and appoints a registrar (with the equivalent rank of a UN assistant Secretary-General) and other registry staff and officers. The ICJ Registry maintains all court records, makes available court publications, communicates with outside organizations, acts as a press office, and maintains a Web site. Appointees to the registry must know both French and English, the official languages of the court.

The World Court should not be confused with the International Criminal Court (ICC), which is located in the same city. The ICC is a relatively new creation, established by the Rome Treaty of 1998, to try war criminals. It applies laws of humanity, as authorized by its contracting states, to individuals who are accused of particularly heinous crimes, such as genocide. As of 2022, 123 nations were parties to the Rome Statute. Once the ICC went into effect in 2002, the UN's Secretary-General signed a bilateral agreement with it, allowing among other actions the referral of cases by the Security Council to the court.

In contrast, the ICJ hears only cases between states that are voluntarily brought to it by one of the adversaries, or it delivers advisory opinions at the request of UN bodies. States are not bound by the ICJ's opinions, nor are they subject to penalties imposed by the court, whereas convicted defendants before the ICC may be incarcerated.

All UN members are parties to the ICJ's statute. Fifteen judges are on the court, elected by the General Assembly and the Security Council for nine-year terms. The procedure of nominating and electing candidates for judgeships on the court is complex and is detailed in Article 4 of the statute (see Resource 4 on the Routledge eResources webpage for the Statute of the ICJ). All nation-states party to the ICJ statute are allowed to put forward candidates, although the nominations are made not by the government, but by a group of four members from the Permanent Court of Arbitration (initiated by The Hague Conference of 1899) who are from the nominating state. If a country is not represented on the Permanent Court of Arbitration, it may still make a nomination through a similar national group of legal experts that would clearly qualify to serve on the arbitration tribunal. Each group can propose as many as four candidates, not more than two of its own nationality. The names are then forwarded to the UN Secretary-General, who submits the names to the General Assembly and the Security Council for vote. For this election, the permanent members of the SC retain no right of veto; the required majority vote for a judge in that body is eight. Both the assembly and the council vote simultaneously but separately. To be elected, a candidate must obtain an absolute majority in both chambers.

The term of office begins on February 6 of the next year. Judges may be reelected, but no two from the same country may serve simultaneously. (If two candidates of the same nationality are elected at the same time, the elder one receives the appointment.) According to Article 16 of the ICJ statute, judges on the court may not engage in other political or administrative employment or in any other professional occupation. Members of the court are independent; they do not represent their governments. Still, they must be qualified for appointment to the highest judicial offices in their respective countries or be recognized as experts in international law. No judge may be dismissed except by the unanimous decision of the other judges. The United Nations has always tried to apportion the judgeships on an equitable geographic basis. (In 2022, the allocation of seats on the court was three African, three Asian, two West European, two East European, one South American, one Middle Eastern, one Caribbean, one from the South Pacific, and one North American.) There is no entitlement to membership, but normally the court has always had judges from the permanent members of the Security Council.

The court deals only with disputes between sovereign states; no private party may present a case. The court is not expected to resolve all international conflicts, but only specific legal disputes brought before it. It has compulsory jurisdiction in cases involving countries that have signed optional clause 36 (paragraphs 2 and 3) of the ICJ's statute, which allows the court to adjudicate legal disputes concerning (a) the interpretation of a treaty, (b) any question of international law, (c) the existence of any fact that may constitute a breach of an international obligation, or (d) the nature and extent of a reparation for such a breach. The two affected states must usually agree to bring the case, and no state may be sued before the court unless it consents to such an action. And bear in mind that a litigant state may request a case be removed from the court's list before a judgment is rendered. Thus, both the effectiveness and the jurisdiction of the court depend on the consent of the states affected.

Cases are normally initiated either by the disputants—who notify the court of a special agreement reached by each to seek court action—or by the initiation of one party, which acknowledges that the opposing party has not recognized the court's jurisdiction but asks the court to still hear the case. Usually, a nation's foreign minister or ambassador to the Netherlands communicates with the court's registrar. Litigants before the court are not required to pay fees or administrative expenses; these costs fall to the United Nations.

Proceedings before the court consist of a written phase, when the parties file and exchange pleadings, and an oral stage, when public hearings are conducted and counsels address the court. The court may hear witnesses and authorize investigations by commissions of experts. The court deliberates in private, but all judgments—arrived at by majority vote—are made public in court chambers. A judge in the minority may file a dissenting opinion, although majority judgments are final; no appeal may be made. Since the court has no power of enforcement, Article 94 of the UN Charter provides recourse to the Security Council for a successful disputant unhappy at noncompliance with a decision. The council may then forward recommendations or take measures to effect the judgment. In fact, however, given the reality of a world of sovereign nations, the court's verdicts depend wholly on the litigants' compliance. Encouragingly for the court's authority, as of 2021 in only two recorded instances had a party disappointed with a decision failed to comply with the court. The first ICJ decision, in the Corfu Channel case of 1946, was rebuffed by Albania when it failed to pay the United Kingdom the £843,947 mandated by the court as compensation for damages suffered. In the second case, the United States, reacting to the 1984 case of *Nicaragua v. U.S.A.*, in which Nicaragua charged the U.S. government with violating international law by mining the harbor at Managua, refused for two years to accept prior compulsory jurisdiction of the court in matters relating to Central America. Following the court's insistence (by a 12–3 majority) that the United States had violated international law and should pay reparations to Nicaragua, Washington blocked any appeal to the SC. Otherwise, the Court's decisions have, by and large, achieved substantial albeit imperfect, compliance.

Article 65 of the statute authorizes the court to deliver **advisory opinions** if requested by another principal UN organ or by a specialized agency. On receiving such a request, the court seeks relevant information and collects written and oral statements on the issue. Advisory opinions are consultative in nature and thus not binding. A nation may simply disregard an advisory opinion, as happened, for example, when in 1948 the court advised the General Assembly that the Soviet Union could not use its veto to deny UN membership to the states of Italy and Finland. Moscow ignored the decision and ultimately struck a compromise with Western nations that resulted in the admittance of the two countries, along with several other nations. Since 1945, the court has rendered just over two dozen advisory opinions concerning various topics, including issues of UN membership, reparation for injuries sustained during service in the United Nations, the territorial status of Namibia and Western Sahara, expenses of various UN operations, the status of human rights special rapporteurs, the legality of the threat or use of nuclear weapons, and the permissibility under international law for Israel to build a wall separating Israeli and Palestinian communities on the West Bank.

During its first seventy-five years, about 150 contentious cases were referred to the court, although several were later removed from the court's list or were considered still pending.[15]

Of the approximately seventy-five countries that had been litigants in these cases, the United States was involved most often (about twenty times); the United Kingdom and the former Yugoslavia ranked second and third.

Three specific cases provide examples of the court's workings. In its first case, the Corfu Channel case (*United Kingdom v. Albania*), the court tendered three judgments. On March 25, 1948, it asserted its jurisdiction over the case involving a British grievance against Albania for explosions in the Corfu Channel in 1946 that had damaged a British warship and killed crew members. Then, on April 9, 1949, it found Albania responsible, under international law, for the explosions. It then assessed Albania a reparation payment to be paid to the United Kingdom. However, as noted previously, Albania refused to observe the judgment.

In the second example, in 1979 the United States requested that the court take the U.S. Diplomatic and Consular Staff in Tehran case (*U.S.A. v. Iran*). Washington brought the case after Iranian militants occupied the U.S. embassy on November 4, 1979 and took its diplomatic and consular personnel hostage. The court immediately held that no requirement for international relations was more fundamental than the inviolability of diplomatic envoys and embassies. In a May 24, 1980, judgment, the court found that Iran had violated obligations to the United States according to international law and under existing conventions. Ultimately, negotiations between Iran and the United States resolved outstanding grievances on both sides, resulting in the establishment of the Iran-U.S. Claims Tribunal to handle claims by nationals of either country.

The third example is the LaGrand case (*Germany v. United States of America*), decided on June 27, 2001. The court determined that the United States had violated international law when it failed to grant consular services to two German brothers executed in Arizona in 1999. Also, the court found that the United States had ignored an ICJ order to stay one of the executions. The two brothers were charged with murder in a 1982 holdup. During the proceedings, Washington conceded that it had neglected the 1963 Vienna Convention on Consular Relations when prosecuting the LaGrand brothers without informing diplomats from their homeland, but insisted that the brothers had received a fair trial and that the verdicts would have been unaffected by consular intervention. ICJ president Gilbert Guillaume, speaking for the court's overwhelming majority, reprimanded the United States for denying defendants their international rights regardless of the likely outcome of a trial. The ruling was noteworthy because it pronounced, for the first time in the court's history, that ICJ provisional orders, such as the ignored injunction against Walter LaGrand's execution, were legally binding.

As these cases demonstrate, the court considers itself an organ of and a contributor to international law. It decides disputes consistent with international law, the sources of which, according to Article 38 of the statute, are international conventions, international custom, general principles of law recognized by civilized nations, judicial decisions, and teachings of the most qualified publicists on the topic.

By the twenty-first century, the ICJ had become part of a remarkably transformed global legal system, featuring a permanent multilateral framework for the resolution of disputes; the preservation of peace; the rules of war; the establishment of war crimes tribunals; financial, economic, environmental, and technological cooperation; and even the promulgation of individual and human rights.

Among other new UN legal structures are the courts founded to deal with dire human rights violations. These courts are discussed in detail in Chapter 7. For now, we simply mention the two special courts set up to handle cases arising from civil wars in the 1990s and the International Criminal Court, whose jurisdiction is more general. The SC created the two geographic-specific courts: the International Criminal Tribunal for the Former

Yugoslavia and the International Criminal Tribunal for Rwanda. The former was the first institution of international criminal prosecution since the end of World War II. They both reflected a renewed interest in the normative tradition in international law. The Rwandan court materialized in late 1994.

SPECIALIZED AGENCIES, PROGRAMMES AND FUNDS, AND OTHER GROUPS

In addition to the UN's six principal organs, other UN-related groups and activities have contributed to the mutable and evolving character of the world organization. We begin our look at these not-so-distant relatives by first examining **specialized agencies**, **programmes**, and **funds**. A listing of these groups can be found in Figure 4.1.

Specialized Agencies

Specialized agencies are autonomous, self-governing entities that, nonetheless, fall under the general rubric of the United Nations; they are specifically mentioned in Articles 57, 63, and 64 of the UN Charter. At some point in time, specialized agencies formally established a contractual relationship with the broader organization, subjecting themselves to the administrative and budgetary rules of the United Nations. They must report to the world body on all aspects of their work and organization. As noted previously, their conduit to the larger organization is the Economic and Social Council. However, ECOSOC's "consultations" with and "recommendations" to the agencies—some with overlapping missions—are less ordered than those in some other UN linkages, because each agency is independent. ECOSOC's oversight is generally limited to making broad suggestions and highlighting certain issues. Still, as of 2022, fifteen (counting the World Bank Group as one) specialized agencies worked with the United Nations via ECOSOC's coordination.

Specialized agencies act in a particular or technical area of international concern, and have, according to Article 57, "wide international responsibilities ... in economic, cultural, educational, health and related fields." They have come into being when the international community has determined that a particular problem or issue requires collaborative action or regulation. The General Assembly created a few of these specialized agencies and UN-sponsored conferences established others. Some came into existence long before the United Nations did. For example, the Universal Postal Union dates from the nineteenth century. The League of Nations originated others, many of which the United Nations ultimately endorsed.

A statute or treaty typically governs a specialized agency, specifying its functions, duties, mandate, voting method, and organizational structure. Specialized agencies are intergovernmental organizations (IGOs) composed of member states. A nation becomes a member by signing and ratifying the relevant treaty. Therefore, not all UN members are *ipso facto* members of all specialized agencies. Specialized agencies also have their own budgets, which are funded by assessment of members or, often, by members' voluntary contributions.

Each agency has an independent governing body, structure, and method of functioning. Usually, a general conference of the agency's members elects the governing body, which includes day-to-day administrative officers (sometimes called a *secretariat*). Whereas decision-making in some agencies conforms to basic democratic procedures (one member, one vote), some agencies depart from this standard. Key exceptions are the International Monetary Fund (IMF) and the World Bank, where weighted voting, based on member states' contributions, determines policy (the IMF and the World Bank are discussed in more detail later in this chapter). Likewise, representatives of government, employers, and labor organizations from each member nation have a vote in the International Labour Organization. Some specialized agencies (e.g., the International Civil Aviation Organization, or ICAO) require nations important to the agency's subject matter (nations with the largest air carriers) to hold seats on the agency's governing body—in this instance, the ICAO council. Other specialized agencies may require general conferences to approve decisions made by governing boards or committees of the agency, although in several, governing boards have considerable leeway in determining rules and making general decisions. Also, specialized agencies may draft treaties or conventions to submit to their member states. Often the GA and ECOSOC will endorse and urge ratification of these international agreements.

Of the growing number of nongovernmental organizations that dot the international landscape, many seek to have an influence on the specialized agencies because the latter deal with matters that NGOs consider vital. Specialized agencies even sometimes need the kind of expertise NGOs offer (comparable to that provided by the perhaps unfairly maligned "interest groups" and lobbyists in congressional or parliamentary systems of government). For example, involved closely with the World Health Organization and other health-related agencies, Médecins Sans Frontières (MSF, "Doctors Without Borders") has developed an ongoing partnership. Its experience and that of other long-standing NGOs have encouraged new organizations to form and seek a voice in agency activities. (In 1999, Médecins Sans Frontières was awarded the Nobel Peace Prize.)

Each specialized agency has established its own mandate and mission. Some of the agencies are chiefly rule-making entities that bring international regulatory norms to common practices—such as the International Civil Aviation Organization, the Universal Postal Union, the International Telecommunication Union, and the International Maritime Organization. Several of the specialized agencies make use of technical experts, who, though appointed by specific member governments, are expected to act without political motivation. Some agencies concentrate on economic and financial matters (World Bank and International Monetary Fund), the rights of labor (International Labour Organization), world food and health issues (Food and Agriculture Organization and the World Health Organization), social and economic development (International Fund for Agricultural Development and UN Industrial Development Organization), stimulation and sharing of scientific advances and preservation of cultural landmarks (UN Educational, Scientific and Cultural Organization), and common cross-national challenges involving weather, the environment and the climate, and protection of intellectual property rights (World Meteorological Organization and World Intellectual Property Organization). All of them are part of the growing functionalist agenda that is central to the United Nations in the twenty-first century.

Programmes, Funds, and "Other Entities"

Of the many other organizations connected with UN pursuits, programmes, funds, and kindred "other entities" hold a singular place. Although confusion about the differences between specialized agencies on the one hand and programmes and funds on the other (e.g., the International Monetary *Fund* and the International *Fund* for Agricultural Development are specialized agencies) can exist, the two are easily distinguished. Specialized agencies are independent bodies, created by distinct treaties; they maintain their own separate administrative boards. In contrast, the General Assembly has expressly established certain programmes, funds, and entities to supervise activities central to UN

UN SPECIALIZED AGENCY LOCATIONS AROUND THE WORLD

Austria

Vienna
   UN Industrial Development Organization (UNIDO)

Canada

Montreal
   International Civil Aviation Organization (ICAO)

France

Paris
   UN Educational, Scientific and Cultural Organization (UNESCO)

Italy

Rome
   Food and Agriculture Organization (FAO)
   International Fund for Agricultural Development (IFAD)

Spain

Madrid
   World Tourism Organization

Switzerland

Berne
   Universal Postal Union (UPU)
   Geneva
   International Labour Organization (ILO)
   International Telecommunication Union (ITU)
   World Health Organization (WHO)
   World Intellectual Property Organization (WIPO)
   World Meteorological Organization (WMO)

United Kingdom

London
   International Maritime Organization (IMO)

United States of America

Washington, DC
   International Monetary Fund (IMF)
   World Bank Group (WBG)
   International Bank for Reconstruction and Development (IBRD) [called the
      World Bank]
   International Development Association (IDA)
   International Finance Corporation (IFC)
   Multilateral Investment Guarantee Agency (MIGA)
   International Centre for the Settlement of Investment Disputes (ICSID)

Charter mandates. While ECOSOC requests annual reports from specialized agencies, UN programmes and funds, as the handiwork of the GA, must report to both the General Assembly and ECOSOC. One similarity is that both specialized agencies and programmes and funds often rely for their funding, for the most part, on members' voluntary contributions and, in some instances, on private organizations and corporations (thus the moniker *fund*).

An executive director at the Under-Secretary-General level heads each fund and programme, and each has an executive board. As of 2022, six UN programmes or funds (plus eight "other entities") were operating. Among the most visible and popular of these—and the only UN body to deal exclusively with children's issues—is the UN Children's Fund (UNICEF), established in 1946 and widely recognized for its sales of greeting cards during the holiday season late each year. The UN Relief and Works Agency for Palestine Refugees in the Near East (UNRWA, under the category "Other Entity"), another of the earliest UN offices, was established in 1949. It provides assistance to Palestinians displaced during the several Middle East wars that have transpired since 1948. A former fund, the United Nations Development Fund for Women (UNIFEM) merged into a new organization, UN Women, in January 2011.

By the second decade of its existence, the United Nations had turned a considerable amount of attention to development issues, and this concentration was mirrored in the GA's initiation of related programs. It established the UN Development Programme (UNDP) to provide technical assistance to developing countries. Four other entities are related to development matters. The UN Population Fund (UNFPA), established in 1969, is the largest multilateral organization offering improved reproductive health programs for women and encouraging family planning. The UN Environment Programme (UNEP), originating in 1972 as a response to the UN Conference on the Human Environment held in Stockholm that year, is the principal UN body involved in attempts to protect the world's environment. The World Food Programme (WFP), dating from 1962, extends food assistance to people living in poverty and, when called on, delivers emergency relief to countries and areas affected by disasters. Finally, the UN Centre for Human Settlements, created in 1978 to coordinate the UN activities in this field, was merged with the Commission on Human Settlements in 2002 to bring about the UN Programme on Human Settlements (UN-HABITAT).

In 1993, reacting to the crisis of escalating numbers of refugees resulting from conflicts, the GA created the Office of the UN High Commissioner for Refugees. With some eighteen thousand personnel scattered around the world (in 132 nations in 2022), UNHCR is a noticeable addition to the UN efforts to aid refugees and protect their rights. About a quarter of UNHCR's expenditures are channeled through over six hundred NGOs, whose chief concern is to provide aid to refugees.

Through many different strategies, the United Nations has supported the empowerment of women. It has sought to encourage gender equality, most importantly through landmark agreements such as the Beijing Declaration and Platform for Action of the Fourth World Conference on Women and the Convention on the Elimination of All Forms of Discrimination against Women (CEDAW). In 2010, the General Assembly pulled together four disparate departments and agencies involved in this work to create UN Women, the United Nations Entity for Gender Equality and the Empowerment of Women, as one of its programmes.

Finally, the United Nations Office on Drugs and Crime (UNODC) was established in 1997 through a merger between the United Nations Drug Control Programme and the Centre for International Crime Prevention. It operates in all regions of the world through a network of field offices. UNODC engages in educational and informational efforts to counter drug use and trafficking, and relies on voluntary contributions, mainly from governments, for 90 percent of its budget.

Other Groups

The plethora of activities we have surveyed seems immense, but is, nonetheless, an incomplete look at the UN System. Before we leave the topic, we should note a few other entities that do not fit precisely into the specialized agencies, and programmes and funds groupings just detailed. Among these are the **research and training institutes**—that is, specialized organizations that engage in consistent research undertakings in their areas of expertise, publish reports, and make available to all nations cutting-edge information about current issues of concern to the UN family. The UN Institute for Training and Research (UNITAR) administers training seminars for new UN staff personnel and concentrates on training individuals from developing countries who aspire to international public service or diplomatic careers. The other institutes are more focused. They include the UN Institute for Disarmament Research (UNIDIR), the UN Interregional Crime and Justice Research Institute (UNICRI), and the UN Research Institute for Social Development (UNRISD).

Still other groups are associated with the United Nations, some more firmly than others. The International Atomic Energy Agency (IAEA) is one of the more recognizable of what the United Nations calls **related organizations**. Related organizations are completely independent of UN administrative requirements. The IAEA is an intergovernmental forum dedicated to the peaceful uses of nuclear technology. The GA established it as an autonomous entity in 1957 in response to President Eisenhower's proposal in his 1953 "Atoms for Peace" address before the assembly. Headquartered in Vienna, the IAEA had a membership of 173 nations in 2022, and it had become the primary UN organ for monitoring compliance with the Nuclear Non-Proliferation Treaty. The IAEA is covered in more detail in Chapter 5.

Among other related organizations are the Comprehensive Nuclear-Test-Ban Treaty Organization and the Organization for the Prohibition of Chemical Weapons. They are administrative units specifically designed to detect possible violations of existing treaties within their competence and to strive to coordinate efforts to uphold these treaties. Last of the related organizations—and most loosely related to the United Nations—is the World Trade Organization, the successor organization to the General Agreement on Tariffs and Trade (GATT), which tries to provide a forum for extensive multilateral negotiation among its 164 members (as of 2022) to lower barriers to international trade. The WTO is examined in more detail later in this chapter.

Finally, the GA established what might be called **other UN entities**, each of which provides a specific service to the world community. One, the UN Office for Project Services, was originated in 1995 to provide harmonized management for UN programmes and funds. Unique among UN agencies, UNOPS must raise its own revenues by marketing its services, and it provides no funding to its clients and partners. Ten UN agencies co-sponsor UNAIDS, the Joint UN Programme on HIV/AIDS, which seeks to reverse and stop the spread of HIV/AIDS. The UN Office for Disaster Reduction (UNISDR) serves the entire UN System. The GA brought the UN High Commissioner for Human Rights (UNHCHR) into being in 1993 in response to the Vienna Declaration on Human Rights issued that year. UNHCHR, whose head the Secretary-General chooses, serves as the secretariat for all treaty bodies involving human rights. Two renowned commissioners were Mary Robinson, former president of Ireland, and her successor, the late Sergio Vieira de Mello.

The surfeit of group names listed in the foregoing sections can induce bafflement; some seem to overlap, while others would reasonably appear to fall under a different rubric. Accordingly, your best recourse may be to revisit the highlighted categories we used under which to subsume these various organs and, at the same time, to take a look at Figure 4.1.

There, you will find these organizations placed, by the UN's preference, under the same labels we used in the preceding descriptions. Finally, having followed the first two suggestions, you may want to think of the United Nations in its newest formulation as a network of IGOs and special bodies that qualitatively marks the emergence of a "new" United Nations, significantly different from that described in the UN Charter.

NEW STRUCTURES ON THE GLOBAL STAGE

Inevitably, new structures surface to complement the work of the various UN groups, as well as to attend to fresh challenges unanticipated by the UN's founders. You have seen the resonance of this generalization in several places in this and previous chapters, including in the elaboration of the evolution of international law in Chapter 3. These diplomatic innovations have been undertaken as pragmatic experiments, often with the result that they have become formal instruments of UN action. Next, we briefly appraise some of these new structures.

World Conferences

World conferences are UN-sponsored international gatherings attended by thousands of individuals representing themselves, governments, international organizations, UN bodies, the media, nongovernmental organizations, and the international scientific and technical community. Although the UN Charter does not specifically authorize the United Nations to convene these conferences, the world body has used the directive in Article 1 of the Charter, calling on it to be a "centre for harmonizing the actions of nations" as the basis for sponsoring conferences. Held at the UN headquarters in New York, in other UN venues, and in cities around the world, these meetings have grown in number, size, and topics covered. The first world conference was held in Havana, Cuba, in 1947–1948 and focused on trade and employment. Meetings held prior to the 1960s were small and infrequent. The UN Conference on Trade and Development (UNCTAD), convened in Geneva in 1964, was the first to attract worldwide attention and to lead to the formation of a formal UN organ, called, appropriately, *UNCTAD*.

Starting with the 1972 Stockholm Conference on the Human Environment, UN world conferences have attracted the involvement of private international interest groups. More than four hundred groups were accredited to the Stockholm meeting. They presented statements to the conference, lobbied delegations, played a critical role in garnering public support for the aims of the conference, and provided important expertise related to the environment.

World conferences have often been defining events in the development of international legal practices and global agendas. The United Nations has used world conferences to concentrate world attention on a number of themes, including the problems and opportunities associated with the issues of human rights, the environment, women, development, human settlements, racism, ozone depletion, natural disasters, education, disarmament, children, population policy, desertification, and sustainable development. A parallel "people's forum" has accompanied each conference held since 1992, allowing nongovernmental groups to present their views and try to mold public opinion. In some past cases, the sponsoring UN body authorized NGOs to participate actively in the conference. Fifty thousand attended the Fourth World Conference on Women in Beijing in 1995.

Both the costs associated with convening world conferences and the usual outcome of the meetings—vague consensual statements—have caused debate about their usefulness. The cost to the United Nations for these meetings has ranged from about $2 million to

$10 million. Yet, official conference expenditures have not included outlays of host countries, which often rival UN spending. Critics have argued that the money could have been better spent ameliorating the problems rather than talking about them. Detractors have also claimed that the meetings were often duplications of efforts being undertaken by specialized agencies or private groups and that the conferences diverted world attention from more serious problems, produced diplomatic compromises with limited commitments of resources, and "politicized" issues that required humanitarian or scientific responses. In contrast, defenders of world conferences, including many nations in the developing world, consider the meetings opportunities to mobilize national, local, and nongovernmental activities to address major global problems, to create international standards that powerful nations cannot ignore, to serve as a fertile ground for new ideas and strategies, and to cut through the UN bureaucracy and world lethargy.

As the new century began, the momentum for convening world conferences had not slackened. Just between 1999 and 2002, the United Nations sponsored seven world conferences. Secretary-General Kofi Annan, an advocate of more such meetings, had conceived and convened the highly publicized Millennium Summit at the New York headquarters in the fall of 2000. New York City also served as the site for the World Conference on Indigenous Peoples in 2014. The three most recent world conferences have dealt with managing disasters and climate risks. The third of these, held in Sendai, Japan in spring 2015, drew 6,500 delegates and 50,000 attendees to the associated Public Forum.[16]

Special Rapporteurs

UN special rapporteurs are part of what is called *Special Procedures* under the aegis of the UN Human Rights Council, which appoints them, and are supported by the High Commissioner for Human Rights. Although the word *rapporteur* derives from Old French, its meaning can be discerned from the English word *report*. In French, it also refers to a *recorder*, as in a court of law.[17] So, a *rapporteur* observes important matters, records them, compiles reports, and presents them to a supervising body. A UN special rapporteur (as well as the somewhat akin "independent expert") should be distinguished from a special representative of the Secretary-General (SRSG), who is chosen by and acts on behalf of, or in place of, the Secretary-General.

We can think of a special rapporteur as being a person commissioned by a UN body through a resolution and charged with preparing a comprehensive report on an area of concern to that body. The report is normally extensive and includes an assessment of the current issue and its historical background; information received from relevant countries; reports of field or site visits; and recommendations for UN action. The United Nations may provide these reports to affected countries for guidance or may use them for crafting discrete policies. Some observers believe that the compendious data compiled by special rapporteurs enhances the development of international human rights law.

Special rapporteurs are experts in the field about which they are chosen to report, and they are often well-respected scholars or professors. The *Special Procedures* of the UN HRC includes the largest body of independent experts in the UN Human Rights system. Despite the extraordinary service special rapporteurs provide, they receive little UN Secretariat assistance. They are not UN staff and are independent from any government or organization. As a rule, they are unpaid volunteers with limited funds and usually no support staff.[18]

Special rapporteurs assume either a *country mandate* (as, for example, the Special Rapporteur on Cambodia), or a *thematic mandate* (addressing a global theme—like rights of privacy, religious liberty, access to safe drinking water, slavery, trafficking in persons, rights of migrants, toxic waste, poverty, and much more). In 2022, there were forty-four thematic and twelve country-specific mandates for which special rapporteurs could be assigned. A total of eighty individuals were serving as special rapporteurs, independent experts, or working group members. In Chapter 7, we will provide more detail on special rapporteurs.

Human Rights Council

The UN General Assembly inaugurated the Human Rights Council on March 15, 2006, as part of the reform program then underway. It replaced the much-maligned Commission on Human Rights, which had been heavily criticized for a membership that included states with some of the worst human rights records and for being a highly politicized body that overlooked some of the worst human rights violations while condemning Israel and Western countries for their policies. Nongovernmental organizations also viewed the establishment of the HRC as a way to give new prominence to human rights throughout the UN System. Lengthy negotiations and a number of compromises proved necessary before agreement was reached between Western and developing nations. Developing nations, with their working majority in the General Assembly, successfully pressed to make the new council a subsidiary body of the Assembly. They also insisted on a broad, regionally balanced membership.

The council has forty-seven members—not much smaller than the fifty-three-member Commission on Human Rights that it replaced. Membership is regionally balanced, but

Photo 4.3 UN Human Rights Council meets in Geneva's Palais des Nations to discuss report on Syria.
Source: UN Photo/Jean-Marc Ferré. Reproduced by permission of the United Nations.

each candidate is voted on separately in a secret ballot and must receive the affirmative votes of an absolute majority of the General Assembly. Each country serving on the HRC is required to undergo a review of its human rights record by the council during its term of membership. Member states are limited to two consecutive terms on the new council and are elected to staggered three-year terms. The GA can suspend the council membership of any state that "commits gross and systematic violations of human rights," though this requires a two-thirds vote.

The council is based in Geneva, where it meets more frequently than its predecessor, with no fewer than three annual sessions for a total of at least ten weeks. It carries a broader mandate than its predecessor did. It has the power (if one-third of the council agrees) to call additional special sessions at the request of any of its members. It works closely with the Office of the High Commissioner for Human Rights. HRC serves as a forum for dialogue on all human rights and seeks to advance international cooperation to enhance the abilities of states to implement human rights commitments. It also "address[es] situations of violations of human rights," and conducts a "universal periodic review" of all UN member states.

An important power of the Human Rights Council is the ability to appoint experts to investigate human rights abuses generally and in particular countries. They are much like the special rapporteurs discussed above. They are known by the antiseptic term "special procedures." They undertake country visits; act on individual cases, bring alleged violations or abuses to the attention of charged states, conduct thematic studies, and engage in advocacy, thus raising public awareness.

Peacebuilding Commission

Like the Human Rights Council, the Peacebuilding Commission (PBC) was the product of lengthy negotiations regarding UN reform. It emerged from the recommendations of the 2004 *High Level Panel on Threats, Challenges, and Change*, Secretary-General Kofi Annan's report, *In Larger Freedom*, and the recommendations of the 2005 UN World Summit. The PBC is considered an advisory body. It reports to both the General Assembly and the Security Council and can only take up issues on which its advice has been requested by one of those two bodies, the Economic and Social Council, or the Secretary-General. Any individual member state can also request the commission's advice about its own situation.

The PBC is directed by an Organizing Committee of thirty-one members. Seven of these members are elected by and from the current Security Council, which will usually include some from the permanent five; seven are elected by and from the current membership of the Economic and Social Council and will tend to be from developing countries. Also included are five of the ten top providers of assessed contributions to the UN, which will include aid donors, the five top providers of military personnel and civilian police to United Nations peacekeeping operations, and, finally, seven members elected by the GA. The council acts through individual country-specific committees (known as *configurations*—each configuration consisting of a dozen or more states, including the country under review, and about the same number of representatives from relevant international and regional organizations). These committees are set up for each post-conflict state or peacekeeping operation.

Recognizing that development is a long-term process, the Peacebuilding Commission seeks to extend the period of attention to post-conflict situations, reconstruction, institution building, and sustainable development. It is charged with identifying resources and financing to establish integrated strategies for post-conflict recovery, both during the presence and after the departure of peacekeeping missions. The commission also compiles best practices from previous efforts, which can be adopted in new crises.

The PBC convened its inaugural session on June 23, 2006. The intended quest of the PBC at the time of its creation was that it would improve the efficiency of assistance programs and attend to the long-term problems of post-conflict states. Unfortunately, as only an advisory group to the Security Council and the General Assembly, the commission has not played a significant role and its companion Peacebuilding Fund to support projects in post-conflict states is often plagued by shortfalls.

In 2015, the United Nations conducted a review of the Peacebuilding Commission. A group of seven experts appointed by the Secretary-General studied the commission and its work. It found:

> [The problems facing the UN's] institutional machinery for building peace are systemic in nature. They result from a generalized misunderstanding of the nature of peacebuilding.... peacebuilding is [often] left as an afterthought: under-prioritized, under-resourced and undertaken only after the guns fall silent.[19]

Among its many recommendations, the panel urged a more effective use of the commission by the Security Council once a peacekeeping mission had achieved sufficient stability, on the ground. And it urged a much larger role for international civil society organizations in peacebuilding. Explaining before the PBC in late October 2021, his announced *Our Common Agenda*, Secretary-General António Guterres emphasized that the commission was expected to play a central role in meeting daunting challenges: "The climate crisis is looming, the pandemic is upending our world and conflicts continue to rage and worsen. The world is experiencing its biggest shared test since the Second World War." Peacebuilding faced, counselled the SG, a formidable task.[20]

Contact Groups

We noted earlier the critical role the Contact Group (CG) consisting of the P5+1 played in the successful negotiation of an agreement with Iran on its nuclear program, and we suggested then that the use of the CG mechanism was a maturing diplomatic procedure in the effort to avoid the glare and contention that too often comes with official Security Council deliberations. Contact groups are not new, but they have attracted new interest as a way to move deliberations forward on the thorniest issues.

Other organizations than the United Nations have used CGs to address difficult threats to peace and security. An example occurred in the 1990s when the G-8 (that grouping of the seven most affluent economies plus Russia) created contact groups (United Kingdom, France, United States, Russian Federation, Germany, Italy) to negotiate and organize peacemaking efforts in Bosnia and Kosovo. As long ago as the late 1970s, a CG addressed South Africa's continuing control of its League of Nations mandate territory, an area that would become the state of Namibia. In May 1977, Pretoria met with the group (United States, West Germany, Canada, Britain, and France) and acknowledged a UN role in the future of Namibia. For the next year, the CG served as a stand-in for the Security Council and achieved a transition agreement.[21]

Secretary-General Boutros Boutros-Ghali's *An Agenda for Peace*[22] in 1992 urged the UN, and particularly the Security Council, to seek "preventive diplomacy" and "peace-making" so as to avoid conflict in the first place. Contact groups have been understood as a diplomatic mechanism within these rubrics. Acting under Chapter VII of the UN Charter, the SC passed four resolutions (1816, 1838, 1846, 1851) in 2008 to deal with the escalating problem of piracy off the coast of Somalia. Experts characterized these resolutions collectively as "the most comprehensive piracy repression guidance promulgated by the UN in their [sic] history."[23] The council's action led to the creation of the most complex contact group so far.

The Contact Group to address piracy included more than eighty countries plus relevant UN agencies, the European Union, the African Union, NATO, the Arab League, and the International Maritime Organization. The group set up five working groups on capacity building, judicial mechanisms for deterring piracy, and cooperation with the commercial shipping industry that used the vital shipping lanes off the coast of Somalia. The contact group and the Security Council worried not only about regional stability and the loss of lives because of pirates in the area, but also that the movement of naval assets by involved states might lead to unintended confrontations.

As the second decade of the twenty-first century proceeded, there were calls for the United Nations and other international organizations to initiate CGs for some of the more persistent international crises. Under the Minsk Agreement (2014) to end the fighting in Ukraine, the Organisation for Security and Co-operation in Europe (OSCE) sponsored a trilateral CG. It consisted of the OSCE Chairmanship, Russian Federation, and Ukraine. For its part, the SC established CGs for Guinea-Bissau (2006), Libya (2011), and the Central African Republic (2013). Proposals as yet unfulfilled have been made for CGs to be formed in order to deal with the Syrian civil war and the Israeli-Palestinian standoff.

GLOBALIZATION, BRETTON WOODS INSTITUTIONS, AND THE UNITED NATIONS

At the end of World War II, diplomats and political leaders, along with financiers and economists, determined to elude the financial and economic policies of economic nationalism that they thought had helped bring on the interwar challenges of economic ruin and international collapse, as well as world war itself. Starting at Bretton Woods, the world finance conference held in New Hampshire in 1944, these leaders created institutions to encourage freer movement of goods, money, and labor; international rules to realize economic liberalization; transparency in economic and financial dealings; the ability to locate and rectify sudden economic troubles in specific areas of the world; and mechanisms to provide necessary capital assistance to nations requiring development financing. The founders of this multilateral, cooperative economic regime saw their efforts as complementary to the simultaneous launching of the United Nations. Post-war planners aimed to bring the world closer together in economic, financial, political, cultural, and social realms, thinking that nationalist and provincial policies—including high protective tariffs—had spawned the collapse of international order in the 1930s. As the world economy grew substantially during the later twentieth century, these efforts appeared to be remarkably successful.

With the end of the Cold War, more and more of the world's nations evinced an interest in joining the expanding, less encumbered economy that until then had characterized chiefly the First World only. These nations had good reasons for such interest. Whereas in 1970 about 3 percent of all manufactured goods were produced in the world's developing nations, by the early 1990s their share was 18 percent, and this percentage rose during the next decade as the mechanisms of international economic and financial integration matured. From 1990 to 1998, the thirteen poor countries with the largest populations realized an impressive average economic growth rate of 7.3 percent, higher than in any prior corresponding time.[24] In 2002, *Foreign Policy Magazine* reported a study indicating that the world's most "globalized" countries had achieved greater income equality.[25]

Still, by 1998, according to the World Bank, some 1.2 billion people lived on less than a dollar a day at 1993 prices. While the occurrence of absolute poverty in the most impoverished areas of the world decreased slightly between 1987 and 1998, the total number of the poor remained about the same, with numbers rising in Africa, parts of Europe and Central Asia, and Latin America and the Caribbean, but falling in East Asia.

In the new era of liberal economic integration, however, the World Bank, the International Monetary Fund (IMF), and the World Trade Organization (WTO) became controversial. They were seen by some socialists, labor activists, environmentalists, government-subsidized businesses, and strong nationalists as promoters of unwelcome globalization that, detractors charged, benefited only large corporations in the richest capitalist nations at the expense of developing countries, laboring people, distinctive native cultures, and the environment. Critics also insisted that self-interested bankers and financiers, not representatives democratically selected by governments, made the key decisions for the World Bank, the IMF, and the WTO. Defenders insisted that these institutions, by bringing the rule of law to the world economy, by providing banking resources for troubled economies, by establishing transparent rules of trade among ever more nations, and by lowering barriers to trade, travel, and investment, offered the best antidote to persistent poverty and the most sensible stimulus to economic growth worldwide.

Bretton Woods Conference

At the UN Monetary and Financial Conference convened in Bretton Woods, negotiators drafted agreements establishing three institutions meant to design a post-war global free trade system and help stabilize international financial relations: the IMF, the International Bank for Reconstruction and Development (IBRD, better known as the World

Photo 4.4 The table in the Gold Room of the Mt. Washington Hotel in Bretton Woods, New Hampshire, at which negotiators created the International Monetary Fund and the World Bank.

Source: Barry Livingstone via Creative Commons Attribution 3.0 license.

Bank), and the General Agreement on Tariffs and Trade (GATT). The last of these was supposed to be an "interim" agreement until an International Trade Organization—which would provide a more ambitious regulatory framework for world trade—could be established. GATT, however, remained in place until January 1, 1995, when the **World Trade Organization** superseded it.

Sponsored by the United States, the Bretton Woods Conference and its negotiated agreements were intended to establish a new international monetary and trade regime that was stable and predictable. Soon after the Bretton Woods institutions came into being, Washington pegged the dollar to gold at $35 an ounce, enacted large foreign aid programs to pump liquidity into the international economic system, and made the largest subscription of funds of any IBRD member to the assets of the World Bank. The IMF, GATT, and the World Bank, while independently administered institutions, since their origin have been considered part of the UN System.

World Bank

The World Bank is a group of five financial institutions headquartered in Washington, DC. These institutions are the IBRD (mentioned just above), the International Finance Corporation (IFC), the International Development Association (IDA), the Multilateral Investment Guarantee Agency (MIGA), and the International Centre for the Settlement of Investment Disputes (ICSID).

The International Bank for Reconstruction and Development began operations in 1946 with a mandate to aid the reconstruction of nations ravaged by World War II and to further the flow of capital around the world. The IBRD and the other institutions in the World Bank Group often find themselves working in close cooperation with the IMF. Since its founding, the World Bank has expanded its activities in ways that have made it even more important but also increasingly controversial. From the initial objective of restoring war-devastated nations, the World Bank Group has broadened its goals to include reducing poverty worldwide, strengthening the economies of poor nations, improving living standards, and promoting economic growth and development. The IBRD is like a global financial cooperative. That is, its member countries effectively own it. Each of its 189 member states (as of 2022) holds shares in the bank based on the size of the country's economy relative to the world's economy. All bank members are represented on the board of executive directors in Washington (developing nations together count close to half the votes). By 2022, the United States continued to hold more shares than any other country (about 17 percent). It was followed in this order: Japan 7.4 percent, China 4.8 percent, Germany 4.3 percent, France and the United Kingdom each about 4 percent, with India, Saudi Arabia, and Russia following, all at about 3 percent.[26] Still, the United States, with 17 percent, held a power of veto over any changes in the bank's articles or policies, because according to the 1944 articles of agreement, 85 percent of the shares are needed to effect such changes.

The bank does not make grants. It lends money to countries—almost always poorer countries that need capital, technical assistance, and sometimes financial and economic policy advice. The loans are repaid. Two types of lending are characteristic of the bank. The first is for developing countries that have an ability to pay market interest rates for the loan. The money for these loans comes from investors around the world who buy bonds issued by the bank. A second type of loan goes to the neediest countries that are unable to pay market interest rates. Because the bank cannot issue bonds to raise money for these loans, lending is done by means of the affiliate International Development Association (IDA), the World Bank Group's "concessional" lending body. The IDA shares the same staff as the IBRD and the same headquarters, reports to the same president (David Malpass in 2022), uses the same financial standards in evaluating projects, and in 2022 had 174 members. The IDA, taking advantage of some thirty countries that provide money needed to extend "credits" to the poorest borrowers, makes loans free of interest. These loans carry a low administrative charge, are long-term, and include five- or ten-year grace period.

Established in 1956, the International Finance Corporation (IFC) is the largest multi-lateral source of loan and equity financing for private-sector projects in the developing world. It promotes sustainable private-sector development. In 2022, it had a membership of 184 nations, all of whom were required to be IBRD members. IFC members appoint representatives to a board of governors that can delegate powers to a board of directors, composed of the IBRD's executive directors. Although the organization has its own articles of agreement, its president is the same as that for the IBRD.

The Multilateral Investment Guarantee Agency MIGA), created in 1988, advances foreign direct investment into emerging economies to reduce poverty and seek improvement of life in the world's poorer areas. MIGA offers political risk insurance to investors and lenders to attract investment into developing countries. In 2022, MIGA had a membership of 181 nations. Membership is open to all World Bank members. It is administered by a council of governors and receives some of its operating capital from the IBRD.

The International Centre for the Settlement of Investment Disputes (ICSID) was established in 1966 under the Convention on the Settlement of Investment Disputes between States and Nationals of Other States. ICSID is an autonomous, international organization with close links to the World Bank. Through arbitration, it mediates when investment disputes arise between private foreign investors and governments, with the parties involved bearing the costs of specific mediations.

The World Bank Group is one of the largest sources of development assistance in the world.[27] In 2019, it provided about $168 billion in grants and loans and was involved in more than one hundred developing economies. Its education funding began in 1963, and as of 2022, the bank was financing educational projects in more than eighty countries. It was also a cosponsor of the Joint UN Programme on HIV/AIDS (UNAIDS), and pioneered global HIV and AIDS financing.

Although critics continue to fault the bank for ignoring challenges such as the environment, distinctive native cultures, the role of civil society, and more, other people find that the bank has added too much to its mandate. In recent years, the bank has expanded its role into social and environmental issues. To ensure that the bank is not working at cross-purposes with other UN bodies, the director sits as a member—along with the directors of both the IMF and the WTO—on the chief executives board of the UN System, chaired by the Secretary-General. From reconstruction efforts in the Balkans to educational programs for young girls in Islamic countries, to the struggle against AIDS, the bank's mission, former managing director Jessica Einhorn once warned, has become unwieldy.[28] The bank, it seems to contrary perspectives, is doing either too much or not enough.

International Monetary Fund

Also created at the Bretton Woods Conference in 1944, the International Monetary Fund (IMF) is a UN specialized agency designed to promote international monetary cooperation; facilitate economic expansion, world trade, high employment, and income growth; promote stability and eliminate restrictions in international money exchange; and assist its members with temporary financial resources to solve balance-of-payment problems

Photo 4.5 World Bank Headquarters in Washington, DC.
Source: Carol M. Highsmith Archive, Library of Congress Prints and Photographs Division.

and other financial difficulties. The IMF, also headquartered in Washington, DC, often finds itself collaborating with the World Bank Group. The economists, financiers, diplomats, and political leaders who forged the post-World War II global structure wanted, in addition to encouraging freer movement of goods, money, ideas, and labor, to avoid the economic and financial pitfalls they believed had helped cause the collapse of international order leading to global conflict. Thus, while seeking transparency in economic and financial arrangements, they also wanted to construct an international ability to locate and rectify sudden economic troubles in discrete areas of the world. By the end of the twentieth century, the IMF became a target of antiglobalization criticisms because of its role in financing debt-ridden nations and imposing stringent conditions on them in return for assistance. Financial crises in Mexico (1995), throughout Asia (1997–1998), in Argentina (2001), and in Greece (2010–2015) led to IMF actions often opposed by some national governments, nongovernmental organizations, other international institutions, and citizens' groups. Critics faulted the IMF for operating in secret, with its decision-making process undemocratically controlled by government finance ministries and large banking interests.

Initially, a primary function of the IMF was to oversee the fixed exchange rate arrangements among the world's countries. The Bretton Woods System fixed foreign currencies' value in relation to the U.S. dollar. As the world's economy changed dramatically following World War II, and as other nations' economies grew, the fixed rate proved unsustainable. In the early 1970s, the Richard Nixon administration announced that the United States would suspend the dollar's convertibility into gold. The consequence was the system we have today of floating exchange rates. Since the abandonment of fixed exchange rates, the IMF has seen its function of surveillance (described below) adapt through changes in its procedures, while its role as a major lender has remained significant and has evolved.

Over time, the IMF has tried to combine several roles that in their complexity, and possible incompatibility, make the institution controversial. It has taken on the role of an international bank, an insurance company, a regulator, and a charity. To begin with, you should think of the IMF exactly as it is named: that is, it is a *fund*. The member countries of the IMF (190 as of 2022) grant an assessed quota to the fund much as individuals deposit money into a bank or a credit union. The quota is based on each member's relative size in the world economy. These quotas determine voting power in the IMF. So, richer nations wield more voting power in IMF decisions. Members pay 25 percent of their quota subscription in international reserve assets (U.S. dollars, euros, Japanese yen, British pound sterling, or the so-called special drawing rights (SDRs), which are defined below). The remaining 75 percent is in the country's own currency. As with a bank or a credit union, members may draw from the general resources of the fund, which are derived from these quota subscriptions. Members with "structural maladjustments" (an inability to meet payments, an accelerating public debt, a dangerously fluctuating currency, a balance-of-trade problem, and so on) may enter into extended arrangements with the IMF. The fund can supplement its resources by borrowing from member countries that have strong economies, allowing it to deal with an immediate problem that threatens international financial stability. Under the IMF's former "Structural Adjustment Facility," funds were made available on "concessional" terms to low-income countries at lower interest rates. Often, these developing countries were engaged in structural reform of their economies. During the late twentieth century, such structural readjustment normally meant moving from a command-style, socialist economy in which outside trade was restricted by protectionist policies, to a free-market economy emphasizing private enterprise, freer trade, and an internationally convertible currency. Such "structural readjustments" were typically the conditions the IMF imposed on the borrowing countries, whose citizens, accustomed to government sustenance, sometimes suffered at least temporary discomfort. In 1999, the Facility was replaced by the Poverty Reduction and Growth Facility (PRGF), partly to meet criticisms such as those mentioned above. The PRGF's core objective was to focus on growth and poverty reduction by integrating more fully macroeconomic programs with poverty reduction and to accentuate a greater degree of national ownership.[29]

Member states govern the IMF. A board of governors is composed of one representative from each member, and an equal number of alternate governors. A governor is usually the minister of finance or the head of the central bank of his or her country. Thus, governors represent their governments. They gather at annual meetings. Otherwise, the governors stay in touch with the IMF executive board stationed at the Washington headquarters. Twenty-four executive directors meet at least three times a week and carry out the policies of the board of governors. A managing director is head of the staff and is Chairman of the IMF's Executive Board.

The so-called special drawing rights (SDRs) are a novel creation of the IMF. The term implies that they can be "drawn" by a member state, much as you would "draw" a loan from a bank in which you had deposits. The IMF's board of directors invented SDRs in

1967. The value of IMF SDRs is measured against a "basket" of a few strong currencies (dollar, yen, pound sterling, and euro) and is based on current market exchange rates. Countries are accorded SDR allotments in the IMF. Technically a paper reserve, SDRs have many of the characteristics of money. For example, SDRs are interest-bearing assets, and interest can be charged on IMF loans made in SDRs. In effect, SDRs represent a movement away from using the dollar as the world's reserve currency, which was implicit in the Bretton Woods System.

The IMF offers *financial assistance*, including credits and loans, to members. With the financial crisis of 2008, the IMF began making loans to affected countries. Many of the loans were provided, as explained above, on concessional terms. The policy was initiated in 1950. Low-income countries do not pay interest for a certain period on these loans. The fund also provides *technical assistance* to its members to help with fiscal and monetary policy and structural reforms.

The IMF does not lend for specific purposes or projects as regional multilateral development banks (MDBs) do. Reserve assets that a member borrows are normally deposited in the borrowing country's central bank and are available to the country as any other international reserves would be. When lending, the IMF provides reserve assets in accepted foreign currencies and SDRs taken from other fund members. A borrower uses its own currency to "purchase" these assets from the fund. To repay, the borrower "repurchases" its own currency with international reserve assets. So, from an accounting perspective, the fund's total resources do not vary. However, financial aid is often linked to specific conditions that the borrowing country must meet. This situation was the case with Mexico and afflicted Asian countries in the mid-1990s and with Argentina in 2001. In each instance, because the world's richer nations—most important, the United States—held the controlling voting power in the IMF and feared instability in world financial markets, the fund, determined to avert a serious world financial crisis, voted to provide "bailout" loans. In the case of Argentina, the IMF arranged a complex $8 billion loan. From 2010 to 2012, the IMF participated in two loan arrangements with Greece.

The Greek situation underscored the IMF's historical evolution. In the beginning, the famed British economist John Maynard Keynes had anticipated an IMF that would be a cooperative fund from which member states could draw the means to maintain economic activity and employment and avoid periodic economic crises. Keynes's idea, derived from his own carefully thought-out economic theories, was that the fund would work like the government-associated Federal Reserve System in the United States. It would act on the basis of global financial and economic needs, rather than on the basis of a bank's profit line. The U.S. banker Harry Dexter White foresaw something different—an IMF that functioned more like a traditional bank, making sure that borrowers repaid debts on time. Most observers thought that the Bretton Woods System incorporated White's more conservative view. Yet, as time has gone on, the Keynes vision has gained traction.[30] For example, in the early 2010s, the fund did participate in the first two (of three) loan agreements with in-arrears Greece, whereby the afflicted country agreed to adopt austerity measures to reduce its deficit. However, the austerity regime only deepened Greece's economic and financial problem, and in 2015, the country had to come back—to the European Union—and seek further relief. This time, the IMF was hesitant to join in the loan bailout; IMF staff thought the Greek government's debt was not sustainable. While the fund recommended conventional structural reforms to enhance economic growth, it also suggested that serious debt relief should be extended to the country in tandem with new loans. That is, there had to be economic growth before further demands for debt repayment could be reasonably expected. This posture had the IMF sounding more Keynesian than in the past. Indeed, recent developments in the fund's practices may be closer to Keynesianism than expected.[31]

World Trade Organization

Joined with the World Bank and the IMF, the World Trade Organization (WTO), headquartered in Geneva, completes the triad of multilateral bodies overseeing the international economy as first projected at Bretton Woods. The WTO is a member-directed negotiating regime that establishes and then administers the rules governing world trade. These rules are designed to facilitate the uninhibited, fair, and predictable flow of international commerce. The WTO was created in 1995 as the result of the so-called Uruguay Round of Multilateral Trade Negotiations (originating in Uruguay and occurring in continuous negotiations during 1986–1994). It acquired authority beyond that of its antecedent General Agreement on Tariffs and Trade (GATT) so that it could better contend with an increasingly complicated system of trade rules. Growing world trade since 1945, assisted by the international rules of first GATT and then the WTO, had been, by the early twenty-first century, one of the main engines of economic development and had contributed, at least according to reliable statistics,[32] to growth in world income and the reduction of poverty.

The WTO's Ministerial Conference, comprising trade ministers or their equivalents from all member countries, meets at least once every two years and is the organization's supreme decision-making body. It sets the WTO's strategic direction. A General Council, made up of ambassadors and heads of delegation in Geneva, convenes regularly to make the necessary day-to-day decisions. The General Council also meets as the Trade Policy Review Body and the Dispute Settlement Body (DSB). The Goods Council, Services Council, and Trade-Related Aspects of Intellectual Property Rights (TRIPS) Council report to the General Council. In addition, specialized committees, working groups, and working

Photo 4.6 Ngozin Okonjo-Iweala takes over as new WTO Director-General, March 1, 2022.
Source: World Trade Organization via Creative Commons Attribution-Share Alike2.0 Generic license.

parties are set up to deal with special issues. A director general is the administrative head of the organization and usually serves a six-year term.

The WTO has six main functions:

- Making available a forum for trade negotiations among all its members.
- Administering the trade agreements thus negotiated.
- Managing specific trade disputes.
- Monitoring national trade policies.
- Providing technical assistance and training on trade policy for developing countries.
- Cooperating with other international organizations on trade issues.

The organization has a modest staff of just over six hundred and a parsimonious budget of slightly more than $200 million (as of 2021). It had 164 member countries as of 2022, accounting for more than 90 percent of world trade. Formerly Maoist China's joining in 2001 was a particularly significant breakthrough, as was the entry of Russia as late as 2012. The world trading system epitomized by the WTO—along with its World Bank and IMF associates—has been assailed in recent years by protest groups representing a congeries of interests (sometimes on opposite ideological waves), including protected businesses (particularly in agriculture), environmentalists (who believe that the expanding trade regimes ignore the environment), labor groups (who fear their members will be replaced by cheaper overseas workers), nationalists (who favor nationalist economic policies), human rights advocates (who anguish over workers' rights in developing countries), socialist-oriented economists (who prefer command to laissez-faire economic strategies), some ethnic groups (who worry about displacement of their language and culture by more economically dominant cultures), and some political activists (who believe that all the advantages from a more open economy extend only to rich capitalist enterprises). The large demonstrations that disrupted the ill-fated third WTO ministerial meeting held in Seattle in November 1999 received worldwide media coverage and underlined the popular resistance to trade liberalization. Since 1999, the WTO arranged designated protest zones in the cities where ministerial meetings took place, in order to accommodate the organized demonstrations that typically accompanied such meetings.

The round of multilateral trade negotiations that was supposed to be launched at Seattle in 1999 never occurred. More than the protests, the main reasons for this failure were disagreements among the United States, the European Union, and Japan over agriculture policies; dissatisfaction among developing countries over the implementation of the previous Uruguay Round WTO agreements; and differing opinions on the use of trade sanctions to enforce labor standards.

The 2001 ministerial meeting in Doha, Qatar (initiating the latest, so-called Doha Round of negotiations) set a goal of January 2005 to complete a further liberalization and boost trade prospects for the world's poorest countries. Prior to the next ministerial gathering—in September 2003 in Cancun—the WTO realized some solid accomplishments: an agreement that more easily allowed impoverished nations to obtain generic medicines for HIV and other diseases, and the imminent accession of Nepal and Cambodia, two of the world's most destitute nations, to membership.

However, by mid-September 2003, the Cancun talks had ended in disarray. The more affluent nations resolved to concentrate initially on issues of cross-border transportation procedures, rules regarding foreign investment and competition, and transparency in awarding government contracts, while the developing nations insisted just as firmly that the first priority was for the wealthier countries to agree to cut their agricultural subsidy programs and thus entertain freer import trade from poorer areas of the world. Led by a new bloc—the "Group of 21," as the media dubbed it—developing nations were resolute that their ideas be given equal billing. The diplomatic standoff could not be bridged, and the conference ended with no progress made toward the Doha goals. Negotiators for the Group of 21 pointed out that while *they* were seeking more liberal international trade, the United States, the European Union, and Japan continued agricultural subsidization for their farmers and disallowed virtually any importation from the developing world. Secretary-General Kofi Annan, presiding in New York over a tense opening of the fall UN season, captured the prevailing mood when he opined about Cancun: "I hope that is not the end of the road and that the parties will go back, and reflect, and then come back in a determined fashion to try and fashion an agreement."[33] Annan, and many others, had a point, because, as a World Bank study had shown, a liberalized trade agreement such as that envisioned at Doha could have lifted as many as 144 million people out of poverty by 2015.[34]

Further, WTO meetings continued up to the twelfth ministerial conference, scheduled for November 2021 in Geneva, which was postponed because of the coronavirus pandemic.[35] There was little progress in addressing the Doha Round disputes, and WTO negotiations stalled. Outside the realm of the ministerial meetings, bilateral and regional multilateral trade arrangements began to surface in lieu of the less satisfying, yet more global, negotiations of the WTO. One of the most ambitious of these was the twelve-nation Trans-Pacific Partnership (TPP), which proposed to link key Pacific Rim countries into a massive trade and finance bloc.

Countervailing Trends

A key part of former U.S. President Barack Obama's Asia policy, the Trans-Pacific Partnership (TPP), would have been the largest free trade arrangement in history. Although technically outside the province of the WTO, it was the first proposed accord to include provisions to protect labor rights and meet environmental concerns. It would have represented a consequential challenge to potential Chinese dominance in trans-Pacific trade and finance, while, according to supporters, boosting the economies of its participants. President Trump, who campaigned against the pact, withdrew the United States from it in January 2017 (his first act as president). With the United States out of the crippled TPP, fifteen countries in Asia, including seven large economies originally slated to be members of TPP, joined in November 2020 with China in her Regional Comprehensive Economic Partnership (RCEP) that then became the largest free trade agreement in history.[36]

This striking veer toward China may have been a harbinger of shifting configurations in international economic (even perhaps political) relations whose impact on the United Nations was, in 2022, unclear, some thought risky. The United States, recall, had been the prime mover of the post-World War II economic settlement. Purposely lodging that settlement within the UN System, the United States maintained singular influence over its operation from Washington, DC, home to both the World Bank and the IMF. As the unparalleled economic power at mid-century, the United States also committed to open global trade via the GATT, then via the WTO. Now, however, a resurgent China seemed to have announced its intent to counterbalance, perhaps displace Washington's global sway.

The full force of China's initiatives was represented by more than the RCEP. President Xi Jinping had ascended to power in 2012 following two predecessors who seemed to deal well with the West, participated tactfully and responsibly in the UN, and presided over unprecedented economic growth that raised China out of poverty and into the upper echelons of world nations. The former two—Jiang Zemin and Hu Jintao—also followed the post-Mao Zedong tradition of serving a ten-year limited term as a president. Xi moved expeditiously into all power positions in the country's hierarchy—General Secretary of the Communist Party, Chairman of the Central Military Commission, and President of the PRC. He also presided over a constitutional change that ended limits on presidential terms, thus qualifying him to be president for life. His flagship foreign policy was the **"Belt and Road Initiative"** (BRI), which set out to spend over one trillion dollars around the world in over one hundred and thirty countries building ports, railways, fiber-optic cables, power plants, and more. Xi saw this policy as promoting global development. In fact, China moved impressively into global development. With the emerging economies of Brazil, Russia, India, and South Africa (along with China, known as the BRICS), she formed in 2014 the New Development Bank (NDB), an international lending institution to aid developing countries. In 2015, China led more than fifty nations in launching the Asia Infrastructure Investment Bank (AIIB), intending to invest in infrastructure projects across Asia. Beijing instituted two unilateral lending projects—its South-South Cooperation Fund (to support climate work in developing countries) and the Silk Road Fund to help underwrite the Belt and Road Initiative.[37] Perhaps these Chinese actions will complement the UN's existing economic and financial structures and their objectives; perhaps they will seriously test them; perhaps, as countervailing trends, they will alter in significant and disquieting ways the UN we have described in this chapter.

SUMMARY

U.S. President Harry Truman once expressed the hope that the UN Charter "would become the Constitution of the world, just as the Constitution of the United States is the Constitution of the 48 states."[38] But constitutions and charters once written ossify and fall out of date unless the entities they authorize find ways to adapt to change and new challenges. While the UN Charter is not a constitution for the world, it has begot a comprehensive international network of organizations that has reasonably evolved to meet the times. Such was not the case for the Covenant of the League of Nations. The League could not respond effectively to the crises of the 1930s. By the first decade of the third millennium, actors within and observers without the UN System, fearing the organization was not evolving fast enough, spoke out on the need for reform. In New York City, Secretary-General Annan worried aloud about the impact on the organization of the inability of its majority and the indispensable, powerful United States to see eye to eye on the challenge of Iraq. An age of reforms, some large, some small, took hold. They added to the already existing evolution in UN institutions that has marked UN history since the commencement of the Cold War.

Debtor nations also worried about the global financial community. In the post-Cold War world, economic liberalism took hold on a global scale, boosting prosperity across the world and actually reducing poverty, yet, in some critics' view threatening weak economies of the South. Trade talks broke down, but new hope always recommenced, leading to a growingly inclusive World Trade Organization and more South-oriented policies from the World Bank and the IMF. The astonishing rise of China and its countervailing financial and trade ventures presented the U.S.-initiated UN with new, problematic challenges.

What seems obvious from an objective distance is that the United Nations is a focus of the news, appearing as a lead story more often than not. It has not been relegated to an obscure limbo in contemporary discourse as happened to the League of Nations. The complicated entity called the *UN System* has bent but not yet broken. This endurance, doubtless, is due in large part to the adaptation of the system to real-world, and frequently novel, trials. The UN's many institutions, at least most of them, have evolved. As it has for almost eighty years, maybe the UN System can consistently renew itself. Most of the world seems to hope so.

KEY TERMS

Advisory Opinions (148)
Belt and Road Initiative (170)
Caucus Groups (132)
Chapter VI½ Provisions (137)
Chief Executives Board (CEB) for
   Coordination (127)
Double Veto (135)
ECOSOC Functional Commissions (142)
Funds (150)
GA Fifth Committee (128)
GA First Committee (128)
GA Fourth Committee (128)
GA Second Committee (128)
GA Third Committee (128)
GA Main Committees (128)
General Committee (129)

Human Rights Council (157)
Important Question (132)
International Monetary Fund (163)
Other UN entities (154)
P5 (135)
Peacebuilding Commission (158)
Programmes (150)
Related organizations (154)
Research and training institute (154)
Secretariat (144)
Special Sessions of the GA (130)
Specialized Agencies (150)
UN System (127)
World Bank (162)
World Conferences (155)
World Trade Organization (162)

DISCUSSION QUESTIONS

How would you explain the "UN System" to a friend who had not read this chapter?
   Is the Security Council relevant or irrelevant in the twenty-first century?
   Is "globalization," as promoted by UN-affiliated organizations, positive or negative in terms of human welfare in the twenty-first century?

RESOURCES FOR FURTHER RESEARCH

Relevant Web Sites

See Resource 4 on the Routledge eResources page for the Statute of the International Court of Justice: www.routledge.com/9781138185807
International Court of Justice (www.icj-cij.org/en)
International Monetary Fund (www.imf.org)
United Nations Human Rights Council
(www.ohchr.org/en/hrbodies/hrc/pages/aboutcouncil.aspxx)
United Nations Peacebuilding Commission (www.un.org/peacebuilding/commission)
World Bank Group (www.worldbank.org)
World Trade Organization (www.wto.org)

Books, Articles, and Documents

Beck, Robert J., and Robert D. Vander Lugt, eds. *International Rules: Approaches from International Law and International Relations.* New York: Oxford University Press, 1996.
Bosco, David L. *Five to Rule Them All: The UN Security Council and the Making of the Modern World.* Oxford: Oxford University Press, 2009.
Economy, Elizabeth, "Xi Jinping's New World Order: Can China Remake the International System?" *Foreign Affairs,* January/February 2022, 52–67.
Fassbender, Bodo. *UN Security Council Reform and the Right of Veto.* The Hague, The Netherlands: Kluwer Law International, 1998.

Moore, John Allphin, Jr., and Jerry Pubantz. *American Presidents and the United Nations: Internationalism in the Balance.* New York and Oxford: Routledge, 2022.

Muldoon, James P., Jr., JoAnn Fagot Aviel, Earl Sullivan, and Richard Reitano, eds. *Multilateral Diplomacy and the United Nations Today.* 2nd Edition. Boulder, CO: Westview, 2005.

O'Brien, Robert, Anne Marie Goetz, Jan Aart Scholte, Marc Williams, Steve Smith, Thomas Biersteker, Chris Brown, eds. *Contesting Global Governance: Multilateral Economic Institutions and Global Social Movements.* New York: Cambridge University Press, 2000.

Peterson, M. J. *The UN General Assembly.* New York: Routledge, 2005.

Power, Samantha. *Chasing the Flame: One Man's Fight to Save the World.* New York: Penguin Press, 2008.

Sievers, Loraine. and Sam Daws. *The Procedures of the UN Security Council.* 4th Edition. Oxford: Clarendon Press, 2014.

Weiss, Thomas G., David P. Forsythe, Roger A. Coate, and Kelly-Kate Pease. *The United Nations and Changing World Politics.* 8th Edition. Boulder, CO: Westview, 2017.

Notes

1 See <unsceb.org/board-member>.
2 <www.un.org/sg/en/content/senior-management-grou>. This number can fluctuate. As of early 2022, there were about four vacancies at the under-secretary level that, if filled, could augment the number in the SMG.
3 This is in Article 18, paragraph 2 of the UN Charter.
4 "Press statement on Baghdad bombing by Security Council president," August 19, 2003, at <www.un.org/press/en/2003/sc7847.doc.ht>.
5 Shashi Tharoor, "Why America Still Needs the United Nations," *Foreign Affairs* (September/October, 2003), 71.
6 See the extended discussion on peacekeeping in Chapter 6.
7 The distinction is elaborated in Chapter 5; in the current context, *peacekeeping* would typically occur in an area where parties in dispute have agreed to invite the peacekeepers; in contrast, *peacemaking*, a much more controversial idea, would result when forces are placed in a violent and still-contentious situation, with the aim of imposing peace before being able to keep it.
8 International Court of Justice, "Chapter I: Organization of the Court," in *Statute of the International Court of Justice*, art. 4, para. 1 (The Hague, the Netherlands: International Court of Justice, n.d.).
9 John G. Stoessinger, *The United Nations and the Superpowers*, 4th Edition (New York: Random House, 977), 3–25.
10 <www.un.org/press/en/2021/sc14743.doc.htm>, and <www.un.org/press/en/2021/sc14750.doc.htm>.
11 See Chapter 8 for a comprehensive discussion of *development*.
12 As of 2022, the United Nations had had nine Secretaries-General. See Resource 6 on the Routledge eResources webpage for the complete list and a brief biography of each: www.routledge.com/9781138185807
13 The Nadia Younes Memorial website is at <nadiayounes.com>.
14 See <www.unglobalcompact.org/about/governance/board/members/bios >, and <www.unglobalcompact.org/news/4836-12-17-2021>.
15 For a list of cases pending before the ICJ, see <www.icj-cij.org/en/pending-cases>.
16 See </www.un.org/press/en/highlights/wcdrr>.
17 *Oxford English Dictionary* (Oxford: Clarendon, 1993). Also see *"rapporteur"* in the French dictionary of *WordReference.com 2015*, found at <www.wordreference.com/fren/Rapporteur>.
18 For full coverage of Special Procedures, see <www.ohchr.org/EN/HRBodies/SP/Pages/Welcomepage.aspx>.
19 Report of the Advisory Group of Experts for the 2015 Review of the United Nations Peacebuilding Architecture, *The Challenge of Sustaining Peace*, June 29, 2015. Found at <www.un.org/pga/wp-content/uploads/sites/3/2015/07/300615_The-Challenge-of-Sustaining-Peace.pdf>.
20 <www.un.org/press/en/2021/sgsm20985.doc.htm>.
21 Robert I. Rotberg, *Suffer the Future: Policy Choices in Southern Africa* (Cambridge, MA: Harvard University Press, 1980), 201, 224.

22 Boutros Boutros-Ghali, *An Agenda for Peace* (New York: United Nations, 1992).
23 James Kraska and Brian Wilson, "Piracy Repression, Partnering and the Law," *Journal of Maritime Law and Commerce* 40, no. 1 (January 2009): 50.
24 J. R. Mandle, "Globalization and Its Critics," *Historically Speaking* 4, no. 1 (September 2002), found at <www.bu.edu/historic/hs/september02.html#mandl>.
25 A. T. Kearney, "Globalization's Last Hurrah?" *Foreign Policy Magazine* (January/February 2002), 128.
26 See <thedocs.worldbank.org/en/doc/284471507050951684-0340022017/original/investorbrief-worldbank2017.pdf>.
27 See <data.worldbank.org/indicator/DT.ODA.ALLD.CD>.
28 Jessica Einhorn, "The World Bank's Mission Creep," *Foreign Affairs* 80, no. 5 (2001): 22–35.
29 See "Key Features of IMF Poverty Reduction and Growth Facility," at <www.imf.org/external/np/prgf/2000/eng/key.htm>.
30 See Eric Zuesse, "The IMF Admits It Was Wrong about Keynesianism," *Business Insider*, January 5, 2013, found at <www.businessinsider.com/imf-admitted-their-economists-were-wrong-2013-1>. And Asad Zaman, "Keynes versus the IMF," *International New York Times*, March 16, 2015, found at <tribune.com.pk/story/853761/keynes-versus-the-imf/>.
31 See the special issue of *Governance*, April 2015, found at <governancejournal.net/2014/10/31/special-issue-has-crisis-changed-the-imf/>. The editors of the journal describe the evolving role of the IMF this way: "Recently, the IMF has been in the headlines as a critic of austerity, inequality and unrestricted capital movements. This is in stark contrast to its conventional pre-crisis image as rigid international bully imposing draconian policies on countries in trouble."
32 World Bank, *World Development Report 2003: Sustainable Development in a Dynamic World: Transforming Institutions, Growth, and Quality of Life* (New York: Oxford University Press, 2002), Chap. 1. Also see John M. Micklethwait and Adrian Woolbridge, *A Future Perfect: The Challenge and Hidden Promise of Globalization* (New York: Crown Business, 2000).
33 "WTO Reeling from Trade Defeat in Cancun," *New York Times*, September 18, 2003.
34 Evelyn Iritani, "WTO Talks Could Derail in Cancun," *Los Angeles Times*, September 7, 2003.
35 For recent ministerial meetings see <www.wto.org/english/thewto_e/minist_e/minist_e.htm>.
36 Peter A. Petri and Michael Plummer, "RCEP: A New Trade Agreement That Will Shape Global Economics and Politics," *Brookings*, November 16, 2020, at <www.brookings.edu/blog/order-from-chaos/2020/11/16/rcep-a-new-trade-agreement-that-will-shape-global-economics-and-politics/>.
37 These two paragraphs have made use of John Allphin Moore, Jr. and Jerry Pubantz, *American Presidents and the United Nations: Internationalism in the Balance* (New York and Oxford: Routledge, 2022), 176–180, and "China's New International Financing Institutions," *The American Progressive*, September 22, 2015, at <www.americanprogress.org/article/chinas-new-international-financing-institutions/>.
38 Public Papers of the Presidents, 1948, 363.

Chapter 5

Maintenance of International Peace and Security

Before 1919, maintaining international peace and security was predicated on countries maintaining a balance of power, forming alliances, and engaging in individual self-defense. After World War I, the Treaty of Versailles introduced the novel notion of **collective security**, which the new League of Nations was to enforce. Following World War II, and upon the League's failure, another group of nations gathered in 1945 and determined, among other things, "to *unite our strength* to *maintain international peace and security*" and "to take effective *collective measures* for the prevention and removal of threats to the peace."[1] These principles would initially define the United Nations (UN) and later reshape it. In this chapter, we discuss the concept of collective security: its evolution as a principle, its role in the United Nations, the effect of the Cold War on it, and its evolving interpretation in the twenty-first century.

HISTORICAL PERSPECTIVE ON INTERNATIONAL PEACE AND SECURITY

Throughout history, human beings and their communities have sought means to improve their mutual relations and to impose order when resorting to force and violence would otherwise be the norm. During the Westphalian era of international politics—so named for its origins in the Treaty of Westphalia (1648), which ended the religious conflict known as the *Thirty Years' War*—the balance of power among sovereign states was the chief means of maintaining peace. Nation-states pursued peace conferences, treaties, alliances, spheres of influence, military deterrence, conventions, bilateral and multilateral negotiations, third-party diplomacy, and even imperial dominion. This approach to peace lasted well into the twentieth century.

The Congress of Vienna, convened at the conclusion of the Napoleonic wars, sought to restructure Europe and modernize its diplomatic practices in a way that would prevent another era of conflict such as had beset Europe during Napoleon's conquests. The ensuing arrangement—the "Concert of Europe" (described in Chapter 2)—marked a notable step in international efforts to achieve peace through permanent organizational vigilance by the great powers; it is often cited as a distant harbinger of the United Nations. It

DOI: 10.4324/9781003281535-6

authorized the use of force to sustain the governments restored after the fall of Napoleon. It sometimes intervened in the internal affairs of European states to defend "legitimate" governments against prospective insurgencies. Despite recurrent opposition, changing circumstances, and the Concert's elementary conservatism, it presided over a Europe that avoided another continent-wide cataclysm for a full century.

The Concert of Europe fully collapsed during the Great War of 1914–1918 (otherwise known as *World War I*). That conflict and the even greater carnage of World War II (1939–1945) convinced many leaders, such as U.S. presidents Woodrow Wilson and Franklin Delano Roosevelt, that the traditional diplomatic methods used to avoid or limit war were no longer sufficient. While not abandoning traditional approaches to peace and security, they sought to maintain international order through new, universal collective security systems, first via the League of Nations (1919), then the United Nations (1945). Creating international organizations such as these—permanent organizations dedicated to resolving crises among their member states and eliminating or greatly diminishing the perceived need to resort to war—emerged as a unique twentieth-century phenomenon.

THE CONCEPT OF COLLECTIVE SECURITY

Alliances and collective defense arrangements are directed outwardly against potential external aggressors who might threaten a group of states. A **collective security** system additionally intends to keep the peace internally among its members. It attempts to guarantee each state's security by considering an attack on one as an attack on all. It obligates each member state first to renounce the use of force against any other member, and, second, to resist aggression by conforming to the rules and procedures of the collective security organization. It works on the assumption that no state would use force against any member of the collective security system because any aggression—since it would be met by overwhelming international force—would be fruitless. Because a collective security system is directed both internally and externally, it subsumes for its members traditional self-help techniques, such as individual and collective self-defense, alliance creation, and declarations of war against an enemy. Members become "state citizens" of a rule-based organization that theoretically defends their legitimate interests against any aggressor.

Keeping world peace through collective security was a novel strategy introduced in the 1919 Treaty of Versailles. This treaty established a League of Nations, the Covenant of which committed its members to foreswear resorting to war to resolve disputes, to reduce their national armed forces "to the lowest point consistent with national defense,"[2] and to act collectively to resist aggression by any state, whether it had joined the League or not. Articles 10, 11, and 16 of the Covenant established the principle of collective security and devised enforcement mechanisms.

LEGAL BASIS FOR COLLECTIVE SECURITY: THE COVENANT OF THE LEAGUE OF NATIONS

Article 10
The Members of the League undertake to respect and preserve as against external aggression the territorial integrity and existing political independence of all Members of the League. In case of any such aggression or in case of any threat or danger of such aggression, the Council [of the League] shall advise upon the means by which this obligation shall be fulfilled.

> **Article 11, paragraph 1**
> Any war or threat of war, whether immediately affecting any of the Members of the League or not, is hereby declared a matter of concern to the whole League, and the League shall take any action that may be deemed wise and effectual to safeguard the peace of nations.
>
> **Article 16, paragraph 1**
> Should any Member of the League resort to war in disregard of its covenants under Articles 12, 13, or 15, it shall ipso facto be deemed to have committed an act of war against all other Members of the League, which hereby undertake immediately to subject it to the severance of all trade or financial relations, the prohibition of all intercourse between their nationals and the nationals of the covenant-breaking State, and the prevention of all financial, commercial, or personal intercourse between the nationals of the covenant-breaking State and the nationals of any other State, whether a member of the League or not.

The most controversial provisions of the League's Covenant were Articles 10 and 16, because they, respectively, raised the thorny issues of naming an aggressor and imposing nondiscretionary mandatory sanctions on a "covenant-breaking" state. Coupled with the requirement for unanimity in the League council, these articles made identifying an aggressor and imposing enforcement measures difficult and meant that the League was unlikely to address serious challenges to the peace.

The Covenant provided no legal or political definition of *aggression*. Neither did the later UN Charter of 1945. Since then, although seemingly critical to a collective security system, reaching agreement on a meaningful definition has proved elusive. One party can always claim that the use of force was provoked by another party's actions. Despite widespread agreement that aggression is wrong, nations engaged in armed conflict consistently contend that they act in self-defense. Even Adolf Hitler claimed that Poland attacked Germany in 1939 at the start of World War II. Often when it is obvious which state attacked another nation, it is still unclear whether the initiation of armed conflict was naked aggression or preemptive defense against an imminent attack. The latter was the justification Israel claimed when it initiated hostilities against its Arab neighbors in 1967. Finally, the opening of military operations in any conflict is usually shrouded in secrecy and confusion, which makes identifying the aggressor and the victim difficult. In 1988, the world community was able to pressure Iran and Iraq to end their unimaginably bloody seven-year war only by, among other things, establishing a commission to investigate who had started the fight. Only twice has the UN Security Council, under the provisions of Article 39 of the Charter, identified an aggressor and then used force to halt the aggression. The first was North Korea in 1950. The second was Iraq in 1990, after that country invaded Kuwait. Argentina was also designated an aggressor in 1982 because of its invasion of the Falkland Islands off the Argentinian coast—called the *Malvinas* by Argentina—but the United Kingdom, not the United Nations, reacted with force in this case. In 1960, an "aggression" was identified in the Congo, but Belgium—the exiting colonial power—was not mentioned as the perpetrator. The United Nations—like the League of Nations—to this day has no working definition of *aggression* that is binding under international law.

Much of the problem for international organizations, under the League then and under the United Nations now, lay with the concept of collective security in a world of sovereign states. If collective security is defined narrowly—in terms of immediately confronting an aggressor state that has crossed an internationally recognized border with military force—and if the definition requires a global response without much regard for individual states' national interests at that moment, successful collective action is likely only in limited circumstances.

A collective security system is built on the presumption that the common interest supersedes, or is at least in harmony with, its members' national interests. The sense of *common interest* might seem obvious in a great conflict, such as either of the twentieth-century world wars, or it might be quite real in an alliance when the members face an extremely dangerous external enemy. For example, from 1949 to 1989 the North Atlantic Treaty Organization (NATO) not only served as a vehicle for confronting the Soviet military threat in Europe, but also—because the threat was immediate and real—provided a mechanism for shading over differences among its European members and between the European allies and the United States. However, once the Soviet Union collapsed, the apparent solidarity in the alliance began to fray as national interests once again asserted themselves. Because a collective security system is also inward looking, trying to maintain peace *among* its members, national interests will often asserted against the common interest when the two are no longer seen as synonymous.

The assumption underlying the concept of collective security is the existence of a community of nations in which each has reasonable trust that the other members of the community will play by the international rules and will use the system to resolves disputes. A community such as this presumes the transformation of independent actors formerly part of an anarchic international environment into partners, or even citizens, operating in a framework of international law and legitimizing (and feasibly democratic) institutions In this sense, collective security mechanisms work best when an overarching sense of government exists, such as one would find in a domestic society. These preconditions are not universally accepted today, which makes the maintenance of an effective collective security system difficult.

Notwithstanding the absence of necessary conditions for collective security as it was understood in the 1930s, the concept can be imagined in broader terms than simply stopping an aggressor at its border, or punishing it once it crosses the border. Many modern threats to international peace and security have taken a guise significantly different from the traditional scenario in which one nation attacks another. Certainly, the latter has occurred, such as in the wars between Israel and surrounding states, between India and Pakistan, and on the Korean peninsula. However, the rise of ethnic and sectarian conflict, civil instability, terrorism, and even pandemic disease has produced a broader, if more ambiguous, understanding of collective security. Rather than a static legal theory, collective security is a "mental construction"[3] that implies a changing meaning as the threats to the community change. Fortunately, the UN Charter does not use the term *collective security*, which has prevented its meaning from becoming ossified in a particular legal definition.

UN efforts to maintain or restore peace and security during the past seventy-five years have widened the meaning of collective security to include "preventive" diplomacy (meant to preclude aggression before it happens), the defense of community values (including human rights, economic well-being, social justice, and a liveable environment), peacekeeping and state-building, and authorization of selected community members to act in the name of all. Its meaning was expanded to include reaction to terrorism the day after the September 11, 2001 attacks. The Security Council passed Resolution 1368, declaring acts of terrorism to be threats to international peace and security. The council applied the same judgment to financing terrorist groups, requiring all member states to take mandatory steps to halt the flow of resources both domestically and internationally for this purpose. In terms of disease, beginning in January 2000, the Security Council held regular sessions on the AIDS epidemic in Africa, finding it to be a threat that, under Chapter VII, the council should address. AIDS became the first health issue discussed by the council as a danger to collective security. Later, the council similarly addressed the 2014 Ebola epidemic in Africa, establishing its first-ever emergency health mission under its authority to end threats to international peace and security.[4]

As interesting, even perhaps as constructive, as the broadened meaning for collective security may be, the evolution occasionally has encountered roadblocks. A telling example occurred when, in December 2021, Russia vetoed a popular Security Council resolution that would have identified climate change as a threat to international peace and security. The resolution would have instructed the Secretary-General to single out climate-related security risks as "a central component" of the UN's conflict prevention efforts. Twelve members of the Security Council voted for the resolution. China, one of the five permanent members, abstained (meaning, as we see in the discussion of the veto in Chapter 4, that the People's Republic would not have stricken down the measure). India, a non-permanent SC member, voted no, and Russia doomed the resolution with its veto. The few opponents argued against tying conflict to climate, and the Russian Ambassador warned that the resolution would give the Security Council a pretext to intervene in any country.[5]

Although the League was a model for the later United Nations, the two organizations differ in important respects. In this chapter, you need to simply recognize that, in some ways, the UN Charter retreated from the League's more robust vision of collective security, as in the following two examples: (a) the League's Covenant disallowed parties to a dispute to vote on how to deal with that dispute, while, bending before power politics, the UN Charter contains no such limitation. (b) a permanent member of the Security Council can block UN action with the veto. The veto did not exist in the League's Covenant.

Unlike the League, the United Nations is a "universal" collective security system.[6] With the admission of Switzerland in 2002, all the world's states had become members (Montenegro, formerly part of Yugoslavia, became a member in 2006, and South Sudan, splitting from Sudan, joined in 2011), and currently the Vatican and Palestine are non-member observer states.

Today, because of universal membership, the UN collective security system is completely an "internal" matter; no external aggressors are left to confront. Precisely because of the inherent tension caused by the inward orientation of collective security in a world of sovereign states, the UN has had difficulty fulfilling its collective security obligations. For example, member states have never met their obligations under Article 43 of the Charter "to make available to the Security Council … in accordance with a special agreement or agreements, armed forces … for the purpose of maintaining international peace and security." The Security Council has had to depend on voluntary contributions of personnel, supplies, and funds through agreements with individual contributing states to undertake peace maintenance or restoration missions. Furthermore, all such actions authorized by the United Nations are subject to the veto power.

COLLECTIVE SECURITY PROVISIONS OF THE UN CHARTER

Article 2, paragraph 4, of the UN Charter stipulates, "All members shall refrain in their international relations from the threat or use of force against the territorial integrity or political independence of any state, or any other manner inconsistent with the Purposes of the United Nations." The nonuse of force by member states, except as they are authorized to do so as part of a UN operation, is a central tenet of the Charter. Although Article 51 grants members "the inherent right of individual or collective self-defense" against an armed attack, this concession to sovereign states to protect their populations and territory, and to regional organizations and military alliances, lasts only until the Security Council can undertake sufficient steps to restore peace. The Charter wording also limits this grant of autonomy by asserting the council's right to investigate and take action on any threat to the peace, even if the states involved in a dispute are opposed to UN involvement.

The Security Council is the body charged with putting the UN's collective security system into practice. The UN's founders made the council the repository of great-power resolve to maintain peace. The General Assembly (GA), while it may discuss any dispute in international affairs, is formally barred from making recommendations to resolve an issue while the council is "seized with the matter." This restriction on the GA means that when the council is addressing an issue on its agenda, its members have decided that the matter is of such critical importance to future peace that resolution of the issue falls solely within the Security Council's jurisdiction under the Charter's Chapter VII.

Any state may bring "any dispute or any situation" that is likely to endanger international peace and security to the council's attention (Article 35). Although the council is not obligated to discuss or act on every complaint brought to it, appeals by nation-states have been one of the usual means by which international conflicts have been placed on its agenda. For this purpose, each Security Council member has representatives in New York

Photo 5.1 Security Council unanimously adopts Resolution 2254 (2015), requesting the Secretary-General to convene representatives of the Syrian government and the opposition to engage in formal negotiations on a political transition.

Source: UN Photo/Eskinder Debebe. Reproduced by permission of the United Nations.

City so that the council may act within twenty-four hours of a request. Iran's complaint in 1946 that, in the aftermath of World War II, Soviet troops still occupied its northernmost province was the first appeal to the council under Article 35. In Africa, states often appealed to the council to end colonialism or to resolve conflicts between neighboring states. Great powers have also used the procedure to obtain UN endorsement for collective or unilateral action against another state. The United States requested sessions of the council at the time of the North Korean invasion of South Korea (1950), the Cuban Missile Crisis (1962), and the Iraqi invasion of Kuwait (1990). Smaller states have appealed to the Security Council to rebuke the actions of major powers. Guatemala in 1954 and Cuba in 1960 used this procedure against the United States, alleging aggression in each case. Since 1948, both Israel and adjacent Arab states have brought complaints about suspected aggression by the other side on many occasions.

The centrality of the Security Council to the UN's collective security system has given the body a unique position in world affairs. It serves as the "legitimizer" or "delegitimizer" for the use of force internationally.[7] The Cold War obscured the legitimizing role as it was used in events such as the Korean War, the wars in the Middle East (1948–1987), and the Cuban Missile Crisis. However, with the end of the East-West confrontation, the council's imprimatur of legitimacy was recognized as critical in the effort to achieve broad support for the use of force. The two Gulf Wars (1991 and 2003), the 1992 use of force in Somalia, and the international efforts in the Balkans during the 1990s all provide evidence of this phenomenon.

The United States' inability to gain Security Council endorsement of its invasion of Iraq in 2003 not only made the invasion more difficult, but also undercut the succeeding occupation and reconstruction of Iraq. The legitimacy of an institution, according to Ian Hurd, is the "subjective feeling on the part of the actors that leads them to behave differently than they otherwise would because they believe the institution requires them to."[8] Arab governments, in particular, have looked to the Security Council to provide legitimacy in the eyes of their own populations when determining their foreign policies in the Gulf region and toward the Israeli-Palestinian dispute. Although none of the permanent members of the Security Council is Middle Eastern, Arab, or Muslim, and three—the United States, Great Britain, and France—are perceived as Western neocolonialist powers in the region, Arab governments have been willing to support actions these powers have undertaken with council endorsement that they would not have supported if the actions had been carried out unilaterally. A recent example was Arab support for the Security Council's endorsement of intervention in the Libyan crisis (2011) to protect civilian populations from their own government forces during the Arab Spring upheavals.

LEGAL AUTHORITY FOR COLLECTIVE SECURITY: UN CHARTER CHAPTERS VI AND VII

To read the Charter of the United Nations is to envision an institution with revolutionary powers and authority in international affairs. The organization is granted not only the traditional instruments of diplomatic intercourse, but also the authority to impose crushing sanctions, to use military force, and to require nation-states to put their troops at the institution's disposal. Chapters VI and VII provide the legal foundation for these sweeping powers. Technically, Chapter VII contains the primary mechanisms for collective security, allowing the organization to undertake all necessary **enforcement measures**, whereas Chapter VI provides for only the traditional means of diplomacy to achieve **pacific settlement** of disputes. However, the distortion of world politics imposed by the Cold War made the use of Chapter VII nearly impossible, because its use required Permanent 5 unanimity in the Security Council. Consequently, from 1945 to the late 1980s, collective efforts to sustain the peace had to be fashioned out of reinterpretations of Chapter VII provisions or creative uses of Chapter VI.

Chapter VII provides more far-reaching powers than those in the ill-fated Covenant of the League of Nations. Article 39 of the Charter gives the Security Council the authority to "determine the existence of any threat to the peace, breach of the peace, or act of aggression" and to "decide what measures shall be taken" to halt the threat or punish the aggressor. Given that the council is the sole defining power determining whether international peace and security have been breached, it has broad latitude. According to Article 2, paragraph 7, which prohibits UN intervention in the internal affairs of states, "peace" in Chapter VII is understood as "international peace."[9] For this reason, actions contemplated by the Security Council must be weighed against the sovereignty of the states that such actions would affect. Not until the turn of the century was the council willing to declare anything other than the use of force by one state against another to be a threat to "international peace and security," the litmus test established in Articles 39, 42, and 43 for collective action.

Chapter VII articulates a number of actions that the Security Council may pursue if it determines that a threat to international peace exists. Article 40 empowers it to take provisional measures to prevent an escalation or aggravation of a dispute, including calling for a cease-fire or an armistice or for the withdrawal of troops. If these recommendations are ignored, coercive nonmilitary or military actions may be taken. In July 1987, the Soviet Union and the United States for the first time joined in a resolution on the Middle East under the provisions of Chapter VII. In Resolution 598, they demanded that Iran and Iraq "observe an immediate cease-fire" in their ongoing war, "discontinue all military actions on land, sea and in the air, and withdraw all forces to the internationally recognized boundaries without delay." Citing Article 40, the council decided "to consider further steps to ensure compliance" if either party refused to accept the UN's demands.

Article 41 enumerates steps that do not involve the use of weapons, such as the cessation of diplomatic relations, economic sanctions, even a blockade, and the full or partial disruption of communications between the outside world and the states responsible for the breach of the peace. If the Security Council believes these measures would be inadequate, it may enforce its decisions with military "air, land, and sea forces" of UN member states, and it may also impose embargoes or any other measures deemed necessary.

Sanctions and embargoes have been used in only a few cases—for example, against Iraq after the Gulf War, in the civil wars of the former Yugoslavia, and against Iran for its apparent violations of the Nuclear Non-Proliferation Treaty. In the Iranian case, the council—which had imposed crippling sanctions on Tehran—agreed to the lifting of the sanctions as part of the 2015 agreement between Iran and the P5+1 (United States, United Kingdom, France, Russia, China, and Germany), by which Iran acquiesced to limiting its nuclear program. You can find a full discussion of the use of sanctions—especially "smart sanctions"—later in this chapter, but for now you should note that their effectiveness in general remains in dispute. Should sanctions or embargoes not be adequate, Article 42 provides for even harsher measures because it authorizes the United Nations to take military action.

According to the original conception of the United Nations as the guarantor of international peace, the organization was expected to command military forces under the Security Council's authority and direction and with the help of a Military Staff Committee. All member states, as charged by Articles 43 and 44, were obliged to contribute troops and equipment to UN-led operations. The Military Staff Committee, consisting of the military chiefs of staff of the council's permanent members, would "advise and assist" the council when it decided to use force. The Military Staff Committee provision was a realization of the wartime Allies' expectation that the great powers would have the responsibility and authority to act militarily through UN machinery to preserve peace in the post-war period. By Article 26, the drafters of the Charter also contemplated the committee's playing a role in the development of UN disarmament programs.

Despite the founders' intentions, the Military Staff Committee, an early victim of the Cold War, was largely ignored after 1946.[10] In 1950, while the USSR was boycotting the Security Council, the committee met briefly to discuss the response to North Korea's invasion of South Korea. The council branded North Korea the aggressor and authorized a military response. Thus, the only military action ever undertaken *under the UN flag* (although with U.S. command) occurred during the Korean War. Once the Soviet delegate returned (from the protest boycott) to the country's permanent council seat, with the weapon of the veto, military action had to be taken by individual member states, at best authorized by pertinent Security Council resolutions or by the recommendations of the General Assembly acting in accordance with the Uniting for Peace Resolution, which is discussed later in this chapter.

LEGAL BASIS FOR COLLECTIVE SECURITY: CHARTER OF THE UNITED NATIONS

Article 25
The Members of the United Nations agree to accept and carry out the decisions of the Security Council in accordance with the present Charter.

Article 39
The Security Council shall determine the existence of any threat to the peace, breach of the peace, or act of aggression and shall make recommendations, or decide what measures shall be taken in accordance with Articles 41 and 42, to maintain or restore international peace and security.

Article 40
In order to prevent an aggravation of the situation, the Security Council may, before making the recommendations or deciding upon the measures provided for in Article 39, call upon the parties concerned to comply with such provisional measures as it deems necessary or desirable. Such provisional measures shall be without prejudice to the rights, claims, or position of the parties concerned. The Security Council shall duly take account of failure to comply with such provisional measures.

Article 41
The Security Council may decide what measures not involving the use of armed force are to be employed to give effect to its decisions, and it may call upon the Members of the United Nations to apply such measures. These may include complete or partial interruption of economic relations and of rail, sea, air, postal, telegraphic, radio, and other means of communication, and the severance of diplomatic relations.

Article 42
Should the Security Council consider that measures provided for in Article 41 would be inadequate or have proved to be inadequate, it may take such action by air, sea, or land forces as may be necessary to maintain or restore international peace and

security. Such action may include demonstrations, blockade, and other operations by air, sea, or land forces of Members of the United Nations.

Article 43
All Members of the United Nations, in order to contribute to the maintenance of international peace and security, undertake to make available to the Security Council, on its call and in accordance with a special agreement or agreements, armed forces, assistance, and facilities, including rights of passage, necessary for the purpose of maintaining international peace and security.

Article 45
In order to enable the United Nations to take urgent military measures, Members shall hold immediately available national air-force contingents for combined international enforcement action. The strength and degree of readiness of these contingents and plans for their combined action shall be determined, within the limits laid down in the special agreement or agreements referred to in Article 43, by the Security Council with the assistance of the Military Staff Committee.

Article 46
Plans for the application of armed force shall be made by the Security Council with the assistance of the Military Staff Committee.

Given the impracticality of mounting a UN military force under the direction of cooperating great powers in the Security Council during the Cold War, a more common practice emerged: the council empowered individual states or other organizations or regional groups to take such action, usually in the form of ad hoc "coalitions of the willing." In this context, the council's role of legitimation is critical. It allows for what Bruno Simma called "another kind of collective security"[11] than the Charter's original plan. Using Article 48, which requires member states, "or some of them," to "carry out the decisions of the Security Council," the body has regularly authorized coalitions "to use all necessary means" to restore peace and stability. The 1991 Gulf War against Iraq was an authorized UN enforcement operation, conducted by a U.S.-led coalition of member states on the basis of Articles 42 and 48. So, too, actions in Somalia, Rwanda, Bosnia and Herzegovina, East Timor, Liberia, Afghanistan, and the Central African Republic were first undertaken under the authorization rubric. However, when the United States invaded Iraq in March 2003 (and in 1999 led NATO forces into Kosovo), it did so without the kind of authorization other actors had received in the examples just cited. That is, non-UN forces, including those from the United States (as in Korea in 1950 and Iraq in 1991), had, in Security Council-authorized situations, represented the UN's wishes. Such was not the case in 2003 in Iraq, which raised a question about the "legitimacy" of the U.S.-led operation.

On paper, Chapter VII worked a revolution in international politics. The Cold War, however, made this revolution more theory than practice. With the Security Council locked in a superpower stalemate, Chapter VII provisions generally could not be implemented when conflicts arose. Instead, council members and the General Assembly were forced to rely on the more traditional methods outlined in Chapter VI in hopes of resolving a dispute or ending hostilities. Chapter VI, comprising Articles 33 through 38 of the UN Charter, describes noncoercive measures for settling disputes between nations peacefully. It provides rules for the implementation of one of the overriding aims of the United Nations as described in Article 1: eliminating threats to global peace and ensuring the settlement or adjustment of potential conflicts that could develop into a threat to international peace and security.

Acting under Chapter VI, the Security Council can decide to investigate a dispute or a situation that could lead to a dispute to ascertain whether it is likely to develop into a threat to international peace and security (Article 34). Although the issue under review has normally been of an international nature, in some instances—such as the control of Rhodesia by a racist minority government after 1966, human rights abuses in collapsing states (e.g., Yugoslavia and Rwanda), the threat of a civilian massacre in Libya by government forces in 2011, and the HIV/AIDS crisis—the Security Council has dealt with problems that did not immediately augur open international violence but were instead internal to a state. Also, the Secretary-General can alert the Security Council to such a case under Article 99. The Secretariat implements Chapter VI decisions, usually with a mandate but with no clear plan from the Security Council.

Once the council establishes that a threat exists, the following options are available to it. First are the measures mentioned in Article 33, paragraph 1: negotiation, mediation, conciliation, arbitration, and judicial decisions, as well as the use of regional institutions and other peaceful means for resolving the threat. The United Nations usually urges the parties to avail themselves of these traditional options under international law and encourages the parties to settle the dispute peacefully themselves by direct bilateral negotiations. Mediation would include a third party, such as the United Nations, to serve as a facilitator. A judicial resolution would require the parties to take the dispute to the International Court of Justice (ICJ). Second, according to Articles 36, paragraph 1, and 37, paragraph 2, respectively, the council can make recommendations about the procedure or method of adjustments and the terms of settlement for disputes. Finally, it can also make more general recommendations if the parties request them (Article 38).

Chapter VI's instruments for preventing war are limited and extend only slightly beyond the diplomatic techniques of the previous two centuries. Thus, alone, Chapter VI provides the council little more than international public persuasion to end disputes. Yet, without the far-reaching remedies of Chapter VII at their disposal, the Security Council and the General Assembly have often turned to broad interpretations of Chapter VI to end a particular conflict. Through this process of reinterpretation, the devices of peacekeeping, observer missions, as well as special political and peacebuilding missions—phenomena not listed in the Charter as part of the UN's arsenal—have come about. In June 1948, the Security Council created the UN Truce Supervision Organization (UNTSO), the UN's first observer mission. UNTSO was directed to assist the UN mediator in his efforts to stabilize a cease-fire in the Arab-Israeli war of that spring. And, acting on the recommendations of Secretary-General Ban Ki-moon, the council in 2013 established the United Nations Assistance Mission in Somalia (UNSOM) to assist the government with nearly all aspects of governance in that war-torn state and in the delivery of needed services to the population.

The uneasy peace following the 1948 Arab-Israeli war lasted until the invasion and occupation of Egypt's Suez Canal by Great Britain, France, and Israel in 1956. An emergency special session of the General Assembly urged a cease-fire, withdrawal of invading forces, and reopening of the canal. Canada's UN representative, Lester Pearson, proposed to the assembly that it replace foreign forces along the canal with a UN force. On November 4, the assembly approved Resolution 998 (ES-1), directing Secretary-General Dag Hammarskjöld to submit a plan "for the setting up, with the consent of the nations concerned, of an emergency international United Nations force (later known as UNEF) to secure and supervise the cessation of hostilities." The operation's intent was to place a neutral force between the combatants and to monitor the cease-fire. Thus, on November 5, 1956, the UN gave birth to its first peacekeeping operation.

UN peacekeeping is discussed fully in Chapter 6, but for now you should note that this fairly common UN device for restoring peace cannot be found in Chapters VI or VII of the Charter. Secretary-General Hammarskjöld coined the term **Chapter VI½** to designate the Charter-based authority for peacekeeping and observer operations. (See the discussion of "Chapter VI½" in Chapter 3). These operations were developed as an action more intrusive than the peaceful settlement provisions of Chapter VI, yet short of Chapter VII provisions authorizing member states to use force. A new "gray area" of UN action emerged somewhat between the two chapters, keeping UN involvement relevant to the resolution of disputes in ways that neither the Charter formally established nor earlier practice by the League of Nations contemplated.

COLLECTIVE SECURITY UNDER COLD WAR CONDITIONS

With the promise of continuing post-war superpower cooperation largely nonexistent by 1946, the UN's ability to respond to international crises depended on its leaders' ingenuity and the great powers' willingness to accept innovations in the application of the Charter. Despite the Charter provisions, UN efforts to secure peace depended on circuitous methods, enhanced roles for the General Assembly and the Secretariat, and expansive interpretations of Chapter VI. Even open aggression could not be addressed through council agreement, as the world discovered in the **Korean War** experience of 1950.

On June 25, 1950, North Korean military forces invaded South Korea. The peninsula had been a source of tension since the end of World War II, with a Communist regime in the north supported by the Soviet Union and the People's Republic of China, and the Republic of Korea (ROK) in the south, recognized by the UN General Assembly as the legitimate Korean government. North Korean aggression was an open challenge to the new United Nations. On June 27, the council determined that a "breach of the peace" had occurred and called on all states, under the authority of Chapter VII of the Charter,

> to furnish such assistance ... as may be necessary to repel the armed attack and to restore peace and security in the area ... [and to] render every assistance to the United Nations in the execution of this resolution.

The council also granted the United States permission to appoint the commander of UN forces. President Truman appointed General Douglas MacArthur to the post. Ultimately, fifteen nations joined the UN coalition, but the bulk of the forces, the strategy, the funding, and the political decisions emanated from Washington, DC, even though the operation was to be under the UN flag.

In contrast to the League's response to aggressive actions in the interwar period, the United Nations proceeded decisively. President Truman saw the crisis as a test of the new organization's collective security capability.[12] However, the strong UN response to North Korean aggression was possible only because of a quirk of UN history: at the time, the Soviet Union was boycotting Security Council meetings to protest the continuing representation of China on the council by the Nationalist government on Taiwan. Mao Zedong's success in winning the country's civil war and installing a Communist regime had led the United States to veto resolutions to switch China's Security Council seat to Beijing. With the Soviet ambassador absent, the USSR could not veto the authorizing resolution for military resistance to the aggression. Chapter VII "worked" only because the unanimity of the permanent council members was not needed.

The war went badly for UN forces in the initial months of combat. However, Seoul—the capital of South Korea—was liberated on September 28. The UN forces drove North Korean troops back across the demarcation line (the thirty-eighth parallel) between the two Koreas, and the Security Council approved the forcible reunification of the peninsula. As described below, North Korea regained momentum in the war and an armistice was finally struck with North and South still divided to this day at the original demarcation line.

Uniting for Peace Resolution

The return of the Soviet ambassador to Security Council sessions made any further council endorsement of allied operations impossible. Council deadlock could now mean a UN military failure in Korea, particularly as Chinese "volunteers" entered the battle on the side of the North Koreans. Anticipating an ineffective Security Council, the United States attempted to shift discussion and authority for measures in Korea to the General Assembly (GA). The USSR argued that such a maneuver violated Article 12 of the Charter, which prohibits the General Assembly from making any recommendations concerning a dispute while the Security Council is deliberating on the matter. With its large working majority in the body, however, the United States easily secured passage of the Uniting for Peace Resolution: fifty-two states voted in favor, five (all from the Soviet bloc) voted against, and two abstained.

The **Uniting for Peace Resolution** (passed on November 3, 1950) "stretched" the Charter, constituting an informal amendment of the document. It gave the General Assembly the authority to discuss a threat to the peace, a breach of the peace, or an act of aggression, and to make recommendations for collective measures whenever "the Security Council, because of lack of unanimity of the permanent members, fails to exercise its primary responsibility for the maintenance of international peace and security." The resolution provided a mechanism to circumvent the anticipated use of the veto—at the time by the Soviet Union, later by other permanent members—to ensure the UN's ability to undertake action to restore the peace. The resolution shifted authority for enforcement measures from the exclusive control of the Security Council to a shared position with the assembly, which now had some legal authority to recommend "the use of armed force when necessary."

Emergency Special Sessions of the General Assembly

The Uniting for Peace Resolution allowed for **emergency special sessions of the General Assembly** to consider recommendations within twenty-four hours of a request by any seven members of the Security Council (nine members after the Charter revisions of 1965). The emergency special session could also be convened at the request of a majority of the assembly's members. The resolution opened a new avenue for maintaining peace or responding to an aggressor when discord between Washington and Moscow appeared to make the UN helpless. The Uniting for Peace innovation represented part of a general Cold War era shift in activity from the council to the larger body, where simple majorities and the absence of the veto made action possible.

On February 28, 2022, at the call of sufficient security council members—and summoned under a "uniting for peace" resolution—the General Assembly convened for its eleventh emergency special session to consider a resolution[13] condemning Russia's invasion of Ukraine only a few days prior. Sponsored by 94 delegations and approved by a vote of 141 to 5 with 35 abstentions, the resolution labeled Russia's intervention as aggression and demanded that it "immediately, completely and unconditionally withdraw all of its military forces from the territory of Ukraine within its internationally recognized borders."

Ironically, the USSR, the Russian Federation's predecessor state, was the first country to use the provisions of the Uniting for Peace Resolution after its passage, joining with Yugoslavia to call for an emergency GA session in 1956 on the Suez Crisis. It used the stratagem again following the so-called Six-Day War in 1967 between Israel and an Arab coalition. In the Suez case, the United Kingdom and France had vetoed Security Council measures calling on them to end their invasion of the canal region. The General Assembly then insisted on an immediate cease-fire and withdrawal of forces from the area. It also directed Secretary-General Dag Hammarskjöld to report within forty-eight hours on the preparation and dispatch of a UN Emergency Force (UNEF) to separate the parties. The end of the crisis and the apparent effectiveness of the UN's first peacekeeping operation seemed to demonstrate the worth of the resolution.

In 1956, a second emergency special session convened to consider the crisis in Hungary and the Soviet invasion of that country. Unfortunately, the session demonstrated one of the two most serious weaknesses of the procedure. In this case, the offender was one of the two superpowers. The General Assembly soon learned that nothing it might do would force the Soviets to change course. A similar impasse occurred in January 1980, when the assembly held its sixth emergency session, this time to consider the Soviet invasion of Afghanistan. All the assembly could do was "deplore" the invasion, call on the USSR to withdraw, and urge the Security Council to find ways to implement the assembly's resolution. Such UN action had little discernible impact on Soviet foreign policy.

Recommendations by the assembly on matters originally thought to be within the sole jurisdiction of the Security Council also raised constitutional concerns for some UN members; as a result, they were unwilling to pay for or support the UN actions that flowed from such recommendations. Following the fourth emergency special session (1960) on the Congolese civil war, both Russia and France refused to pay their assessments for peacekeeping operations that the General Assembly had recommended. The result was a financial crisis that brought the world body to the verge of bankruptcy. The Congolese experience made the Uniting for Peace Resolution far less appealing. It was not invoked again until 1980.

Emergency Special Sessions of the UN General Assembly Authorized by the Uniting for Peace Resolution

First	Suez Crisis	November 1–10, 1956
Second	Hungarian Crisis	November 4–10, 1956
Third	Lebanon and Jordan	August 8–21, 1958
Fourth	Congo Question	September 17–19, 1960
Fifth	Middle East War of 1967	June 17–September 18, 1967
Sixth	Afghanistan	January 10–14, 1980
Seventh	Palestine	July 22–29, 1980;
Eighth	Namibia	April 20–28, June 25–26, August 16–19, September 24, 1982
Ninth	Occupied Arab Territories	September 3–14, 1981
Tenth	Occupied East Jerusalem and the Rest of the Occupied Palestinian Territories	January 29–February 5, 1982
Eleventh	Illegal Israeli Actions in Occupied East Jerusalem and the Rest of the Occupied Territories	April 24–25, July 15, November 13, 1997; March 17, 1998; February 5, 8, and 9, 1999; October 18–20, 2000; December 20, 2001; May 7, August 5, 2002; September 19, October 20–21, December 8, 2003
	Russia's invasion of Ukraine	July 16–20, 2004 November 17, December 15, 2006 January 15–16, 2009 December 21, 2017 and June 13, 2018 February 28–March 2, 2022

The UN General Assembly convened eleven emergency special sessions, half of them concerning Middle East conflicts, in the organization's first seventy-seven years. The more recent sessions demonstrated an evolution in the use of the device. During the Cold War, one or more permanent members of the Security Council would usually organize the necessary majority to convene the General Assembly, hoping to find support in the face of a veto by one of the other P5. Beginning in the 1990s, a more common occurrence was for groups of smaller states to call an emergency special session. The tenth emergency session, first convened in April 1997 to address Israeli occupation of East Jerusalem, the Gaza Strip, and the West Bank, met several times during the next twenty years at the behest of the Arab and non-aligned caucuses in the General Assembly. In most cases, it met in response to a U.S. veto of a proposed Security Council resolution criticizing Israeli actions.

In the fall of 2003, representatives to the GA reopened the tenth emergency special session to discuss provocative decisions by the government in Tel Aviv, one of which was to build a security wall between Israeli and Palestinian communities in the West Bank, and between Israel proper and the occupied territories. The emergency session took the unusual step of referring the matter to the International Court of Justice (ICJ) in The Hague for an advisory opinion on the legality of the barrier. The court agreed to hear the case. By a vote of 14 to 1, the judges of the ICJ held that the wall was illegal under international law and must be removed. The court called on the General Assembly and the Security Council to "consider what further action is required to bring to an end the illegal situation resulting from the construction of the wall and the associated regime."[14] Days later, the General Assembly, by a vote of 150 to 6, with 10 abstentions, urged all member states to acknowledge the illegality of the wall and to render no aid to the Israeli project.

In its opinion, the court held that it had jurisdiction in the case because the General Assembly had authority to request an advisory opinion, even though the Security Council remained seized with the matter. The ICJ noted:

> There has been an increasing tendency over time for the General Assembly and the Security Council to deal in parallel with the same matter concerning the maintenance of international peace and security (see, for example, the matters involving Cyprus, South Africa, Angola, Southern Rhodesia, and more recently Bosnia and Herzegovina and Somalia).[15]

At least according to one observer, the court's decision opened up another avenue to circumvent a veto by a permanent member of the Security Council—that is, by court decision declaring an act in violation of international law and a threat to international peace and security.[16] That being said, in the twenty-first century only the emergency session on the Ukraine crisis has been convened to address issues deadlocked by the veto, and so no UN action was taken when the United States intervened in Iraq (2003), Russia annexed Crimea (2015), Ukraine fell into secessionist civil war (2014), or when Russia and China repeatedly blocked resolutions authorizing collective action in the Syrian civil war.

Peacekeeping and Military Observer Groups

Conflict in the Middle East has been not only the UN's longest-running challenge to collective security, but also the cauldron in which the world organization has had to devise its most important innovation to preserve peace and stability—the peacekeeping mission.[17]

As we noted previously, the 1948 war between the new state of Israel and several Arab states led to the creation of the UN's first observer mission (UNTSO), and the 1956 Suez Crisis brought about the first peacekeeping force (UNEF).

As would be the case for nearly all early UN peacekeeping efforts, the placement of the emergency force along the Sinai in November 1956 was contingent on approval by the sovereign state involved, in this case Egypt. UNEF patrolled the border and monitored the cease-fire until 1967. In the spring of that year, Egyptian incursions in the Gaza Strip and Sharm El-Sheik, plus moves by other Arab states, convinced the Israelis that an attack was imminent. Of particular moment was Egyptian president Gamal Abdel Nasser's insistence that the UN "Blue Helmets" (i.e., the UNEF group) be removed in order to open the Sinai for any projected attack. Secretary-General U Thant withdrew the force. Shortly thereafter, the Middle East War of 1967 broke out. Following the war, UNEF II patrolled a new cease-fire. By the time of its termination in 1979, the effort had resulted in the loss of thirty-six peacekeepers' lives from hostile action.

Generally subsumed under the nomenclature of **peacekeeping**, a term not found in the UN Charter, the insertion of outside personnel under UN command to separate warring parties, to monitor a cease-fire, or to provide neutral administration has become a hallmark of the UN's role in world affairs. During the latter half of the twentieth century, the distinctive blue helmet that the UN peacekeepers wore became a symbol of the international security system: the Blue Helmets provided an important mechanism for preserving the global order, ensuring the survival of small states, protecting human rights, and undertaking nation-building in failed states. Peacekeeping is a concept that has evolved through the years, and in the next chapter, we describe the UN peacekeeping's critical, and amplified, role in the twenty-first century.

DISARMAMENT AND ARMS CONTROL

Far more central to the notion of collective security than peacekeeping, however, was the conviction that conflict and general war could be eliminated only by a vast reduction in the world's military arsenals. While the UN Charter says nothing about peacekeeping, it specifically cites "disarmament and the regulation of armaments" as one of the "general principles" on which international peace and security are based.[18] It also charges the Security Council with proposing plans for arms control.[19] From its earliest days, the United Nations sought to facilitate the reduction and control of the most destructive weapons. This effort was given an urgency by the dawning of the nuclear age just as the United Nations was coming into being.

Disarmament is neither a requirement of nor a necessary condition for collective security. A case can be made that international peace and security require the maintenance of sufficient military force to repel any aggressor or to enforce the world community's decisions. Nonetheless, beginning with World War I, leaders like U.S. president Woodrow Wilson believed that collective security could succeed only if it was accompanied by deep reductions in, and even the elimination of, national military arsenals. Arms races were perceived as destabilizing. Both the League's Covenant and the UN Charter committed their respective organizations to fostering world disarmament. The rise of military dictatorships in Europe and Asia in the 1930s reinforced the opinion that reduction of armaments was essential to the maintenance of peace and to the replacement of the use of force with the rule of law.

During the Cold War, the UN's preoccupation was with weapons of mass destruction (WMDs) owned by the world's major powers. The proximity of events in 1945 made this preoccupation inevitable. The conclusion of the San Francisco Conference in June of that year, the immediate submission of the Charter to the U.S. Senate for ratification with the public belief that the new organization would be able to address the most serious problems, and only two months later, the American detonation of the world's first atomic bomb over Hiroshima, Japan, put extraordinary pressure on the United States and other major powers to place atomic energy under UN control. The General Assembly's first resolution, passed on January 24, 1946, created the UN Atomic Energy Commission (UNAEC) to make recommendations to the Security Council on methods to "deal with the problems raised by the discovery of atomic energy." The Security Council members, plus Canada when it was not a council member, were appointed to the commission.

At the inaugural meeting of UNAEC, the United States submitted a proposal to place all uranium mines, processing facilities, and fissionable materials worldwide under UN ownership in a new agency called the *Atomic Development Authority* (ADA). The ADA would then distribute "denatured" nuclear materials to national governments for peaceful uses. The United States envisioned the transfer of American, Soviet, and all other national nuclear assets to the United Nations in a phased process. The U.S. representative to UNAEC, Bernard Baruch, put forward the *Baruch Plan*, calling for penalties against states that violated ADA authority. The United States promised to destroy its stockpile of weapons and to turn over its scientific information to the ADA once a system of inspections and controls was put in place. The proposal met immediate Soviet opposition, which demonstrated that the emerging Cold War antagonisms were likely to make UN progress on disarmament extremely difficult. The USSR argued that the U.S. initiative was simply an attempt by the United States to maintain its nuclear advantage. The Soviets insisted that the U.S. nuclear arsenal had to be destroyed before any controls or UN ownership could be set up. While the commission approved the U.S. plan by 10 to 0 in December 1946, the Soviet Union abstained, which made any practical creation of a UN agency with the designated powers impossible.

In December 1953, President Dwight Eisenhower revised the U.S. position, calling on nuclear powers to transfer a small percentage of their nuclear materials to a new International Atomic Energy Agency (IAEA) under the ultimate authority of the United Nations but largely independent of its control. In the intervening years between the Baruch Plan and Eisenhower's proposal, the Soviet Union detonated its first atomic device (1949) and quickened its nuclear efforts. The United States, for its part, had decided to establish a nuclear arsenal and delivery systems capable of guaranteeing deterrence based on a credible second-strike capability against any surprise attack. Although the Soviet Union rejected the proposal, Eisenhower's initiative led to the inauguration of the IAEA in 1957. Of note for this discussion was the framing of the IAEA's safeguards inspection system, which was meant to guarantee that nations without nuclear weapons were not diverting nuclear energy materials intended for peaceful purposes to weapons use.

The UN's impact on disarmament in the 1950s was negligible. In 1952, the Atomic Energy Commission and the UN's Commission on Conventional Armaments were merged into the UN Disarmament Commission. However, this forum served as little more than a setting for Soviet and U.S. propaganda bombasts, the former power calling for "general and complete disarmament," the latter insisting on verifiable and intrusive inspection as part of any disarmament plan. Serious discussions within the Disarmament Commission occurred only in the Commission's subcommittee on disarmament, established in 1954 and made up of the United States, the Soviet Union, the United Kingdom, France, and Canada. These states conducted their talks in secret. To be sure, the growing number of new UN members from the developing world, and the desire to maintain influence in these countries, led the superpowers to make organizational concessions to the UN membership; but the nuclear powers still monopolized the substantive issues. The subcommittee was eventually expanded to ten and then eighteen, but the only serious negotiations were conducted in bilateral contacts between Washington and Moscow.

A number of agreements were concluded in the 1960s and early 1970s as a result of U.S.-USSR talks. Following the dangerous confrontation in the Cuban Missile Crisis, the two sides agreed to the 1963 Partial Test Ban Treaty and a communications hotline between the two capitals to ensure no misunderstandings on the deployment or use of weapons and personnel. In 1972, they reached agreement on the Anti-Ballistic Missile Treaty.

The UN negotiations were relegated to what were then seen as peripheral matters. Two topics dominated UN weapons diplomacy: nuclear weapons–free zones (NFZs) and nuclear non-proliferation. The Antarctic Treaty of 1959 was the first agreement to ban nuclear weapons on a regional basis. The treaty prohibited weapons or weapons testing on the Antarctic continent. Signatories pledged to demilitarize Antarctica. To protect the environment, the treaty banned the dumping of radioactive wastes. NFZ agreements were also achieved for Latin America (Treaty of Tlatlelolco, 1976), Africa (Treaty of Pelindaba, 1996), Southeast Asia (Treaty of Bangkok, 1995), the South Pacific (Treaty of Rarotonga, 1985), and Central Asia (2009, with an additional protocol signed by other major nuclear powers in 2014 respecting the NFZ). In 1979, following successful negotiations, the United Nations effected the prohibition of weapons on the moon and other celestial bodies.

The UN's single greatest achievement in restraining the nuclear arms race was the Treaty on the Non-Proliferation of Nuclear Weapons, usually referred to as the **Nuclear Non-Proliferation Treaty (NPT)**. This treaty was opened for signature on July 1, 1968, and entered into force in 1970. It grew out of negotiations in the Eighteen-Nation Disarmament Committee (ENDC). In August 1967, for the first time, the United States and the Soviet Union submitted a joint draft agreement. The superpowers hoped to halt the spread of nuclear weapons by convincing states without such weapons to foreswear their acquisition and to bar existing nuclear weapons states from transferring these weapons to any nonnuclear state or assisting any nonnuclear state in manufacturing them. A state adhering to the NPT was obligated to subject its entire peaceful nuclear program to the International Atomic Energy Agency's safeguards inspection regimen and to pledge to acquire nuclear materials and equipment only for peaceful purposes.

Many nonnuclear states balked at the U.S.-Soviet draft because it appeared to cement the existing power structure permanently, with the nuclear states—at the time the five permanent members of the Security Council only—in a position to dominate world affairs indefinitely. Several ENDC delegations, led by Nigeria and Brazil, indicated that they would not freeze their nuclear development programs, while the superpowers continued to stockpile and modernize their weapon systems. These delegations insisted that the United States and the USSR move toward ending their "vertical" proliferation before nonnuclear states pledged to halt the "horizontal" proliferation of these weapons.

Without the signatures of the states that were on the threshold of developing nuclear weapons, the NPT would have been worthless. Recognizing this, the superpowers added an article to the draft treaty that committed them to "pursue negotiations in good faith on effective measures relating to the cessation of the nuclear arms race at an early date and to nuclear disarmament" (Article VI). Disarmament was no longer simply an East-West issue but also a North-South issue; the developing world used its political clout to pressure the superpowers into concessions. The commitments made in the NPT meant that the U.S.-USSR negotiations on arms control would have to show some progress or critical nonnuclear states would not sign the treaty. This incentive encouraged the opening of Strategic Arms Limitation Talks (SALT) between Moscow and Washington, resulting in the SALT agreements of 1972: the five-year Interim Agreement on Certain Measures with Respect to the Limitation of Strategic Offensive Arms, which curtailed the growth of missile delivery systems on both sides, and the Treaty on the Limitation of Anti-Ballistic Missile Systems (ABM Treaty). The latter limited the number of defensive systems each side could maintain.[20] The UN negotiations on non-proliferation had contributed to slowing the superpower arms race.

The NPT called for a conference twenty-five years from entry into force. Held at UN headquarters in 1995, that conference reached a consensus on extending the NPT indefinitely. The parties also agreed to an "enhanced" review process to hold all governments "accountable" for their NPT obligations. The nuclear weapons states, moreover, committed to achieve a Comprehensive Nuclear-Test-Ban Treaty (CTBT). During the 1990s, adherence to the NPT accelerated as long-time holdouts like France (1992), China (1992), and South Africa (1991) signed and ratified the treaty. By 2021, only four states stood outside the framework of the treaty: India, Pakistan, Israel, and North Korea, which initially joined the treaty but then announced its withdrawal in 2003.

Following the adoption of the NPT, the ENDC evolved into the Conference on Disarmament (CD). It aspired to become the world's principal multilateral disarmament negotiating forum. However, the size of the Conference (65 member states) and the requirement that it reach decisions by consensus, coupled with the centrality of nuclear weapons to the strategic interests of the major powers, meant that this Geneva-based body had a diminishing impact on disarmament efforts. The Conference's last successes were the Chemical Weapons Convention (1992) and the Comprehensive Nuclear-Test-Ban Treaty (1996). Generally, countries avoid the body as they pursue arms control.

The plight of the Conference on Disarmament was emblematic of the difficulty a universal international organization dedicated to collective security has in addressing an issue when it touches on matters critical to the most powerful states' national security interests. These states are unlikely to relinquish their control over the negotiating process or to subject their armaments to international regulation without clearly controllable benefits to themselves. In the United Nations, this dilemma meant that the Security Council was unable to put forward a meaningful disarmament program during the Cold War, and the GA was relegated to admonishing the nuclear powers about their responsibilities and to concocting structures and initiatives to exhort world public opinion on the merits of disarmament, and convening three special sessions on disarmament (1978, 1982, and 1988) prior to the end of the century and committed to a fourth gathering once an agenda and format could be agreed upon. To its credit, the GA meetings were the first global general conferences on disarmament since the World Disarmament Conference sponsored by the League of Nations in 1932.[21]

The 1978 special session set up the UN Institute for Disarmament Research (UNIDIR), an autonomous intergovernmental organization within the UN System. The institute's small, permanent staff is located in Geneva. It is funded by voluntary contributions and the regular UN budget. Its purpose is to provide the international community with data on and analyses of problems related to the arms race, particularly in the nuclear field.

Changing Disarmament Priorities

Nuclear Weapons

The United States and the Soviet Union signed the Intermediate Nuclear Forces Agreement (INF) in 1987. Mikhail Gorbachev had succeeded to the leadership of the Soviet Communist Party in March 1985, promising a restructuring of the Soviet economic system and "new thinking" in foreign policy. He moved quickly to open serious arms negotiations with Washington.

The thaw in U.S.-USSR relations and then the collapse of the Soviet empire by the end of 1991 opened the way to new arms accords between Washington and Moscow. The INF was the first arms control agreement between the two sides to reduce and dismantle nuclear weapon delivery systems. In 2002, the two sides signed the Strategic Offensive Reductions Treaty (SORT) that called for the two countries to cut their nuclear arsenals to less than 2,200 warheads by 2012. Those limits were extended several more years in the "New START" treaty concluded in 2011.[22]

The end of the Cold War also shuffled the world community's disarmament priorities. Proliferation of nuclear weapons to nonnuclear states became a prime concern. The focus of the UN Security Council was on North Korea and Iran. Having announced in 2003 it would leave the NPT, the North Korean government carried out its first nuclear tests in 2006, prompting the council to pass Resolution 1718, imposing a trade ban on luxury imports and on weapons-related materials. Later tests led to further sanctions on North Korean financial assets and banking transactions. The European Union (EU) followed suit, banning imports from the country and prohibiting official travel between the EU and North Korea. Sanctions escalated in 2009 when the North launched a satellite, testing the needed technology for an intercontinental ballistic missile. Despite international pressure, the government continued its missile launches and tests over the next decade. By then, unanimity among the council's five permanent members on how to address the proliferation threat eroded, with Russia and China seeking a lifting of the sanctions in 2019 and again in 2021. A proposed resolution in this regard was bound to fail because of a threatened veto by the United States, which unilaterally continued to alternately cajole and threaten North Korea during the Obama and Trump administrations, hoping to make progress on nuclear disarmament in the reclusive nation.

Iran, a signatory of the NPT, was cited by the International Atomic Energy Agency in 2004 for violating the agency's safeguards system that monitors nonnuclear states to be sure that they are not developing nuclear weapons. The IAEA claimed that Iran was hiding elements of its program, enriching uranium to weapons grade levels, and not turning over required data. The Security Council responded with sanctions. For nearly a decade, the P5 had demanded through binding resolutions that Iran suspend uranium enrichment and heavy-water-related projects that could lead to it acquiring a nuclear bomb. Beginning in 2006, the powers proposed comprehensive limitations on Iran's program, and when Iran balked, the council imposed damaging sanctions on the Iranian economy. Over the next few years, when negotiations faltered between Iran and the IAEA, the Security Council tightened the sanctions. In an effort to end the sanctions, Tehran agreed to talks with the five Security Council permanent members (France, United States, China, Russia, United Kingdom) plus Germany (**P5+1**).

After 2009, most of the negotiations between the P5+1 and Iran gravitated between the UN facilities in Geneva, Switzerland, and Vienna, Austria. In mid-March 2015, the respective foreign ministers reached an intensely negotiated framework agreement that would lead, on July 14, to a comprehensive document being signed by all negotiating parties. The Joint Comprehensive Plan of Action (JCPOA) called for Iran to reduce its uranium stockpile by 97 percent and limit its enrichment to 3.67 percent, below what is needed to develop a nuclear bomb, to drastically reduce its supply of centrifuges for enrichment, to reconfigure its research reactor to cut the amount of plutonium produced, and to allow intrusive IAEA inspections not only of nuclear facilities but also uranium mines and mills. In return, sanctions would be lifted and time limits of 10–25 years would allow Iran eventually to get out from under the JCPOA's strictures.

Monitoring by the IAEA affirmed that Iran was meeting its obligations, but the United States, once President Trump came to office, withdrew from the JCPOA. Iran used the

U.S. withdrawal to explain its subsequent decision to begin enriching uranium beyond the agreement's limits.

The long, disappointing history of the United Nations and great powers trying to restrict nuclear weapons development in Iran and North Korea raises the fundamental question whether the world community has the tools to stop any nation fully committed to acquiring nuclear weapons. Even when the permanent members of the Security Council have acted in unity or, at least, acquiesced in sanctions, diplomatic pressure, or negotiations with North Korea and Iran over the last two decades, progress has been hard to demonstrate. Despite nuclear disarmament being the first, and in some aspects the most important, issue addressed by the UN since its founding, it has been unable to come up with effective instruments to achieve its goals with governments, whether they be great or lesser powers.

Because of this conundrum, it is not surprising that the United Nations in the post-Cold War environment has turned much of its disarmament attention to other aspects of the global arms buildup, such as chemical weapons, landmines, arms trafficking, and conventional weapons. By the turn of the millennium, a virtually unlimited supply of even the most modern weapons in the hands of large and small states, ethnic groups, and terrorist organizations meant that all wars held the potential to endanger the lives of millions. Faced with an estimated five hundred million small arms in circulation worldwide, and new types of WMDs, the United Nations turned its attention to a broader weapons agenda.

Chemical Weapons

The use of chemical weapons by Iraq against the Iraqi Kurds (in Halabja in 1988) and during the Iran-Iraq War revived old images of World War I gas warfare. On November 30, 1992, the UN General Assembly adopted the Convention on the Prohibition of the Development, Production, Stockpiling and Use of Chemical Weapons and on Their Destruction (Chemical Weapons Convention, or CWC). As of 2021, only three states (Egypt, South Sudan, North Korea) had not become parties to the treaty, while Israel had signed but not ratified the convention. The CWC was the first with the goal of eliminating an entire category of WMDs.

To enforce its provisions, the convention established the Organisation for the Prohibition of Chemical Weapons (OPCW). Each government signing the agreement obligated itself to destroying all chemical weapons it owned or any that it had abandoned in another country, as well as any facilities used to produce these weapons. The OPCW was authorized to carry out surprise inspections, with trained experts, not only of suspected chemical weapons sites, but also of industrial facilities.

The dual-use nature of chemicals and the ease of their production make the exclusion of chemical weapons from the world's arsenals nearly impossible. This became abundantly apparent during the Syrian civil war when the government launched aerial chemical attacks on its own civilian population in 2013, only acceding to the treaty *after* the UN Secretary-General instituted an investigation and the United States threatened military reprisals for the attacks. The convention also does not diminish the danger of chemical attacks by terrorist or non-state groups, such as the sarin chemical attack on the Tokyo subway in 1995.

Still, in a promising breakthrough, Libya joined the OPCW in February 2004 and disclosed that it had stockpiled twenty-two tons of mustard gas. It agreed to eliminate all such weapons. This new and welcome cooperative policy led Libya to work with IAEA inspectors to fully dismantle the nation's nuclear arms program. Consequently, when the country fell into civil war after 2011, there were no meaningful stockpiles of chemical weapons in Libya that could fall into the hands of combatants or encroaching non-state terrorists.

More recently, the OPCW sent a technical team to Germany to gather information concerning the alleged chemical poisoning in August 2020 of Mr. Alexei Navalny, a public opponent of Russian president Vladimir Putin. The experts collected biomedical samples from Navalny and sent them for independent analysis. The results confirmed that he had been poisoned with Novichok, a Soviet-era nerve agent, a chemical prohibited by the CWC. Two UN special rapporteurs later concluded that the attempted extrajudicial execution had been ordered by the Russian government. Navalny's case was only one of several over the previous decade that indicated governments' willingness to use chemical weapons to kill individuals they believed threatened their interests.

Biological Weapons

The United Nations has also taken a renewed interest in biological weapons, reinforced by the emergence of highly organized and well-financed terrorist groups. Biological weapons are living organisms, most commonly bacteria and viruses, deliberately disseminated to cause death or disease in humans, animals, or plants. They are considered weapons of mass destruction because their potential to destroy life is equaled only by nuclear weapons. Deaths in the United States from anthrax sent through the postal system shortly after the terrorist assaults on New York City and Washington, DC, in 2001 demonstrated the panic and destruction that a coordinated biological attack could cause.

The 1925 Geneva Protocol prohibited the use of biological weapons in warfare. The 1972 Convention on the Prohibition of the Development, Production and Stockpiling of Bacteriological (Biological) and Toxin Weapons and on Their Destruction (Biological Weapons Convention, or BWC) went further by prohibiting their development and possession. Fifty years after its negotiation, 183 countries were parties to the Convention. The UN Secretary-General has authority under the treaty to investigate the alleged use of biological weapons and report the findings to member states.

Concerns about these types of weapons grew dramatically following the 1991 Gulf War. Persuasive evidence indicated that the Iraqi regime had developed an offensive biological weapons capability. After the war, the Security Council required the unconditional destruction of its biological arsenal and the capacity to produce it. Until their forced departure from Iraq in 1998, the UN inspectors regularly catalogued and destroyed facilities and munitions.

The continuing danger demonstrated the most serious weakness in the Biological Weapons Convention: the absence of a binding verification regime that could assure countries that suspected producers were not building stockpiles. At a special conference held in April 1994, the parties to the convention established an ad hoc working group to draft an inspection protocol, but little came of it. The United States, in particular, resisted the proposed verification regime.

Conventional Weapons

The expanded use of conventional weapons—such as landmines and small arms—especially in sectarian violence in Africa, Asia, and Eastern Europe has caused heightened concern at the United Nations. It also generated a strong response by the nongovernmental community; NGOs have pressured their governments and the UN to address the humanitarian disaster these weapons cause.

Since the 1970s, the United Nations had been involved in the movement to ban landmines. However, frustration with the slow pace of developing a specific landmine agreement in the Conference on Disarmament led several states and NGOs to pursue negotiations outside the UN structure. In October 1996, Canada and Belgium launched the Ottawa Process. The resultant International Campaign to Ban Landmines (ICBL) was led by the nongovernmental community, including organizations such as Doctors Without Borders and the International Committee of the Red Cross. A land-mines convention was crafted in 1997. It prohibited in all circumstances any use of antipersonnel landmines. It also required the destruction of stockpiles within four years after the treaty entered into force and mandated that mines already in the ground be destroyed within ten years. By 2021, 164 states had signed or acceded to the convention. In support of the treaty, the United Nations made demining one of its important functions in peacekeeping operations. But still today, landmines litter the battlefields of past conflicts. To address the problem, fourteen UN departments, agencies, programmes, and funds instituted a cooperative initiative to assist in mine-action programs in thirty countries and three territories. As a sign of the growing role of international civil society in UN work, much of the actual demining and mine-risk education has been turned over to nongovernmental organizations. Other intergovernmental, international, and regional organizations, as well as international financial institutions, also support mine action by funding operations or providing services to individuals and communities affected by landmines. Among the states notably absent from the list of signatories to the Landmine Convention are the United States, China, Pakistan, India, Israel, and the Russian Federation. (However, in 2004, the United States announced that it would end the production and use of "persistent" antipersonnel and antitank mines after 2010. Washington committed to use only landmines that would render themselves inert within days of their deployment. The United States also promised to produce only those that are detectable by metal detectors.

Conflicts in the post-Cold War era have been fought almost exclusively with light or small arms. The civil wars of Africa and Latin America, the secessionist efforts in southeast Europe, and the ethnic struggles in both Asia and Africa have been between peoples and governments with limited resources. They have obtained their weapons largely from clandestine arms brokers in the growing weapons black market, or from states anxious for revenues from arms sales. The disintegration of states and the weakening of central control over national arsenals have also produced a huge dispersion of these armaments. The United Nations estimated in 2018 that more than eight hundred million small arms and light weapons (SALW) were in circulation worldwide.[23] Several countries, notably Mexico and Kenya, led a diplomatic campaign in 2021 to elevate the Security Council's role in slowing the illicit trade in SALW, arguing that the trade was undermining international peace and security in conflict zones. Russia and the United States opposed any council action, hoping to divert the matter to the UN General Assembly. Not coincidentally, neither country had joined the Arms Trade Treaty (ATT), which was intended to promote appropriate governmental regulation of the cross-border trade of conventional arms.

The Arms Trade Treaty came into effect in 2014 and had 110-member state parties by the end of the decade. The ATT seeks to promote appropriate governmental regulation of the cross-border trade of conventional arms. The treaty calls on its signatories to pass national legislation to license and strictly regulate the transfer of small arms as well as battle tanks, armored combat vehicles, large-caliber artillery systems, combat aircraft, attack helicopters, warships, missiles, and missile launchers. Signatories are also required to prohibit the export of the ammunition and munitions used by these weapons.[24]

States have found it difficult to arrive at a consensus on how to cut small-arms quantities or how to regulate their movement. Many states argue that the regulation of small arms should be solely an issue for national governments. In the late 1990s the General Assembly adopted, by consensus, a resolution calling for "practical disarmament measures" (PDMs). These measures included provisions for the destruction of SALW and of ammunition and explosives, as well as the demobilization of forces in civil conflicts with concurrent disarmament of armed personnel, pilot projects for voluntary weapons collection, demining, and harmonization of national legislation on illicit arms traffic. In addition, the United Nations inaugurated the Register of Conventional Arms to contribute to confidence building and transparency. These actions were limited steps, but they set the stage for the successful negotiation of the Arms Trade Treaty.

POST-COLD WAR COLLECTIVE SECURITY

During the last decade of the twentieth century, the United Nations faced both the opportunity and the burden of meeting threats to collective security through the original provisions laid down in the Charter. The collective action taken against Iraq in 1991 marked the first use of Chapter VII enforcement measures since the "police action" in the Korean War (1950–1953), and it went much further than any previous peacekeeping effort. Between August—when Iraqi forces invaded and occupied Kuwait—and November, the Security Council passed ten resolutions meant to isolate Iraq and to prepare the legal groundwork for collective military action.[25]

As in the case of Korea, the United Nations did not put its own forces in the field under Security Council command. Instead, it authorized a coalition of states led by the United States to use "all necessary means ... to restore peace and security in the area." Unlike Korea's police action, the troops did not fight under the UN flag. In practical terms, the United Nations "subcontracted" its collective security duties to an international coalition. The procedure of **subcontracting**—authorizing a state or group of states to act on behalf of the world community to restore peace and stability—became a regular feature of Security Council action at the turn of the millennium. It would be used in Somalia, Rwanda, Bosnia, Kosovo, East Timor, Libya, and the Central African Republic. The rapid success of coalition forces in the 1991 war and the imposition of near-mandate conditions on Iraq seemed to augur a new era of promise for the United Nations. U.S. president George H. W. Bush opined that maybe now, in the wake of the Cold War stalemate, the United Nations could live up to its founders' vision of its being the "last best hope for peace."[26] Bush and the leaders of the other permanent Security Council members worked assiduously to maintain unanimity not only on the Iraq crisis but also on other challenges to collective security.

In this "summer" of collective unanimity among the great powers, the Security Council encouraged Secretary-General Boutros Boutros-Ghali to draft proposals on "ways of strengthening and making more efficient within the framework and provisions of the Charter the capacity of the UN for preventive diplomacy, for peacemaking and for peacekeeping."[27] The Secretary-General outlined his recommendations in *An Agenda for Peace*. He encouraged the council to act early to assist "states at risk" and urged member states to earmark military contingents for quick UN activation. The report outlined problems in the less developed countries and the need for a humanitarian, political, economic, and military response by the United Nations.

The Secretary-General's report contained a tacit assumption that collective security implied something more than the absence of war between two recognized nation-states. Therefore, collective security could not be ensured solely by separating combatants or, in the worst case, driving back an aggressor to its antebellum borders. The definition of the UN's purpose in this regard now included addressing traditionally internal domestic issues, previously thought to be beyond the Charter's reach. As suggested previously in this chapter, collective security is an intellectual construct, undefined by the Charter. As such, in the new world of post-Cold War politics, and in the conception of the post-Gulf War Security Council membership, collective security required innovations and a revision of UN mechanisms.

Immediately affected by the new understanding of collective security was the forty-year-old practice of peacekeeping. As a result of Boutros-Ghali's *Agenda for Peace*, three new terms—*preventive diplomacy, peacemaking,* and *postconflict peacebuilding*—entered the UN lexicon. **Preventive diplomacy** attempts either to resolve intra- and inter-state conflicts before violence erupts or to limit the spread of violence; it is intended to be proactive peacekeeping. **Peacemaking** seeks to bring hostile parties to agreement through negotiation and mediation before or after the intervention of UN peacekeeping forces. **Peacebuilding** aims to construct an environment that sustains durable peace, often by UN administration. It also includes addressing the economic, social, cultural, and humanitarian problems that underpin violent conflict. Taken together and coupled with the long-standing UN practice of peacekeeping, these innovations amount to a UN effort at sustaining and rebuilding nations torn apart by internal violence or govern-mental collapse. They represented a theoretical foundation for subsequent UN efforts at nation-building and for promotion of the idea that the international community has the "responsibility to protect" domestic populations from the egregious violation of their human rights by their own government. Critics of Boutros-Ghali's report suggested that an expansion of the UN role in these ways was first and foremost beyond the UN's financial and political capabilities and, second, a form of international neocolonial-ism reminiscent of the League's old mandate system. (A full description of what came to be called *second-generation peacekeeping*—and later nation-building—is provided in Chapter 6.)

Smart Sanctions

Shortly after the turn of the century, the Security Council addressed the weaknesses of another instrument of collective security: international sanctions against a state that threatens world peace and security. Article 41 of the UN Charter authorizes the Security Council to impose mandatory sanctions, including "complete or partial interruption of economic relations and of rail, sea, air, postal ... and other means of communication, and the severance of diplomatic ties." All member states are obligated to enforce the Security Council's decision. The tradition of using these draconian measures short of the use of force in order to punish a state and change its behavior dates from the League's Covenant. Since 1919, the imposition of sanctions has been promoted as a step short of war that will penalize the wrongdoer sufficiently for it to alter its policy.

Unfortunately, little evidence indicates that sanctions—economic, military, or diplomatic—produce the desired result. Often, enforcing imposed sanctions is difficult because individual states sometimes find the economic incentives to continue trade with the offending government more in their national interest than maintaining solidarity with the rest of the world. States under sanction have generally pursued policies that have other motivations than those that would be amenable to change under international economic pressure. Their governments, as well, can make the case to the domestic population that any hardships currently experienced are the product of "unjust" international sanctions, not the product of the government's policies. Often, the effect of sanctions is to worsen the humanitarian situation while imposing no hardships on the leadership. For several of these reasons, the League of Nations' record on the use of sanctions was disappointing. As early as the Japanese invasion of Manchuria in 1931, the League could not mold sufficient international unity to impose sanctions. Then, in 1935, Mussolini's Fascist Italy invaded Ethiopia and all that the League could muster were "voluntary" economic sanctions against the invader. They had no effect on Rome's policy.

The UN record has been only slightly better. The ability to impose sanctions is limited by the veto in the Security Council, and, conversely, the power to end them is also restricted by the right of one of the P5 to block such action. Thus, UN sanctions are never used against a major power. The Security Council imposed mandatory economic sanctions for the first time in November 1965 against the racist regime of the self-declared independent state of Rhodesia. Nearly three years later, the council needed to make the sanctions "comprehensive" because they had had little apparent effect on the regime. Sanctions were also imposed on Iran following the 1979 hostage-taking of diplomatic personnel at the U.S. embassy in Tehran, and again in 2006 (Security Council Resolution 1737) for its nuclear enrichment and reprocessing activities. Some observers have noted that Tehran *did* come to the negotiating table to seek sanctions relief and did sign the P5+1-negotiated Joint Comprehensive Plan of Action, formally promising not to develop a nuclear weapons capability and yielding to intrusive international verification of its compliance with the agreement's restrictions, suggesting a major, if rare, success of SC-imposed sanctions.

Prior to this 2015 agreement between the P5+1 and Iran, the case of sanctions against the South African government meant to end its practice of apartheid was often cited as perhaps the only successful operation of this kind. South Africa's racial policies were first debated in the UN General Assembly in 1946. South Africa's apartheid laws mandated formal and severe racial segregation; the minority white population was in control of the government and all important institutions and economic activities. The black majority had limited rights of movement, exercised few political rights, and lived in poverty. In 1960, the GA declared apartheid "reprehensible and repugnant to human dignity." And in 1962, it placed "voluntary" sanctions on South Africa, including breaking diplomatic relations, boycotting South African goods, and refusing landing rights to South African aircraft. Six years later, it discouraged immigration into the country and advocated the end of economic links with the outside world. The United States, Great Britain, and France refused to support mandatory sanctions, citing Cold War concerns. Though voluntary, the sanctions heightened South Africa's ostracism from the global community. Attention on South Africa's policy led to private corporate and individual government decisions that hurt the country's economy and may have hastened the release of Nelson Mandela and the transfer of power from the white minority government.

The growing consensus among the permanent members of the council in the 1990s, coupled with the outbreak of serious ethnic and religious conflict in many parts of the world, produced a new interest in sanctions. Short of military intervention, economic penalties seemed a reasonable first step to punish a violator of collective security intent, whether it was a government violating its citizens' human rights, conducting genocide, blocking legitimate self-determination, or actually committing a cross-border transgression, or whether it was a non-state actor that did not live up to its agreements or had committed an international atrocity, such as al-Qaeda did in September 2001. Since 1966, the Security Council has imposed 30 sanctions regimes.[28]

The most severe sanctions were imposed on Iraq after the 1991 Gulf War and included both economic and military restrictions. U.S. administrations and their allies in the Security Council insisted that these sanctions were necessary to prevent Saddam Hussein from replenishing his arsenal of weapons of mass destruction. The Iraqi leader used the unpopularity of the sanctions to maintain his grip on power in Iraq. Faced with growing public criticism and no apparent progress on removing Hussein from office, the council adjusted the sanctions, creating the "oil-for-food" program to allow the sale of Iraq's most important resource in order to purchase needed humanitarian supplies. The sanctions, however, remained unpopular with many governments. Black market and government-sponsored violations of the sanctions occurred without a way to penalize the violators.

In April 2000, the Security Council established a working group to consider the troublesome issues surrounding the use of sanctions. The product of these deliberations and of a series of separate expert conferences was the innovation of **smart sanctions**. These were tailored to "have a high probability of directly hurting those responsible for the targeted policies while sparing the general population."[29] They included freezing the financial assets of the nation's leaders and blocking the transfer of such assets, restricting the leadership's travel outside the country, and embargoing key commodities needed to carry out the objectionable activities. As an example, in July 2000, the Security Council banned the importation of diamonds from Sierra Leone that were not certified by the government. The production and sale of "conflict diamonds"—diamonds sold to finance military operations by rebel or separatist groups—had become a problem throughout sub-Saharan Africa.[30]. By 2021, more than 1,000 individuals and entities were under UN smart sanctions.[31]

Smart sanctions allow humanitarian assistance and limited trade to continue. Of importance, they carry sunset provisions so that sanctions cannot be frozen in place beyond their usefulness. This proviso caused strains in the first decade of the twenty-first century as the United States and Great Britain refused to lift sanctions against Iraq. Russia and China regularly blocked new sanctions regimes, for example, in 2021 to address Myanmar's military leaders' harsh crackdown on domestic opponents and their treatment of the Ruhingyan population. China claimed that sanctions would "aggravate tension and confrontation and further complicate the situation."[32]

Difficulties with the new type of sanctions remain that may make them not much more effective than those attempted since the 1920s. Freezing assets requires nations other than the targeted country to change national legislation, alter import and export policies, and subject their domestic laws to the Security Council's diktats. Since the council cannot force such revisions, smart sanctions, even if "mandatory," require voluntary acquiescence by the UN's member states.

New Role for Regional Organizations

Post-Cold War collective security has depended more and more on the active engagement of regional intergovernmental organizations. They have carried out peacekeeping operations, worked closely with UN agencies to deliver humanitarian assistance, provided mediation and negotiation services to conflicting groups, and organized collective responses to threats in their regions. Both the Millennium Summit in 2000 and the 2005 World Summit endorsed an active involvement of regional organizations in cooperation with the Security Council on critical issues such as the "responsibility to protect" populations in their respective regions from genocide and crimes against humanity.

Regional organizations provide an alternative to direct UN involvement, share costs in peacekeeping and other activities, and have a clearer knowledge of the issues involved in a regional conflict. The **African Union** (AU) is an example of a regional organization that has played a serviceable role cooperating with the United Nations in addressing civil and international conflicts on the African continent. It intervened with troops in the Darfur region of the Sudan in 2004. Limited in resources and finances, the AU indicated that it would remain only until a UN peacekeeping operation could take its place. In June 2007, the Sudanese government gave its initial approval to a joint AU-UN force, but insisted that the majority of peacekeepers be Africans. The joint force officially ended operations in December 2020. Also on the continent, the **Economic Community of West African States** (ECOWAS) has conducted its own peacekeeping operations. Moreover, from the 1990s through the first two decades of the twenty-first century, the United Nations engaged in co-deployments and joint peacekeeping operations with ECOWAS in several countries.

During the twenty-first century, regional organizations have also acted independently where UN Security Council unanimity did not exist. The **Association of Southeast Asian Nations** (ASEAN), faced with Chinese claims of sovereignty over the South China Sea, resisted those claims and sought to negotiate a Code of Conduct for the region with Beijing. The **Organisation for Security and Cooperation in Europe** (OSCE) took the lead to negotiate the outstanding issues in the dispute between Russia and Ukraine following the former's annexation of Crimea and its support for separatists in the eastern region of Ukraine.

Secretaries-General Kofi Annan and Ban Ki-moon were strong advocates for the engagement of regional organizations in UN activities, peacekeeping and otherwise. In 2021, their successor, António Guterres, lauded the cooperation between the UN and regional organizations, calling it a "key priority" for the world body. He cited their work in Mali, Libya, Ethiopia, even Colombia, in providing "complementarity" to the UN's efforts at peacebuilding.[33]

R2P—Responsibility to Protect

Many of the conflicts regional organizations addressed in the twenty-first century were upheavals *within* states, not *between* them, and most direct interventions were brought on by reports of egregious violations of human rights. After the Cold War, growing concern with human rights abuses led to an evolution in the understanding of the UN's mandate to "maintain international peace and security," expanding it to allow for, even require, intervention in the domestic affairs of states, particularly where governments threatened their own populations. In 2000, UN Secretary-General Kofi Annan made the case for "individual sovereignty" taking precedence over state sovereignty when the state could not or would not guarantee the human rights of its citizens. The developing concept at the UN and in international law of a "Responsibility to Protect" was a logical extension of new moral sensibilities deriving from heightened interest in an individual's human rights.

The UN's 2005 World Summit affirmed that "every sovereign government has a 'responsibility to protect' its citizens and those within its jurisdiction from genocide, mass killing, and massive and sustained human rights violations." If the government does not carry out its responsibility, the World Summit's Outcome document stated:

> The international community, through the United Nations, also has the responsibility to use appropriate diplomatic, humanitarian and other peaceful means, in accordance with Chapters VI and VIII of the Charter, to help protect populations from genocide, war crimes, ethnic cleansing and crimes against humanity. In this context, we are prepared to take collective action.[34]

Examples that underscored the growing demand for international intervention in state matters were the violence of the civil wars in the Former Yugoslavia (1990s), genocide in Rwanda (1994), brutality in Timor-Leste (1999), serious human rights violations in the Democratic Republic of the Congo (ongoing in the twenty-first century), the bloodbath in Darfur (2006–2007), the threat by the Libyan government to destroy oppositionist civilian populations (2011), and atrocities in the Syrian civil war (2011–2021). Although there are critics of R2P—including some leaders of developing countries who fear that the new notion might lead to renewed colonial intervention in their countries, and First World "realists" who continue to privilege sovereignty and oppose foreign policies based on morality instead of national interest—there was budding support for upholding the new principle in the early 2000s.

The Security Council, on March 11, 2011, made the first practical use of the principle when it passed resolution 1973 authorizing intervention in Libya and the imposition of a no-fly zone for the limited purpose of ensuring "the protection of civilians and civilian populated areas." The resolution noted the "widespread and systematic attacks" by the government on its own citizens, calling them likely crimes against humanity. France and Germany pressured the United States to support council action to end the threat to civilians.[35] The Arab League also called on the Security Council to take action. The United States acceded, but President Barack Obama directed his ambassador at the UN to seek amendments to the resolution allowing for "all necessary means" to halt Gaddafi.[36] Obama directed that the United States enforce the no-fly zone once approved, but leadership of the military effort in Libya should fall to others, specifically to NATO and Arab League members.[37] The Security Council resolution authorized intervention by member states "acting nationally or through regional organizations or arrangements…to take all necessary measures." Because the R2P principle frowns upon *unilateral* intervention (as exemplified by the U.S. invasion of IRAQ in 2003), the most difficult challenge to the new doctrine has been to achieve agreement among the "permanent five." Russia and China abstained on the final vote. Always worried about violations of state sovereignty, they demanded that the resolution be narrowly limited to the humanitarian goal with a specific reference to Resolution 1738.

The center of the Libyan uprising was in the town of Benghazi that soon came under threat from Gaddafi's security forces. As the military mission developed, the United States and several of its European allies cited the resolution as their authority for aerial bombardments on Gaddafi's forces, in effect aiding the rebel cause, blurring the line between humanitarian intervention and regime change. Gaddafi fled Tripoli and was captured and executed shortly thereafter. A transitional government was put in place in October. Russia viewed the overthrow in Libya as a misuse of UN authority by the United States and the West.

Partly because of the evolution of events in Libya, China and Russia opposed any similar resolutions concerning Syria or other civil conflicts. Their opposition demonstrated the limited viability of R2P as a pragmatic evolution of the UN's collective security doctrine. Without consensus or at least acquiescence among the permanent members of the council, R2P could not be used in situations where egregious human rights violations were underway. Moreover, some group of states would have to take on the costs of intervention. None were willing to do that during the second decade of the twenty-first century in Yemen or Myanmar, for example, where civilian populations were under indiscriminate bombing or being forced out of their homes into refugee status.

TWENTY-FIRST-CENTURY CHALLENGES TO COLLECTIVE SECURITY

Russia's and China's hostility toward the further use of the "Responsibility to Protect" principle reflected the growing sclerosis of the Security Council. Just as the Cold War had diminished optimism for great power cooperation, the council's repeated inability to act in the early twenty-first century raised memories of that earlier period. The conflicts between 2003 and 2014 in Iraq, Georgia, and Ukraine, rising great-power rivalry among the United States, Russia, and China, coupled with long-continuing Middle East tensions, all spawned doubts about the efficacy of collective security under council direction.

The 2003 Iraq War

The American decision to go to war in Iraq in 2003 with only a "coalition of the willing" fundamentally challenged the collective security arrangement and the institutions of post-World War II global order crafted by the United States and its allies in the 1940s. You will recall from Chapter 3 that then-Secretary-General Kofi Annan believed that the U.S. intervention without an authorizing Security Council resolution made the war illegal and threatened the foundational principles of the United Nations Charter. It broke with precedent on a scale that raised issues of international legality and prompted global perceptions of the United States as a rogue actor in the existing international order.

This, of course, was not President George W. Bush's sense of what he was doing in Iraq. The administration argued that the American policy was an endorsement of the collective security principle itself, since military action would enforce mandatory Security Council resolutions approved at the conclusion of the first Gulf War and ignored by Saddam Hussein ever since. He told the American Enterprise Institute, "In confronting Iraq, the United States is also showing our commitment to effective international institutions. We believe in the Security Council so much that we want its words to have meaning." He would make the same argument at the United Nations. In his 2002 General Debate speech, he scolded and challenged the UN on the matter of Iraq.

> All the world now faces a test, and the United Nations is at a difficult and defining moment. Are Security Council resolutions to be honored and enforced, or cast aside without consequence? Will the United Nations serve the purpose of its founding, or will it be irrelevant?

The administration did attempt to obtain a Security Council authorization for war. The negotiations at the UN lasted into November and produced Resolution 1441, a classic example of diplomatic obfuscation that would be interpreted by Washington as an approval for war, delayed only by additional time given to Iraq to abide by past resolutions, and understood by the opponents of war, particularly Germany, France, and Russia, as requiring further council action. France insisted that a report of clear violations of earlier resolutions would be needed before enforcement measures could be employed.

The council decided in Resolution 1441 that Iraq had been "and remains in material breach of its obligations under relevant resolutions," but decided "to afford Iraq a final opportunity to comply" or face "serious consequences" for non-compliance. This was not the usual language of the council when taking collective security action against an offending state. Both before and after the passage of Resolution 1441 the Security Council, addressing other threats to peace, authorized force in the exercise of collective security using a formulaic pronouncement, finding a "threat to international peace and security" and authorizing states "to use" or "to take all necessary measures" to rectify the transgression.[38] In the negotiations on a draft resolution, the United States proposed language that fashioned a clear trigger between "*a material breach*" and "*all necessary means*" being taken, but U.S. Secretary of State Colin Powell reported to the president that with that language the resolution would fail by a vote of 1 to 14. In this case, the Bush administration latched onto the phrase "material breach" for its legal justification of military action, while the opponents argued that an authorization to actually use force would have to

204 Maintenance of International Peace and Security

come after the latest UN arms inspection team reported back on Iraqi compliance or non-compliance.

President Bush signaled as early as 2002 that the United States was willing to go to war with Iraq even without a UN endorsement. He asserted that his government would do so under his new doctrine of preemption—the right to launch preventive war when an overwhelming potential threat faced the country. The Bush administration's *National Security Strategy* of 2002 insisted:

> While the United States will constantly strive to enlist the support of the international community, we will not hesitate to act alone, if necessary, to exercise our right of self-defense by acting preemptively against such terrorists, to prevent them from doing harm against our people and our country.[39]

Most international legal scholars sided with the opponents of intervention, seeing unilateral U.S. action as a violation of collective security. International jurists pointed specifically to the Security Council practice of mandating "all necessary means" to make military action legitimate.[40] President Bush, however, decided to go ahead with military operations, telling the American people on the eve of war, "the United Nations Security Council has not lived up to its responsibilities, so we will rise to ours."

Crises in Georgia and Ukraine

The fear at UN headquarters was that the Bush doctrine of preemption, as used in Iraq, could become a precedent for unilateral action by powers that perceived serious threats to their national interests, undercutting further the UN's bedrock principle of collective security. Russia's military intervention in Georgia and its annexation of Ukraine's Crimea fit the new pattern. In August 2008, Russia sent forces into Georgia's breakaway provinces of Abkhazia and South Ossetia, regions of the country with a minority of ethnic Georgians, and in which separatists had long sought Russian support for independence from the national government. As part of the previous Soviet Union, and lying along the Transcaucasian region between the Russian Federation and the Middle East, Georgia was perceived by the Russian government as of critical geopolitical importance. For several years leading up to the Russian intervention, a UN contact group, the Group of the Friends of the Secretary-General (Germany, France, Russian Federation, United Kingdom, and the United States) had attempted to ease tensions and resolve, without much progress, the outstanding issues between the government in Tbilisi and the provinces.

Following Russian intervention, Moscow recognized both Abkhazia and South Ossetia as independent states and continued what it called its "peace enforcement operation" with a heavy investment of Russian troops and materiel. Despite condemnation by other major powers, regional organizations, and world leaders, the United Nations, given the Russian veto in the Security Council, could do little beyond the provision of humanitarian and refugee assistance, and the offer of the institution's good offices.

Again, in spring of 2014, Russia's president Vladimir Putin used unilateral military power in another sovereign state, ostensibly to protect ethnic Russians and to reclaim territory illegitimately separated, in his view, from Russia at the conclusion of the Cold War. The February overthrow of the Russian-friendly Ukrainian president provided the context for Russian intervention. Ethnic Russians not only in Crimea but also in the eastern provinces of Ukraine sought autonomy from Kyiv and Russia's help in achieving it.

Russia already maintained a major naval base in Crimea. As political events unfolded in Ukraine, Russian military and intelligence forces, operating covertly, joined with Crimean separatists to take over the Crimean parliament that, in turn, declared an independent Republic of Crimea and called for a referendum on the future of the peninsula. The international community, including the UN General Assembly, largely rejected the idea of a referendum, which Ukraine called illegal. Russia vetoed a similar resolution in the Security Council. Voters in Crimea overwhelmingly approved the territory joining the Russian Federation, which was effectuated by a treaty signed in Moscow in March.

With the United Nations unable to take action because of the Russian veto power, the United States and Western European powers collectively decided to impose economic sanctions on Russia without referral to the UN. Coupled with falling oil prices at the time, the sanctions had a significant impact on the Russian economy. There was a concerted effort through regional organizations, among them the European Union and the Council of Europe, to isolate Russia and to block any expansion of Russian involvement in other parts of eastern Ukraine. But President Putin was not deterred. In the winter of 2021–2022, Russia massed nearly 190,000 troops and materiel on the Ukrainian border, demanding Ukraine demilitarize and renounce any future desire to join the North Atlantic Treaty Organization. Suggesting the country was run by neo-Nazis who had carried out genocide against the people in its eastern provinces, President Putin launched military operations in Ukraine on February 24 despite multilateral efforts to blunt such a move. While Western nations imposed unprecedented sanctions on Russia, at the UN, with a Russian veto looming in the Security Council, the General Assembly convened the emergency special session described above to condemn Russian actions. As the war proceeded into the spring, the UN Security Council met regularly in emergency sessions. In response to alleged war crimes committed in Ukraine by Russian troops, the General Assembly in early April voted 93–24, with 58 abstentions (thus achieving the necessary two-thirds super majority) to suspend Russia from the Human Rights Council.[41]

THE UN'S LONGEST COLLECTIVE SECURITY CRISIS: MIDDLE EAST CONFLICTS

The League of Nations was the first international organization to address the turmoil of the Middle East. Following the collapse in World War I of the far-reaching, seven-hundred-year-old Ottoman Empire, allied powers at the Versailles Peace Conference formulated a Mandate System under the authority of the League. The Mandates were a compromise between European states that sought new colonial possessions in the region and the United States, which supported self-determination for the various peoples of the now-gone empire. European states were granted supervisory authority over designated territories, an authority that was meant to last until national populations were deemed ready to form and maintain stable nation-states. In some cases, the Mandates remained in place beyond the practical life of the League, and in other cases the end of the Mandates brought weak new governments to power. World War II brought the end of the League and no clear solutions to the many problems of the Middle East.

Arab-Israeli Dispute

The British government was the first Mandate power to hand a portion of the Middle East crisis to the fledgling United Nations when it announced in 1947 that it would end its administration of Palestine the following year. The United Nations established the UN

Special Commission on Palestine (UNSCOP) to find a way to end the growing conflict between the indigenous Palestinian population and the large number of Zionist Jews who sought their own independent state. UNSCOP recommended partitioning Palestine into Jewish and Arab states and placing Jerusalem under international administration. The General Assembly accepted this formula in Resolution 181,[42] which the Security Council endorsed. Zionist leaders accepted the plan, but Palestinians and regional Arab leaders rejected it as the "theft" of Palestinian land.

On May 14, 1948, Zionist leaders declared the independence of Israel within the borders assigned by Resolution 181. The Arab states of Egypt, Transjordan, Iraq, and Syria responded with military intervention. Despite their overwhelming advantage in numbers, the Arab militaries proved no match for the determined Israelis. The United Nations attempted to establish a cease-fire through the diplomacy of its mediator, Count Folke Bernadotte of Sweden. Tragically, Bernadotte was assassinated in Jerusalem on September 17 by Israeli ultranationalists. His successor, Ralph Bunche, finally achieved an armistice in the spring of 1949. By the time the fighting ended, Israel's forces were in control of nearly all of Palestine, except East Jerusalem, the West Bank of the Jordan River, parts of the Golan Heights, and the Gaza Strip.

In the course of successive wars in 1948, in 1956 during the Suez Crisis, and in June 1967, the United Nations served as the locus of negotiations for repeated cease-fires and for the provision of peacekeeping forces to separate combatants. Equally important, it responded to the huge flows of Palestinian refugees, who numbered nearly seven hundred thousand in 1948. The General Assembly created the UN Relief for Palestine Refugees (UNRPR) in that year, and gave the effort nine months to assist the refugees. When the assembly realized that refugee assistance would have to extend well into the future, it replaced UNRPR with the UN Relief and Works Agency for Palestine Refugees in the Near East (UNRWA), which continues its work of providing education and work projects in addition to humanitarian assistance into the twenty-first century's third decade.

The uneasy peace following the 1948 war lasted until 1956, when the nationalist Egyptian leader, Gamal Abdel Nasser, announced his intentions to nationalize the Suez Canal. The October invasion of the Canal Zone by Great Britain, France, and Israel brought about the UN General Assembly's first emergency special session and the creation of UNEF (the UN Emergency Force). UNEF's presence on Egyptian soil ended a direct conflict between Israel and its most important Arab neighbor. The next decade witnessed violent terrorist attacks, bombings, and brief border skirmishes. The Arab states sponsored new Palestinian organizations. Nasser took the lead in organizing the Palestine Liberation Organization (PLO) in 1964. With Arab support, Palestinian groups such as al-Fatah launched increasingly severe assaults on Israeli domestic sites.

Hostilities reached a critical point between Israel and two of its foes, Egypt and Syria, in the spring of 1967. On May 16, Nasser asked UN Secretary-General U Thant to remove UNEF from the Sinai. Thant consented, much to the consternation of many world leaders. On May 22, Egypt closed the Strait of Tiran and the Gulf of Aqaba, which put a death grip on Israel's economy. Israel responded with a preemptive attack on Egypt, Iraq, Jordan, and Syria. Israeli forces seized the Sinai Peninsula, Syrian territory in the Golan Heights, and the land designated by the 1947 UN partition plan as the space for the Arab state in Palestine—most important, the West Bank and East Jerusalem. The fighting ended in a cease-fire on June 10. Not until November was the Security Council able to arrive at a resolution acceptable to all the parties. **Resolution 242**, adopted unanimously on November 22, called for a withdrawal of Israel's forces from occupied territories, a termination of the state of belligerency, and mutual recognition, freedom of navigation, and a settlement of the refugee problem. The resolution was premised on the idea of "land for peace."

Later, the parties would spar over the meaning of Resolution 242, specifically concerning whether it required the Israelis to withdraw from *all* occupied territories or from only those that would not jeopardize Israel's security. Nevertheless, this resolution became the cornerstone for all subsequent peace negotiations.

The growing developing-world majority at the United Nations saw Israel as the aggressor and an illegal occupier of Arab lands. The world body steadily shifted toward support for the Palestinian cause, which culminated in recognition of the PLO as the "legitimate representative of the Palestinian people" in 1974 and its achievement of "observer status" at the United Nations. Anti-Israeli sentiment peaked with the passage of a resolution in November 1975 equating Zionism with racism. The pro-Palestinian tilt of the United Nations convinced the most powerful member of the body—the United States—that the United Nations was aggravating the Arab-Israeli crisis.

The hesitant peace after the 1967 war lasted only until October 6, 1973. On Yom Kippur, the Day of Atonement in the Jewish calendar, Syria and Egypt opened two fronts against Israel, seeking to liberate lands captured in the previous conflict. Within ten days, however, the balance of forces had shifted, and both Syria and Egypt were in retreat. At the United Nations, the USSR offered a draft Security Council resolution, and after lengthy negotiations between the Soviet and U.S. governments, the Security Council called for a return to the original cease-fire lines. Following a meeting in the Sinai between Israeli and Egyptian negotiators, under UN auspices, a cease-fire was restored.

The war marked the last time the United Nations would serve as the arena for Arab-Israeli peace initiatives. The U.S. administrations after 1973 used their diplomatic resources to monopolize the peace process. President Nixon's secretary of state, Henry Kissinger, engineered a military disengagement between the Egyptians and the Israelis on the Sinai Peninsula (January 1974) and a similar agreement between the Israelis and the Syrians in the Golan Heights (May 1974). As part of the latter accord, the United Nations acquired the limited role of placing military observers between the two sides in the Golan Heights (UN Disengagement Observer Force, or UNDOF). U.S. domination of international efforts to resolve the Arab-Israeli dispute continued into Jimmy Carter's presidency. Carter played the central role in the negotiation of the Camp David Accords, which included a "Framework for Peace" between Israelis and Palestinians and a peace treaty between Israel and Egypt.

The Carter-negotiated framework, based on UN Resolutions 242 and 338, recognized the right of Palestinian representatives to participate in negotiations aimed at establishing a Palestinian self-governing entity in the West Bank and Gaza. The framework called on the UN Security Council to ensure that its provisions were carried out.

Attempting to disrupt the Camp David Accords, the PLO stepped up guerrilla attacks on Israel from southern Lebanon and from Syrian territory. In June 1982, the Israeli government conducted a full-scale invasion of Lebanon. In response, the UN Security Council passed Resolution 509, demanding that "Israel withdraw all its military forces forthwith and unconditionally to the internationally recognized boundaries of Lebanon." Ignoring the UN action, Israeli forces advanced to the outskirts of Beirut. The UNIFIL (UN Interim Force in Lebanon) forces that had been in the country since 1978 could do little but stand aside and report to New York on the invasion.

The U.S.-orchestrated peace process was given a boost by the allied victory over Saddam Hussein in the 1991 Gulf War. Secretary of State James Baker shuttled between capitals in hopes of a breakthrough, an effort culminating in the Madrid Conference in 1991. PLO representatives from the occupied territories joined Israeli government officials and representatives of the Arab states at the negotiating table with President George H. W. Bush and Soviet president Mikhail Gorbachev. The United Nations was granted a

SECURITY COUNCIL RESOLUTION 242

[UN Security Council Resolution 242 was adopted unanimously on November 22, 1967, following the cessation of the Middle East War of 1967 (June 5–10). It was the most significant, albeit belated, UN response to the war.]

The Security Council,

Expressing Its Continuing Concern with the Grave Situation in the Middle East,

Emphasizing the inadmissibility of the acquisition of territory by war and the need to work for a just and lasting peace in which every State in the area can live in security,

Emphasizing further that all Member States in their acceptance of the Charter of the United Nations have undertaken a commitment to act in accordance with Article 2 of the Charter,

1 *Affirms* that the fulfillment of Charter principles requires the establishment of a just and lasting peace in the Middle East which should include the application of both the following principles:

   i Withdrawal of Israel armed forces from territories occupied in the recent conflict;
   ii Termination of all claims or states of belligerency and respect for and acknowledgment of the sovereignty, territorial integrity and political independence of every State in the area and their right to live in peace within secure and recognized boundaries free from threats or acts of force;

2 *Affirms further* the necessity

   a For guaranteeing freedom of navigation through international waterways in the area;
   b For achieving a just settlement of the refugee problem;
   c For guaranteeing the territorial inviolability and political independence of every State in the area, through measures including the establishment of demilitarized zones;

3 *Requests* the Secretary-General to designate a Special Representative to proceed to the Middle East to establish and maintain contacts with the States concerned in order to promote agreement and assist efforts to achieve a peaceful and accepted settlement in accordance with the provisions and principles in this resolution;

4 *Requests*, the Secretary-General to report to the Security Council on the progress of the efforts of the Special Representative as soon as possible.

Adopted unanimously at the 1,382nd meeting.

---

meager "observer" status. Of importance, the Madrid Conference provided the umbrella structure for secret talks between the PLO and the Israeli government. These talks led to the **Oslo Accords** of 1993, which formally accepted the long-endorsed UN principle of partition in Palestine. The accords were signed, however, on the White House lawn without the slightest verbal or ceremonial nod to the United Nations. As part of the accords, the PLO conceded Israel's right to exist and Israel recognized the Palestine Liberation Organization as the representative of the Palestinian people. The Declaration of Principles established a Palestine Authority (PLA) in the Gaza Strip and in the West Bank city of Jericho, where Yasser Arafat then established his new government. The accords contemplated the eventual transfer of most of the occupied territories to Palestinian control.

The peace process sustained a severe blow with the election of Israeli Prime Minister Benjamin Netanyahu in 1996. His government opposed further concessions to the Palestine Authority. Netanyahu emphasized security and settlements in the territories, the latter of which the UN General Assembly regularly declared illegal. In the spring of 1997, the United States vetoed a Security Council resolution condemning the construction of an Israeli settlement at Har Homa. President Clinton explained the veto, arguing that the insertion of the United Nations into the issue could jeopardize the ongoing peace negotiations between the Israelis and the Palestinians.

Clinton convened a second Camp David Summit in the summer of 2000, bringing together Arafat and Ehud Barak, Netanyahu's successor. Unfortunately, the meeting ended in failure. The collapse of the summit prompted new violence. As hostilities grew in the West Bank, for the first time since 1973, a U.S. administration sought the active leadership of the UN Secretary-General. Kofi Annan, who had been shuttling among Jerusalem, Tel Aviv, and Gaza City, and traveling elsewhere in the Middle East in a quest to ease tensions, stepped into the U.S.-Israeli-Palestinian standoff. He persuaded Palestinian and Israeli leaders to join Egyptian president Hosni Mubarak in a summit at Sharm El-Sheik on October 14, 2000.

At Sharm El-Sheik, Israel agreed to withdraw military forces to positions held before the beginning of the unrest, to lift the closure of the West Bank and Gaza, and to reopen the Gaza airport. Security forces from both sides agreed to resume a dialogue that had been interrupted by the crisis. President Clinton appointed a U.S.-controlled fact-finding committee (the Mitchell Commission, named for its chair, former U.S. Senator George Mitchell) after consulting with the parties and Annan. The text of the commission's report, then, was to be shown to Annan and UN officials before publication, and the United States was to make the final decision on the wording of the report. A brief triangulation had emerged among the White House, UN headquarters, and Middle East leaders.

The Annan-U.S. cooperation continued into the early days of President George W. Bush's administration. Bush sent Secretary of State Colin Powell to the region and announced a change in the U.S. policy, endorsing the placement of an observer mission to monitor a cooling-off period until peace negotiations could resume.

Despite concerted UN and U.S. diplomacy, violence escalated during the summer with suicide bombings orchestrated by Palestinian groups and reprisal military assassinations of Palestinian leaders on the West Bank and the Gaza Strip. Under intense international pressure, in June 2002, President Bush announced his support for a Palestinian state living side by side with Israel, and he expressed America's interest in developing a "Road Map" to bring about a final resolution. Working with the United Nations, the EU, and Russia, the United States joined "**The Quartet**," which produced a "performance-based roadmap to a permanent two state solution." The Road Map called for a series of parallel steps by both sides toward the vision of creating two independent states by 2005.

The Quartet's roadmap to peace remained elusive. In Israel, growing consternation over continuing terrorist attacks undermined support for it and the Palestinians protested Israel's construction of a 625-mile security fence. Much of the world saw the fence as a new form of apartheid. The GA took the unusual step of seeking an advisory opinion from the International Court of Justice on the legality of the barrier. A court decision declaring the wall illegal and condemnations of its construction in the United Nations fell on deaf ears in Tel Aviv. Tensions rose, and when Palestinian radicals abducted an Israeli soldier, the Israelis moved troops into northern parts of the Gaza Strip. Hezbollah militants from Lebanon then seized two Israeli soldiers in cross-border raids. Israel responded with air and land attacks on southern Lebanon. UN Secretary-General Annan called for the release of the soldiers and condemned Israel's retaliatory strikes. The Lebanese war lasted a full month before the UN was able to orchestrate a cease-fire.

Renewed hope for a multilateral peace process emerged in 2009 with the election in the United States of President Barack Obama. That summer, in a ground-breaking speech in Cairo, Egypt, he encouraged the Arab and Muslim world to expect the United States would address the just demands of Palestinians and push the Israeli government to end policies so deeply despised by the Palestinian community. His first steps were heartening in that his government diplomatically achieved an Israeli freeze on new settlements and a revival of talks between Israeli Prime Minister Benjamin Netanyahu and Palestinian President Mahmoud Abbas. The talks, however, broke down when the settlement freeze ended and Netanyahu demanded that the Palestinian government recognize Israel as a *Jewish* state.[43] The early optimism further gave way when relations between the president and Netanyahu soured. Nevertheless, in his 2010 speech to the UN General Assembly, President Obama expressed hope that Palestinian statehood and Middle East peace would be achieved in the succeeding twelve months through hard work at the negotiating table. He opined, "When we come back here next year, we can have an agreement that will lead to a new member of the United Nations, an independent, sovereign state of Palestine, living in peace with Israel."[44] That public prediction would embolden Palestinian leaders and dampen the Israeli government's willingness to make concessions.

Photo 5.2 Benjamin Netanyahu, Prime Minister of Israel, addresses the General Assembly's seventieth session.

Source: UN Photo/Cia Pak. Reproduced by permission of the United Nations.

By 2011, Palestinian leaders concluded that achievement of a state and the end of occupation could not come through negotiations. Faced with no hope of successful negotiations with Tel Aviv, they decided to push for statehood recognition by the United Nations and membership in the world body. By March of that year, 112 countries had recognized the state of Palestine, including several European governments. In September, President Abbas formally submitted Palestine's application for membership. Palestine was admitted to the UN Educational, Scientific and Cultural Organization (UNESCO), but admission to the General Assembly would constitute formal statehood recognition by the UN, a step that would meet with forceful opposition from the United States, Israel, and other major actors. The U.S. representative threatened that the admission of Palestine as a state, without a peace settlement in place, would lead to a cut-off of U.S. contributions to the UN. With membership stalled, the Palestinian government switched tactics and asked for an upgrade in status from "observer entity" to "non-member observer state." The General Assembly agreed by a vote of 138 to 9. The vote constituted a *de facto* recognition of Palestine as a state.

Photo 5.3 Mahmoud Abbas (center), president of the State of Palestine, presents Palestine's flag to be raised for the first time at UN Headquarters in New York, September 30, 2015.

Source: UN Photo/Mark Garten. Reproduced by permission of the United Nations.

Palestine's diplomatic victory did not change things for the better in the territories. Rocket attacks on Israel by militants in Gaza, the continuing blockade of the Strip by Israel, and recriminations over kidnappings in the West Bank all led to open warfare in the summer of 2014. Seven weeks of war left twenty-one hundred people dead. A cease-fire took hold in late August. More than ten thousand Gazans were wounded in the conflict. Sixty-six Israeli soldiers and five Israeli civilians died. The UN Office for the Coordination of Humanitarian Affairs reported that five hundred and twenty thousand Palestinians had been displaced. Demonstrating a new level of tension in the Israeli-Palestinian quarrel, beleaguered Palestinian Authority President Mahmoud Abbas announced in his UN speech of September 30, 2015 that Palestinians no longer would be bound by any mutual agreements with Israel, including the Oslo Peace Accords.

The near-complete exclusion of the United Nations from the Israeli-Palestinian peace process and even a threat to its seventy-year humanitarian role in the Palestinian community came with the election of U.S President Donald Trump. His approach to the Middle East, and specifically to the Israeli-Palestinian puzzle, deviated from the conventional UN-backed formula, based on Security Council Resolution 242 of 1967. Trump committed to the Israeli right-wing Likud party stance, which envisioned a Greater Israel in Palestine.

In mid-May 2018, the American administration relocated its embassy from Tel Aviv to Jerusalem.[45] Since Jerusalem was a contested site between Israelis and Palestinians, both claiming it as their capital, the UN and international consensus had considered that such a transfer should await a permanent peace between the claimants. In early September, the United States canceled $200 million earmarked for programs based in Gaza. The administration closed the Palestinian Mission office in Washington, supported Israeli annexation plans in the territories, and recognized the Golan Heights as part of Israel.[46] It also withdrew from the UN Relief and Works Agency (UNRWA), which had been supported by every American president since its establishment in 1949. As of 2019, more than 5.6 million Palestinians were registered with UNRWA as refugees. In the aftermath of Washington's move, European and Arab countries pledged to support the agency and Germany promised increased financial backing.[47]

The Trump policies reflected a general demotion of the Palestinian-Israeli conflict in American foreign policy, which was mirrored as well in Arab foreign policies. Palestinians' cause became less of a priority as their prospects of achieving a state receded and as other Middle East issues, particularly the perceived threat of Iran, escalated. Measuring their self-interest, several Arab governments moved closer to Israel, first secretly, then in a public diplomatic agreement. In August 2020, President Trump announced the "full normalization of relations" between Israel and the United Arab Emirates, and by the end of the year, Bahrain, Sudan, Yemen, and Morocco joined the UAE in what came to be called the Abraham Accords, establishing regular diplomatic, economic, and travel relations with Israel.

The dam of Arab opposition to Israeli occupation policies was broken by the Abraham Accords. The Palestinians found themselves without significant allies in the region. It seemed unlikely that the world could return to a two-state solution. The ruling Israeli government was realizing the dream of a Greater Israel; the United States had endorsed the move; a mushrooming number of Arab states was accepting the reality and opening up embassies in Israel. Was there now to be only "one state," as it happens, with a growing population of Palestinians? If so, how would the international community (and the UN) now perceive and address the situation? There were in 2020 approximately 2.7 million Palestinians in what could be called "Greater Israel." (There were an additional two million in Gaza.) That compared to about 6.5 million Jews.[48] The international community and the United Nations were now faced with a new reality that could not respond to older proposed solutions.

Iran, Nuclear Weapons, and Gulf Crises

We will not rehearse here the detailed discussion earlier in this chapter of the two Gulf Wars of the 1990s and early 2000s. Both conflicts were part of a general rise in tensions following the 1979 Iranian revolution that toppled the Shah of Iran and brought to power a radicalized Shiite government in Tehran. The revolution and the foreign policy pronouncements of Iran's new leader, Ayatollah Ruhollah Khomeini, exacerbated historical tensions between Shiites and Sunnis in the region. The revolution initially weakened Iran and gave an opportunity to Iraq's dictator, Saddam Hussein, to seek to alter the balance of power. War broke out between the two countries in 1980. It was one of the longest and most costly conflicts of the twentieth century, with casualty estimates as high as two million people.[49] The UN Security Council passed more than 15 resolutions calling for end to the fighting, but with little impact. Not until its passage of Resolution 598 in July 1988, jointly sponsored by the United States and the Soviet Union, insisting on a cease-fire and threatening retaliation against either combatant refusing to comply, did the parties halt their military operations.

The Iran-Iraq War shifted the United Nations' and the world's attention from the almost exclusive four-decade preoccupation with Palestinian-Israeli tensions as the epicenter of Middle East conflict to the threats to international peace and security in the Gulf. The two warring countries used the cease-fire hiatus to rearm and prepare for future hostilities. As part of his strategic policy, Iraq's president launched the invasion of Kuwait, triggering the first Gulf War. As noted earlier, while the United States led the multilateral force that liberated Kuwait, it did so with the concurrence of the UN Security Council, and it conducted the war within the confines of SC resolutions. Subsequently, the UN imposed heavy sanctions on Baghdad and prohibitions on Saddam's development of weapons of mass destruction and the use of his military. The second gulf war (2003) had no Security Council imprimatur. The UN was sidelined by the American leadership and only invited to play a role in the situation after the U.S. occupation of Iraq.

The Bush administration had labeled both Iraq and Iran members of an "axis of evil." While confronting and then occupying Iraq over its supposed possession of weapons of mass destruction, it simultaneously belabored the UN over its inability to constrain Iran's nuclear ambitions. For nearly a decade, the Security Council had demanded through binding resolutions[50] that Iran suspend uranium enrichment and heavy-water-related projects that could lead to it acquiring a nuclear bomb. Beginning in 2006, the powers proposed comprehensive limitations on Iran's program, and when Iran balked, the council imposed damaging sanctions on the Iranian economy. Over the next few years, when negotiations faltered between Iran and the International Atomic Energy Agency (IAEA), the Security Council tightened the sanctions.

After 2009, most of the negotiations between the P5+1 and Iran gravitated between the UN facilities in Geneva, Switzerland, and in Vienna, Austria. But in spring 2015, as self-imposed deadlines approached to reach a deal, the parties, hosted by the Swiss government and with the European Union serving as the interlocutor, agreed to meet in Lausanne. On April 2, they announced a framework agreement that would lead, on July 14, to the comprehensive document—the JCPOA, discussed in detail earlier in this chapter—being signed by all negotiating parties in Vienna.

The Arab Spring and Its Aftermath

Around 11:30 am local time on December 17, 2010, in the small rural Tunisian town of Sidi Bouzid, a young man set fire to himself in the middle of a busy street in front of the provincial governor's office. The victim was Muhamad Bouazizi, a 27-year-old street vendor whose sole income came from the sale of mainly vegetables gathered from his family's meager plot and from a food distribution center, paid for with borrowed money. His self-immolation was a protest against years of harassment by local police seeking bribes. Earlier that day, his cart had been overturned and then seized by authorities for supposedly not having a permit.

Bouazizi's desperation and death triggered the largest upheaval of Arab governments since the end of World War II. It immediately led to protests in the streets of Tunisia against the corrupt government of strongman President Ben Ali. Within a month, he had fled the country. The fever of the "Arab Spring" spread quickly to Libya, Egypt, and Yemen, where massive protests brought down long-standing governments, leading ultimately to civil chaos, not the democracies most protesters sought. Shiite protesters against the Sunni monarchy in Bahrain were crushed by Saudi forces. In Syria, the Arab Spring sparked opposition to President Bashir Assad, leading to a decade of bloody civil war, refugee flows, and massive humanitarian problems.

For international organizations, particularly the United Nations, the EU, the Gulf Cooperation Council, and the League of Arab States, the Arab Spring presented unprecedented challenges, all seeking to restore stable governments, feed and shelter large populations, end region-wide violence, and provide resources for economic development. During the Syrian conflict, civilians fleeing into neighboring Turkey and Lebanon filled a string of refugee camps that looked like a pearl necklace on the map. More than two dozen camps in all, established by the Lebanese and Turkish governments, were largely provisioned and financed by the UN's primary refugee agency, the UN High Commissioner for Refugees (UNHCR). They were safe havens for more than 200,000 of the estimated 850,000 Syrian refugees in Turkey. To pay for the costs of humanitarian aid, the UNHCR appealed for $6.5 billion, the largest amount ever requested for a single humanitarian emergency. Of the total, $2.3 billion was earmarked for UNHCR's sister UN organization, the Office for Coordination of Humanitarian Aid (OCHA). In all, more than four million Syrians escaped the country. Another 7.6 million were internally displaced, with 12.2 million in need of humanitarian assistance. Secretary-General Ban Ki-moon appointed a special envoy for Syria, Staffan de Mistura, a seasoned UN diplomat, to seek a negotiated solution to the conflict. He traveled to Damascus, other capitals in the region, Moscow, Geneva, New York, and other venues urging a cease-fire in the civil war to no avail.

In Yemen, the Arab Spring brought down President Abdullah Salah's government in June of 2011, when opposition forces bombed his palace, injuring Salah. By 2014, the country was in ruins from a civil conflict that led to a proxy war between Saudi Arabia and Iran, the former backing Sunni forces and Iran supporting Shiite Houthi tribesmen. Early in the war, the UN Secretary-General appointed yet another a special envoy to seek a negotiated peace. Those efforts led to the Stockholm Agreement (December 13, 2018), lifting the blockade of major ports so that humanitarian goods and food could reach the population. It also allowed for a prisoner exchange. However, the presence of al-Qaeda in Arabia, the continuing tensions between Saudi Arabia and Iran, and the rebel hold on the capital all worked to undermine a lasting peace. In February 2021, the Security Council was still calling for a "cessation of hostilities" (Resolution 2565), couching it in the effort to halt the spread of COVID-19.

SUMMARY

Universal collective security is the principle on which the United Nations was founded. It was meant to replace the older and more traditional methods—the balance of power, alliances, and individual self-defense—for keeping the peace and avoiding another war like the two that so traumatized the world in the twentieth century. Collective security presumes a group of citizen states committed to defending the community against any violator of its rules. In the Cold War, this environment did not exist. The United Nations had to develop substitutes for the Charter's collective security provisions or face the same fate as that of the League of Nations in an earlier time. It responded with peacekeeping and Chapter VI½ innovations. Only the new United Nations of the early post-Cold War era was able to approach its founders' intent. The brief "spring" of great-power cooperation gave way just a few years into the new millennium, requiring new, less formal mechanisms outside the direct control of the Security Council to attempt to address threats to peace and security, and yet, as the Middle East demonstrates, the goal remains elusive.

KEY TERMS

African Union (200)

Association of Southeast Asian Nations (201)

Chapter VI½ (185)

Collective Security (175)

Economic Community of West African States (201)

Emergency Special Sessions of the General Assembly (186)

Enforcement Measures (180)

Korean War (185)

Nuclear Non-Proliferation Treaty (NPT) (191)

Organisation for Security and Cooperation in Europe (201)

Oslo Accords (208)

P5+1 (193)

Pacific Settlement (180)

Peacebuilding (198)

Peacekeeping (189)

Peacemaking (198)

Preventive Diplomacy (198)

Regional Organization (200)

"The Quartet" (209)

Resolution 242 (206)

Smart Sanctions (200)

Subcontracting (197)

Uniting for Peace Resolution (184)

DISCUSSION QUESTIONS

Compare the provisions listed in the figure titled "Legal Basis for Collective Security: The Covenant of the League of Nations" with those listed in the figure "Legal Basis for Collective Security: Charter of the United Nations." What differences do you note? What factors explain the difference in approach to collective security in the two documents?

Is it appropriate in your view for the UN Security Council to use the principle of collective security to intervene in the internal affairs of an admittedly sovereign state to address what it sees as a threat to international peace and security?

Is the "Responsibility to Protect" (R2P) principle a reasonable response by the international community to egregious violations by a government of its citizens' human rights or is it, itself, a fundamental violation of state sovereignty and of the UN Charter?

How might collective security be reconceptualized in the twenty-first century to ensure that unilateral military action, such as the 2003 U.S. intervention in Iraq or the 2008 Russian intervention in Georgia, does not happen without UN approval, while at the same time acknowledging the need for states to confront perceived serious threats to their national well-being when the Security Council is unlikely to deal with the threat?

RESOURCES FOR FURTHER RESEARCH

Relevant Web Sites

International Atomic Energy Agency (www.iaea.org)
Organisation for the Prohibition of Chemical Weapons (www.opcw.org)
Comprehensive Nuclear-Test-Ban Treaty Organization (www.ctbto.org)
UN Institute for Disarmament Research (www.unidir.org)
UN Mine Action Service (www.mineaction.org/)
UN Office for Disarmament Affairs (www.un.org/disarmament/)
UN Security Council (www.un.org/securitycouncil/)

Books, Articles, and Documents

A More Secure World: Our Shared Responsibility. Report of the High-level Panel on Threats, Challenges and Change. United Nations. A/59/565, December 2, 2004.

Bosco, David L. *Five to Rule Them All: The UN Security Council and the Making of the Modern World.* Oxford: Oxford University Press, 2009.

Butler, Richard. *Iraq, Weapons of Mass Destruction, and the Growing Crisis of Global Security.* New York: Public Affairs, 2000.

Claude, Inis. *Swords into Plowshares: The Problems and Promise of International Organization.* 2nd Edition. New York: Random House, 1959.

Cortright, David. *The Sanctions Decade: Assessing UN Strategies in the 1990s.* Boulder, CO: Lynne Rienner, 2000.

Mohler, Bjorn. *The Pros and Cons of Subsidiarity: The Role of African Regional and Subregional Organizations in Ensuring Peace and Security in Africa.* Copenhagen: Danish Institute for International Studies, 2005.

Moore, John Allphin, Jr., and Jerry Pubantz. *American Presidents and the United Nations: Internationalism in the Balance.* New York and London: Routledge, 2022.

Pubantz, Jerry. "George W. Bush and the United Nations: Idealism's Departure from Collective Security," *The George W. Bush Presidency: Foreign Policy*, edited by Meena Bose and Paul Fritz. New York: Nova Science Publishers, 2016, 69–79.

Simma, Bruno, ed. *The Charter of the United Nations: A Commentary.* Munich, Germany: C. H. Beck, 1995.

Thakur, Ramesh. *The United Nations, Peace and Security: From Collective Security to the Responsibility to Protect.* Cambridge: Cambridge University Press, 2006.

Tucker, Jonathan B., ed. *Toxic Terror: Assessing Terrorist Use of Chemical and Biological Weapons.* Cambridge, MA: MIT Press, 2000.

United Nations Office for Disarmament Affairs. *Fact Sheet: Chemical Weapons*, 2021 at front. un-arm.org/wp-content/uploads/2021/07/CW-Fact-Sheet-July2021.pdf

Weapons of Mass Destruction Commission. *Weapons of Terror: Freeing the World of Nuclear, Biological and Chemical Arms.* Stockholm, Sweden: Weapons of Mass Destruction Commission, 2006.

Notes

1 United Nations, "'Preamble' and 'Chapter I: Purposes and Principles'," in *Charter of the United Nations*, art. 1, para. 1 (italics added) (New York: United Nations, 1945).
2 League of Nations, *The Covenant of the League of Nations* (Geneva, Switzerland: League of Nations, 1919), art. 8.

3 Brian Frederking, "Constructing Post–Cold War Collective Security," *American Political Science Review* 97, no. 3 (2003): 363.

4 Security Council Resolution 2177, September 18, 2014.

5 "Security Council Fails to Adopt Resolution Integrating Climate-Related Security Risk into Conflict-Prevention Strategies," 13, December 2021, at <www.un.org/press/en/2021/sc14732.doc.htm>.

6 The League reached nearly universal membership during its lifetime, having a minimum of sixty members at any one time and a maximum of sixty-three.

7 Inis Claude, "Collective Legitimation as a Political Function of the UN," *International Organization* 20, no. 3 (1966): 367–379.

8 Ian Hurd, "Legitimacy, Power and the Symbolic Life of the Security Council," *Global Governance* 8, no. 1 (2002): 38.

9 Bruno Simma, ed., *The Charter of the United Nations: A Commentary* (Munich, Germany: C. H. Beck, 1995), 572.

10 The final debate among the permanent members about the creation of a UN force occurred in August 1948. After that, the representatives of each country's chief of staff met biweekly for five to fifteen minutes, ceremonially marking the existence of the committee. Only once, at the time of the Iraqi invasion of Kuwait, was a meeting of the full Military Staff Committee held in which serious discussions took place about military operations. However, no actions ensued from those discussions.

11 Simma, *The Charter*, 575, note 25.

12 John Allphin Moore, Jr., and Jerry Pubantz, *To Create a New World? American Presidents and the United Nations* (New York: Peter Lang, 1999), 71–73.

13 A/ES-11/L.1, March 1, 2022.

14 International Court of Justice, "The Court Finds that the Construction by Israel of a Wall in the Occupied Palestinian Territory and Its Associated Régime Are Contrary to International Law," press release, 2004/28, July 9, 2004.

15 International Court of Justice, *Legal Consequences of the Construction of a Wall in the Occupied Palestinian Territory*, General list no. 131, advisory opinion, July 9, 2004, para. 27.

16 Gregory Khalil, "Just Say No to Vetoes," *New York Times*, July 19, 2004.

17 Former Secretary-General Kofi Annan has written, "The Most Original Contribution the UN has made to Conflict Prevention is the Invention of Peacekeeping." *We the Peoples: A UN for the 21st Century* (Boulder, CO: Paradigm, 2014), 8.

18 United Nations, "Chapter IV: The General Assembly," in *Charter of the United Nations*, art. 11, para. 1 (New York: United Nations, 1945).

19 Ibid., "Chapter V: The Security Council," art. 26.

20 Jerry Pubantz, "Strategic Arms Limitation Talks," in *The Modern Encyclopedia of Russian and Soviet History*, eds. George N. Rhyne and Joseph L. Wieczynski, 37:173 (Gulf Breeze, FL: Academic International Press, 1984).

21 A. LeRoy Bennett, *International Organizations: Principles and Issues*, 4th Edition (Upper Saddle River, NJ: Prentice Hall, 1988), 322.

22 In February 2019, President Trump withdrew the United States from the INF treaty and threatened to do the same with the New START treaty.

23 Ibid.

24 The treaty and information about it can be found at <www.un.org/disarmament/ATT/>.

25 Among the most important were Resolutions 660 (a condemnation of the invasion), 661 (the imposition of mandatory economic sanctions), 662 (a declaration that the annexation of Kuwait was null and void), and 678 (which gave Iraq forty-eight days to withdraw from Kuwait or face military retaliation).

26 Moore and Pubantz, *To Create a New World*, 296–297, 304–305.

27 Boutros Boutros-Ghali, *An Agenda for Peace*, UN document A/47/277-S/2411 (New York: United Nations, June 17, 1992), para. 1, <www.un.org/ruleoflaw/files/A_47_277.pdf>.

28 See <www.un.org/securitycouncil/sanctions/information>.

29 Michael Brzoska, "From Dumb to Smart? Recent Reforms of UN Sanctions," *Global Governance* 9, no. 4 (2003): 522.

30 To address the problem of "conflict diamonds" generally, in December 2000, the General Assembly adopted a resolution supporting the creation of an international certification scheme for rough diamonds. By November 2002, the world community had established the Kimberley Process Certification Scheme that regulates rough diamond production and trade.

31 Fact Sheet, United Nations Security Council Subsidiary Organs, at <www.un.org/securitycouncil/sites/www.un.org.securitycouncil/files/subsidiary_organs_factsheets.pdf>.

32 Chris Barrett, "'A bloodbath is Imminent' in Myanmar but China Blocks UN Sanctions," *The Sydney Morning Herald*, April 1, 2021, at <www.smh.com.au/world/asia/a-bloodbath-is-imminent-in-myanmar-but-china-blocks-un-sanctions-20210331-p57fuw.html>.

33 António Guterres, "Remarks to the Security Council - on Enhancing Cooperation between the United Nations and Regional and Subregional Organizations in Enhancing Confidence Building and Dialogue in Conflict Prevention and Resolution," April 19, 2021.

34 A/Res/60/1 (2005).

35 James Mann, *The Obamians: The Struggle inside the White House to Redefine American Power* (New York: Viking, 2012), 290.

36 Ibid., xiii.

37 Chris J. Dolan, *Obama and the Emergence of a Multipolar World Order: Redefining U.S. Foreign Policy* (Lanham, MD: Lexington Books, 2018), 158–159.

38 See, for example, Security Council Resolutions 678 (Kuwait, November 29, 1990), 816 (Bosnia and Herzegovina, March 31, 1993, also res. 836, June 4, 1993), 1244 (Kosovo, June 10, 1999), 1264 (East Timor, September 15, 1999), 1386 (Afghanistan, December 20, 2001), 1497 (Liberia, August 1, 2003), 1511 (Iraq, October 16, 2003—the Security Council's first collective security action on Iraq, authorizing a multinational force under unified command), 1546 (Iraq, June 8, 2004, continuation of the multinational force), 1529 (Haiti, February 29, 2004), and 1851 (Somalia, December 16, 2008).

39 *National Security Strategy of the United States*, September 2002. <www.whitehouse.gov/nsc/nss.pdf>.

40 The most detailed legal study was commissioned by the Dutch government. See Report of the Dutch Committee of Inquiry on the War in Iraq. *Netherlands International Law Review*, 2010, 81–137. Also see Steven J. Barela, "Preemptive or Preventive War: A Discussion of Legal and Moral Standards," *Denver Journal of International Law and Policy* 33, no. 1: 32–41.

41 <news.un.org/en/story/2022/04/1115782>.

42 UN General Assembly, *Resolution 181 (II): Future Government of Palestine*, A/RES/181(II), November 29, 1947.

43 Moore and Pubantz, *The New United Nations*, 202.

44 Remarks to the United Nations General Assembly in New York City, September 23, 2010, *Public Papers of the Presidents of the United States* (Washington, DC: U.S. Government Printing Office, 2010), Book II, 1410.

45 "President Donald J. Trump Keeps His Promise to Open U.S. Embassy in Jerusalem, Israel," May 14, 2018, at <www.whitehouse.gov/briefings-statements/president-donald-j-trump-keeps-promise-open-u-s-embassy-jerusalem-israel/>.

46 John Allphin Moore, Jr. and Jerry Pubantz, *American Presidents and the United Nations: Internationalism in the Balance* (New York and London: Routledge, 2022), 171.

47 Peter Beaumont and Oliver Holmes, "Trump Poised to Cut All US Funding for Key UN Palestinian Refugee Programme," *The Guardian*, August 31, 2018, at <www.theguardian.com/world/2018/aug/31/trump-to-cut-all-us-funding-for-uns-main-palestinian-refugee-programme>.

48 Jeffrey Heller, "Jews, Arabs Nearing Population Parity in Holy Land," *Reuters*, March 26, 2018, at <www.reuters.com/article/us-israel-palestinians-population/jews-arabs-nearing-population-parity-in-holy-land-israeli-officials-idUSKBN1H222T>; "Palestinians to Outnumber Jewish Population by 2020, Says PA Report," *Haaretz*, December 31, 2012, at <www.haaretz.com/pa-palestinians-to-outnumber-jews-by-2020–1.5285402>.

49 John Allphin Moore, Jr., and Jerry Pubantz, *Encyclopedia of the United Nations*, 2nd Edition, Vol. I (New York: Facts on File, 2008), 251.

50 UN Security Council Resolutions 1696 (2006), 1737 (2006), and 1747 (2007).

Chapter 6

Peacekeeping and Nation-Building

When you think of the United Nations (UN) today, you might envision an organization engaged in peacekeeping and nation-building operations. Many twentieth- and twenty-first-century UN missions in countries around the world have been devoted to these objectives. The ramifications of these UN missions have been enormous and have resulted in a redefinition of the entire UN organization. Former Secretary-General Kofi Annan once wrote, "The most original contribution the UN has made to conflict prevention is the invention of peacekeeping."[1] Particularly with the decline in inter-state wars and the rise in ethnic and religious civil conflict, peacekeeping missions have escalated in number and expanded in their mandates, moving beyond separating combatants and monitoring truces toward the goal of reconstructing domestic governments and civil societies along democratic lines. United Nations Secretary-General Boutros Boutros-Ghali spelled out this ambitious program of UN-sponsored democratic nation-building in his report *An Agenda for Peace*. He urged the United Nations to identify "at risk" states and to act early in order to avoid the collapse of state sovereignty and internal order.[2] In this chapter, we discuss many of the peacekeeping and nation-building missions that have contributed to the evolution of the UN's role in the world.

THE ORIGIN OF PEACEKEEPING IN THE UNITED NATIONS

The founders of the United Nations did not envisage anything like the recent practice of peacekeeping. The idea of using a neutral international force to facilitate peace was a novel innovation, requiring the development of an entirely new method of operation without the benefit of previous precedents that normally govern international activity. Entering its seventy-seventh year, the United Nations had undertaken seventy-one peacekeeping operations, costing more than 4,100 fatalities among the peacekeeper contingents. At its zenith in 2015, nearly 133,000 peacekeepers were serving in sixteen missions at an annual cost of $85 billion. The nature of these missions had evolved dramatically from their initial character to include humanitarian assistance, civil administration, combatant separation, truce observation, peacemaking, refugee repatriation, election administration, disarmament, and nation-building.

DOI: 10.4324/9781003281535-7

As initially conceived in 1948 and 1949—and practiced for the first forty years of the United Nations—peacekeeping was a narrowly focused process with limited and specific purposes. During the Cold War, peacekeeping operated according to fairly clear rules. **Ralph Bunche**, under-secretary-general for special political affairs and the highest-ranking American in the UN administration, developed most of these rules in the 1950s. Peacekeeping involved an international effort to end a war between states by placing UN-authorized observers or military personnel into a conflict region as part of an agreement to end hostilities. It was always carried out with the express permission of both sides to the conflict. Only military from small or relatively neutral states were included in the peacekeeping force. Neither the superpowers nor any of the other permanent members of the Security Council contributed personnel. Authorized by a Security Council resolution or an emergency special session of the General Assembly, a peacekeeping operation was supervised by the Secretary-General or his designee. Peacekeepers arrived after both parties had negotiated a settlement. They positioned themselves between the combatants. The sole purpose of early peacekeeping was to supervise the implementation of truce agreements and specifically to verify that both sides took appropriate actions to carry out the agreements already reached. Although military personnel were involved, they carried no more than light arms. Peacekeepers had no enforcement powers and were directed to use force just to defend themselves. Peacekeepers were sent only after the UN Secretariat negotiated a Status of Forces Agreement (SOFA), by which the host state—since it remained a sovereign nation—granted permission to use its territory. The agreement also defined the peacekeepers' powers, their access to facilities, and the specific territory in which they would operate.

Beginning with the UN Emergency Force (UNEF) in 1956, the United Nations found that the most serious administrative problem with regard to putting a peacekeeping force in the field was obtaining the financial resources to support it. Dispatched as part of the resolution of the Suez Crisis, UNEF was placed along the Suez Canal on Egyptian territory, replacing British, French, and Israeli troops that had invaded the area. At that time, Secretary-General Dag Hammarskjöld proposed that the expenses be paid out of the regular UN budget, citing Article 17 of the Charter, which obligates member states to pay "the expenses of the Organization." This type of payment had already been made in the case of the UN Truce Supervision Organization (UNTSO), described in the last chapter. The Soviet Union and several Arab states objected, demanding that the "aggressors"—Great Britain, France, and Israel—pay the costs. In 1960, when the General Assembly authorized a peacekeeping force to intervene in the Congolese civil war, France joined the states refusing to pay assessments associated with the operation. The French argued that only the Security Council, under Chapter VII of the Charter, could obligate the organization and its members to fund such operations. Despite an advisory opinion from the International Court of Justice in July 1962 that peacekeeping expenses are expenses of the organization within the meaning of the Charter, raising sufficient funding for these operations remained problematic. By 1964, member states' neglect in paying their peacekeeping assessments put the United Nations in the first of its periodic financial crises.

As a result, stopgap measures were instituted to pay for peacekeeping.[3] Although a peacekeeping budget was established as one of the "regular" budgets of the organization, the United Nations depended heavily on voluntary contributions. At various times, it also floated bond issues to cover expenses. With fluctuating annual costs reaching more than $3.5 billion at different times during the 1990s, and arrears in assessed contributions topping $1.5 billion, the organization was often unable to reimburse governments that contributed troops and equipment.

IMPORTANT COLD WAR PEACEKEEPING MISSIONS

UN Military Observer Group in India and Pakistan

In 1948, the United Nations sought to sustain a cease-fire between the newly independent states of Pakistan and India. Claims between the two states to the territory of Kashmir and Jammu dated from the partition of the Asian subcontinent and the departure of British colonial administration. The 1947 partition plan allowed the disputed region to join either state. Following its accession to India, an act Pakistan impugned, fighting broke out between Muslim Pakistan and majority-Hindu India. In January, India and Pakistan accepted UN observers to monitor a cease-fire. UN Military Observer Group in India and Pakistan (UNMOGIP) personnel arrived in January 1949 and continued their presence even during outbreaks of hostility in 1965 and 1971, which demonstrated the fecklessness of early peacekeeping missions to halt open warfare. In July 1972, the two sides agreed to a "line of control" in Jammu and Kashmir that approximately corresponded to the cease-fire line established in 1949. With this agreement, India then argued that the UN mission was no longer needed, and New Delhi thus opposed its continuation. Succeeding UN Secretaries-General, nonetheless, took the position that only the Security Council could terminate the operation, which it had not done by the winter of 2021. The budget that year was approximately $10 million.

UN Operation in the Congo

The United Nations first became involved in the Congo when the Belgian colony achieved independence in July 1960. On July 4, the Armée Nationale Congolaise (ANC) mutinied against its Belgian officers and began attacking European civilians. Against the Congolese government's wishes, Belgium sent ten thousand paratroopers to restore order. On July 11, the mineral-rich Katanga Province seceded. Heavy fighting between Belgian and Congolese troops led both the country's prime minister, Patrice Lumumba, and the Belgians to request the dispatch of UN peacekeepers. Foreshadowing what would become an initiative to expand on the peacekeeping role developed so far by the UN Secretariat, Secretary-General Hammarskjöld invoked Article 99 of the Charter to bring the crisis to the Security Council's attention. The council established the UN Operation in the Congo (ONUC) to replace the Belgian troops and to support the central government against rebel and secessionist challenges.

The United Nations became more involved in the civil war after a constitutional crisis in late 1960, during which Lumumba was murdered. On February 15, 1961, Hammarskjöld declared that ONUC could act to investigate the assassination, protect civilians, prevent clashes between armed units, reorganize the army, and remove Belgians from Katanga. The Security Council authorized the use of force, if necessary, to prevent civil war. In response to an increasingly radical and violent secessionist movement, the council extended ONUC's authorization to detain and apprehend mercenaries and confiscate their arms. In December 1961, the Katangans attacked the Elisabethville airport, and ONUC retaliated, killing fifty civilians.

In the Congo, the United Nations attempted to expand the meaning of peacekeeping by going beyond simply separating two independent states and monitoring an armistice or a cease-fire. The original model of peacekeeping could be rationalized as an extension of collective security, because it was intended to secure the peace between UN member states when Chapter VII measures were not available as a result of divisions in the Security Council. However, in this case, Secretary-General Hammarskjöld's forces were inserting themselves into an internal dispute and taking sides, albeit, in this instance, the side of the central government.

Some UN member states criticized ONUC's operations as inappropriate because the Security Council had not authorized them. The French adopted such a position, which led Paris to refuse to pay its assessment for the mission. Given that the costs of the operation exceeded the rest of the UN budget at the time, nonpayment by France and other states created a financial crisis for the United Nations from which it did not recover during the twentieth century. Nations in the Soviet bloc, led by the USSR, objected to the operation altogether. Soviet leaders contended that UN actions were little more than operations in support of U.S. interests in the Congo. ONUC thus became a matter of contention between Washington and Moscow, which jeopardized the UN's effectiveness and legitimacy in general. Even mild Soviet support for the UN policy had reached a breaking point when the Soviet-sponsored Congolese leader Lumumba was assassinated after being released from UN protective custody. The Soviet UN delegation refused to have any further working relationship with the Secretary-General and stepped up its efforts to replace him with a *troika*—a constitutional revision of the Charter that would have replaced the Secretary-General with a committee of three secretaries, two representing the paramount ideological blocs in the Cold War and the remaining one representing the neutral states.

Dag Hammarskjöld died in a 1961 plane crash in a remote part of Northern Rhodesia (now Zambia) while on an inspection trip to the Congo. A year later, ONUC forces left the country. From 1960 to 1964, more than ninety-three thousand troops served in ONUC; twenty thousand were present at any one time. The total cost of military operations was $402 million. In the 1990s, UN forces would return to the Congo with a different type of mission, reflecting novel post-Cold War requirements. This changed form of UN peacekeeping operation is described later in the chapter as part of our discussion on "second-generation" and nation-building peacekeeping in the aftermath of the Cold War.

The initial Congo mission raised constitutional questions about peacekeeping and military enforcement under Chapters VI and VII of the UN Charter, as well as about the role of the Secretary-General in peace and security issues. The mission was generally perceived as a UN failure because it entangled the United Nations in the Cold War rivalry of the time, cost far too much, and was too ambitious in its goals. This mission turned into an early experiment in nation-building—an undertaking that went beyond the existing understanding of the Charter. Nonetheless, the effort did introduce some elements of *future* peacekeeping missions, many of which remained dormant until Cold War hostilities receded. For instance, for the first time, UN civilian police contingents were introduced into a peacekeeping mission. By the turn of the century, many peacekeeping missions would have far more police personnel than military troops. The preeminent role of the Secretary-General and his staff, challenged by the Soviet bloc at the time, increasingly became a hallmark of later missions, and the insertion of UN forces in a *domestic* conflict became an accepted mechanism by the 1990s.

UN Peacekeeping Force in Cyprus

Controlled by the Turkish Ottoman Empire from the sixteenth century, Cyprus, the third largest island in the Mediterranean Sea, was annexed by Great Britain during World War I. For centuries, the majority ethnic Greek population considered Greece the mother country. Cyprus became independent in 1960, and full rights were promised to its minority Turkish population. In 1964, communal clashes occurred between Greek and Turkish

Cypriots, and a temporary UN peacekeeping force—the UN Peacekeeping Force in Cyprus (UNFICYP)—was sent to the island to help end the dispute.

In 1974, Archbishop Makarios, the Cypriot president, was overthrown by a military coup apparently seeking to merge the island with Greece. Turkey responded with an invasion to protect the Turkish minority. The United Nations augmented UNFICYP to supervise a buffer zone (ranging from a few yards to several miles cutting completely across the island) between the Greek Cypriot National Guard and Turkish forces. Turkey controlled about 40 percent of the country and in 1983 proclaimed a separate "Turkish" republic. The Security Council declared this action invalid, and the Secretary-General and his special adviser on the island tried to draw the opposing forces into direct discussions to end the long stalemate and initiate meaningful negotiations leading to a comprehensive settlement. As of 2022, UNFICYP continued its work.

Ironically, the lengthy presence of UNFICYP lessened incentives for reunification. Talks aimed at that result commenced in 1999. Driven by Cypriot interests in joining the European Union (EU) and the EU's acceptance of Cyprus conditioned on progress toward reunification of the island, a peacemaking impetus emerged early in the twenty-first century. Secretary-General Annan put forward the *Annan Plan* in 2003, based on his provision of "good offices" in talks conducted between the two sides. The plan called for a referendum on reunification under a federal arrangement. It urged territorial adjustments, a new property regime, and the creation of a reconciliation commission. After additional negotiations, Annan was authorized, on his own, to make adjustments in the plan and to submit it for a vote. When he did so in April 2004, Turkish voters approved the plan, but the Greek Cypriots rejected it by 3 to 1.

Partly driving Annan's personal attempt to bring final resolution to the Cypriot crisis was the mounting cost of the status quo for UNFICYP. Through the years, the mission had added humanitarian and policing functions to its tasks. It created bureaucratic subdivisions to cover public information duties, civil affairs, and even emergency helicopter services, such as medical evacuations. Voluntary contributions—mainly from Greece and the Cypriot national government—financed much of this activity, but remaining costs added to the UN financial crisis. The financial problem led countries such as Sweden and Finland to withdraw from the force. The Danes, British, Canadians, and Austrians reduced their contingents. The shift to nation-building functions by UNFICYP, along with Annan's direct involvement in the negotiations between Turkish and Greek communities on the island, brought about an evolution in the nature of the UN operation. Increasingly, it moved from a *peacekeeping endeavor* to a *peacemaking initiative.*

The global economic slowdown in 2010 hurt both the Greek and Turkish communities on the island. In 2013, the European Union and the International Monetary Fund (IMF) provided a ten billion euro bailout, requiring extensive structural reforms from the Cypriot government in return. Coupled with a suggestion by Secretary-General Ban Ki-moon that no one should take for granted that UNFICYP would be renewed long into the future, financial circumstances moved the two sides toward negotiations. In the spring of 2021, the UN sponsored peace talks between the two sides, but they quickly broke down with Turkish Cypriot leaders insisting on the recognition of their independent state and Greeks insisting on unification.

UN Disengagement Observer Force

In October 1973, war broke out between Israel and Egypt in the Sinai Peninsula and between Israel and Syria in the Golan Heights, a barrier range—and, at the time, a Syrian territory—between the two states. With the achievement of a cease-fire in the war, the

Security Council hurriedly returned UNEF to the Suez Canal region. By the following May, Israel and Syria reached a disengagement agreement that included a provision for the insertion of a UN military observer force. For the first time, a UN force was used to maintain an area of separation between two warring nations. For four decades, UN Disengagement Observer Force (UNDOF) troops were the only military presence allowed in a region of the Golan stretching more than fifty miles long and varying between one and seven miles wide. The force established permanently manned installations, turned back any incursions by personnel from either side, conducted mine clearing, and inspected "areas of limitation" outside the separation zone for illegal armaments or military activity. At the end of 2021, UNDOF still had more than eleven hundred military personnel. In essence, the force served as a trip wire against either combatant's launching a surprise attack and as a guarantee against an accidental reigniting of the Syrian-Israeli conflict. This mandate was becoming more precarious with the simultaneous threats of the Syrian civil war on the edges of the Golan and Israel's claims to sovereignty over the Heights.

UN Interim Force in Lebanon

Established by the Security Council in 1978, the UN Interim Force in Lebanon (UNIFIL) was sent to the Middle East to confirm withdrawal of Israeli forces that had invaded southern Lebanon in response to an earlier Palestinian commando attack. UNIFIL's mandate included restoration of peace and security and assistance to the Lebanese government in returning its effective authority to its southern region. The force, still in that country in 2022, long ago ceased to be an "interim" operation. Over its forty-plus-year history, UNIFIL peacekeepers monitored the process, the activities of the various, virtually autonomous, militias in the country, the initial withdrawal of Israeli forces from Lebanese territory and then its invasion again in 1982, this time driving all the way to Beirut. UNIFIL found itself behind Israeli lines and limited to providing humanitarian assistance.

Once Israel finally withdrew in July 2000, "in full accordance with Security Council Resolutions 425 and 426," UNIFIL's challenges lingered. Mine clearance was an acute problem. Numerous minor violations of the line of withdrawal (the so-called Blue Line) continually took place on both sides. Renewed hostilities between Hezbollah, the primary Islamic party and militia in Lebanon, and Israel in 2006 led the council to expand UNIFIL's duties. Among other responsibilities, the peacekeeping operation was called on to accompany and support the Lebanese armed forces (LAF) as they deployed throughout the south of Lebanon, to help ensure humanitarian assistance to the civilian population, and to oversee the safe return of displaced persons. The LAF still had not secured the southern part of the country sufficiently by 2022 that would allow UNIFIL to withdraw. Moreover, the precarious state of the national government and the influx of Syrians fleeing their civil war argued for a continuing UN presence.

As late as 2022, more than ten thousand peacekeepers were serving in UNIFIL from forty-six countries. Interestingly, that number included peacekeepers from major nations, including China, France, and Germany. We noted earlier that early peacekeeping efforts never included troops from major powers. But with the changing duties of peacekeeping operations and the changed atmosphere of the post-Cold War era, UNIFIL came to represent an evolution in the composition of UN peacekeeping forces. Since its inception, the force has sustained more than 313 fatalities.

In its mandated lifetime, UNIFIL, like UNFICYP, bridged the eras of international politics that dominated the last half of the twentieth century. Children of the Cold War, both peacekeeping missions evolved in the post-Cold War era as politics at the United Nations and in the world shifted. As discussed below, the end of the Cold War brought a metamorphosis in peacekeeping—the introduction of "second-generation" missions, even nation-building—that made these earlier efforts in some ways relics of a time when the United Nations could not live up to its obligation to maintain peace and security in the world.

NATION-BUILDING

The 1990s saw the launching of almost three times as many peacekeeping missions as were initiated during the previous forty years. This growing number reflected increasing security crises and greater reliance on the United Nations to address domestic upheavals. The new missions were significantly different in their mandates and in their day-to-day operations, constituting what came to be known as *robust peacekeeping*, or **second-generation**

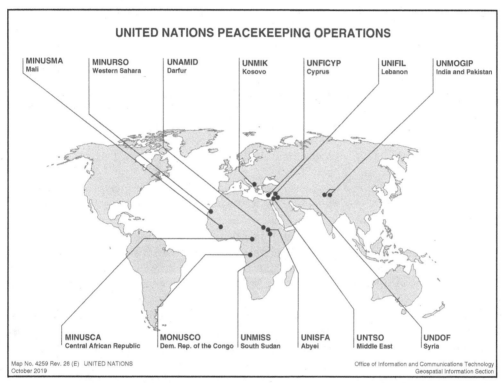

MINURSO	United Nations Mission for the Referendum in Western Sahara	established: 1991
MINUSCA	United Nations Multidimensional Integrated Stabilization Mission in the Central African Republic	established: 2014
MINUSMA	United Nations Multidimensional Integrated Stabilization Mission in Mali	established: 2013
MONUSCO	United Nations Organization Stabilization Mission in the Democratic Rep. of the Congo	established: 2010
UNAMID	African Union-United Nations Hybrid Operation in Darfur	established: 2007
UNDOF	United Nations Disengagement Observer Force	established: 1974
UNFICYP	United Nations Peacekeeping Force in Cyprus	established: 1964
UNIFIL	United Nations Interim Force in Lebanon	established: 1978
UNISFA	United Nations Interim Security Force for Abyei	established: 2011
UNMIK	United Nations Interim Administration Mission in Kosovo	established: 1999
UNMISS	United Nations Mission in South Sudan	established: 2011
UNMOGIP	United Nations Military Observer Group in India and Pakistan	established: 1949
UNTSO	United Nations Truce Supervision Organization	established: 1984

Figure 6.1 United Nations peacekeeping operations. (See Resource 3 (print) and Resource 8 (online) for acronyms.)

Source: Map No. 4259 Rev. 27(E), March 2021. Department of Field Support, Cartographic Section. Reproduced by permission of the United Nations.

peacekeeping. Only thirteen peacekeeping missions were authorized prior to 1988. From 1988 through 2000, more than thirty-six operations were undertaken. As we noted in Chapter 3, the financial burden of robust peacekeeping was one of the factors pressing the United Nations toward significant internal reform. In 1988, fewer than 10,000 peacekeepers were on duty, costing the organization $364 million annually.[4] By 1993, the number was approaching eighty thousand personnel, and the peacekeeping budget had risen to $4 billion. Other challenges included providing adequate training and equipping and transporting troops pledged by various nations (Figure 6.1).

UN Department of Peace Operations

To manage the escalating mission and size of UN peacekeeping, the Department of Peacekeeping Operations (DPKO) was created in 1992 as an integral part of the executive office of the UN Secretary-General, and was reorganized as the Department of Peace Operations (DPO) in 2019. DPO has administrative, managerial, planning, and preparation responsibilities for all peacekeeping missions. It is headed by the USG for peace operations and has divisions for distinct regions of the world.

Apparent peacekeeping successes in Angola and Namibia, which are described later in this chapter, encouraged confidence that the United Nations could intervene effectively in disintegrating states, not only to restore peace but also to undertake state-building. However, failures in Somalia (1993) and Rwanda (1994) induced strong pressures for an evaluation of DPKO operations and the UN peacekeeping function in general. The department struggled with inadequate resources, trying to meet new mandates that went far beyond the original idea of peacekeeping.

In March 2000, Secretary-General Annan appointed a panel of experts to study the new challenges faced by UN peacekeeping. He appointed former Algerian foreign minister Lakhdar Brahimi to chair the group. Brahimi had previously served as Annan's special representative to Afghanistan and would return to that role following the overthrow of the Taliban government in 2001. The Secretary-General asked Brahimi to prepare frank and specific recommendations that would narrow the gap between the UN's burgeoning peacekeeping responsibilities and its limited financial and organizational resources.

Brahimi's Panel on UN Peace Operations published a seventy-page report calling for dramatic reform of the UN's peacekeeping missions, its Department of Peacekeeping Operations, the process by which the Security Council and the Secretary-General implemented decisions to intervene in conflicts, and the funding mechanisms for peacekeeping efforts.[5] The panel made nearly sixty recommendations. One of the most significant was to establish for each mission an integrated task force combining political analysis, military operations, civilian police, electoral assistance, aid to refugees, transparent financing, logistics, public information, and streamlined procurement procedures. The panel also urged that definitions of *self-defense* be stretched to allow UN peacekeepers to take a more offensive posture in dangerous situations. It proposed that traditional UN "impartiality" between combatants in a conflict not be allowed to "amount to complicity with evil." According to the panel, the credibility of UN peacekeeping depended on being able "to distinguish victim from aggressor."[6] Coming on the eve of the Millennium Summit, the **Brahimi Report** recommendations elicited the most earnest and sustained discussion among the attending heads of government.

The panel recommended that to fund rapid deployment the Secretary-General be authorized to commit as much as $50 million in advance of a contemplated Security Council decision to undertake a new operation. The panel encouraged "a substantial increase in resources for Headquarters support of peacekeeping operations." Annan welcomed the panel's findings and requested that the General Assembly authorize the expenditure of $22 million to carry out all the recommendations. In January 2001, the assembly granted a first installment of $9.5 million.

Initial reaction to the report among developing states was cool; they feared the new rules for peacekeeping might amount to a form of UN "colonialism." Among the permanent Security Council members, this concern was initially reflected by the demur of Chinese president Jiang Zemin and Russian president Vladimir Putin. A vigorous public relations effort by Annan and Brahimi, combined with the promise of U.S. funding if the recommendations were accepted, ended the opposition. By the spring of 2001, most national leaders supported the activist peacekeeping vision of Secretary-General Annan and Ambassador Brahimi.

Importantly, at the time of the seventieth anniversary gathering of the UN General Assembly, the commitment to comprehensive peacekeeping was given a boost by major powers' authorization of their own troops to UN missions, breaking with the Cold War practice against major country participation. U.S. President Barack Obama convened a peacekeeping summit on the side of other official UN meetings going on in New York City in September 2015. More than fifty nations committed to provide an additional fifty thousand personnel to peacekeeping. The United States agreed to double its contribution of U.S. military officers. China said that it would assemble a standby force of eight thousand troops for peacekeeping and increase its financial contribution. Great Britain also raised the number of peacekeepers it would contribute.

Early Second-Generation Peacekeeping Missions

The conflicts brought to the United Nations after 1988 mainly involved domestic turmoil— that is, internal civil wars, several disputing the legitimacy of an existing government or assaulting ethnic, religious, and minority groups. Although these conflicts often affected, or potentially affected, international peace and security, they were outside the UN's original scope, which dealt typically with international disputes and interstate warfare. Consequently, UN intervention in the guise of peacekeeping necessarily involved the world organization in domestic administration, the provision of humanitarian assistance, and the reconstruction of civil society.

The new collection of activities now the responsibility of the UN operation was reminiscent of the old mandate system of the League of Nations, although state administration was now internationalized and the United Nations was becoming something equivalent to the League's mandatory power. This UN role produced a new generation of peacekeeping that challenged the bedrock international principle of national sovereignty. In so doing, it reinterpreted the UN Charter, which does not provide explicit authority for the United Nations to act contrary to the full sovereignty of a member state. Originally, UN intervention in a state's internal affairs was considered acceptable only with that government's permission. This premise seemed to follow the intent of the Charter language in Article 2, paragraph 7: "Nothing contained in the present Charter shall authorize the United Nations to intervene in matters which are essentially within the domestic jurisdiction of any state." However, the same paragraph contains a delicate caveat: "but this principle shall not prejudice the application of enforcement measures under Chapter VII." Furthermore, because at least one of the parties involved in these new disputes was likely a rebel movement, the United Nations (specifically the Security Council, which is authorized to act under Chapter VII of the Charter) found itself in nearly every case intervening without the approval of all parties to the dispute, which violated one of the "rules" of peacekeeping operations established in the earliest UN missions.

In these civil conflicts, peacekeepers became involved in **nation-building**, which can be defined as a purposeful effort "to install or construct the institutions of national government and civil society in a dysfunctional state."[7] They were often asked to protect refugees and guard the delivery of humanitarian aid, as well as to investigate and seek to prevent violations of the human rights of the populace. Once peacekeepers attempted to protect victims or segments of the population, the neutrality on which their actions had previously been based was compromised, and they could be perceived as parties to the conflict by at least one side. Efforts to protect civilians involved unprecedented cooperation of peacekeeping forces with specialized agencies and nongovernmental organizations. In addition, the new mandates often involved lengthy deployments that included not merely troops but also police officers and legal officials, economic advisers, and humanitarian workers.

Three early second-generation peacekeeping missions—in Namibia, Angola, and Cambodia—produced varied results but also provided models for later, more comprehensive operations.

Namibia

Namibia, known until 1968 as *South-West Africa*, became a colony of Germany in 1884. With Germany's defeat in World War I, the League of Nations categorized Namibia as a class "C" mandate administered by the Republic of South Africa. In 1946, the UN General Assembly encouraged all mandatory states to end their trusteeship agreements. South Africa refused to end its control. Despite a series of General Assembly resolutions adverse to South African supervision and legal proceedings in the International Court of Justice, the region remained under Pretoria's domination into the 1980s.

During the last twenty years of South African control, a UN-recognized rebel organization known as the South-West Africa People's Organization (SWAPO) emerged. As violence in the region escalated in the late 1970s, the Security Council passed Resolution 435 (1978), which called for Namibia's independence and for free elections based on universal suffrage. Cold War politics enabled South Africa to stall Namibian independence for more than a decade. However, by 1988, the high human and monetary costs of war and the changing relationship between the United States and the USSR led the parties to reach an agreement on a cease-fire, the withdrawal of foreign forces, and free elections in Namibia.

The Security Council designed the UN Transition Assistance Group (UNTAG) to assist with the independence process. UNTAG educated and registered voters, oversaw the 1989 elections for a constituent assembly, assisted in Namibian refugee repatriation, and confirmed that troops were confined to bases. UNTAG deployed 1,500 police monitors, 2,000 civilian administrators, and 4,650 military personnel. It declared the elections—in which 96 percent of eligible Namibians voted and SWAPO won a majority—to be free and fair. On March 21, 1990, Namibia achieved full independence and UNTAG left the country. Independent Namibia became a UN member in April 1990. With a total cost of $368 million, UNTAG was seen as a harbinger of a new and vital role for the United Nations.

Angola

The agreements on Namibia opened an important opportunity to realize peace in Angola as well. In 1991, the two major contenders for power, the MPLA (Movimento Popular de Libertação de Angola) and UNITA (União Nacional para a Independência Total de Angola) negotiated a set of peace accords that were intended to lead to national reconciliation and democratic elections. Elections were finally held in 1992, under UN observation;

however, UNITA's Jonas Savimbi alleged widespread electoral fraud and refused to accept the results, which clearly favored the MPLA over UNITA.

Between 1988 and 1999, the United Nations initiated three "verification" missions to the country and one observer mission (UN Observer Mission in Angola, or MONUA). MONUA, which commenced operations in mid-1997, had the mandate to verify the neutrality of the Angolan national police force, monitor the collection and destruction of weapons, and oversee the security of UNITA leaders. As the security situation deteriorated, the Security Council extended the mission several times, finally to February 1999. During the last week of 1998, rebel forces shot down two MONUA airplanes, killing more than twenty passengers and crew. When UN officials were denied access to the crash site, the Security Council ordered all UN workers out of the country. UN operations totaled costs of $1.5 billion and the loss of sixty staff members in a failed attempt to bring peace to the country. Subsequently, Jonas Savimbi died in combat with government forces in February 2002, effectively, if violently, ending the twenty-seven-year-old civil war. The two factions shortly thereafter reached a cease-fire. President and MPLA leader Jose Eduardo Dos Santos sponsored a new constitution in 2010. Elections in 2012 confirmed Dos Santos as the president. Angola assumed a nonpermanent seat on the UN Security Council for the 2015–2016 term.

Cambodia

Cambodia was left in internal chaos following the U.S. debacle in Vietnam. In 1975, the particularly vicious government of the Khmer Rouge, a Communist guerrilla movement led by Pol Pot, came to power. It carried out a massive genocide of whole classes in Cambodian society and imposed totalitarian rule, closing the country off from the outside world.[8] Vietnam invaded Cambodia in December 1978 and replaced the Pol Pot government with the Heng Samrin—Hun Sen regime. Three Cambodian factions opposing the Hun Sen government quickly emerged, including the remnants of the Khmer Rouge movement.

The United Nations was involved early in seeking a political settlement of the conflict that followed the installation of the Hun Sen government. While the General Assembly convened an international conference in 1981, a significant UN role became possible only in August 1990, when the Security Council's permanent members reached agreement, acceptable to the Cambodian parties, on a framework for a political settlement. The Security Council created the UN Transitional Authority in Cambodia (UNTAC) to impose the UN plan. UNTAC took on an unprecedented set of responsibilities. It managed daily administration of Cambodian foreign and defense policy, provided domestic government services, and stationed more than twenty thousand UN personnel in the country.

Elections took place in May 1993 under UNTAC supervision and were declared free and fair. Despite the elections and UN efforts, differences among the various Cambodian factions lingered. In 1997, Hun Sen executed a coup, removing his opponents from the power-sharing arrangement then in place. Intricate internal negotiations ensued, and in July 1998, again with international monitors present, another controversial election took place, won by Hun Sen.

The departure of UNTAC and the domination of Cambodian politics by the authoritarian Hun Sen government left Cambodia unstable and ill-equipped to come to grips with the reality of the one and a half million Cambodians who were executed or who died from starvation and disease during Khmer Rouge rule. Through further negotiations between Cambodia and the UN, a Khmer Rouge Tribunal (officially the Extraordinary Chambers in the Courts of Cambodia—ECCC) was established in 1997 to try senior leaders of the former regime and "those most responsible" for alleged violations of international law, including genocide, war crimes, and crimes against humanity.[9] The UN-Cambodia agreement called for both Cambodian and international judges to serve on the court and for the prosecution also to be conducted by both Cambodian and international personnel. The UN paid the lion's share of the court's budget. Following the conviction and incarceration for life of several Khmer Rouge leaders, the ECCC held its final public session in August 2021. After a quarter of a century of the Tribunal's existence, the Cambodian government showed little interest in further pursuing charged individuals still free from detention.

Results of Second-Generation Peacekeeping Missions

These early transitional peacekeeping missions, despite their checkered record of success, set the stage for several comprehensive nation-building operations from the 1990s into the twenty-first century. Faced with the "return of history" in Eastern Europe, the Middle East, and Africa, the great powers looked for multilateral mechanisms to maintain an uneasy peace among warring ethnic and religious communities and to help establish stable governments that could meet international standards for human rights and democracy.[10] Collective security was now recognized to include these domestic conditions, as well as refugee repatriation, humanitarian assistance, and the elimination of weapons of mass destruction. The new missions were all undertaken under the unique powers of the Security Council, which emerged as the "legitimizer"[11] for the practical operating definition of collective security in the new millennium.

Two particular conflicts in the 1990s tested the limits of what second-generation peacekeeping could achieve. In decaying Yugoslavia, the United Nations was faced with the disintegration of one of its founding members, accompanied by acts of brutality and bloodshed not seen in Europe since the end of World War II. The UN's inability to achieve a peaceful solution and its apparent ineffectiveness even to protect innocent civilians strengthened critics' arguments that the world body was not able to address the major conflicts of the current era. Likewise, in central Africa, the UN's inactivity was blamed for the scope of the genocide that ravaged Rwanda in 1994.

Former Yugoslavia

The state of Yugoslavia emerged after World War I out of Balkan territories of the former Ottoman and Austrian empires, bringing together a number of groups of Slavic ethnic peoples, each with its own desire for independent statehood. The new nation was the creation of the powers that drafted the 1919 Treaty of Versailles. Through most of its history, authoritarian governments forcibly united the country. When its Communist leader, Josep Broz Tito, died in 1980, Yugoslavia slowly began to unravel. Its disintegration accelerated in 1987 when Slobodan Milosevic became the leader of the Serbian ultranationalist movement. As Serb dominance of the federal government escalated, restive Yugoslav republics moved toward declarations of independence. Slovenia was the first to do so, followed by Croatia.[12]

Milosevic responded with force, first in Slovenia, then with **ethnic cleansing** in Serb-dominated parts of Croatia. Croats and Serbs had been bitter enemies in World War II. The Croatian Ustache militia had, with the help of the German army, rounded up Serbs and placed them in the Jasenovac concentration camp. This history served as the backdrop for the post-Cold War violence in which Serb military units "cleansed" areas of Croats, killing many and driving others into refugee status.

The Security Council imposed an arms embargo on Yugoslavia in September 1991. The Secretary-General then appointed a personal envoy, former U.S. secretary of state Cyrus Vance, to coordinate UN cooperation with European Union peace efforts, led by veteran British diplomat Lord Owen. The Vance-Owen Plan that materialized envisioned the cantonization of Bosnia, dividing the republic among Bosnian Muslim, Bosnian Serb, and Croatian communities. None of the parties was willing to accept the proposed subdivisions, and the mission failed.

Bosnia proved to be the battleground for the most brutal Balkan fighting and the most violent war crimes in Europe since World War II.[13] Bosnia and Herzegovina declared independence in March 1992 and became a member of the United Nations on May 22, 1992. In ethnically mixed Bosnia, Serb militias moved to drive out Muslims from areas that would then have a Serb majority. These militias, led by General Ratko Mladic, under the political leadership of Radovan Karadzic, killed Muslim men, women, and children; carried out a systematic campaign of rape and terror; and created death and detention centers. Images of these camps, displayed in the Western media, reminded the international community of Nazi concentration camps and produced demands for intervention.

Bosnian Muslim calls for stronger action were met largely with international indifference. A peacekeeping force, the UN Protection Force (UNPROFOR)—established by the Security Council in early 1992—sent to Yugoslavia proved ineffective. The Muslim populations moved from the countryside to UNPROFOR "protected areas," or safe havens, in Mostar, Gorazde, Srebrenica, and elsewhere, believing in the UN promise of protection, only to find the peacekeepers unable to fight off the Serb militias. At Srebrenica, Mladic's forces gathered up men and boys, marched them out of the town as UN peacekeepers were held hostage, and summarily executed the civilians in the surrounding fields.[14]

By 1994, a quarter-million people may have fallen to the war in the Balkans, and more than two and a half million had been displaced. The United Nations demonstrated, by its ineffectiveness, the limits of the institution in the new post-Cold War world. The "promise" that had appeared evident in the afterglow of the first Gulf War was dissipating. Although the old veto crisis on the Security Council that had persisted for forty years had receded, national interests among the five permanent members and a determined enemy in the hills of the Balkans made the United Nations a less attractive venue for resolving the conflict.

After a brutal mortar attack on the marketplace in Sarajevo, NATO, pressured by the American administration, bombed Serb positions around the capital in August 1995. Coupled with a successful Croatian offensive that reclaimed large territories held by the Serbs, the long-awaited NATO action forced Milosevic to the bargaining table. Invited by President Clinton to Dayton, Ohio, the leaders of Serbia, Croatia, and Bosnia hammered out an agreement, the **Dayton Peace Accords** (November 1995), ending the war and providing that the United Nations monitor the agreement through the Implementation Force (IFOR) made up of NATO troops, to be replaced later by a Stabilization Force (SFOR).

All parties agreed to establish a permanent cease-fire in Bosnia, repatriate refugees, and create a multiethnic state with a tripartite presidency and autonomous ethnic enclaves. Most important, the accords inserted NATO ground forces in support of a contemplated UN peacekeeping operation. Clinton committed twenty thousand U.S. troops to the multinational force, noting that unlike the UN forces, the new contingent would be heavily armed and ready "to respond immediately ... with overwhelming force ... to any violations"[15] of the peace agreement. Bosnia demonstrated the United States' unique position and role in contemporary international affairs. It also made clear the limitations of UN-sponsored solutions.

As NATO forces arrived in Bosnia, calls were made for them to search out, capture, and send to The Hague the Bosnian Serb leaders who had been charged with war crimes. In

1993, the Security Council had created the International Criminal Tribunal for the Former Yugoslavia (ICTY) as the first institution of international criminal prosecution since the end of the World War II. It was charged with indicting and trying suspected war criminals for crimes against humanity. The ICTY issued its first indictment on November 11, 1994, for Dragan Nikolic, a Bosnian Serb who was allegedly the commander of a small prison camp in eastern Bosnia. In October 2001, the parliament of the Bosnian Serb enclave approved the arrest of individuals under indictment by the international tribunal in The Hague. In July 2004, it directed its own government to hunt for the indicted individuals.[16]

The creation of the ICTY and the eventual indictment and trial of Slobodan Milosevic were the few bright highlights in the UN's performance during the Bosnian crisis. The United Nations was given a minor role in post-conflict Bosnia, and it received little cooperation from local ethnic leaders in pacifying and reconstructing the country. The Security Council established the UN Mission in Bosnia and Herzegovina (UNMIBH), but its limited responsibilities were to reform the local police and assess the Bosnian judicial system. Real power was placed in the hands of the High Representative, a post created directly by the Dayton Accords. The UN mission completed its job in 2002, turning over police oversight to a European Union police mission, but the High Representative continued the hard work of trying to create a multiethnic and peaceful state among highly distrustful Serb, Muslim, and Croat communities.

Rwanda

In Yugoslavia, the United Nations responded ineffectively and late to rising ethnic tensions, allowing Milosevic's forces to carry out horrendous human rights violations that led to the deaths of hundreds of thousands of people. The UN failure in Rwanda at approximately the same time as the Balkan debacle may have been even more regrettable, in that the UN actions actually contributed to the human suffering and death in that African nation.[17] When ethnic tensions rose dramatically in Rwanda in 1994, Security Council members, particularly the United States, cautioned against UN intervention. The genocide of nearly eight hundred thousand ethnic Tutsis ensued, and Rwandans (both Tutsi and Hutu) fled the country into makeshift refugee camps in the Congo and other surrounding states.

Fighting between the Hutu majority government of Rwanda and Tutsi rebels commenced in 1990. Several cease-fire agreements were reached; the most important was the Arusha Agreement in 1992. To monitor the cease-fire and assist in the creation of a transitional government, the Security Council created UNAMIR—the UN Assistance Mission for Rwanda. Belgian and Bangladeshi forces—the only contingents offered by the world community—were stationed in Kigali, the nation's capital.

The crisis that sparked the planned genocide of Tutsis by Hutu militia occurred in April 1994 when the presidents of Rwanda and Burundi were killed in a plane crash arriving at Kigali airport. Among those killed in the succeeding slaughter were the Rwandan prime minister, several cabinet members, and Belgian peacekeepers protecting the government officials. The Security Council's immediate response was to reduce UNAMIR's presence from more than 2,500 peacekeepers to 270. Another six months would pass before UN forces in sufficient numbers were introduced into the maelstrom to secure an end to the fighting and restore stability. In the meantime, nearly three and a half million people were killed, and two million fled to refugee camps outside Rwanda.

In April 1998, Secretary-General Annan traveled to Rwanda. Before that country's parliament, he sought to repair an abiding ill will by acknowledging the UN's delinquency in responding to the horrific Tutsi massacre. A year later, the Secretary-General appointed an independent commission to look into the UN actions at the time of the Rwandan disaster. The inquiry found that "the failure by the United Nations to prevent, and subsequently, to stop the genocide in Rwanda was a failure by the United Nations System as a whole."[18] It cited a lack of resources and political will on the part of the major powers on the Security Council as contributory factors to the high death toll. It noted that the Nigerian president rightly assessed the situation when he suggested that the council "risked becoming the laughing stock of the world"[19] if it did not act. The Secretary-General was also criticized: the commission asserted that "he could have done more."[20]

Later Nation-Building Missions

The bitter peacekeeping experience in Bosnia and Rwanda did not dissuade the UN from attempting far-reaching democratic nation-building missions in the new century. A product of the Brahimi Report recommendations, of Secretary-General Annan's commitment to "personal" sovereignty in opposition to the state's sovereignty where the citizen's well-being and human rights are threatened, and of the growing UN commitment to democracy promotion in conflict-riven states, nation-building strategies were developed in many different settings.

East Timor/Timor-Leste

Indonesian forces occupied East Timor when Portuguese colonial rule ended in the 1970s. East Timorese regularly sought UN assistance in their push for independence. A 1999 referendum overwhelmingly endorsed separation, and a coalition of forces led by Australia entered the country to ensure the wishes of the local population. Following the transfer of power to a newly elected "Timor-Leste" government in May 2002, violence did not abate. Gang activity, Indonesian-backed raids from West Timor, grinding poverty, and corruption all contributed to a weak transitional democracy. The crisis reached a crescendo in 2006. It was at that point that a coalition of Timorese civil society organizations (CSOs) and international NGOs demanded renewed UN intervention to establish security.

The UN responded by creating UNMIT (United Nations Mission in Timor-Leste) with a mandate to "provide support to the national police and assist in conducting a comprehensive review of the role and needs of the security sector; [and] assist in further strengthening the national capacity for the monitoring, promotion and protection of human rights."[21] UNMIT was further enhanced in 2008 in response to a failed assassination attempt on the lives of Timor-Leste's president and prime minister.

In late 2010, two thousand UN personnel from more than thirty nations remained in the country. Their task, as required by Security Council Resolution 1704 (2006), was to support the government in "consolidating stability, enhancing a culture of democratic governance, and facilitating political dialogue among Timorese stakeholders, in their efforts to bring about a process of national reconciliation and to foster social cohesion." Producing social cohesion proved the most difficult to resolve. Democratic society requires some common thread of citizenship to override religious, ethnic, racial, and other "accidental" divisions in society. The government and UNMIT signed a Joint Transition Plan to guide planning and to transition required governmental tasks from the nation-building operation to the national government. This was successfully completed by the end of 2012 and the UN mission was closed down.

Photo 6.1 Members of the United Nations transitional administration in East Timor (UNTAET), accompanied by a group of local children as they conduct a security patrol.

Source: UN/DPI Photo/Eskinder Debebe. Reproduced by permission of the United Nations.

Kosovo

Unfortunately, the wave of self-determination politics that swept Eastern and Central Europe in the 1990s proved a formula corrosive to democratic stability in Kosovo, a province of Serbia appreciably populated by ethnic Albanians. Ethnic hostility reached a state of war in 1999 between the central Serbian government (representing the Orthodox Christians of Serbia) and the Albanian majority (overwhelmingly Sunni Muslims). Under the umbrella of a peace agreement negotiated between the Serbs and NATO/European Union/United Nations negotiators, international military and civilian forces moved into Kosovo to protect the population and to administer the province, which nonetheless remained ostensibly part of sovereign Serbia.

Security Council Resolution 1244 (June 1999) authorized the UN Interim Administration in Kosovo (UNMIK) to carry out unprecedented powers of governance and administration, providing essential services, repatriating one million refugees, and facilitating a political process that would lead to autonomy and self-governance. These duties were to be conducted within a province of a sovereign state that had not requested, in fact had battled, foreign intervention. Neither Kosovars nor the central government was left with determining the destiny of the territory.

In March 2008, the Kosovo Assembly unilaterally declared independence for the province. While an International Court of Justice judgment found that autonomy decision to be consistent with international law, the declaration did not remove UNMIK or the other international organizations operating in Kosovo. The declaration of independence only complicated the situation by inflaming the passions of the large Serbian population in the northern part of the province. The hope for social peace in Kosovo that eluded the international community was based on the same expectation as in Timor-Leste; that is, that a vibrant civil society could be formed. However, Kosovo suffered from there being no tradition of civil society organizations (CSOs) playing a role in Yugoslav or Serbian politics.

Upon intervening, several EU nations collaborated to address the inter-ethnic divide in Kosovo through civil society action. After 2002, when the Kosovo Assembly came into being, the European Centre for Minority Issues (ECMI) mobilized civil society activists, young political party members, and influential Kosovars to lobby the Assembly on such issues as equal access to justice, education, economic policy, health, and social services. The Organization for Security and Cooperation in Europe (OSCE), UN Educational, Scientific and Cultural Organization (UNESCO), and the European Union Rule of Law Mission in Kosovo (EULEX) also engaged with the Kosovo community. The World Bank established a Civil Society Fund to finance the development of local organizations. Meantime, individual states initiated programs, the largest being those administered by the U.S. Agency for International Development (USAID). UNMIK served as the meta-state and responded not to the local population but to the administrative structure at UN Headquarters in New York City, and specifically to the UN Secretary-General.[22] Since Kosovo's declaration of independence, UNMIK's security responsibilities passed to the Kosovo government and EULEX took up its remaining civil administration tasks. Yet, given recurrent violence, the Security Council remained reticent as late as 2022 to end the mission.

Afghanistan

The Security Council created the United Nations Assistance Mission in Afghanistan (UNAMA) following the U.S.-led invasion of Afghanistan. The United States and the Afghan Northern alliance toppled the Taliban government in Kabul in 2001 and attacked installations of the al-Qaeda terrorist network. The council's decision amounted to a tacit approval of the U.S. action and an internationalization of the post-war political and economic reconstruction of Afghanistan.

Secretary-General Annan sent the reliable Lahkdar Brahimi as his special representative, with a mandate to coordinate all UN activities in the country and to work with indigenous political groups and the occupying forces to establish a viable working democracy in Afghanistan. UNAMA also worked with the International Security Assistance Force (ISAF), the multinational military operation in the country put in place after the invasion. In this regard, the operation reflected the UN's growing willingness to work closely with regional and military organizations.

Attempting to "rebuild" Afghanistan, the United Nations sponsored the Bonn Conference in 2002 to put in place a provisional government and to draft a constitution, approved in 2004, effectively providing an international mandate for nation-building. Meanwhile, the international Tokyo Conference raised pledges of economic assistance. UNAMA worked to implement the will that emerged from these gatherings. It also coordinated much of the NGO assistance in the country, addressed human rights issues left by the previous fundamentalist regime, and created civil society institutions that were meant to undergird democracy and the rule of law.

A significant international nongovernmental organization presence already existed in the country prior to the events of 2001. An impoverished nation afflicted by invasion and internal conflict for more than two decades, Afghanistan was the venue for the activities of humanitarian organizations and UN specialized agencies. As early as 1991, the Afghan NGO Coordination Bureau (ANCB) was created to harmonize myriad international initiatives among the engaged INGOs and IGOs, and with the Afghan government and civil society.

After the overthrow of Taliban rule, Afghanistan became a test case for how a large number of INGOs could work alongside an international military operation and could turn non-state actor activity in cooperation with international organizations to state-building tasks. There was a quick increase in the number and types of private organizations that opened operations in the country. By 2006, more than 1,000 INGOs and domestic NGOs were attempting to work together to build the new state.[23] It was sometimes difficult to dissociate in Afghan minds local CSOs from both the INGO and international organization operatives. Foreign governments and international organizations contracted with INGOs to encourage democracy, conduct development, and promote human rights in Afghanistan. For example, USAID, the World Bank, European Commission, and Asian Development Bank all let contracts to private groups to reconstruct the Afghan public health system with the goal of using the new system to support state-building.

Much as was the case in Kosovo, civil society construction and participatory politics in Afghanistan were primary goals of UNAMA and other international agencies. As the United Nations celebrated its seventieth anniversary in 2015, the "UN family" of more than twenty agencies working in Afghanistan included among others the International Labour Organization, the Office of the High Commissioner for Human Rights, UN Women, the World Health Organization, the World Food Programme, the World Bank, the UN Children's Fund, and the UN Office on Drugs and Crime.

Yet, the governmental structures, economic architecture, and social programs put in place by the UN and the international community over twenty years quickly collapsed when the United States and its military allies withdrew from Afghanistan in August 2021 and the Taliban suddenly reclaimed power. Faced with a downward spiral in the Afghan economy, renewed threats to the human rights of girls and women, the specter of starvation and new refugee flows, the Security Council renewed UNAMA's mandate, calling upon it to coordinate whatever international humanitarian assistance could be practically introduced in Afghanistan.

Peacebuilding

Second-generation peacekeeping and nation-building, although far more intrusive than earlier UN operations, are implicit acknowledgments that much more is required than simply restoring peace if the world community wants to ensure that a fissured domestic society will not fall back into a state of anarchy and violence. Yet, the UN Charter provides no guidelines or directives on how to prevent a return to war. Even in a promising new era, the UN's options remain limited with regard to ending conflict or preventing the outbreak of war. Its dependence on subcontracting the use of force confirms this assessment.

The United Nations has attempted to reduce the chances of regression to the conditions that brought on conflict in the first place by creating "peacebuilding" and political support offices, not only where peacekeeping missions are under way, but also in states and regions where a likely threat of violent instability exists. In his 2003 report to the General Assembly, Secretary-General Annan noted that "even when apparently successful in repairing war-torn States, the international community can ill-afford to declare 'victory' prematurely."[24] Usually, these offices are headed by the special representative of the secretary-general (SRSG), who will normally head the peacekeeping operation as well. By the twenty-first century, more than four dozen peacebuilding, political, nation-building, and second-generation peacekeeping operations had been undertaken. They could be found on every populated continent except North America. (See Resource 8 on the Routledge eResources webpage for a full list of these operations; Figure 6.2.)

ONGOING POLITICAL AND PEACEBUILDING MISSIONS

BINUH — Haiti
UNOWAS — West Africa and the Sahel
UNSMIL — Libya
UNSCO — Middle East
UNSCOL — Lebanon
UNRCCA — Central Asia

UN Verification Mission in Colombia — Colombia
UNIOGBIS — Guinea-Bissau
UNOCA — Central Africa
UNSOM — Somalia
UNAMI — Iraq
UNAMA — Afghanistan

Map No. 4147 Rev. 48(E)   UNITED NATIONS
October 2019

Office of Information and Communications Technology
Geospatial Information Section

BINUH	United Nations Integrated Office in Haiti	established: 2019
UNAMA	United Nations Assistance Mission in Afghanistan	established: 2002
UNAMI	United Nations Assistance Mission for Iraq	established: 2003
UNIOGBIS	United Nations Integrated Peacebuilding Office in Guinea-Bissau	established: 2010
UNOCA	United Nations Regional Office for Central Africa	established: 2011
UNOWAS	United Nations Office for West Africa and the Sahel	established: 2016
UNRCCA	United Nations Regional Centre for Preventive Diplomacy for Central Asia	established: 2007
UNSCO	Office of the United Nations Special Coordinator for the Middle East Peace Process	established: 1999
UNSCOL	Office of the United Nations Special Coordinator for Lebanon	established: 2007
UNSMIL	United Nations Support Mission in Libya	established: 2011
UNSOM	United Nations Assistance Mission in Somalia	established: 2013
	United Nations Verification Mission in Colombia	established: 2017

Figure 6.2 Ongoing political and peacebuilding missions. (See Resource 3 (print) and Resource 8 (online) for acronyms.)

Source: Map No. 4147 Rev. 49(E), March 2021. Department of Field Support, Cartographic Section. Reproduced by permission of the United Nations.

Often the political and peacebuilding offices are in distant corners of the globe that have gained little world attention but could straightaway find themselves on the front pages of the world's press with the outbreak of internal violence. Bougainville is a fair example. An island in the southwestern Pacific Ocean, Bougainville is a province of Papua New Guinea. A former French, then German, then Australian colony, it was merged with Papua New Guinea against much of the local population's wishes. By the late 1980s, separatists had formed the Bougainville Revolutionary Army and were attacking the central government's defense forces and non-Bougainvillean economic interests on the island. Meanwhile, anti-independence Bougainvilleans formed their own army to attack the rebels, which led to a three-way battle and the general destruction of life in Bougainville, resulting in more than fifteen thousand deaths. In 1989, the UN Secretary-General opened the UN Political Office in Bougainville (UNPOB) with a mandate to encourage a peace process, to help implement agreements reached between the warring groups, to restore services and the economy in Bougainville, and to achieve an agreement among the groups on holding elections under a new constitution. The UN operation contributed to the signing of several peace agreements and the imposition of a regional peace-monitoring group including personnel from Fiji, New Zealand, Australia, and Vanuatu. UNPOB and an observer mission created by the Security Council directed the disposal of weapons used in prior conflicts, which diminished the chances of a revival of open warfare. On June 15, 2005, Bougainville inaugurated a new, autonomous government.

Political and peacebuilding offices similar to UNPOB were established in Côte d'Ivoire, Angola, Burundi, and the Great Lakes Region on the African continent. Elsewhere, they could be found in the Palestinian territories, Haiti, and Tajikistan. The Palestinian mission (UNSCO) initially established in 1994 by the Secretary-General emerged from events put in train by the 1993 Oslo Accords between Israel and the Palestine Liberation Organization. It was meant to facilitate the peace process. But, as the prospects of peace receded, UNSCO, as a field mission of the UN Department of Political and Peacebuilding Affairs, by 2022 had become solely the coordinating agency for the humanitarian and development activities of more than twenty UN agencies, funds and programmes for the Palestinians.

Political and peacebuilding operations are part of a sliding scale of UN involvement. In some cases, such as Bougainville, they can lead to the apparent restoration of a legitimate government and the resolution of internal conflicts, which allows the United Nations to withdraw its mission. However, if the political office is unsuccessful, the Security Council must consider increasing direct UN involvement. We will see this pattern playing out in the specific cases described as we proceed with this chapter.

The Promotion of Holistic Democracy

The failed state presents the twenty-first century with one of its more consequential threats to global security. For three decades, major international organizations, led by the United Nations, have attempted to address this threat through direct intervention and the promotion of democratic nation-building. The effort has extended from Namibia and Angola to Timor-Leste, Cambodia, Kosovo, Bosnia, Afghanistan, Somalia, Haiti, Rwanda, Liberia, South Sudan, and Libya, among other hot spots. Increasingly, these missions were premised on a democratic template that went well beyond traditional Western philosophical traditions. A thickened definition of democracy emerged out of neo-Kantian roots that contemplated democracy as a civil order combining political arrangements, economic development, human rights protection, gender sensitivity, civil society empowerment, and the protection of diverse cultures.

In 2009, UN Secretary-General Ban Ki-moon spelled out this conception of democracy in his notable *"Guidance Note on Democracy."*[25] Secretary Ban's framework accepted the "internationally agreed normative content" of the international democratization project as it had emerged over the post-Cold War era, and asserted that the world organization "advocated a concept of democracy that is holistic." ***Holistic democracy promotion*** has become the strategy not only of the UN but also of the EU, the Organization for Economic Cooperation and Development, the Association of East Asian Nations, the African Union (AU), other regional organizations, and regional development banks.

The "Responsibility to Protect" doctrine that the 2005 World Summit ratified reinforces the commitment to holistic democracy. It requires intervention in the domestic affairs of states not just to bar immediate threats to individuals' personal survival, but also on behalf of perceived legitimate ends: security, human rights, democracy, and development.

The establishment of R2P, according to Secretary-General Ban Ki-moon, "affirmed the role of the international community in assisting States to protect their populations from these crimes, including by assisting those which are under stress, before crises and conflicts break out."[26] He made clear in his 2012 report on the topic to both the Security Council and the General Assembly that "one should not draw too sharp a distinction between prevention and response." In his view, peacekeeping and nation-building built on internationally sponsored inclusive democratic politics are critical components of the R2P principle.[27] He cited as success stories Sierra Leone, Côte d'Ivoire, Guinea, and Tunisia. And in a case like South Sudan, where conflict resumed despite the international community's best efforts, he argued that the UN should have used greater "incentives and pressure" to ensure the "non-violent management of political tensions." Under the umbrella of the Responsibility to Protect, IGOs and international nongovernmental organizations regularly engage in holistic democracy promotion through funding projects, state-building dedicated to democratic politics, and the delegitimization of state leaders and policies that violate these normative goals.

Africa

Collective security is a legacy of great European wars, both those fought on the continent in the eighteenth, nineteenth, and twentieth centuries and those fought around the world by European powers. Europe has been a dangerous continent ever since the nation-state system was born. In the twentieth century alone, the continent absorbed the most violent and deadly wars in history. At the end of World War II, in response to conflict, instability, and colonialism, the great powers sought a new formula for peace through the concept of collective security established first in the League of Nations.

The irony in the new millennium is that Europe remained generally at peace until the intervention of Russia in Ukraine in 2014 and its threats to that country in 2022, and the devices created more than half a century ago to keep the peace, now implemented by the United Nations, are mostly directed elsewhere. As the many examples presented in this chapter demonstrate, those efforts have been directed particularly toward Asia and Africa. The problems of grinding poverty, disease, sectarian strife in postcolonial multiethnic states, artificial borders imposed by colonial powers, religious division, and authoritarianism have made sub-Saharan Africa a focal point of world conflict and will probably keep it in upheaval for years to come. Many UN second-generation peacekeeping, nation-building, and peacebuilding operations have been established in Africa in hopes of ameliorating human suffering and ensuring that Africa does not become the new "tinderbox" for wider conflagration.

Somalia

In December 1992, Security Council members found the instability in Somalia to be a threat to international peace and authorized intervention under U.S. leadership. After long-time dictator Siad Barre was deposed in 1991, civil war erupted between Somalia's different clans and factions. In addition to attacking each other, private armies harassed UN and NGO relief efforts. To help ease the suffering of the population, the Security Council established the first UN Operation in Somalia (UNOSOM I) in April 1992. The council hoped that the warring factions would respect the UN peacekeepers as they attempted to deliver critical food and humanitarian assistance, but even food warehouses in the capital, Mogadishu, came under regular attack. In the fall, Secretary-General Boutros-Ghali wrote to President George H. W. Bush, asking for U.S. military assistance. The president agreed to act and requested a Security Council resolution authorizing U.S. military intervention. On December 3, the council passed Resolution 794, invoking Chapter VII and accepting the offer "by a member state" to put together an international coalition (UNITAF, or Unified Task Force) to protect the distribution of humanitarian supplies. For the first time, the United Nations had expressly subcontracted a peacekeeping operation.

Although the deployment of UNITAF did much to pacify the situation and make humanitarian assistance by the United Nations and other groups possible, the needed "secure environment" could not be established. Somalia remained without a functioning and effective central government. In early 1993, the Security Council set up UNOSOM II. Its mandate included disarming the warring factions, demining, assisting in the reconstruction of the Somali economy and political institutions, repatriating refugees, and building the social infrastructure of the country. UNOSOM II undertook no less than the salvation of a "failed" state. The Security Council committed twenty-eight thousand military and police personnel to the task.

UNOSOM II left in early March 1995, having sustained 147 casualties during its mission, at a cost of $1.6 billion. The experience in Somalia demonstrated the limits of robust peacekeeping. It could not succeed where indigenous clans sought to undermine national reconciliation. Well through the first quarter of the twenty-first century, the Somali transitional government faced intrastate instability and large humanitarian needs. In 2006, the government was forced to withdraw from the capital of Mogadishu by the rebel group known as the Islamic Courts Union (ICU). Responding to the ICU threat, the African Union put its own peacekeeping operation in the country, albeit with the formal approval of the UN Security Council. Other terrorist groups such as the radical Islamic organization known as al-Shabaab carried out attacks on villages and urban communities.

The departure of UNOSOM II did not end the UN's political involvement. In February 2000, the United Nations facilitated a peace conference in Djibouti that led to the election of a new Somali president and national assembly and to the creation of a transitional national government in August. The UN moved from peacekeeping to UN peacebuilding. Specialized agencies and programmes increased their presence to address humanitarian needs. Among them were the Food and Agriculture Organization; the UN Development Programme; the UN Educational, Scientific and Cultural Organization (UNESCO); the UN High Commissioner for Refugees; the UN Children's Fund; the UN Development Fund for Women (now part of UN Women); the World Health Organization; and the World Food Programme.

While a declaration of principles—known as the *Eldoret Declaration*—among the most important clan leaders and the transitional national government about the restoration of peace in Mogadishu was achieved early in the century, it was regularly undermined by violent outbreaks in the cities of Somalia, many of them fueled by the flow of illegal weapons and ammunition into the country. On December 16, 2003, the Security Council, acting under Chapter VII, unanimously established a monitoring group to investigate violations of the mandatory arms embargo in Somalia. The council threatened to impose "possible future measures" against states and groups that violated the embargo.

Ethiopian troops intervened in Somalia in 2006 to drive the Islamic Courts Union from power and Kenya invaded several years later to tamp down the terrorist threat. The United Nations continued an assistance mission well into 2022 with the goals of enhancing the rule of law, promoting human rights, and coordinating international assistance, but the world body was eclipsed by national foreign policies that sought to eliminate the threats from radical groups and general instability in the country. In 2017, the United States expanded its counterterrorism capabilities in the country, while remnants and splinter groups from the defeated ICU turned to suicide bombings and attacks on civilians, particularly in the southern part of the country.

Democratic Republic of the Congo

The second period of UN involvement in the Congo was precipitated by the 1994 Rwandan genocide and the consequent exodus of one million primarily Hutu ethnic refugees into temporary camps in eastern Congo (then called *Zaire*). These camps became staging grounds from which Hutu extremists attacked Rwanda and Uganda. Zaire's long-time dictator, Mobutu Sese Seko, was unable to control the camps and faced rebel movements in eastern Zaire. With the help of outside forces, Laurent Kabila's Alliance of Democratic Forces for the Liberation of Congo (ADFL) overthrew President Mobutu in May 1997. In the process, ADFL forces attacked the refugee camps and killed more than two hundred thousand people.

Kabila proved to be no more popular than his predecessor. His government faced opposition from neighboring countries that, in turn, aided anti-Kabila rebel groups. Past allies of Kabila, Rwanda and Uganda, were disappointed that the new president had not secured the borders of eastern Congo. Angola, Zimbabwe, and Namibia sent troops to aid Kabila, and Chad and Sudan sent military advisers, which created Africa's "first war." In Lusaka, Zambia, on July 10, 1999, the Democratic Republic of the Congo (DRC), Angola, Namibia, Rwanda, Uganda, and Zimbabwe, at the urging of the Security Council and with the help a Special Envoy from the Secretary-General, signed the **Lusaka Agreement**, which imposed a cease-fire and called for the disarmament of Congolese militias. In response, the council created the UN Organization Mission in the DRC (MONUC), later replaced by MONUSCO (the United Nations Organization Stabilization Mission in the Democratic Republic of the Congo). The council initially authorized a mission force of 5,537 military personnel, but that had grown to more than 14,000 troops by 2022 and 230 of its personnel had been killed. In a departure from past peacekeeping operations, the council decided in 2014 to establish an "intervention brigade," consisting of three infantry battalions, one artillery, and one special force and reconnaissance company to operate under direct command of the MONUSCO Force Commander, with the responsibility of neutralizing armed groups and contributing to civilian security in the eastern section of the country. While the council specifically said the intervention brigade should not be seen as a precedent, the creation of a war-fighting unit on behalf of the central government was clearly in line with the recommendations of the earlier Brahimi Report.

The United Nations used its military forces to combat ethnic rebel groups, particularly in the eastern part of the country. The city of Bunia in the Ituri District and Goma, a city of more than one million people, came regularly under attack by the rebel group known as M23, reportedly supported by Rwanda. As many as fifty thousand civilians may have lost their lives during the fighting in the region. It was also the site of ethnic massacres; one of the most brutal reported in mid-January 2004, when a local militia rounded up men and boys in the village of Gobi, just north of Bunia. At least one hundred were systematically executed. In Bunia itself, foreigners and UN forces were regularly attacked. Goma was seized by the rebels in November 2021.

Sixty years earlier, a UN peacekeeping mission to the Congo had also tried to expand its mandate beyond simply supervising a cease-fire to include nation-building in the midst of a civil war. It had proved a disaster both for the Congo and for the UN's peacekeeping role in the world. MONUSCO's efforts test how much world affairs has changed in the intervening period, as well as the limits of the new robust peacekeeping.

Photo 6.2 UN Secretary-General Ban Ki-moon on his way to visit Mungote IDP (Internally Displaced Persons) Camp, in the Democratic Republic of the Congo.

Source: UN Photo/Eskinder Debebe. Reproduced by permission of the United Nations.

Sierra Leone and Liberia

Situated on the west coast of Africa, between Guinea and Liberia, Sierra Leone had gone relatively unnoticed in the three decades following its independence from Great Britain in 1961. It came to the public's attention because of a ruinous civil war in 1991. The country had suffered under the one-party dictatorship of Siaka Stevens and his successor, Joseph Momoh. The regime was a classic example of inept economic stewardship and political repression on the African continent. By the close of the 1980s, the International Monetary Fund (IMF) had declared Sierra Leone in a state of economic emergency and ineligible for further IMF lending.

The country was further weakened in 1991 when armed rebels attacked government forces, initiating the civil war that ravaged Sierra Leone and destabilized neighboring Liberia. The rebels, known as the Revolutionary United Front (RUF), were led by Foday Sankoh and supported by Liberian president Charles Taylor. As in the case of other African conflicts, such as in Angola, the RUF capitalized on Sierra Leone's vast resources of alluvial diamonds to fund its activities.

In 1992, dissatisfied members of the Sierra Leone army carried out a coup. Although it initially enjoyed popular support, within two years the people were demanding a return to civilian government. In 1995, UN Secretary-General Boutros-Ghali appointed Berhanu Dinka as his special envoy to aid negotiations that would lead to democratic elections. Mr. Dinka worked closely with both the Organization of African Unity (OAU—renamed the African Union, or AU, in 2001) and the Economic Community of West African States (ECOWAS) to facilitate a return to civilian rule. Elections took place in 1996, and Ahmed Tejan Kabbah was elected the president. However, in the spring of 1997, this time in collaboration with the RUF, the military ousted the Kabbah government.

In response to the coup, the UN Security Council imposed an arms and oil embargo. It authorized ECOWAS to administer the sanctions through its own peacekeeping force, comprising mostly Nigerian troops. The council's decision to work with ECOWAS reflected the new UN premise of regionalizing peacekeeping responsibilities: collective security need not be imposed directly from UN headquarters but could be approached by **subcontracting** international authority to a regional organization. The council also pursued this strategy in Bosnia and Herzegovina, where the UN operation worked closely with NATO, and in Georgia, where the corresponding organizations were the OSCE and the Commonwealth of Independent States (CIS).

President Kabbah successfully regained power in the spring of 1998, and in June the Security Council authorized the UN Observer Mission in Sierra Leone (UNOMSIL) to encourage disarmament, to report on human rights violations, and to restructure Sierra Leone's security forces. Subsequently, a joint UN-ECOWAS-Sierra Leone government coordination mechanism was established for conflict management in Sierra Leone.

The RUF and the government of Sierra Leone reached a comprehensive peace accord (known as the **Lomé Agreement**) in July 1999. It established the legal provisions for the RUF to become a political party in Sierra Leone and for its members to hold important cabinet positions within the government. UNOMSIL was replaced by the UN Assistance Mission in Sierra Leone (UNAMSIL), which included the deployment of 11,500 armed forces (with a maximum authorization of 17,500). Its primary purpose was to assist the central government in restoring peace and security. During the war, nearly 700,000 people were displaced, 75,000 died, and thousands were purposefully maimed through brutal amputations conducted by the RUF.

Peace and reconciliation seemed to be within reach with the Lomé Agreement; however, the RUF failed to comply with the terms of the agreement, and intermittent fighting and terrorist acts were still too common as the century turned. Parts of Sierra Leone continued to be under rebel control. In June 2000, to address the perceived illegal intervention in Sierra Leonean affairs by the Taylor government of Liberia, as well as the human rights abuses perpetrated by the RUF, President Kabbah asked Secretary-General Kofi Annan to establish a tribunal to try suspected war criminals. He hoped for an international tribunal like the tribunals established for Rwanda and the former Yugoslavia. In January 2002, the Special Court for Sierra Leone came into being, featuring a mixed composition of international and Sierra Leonean jurists. This special court is discussed in more detail in Chapter 7. The court indicted, among other people, Liberia's Charles Taylor for his support of the RUF.

The interconnections between Sierra Leone and Liberia at the turn of the century ran deeper than simply Taylor's involvement in Sierra Leone's civil war. At times, the future stability of all West African nations appeared to depend on how these two countries' troubled histories, in tandem, would evolve. For this reason, the Economic Community of West African States took the lead in promoting the peace process, working closely with the United Nations, even introducing regional troops into both states. In the case of Liberia, ECOWAS first introduced military observers in 1990. It also negotiated the first peace agreement in the ongoing civil war in 1993, which led to the introduction of the UN Observer Mission in Liberia (UNOMIL). This UN peacekeeping operation was the first to be undertaken in cooperation with a peacekeeping mission already established by another organization.

UNOMIL and ECOWAS worked together to implement a 1993 peace agreement, which ultimately brought Charles Taylor to power. As the Taylor regime became increasingly oppressive and human rights abuses mounted, new rebel movements emerged. Both sides funded their military operations with the illegal sales of "conflict diamonds." The escalating bloodshed took as many as one hundred thousand civilian lives.

In July 2003, the Security Council created UNMIL (UN Mission in Liberia), authorizing a force of fifteen thousand troops. President Taylor was also under broad international pressure to resign, which he did on August 11. ECOWAS peacekeepers serving in Liberia were "rehatted" as UN peacekeepers in October. These forces came from eight West African countries. Additional personnel were soon added from other African states and from all the permanent Security Council members except Russia. Peacekeepers were deployed out of the capital of Monrovia to disparate parts of the country. Their primary task was to disarm the warring groups. Politically, the hope was that UNMIL could help the new transitional government restore normal services and civil society.

The first free and fair elections in Liberian history occurred in 2005. The electorate chose Ellen Johnson Sirleaf as president, the first female ever to be elected president in any African country. President Sirleaf was reelected in the peaceful and fair election of 2011 (and awarded the Nobel Peace Prize jointly with two others that same year for her nonviolent work on behalf of women's safety and their right to full participation in peace-building). Prior to that, she had requested the extradition of Charles Taylor, who was turned over for trial in The Hague. With Sirleaf's election, UNMIL's mission changed but did not end until July 2016, when peacekeeping duties were turned over to the Liberian government. UNMIL and the peacekeeping operation in Sierra Leone were both lauded as among the most successful missions ever launched by the United Nations.

The Liberian people faced a different kind of threat soon after the restoration of civilian government. It was to be confronted with a major health crisis. An epidemic of Ebola virus disease broke out in Guinea in December 2013 and spread quickly to Sierra Leone and Liberia. The epidemic caused significant loss of life in northwest Africa. On September 18, 2014, the Security Council declared the outbreak a "threat to international peace and security," and unanimously adopted Resolution 2177. The resolution brought into being the UN Mission for Ebola Emergency Response (UNMEER). UNMEER was immediately deployed to Guinea, Liberia, and Sierra Leone, as well as to Ghana, where it established mission headquarters. It was tasked to coordinate all relevant UN actors and to work with governments and the African Union and the Economic Community of West African States, in order to ensure a rapid and effective response to the crisis. UNMEER also worked closely with the World Health Organization, which, in summer 2015, assumed oversight of the UN System's Ebola emergency response.[28] While the threat of the virus remained, its spread was considerably contained. In mid-2015, Liberia announced that there were zero Liberians being affected (although, the threat continued, and an occasional victim was isolated).

Central African Republic

During most of this century, the Central African Republic (CAR) has been torn by civil war and religious division. A former French colony, the CAR has experienced little but dictatorial rule and coups since independence. The first internal war of the new millennium ended in 2008 with the formation of a unity government under François Bozizé. His government lasted until 2013 when he was forced to flee, as the capital of Bangui was seized by the rebel, and largely Muslim, group Séléka. The leader of Séléka, Michel Djotodia, declared himself the president, suspended the constitution, and dissolved parliament. The Djotodia government lasted less than a year as the country descended into internecine carnage between Séléka and a Christian militia known as anti-balaka (translated as "anti-machete," meaning essentially "anti" the bullets of the Séléka). In addition to thousands of brutal civilian deaths, the fighting produced large refugee flows, totaling more than three hundred thousand people by 2014.

When the civil war accelerated, the United Nations pulled all nonessential personnel from the country. As the situation grew more serious, the UN Security Council authorized an AU mission to the CAR. It was joined by French peacekeepers hoping to quell the violence. Secretary-General Ban Ki-moon addressed the Security Council on February 20, 2014, asking for UN reinforcements to bolster the AU and French troops. In April, the council established the UN Multidimensional Integrated Stabilization Mission (MINUSCA), with a force ceiling of ten thousand personnel. By 2022, the force had grown to 17,500 personnel.

MINUSCA was successful in establishing peace in sections of the country, but Christian-Muslim violence remained the norm, even in the capital. The UN operation organized the Bangui Forum for National Reconciliation in May 2015, bringing together more than seven hundred leaders in CAR life. The forum produced three agreements—to disarm Séléka and anti-balaka forces before national elections, to release all 6,000–10,000 child soldiers, and to establish a timeline for new elections.[29] The hope was to bring about a transitional government in the Central African Republic. The UN's role in the conflict, however, was marred by reports of sexual abuse of local citizens by UN peacekeepers. Secretary Ban moved quickly to investigate the charges and made clear the UN would remain in the country to carry out essential tasks, including the repatriation of refugees and the mediation of political divisions.

While the Bangui Forum held out hope for a transition to peace and a normal political process, murders, looting, and violence continued through the rest of the year. By fall of 2015, serious conflicts were increasing. The Security Council responded by imposing an

Photo 6.3 Lieutenant General Maqsood Ahmed (second from left), UN Military adviser for peacekeeping operations, and Brigadier General Frédéric Hingray (center right), Force Chief of Staff for MINUSCA, jointly visit a military base of the African-led International support mission in the Central African Republic (MISCA).

Source: UN Photo/Catianne Tijerina. Reproduced by permission of the United Nations.

asset freeze and travel ban—smart sanctions—on those engaging in acts that undermined the peace process. It reiterated its support for the transitional authorities created after the forum, under the leadership of Catherine Samba-Panza as the transitional head of state.

The two major parties, however, could not agree on modalities for the scheduled October 2015 elections, which were then delayed. Interim President Samba Panza rushed home from the annual 2015 General Assembly meeting in New York as fighting resumed in the country. Again following a contested 2020 presidential election fighting broke out. This time the central government turned not to the UN but to Russian mercenaries and Rwandan military forces to push back early successes by the rebels. The Central African Republic, like Somalia, demonstrated the growing willingness of other actors to assert their interests in crises that had been left to the UN in the immediate post-Cold War era.

AFRICAN UNION—UNITED NATIONS HYBRID MISSION IN DARFUR

Peacekeeping is an innovation in the application of collective security, a central tenet of the UN Charter. It was invented and implemented initially through the UN apparatus in New York City and remained a centralized function through the end of the twentieth century. But in the twenty-first century, the peacekeeping task has often devolved to regional international organizations, either authorized and conducted solely within their domain, such as OECD's operations in Ukraine, or in conjunction with UN efforts, as in the Darfurian case described below.

Reports of genocidal attacks on villagers in the western section of Sudan—a region known as Darfur—started to appear in the world press in 2003. Long-simmering ethnic animosities toward the minority Darfuris by the Arab majority combined with increased tensions over limited resources, particularly water, led to the attacks. They were carried out by Arab gangs, most conspicuously by a group known as the janjaweed, which seemed to have the backing of the Sudanese government in Khartoum headed by President Omar al-Bashir.

As the killings increased, AU members took the decision in 2004 to insert an AU peacekeeping force (AMIS). The peacekeeping operation was endorsed by the UN Security Council. For three years, the AU force of 7,000 troops was the only meaningful intervention. By 2007, however, due to a lack of funds and attacks on its personnel, including hostage-taking, by Sudanese rebel groups, the organization sought UN intervention. Faced with the possible dissolution of AMIS, the Security Council passed Resolution 1,769 creating the United Nations Assistance Mission in Darfur (UNAMID) that absorbed the AU operation into a hybrid peacekeeping effort.

The prosecutor for the International Criminal Court in 2009 charged President al-Bashir with five counts of crimes against humanity and two counts of war crimes for the government's support of the groups carrying out the attacks in Darfur. Until his overthrow in 2019, there was little chance al-Bashir would be extradited to The Hague. The transitional military-civilian government considered the possibility but decided to keep him under house arrest. Meanwhile, the prospect of a more democratic government augured for more peaceful conditions in Darfur. UNAMID ended its mission at the close of 2020, expecting the central government to provide regional security. The hybrid mission was replaced with a new political mission, the UN Integrated Transition Assistance Mission in Sudan (UNITAMS). Almost immediately, new atrocities were reported in Darfur, many with evidence of Sudanese military backing, producing more internally displaced persons and refugees fleeing to surrounding countries.

SUCCESS AND FAILURES

Contemporary UN peacekeeping came about through innovation and lessons learned. It has been buffeted by the changing international environments of Cold War, unipolar Western optimism, and rising ethnic and sectarian nationalism. Early efforts separated adversaries, reaching from Kashmir to the Suez Canal. Under the experienced eyes of UN leaders like Dag Hammarskjöld, Lester Pearson, and Ralph Bunche, the basic structures of peacekeeping took shape. Missions were successful in monitoring cease-fires and giving time for negotiation to lessen tensions. But they also were caught up in the Cold War rivalry between the Soviet Union and the United States. Hammarskjöld's foray into nation-building in Congo not only failed to deliver a peaceful resolution but nearly brought the UN to financial ruin.

Boutros Boutros-Ghali and Kofi Annan recognized the possibilities opened up by the end of superpower confrontation, but they also grappled with the budgetary realities that the United Nations could not address all of the world's conflict zones, and they understood that those conflicts were increasingly intra-state rather than inter-state. It was no longer a matter of separating national combatants, but rather required intervening in sovereign, albeit failed, states to protect populations and their human rights, sometimes from their own governments. There were successes in this regard, from El Salvador to Sierra Leone, Liberia, Namibia, Côte d'Ivoire, Angola, Timor Leste, and Cambodia.

In 2018, Secretary-General António Guterres congratulated the world on these successes, noting, "At its best, UN peacekeeping is a remarkable enterprise of multilateralism and international solidarity."[30] But he also said, "We are damaging the instrument of peacekeeping, and indeed multilateralism itself, in creating unrealistic expectations. Lives and credibility are being lost."[31] He acknowledged the failures in the Democratic Republic of the Congo, the Central African Republic, Mali, Haiti, and South Sudan. We could also add Rwanda and Afghanistan to that list. Sometimes the wounds were egregiously self-imposed. Charges of sexual abuse against peacekeepers in the Central African Republic, Haiti, and Côte d'Ivoire marred the UN's reputation and effectiveness. Haitians also experienced the introduction of cholera emanating from peacekeeper encampments. Ban Ki-moon and Guterres were forced to consider reforms to the peacekeeping process. As we described in Chapter 3, Guterres undertook the most extensive revisions in peacekeeping since Annan and Lakdhar Brahimi proposed the protection of individual sovereignty and taking sides in UN operations. The Secretary-General reorganized the bureaucracy in New York, placed mission responsibility on the UN resident director in each country, and launched his A4P initiative that was meant to bring greater accountability and better training to the peacekeeping exercise.

Endorsed by NATO, the EU, the AU and other international organizations, "Action for Peacekeeping" aimed at advancing political solutions to conflicts into which peacekeepers might otherwise be inserted. Guterres emphasized the "primacy of politics" as the best strategy for reducing even the need for large-scale peace operations. A4P sought more collaboration with regional organizations and even subregional actors. However, even if Guterres's reforms refurbished the UN peacekeeping apparatus and mission capabilities, there was little sign as he entered his second term that the major powers were much interested in expanding peacekeeping in the foreseeable future; this despite the serious threats to peace and security then present in Syria, Myanmar, Ethiopia, Ukraine, and other hotspots.

SUMMARY

The term *peacekeeping*, like *collective security*, cannot be found in the UN Charter. Yet, during the past sixty-five years, peacekeeping operations have been the most visible expression of the UN's commitment to maintaining peace and security. Created as a pragmatic innovation existing legally somewhere between Chapters VI and VII of the Charter, peacekeeping has evolved from the placement of a neutral force between consenting combatant governments to a comprehensive project, often including the involvement of troops from major powers, meant to reconstruct failed states as stable democracies. The Security Council and the General Assembly have authorized operations, or subcontracted missions to member states, first in the Middle East, then in Latin America, Asia, and most recently Africa, in hopes of ending violent conflicts.

By its nature, peacekeeping in the new millennium is significantly different from the missions created during the Cold War. Second-generation peacekeeping, nation-building, and holistic democracy promotion challenge the fundamental principle of state sovereignty on which the United Nations was originally built. It places the new United Nations directly in the internal affairs of disintegrating nations. In so doing, peacekeeping has become one of the UN's most important successes, but also its largest financial and administrative burden. It has also risked the UN's credibility, albeit for a worthy cause. It has forced the world body and its members to reconsider and expand the definition of collective security to include the defense of citizens' rights and well-being within their own nation. Consequently, it has contributed to a redefinition of the organization from solely an intergovernmental organization to, as well, a central institution in the construction of domestic societies.

KEY TERMS

Annan Plan (223)
Brahimi Report (226)
Dayton Peace Accords (231)
Ethnic Cleansing (230)
Holistic Democracy Promotion (238)
Lomé Agreement (243)

Lusaka Agreement (241)
Nation-Building (228)
Ralph Bunche (220)
Second-Generation Peacekeeping (225–6)
Subcontracting (243)

DISCUSSION QUESTIONS

Is nation-building an appropriate task for UN peacekeeping operations given the Charter's admonition that the United Nations not "intervene in matters which are essentially within the domestic jurisdiction of any state"?

Is the "Responsibility to Protect" doctrine a fundamental violation of state sovereignty as understood in international law?

Should the world community, largely through Security Council decisions, intervene as broadly as it has in the myriad of African conflicts, or should these be left to the African Union and other regional organizations?

RESOURCES FOR FURTHER RESEARCH

Relevant Web Sites

See Resource 8 on the Routledge eResources page for current information on UN Peacekeeping and Nation-building operations: www.routledge.com/9781138185807
   An Agenda for Peace: Preventive Diplomacy, Peacemaking and Peace-Keeping
   (www.un.org/ruleoflaw/files/A_47_277.pdf)

Report of the Panel on United Nations Peace Operations
(peacekeeping.un.org/en/report-of-panel-united-nations-peace-operations-brahimi-report-a55305)
UN Department of Peacekeeping Operations (www.un.org/en/peacekeeping/)

Books, Articles, and Documents

Ban Ki-moon. *Guidance Note of the Secretary-General on Democracy.* New York: United Nations, 2009, found at Roland Rich, Special Report, <muse.jhu.edu/article/379589/pdf>.

Boulden, Jane. *The United Nations Experience in Congo, Somalia, and Bosnia.* Westport, CT: Praeger, 2001.

Boutros-Ghali, Boutros. *Supplement to an Agenda for Peace.* New York: United Nations, 1995.

Ciorciari, John D. and Anne Heindel, *Hybrid Justice: The Extraordinary Chambers in the Courts of Cambodia.* Ann Arbor, MI: University of Michigan Press, 2014.

Hirsch, John L., and Robert B. Oakley. *Somalia and Operation Restore Hope.* Washington, D.C.: United States Institute of Peace Press, 1995.

Pubantz, Jerry, and John Allphin Moore, Jr. *Is There a Global Right to Democracy? A Philosophical Analysis of Peacekeeping and Nation Building.* Lewiston, NY: Edwin /Mellen Press, 2012.

Report of the Secretary-General. *Peacebuilding in the Aftermath of Conflict.* A/69/399-S/2014/694, September 23, 2014.

UN Department of Public Information. *The Blue Helmets: A Review of United Nations Peacekeeping.* 3rd Edition. New York: United Nations, 1996.

UN Department of Public Information. *The UN and Somalia: 1992–96.* Vol. 3. UN Blue Book Series. New York: United Nations, 1996.

UN Department of Public Information. *UN Peacekeeping: 50 Years, 1948–1998.* New York: United Nations, 1998.

Weiss, Thomas G. *Humanitarian Intervention: Ideas in Action.* Malden, MA: Polity, 2007.

Notes

1 Kofi Annan, *We the Peoples: A UN for the 21st Century* (Boulder, CO: Paradigm, 2014), 8.

2 Boutros Boutros-Ghali, *An Agenda for Peace* (New York: United Nations, 1992).

3 See A. LeRoy Bennett, *International Organization: Principles and Issues,* 4th Edition (Upper Saddle River, NJ: Prentice Hall, 1988), 94–97; United Nations, *Basic Facts about the United Nations* (New York: United Nations, 2004), 19–20; and Diana Ayton-Shenker, ed., *A Global Agenda: Issues before the 57th General Assembly of the United Nations* (Lanham, MD: Rowman & Littlefield, 2002), 277.

4 Senate Committee on Foreign Relations, *Reform of the United Nations Peacekeeping Operations: A Mandate for Change* (Washington, D.C.: U.S. Government Printing Office, 1993), viii.

5 United Nations, *Report of the Independent Inquiry into the Actions of the United Nations during the 1994 Genocide in Rwanda,* UN document S/1999/1257 (New York: United Nations, December 16, 1999), 23. The Brahimi Report can be found at <www.un.org/en/ga/search/view_doc.asp?symbol=A/55/305>.

6 UN *Report of the Independent Inquiry,* 37.

7 Jerry Pubantz and John Allphin Moore, Jr., *Is There a Global Right to Democracy? A Philosophical Analysis of Peacekeeping and Nation Building* (Lewiston, NY: Edwin /Mellen Press, 2012), 203.

8 Samantha Power, *A Problem from Hell: America and the Age of Genocide* (New York: Basic Books, 2002), 107–127.

9 For a full history and analysis of the Court's work, see John D. Ciorciari and Anne Heindel, *Hybrid Justice: The Extraordinary Chambers in the Courts of Cambodia* (Ann Arbor, MI: University of Michigan Press, 2014).

10 Brian Frederking, "Constructing Post–Cold War Collective Security," *American Political Science Review* 97, no. 3 (2003): 374–375.

11 Ian Hurd, "Legitimacy, Power and the Symbolic Life of the Security Council," *Global Governance* 8, no. 1 (2002): 38.

12 Slovenia and Croatia each joined the UN in 1992.

13 For a full discussion of the war in Bosnia and the UN's role in its resolution, see, among other works, Jasminka Udovicki and James Ridgeway, eds., *Burn This House: The Making and Unmaking of Yugoslavia*, revised and expanded edition (Durham, NC: Duke University Press, 2000); Richard Holbrooke, *To End a War* (New York: Random House, 1998); and Power, *A Problem from Hell.*

14 This discussion of events in Bosnia is drawn in large measure from two other works by the authors. See John Allphin Moore, Jr., and Jerry Pubantz, *Encyclopedia of the United Nations* (New York: Facts on File, 2002), 30–31, 114–117; and John Allphin Moore, Jr., and Jerry Pubantz, *To Create a New World? American Presidents and the United Nations* (New York: Peter Lang, 1999), 321–324.

15 "Address to the Nation on Implementation of the Peace Agreement in Bosnia-Herzegovina," November 27, 1995, *Public Papers of the Presidents of the United States.*

16 Reuters, "Bosnia Serb Parliament Urges Karadzic to Surrender," July 20, 2004.

17 United Nations, *Report of the Independent Inquiry (Brahimi Report)*, 3, 21, 23, 35.

18 Ibid., 3.

19 Ibid., 23.

20 Ibid., 37.

21 Security Council Resolution 1704, August 25, 2006.

22 Harry Blair, Lorel Donaghey, and Dardan Velija, *Kosovo Civil Society Sector Assessment, Final Report* (Washington, DC: Management Systems International, 2004), iv.

23 Lara Olson, "Fighting for Humanitarian Space: NGOs in Afghanistan," *Journal of Military and Strategic Studies* 9, no. 1 (Fall 2006): 1.

24 UN General Assembly, *Implementation of the United Nations Millennium Declaration: Report of the Secretary-General*, UN document A/58/323 (New York: United Nations, September 2, 2003), para. 42.

25 Ban Ki-moon, *Guidance Note of the Secretary-General on Democracy* (New York: United Nations, 2009), found at Roland Rich, Special Report, <muse.jhu.edu/article/379589/pdf>.

26 Report of the Secretary-General, *Responsibility to Protect: Timely and Decisive Response.* A/66/874—S/2012/578, July 25, 2012.

27 Report of the Secretary-General, *Peacebuilding in the Aftermath of Conflict*, A/69/399-S/2014/694, September 23, 2014.

28 See </ebolaresponse.un.org/un-mission-ebola-emergency-response-unmeer>.

29 Matthew Mitchell, "Central African Republic: MINUSCA Too Little, Too Late?" Paper for presentation at the International Studies Association-South Conference, October 24, 2015, 6.

30 António Guterres, "Secretary-General's Remarks to Security Council High-Level Debate on Collective Action to Improve UN Peacekeeping Operations," 28 March 2018. Available at <www.un.org/sg/en/content/sg/statement/2018-03-28/secretary-generals-remarks-security-council-high-level-debate>.

31 Ibid.

Chapter 7

Making Global Public Policy

Promoting Civil Society, Human Rights, and Women

Besides maintaining international peace and security, the Charter of the United Nations commits the organization to international cooperation "in solving international problems of an economic, social, cultural, or humanitarian character, and in promoting and encouraging respect for human rights and for fundamental freedoms for all" (Article 1). This injunction has become increasingly important in the twenty-first century, as public policy issues have found a shared ground between domestic and international jurisdictions. As a product of globalization and the communications revolution, the diminished monopoly of national governments over all issues touching their citizens' lives has opened a space for international organizations to become actors in their own right on policies that affect people in many parts of the globe. More than simply the creatures of their founding states, institutions like the United Nations (UN) promote their own agenda, organize a world community of supporters for their purposes, marshal large bureaucracies to implement policies, and convene world events that cannot be ignored by national governments. International organizations may not yet be "parliaments" for world citizens, but in the twenty-first century, they are far more than cooperative forums in the service of members' exclusive national interests.

The United Nations in the current era finds itself creating, promoting, and enforcing public policy on various topics of human concern, and in doing so, it continues to expand its reach and the frequency and depth of its participation with non-state actors. The UN's engagement with nongovernmental organizations (NGOs) and other private actors in the process of global policy making is yet another indicator that the organization has become a *transnational* body. In this chapter, we cover how the United Nations has been responding to thematic issues, such as human rights and women's empowerment, and, in the process, has become a central policy maker in the lives of people around the world.

DOI: 10.4324/9781003281535-8

EMERGING GLOBAL DEMOCRATIC GOVERNANCE AND GLOBAL CITIZENSHIP

In the twenty-first century, international affairs are not the politics of the global village. Yet, in today's world, we are on *shared* ground, where states and their power are very real, even predominant, but are nonetheless challenged by external and internal forces that are both new and old, and collectively different from what has come before. These forces are representative of the empowered individual, of communications technology that has made a qualitative leap, of huge reservoirs of wealth controlled overwhelmingly by private corporations, and of great disparities of power in a world of uneven development. Global actors like the United Nations play a critical role on many issues that weave together domestic and international characteristics.

We sometimes consciously take notice of the transboundary connections that challenge sovereign governments' autonomy regarding their domestic policies. For example, when we fill our cars with gasoline that has doubled in price very quickly due to a crisis in the Middle East, the connection between the global and the local is clear. At other times, the links are real but not apparent. Beyond trade, international issues that now have a high impact on domestic life are immigration and emigration, human rights, drug trafficking, climate change, health pandemics, and terrorism. In the case of terrorism, as one clear example, we have come to understand that to protect our personal safety in our neighborhoods, it is necessary to act internationally against nontraditional participants in the global system.

If the state is increasingly challenged in the international arena, who and what have been empowered at its expense? Non-state actors, even individuals, seem to be among the beneficiaries. So too do international organizations and collective governance networks that include national governments as participants but also include multinational corporations, advocacy groups, experts, subnational communities with access to international bodies, and social movements.

Through these entities, state citizens have found new platforms and channels on the world stage to pursue effective participation. They have been able to transfer the methods of national citizenship to the larger arena, often engaging in activities that intrude into the domestic affairs of states that are not their own. People, individually and in association with others, have the power, and growing authority, to play key roles in the processes of norm setting and policy formation at the global level. In terms of self-identification, many have become global citizens attempting to address the development of international and enforceable policies on what previously were considered domestic issues (e.g., the environment, criminal justice, health, electoral security, and human rights). The United Nations and other international organizations have become nodal points in the broad networks that are the focus of individuals and groups who wish to have an impact on global norms and policies.

While much of what we describe here is a burgeoning phenomenon of contemporary times, from its beginning the United Nations has had a mandate to address issues that by their nature impinge on the internal life of states. At the San Francisco Conference in 1945, delegations from newly independent nations, as well as from Latin America and the United States, urged a mandate for the United Nations that would be wider than solely the immediate preservation of international peace and security. The delegations argued that only by addressing the underlying social and economic problems faced by the world's people could long-term peace be achieved. Their success in including this broader authority became particularly meaningful as Cold War deadlock materialized in the council. The General Assembly, with its expanding membership from the developing world, increasingly found itself focusing on economic development and other distinct challenges in the developing world.

In the decades following 1960, a **thematic diplomacy** emerged that emphasized international cooperation to solve human problems of a global character. These problems might be of a domestic intrastate nature as much as they might be the basis for disputes between states. Often dubbed the *Other United Nations* during the Cold War—because it addressed "soft" or "peripheral" issues—thematic diplomacy emerged by the close of the millennium as a central mission of the world body. The Charter also identified some thematic areas critical to world peace, such as disarmament, decolonization, international law, and human rights. Furthermore, many intergovernmental organizations that were founded long before the United Nations took as their missions the amelioration of human suffering and the betterment of living conditions. As you learned in Chapter 4, many of these international governmental organizations (IGOs) were brought into the UN System as UN specialized agencies.

After the Cold War, the United Nations expanded its role in developing global public policies by providing the framework, initiative, and resources needed to address a broad range of human issues. The election of Kofi Annan as the Secretary-General accelerated the process. His efforts at UN reform included a new, inclusive approach to the private sector. By the time of the UN's Millennium Summit in 2000, Annan could report the "forging of global partnerships that would hardly have been conceivable a decade ago."[1] These partnerships included ties to the business community, civil society organizations, and philanthropic foundations. Coordinated through the UN Fund for International Partnerships (UNFIP), collaborative arrangements were struck with a wide range of organizations, including the Rockefeller Foundation, the Bill and Melinda Gates Foundation, the Coca-Cola Company, Cisco Systems, United Way International, and Ericsson Corporation. Secretary-General Annan pursued a "stakeholder" strategy, attempting to engage three broad categories of non-state participants: nongovernmental organizations (NGOs); civil society members (including private individuals and subnational organizations); and the world business community.

Together, these three components created a strong advocacy group for addressing thematic issues. They also marked an evolution in the UN's role as an intergovernmental organization. This change in organizational character had the salutary effect of bringing the United Nations into a closer working relationship with international civil society. It also posed the risk that UN leaders and agencies might misjudge the willingness of governments to dilute their monopoly on the policy process. In the end, the United Nations could involve private entities in its work only to the extent that member states—particularly those that were large and powerful—were willing to allow it.

THE AGE OF THE NONGOVERNMENTAL ORGANIZATION

Somewhere between the realities of state-dominated international politics and the first signs of a meaningful international civil society, NGOs have carved out an important role for themselves in the discursive politics of contemporary international relations. In the current international governance structure, NGOs contribute to international agenda setting, decision-making, and policy implementation. They are the policy advocates playing the roles at the international level served by interest groups within domestic society. NGOs are "citizen organizations" in international life. They are sociologist Jürgen Habermas's "nodal points" in the international communications network, part of international civil society, advancing the salient issues, possible solutions, and constructed values of a vibrant democratic process into the public sphere, where global consensus formation is possible.[2] In the view of Stanford professor Jessica Matthews, NGOs' newfound power marks a "power shift" in international relations[3] away from the nation-state and toward non-state actors. For supporters of this movement, the shift means a democratization of international relations, allowing those traditionally excluded from the process to have a meaningful voice. However, the expansion of NGOs' role in international affairs is not universally lauded, nor is it seen in some quarters as particularly democratic. Traditional diplomats, who speak for national governments, point out that NGO representatives are unelected and often do not reflect majority opinion either internationally or in the countries of their origin. Only representatives of sovereign democratic states may make that claim, say these critics. Even if the criticisms are true, the very need to make them reflects recognition of the new presence of this community in international relations.

The inclusion of non-state actors in the work of UN bodies has contributed to the UN's augmented role in shaping thematic policy and has provided conduits beyond traditional member state agencies for implementing this policy. Article 71 of the Charter allows **nongovernmental organizations** to establish "consultative status" with the Economic and Social Council (ECOSOC). Starting in the late 1980s, NGO participation in the United Nations changed in quantity and quality. The statistics on NGOs granted consultative status are telling: 41 in 1948; 377 in 1968; 2,200 in 2003; and 4,045 by early 2022. The growth in numbers and participation has led UN bodies to identify NGOs as recognized entities of emerging international "civil society." They have become "citizen organizations" within the UN System, advocating particular goals and mobilizing support for and against UN initiatives.

In 1996, ECOSOC enhanced the role NGOs could play in its work (Resolution 31), designating some as eligible to propose items for its agenda. Those granted "general" consultative status were allowed to designate representatives to sit as observers at ECOSOC meetings and to submit written statements to both the council and subsidiary bodies. By 1997, NGOs could address the council on subjects of interest, a step that reflected the democratization of UN procedures.

The ECOSOC decision was part of an expanding acceptance of NGOs in the daily work of UN bodies, conferences, and agencies, and it accelerated their participation in other sectors of the UN System. Nearly all General Assembly committees introduced procedures for NGO participation, including the First Committee (Disarmament) and

---

NONGOVERNMENTAL ORGANIZATION PARTICIPATION IN THE UN SYSTEM

The United Nations system, including international finance and development agencies, and all intergovernmental organizations and forums should ... take measures to ... review and report on ways of enhancing existing procedures and mechanisms by which non-governmental organizations contribute to policy design, decision-making, implementation and evaluation at the individual agency level, in inter-agency discussions and in United Nations conferences.

—United Nations, "Strengthening the Role of Non-Governmental Organisations: Partners for Sustainable Development," in *The Earth Summit 1992: Agenda 21* (New York: United Nations, 1992), Chap. 27, para. 27.9.

the Sixth Committee (Legal), which have historically been dominated by government representatives protecting the highest state interests. In the latter case, NGOs played a critical role in the negotiations leading to the creation of the International Criminal Court (ICC). NGOs also provide participants for panels of experts; serve on agencies such as the Joint UN Programme on HIV/AIDS (UNAIDS); and develop program proposals for disease control, poverty eradication, and other social improvements in poorer parts of the globe. In an unprecedented step, representatives of three NGOs—Oxfam, CARE, and Médecins Sans Frontières (Doctors Without Borders)—gave an informal briefing to the Security Council in February 1997 on the humanitarian crisis in Africa. Since then, an NGO consultation group has met regularly with the Security Council president to provide advice on matters before the council.

All UN-sponsored world conferences since the early 1970s have incorporated companion NGO forums in an effort to generate public support for the programs launched by the conferences. At these meetings, NGOs have often been allowed to present statements and to lobby delegations. Maurice Strong, Secretary-General of the 1972 UN Conference on the Human Environment (UNCHE), held in Stockholm, believed NGO participation to be critical not only to the success of the conference, but also to the implementation of its initiatives. In its final report, the conference called on not only states but also "citizens and communities ... enterprises and institutions at every level [and] ... [g]overnments and peoples to exert common efforts for the preservation and improvement of the human environment."[4] By the close of the 1990s, the UN General Assembly routinely required the participation of NGO representatives in the "PrepComms"—preparatory committees— for UN-sponsored global meetings, and in the subsequent plenary sessions. In October 2021, for example, more than 9,700 NGO and 2,600 media representatives gathered in Glasgow, Scotland, for the first follow-up meeting (COP26) to the Paris Agreement on Climate Change signed in 2016.[5]

Nongovernmental organizations bring community concerns to UN bodies, monitor global policies and international agreements, provide analysis and expertise, serve as early warning mechanisms, and generally act as interest groups within the UN System. They are critical to the local implementation of UN programs, where subnational and private organizations are best suited to provide the workforce and public support for UN efforts. Often, NGOs and UN agencies partner to undertake joint projects, as we have seen in the previous chapter, regarding various nation-building operations.

NGOs at the United Nations have established several bodies to coordinate their activities, three of which deserve special mention. First, CoNGO, the Conference on Non-Governmental Organizations in Consultative Status with the Economic and Social Council, serves as a representative voice of NGOs. Its aims are to ensure that NGOs enjoy the fullest opportunities and appropriate facilities for performing their consultative functions, to provide a forum on the consultative process, and to convene meetings of member organizations to exchange views on matters of common interest. Second, the NGO community elects an executive committee to act in an advisory and liaison capacity to channel information and represent its interests in the UN's Department of Global Communications (DGC). Each year, the committee and the DPI stage the largest NGO conference convened by the world body. In 2018, it attracted more than two thousand people and over 300 NGOs to the UN headquarters in New York. Finally, the UN Non-Governmental Liaison Service (NGLS) promotes partnerships between the United Nations and civil society organizations on development and other issues currently on the international agenda. NGLS organizes meetings and briefings that bring together relevant private groups and UN offices.[6]

Although Article 71 links NGOs only to ECOSOC, other principal UN organs, and most specialized agencies, have created consultative status for relevant private groups.

Among the agencies to have done so are the International Labour Organization (ILO), the UN Conference on Trade and Development (UNCTAD), the World Intellectual Property Organization (WIPO), the International Telecommunication Union (ITU), the World Health Organization (WHO), the Food and Agriculture Organization (FAO), and the International Maritime Organization (IMO).

NGOs also play a role in the work of the UN's Human Rights Council. They may submit written statements, make oral interventions, and participate in debates, panel discussions, interactive dialogues, and the Universal Periodic Review, which involves a review of the human rights records of all 193 United Nations member states once every four years. As in all public policy settings, NGOs associated with the Human Rights Council and other UN bodies bargain for enhanced power and influence, criticize agency policies, publicize perceived organization failures, create alliances with like-minded interest groups and sympathetic UN officials, and lobby individual national delegations on behalf of desired policies. When NGOs are not successful in one UN setting, they often seek other avenues to influence the world community. They add complexity to international policy and UN policy making, but they also ensure broader consensus for adopted policies than would otherwise be expected.

The first intergovernmental organization to incorporate popular participation in decision-making was the International Labour Organization (ILO). This post-World War I agency grants each member state four representatives, only two of whom are government delegates. The other delegation members are employer and worker representatives. Delegation members are not required to speak or vote with one national voice, but they may and do cast differing votes on issues brought before the organization. UNAIDS was the first UN "programme" to welcome NGO representatives to full membership on its coordinating board. The board includes delegates from twenty-two governments from all regions of the world, seven representatives from participating agencies, and five representatives from NGOs, which include associations of people living with AIDS. The UN Children's Fund (UNICEF), the UN High Commissioner for Refugees (UNHCR), the UN Population Fund, and the World Food Programme also make extensive use of NGOs.

Their operational competence, flexibility, and knowledge of local conditions, as well as the complementary resources that they bring to humanitarian programs, make NGOs key partners and implementing agents. In April 2003, for example, the UN Development Programme (UNDP) entered into a global partnership with the WWF (formerly known as the World Wildlife Fund) to combat environmental problems such as deforestation, climate change, and desertification. With more than twenty-eight national organizations, twenty-four program offices, and a history of investing more than $1 billion in 130 nations since 1985, the WWF was in a particularly strong position to assist the UNDP, and, conversely, affect the agency's agenda and policies. In a particular partnership project, UNDP and the WWF signed an agreement with Bhutan to protect that nation's "green corridor" of forest and mountain ecosystems. The $1.8 million price tag was to be paid by the World Bank's Global Environment Facility (GEF), Bhutan, and the WWF.

In cases when IGOs have failed to follow the UN lead in welcoming NGO participation, they have often faced demands for "democratization" of their institutions and procedures. The most dramatic expression of these "people's demands" has come in connection with the internal decision-making processes of the World Trade Organization (WTO) and the World Bank. The Marrakesh Agreement replacing GATT with the WTO makes specific reference to NGOs. However, neither the WTO nor the World Bank has been as proactive as other parts of the UN System in co-opting NGOs, which has produced broad criticism of these two institutions and demands for greater private participation. Anger at the closed methods the Bretton Woods institutions use spilled over in the 1990s into street protests and petitions for greater inclusion.

THE MODEL UNITED NATIONS EXPERIENCE

One interesting NGO affiliated with the United Nations is the National Model United Nations (NMUN), which prides itself on being the oldest student simulation of the UN.[7] The organization is officially accredited with the UN Department of Global Communications. The NMUN is but one of many Model UN (MUN) simulations that bring together students from middle school, high school, and college to engage in imitating real world international diplomacy. The Model UN learning experience, because it does attract students from around the world, is an example—for a theme of this chapter—of promoting international civil society.

There is no overarching administrative body that manages all Model UN activities. Independent MUN conferences may be organized in a regional or local venue, anywhere in the world—there is an accelerating growth of such conferences around the globe—or, as the case with the NMUN, in New York, in the environment of the actual United Nations headquarters. Conferences are usually organized and administered far in advance by a student staff (sometimes replicating UN Secretariat positions; for example, the lead student staff officer is often called the Secretary-General), or by a university or other educational organization.

Delegates to Model UN conferences typically come from an extracurricular MUN student club or from a specific class at their school or college, often accompanied by a faculty adviser who has taught them in a class scheduled prior to the conference. Their delegation is assigned a specific country by the conference's organizers, and they must study the culture, politics, history, and foreign policy of that country so as to represent with as much accuracy as possible the position of the country in the United Nations.

Usually, the conference emulates some of the main organs of the UN, a number of General Assembly committees, and perhaps specialized agencies, programmes and funds, or related organs, even other related IGOs (like NATO, the Arab League, the Organization of American States, or the European Union), and, importantly as the world governance network evolves, significant NGOs. School delegations assign individual members of their group as delegates to these organs or committees, representing their designated country. For the full conference, simulating the UN's procedures for establishing its annual agenda, student delegates prepare for a set number of specific topics that will be considered by their committee or organ (usually about three current international issues). In preparing, students may benefit by a *background guide*, produced by the conference's voluntary student staff (as is the case with the NMUN), for each committee being simulated.

Beginning in the interwar period as a simulation of the League of Nations, the NMUN was chiefly a student-organized national meeting intended to have student delegates impersonate the actual workings of the UN, using the tools and procedures of diplomatic practice. The NMUN grew significantly from its beginnings. The annual conference, held in New York City each spring, currently includes two overlapping meetings to accommodate the growing numbers of delegates at the UN building and other city venues. The NMUN also administers conferences overseas and in Washington, DC.

Student delegates come from colleges and universities throughout the United States, as well as from several other countries, making the New York conference international in scale. Delegations benefit from the NGO status of the NMUN, meaning that most delegations can receive in-depth briefings by the diplomatic mission of the country they are representing. The New York-based organization also often meets for a concluding session in the great hall of the General Assembly.

Photo 7.1 Model United Nations delegates gather at UN headquarters.
Source: NMUN. Reproduced with permission of National Model United.

MUN conferences are, then, educational simulations where students can learn about diplomacy, international relations, contrasting cultural views, and, of course, about the United Nations. The MUN exercise typically emphasizes research competence, critical thinking, public speaking, debating, writing skills, and interpersonal tact. Some conferences require that delegates submit preliminary "position papers" on the topics established for their committees, showing that the delegates fully understand the topics before their committees and their country's foreign policy positions. Student delegates must as well become familiar with the *rules and procedures* of the Model UN conference they are attending. These rules are important for keeping order so that a committee can make progress. *Caucusing*, or informal negotiation, is an integral part of MUN conferences; it requires problem solving, collaboration, and compromise. Composing *resolutions* usually takes place at the conference, since delegates must achieve compromise (just as at the real United Nations) in order to craft resolutions acceptable to a majority of countries.

Students must learn the role of sponsors and signatories in the resolution-writing process. All of these rules, procedures, informal negotiations, and drafting exercises mirror the "parliamentary" character of the United Nations and nearly all international organizations. For example, the outcome of deliberations in international bodies usually is a formal resolution that has distinct sections that follow traditional formulations and vocabulary, and is then passed or rejected in a formal open session of the organization. In MUN, students, therefore, learn about the use of preambulatory and operative clauses as well as how to amend a resolution. Delegates are also obliged to wear *business attire* to conference sessions, to underscore the expected decorum of the exercise.[8]

Photo 7.2 Student delegates caucus at the 2015 national model UN in New York City.
Source: NMUN. Reproduced with permission of National Model United Nations

At the conclusion of some conferences, exemplary delegations and individual delegates receive awards as recognition for excellent performance in all aspects of the conference. MUN alums tend to savor their experience, remembering it as a highlight of their school days and as an introduction early in their lives to a meaningful touch with international civil society.

SPECIAL RAPPORTEURS

Private individuals and NGO representatives have been inducted into the UN decision-making process. They serve as individuals on important committees and are given access to UN officials and agencies. In fact, they are often appointed as UN **special rapporteurs**, a topic we first discussed in Chapter 4. As we saw in that chapter, UN special rapporteurs are part of *Special Procedures* within the Human Rights Council (which replaced the Commission on Human Rights in 2006). "Working Groups" and "Independent Experts" are also commissioned by the Human Rights Council and are part of *Special Procedures.*

Special rapporteurs assume either a *country mandate* or a *thematic mandate.* They undertake country visits, compile relevant information, act on individual cases of alleged violations of human rights, and contribute to the development of international human rights standards. All Special Procedures appointees report annually to the Human Rights Council and to the General Assembly. By 2022, including *all* Special Procedures activities, there were forty-four thematic and twelve country-specific mandates (most of these being special rapporteur mandates).[9] The most intrusive aspect of UN Special Procedures operations, particularly for special rapporteurs, is the "country visit." By UN direction, mandate-holders are to be given wide-ranging guarantees within visited countries: freedom of movement in the whole country, including in restricted areas; freedom of inquiry, including access to all prisons, detention centers, and places of interrogation; full contact with national and local branches of government; full access to NGOs, private institutions, and media; confidential and unsupervised contact with witnesses and other private persons, including persons deprived of their liberty; and full access to all relevant documentary material. No person who has been in contact with a specific special rapporteur (or other Special Procedures representative) is to suffer harassment, punishment, or adverse judicial proceedings for cooperating with the UN-authorized expert.[10]

The findings of special rapporteurs can be critical to the avoidance of future human rights violations and threats to international security. In April 1993, the Special Rapporteur on Summary Executions warned the UN that genocide was imminent in Rwanda. Unfortunately, his report went unattended outside the Commission on Human Rights, leaving the world body unprepared for the massacres that occurred a year later. Fortunately, the report of Roberto Garretón, Special Rapporteur on Human Rights in the Democratic Republic of the Congo (a *country* mandate), fared better. Mr. Garretón was invited in January 2000 to brief the Security Council as it addressed the deteriorating situation in that country. Using the "**Arria Formula**"—a procedure by which the Security Council hears from non-state representatives—the special rapporteur reported to the council on three occasions. Subsequent briefings were given by other experts, such as the Special Rapporteur on Burundi, as the council contemplated peacekeeping operations in troubled regions of the globe.[11]

Special rapporteurs address delicate issues formerly seen as tangential to the exploration of peaceable relations between and among nation-states. The unique role of the Human Rights Council—associated special rapporteurs has been to document, even advocate for, and bring to the discussion table issues affecting marginalized peoples, such as migrants, women, the internally displaced, religious and ethnic minorities, and victims of arbitrary detention. Also, as we see above in reference to the Special Rapporteur for the Democratic Republic of the Congo, rapporteurs may now report directly to the Security Council under the so-called Arria Formula, an informal arrangement named for Ambassador Diego Arria of Venezuela, that, since the mid-1990s, has allowed the Security Council greater flexibility to be briefed about international peace and security issues. Thus, the role of the special rapporteur may transcend the sovereign command of the nation-state. The reports issued by special rapporteurs document affairs within specific countries (acceding to *country mandates*) as well as human rights infringements worldwide (acceding to *thematic mandates*). Since the appointment of the first special rapporteur in 1980, these reports have provided informative grist for policy makers and academics interested in the all-embracing pursuit of international peace and the advancement of human rights.

By illustration, we now look at one particular special rapporteur with a *thematic mandate* on a topic that the international news media covered extensively during and beyond the second decade of the twenty-first century—the situation faced by migrants. In 1999, the now-defunct UN Commission on Human Rights created the mandate of the Special Rapporteur on the Human Rights of Migrants. The Commission renewed and expanded the mandate in 2002 and 2005, and the new Human Rights Council continued and strengthened the mandate up to 2022.[12] In 2017, the Council appointed Felipe González Morales as Special Rapporteur on the Human Rights of Migrants. When appointed, he was a professor of International Law at the Diego Partales University in Santiago, Chile and taught international human rights law since 2003 at several universities in Spain and in the United States, as well as in Chile. He holds a Doctorate and a Master's degree in

Advanced Human Rights from University Carlos III and an LL.M. in International Legal Studies from American University in Washington, DC.[13] It is fair to say that Dr. Morales is representative of the caliber of individuals receiving assignment as special rapporteurs.

The late twentieth and early twenty-first centuries encountered an astounding migration challenge, much of it violently and unrelentingly pressed upon the ill-fated. In December 2015, the UN High Commissioner for Refugees reported that the global refugee total had passed the twenty million threshold for the first time since 1992. Meantime, the Western world suddenly felt the painful sting of human movement, partly as a consequence of the aftermath of the "Arab Spring" uprisings—including the rise of militant terrorist groups in the area from Libya sweeping east into the setting of ancient Mesopotamia as far as Afghanistan, and most particularly the ongoing Syrian civil war that commenced in spring 2011.

From the beginning of these heartrending human movements, the United Nations found itself in the mix. The organization struggled to cope with the accelerating exodus from northern Africa and the Middle East. The last day of September 2013, as the United Nations was meeting in New York for its opening fall session, Secretary-General Ban Ki-moon convened a high-level meeting on the migrant issue and outlined eight guiding principles to enhance preparedness. The hand of the then Special Rapporteur François Crépeau (predecessor to Dr. Morales) was discernible in what followed. His reports and public comments provided the kind of guidance that forwarded the high-level meeting. Delegations that fall began their work with the unanimous adoption of a Declaration by which the 193-member Assembly decided to work toward an effective and inclusive agenda on international migration that integrated development and respected human rights by improving the performance of existing institutions and frameworks. Secretary-General Ban called on member states to accede to the Declaration's eight principles: (1) to protect the human rights of every migrant (encouraging all states to ratify all relevant international agreements and instruments), (2) to reduce the cost of labor migration, (3) to eliminate migrant exploitation, including human trafficking, (4) to address specifically the plight of stranded migrants, (5) to improve public perceptions of migrants, (6) to integrate migration into the development agenda, (7) to strengthen the migration evidence base, and (8) to enhance migration partnerships and cooperation.[14]

The UN's move into crisis prevention mode by mid-decade emerged, in part, due to information compiled by the special rapporteur. In October 2020, Secretary-General António Guterres transmitted to the General Assembly's 75th session the exhaustive and important report on migrant children that Dr. Morales had compiled following input from thirty-three countries, six intergovernmental organizations, and numerous civil society and human rights organizations. The report identified good practices and concluded that immigration detention of children was effectively avoidable. The Special Rapporteur recommended that states shift from a focus on enforcement and coercion toward providing human rights-based alternative care and reception for all migrant children and their families.[15] In spring 2021, the Special Rapporteur issued a comprehensive report for the High Commissioner for Refugees on current views regarding the legal and necessary means to address the human rights of migrants. That summer his required report to the Human Rights Council detailed his exhaustive agenda, which included, among innumerable activities, participation in a conference at the University Carlos III of Madrid on defending migrants' human rights during the COVID-19 pandemic, presenting a lecture at Columbia University in New York at the conference "COVID-19, Migration, and Human Rights Impact and Solutions," plus participating in several webinars and scholarly forums, while maintaining his consultation schedule.[16]

We may tentatively suggest that the *ongoing* work of UN special rapporteurs, as seen in the dedicated efforts of François Crépeau and Felipe González Morales, offer an opportunity for us to think anew about the UN. While the new Human Rights Council has been the recipient of harsh criticisms not unlike those leveled at its predecessor Commission on Human Rights, the Special Procedures project, including specifically the work of special rapporteurs, heralds a new, perhaps more satisfying, future course.

GLOBAL CIVIL SOCIETY

What you can see in the UN's use of special rapporteurs and its extensive involvement with nongovernmental organizations are examples of the new United Nations acting transnationally, going beyond its traditional membership of nation-states to engage private entities in its work. Begun as an intergovernmental organization, the United Nations has, in truth, become a *transnational* body, with a large part of its budget and institutional structure committed to addressing policy issues in cooperation with non-state actors, who are, in turn, members of an emerging international civil society.

In 1997, Secretary-General Kofi Annan defined international civil society as the

> sphere in which social movements organize themselves around objectives, constituencies and thematic interests. These movements include specific groups such as women, youth and indigenous people. Other actors ... include local authorities, mass media, business and industry, professional associations, religious and cultural organizations and the intellectual research communities.[17]

During his tenure, he encouraged greater participation of these groups in UN activities. Annan had a particular interest in engaging private enterprises in UN activities. To this end, he created the Global Compact in his office (as we saw in Chapter 4). Corporations that join the Compact—of which there were about twelve thousand participants from one hundred sixty countries in 2022—commit to ten principles established in important UN conventions, and in so doing are given recognition and involvement in the work of the world body. The Global Compact set as its overall goals the promotion of international corporate citizenship and social responsibility and the establishment of corporate "good practices." The Secretary-General also wanted to make these corporations stakeholders in UN initiatives.

In February 2003, the Secretary-General appointed a panel of eminent persons, headed by Fernando Henrique Cardoso, the former president of Brazil, to look at UN-international civil society relations and to make recommendations on how they might be improved. In the final **Cardoso Report**, panel members called for a "paradigm shift" in the work of the UN. The panel urged the UN to become an "outward-looking organization," serving as the "convener" of multiple constituencies.[18]

The panel asserted that the UN needed to go beyond its intergovernmental nature and become an actor itself in international civil society, arguing that the United Nations should accept a role in global governance, emphasizing "participatory democracy" and "accountability." The report contained thirty discrete proposals, which led to major UN bodies, such as the General Assembly, finding ways to engage international civil society organizations in their work.

Mindful consideration of the private sector in the international arena is recognition by the UN leadership that an emerging international civil society exists and that it will have a significant impact on the success or failure of UN initiatives. With limited resources, the United Nations has widened its scope by including private components of the international community. Among the benefits of such inclusion is one of special note: the world body has been allowed to extend its reach through **subsidiarity**—a concept of governance that places responsibility for policy making and implementation at the lowest and most decentralized level commensurate with the ability to perform assignments effectively and efficiently. Subsidiarity allows for burden sharing between UN agencies and private entities. It encourages expansive relationships among sovereignty-free actors, civil society, regional and transregional organizations, UN specialized agencies, and principal UN organs. Such burden sharing can protect the United Nations from overload, and it attracts support for UN policies by lowering the locus of decision-making to the level where the costs and benefits of decisions are most immediately experienced.

As part of international civil society, the United Nations has taken on specific functions. Thematic diplomacy, which we described earlier in this chapter, has opened the door for a comprehensive global policy process with the United Nations as a central actor in it. This process also includes national governments, other international organizations, world markets, NGOs, and individuals. The United Nations not only employs and interacts with these entities, but is also deeply affected by them. Non-state actors have many centers of policy making within the UN System that they can target in their effort to influence global policy. The General Assembly, the Security Council, the Economic and Social Council, specialized agencies, regional economic commissions, the World Bank and the WTO, UN world conferences, and development programs all provide entry points into policy making. The result is a comprehensive international public policy process in which the United Nations serves as both arena and actor, producing with time global policy on some of the most important thematic issues of the twenty-first century. We look at several of these policy areas in this chapter as well as in Chapter 8.

HUMAN RIGHTS

The Policy Process

Tuesday, April 29, 2003: Slobodan Milosevic, former dictator of Yugoslavia, sat in Trial Chamber III. Judge Richard George May was presiding as Milosevic prepared, as he had done many times in the previous six months, to cross-examine a witness testifying against him. Milosevic stood accused of war crimes and genocide against the peoples of Croatia and Bosnia. He was being tried in the International Criminal Tribunal for the Former Yugoslavia (ICTY) in The Hague. He was the ultimate "prize," the person everyone, except for ultranationalist Serbs, wanted to see tried for the heinous Balkan barbarism of the previous decade. The session had begun at 9:03 that morning with witness C-048. The prosecutor had brought the witness to the stand to inquire about killings ordered by the Yugoslav security services, of which C-048 had knowledge. Milosevic was representing himself and contesting the right of the court to try him, firmly believing that because the actions for which he was indicted had been carried out when he was the president of a sovereign state, the charges were unwarranted. Thus, he aggressively challenged all the witness's contentions. At one point, the following exchange occurred:

> Milosevic   All right. You're claiming that in the former Yugoslavia, in the Socialist Federal Republic of Yugoslavia, in fact, when it existed that a decision could be made at the meeting of the federal minister and of his republican ministers to kill somebody. Is that what you're claiming?
> C-048   Yes, of course.

Milosevic Fine. Now, who gave instructions? Who gave the order? ... Who gave instructions in March 1990 for this killing, the killing that you're talking about? Who gave the order? You must know that, if you know that an order was given by the service as you say.

C-048 Well, I know that the order was given by the service....

Milosevic So who gave the order?

C-048 [My informant] didn't mention that.

Milosevic Ah. He didn't mention a name. Right.... [19]

The world had not seen such drama since the Nazi war crimes trials at Nuremberg in 1945. Security Council Resolution 827, in May 1993, had established The Hague tribunal to indict, try, and punish individuals responsible for a long list of war crimes that had occurred during the bloody breakup of Yugoslavia. Soon thereafter, the United Nations created an equivalent court to try human rights abuses committed during the 1994 civil war in Rwanda.

Although the Rwandan and Yugoslav tribunals emerged only in the wake of the Cold War, human rights have been a concern of the United Nations since its founding. Before World War II, human rights were rarely addressed in international relations. Only a few international human rights agreements had been realized, such as the Slavery Convention of 1926 and The Hague Convention of 1907, which dealt with a government's treatment of foreign nationals. However, nothing had been said about a nation's treatment of its own citizens. Under the principle of sovereignty, the relations between a government and its people were considered an internal matter.

The preamble of the UN Charter, however, raises international concern for human rights to a new level of significance. It declares that one of the organization's purposes is "to reaffirm faith in fundamental human rights, in the dignity and worth of the human person, in the equal rights of men and women and of nations large and small." The Charter contains several references to human rights (Articles 13, 55, 56, 62, 68, and 76) but does not define the term.

Authorized by the Charter, the Economic and Social Council created the **Commission on Human Rights** in 1946. At its initial session, the commission established a small drafting group to prepare the **Universal Declaration of Human Rights (UDHR)**. Eleanor Roosevelt, widow of U.S. president Franklin D. Roosevelt, chaired the drafting committee. On December 10, 1948, the General Assembly adopted the Universal Declaration as "a common standard of achievement." Reflecting the predominantly Western membership of the United Nations in 1948, twenty-two of the declaration's thirty articles deal with individual, civil, and political rights, and only six articles deal with economic, social, and cultural rights. The declaration stresses the "inherent dignity" of the individual; the principle of equality; and the three interrelated fundamental rights of life, liberty, and the security of the person. The declaration accepts the principle that states can limit human rights only when such laws are "solely for the purpose of securing due recognition and respect for the rights" of others and establishing "the just requirements of morality, public order and the general welfare in a democratic society."

The Universal Declaration set the direction for all later agreements in the field of human rights. However, it required elaborate negotiations spanning another eighteen years to produce the other two documents that, with the Universal Declaration, compose the composite **International Bill of Human Rights**. The General Assembly adopted the much more specific **International Covenant on Civil and Political Rights (ICCPR)** and the **International Covenant on Economic, Social and Cultural Rights (ICESCR)** much later, in 1966. These two covenants were written in the form of treaties, requiring ratification by the member states and consequently instituting legally binding obligations. The ICCPR detailed the freedoms of speech, press, worship, and assembly; the security of person and property; free political participation; and procedural due process, protecting the individual against arbitrary and unreasonable government action. Each state assumed the obligation to submit regular reports to a new UN Human Rights Committee, which would review them in detail and make recommendations to governments for improvement and additional legislation. The ICESCR provided guarantees of "the right of everyone to the enjoyment of an adequate standard of living for himself and his family, including adequate food, clothing, and housing, and to the continuous improvement of living conditions." It also guaranteed access to adequate education, social security, medical care, employment, shelter, mental health, and leisure, requiring an expansion of governmental functions. At the insistence of the developing nations, which by 1966 made up a majority of UN membership, both documents recognized the right of self-determination. By 2021, about 85 percent of UN member states had ratified the two covenants.

The effort to produce these agreements was arduous because of differing views among countries over what constitutes a human right. On the one hand, Western states and their citizens, drawing on a tradition of liberal politics that accentuates the primacy of the individual, placing strong emphasis on civil and political rights. That is, they stress the rights of the person and view human rights as protecting the individual from actions by the state. They emphasize protection of minority groups against majority power. This viewpoint advocates the use of the judicial process to protect human rights. Such an outlook emphasizes rights such as free speech, freedom of religion, freedom of assembly, specific rights of the accused, and the right to organize. On the other hand, developing nations emphasize economic, social, and cultural rights, considering them prerequisite to the exercise of political rights. Western nations object to the inclusion of these elements, contending

Photo 7.3 Eleanor Roosevelt and *The Universal Declaration of Human Rights.*
Source: UN/DPI Photo. Reproduced by permission of the United Nations.

they are "goals" rather than "rights." In part, the developing world's viewpoint is based on living conditions and the culture in these states. Theirs is a collective outlook that holds that societies, as groups, have rights and that the rights of the group as a whole supersede individual rights. This approach requires government action to provide citizens with the conditions and facilities essential for the full realization of rights. Developing nations view economic rights, particularly the right to development, as creating obligations for the international system as well, including the provision of needed resources for development. Developing nations have emphasized the primacy of rights such as adequate food, tolerable living standards, and requisite shelter. The developed world has resisted elevating economic rights to a position of primacy because it views doing so as an effort to redistribute wealth to its disadvantage.

Despite the difference in outlook by member states, the United Nations has negotiated and adopted a long list of conventions and declarations that have sought to extend and clarify the meaning of *human rights.* The Commission on Human Rights, the predecessor to the current Human Rights Council, drafted some, other bodies drafted some, and several resulted from UN conferences or came from specialized agencies. Among the principal documents on the long list are the conventions on the Prevention and Punishment of the Crime of Genocide (1948), the Elimination of All Forms of Racial Discrimination (1965), the Suppression and Punishment of the Crime of Apartheid (1973), the Political Rights of Women (1952), the Elimination of All Forms of Discrimination against Women (1979), the Suppression of the Traffic in Persons and of the Exploitation of the Prostitution of Others (1949), the Status of Refugees (1951), the Status of Stateless Persons (1954), Torture and Other Cruel, Inhuman or Degrading Treatment or Punishment (1984), the Rights of the Child (1989), and the Protection of the Rights of All Migrant Workers and Members of Their Families (1990). Declarations have dealt with the Eradication of Hunger and Malnutrition (1974), the Protection of Women and Children in Emergency and Armed Conflict (1974), the Rights of Disabled Persons (1975), the Right to Development (1986), the Rights of Persons Belonging to National or Ethnic, Religious and Linguistic Minorities (1992), and two conventions added in 2006 on the Rights of Persons with Disabilities and on the Protection of All Persons from Enforced Disappearance. Additional protocols have been added to several of the existing covenants.

Many agencies and organizations within the UN System have also negotiated agreements relating to human rights. The International Labour Organization has formulated several treaties regarding the rights of labor, including the right to organize. Other agencies that have drafted and approved agreements include the UN Children's Fund, the UN Commission on the Status of Women (CSW), and the UN High Commissioner for Refugees (UNHCR). All set standards and require reporting by governments. Together, these agreements and conventions constitute a body of growing international law on human rights.

The UN institutional structure within which these agreements and the international human rights regime have been negotiated consists of the Human Rights Council and the Human Rights Committee mentioned previously, as well as ten other committees individually established to monitor the implementation of specific important conventions. Among them are the Committee against Torture; the Committee on the Elimination of Racial Discrimination; the Economic, Social and Cultural Rights Committee; the Committee on the Elimination of Discrimination against Women; and the Committee on the Rights of the Child.

Until its demise in 2006, the Commission on Human Rights had a long record of proposing new conventions, declarations, and conferences attending to specific human rights issues or to the rights of specific vulnerable groups. But its work was not without

LANDMARKS IN THE DEVELOPMENT OF HUMAN RIGHTS INTERNATIONAL LAW

International Bill of Human Rights

The Universal Declaration of Human Rights	December 10, 1948
International Covenant on Civil and Political Rights	December 16, 1966
International Covenant on Economic, Social and Cultural Rights	December 16, 1966

Important UN Human Rights Instruments

Convention on the Prevention and Punishment of the Crime of Genocide	December 9, 1948
Convention on the Political Rights of Women	December 20, 1952
International Convention on the Elimination of All Forms of Racial Discrimination	December 21, 1965
Convention on the Elimination of All Forms of Discrimination against Women	December 18, 1979
Convention against Torture and Other Cruel, Inhuman or Degrading Treatment or Punishment	December 10, 1984
Declaration on the Right to Development	December 4, 1986
Convention on the Rights of the Child	November 20, 1989
International Criminal Tribunal for the Former Yugoslavia	May 25, 1993
Vienna Declaration on Human Rights	June 25, 1993
UN High Commissioner for Human Rights	December 20, 1993
International Criminal Tribunal for Rwanda	November 8, 1994
Rome Statute of the International Criminal Court	July 17, 1998
International Criminal Court	July 1, 2002
International Convention on the Rights of Persons with Disabilities	December 13, 2006
International Convention for the Protection of All Persons from Enforced Disappearance	December 20, 2006

controversy, particularly because some of its elected members had questionable human rights records. The chorus of criticism led to Secretary-General Annan's proposal that the commission be replaced by a smaller but more respected human rights council, its members elected at large by two-thirds vote of the member states in the General Assembly. We urge you to return to Chapter 4 to review the membership, duties, and work so far of the Human Rights Council.

In 1967, ECOSOC authorized the Commission on Human Rights to move beyond general discussion and to consider human rights violations in individual countries. It was allowed to entertain specific complaints by individuals against their own government. The new Human Rights Council has taken on this authority as well. After review by two working groups, the council decides whether to make public the human rights violations made in the complaints, and can refer the matter to the Secretary-General. Public opinion can be mobilized against a government that systematically violates the rights of its citizens. Although no enforcement is possible, both the council and the General Assembly can pass resolutions condemning the worst abuses on a country-specific basis. The Human Rights Council has given high visibility to the work of special rapporteurs, as we note earlier in this chapter. This procedure ensures discussion of the specific abuses and often leads to resolutions criticizing the offending state. The council's approach has been replicated by most of the human rights monitoring bodies.

UN human rights bodies are assisted by a large number of NGOs that serve as advocates of human rights and work to protect these rights. At times, the NGOs intervene to protect individuals who are denied their rights. These NGOs monitor the situation in each of the world's nations and submit informative reports to the various monitoring bodies. While functioning separately, they therefore are indirectly a part of the global monitoring system for human rights.

The issue of human rights is an area of concern for one of the largest blocs of nongovernmental organizations. Among the most influential in the UN policy process are Amnesty International and Human Rights Watch. Nearly all UN human rights committees actively solicit NGO participation. Materials submitted by NGOs are regularly distributed to committee members. Each committee, depending on its specific rules of procedure, allows NGOs to address the plenary session, working groups, or informal sessions of the body. Private representatives also lobby members between sessions and throughout the year. In many ways, these private international interest groups set the general human rights agenda for the world community to address through the UN structures.[20]

In 1993, the United Nations convened the World Conference on Human Rights, known as the **Vienna Conference**. Its charge was to conduct a global review of human rights and UN efforts in this area. The Vienna Declaration and Program of Action, adopted by the participants, who represented 171 nations, highlighted the links among development, democracy, and the promotion of human rights, bridging the differing interpretations of the West and the developing nations. It emphasized the universality, indivisibility, and interdependence of civil, cultural, economic, political, and social rights, declaring all to be the responsibility of governments and requiring governments to promote all human rights and fundamental freedoms. The declaration reaffirmed the right to development as a universal, inalienable, integral, and fundamental part of human rights. The signatories of the Vienna Declaration agreed that the development of the poorest nations was the collective responsibility of the international community. The final document asserted that extreme poverty and social exclusion constituted a "violation of human dignity." The declaration emphasized the rights of all vulnerable groups, especially women, and extended this protection to indigenous peoples.

The Vienna Declaration also recommended the creation of the position of **UN High Commissioner for Human Rights (UNHCHR)** to advocate human rights and to coordinate UN programs, agencies, and offices involved in this field. The creation of a central office for UN human rights efforts had become a necessity by 1993. With a plethora of institutions and a vibrant NGO community involved in the policy process, as well with a new realization that human rights protection was a critical aspect of maintaining international peace in a world of growing ethnic and religious separatism, the General Assembly acceded to the conference proposal.

The high commissioner serves as the focal point for all UN human rights activities and acts as the secretariat for all treaty bodies monitoring compliance with human rights covenants and agreements. Located in Geneva, the UNHCR has several divisions that, in turn, conduct studies and provide recommendations, information, and analysis to all UN organs dealing with human rights issues, oversee regional offices around the world, monitor human rights treaty compliance, and provide services to the Human Rights Council. The UNHCHR carries out its mission by promoting international agreements that set standards and then urges member states to report on their progress. The United Nations supplies information and assists nations in meeting human rights standards through technical missions and by developing model codes and programs.

UN Secretaries-General have given high visibility to the post, encouraging and receiving direct reports from the high commissioner. Particularly with the appointment in 1997 of Mary Robinson, the former president of Ireland, who traveled widely to conflict areas and made public indictments of rights violators, the UNHCHR became an independent voice in the policy arena. The importance accorded to the position continued to be highlighted with the appointment in 2018 of Michelle Bachelet, the first woman to be president of Chile (a post she held for two separate terms), as well as the first elected female leader in South America. Before becoming High Commissioner for Human Rights, she served as the first Executive Director of the newly created UN Entity for Gender Equality and the Empowerment of Women. She is often mentioned as a possible candidate to be the first woman Secretary-General for the UN. On August 31, 2022, her last day as High Commissioner and despite extraordinary pressure from Beijing not to publish it, Bachelet issued a scathing UN report accusing China of massive human rights violations against its Uyghur Muslim population in the Xinjiang region. The report detailed incidents of torture, rape and arbitrary detention in the government's Uyghur "re-education" facilities that provided credible evidence, the report said, of crimes against humanity. These camps often separated families and resulted in the long-term disappearance of men, women, and children.

The Judicial Process

During the past three-quarters of a century, society has witnessed an advancing acceptance of the idea that individuals may be held criminally responsible for what had previously been considered acts of state. Since the days of royal absolutism and the acceptance of state sovereignty in the seventeenth century, public leaders could cite their role as political figures and have little fear that they would face legal prosecution for their acts. However, after World War II, the Allies successfully tried the German and Japanese leadership for war crimes. The tribunals at Nuremberg and Tokyo included a new charge: "crimes against humanity." For the first time, the international community asserted that an individual leader could be tried in an international court for crimes committed against the domestic population. At Nuremberg, the four victorious powers—the United States, the United Kingdom, France, and the Soviet Union—served as judges. The highest leaders under indictment received the death penalty from both tribunals. Each court cooperated with the UN War Crimes Commission, but the trials were military rather than UN trials.

In the course of developing human rights treaties, the United Nations adopted the Nuremberg Tribunal Charter. This charter defined *crimes against humanity* as crimes of "murder, extermination, enslavement, deportation, and other inhumane acts committed against any civilian population, before or during a war ... whether or not in violation of the domestic law of the country where perpetrated." In so doing, the United Nations established an inherent tension between its commitment not "to intervene in matters which are essentially within the domestic jurisdiction of any state or [to] require the Members to submit such matters" for settlement (Article 2, paragraph 7) and the promotion of human rights and fundamental freedoms, which was also part of the UN's mission listed in its Charter (Articles 1, 13, and 55).

The International Criminal Tribunal for the Former Yugoslavia, in The Hague, and the International Criminal Tribunal for Rwanda (ICTR), with headquarters in Arusha, Tanzania, dealt with this kind of crime. Each had jurisdiction involving only the specified country, and in the Rwandan case, for Rwandan citizens who may have committed war crimes in neighboring states. The creation of these tribunals was an expression of the wide-reaching horror at the genocide practiced in both crises. The relative success of the two tribunals encouraged authorities in Sierra Leone to request a similar UN court for persons charged with crimes in its ongoing civil war and with violations of international humanitarian law against UN personnel in the country. After negotiations between the government and the UN Secretariat, the Special Court for Sierra Leone was established in the fall of 2000. These three tribunals responded to particular atrocities occurring in specific civil conflicts. However, their ad hoc nature left many governments with the conclusion that the long-term response to human rights crimes should be a permanent court to which suspected violators could be remanded for trial. Although an old idea, [21] it was given a new impetus by the encouragement of U.S. president Bill Clinton. In 1998, a conference of one hundred countries approved the Rome Statute of the **International Criminal Court (ICC)**, establishing a permanent body to investigate and decide cases involving individuals responsible for the most serious crimes of concern to the international community—genocide, crimes against humanity, and war crimes. After we present the groundbreaking work of the ad hoc tribunals created by the United Nations between 1993 and 2002, we will look at the launching of a permanent ICC.

For the innocent civilians who suffered through the commission of genocidal acts and war crimes in the Balkans in the 1990s, the establishment of the international tribunal in The Hague provided an opportunity to hold accountable those culpable for the massive violation of human rights. Article 1 of the ICTY statute stated, "The International Tribunal shall have the power to prosecute persons responsible for serious violations of international humanitarian law committed in the territory of the former Yugoslavia since 1991" until the UN Security Council decides to withdraw its mandate. The crimes it was specifically empowered to prosecute were grave breaches of the 1949 Geneva Convention, violations of the laws and customs of war, genocide, and crimes against humanity, very similar to the jurisdiction of the ICC. The ICTY could also prosecute persons already under accusation in a national court if the accused was charged only with an "ordinary" offense (i.e., not a war crime) or if the national trial had not been impartial.

The Security Council, upon recommendation of the Secretary-General, selected the judges and the lead prosecutor for the tribunal. The council was careful to include broad multinational representation among the judges and prosecutors. The International Criminal Tribunal for the Former Yugoslavia could not try defendants in absentia, but a Rule 61 proceeding allowed the prosecutor to present evidence publicly and to call witnesses. The stated purpose for this allowance was to reconfirm the indictment against the defendant and to permit the judges to issue an international arrest warrant. Thus, the tribunal could publicly air the charges against the individual being sought, and increased pressure was placed on alleged war criminals, who would not be able to travel out of the country without fear of detention by a UN member.

Although the indictment, arrest, and trial of Slobodan Milosevic may have marked the high point of the tribunal's activities, during its first decade eighty-eight accused persons appeared before the court. The ICTY issued its first indictment on November 11, 1994, for Dragan Nikolic, a Bosnian Serb who was alleged to have been the commander of a small prison camp in eastern Bosnia. The first conviction was for Dusko Tadic, who was convicted of every count established by the statute except genocide. Other notable indictments included Bosnian Serb leaders Radovan Karadzic and General Ratko Mladic. The tribunal convicted Karadzic in March 2016 of genocide for the massacre of Muslim men and boys at Srebrenica, and of war crimes and crimes against humanity during his leadership of the Bosnian Serb forces in the civil war.

During its lifetime, the tribunal publicly indicted 162 individuals, tried all but thirty-six of them, and sentenced eighty for their crimes. Of those found guilty, Radislav Krstic (chief of staff of Bosnian Serb forces that attacked civilians and UN personnel in the safe haven of Srebrenica) received a sentence of forty-six years' imprisonment for genocide, crimes against humanity, and violations of the laws of war. Zdravko Tolimir, an assistant commander of the Bosnian Serb Army, received a life sentence for his role in the murders of men and boys in the supposed UN safe havens of Srebrenica and Žepa. The ICTY relied on other institutions, most notably the North Atlantic Treaty Organization (NATO), to apprehend and extradite indicted individuals. Once sentenced, defendants would serve their terms in nations that volunteered prison space and were approved by the tribunal. Of the first ten individuals convicted by the tribunal and sentenced to serve active sentences, all were placed in European prison systems.

The UN Security Council created the International Criminal Tribunal for Rwanda on November 8, 1994 (Resolution 955). The ICTR had a limited time jurisdiction (calendar year 1994), but its mandate extended beyond the borders of Rwanda to incorporate crimes against Rwandans in refugee camps in the Republic of the Congo and in Burundi. The crimes it was empowered to prosecute were much the same as those before the Yugoslav tribunal, as were its structure and procedures.

The ICTR issued its first indictments, charging eight persons, on November 28, 1995. The tribunal also charged Jean-Paul Akayesu, a high government official, with inciting other persons to commit rape—the first time in history this offense was recognized as a "war crime." Former Rwandan Prime Minister Jean Kambanda was tried and convicted in September 1998. The first head of government to be convicted for such crimes, Kambanda was sentenced to life imprisonment. The convictions of Akayesu and Kambanda were the first ever rendered by an international court for genocide. Despite these convictions, many NGOs—among them Human Rights First, Human Rights Watch, War Criminal Watch, Africa South of the Sahara, and the International Commission of Jurists—criticized the court for the slow pace of the trials and its apparent leniency toward many individuals who were charged.

At a cost of $2 billion, over twenty-one years the Rwandan court heard ninety-three cases. These people included the former Rwandan ministers of defense, interior, and finance, as well as the chief of staff of the army and the president of the national assembly. Private citizens were not immune from charges; religious leaders, businesspeople, and students were also detained. Mali was the first country to provide prison facilities for the enforcement of the tribunal's sentences. The ICTR was authorized to give a maximum punishment of life in prison, but no death penalty.

After two decades of reasonable prosecutorial success, the Security Council decided to wind down the work of both tribunals by creating the Mechanism for International Criminal Tribunals (MICT), which was authorized to complete any remaining appeals from convicted defendants and to hear any retrials based on the outcome of those appeals. It was also charged with seeking the arrest and prosecution of the nine remaining fugitives associated with the Rwandan massacre, supervising the enforcement of sentences, maintaining the courts' archives, and protecting victims and witnesses from reprisal.

The apparent success of the tribunals for Yugoslavia and Rwanda strengthened the case for a permanent criminal court and led to the consideration of additional ad hoc panels in countries where conflict had produced human rights abuses. By 2000, **judicial diplomacy** had emerged as a reasonable way for the world community to punish political leaders who violated their citizens' rights and to dissuade others with the sure expectation of criminal responsibility. Sierra Leone provided such a venue. Wracked by civil war from 1991 onward despite two fragile peace agreements between the central government and the Revolutionary United Front (RUF), Sierra Leonean president Alhaji Ahmad Tejan Kabbah asked the international community to establish a tribunal to try suspected war criminals. After considering a letter Kabbah sent to Secretary-General Annan in June 2000, the Security Council directed Annan to negotiate the terms of a court for this purpose. An agreement was reached in January 2002.

Unlike the international tribunals in The Hague and Arusha, the Special Court for Sierra Leone was not a subsidiary organ of the United Nations, but rather a treaty-based court of mixed composition and jurisdiction—both national and international. Created by agreement between the United Nations and the national government, this court was charged with prosecuting "persons who bear the greatest responsibility for serious violations of international humanitarian law and Sierra Leonean law committed in the territory of Sierra Leone since 30 November 1996." The court's jurisdiction extended to the following:

> The most egregious practices of mass killing, extrajudicial executions, widespread mutilation, in particular amputation of hands, arms, legs, lips, ... sexual slavery, abduction of thousands of children and adults, ... forced recruitment into armed groups, looting and setting fire to large urban dwellings and villages.[22]

The court indicted several prominent politicians, including Brima "Bazzy" Kamara, the commander of the military junta that seized power in 1997. Kamara was charged with terrorizing civilians, attacking UN personnel, and sexual violence. However, the June 2003 indictment of Liberian president Charles Taylor for his support of the RUF demonstrated the limits of using judicial process to end conflicts and discourage human rights abuses. At the time of his indictment and the issuance of an international arrest warrant, President Taylor was in Ghana, participating in delicate peace negotiations to end the violence then under way in Liberia. Instead of arresting Taylor, Ghanaian and UN officials let him leave the country. The court's chief prosecutor expressed outrage. Kofi Annan's spokesman indicated that the Secretary-General supported the work of the court but also attached "great importance to the peace process" in Liberia, and implied that Taylor was not arrested because of the political need to keep Taylor engaged with that process.

Peace diplomacy temporarily trumped human rights proceedings, which demonstrated the fine distinctions that so often must be made in pursuing the desired, complex, but not always complementary goals of the international community.[23] In March 2006, the newly elected president of Sierra Leone, Ellen Johnson Sirleaf, requested the transfer of Taylor from Nigeria to her country for trial. After a number of missteps, Taylor's arrest was accomplished. Following negotiations, he was transferred to The Hague for trial in the ICC. In 2012, the court convicted him on eleven counts and sentenced Taylor to fifty years imprisonment in a British maximum-security prison.

While the Yugoslav, Rwandan, and Sierra Leonean courts were distinct responses to specific crises, a milestone in human rights policy was reached on July 17, 1998, with the adoption of the **Rome Statute**, which established the permanent International Criminal Court. The Rome Statute extended the court's jurisdiction to genocide, war crimes, and crimes against humanity, and it provided definitions for these crimes. The statute, however, did not authorize the court to hear cases involving alleged terrorism. We must remember that the Rome Statute was drafted and approved prior to the events of 9/11. But even now it would be difficult to find a consensus on the definition of terrorism and how to charge and try alleged terrorists or their organizations. Some legal scholars have argued that terrorism could be added to the current statute as a separate crime or could be included in the already covered "crimes against humanity." However, the legal, procedural, and substantive hurdles to obtaining a conviction in the ICC have seemed too great by most governments, and, thus, there has been no political will to expand the Court's jurisdiction.[24]

The ICC began operations in the summer of 2002 with the charge of investigating and bringing to justice individuals, not countries, who commit the most serious crimes of concern to the international community, including widespread murder of civilians, torture, and mass rape. Unlike the International Court of Justice, the ICC supersedes the usual limitations of sovereignty by having persons, not states, before it and by bringing cases against involuntary parties. Its jurisdiction complements national legal systems by taking cases that states refuse or are unwilling to undertake against their own nationals. Cases may be referred to the ICC by the Security Council under Chapter VII of the Charter, by one of the parties to the Rome Statute, or by the chief prosecutor with the approval of three judges. The court has no restrictions in terms of geography or time, which remedies a weakness in the ad hoc tribunals.

One hundred sixty countries participated in the UN Diplomatic Conference of Plenipotentiaries on the Establishment of an International Criminal Court (June 15–July 17, 1998), along with 124 NGOs, 17 intergovernmental organizations, and 14 UN specialized agencies and funds. By April 2002, the sixty ratifications necessary to bring the court into existence had been achieved. However, initiation of the court did not occur without controversy. In particular, the United States objected to the court's jurisdiction, fearing that U.S. military personnel and peacekeepers could be subject to unwarranted charges and hauled before the international forum. The United States not only declared that it would ratify the statute only if its jurisdiction were limited to cases referred to it by the UN Security Council, but also brought considerable pressure to bear on governments specifically to exempt U.S. personnel. The statute, as opened for signature in 1998, had no such provisions and claimed universal jurisdiction on the basis of international law. U.S. president Bill Clinton signed the Rome Statute but noted the need for amendments to it. Clinton's successor, President George W. Bush, withdrew the statute from Senate consideration for ratification until Washington's concerns were met. Within the Security Council, the United States pressed for and achieved yearly exemptions from the court's jurisdiction over UN peacekeepers. It was successful because of support from Russia and China, each of whom had not acceded to the Rome Statute (still true as of 2022). In the summer of 2004, however, the United States dropped its effort to renew its exemption, when, faced with the scandal of U.S. abuse of prisoners in occupied Iraq and the strong objection of Secretary-General Annan, other council members made clear they would accept no language that gave special treatment to U.S. military personnel.

Although the United Nations shepherded the creation of the court, the ICC is not a subordinate agency. It is an independent international organization with a diplomatic agreement on the modalities of its relationship with the United Nations. Its eighteen judges are elected to nine-year terms by the Assembly of the Statute's state parties; no two judges come from the same country. The assembly also elects the chief prosecutor. The judges elect the president of the court. The ICC has pretrial, trial, and appeals divisions. The court may impose fines, forced compensation to victims, or imprisonment. It may not impose the death penalty. During its first year in operation, the ICC received more than two hundred complaints seeking court action.

The International Criminal Court breaks new ground in international law. Not only does it limit claims of state sovereignty and make persons, not states, the subjects of international legal standing, but also for the first time in history it allows the direct participation of alleged victims. Victims may make written submissions to the court, participate at every stage of the criminal proceedings, be represented by counsel of their own choosing before the court, and seek compensation for the human rights abuses they have suffered. For the first time in history, an international court has the authority to order an individual to compensate another individual. It may do so to provide restitution, indemnification, or rehabilitation. Ordered compensation is paid through the Victims Trust Fund established in the Rome Statute. The fund can be augmented further by contributions from nation-states, private individuals, and other international organizations.

Contemporary Rights Challenges

Taking on human rights, especially as the topic has evolved since World War II, the UN faces continual trials, even beyond those we have described from the late twentieth century and early years of the present century. State sovereignty, as we have noted, is always a complicating factor. Additionally, while "democratic" rights mean that a majority should have the right of self-government, minorities and individuals are still expected to retain rights. Two other related factors that sometimes befog the UN's efforts are ethnic and religious differences.

Myanmar provides a troublesome example of these differentiations. A south Asian country once called Burma (which joined the UN in 1948 following its independence from Britain, and changed its name in 1989), the country reveals despairing ethnic and religious divergences which cloud, but inform, the dilemma of separate "ethnic" rights, "religious" rights, and "democratic" rights—all of concern to the UN. The overwhelming majority of Myanmar's population is Buddhist and ethnically Burman. Within the country, however, is found a despised minority group of Muslim-practicing Rohingya, who, according to a Human Rights Council fact-finding report, have, since 2017, suffered "a textbook example of ethnic cleansing....with genocidal intent" at the hands of Myanmar's Buddhist and Burman military. In January 2020, the International Court of Justice ordered Myanmar (at that time a democratic government) to take measures to protect members of its Rohingya community from genocide. Secretary-General António Guterres described the Rohingya as "one of if not the, most discriminated people in the world." Myanmar insisted that it was fighting militants and even its democratic leader, Aung San Suu Kyi (recipient of the Nobel Peace Prize), denied the allegations, despite confirmation by the UN and other independent sources (Amnesty International and Human Rights Watch, for example).

To complicate matters further, until 2011, a military junta hostile to "democratic" rights ruled Myanmar. In late 2011, the junta, under international pressure, released Aung San Suu Kyi from house arrest and granted general amnesty for political prisoners. By 2016, trustworthy elections had been held and Suu Kyi had become prime minister. But on February 1, 2021, a military coup returned non-democratic rule to the country. Aung San Suu Kyi and others were again placed under house arrest and faced serious charges. The Secretary-General immediately condemned the coup. Although Russia and China had consulted with Myanmar's military leaders before the power seizure, neither used its veto to restrain the Security Council's resolution calling for the release of detained democratic leaders. In September, Michelle Bachelet, High Commissioner for Human Rights, issued a blistering warning of a human rights catastrophe as a consequence of the coup and the large-scale abuse of human rights accompanying it. "The international community must redouble its efforts to restore democracy and prevent wider conflict before it is too late," she urged. Simultaneously, Tom Andrews, Special Rapporteur on Human Rights in Myanmar, while echoing the High Commissioner's alarm, shrewdly added that the military junta was *continuing* to deny the existence of the Rohingya minority, as it happens, a policy like that pursued during the brief democratic interregnum.[25] That is, the UN, dealt a difficult hand in Myanmar, strove diligently to address comprehensively the discrete issues of "ethnic," "religious," and "democratic" rights, all appearing in the same despondent place.

While this is but one example of the kinds of irritants the UN encounters as it toils to uphold and advance human rights, it may provide a heuristic case study, useful when considering human rights problems such as the Tigray War in Ethiopia, where minority Tigrayans (about 6 percent of the country's population) began resisting central government forces in November 2020; all sides in the brutal conflict were accused of unlawful killings, torture and sexual violence, clearly violating international human rights.

WOMEN'S RIGHTS

Securing Group Rights through Public Mobilization

In the Western philosophical tradition, human rights have been considered primarily individual rights. They arise from the "self-evident" condition of equality. The persistence of inequality, however, means that identifiable groups of human beings are often mistreated, exist in a condition of second-class citizenship, or are unable to share in the full benefits of society as others do. Certainly, the largest "minority" to experience unequal treatment in nearly all societies is women, who, in fact, make up a majority of the human population. In 1945, the UN Charter became the first international document in history to acknowledge the role of women in the world and to accentuate gender equality as a fundamental human right. One of the UN's first acts was to create the Commission on the Status of Women (CSW) in 1946 as the first functional commission of ECOSOC. Many of the UN's strategies, first employed on behalf of women, have also been used to improve the lives of children, the elderly, indigenous peoples, and ethnic minorities. In so doing, the United Nations has elevated "group" rights to comparable status with individual human rights.

Successful UN human rights initiatives have necessarily generated global policy affecting particular groups within the universal human family. The promotion of legal standards through binding conventions and treaties, the judicial defense of personal rights against human rights abuses, and the budding endorsement of personal sovereignty as a limitation on state sovereignty have provided a rationale for group rights. In the UN endeavor to secure these rights, however, the organization has not stressed primarily legalist and judicial policy-making strategies. This fact is particularly true with regard to international gender policy that has been directed toward enhancing women's rights and power. The United Nations has employed three additional strategies that have generally eclipsed the "judicial diplomacy" used in the defense of individual rights: mobilization of public opinion through world conferences and public forums; enhancement of research on women, with the goal of permanent empowerment; and provision of assistance for women in areas traditionally underfunded or ignored by national governments, such as health, child rearing, education, development, and environmental safety. These strategies cumulatively constitute a "campaign," organized and promoted by the United Nations on behalf of women and their empowerment—economically and politically—within their own societies and internationally. In addition to providing legitimacy and an institutional arena in the global effort to achieve gender equality, the United Nations is cheerleader, interest group, and fundraiser, with a particular set of goals—some of them controversial—that it has pursued with member states, NGOs, and other IGOs.

To be sure, the United Nations has created several legal instruments intended to enhance the status of women. These documents address a number of issues, including prostitution (Convention for the Suppression of the Traffic in Persons and of the

Exploitation of the Prostitution of Others, 1949), equal pay for men and women for work of equal value (International Labour Organization Convention Concerning Equal Remuneration for Men and Women Workers for Work of Equal Value, 1951), the ability to vote and hold public office (Convention on the Political Rights of Women, 1952), marital rights (Convention on Consent to Marriage, Minimum Age for Marriage and Registration of Marriages, 1962), the right to equal education (UNESCO Convention against Discrimination in Education, 1960), the end to gender discrimination (UN Convention on the Elimination of All Forms of Discrimination against Women, or CEDAW, 1979), and the end to violence against women, including pernicious practices such as the honor killings and trafficking of women (UN Declaration on the Elimination of Violence against Women, 1993).

The campaign on behalf of women's rights, however, has been far more a media, public opinion, and development assistance effort than an exercise in international law formation. Beginning with the UN Decade for Women (1976–1985), which encouraged governments, nongovernmental organizations, and UN units to focus on women's conditions in various parts of the world, the United Nations has directed media attention toward women's issues. It has also hosted four major world conferences on women (Mexico City, 1975; Copenhagen, 1980; Nairobi, 1985; and Beijing, 1995) and a follow-up General Assembly special session (Beijing+5, 2000) to outline the challenges to gender equality and the actions needed to remove these barriers. These conferences served to mobilize other actors both internationally and domestically and to raise awareness about the conditions of women and girls around the world. Other UN conferences, such as the 1993 World Conference on Human Rights and the 1995 World Social Summit in Copenhagen, emphasized the critical needs and roles of women in their societies.

Delegations from 133 governments took part in the first world conference on women held in Mexico City in 1975. Organized by the CSW, the conference debated and then adopted a World Plan of Action for addressing the issues of equality, development, and peace. The momentum of this meeting led to the creation of the Voluntary Fund for development projects related to women, later known as the *UN Development Fund for Women (UNIFEM)*. Also, a special UN research agency known as *INSTRAW (International Research and Training Institute for the Advancement of Women)* was established. In Copenhagen four years later, 145 governments participated and nearly eight thousand individuals attended a concurrent NGO forum. A redefined Plan of Action was adopted that drew attention to problems of employment, health, and education.

The first two conferences highlighted a normal characteristic of policy making: debate over priorities and methods for achieving accepted goals. In Mexico City and Copenhagen, differences emerged between countries of the North and those of the South; the developing world suggested that the important issues for women were those imposed by the economic and political neocolonialism of the developed states. Representatives from developed states emphasized challenges to women in the workplace and the political arena.[26] This debate carried over to the third world conference, held in Nairobi, Kenya, in 1985. There, attention was once again given to themes of equality, peace, and development. The final document of the conference, known as the **Nairobi Forward-Looking Strategies for the Advancement of Women**, called for new recognition that women and children are often the groups most harmed by poverty, drought, armed conflict, family violence, and marginalization caused by refugee, migrant, or ethnic minority status. Strategies were devised to accelerate fulfillment of women's rights issues during the last fifteen years of the twentieth century. According to the United Nations, in the last ten years of the century, approximately one hundred twenty governments reported progress in meeting the targets established at Nairobi.

CHRONOLOGY OF UN EFFORTS ON BEHALF OF WOMEN

June 26, 1945	UN Charter signed in San Francisco
June 21, 1946	Commission on the Status of Women created
December 20, 1952	Convention on the Political Rights of Women adopted
November 7, 1967	UN Declaration on the Elimination of Discrimination against Women
June 19–July 2, 1975	First World Conference on Women (Mexico City)
December 18, 1979	Convention on the Elimination of All Forms of Discrimination against Women (CEDAW) adopted
Summer 1980	Second World Conference on Women (Copenhagen)
April 6, 1982	CEDAW Committee created
August 11, 1983	International Research and Training Institute for the Advancement of Women (INSTRAW) opens
December 14, 1984	UN Development Fund for Women (UNIFEM) created
July 15–27, 1985	Third World Conference on Women (Nairobi)
April 20, 1987	Nafis Sadik becomes the first woman to head a major UN program—UN Population Fund
December 21, 1990	Secretariat sets 1995 targets for the employment of women: 25 percent in senior posts
February 7, 1992	Margaret Joan Anstee becomes first woman to head a peacekeeping mission and to be appointed a special representative of the Secretary-General (to Angola)
December 20, 1993	UN Declaration on the Elimination of Violence against Women
July 12, 1995	Rosalyn Higgins is elected the first woman judge to the International Court of Justice
September 4–17, 1995	Fourth World Conference on Women (Beijing)
March 2, 1998	Louise Fréchette becomes the first deputy Secretary-General
June 5–19, 2000	Beijing +5 special session convenes in New York
September 18, 2000	Millennium Declaration approved, calling in three out of eight goals for specific improvements in women's lives
April 26, 2002	Secretary-General appoints M. Patricia Durrant the first ombudsman
February 25, 2008	Secretary-General launches global "UNiTE to end violence campaign against women" campaign
January 1, 2011	UN Women begins operations, merging INSTRAW, DAW, UNIFEM, and the Office of the Special Adviser on Gender Issues
April 17, 2012 September 27, 2015	UN Chief Executives Board approves system-wide plan on gender equality and women's empowerment World Summit approve 17 Sustainable Development Goals (SDGs). SDG #5 calls for gender equality globally by 2030.

In 1995, the seminal fourth World Conference on Women was held in Beijing. Representatives of 189 governments attended the meeting, and a new five-year global action plan affirming the themes of equality, peace, and development was adopted. The **Beijing Declaration** and **Platform for Action (PFA)** identified twelve critical areas of concern for women's advancement and empowerment: poverty, education and training, health, violence, armed conflict, economy, decision-making, institutional mechanisms, human rights, media, environment, and the girl child. Five years after the Beijing conference, a special session held in June 2000, known as *Beijing +5*, gave government representatives and NGOs an opportunity to assess progress on the platform. Three months later, the Millennium Summit would codify in the Millennium Declaration many of the major initiatives launched by these earlier conferences. The effort continued with the fifth goal of 2015's Sustainable Development Goals (SDGs): to "Achieve gender equality and empower all women and girls." UN Women has since then reported regularly on progress; its 2018 flagship summary was entitled "Turning promises into action: Gender equality in the 2030 Agenda."[27]

Notably, as early as the Beijing meeting, a rift in the world community's approach to gender issues became evident. Conservative religious forces, particularly right-to-life NGOs, the Vatican, Islamic delegations, and nations with sizable Roman Catholic populations, opposed any language in the final conference statement that might imply endorsement of abortion or that might disrupt traditional national custom and law concerning the role of women in society. Using compromise language, the Beijing Platform for Action affirmed

> the right of men and women to be informed and to have access to safe, effective, affordable and acceptable methods of family planning of their choice, as well as other methods of their choice for the regulation of fertility *which are not against the law.*

The clash between secularists and traditionalists had first caught the public's attention at the UN's International Conference on Population and Development (ICPD) in Cairo in September 1994. The Cairo meeting was the fifth global conference on population, but the first to end in strong ethical controversy. It endorsed the rights of all people to reproductive freedom, and it encouraged policies that would slow population growth, including the empowerment of women, expanded educational opportunities, gender equality, and poverty reduction. This stance was a significant shift from the usual conference goals of setting targets for demographic growth and reflected the persuasive influence of moderate women's NGOs arrayed between conservative forces represented by Catholic and Islamic groups on one side and feminist groups at the other end of the spectrum.[28] With regard to abortion and family planning, all the conference could do was endorse ambiguous compromise language. It urged governments "to deal with the health impact of unsafe abortion as a major public health concern and to reduce the recourse to abortion through expanded and improved family planning services." It also declared that "in no case should abortion be promoted as a method of family planning."

In addition to the Beijing women's conference and the Cairo meeting on population, the World Summit on Social Development (WSSD; March 1995) emphasized the importance of women in the development process and the need to create equity between men and women in all aspects of social life. Despite differences between developed and developing states, and between religious and secular forces, the UN sessions that convened in the mid-1990s announced the agenda for progress on women's issues. Women's NGOs played the critical role of "framing" these issues for subsequent UN action. As a result, the General Assembly was able to set benchmarks for measuring progress. It recommended, among other goals, that the 1990 illiteracy rate for women and girls be halved by 2005, that the primary school enrollment ratio for all children be increased to 90 percent by 2010, and that 100 percent of all family planning facilities offer comprehensive services by 2015. In 2000, these would become official targets in the Millennium Development Goals (MDGs).

Research on Women

The United Nations collects statistics on women. Few countries keep separate records on women or attempt any statistical analysis of women's lives and work. Since the late 1970s, the UN Statistical Office, INSTRAW, and the ILO have created methodologies appropriate for studying women. The UN's Department of Economic and Social Affairs' Statistical Division publishes every five years *The World's Women*, most recently in 2020, which provides data on and analysis of women's experiences around the globe. The Division's studies highlight the effects of long-term inequalities and encouraged governments as well as the United Nations to take action to prevent them. Starting in the 1990s, UN advocacy for women fostered training programs and development projects all aimed at raising awareness and improving women's lives.

The Economic and Social Council created the International Research and Training Institute for the Advancement of Women in 1976 as the primary agency for data collection and dissemination of information on women. It was subsumed into a new umbrella agency, **UN Women**, in 2011, along with the Division for the Advancement of Women (DAW) and the UN Development Fund for Women. UN Women, in turn, established a training center, featuring a comprehensive e-learning platform sponsored by Denmark, Estonia, and Switzerland. For all of its programs, UN Women annually raises more than $500 million from donor governments and private sources.

The Division for the Advancement of Women, now also part of UN Women, has existed within the UN Secretariat in one form or another since 1946. In 1995, it served as the substantive secretariat for the world conference in Beijing, and after the meeting it prepared analytical studies on the priority areas identified in the Beijing Declaration. Its Gender Analysis Section organized panels of experts and workshops on emerging women's issues.

Development Assistance for Women

Three of the eight Millennium Development Goals approved in 2000 spoke directly to the empowerment of women through UN development strategies (Goals 2, Achieve universal primary education for both boys and girls; Goal 3, Promote gender equality and empower women; Goal 5, Improve Maternal Health). Over the next fifteen years, the United Nations, through agencies such as the UN Development Programme and UN Women, targeted its efforts with much success on bringing women into the mainstream of national life. UNDP and other UN bodies focused on bringing women into active participation through civil society and electoral politics. The centrality of women in the UN's development policies was put in high relief with the adoption of the SDGs in 2015, referenced earlier in this chapter, which included a commitment to complete gender equality globally by 2030. We will have much more to say about the SDGs in the next chapter.

The United Nations directly or through its specialized agencies assists women in areas such as health, education, family planning, investment, combating gender violence, political empowerment, employment training, and the environment. Prominently, the UN Children's Fund, the World Food Programme, and the World Health Organization have provided assistance to women and girls in most countries of the world. In the case of WHO, the organization has made a special effort to focus international attention on the effects of AIDS on women and girls. After the Beijing conference, the central agency for UN women's assistance programs was the UN Development Fund for Women.

UN Women has developed close working relationships with activist NGOs, particularly in Africa and Latin America, to achieve its goals. One of its core strategies in the new millennium is forging partnerships among the main stakeholders addressing women's issues, including governments, the UN System itself, and the private sector. UNIFEM first made use of NGOs as implementing agencies for its projects in the 1980s, a practice UNDP and other UN development bodies soon followed. UN Women maintains a Global Civil Society Advisory Group of twenty-five members and as many as forty regional, national, and multi-country advisory groups in order to give NGOs a voice in the work and implementation programs of the organization. Through these groups and its programs, UN Women has aimed at strengthening women's economic capacity as entrepreneurs and producers, enhancing their role in governance and leadership within their societies, and advocating for women's human rights. Its programs mirror the broader public policy debate under way in the United Nations, focusing primarily on achieving the organization's sustainable development goals. Its engagement with NGOs in its programs also reflects the ever-growing UN involvement with international civil society in the policy process.

Of course, declarations, resolutions, and pronouncements do not ensure that policy is made and implemented. Formal institutional structures and procedures are usually responsible for those tasks. In this regard, within the UN System an important moment for the empowerment of women came with the approval of the system-wide action plan on gender equality and the empowerment of women (UN-SWAP) in 2012. Approved by the UN Chief Executives Board, UN-SWAP for the first time assigns common performance standards for the gender-related work of all UN entities. UN Women has a leading role in supporting the implementation of the plan, which uses a framework with fifteen performance indicators based on intergovernmental mandates. Under UN-SWAP, all UN bureaucracies must adopt policies on gender equality and women's empowerment in their planning documents and activities that meet one or more of the fifteen objectives in the program. They are held accountable through performance reporting requirements and assessment measures. By way of SWAP, the UN has moved beyond a campaign on behalf of women and has made women-centric policies central to its regular operations.

By 2022, more girls were going to school worldwide, fewer girls were forced into early marriage, more women were serving in parliament and positions of leadership, and laws were being reformed to advance gender equality. Still, activists continued to urge attention to women's rights and to meeting the Sustainable Development Goal number 5, as well as other SDGs relevant to the welfare of women and girls. Of particular concern was the plight of women and girls following the return of Taliban rule in Afghanistan as U.S. and NATO troops left the country in late summer 2021. As you read in the Introduction, the Security Council responded by extending the mandate of the UN Assistance Mission in Afghanistan and emphasizing the "importance of the full, equal and meaningful participation of women." UN Women committed to staying in the country, working to ensure that women's rights were protected and promoted, and engaging with women's civil society and the Afghan women's movement.[29] From the perspective of 2022, Afghanistan could prove a most demanding test, even a prototype, for one of the UN's most accented stances.

SUMMARY

The United Nations was founded as an intergovernmental organization of sovereign member states primarily dedicated to keeping the peace through collective security measures. Its Charter, however, authorizes it to protect human rights and to better the lives of people around the world. During the past three-quarters of a century, the effort to respond to thematic issues relevant to individuals' lives has led the United Nations into a central policy-making role separate from the immediate causes of peace and war, and into a complex relationship with non-state actors of all types. As such, the United Nations has become a key player on the international, national, and subnational levels of the public policy process. In this chapter, we discussed how the United Nations has been central to the judicial and legal definition and enforcement of the world's conception of human rights and how it has mobilized public opinion on behalf of an international women's agenda. In Chapter 8, we look at international economic development and global environmental policy, respectively, and explain that the United Nations also serves as a conduit for particular states' objectives for the international community and as the initiator of public policy processes that go beyond the institution itself to involve other multilateral forums.

KEY TERMS

Arria Formula (260)
Beijing Declaration (277)
Cardoso Report (262)
Commission on Human Rights (264)
International Bill of Human Rights (264)
International Covenant on Civil and
  Political Rights (ICCPR) (264)
International Covenant on Economic, Social
  and Cultural Rights (ICESCR) (264)
International Criminal Court (270)
Judicial Diplomacy (271)
Nairobi Forward-Looking Strategies for
  the Advancement of Women (276)

Nongovernmental Organizations (254)
Platform for Action (PFA) (277)
Rome Statute (272)
Special Rapporteurs (259)
Subsidiarity (263)
Thematic Diplomacy (253)
UN High Commissioner for Human
  Rights (UNHCHR) (268)
UN Women (279)
Universal Declaration of Human Rights
  (UDHR) (264)
Vienna Conference (268)

DISCUSSION QUESTIONS

Are human rights relative and culturally determined or universal in nature?

May the United Nations and/or the international community legitimately enforce human rights standards and norms in today's world?

What role should nongovernmental organizations play in the work of the United Nations, given it is an intergovernmental organization made up of sovereign states?

RESOURCES FOR FURTHER RESEARCH

Relevant Web Sites

Human Rights Council (www.ohchr.org/en/hrbodies/hrc/pages/home.aspx)
  International Criminal Court (www.icc-cpi.int)
  NGO Branch, UN Department of Economic and Social Affairs (csonet.org/index. php?menu=14)
  Office of the UN High Commissioner for Human Rights (www.ohchr.org/EN/pages/ home.aspx)
  UN Office for Partnerships (www.un.org/partnerships/)
  UN Women (www.unwomen.org/en)
  WomenWatch (www.un.org/womenwatch/)

Books, Articles, and Documents

Alger, Chadwick. "The Emerging Roles of NGOs in the UN System: From Article 71 to a People's Millennium Assembly." *Global Governance* 8, no. 1 (January/March 2002): 93–117.
Anheier, Helmut. *Global Civil Society*. Oxford: Oxford University Press, published annually.
Becker, Jo. *Campaigning for Justice: Human Rights Advocacy in Practice*. Palo Alto: Stanford University Press, 2013.
Dany, Charlotte. *Global Governance and NGO Participation: Shaping the Information Society in the United Nations*. London and New York: Routledge, 2013.
Forsythe, David P. *Human Rights in International Relations*. New York: Cambridge University Press, 2000.
Glendon, Mary Ann. *A World Made New: Eleanor Roosevelt and the Universal Declaration of Human Rights*. New York: Random House, 2001.

Jones, John R.W.D. *The Practice of the International Criminal Tribunals for the Former Yugoslavia and Rwanda.* Irvington, NY: Transnational, 1999.

Kant, Immanuel. *Perpetual Peace*, ed. Lewis White Beck. New York: Bobbs-Merrill, 1957.

Korey, William. *NGOs and the Universal Declaration of Human Rights: A Curious Grapevine.* New York: St. Martin's Press, 1998.

Moore, John Allphin, Jr., and Jerry Pubantz. *Encyclopedia of the United Nations.* 2nd Edition. New York: Facts on File, 2008.

Panel of Eminent Persons on United Nations-Civil Society Relations. *Report: We the Peoples: Civil Society, the United Nations and Global Governance.* June 21, 2004, A/58/817.

Pietilla, Hilkka, and Jeanne Vickers. *Making Women Matter: The Role of the United Nations.* London: Zed Books, 1996.

Weiss, Thomas G., and Leon Gordenker, eds. *NGOs, the UN and Global Governance.* Boulder, CO: Lynne Rienner, 1996.

Zoelle, Diana. *Globalizing Concern for Women's Human Rights.* New York: St. Martin's Press, 2000.

Notes

1 UN General Assembly, *Report of the Secretary-General on the Work of the Organization*, UN document A/55/1 (New York: United Nations, 2000).

2 Jürgen Habermas, *Between Facts and Norms: Contributions to a Discourse Theory of Law and Democracy* (Cambridge: MIT Press, 1996).

3 Jessica Matthews, "Power Shift," *Foreign Affairs* (January/February 1997): 50–66.

4 UN Environment Programme, *Declaration of the United Nations Conference on the Human Environment* (Geneva, Switzerland: UN Environment Programme, June 16, 1972), preamble, para. 7.

5 <unfccc.int/sites/default/files/resource/cp2021_inf03p01_adv.pdf>.

6 An example of ongoing NGO efforts in 2021 occurred when, responding to the COVID-19 crisis in Africa, UNHCR, the International Council of Voluntary Agencies (ICVA), and international and national NGOs convened region-wide, multi-day, consultations in northeastern and southern Africa. See <www.unhcr.org/afr/2021-regional-ngo-consultations-ehagl.html>.

7 See the NMUN Web site found at <www.nmun.org>.

8 See the UNA/USA's Web site, "Model UN Preparation," found at <www.unausa.org/global-classrooms-model-un/how-to-participate/model-un-preparation>.

9 For full coverage of Special Procedures, see <www.ohchr.org/EN/HRBodies/SP/Pages/Welcomepage.aspx>.

10 UN Human Rights; Office of the High Commissioner, at <www.ohchr.org/EN/HRBodies/SP/Pages/CountryandothervisitsSP.aspx>.

11 Report of the United Nations High Commissioner for Human Rights and Follow up to the World Conference on Human Rights. Effective Functioning of Human Rights Mechanisms. E/CN.4/2000/14, 11 September 2001, at ≤undocs.org/pdf?symbol=en/E/CN.4/2001/2≥.

12 For full explication, see <www.ohchr.org/EN/Issues/Migration/SRMigrants/Pages/SRMigrantsIndex.aspx>.

13 For Dr. Morales' biography, see <www.ohchr.org/EN/Issues/Migration/SRMigrants/Pages/FelipeGonzalezMorales.aspx>.

14 "Making migration work: An eight-Point Agenda for Action," High-Level Dialogue on International Migration and Development, October 3–4, 2013, United Nations, New York, found at <www.un.org/en/ga/68/meetings/migration/pdf/migration_8points_en.pdf >.

15 <www.ohchr.org/EN/Issues/Migration/SRMigrants/Pages/CallEndingImmigration-DetentionChildren.aspx>.

16 See <reliefweb.int/sites/reliefweb.int/files/resources/A_HRC_47_30_E.pdf>.

17 Kofi Annan, Report of the Secretary-General, *In Larger Freedom: Towards Development, Security and Human Rights for All*, March 21, 2005, A/59/2005.

18 Panel of Eminent Persons on United Nations-Civil Society Relations, *Report: We the Peoples: Civil Society, the United Nations and Global Governance*, June 21, 2004, A/58/817.

19 The exchange can be found at <www.icty.org/x/cases/slobodan_milosevic/trans/en/030429ED.htm>.

20 See Jutta Joachim, "Framing Issues and Seizing Opportunities: The UN, NGOs, and Women's Rights," *International Studies Quarterly* 47, no. 2 (2003): 247–274.

21 As early as October 1946, participants in international legal meetings discussed the possibility of a permanent war crimes tribunal to sustain the momentum created at Nuremberg and Tokyo. In 1948, the International Law Commission of the United Nations began discussions for the creation of a criminal court, and this sentiment was given greater momentum with the signing of the Geneva Conventions on December 9, 1948. The issue remained on the commission's agenda throughout the Cold War.

22 UN Security Council, *Report of the Secretary-General on the Establishment of a Special Court for Sierra Leone*, UN Document S/2000/915 (New York: United Nations, October 4, 2000), 1.

23 Michael P. Scharf, "The Special Court for Sierra Leone," *International Peacekeeping* (July/December 2000): 156–158.

24 For a full discussion, see Aviv Cohen, "Prosecuting Terrorists at the International Criminal Court: Reevaluating an Unused Legal Tool to Combat Terrorism," *Michigan State International Law Review* 20, no. 2 (2012): 219–257.

25 Internet sources used for these paragraphs: <news.un.org/en/story/2020/01/1055841>;<news.un.org/en/story/2020/01/1055841>; <www.ohchr.org/EN/NewsEvents/Pages/DisplayNews.aspx?NewsID=27521&LangID=E>; and <news.un.org/en/story/2021/09/1100752>.

26 Joachim, "Framing Issues," 256.

27 <www.unwomen.org/en/news/in-focus/women-and-the-sdgs>.

28 Joachim, "Framing Issues,"247, 268.

29 See UN Women, 12 October 2021 at <www.unwomen.org/en/news/stories/2021/10/experts-take-gender-equality-is-critical-for-the-afghanistans-future>.

Chapter 8

Economic Development, the Environment, and Health Policy

Besides making and promoting policy on human rights and women's issues, the United Nations (UN) has been actively engaged in pursuing development policy, and examining and addressing economic, environmental, and health issues affecting the world. In this chapter, we discuss mainly economic development in poorer nations, but also global environmental politics, the battle with HIV/AIDS, climate change, the coronavirus pandemic, and the concepts of *sustainable development* and *sustainable* human *development*.

BACKDROP TO ECONOMIC DEVELOPMENT POLICY

As we noted in the last chapter, the first article of the UN Charter calls on the United Nations to address "international problems" of an economic and social character. The UN's founders recognized that challenges to international peace and security could come in forms other than solely military threats. The Charter committed its members to provide "higher standards of living, full employment, and conditions of economic and social progress and development ... [and] solutions of international economic, social, health, and related problems" as *preconditions* to continuing global "stability and well-being" (Article 55). The following Article 56 made a general pledge on behalf of the UN's members to "take joint and separate action" to achieve these ends.

The idea of improving people's social and economic lives as a route to ensuring international order was not new when delegates gathered in San Francisco in 1945. It had already been embodied in the functional international organizations initiated in the nineteenth century, such as the Central Commission for Navigation on the Rhine and the International Telegraph Union. While these early international organizations did not address specifically modern issues of economic and human development, they did represent a first effort to address common social problems beyond issues of war and conflict. Later, President Woodrow Wilson's famous 1918 speech laying out "Fourteen Points" to guide the reconstruction of the world after the Great War implicitly acknowledged that all nations should advance the living standards and human circumstances of their populations. This element of emerging international discourse was included in the Covenant of the League of Nations and manifested by the League's creation of agencies such as the International Labour Organization.

DOI: 10.4324/9781003281535-9

Much of the post-war planning in the 1940s for a new international order included what political scientists would call the "articulation" of economic, social, and human rights interests as critical components of the proposed United Nations.[1] Parallel organizational efforts were being made to aggregate these interests and to develop institutional and policy responses to these perceived needs. Among such efforts were the convening of the Bretton Woods Conference, which led to the founding of the World Bank as a source of financing for development, and the 1943 meeting in Hot Springs, Virginia, that established the Food and Agriculture Organization to meet the overwhelming humanitarian food needs of the time, to enhance living conditions in the world's rural areas, and to elevate agricultural productivity.

The commitment to social and economic development by the authors of the UN Charter was as central a tenet of the new organization as were efforts to make peace, ensure self-determination, and protect human rights.[2] In 1945, however, long-term amelioration of living conditions was not considered a priority item for UN action; the world looked to the new body to deal with more immediate threats of conflict. Nonetheless, spurred by the initiatives of important member states—particularly the United States—and faced with the abysmal poverty of millions of people in immediate post-war Europe (and for the years following in Africa, Asia, and Latin America), economic development and global social policy became key tasks of the world organization. By the 1960s, the UN's newly independent members from the developing world used their voting majority in the General Assembly to encourage even greater efforts in these areas. The twin pressures of the East-West confrontation during the Cold War and North-South tensions then and since served as the primary motivating forces inspiring UN development policies and institutions. Poorer states used the United Nations as their public relations platform to criticize aid policies instituted by industrialized nations. With a working majority, they were able to launch UN initiatives and expand the parameters of the global development debate. The give-and-take between donor and recipient nations resulted in the creation of major UN development agencies, the setting of policy terminology and direction, and the establishment of a world economic development agenda. Today, myriad UN specialized agencies, "programmes," and "funds" are headquartered in New York City, Geneva, Nairobi, and many cities in the developing world, providing a comprehensive global system of economic and social development aid for the world's poor.

In his State of the Union Address to Congress in spring 1949, U.S. president Harry Truman made a direct appeal for funds to improve the lives and economies of peoples in the impoverished nations of Africa, Asia, and Latin America. Called the **Point Four Program**, Truman's plan proposed that the resources be administered through the United Nations.[3] The president rationalized his proposal to Congress by avowing that it would blunt the growing threat of worldwide Communism; however, it also reflected the U.S. commitment to bolster the process of self-determination then under way in the collapsing colonial empires. Congress provided the funds by June, and within a year, the UN Economic and Social Council, with new prospective funding, established the Expanded Program of Technical Assistance (EPTA). Financed by voluntary contributions—60 percent of its $20 million budget coming from the United States—EPTA was the largest UN program at the time.

Truman's immediate successors in the White House, Dwight Eisenhower and John Kennedy, also urged greater economic development efforts in the "Third World" under UN auspices. The motive for their encouragement turned to the U.S. desire to diminish Soviet influence in developing countries. President Eisenhower also couched the U.S. proposals for expanded aid in the context of the nuclear arms race. In what came to be known as his *Chance for Peace* speech, delivered to a group of newspaper editors in April 1953, Eisenhower called on Soviet leaders to accept a broad reduction in armaments on both sides. He argued that the resources saved from reduced military budgets of the superpowers by an agreed arms-control regime could then be put to the task of meeting the human needs of people in the poorest parts of the world. With a passion that would seem uncharacteristic of later presidents, Eisenhower made his point: "Every gun that is made, every warship launched, every rocket fired signifies in the final sense, a theft from those who hunger and are not fed, those who are cold and are not clothed."[4] While the president saw the value to a U.S. foreign policy of providing bilateral aid directly from Washington to less affluent states, he regularly promoted UN administration of disarmament savings on behalf of the "700 million people ... who have won full independence since World War II."[5]

The American call for greater economic assistance to the developing world and the creation of the EPTA met with enthusiasm among the postcolonial member states of the United Nations. However, the EPTA focused mostly on providing technical assistance and experts rather than on shifting capital from the industrialized states to poor countries. To encourage the latter, the General Assembly established the Special UN Fund for Economic Development (SUNFED) in 1957. Marking the first confrontation in what would become the **North-South debate**, the developing states of the Third World, located mostly in the Southern Hemisphere, hoped SUNFED would attract $250 million in contributions from wealthier states in the Northern Hemisphere. Many governments demanded that the industrialized states give as much as 1 percent of their gross national product to the fund, citing the need to build roads, schools, hospitals, electrical power plants, and other essential infrastructure for further economic development.

The financial response by rich nations was tepid. Several European countries contributed a few million dollars, and the United States agreed to match two-thirds of the total amount collected, but SUNFED never achieved its funding goals. In part, this failure was due to the continuing competition between the United States and the Soviet Union. Each was suspicious of UN development projects and investments that might be intended to curry favor by its opponent. Such suspicion was particularly the case once Nikita Khrushchev took over the undisputed reins of Soviet leadership in 1956. He reversed Stalin's policy of Soviet noninvolvement in Third World politics, agreeing to provide significant bilateral aid to "non-aligned" nations in Asia, the Middle East, and Africa. Aid programs to India and Egypt in particular were seen in the West as attempts to spread Communist influence. The United States, under President John Kennedy, countered the Soviet initiative with its own expanded aid programs—military and economic. Kennedy suggested that the struggle between the "free" world and Communism would be won or lost largely through foreign aid to impoverished places in Africa, Latin America, and Asia.

Superpower foreign aid competition poured funds into the developing world, but these resources did not fully address the conditions or meet the recipient states' desired needs. Tied to specific terms of trade, and largely given to advance U.S. or Soviet foreign policy goals, the aid was often spent inefficiently with little long-term stimulus to economic improvement. Developing countries preferred that assistance come through the United Nations, where their growing numbers would ensure multilateral coordination and little direct influence from donor nations in the administration of the aid.

Once the deadlock on UN membership expansion was broken in 1955, a large number of developing states were quickly admitted into the organization, and by the early 1960s, they had become a majority in the General Assembly. With the focus of UN activity shifting from the Security Council—because of continuing confrontation between the United States and the USSR—to the assembly, these new members used the forum to highlight North-South differences over economic development. They criticized aid and trade policies controlled by the prosperous nations and urged a new global economic system in which "fair" trade and the redistribution of global wealth to the developing world would be hallmarks. In essence, the South was demanding an overhaul of the Bretton Woods system.

Beginning in 1961, the General Assembly established four consecutive **Development Decades** to bring attention to the plight of poor countries. These decades gave visibility to UN efforts to assist the least developed countries (LDCs) and to inspire increased foreign assistance. Central to the message of the Development Decades was the perennial demand that the developed world transfer a larger percentage of its GDP to the Third World. Particularly during the Second and Third Decades (1971–1990), the General Assembly made a concerted effort to promote the agenda of the confrontational New International Economic Order (NIEO), which we describe later in this chapter.

In the Third Development Decade, the United Nations adopted the Substantial New Programme of Action (SNPA) for least developed countries and the New Industrial Development Strategy. These programs marked a shift in Third World tactics by encouraging LDCs to move toward economic liberalization, to end corruption, and to provide greater transparency and consistency in economic policies. The confrontation with the richer North having produced little improvement in their economic fortunes, poor nations sought global assistance to bring their economies into the processes of globalization and to end pernicious debt owed to world financial institutions and donor states.

UN CONFERENCE ON TRADE AND DEVELOPMENT

During the First Development Decade, the UN majority initiated two structural innovations that dominated development policy for the rest of the century: the **UN Conference on Trade and Development (UNCTAD)** and the UN Development Programme (UNDP). The initiative for a conference on trade and development first came from the **Non-Aligned Movement (NAM)**, a group of states self-characterized as neutral in the East-West conflict. NAM originated with a conference of Asian and African nations in Bandung, Indonesia, in 1955. Later, partly in response to NAM's urging, the UN Economic and Social Council voted to convene a world conference. UNCTAD met in Geneva from March 23 to June 16, 1964. It would meet regularly every four years after that in a different city—the next three convening in cities of the global South: New Delhi, India; Santiago, Chile; and Nairobi, Kenya, which was also the site of the fourteenth UNCTAD quadrennial session in June 2016.[6]

The first UNCTAD meeting was expected to be only a conference, but at that meeting delegates recommended making it a permanent organization within the UN System, with Raúl Prebisch of Argentina as its first Secretary-General. The General Assembly followed suit and established UNCTAD as one of its subsidiary organs, with headquarters in Geneva.

With a universal membership, UNCTAD is an intergovernmental organization committed to ameliorating the economic problems of underdevelopment in the global South by negotiating with the industrialized nations, particularly on trade issues. In 2020, UNCTAD's total budgetary resources were more than $88 million. UNCTAD assists needy countries in attracting investors by means of reliable and transparent financial information at the corporate level. It has also undertaken responsibilities for the implementation of the UN's sustainable development program in the developing world.

UNCTAD's relatively nonpolitical character in the new millennium represents a shift in image and policy since the confrontational era of the 1960s and 1970s. Raúl Prebisch, in contrast to other heads of UN organs, was an activist on behalf of the developing nations of the South. The major initiatives undertaken during his tenure included commodity agreements and the establishment of a General System of Preferences (GSP) to open the markets of developed states to goods from developing countries. *Commodity agreements* are arrangements among producing nations, sometimes including consuming nations, to cooperate in marketing raw materials. The objective of these agreements is to stabilize prices. An alternative approach is for the producing nations to establish marketing quotas that limit the amount of a given product in world trade, which would thus prevent prices from falling below the cost of production. Prebisch's UNCTAD secretariat also promoted the Common Fund, which would support price stabilization.

Prebisch had broad support among the LDCs participating in UNCTAD. Most importantly, a Third World caucus known as the **Group of 77 (G-77)** coalesced around Prebisch's leadership and put together a set of consensus demands. During the half-century following its initiation in 1964, the G-77 grew to 134 nations, finding in their cohesion the voting strength to dominate UNCTAD's agenda. Success in passing resolutions, however, does not automatically translate into a new policy in an intergovernmental organization. In this case, it would require convincing the sovereign donor states and stakeholders in the Bretton Woods system to alter policy. The G-77 regularly found that it could not overcome the opposition of the United States and other capitalist member states to policies they saw as restrictive of a free market world economy.

One of the most controversial proposals the G-77 and UNCTAD put forward was known as the **New International Economic Order**, a plan to radically reform and even replace large components of the world trade system put in place at the close of World War II, and to require the world's industrialized states and multinational corporations to conform their aid and investment policies to UN-approved guidelines. The Group of 77 proposed the NIEO as a way to redress global trade imbalances, which it perceived as unfair to the developing states. The plan was based on Prebisch's **theory of "dependency"** (see the discussion in Chapter 1 of "dependency theory"), which asserted that the industrialized nations had manipulated the rules to keep less fortunate nations permanently impoverished and "dependent" on developed nations for goods and support. A special session of the General Assembly approved the G-77's proposal in 1974.

The NIEO called for a radical reform of the world trade system with a new set of rules, including more favorable terms of trade for primary commodities, the transfer of technology to developing countries, a charter establishing the economic rights and duties of states in the international system, more-liberal aid policies, and a code of conduct for multinational corporations. The overall goal of the NIEO was a global redistribution of wealth, believed by its advocates to be the only hope for LDCs to escape poverty.

Most developed countries criticized the NIEO as an inappropriate regulation of international free trade, likely to limit, not encourage, foreign direct investment. Despite special sessions of the General Assembly convened in 1975, 1980, and 1986 to deal with development issues, and despite recurring calls for the implementation of NIEO at UNCTAD gatherings, wealthy nations made few concessions beyond granting preferences for imports from specific LDCs.

Yet, by the 1980s, the NIEO agenda was politically dead, superseded by a new concern for the growing debt levels maintained by developing states. The NIEO's recommendations were also becoming irrelevant because of the rapid expansion of free markets as the Cold War came to an end. The collapse in commodity prices worldwide early in that decade limited the effectiveness of NIEO-endorsed commodity agreements. Increasingly, governments in LDCs sought foreign investment and debt reduction or forgiveness, jettisoning the more radical NIEO proposals. However, they still demanded tariff exemptions, protection for newly created domestic industries, development assistance, export diversification, and guaranteed access to the markets of industrialized countries. That is, the G-77 became more practical, diplomatic, and pragmatic in its proposed solutions to the problems of development.

Although the success of neoliberal free market policies undermined the initial thrust of UNCTAD, the relative decline of developing countries' economies during the 1990s revived interest in the role of the organization. In 1996, at UNCTAD IX, held in Midrand, South Africa, the organization adopted a number of reforms to its structure and procedures and committed itself to helping less fortunate nations deal with the challenges presented by globalization. Issues of particular importance to UNCTAD included the plight of least developed, landlocked, and island countries; development and poverty alleviation in Africa; empowerment of women; and economic cooperation among developing nations. It also encouraged the growing trend by transnational corporations to transfer their regional and global headquarters to developing countries.

The acceptance of globalization as a fait accompli did not prevent UNCTAD from being critical of the World Bank and donor states for neglecting the continuing "unfair" aspects of world trade. At the Midrand meeting, many delegations noted the inequities imposed by globalization in the developing world and the many states that had not benefited from the liberalization of trade. In particular, the World Trade Organization was criticized for ignoring the development concerns of LDCs and other poor nations. Delegates urged greater inclusion of the developing world in the decision-making processes of international financial organizations.[7] UNCTAD also criticized the International Monetary Fund (IMF) and the World Bank for changing their structural adjustment requirements on conditional lending to poor countries, by giving new emphasis to domestic poverty reduction strategies in those states.[8] True to its ideological origins, UNCTAD called on financial institutions to correct inequities in the world trading system, newly exacerbated by global economic liberalization.

At the end of the second decade of the twenty-first century, UNCTAD's membership turned its attention to supporting the UN's sustainable development goals (SDGs) and their achievement by 2030 and helping developing countries with digital trade, trade integration, investment and their continuing debt problems.[9] Development remained the heart of the organization's work, as it persisted in promoting macroeconomic policies best suited to ending global economic inequalities and offered direct technical assistance to economies in transition.

UN DEVELOPMENT PROGRAMME

The General Assembly replaced the Special UN Fund for Economic Development and the Expanded Program of Technical Assistance with a new organization—the **UN Development Programme (UNDP)**—in 1965. Like UNCTAD, UNDP is an outcome of the First Development Decade and a subsidiary organ of the General Assembly. Headquartered in New York City, it serves as the lead agency for all UN development efforts. It maintains a network of national and regional offices in more than 170 countries and territories. About 90 percent of UNDP's resources—derived primarily from voluntary contributions and amounting to the largest item in the UN budget—go to about sixty-five nations with nearly 90 percent of the world's poorest people. More than 80 percent of all UNDP staff serve in local offices in developing countries. The offices work closely with the national governments and civil societies of these countries and often function as the local contact and coordination office for the entire UN System. UNDP prepares publications, among them the annual *Human Development Report*. This report is a compilation of statistics based on comparative country data that provides information on specific countries as well as on world and regional trends.

Following the 1992 Earth Summit (the **UN Conference on Environment and Development**), UNDP took on expanded responsibilities for implementing many of the new UN initiatives directed at sustainable development. The conference's Agenda 21 called for UNDP to join with the UN Environment Programme, the World Bank, UNCTAD, the Global Environment Facility (GEF), the International Development Association (IDA), and regional development banks to carry out more than one thousand specific recommendations. In fulfilling its new tasks, reinforced in 2015 by its assigned responsibilities to implement the sustainable development goals, UNDP has come to play a coordination role among UN agencies, and particularly between recipient nations and the Bretton Woods financial institutions. It distributes most of the technical assistance resources provided by the UN System.

UNDP expanded its mission statement in the early 1990s to encompass humanitarian assistance and social development. UNDP has become increasingly active in diverse fields—from establishing solar power energy supply systems and natural disaster management to supporting elections in transitional states. To attain the larger goal of sustainable *human* development, UNDP has focused on poverty eradication, democratic governance projects, information and communications technology, energy and the environment, and crisis prevention and recovery. To move the development process forward as expeditiously as possible, UNDP has sponsored a "roundtable process" that brings together governments that receive assistance with the donor community to address the priority items on the agency's agenda. Seeking to promote the SDGs and their predecessor Millennium Development Goals (MDGs) in all parts of its work, UNDP engages in, for example, women's empowerment and gender equality programs, in the event coordinating activities with, and interviewing and hiring staff for, UN Women.[10]

UN DEVELOPMENT PROGRAMME AT A GLANCE

Origin	Created in 1965 by General Assembly Resolution 2029; subsumed the Expanded Program on Technical Assistance, and the Special UN Fund for Economic Development
Headquarters	New York City
Administrator	Achim Steiner (2021–); member of Secretary-General's Senior Management Group
Governing Body	Executive board of thirty-six members; also administers the UN Capital Development Fund and the UN Volunteers
Voluntary Contributions (2019)	$4.7 billion
Thematic Trust Funds	Crisis Prevention and Recovery
	Democratic Governance
	Environment & Energy
	Poverty
	Gender
	HIV/AIDS
Offices	In 177 nations
Oversees	UN Office for South-South Cooperation
	UN Capital Development Fund
	UN Volunteers
Implementation Responsibilities	Global Environment Facility
	Agenda 21
Strategic Plan Focus	How to adopt sustainable development pathways
	How to build and/or strengthen inclusive and effective democratic governance
	Resilience building, including peacebuilding and state-building in post-conflict and transition settings; and disaster risk reduction, preparedness, response, and recovery
Publications	*Human Development Report* (annual)

In all its work, UNDP has given special emphasis to full equality between men and women and to enhancing the power of women in their countries. It joined with UNIFEM and UNCTAD in July 2003 to create a special UN task force on "gender and trade," hoping to "sensitize" policy makers to issues of international trade that affect women's lives and their roles in the development process.[11] The task force found that increased trade and investment in the labor-intensive sectors of developing countries expand employment opportunities for women. It also warned that economic liberalization, particularly of a country's service sector, worsens inequities in women's access to basic resources and services. It called for global attention to the needs of women in the workplace and to employment conditions that ensure gender equality.[12]

UNDP is also responsible for the UN Volunteers (UNV); the UN Capital Development Fund (UNCDF), which provides credit for the poor in LDCs and encourages sustainable uses of natural resources; and the Drylands Development Centre (UNDP-DDC), which spearheads efforts to reverse desertification and the consequences of drought. UNDP has formed partnerships with other UN programs and specialized agencies to address specific issues such as HIV/AIDS and environmental degradation. It has placed the fight against HIV/AIDS at the center of its work with governments in the developing world, serving as one of the implementing agencies of the Global Programme to Combat HIV/AIDS.

THE RIGHT TO DEVELOPMENT AND THE LEAST DEVELOPED COUNTRIES

The establishment of UNCTAD and UNDP were significant victories for states residing mostly in the Southern Hemisphere, but these organizations did not produce immediate meaningful changes in the development policies of donor states. Developed nations often criticized UN development efforts to the extent that they were bound up with the proposals of the New International Economic Order, violated free trade principles, or seemed to be politicized by the overlapping confrontation between the capitalist West and the socialist bloc. In the view of major Western nations, any moral claim to resources from the industrialized North by the postcolonial world was specious. Economic development could best be achieved by full participation in the world trade system and the operation of free market economies at home. Some Western European states also expressed concern that unfettered industrial development in the Third World could do irreversible damage to the environment.

In December 1986, the General Assembly declared development to be an inalienable human right by virtue of which each person and all peoples are entitled to participate in, contribute to, and enjoy economic, social, cultural, and political development, an essential condition for all human rights and fundamental freedoms to be fully realized.[13] Several world conferences subsequently reaffirmed the principle in their final documents. Among them, the most important were the Rio Declaration (Principle 3) of the 1992 Earth Summit, the 1993 Vienna Declaration and Programme of Action at the World Conference on Human Rights, and the Declaration of the Third UN Conference on the Least Developed Countries in 2001. The Right to Development was also highlighted in the Millennium Declaration (2000), the 2002 Monterrey Consensus, the 2005 World Summit Outcome Document, and the 2007 Declaration on the Rights of Indigenous Peoples. It is a core feature of the Sustainable Development Goals.

Declared principles require policy initiatives to make them meaningful. After four years of deliberation, the General Assembly, in June 1997, adopted the Agenda for Development. The idea for an agenda emerged in 1992 in response to Secretary-General Boutros

Boutros-Ghali's elaboration of *An Agenda for Peace.* At that time, many nations in the global South worried that the international community was downgrading development concerns in favor of concentrating on the traditional issues of peace and security. Also fearing that UN agencies had become marginalized by the Bretton Woods institutions, they saw the core thrust of the agenda as reaffirming the importance of development and resituating the world organization's central role in that process. The agenda addressed the familiar components of development—such as economic growth, trade, finance, science and technology, poverty eradication, employment, and human resource development—and placed new emphasis on the role of democracy, human rights, popular participation, good governance, and the empowerment of women.

Between 1980 and 2022, the United Nations convened five world conferences on the plight of least developed countries, acknowledging at each meeting that the many international efforts to lift impoverished countries out of the depths of privation had largely failed. Conference declarations noted that the world economy marginalized poor countries; in fact, in many cases, these countries' per capita incomes were decreasing, even in absolute terms. The growing international debt crisis of the 1980s aggravated their plight. Each conference called for new types of aid and for economic reforms in LDCs that would make these states more competitive in world trade and more efficient at home.

The first UN Conference on Least Developed Countries (UNLDC-I) occurred in Paris in 1981. The conference adopted the "Substantial New Programme of Action" noted previously which emphasized the decentralization of LDCs' economies, political democratization, and financial transparency. When UNLDC-II convened nine years later in Paris, little evidence indicated that SNPA had halted the slide into extreme poverty. LDCs had declined in all areas of per capita measurement. They had also taken on huge debt burdens that eliminated resources for investment and discouraged foreign direct investment. The one hundred fifty governments in attendance approved the Paris Declaration. It established as its basic principle "shared responsibility and strengthened partnership" between LDCs and all other groups—developed states, NGOs, other developing states, international financial institutions, and the private sector. The conference charged UNCTAD with the implementation of the conference's recommendations and called on the World Bank and UNDP to monitor and encourage country-level efforts.

Although economic conditions did not improve noticeably in the least developed states during the 1990s (only one LDC—Botswana—"graduated" from the official list of forty-nine nations in this category), the UN conferences had generated new international and domestic initiatives to solve LDCs' problems. Lending states evinced a new interest in debt relief, as evidenced by the World Bank's and IMF's creation of the Heavily Indebted Poor Country (HIPC) Initiative in 1996. Faced with the reality that many poor countries spend several times more on servicing accumulated international debt than on the problems facing their people, the initiative sought to achieve "debt sustainability" in these states and overall poverty reduction. "HIPC" nations that are willing to implement economic reform programs aimed at reducing poverty receive special assistance and debt relief from the world community. HIPC efforts have been reinforced by additional funding and concessions from the major economic powers, known as the *G-7*.[14] In June 2005, the major economies reached agreement on a $40 billion write-off of debt owed by eighteen of the world's poorest countries and owed mostly to the IMF, the World Bank, and the African Development Bank.

In addition to the World Bank Group institutions, the four UN regional development banks contribute financial support and expertise to economic development activities in the developing world. Along with the World Bank, subregional banks, and Multilateral Financial Institutions (MFIs), these banks make up a complex lending structure directed at development. They are the African Development Bank, created in 1964; the Asian

Development Bank (1966); the Inter-American Development Bank (1959); and the newest of the four, the European Bank for Reconstruction and Development, established in 1991. Each bank has its own mandate, board of directors, and independent status but is part of the UN System. The banks have overlapping members, including both borrowing countries and developed states that invest in the institutions, and work closely with other multilateral financial institutions, the most important of which are the European Investment Bank, the International Fund for Agricultural Development (IFAD), the Islamic Bank, the Nordic Development Fund, the Nordic Investment Bank, and the OPEC (Organization of Petroleum Exporting Countries) Fund for International Development. The banks are also closely associated with regional organizations in their area. For example, the African Development Bank and the Islamic Development Bank entered into an agreement with the Economic Community of West African States (ECOWAS) to finance projects both for regional and nonregional entrepreneurs and for microenterprises. Each regional bank provides several types of assistance: long-term loans to developing countries in their region at market rates, extended long-term loans—referred to as *credits*—at interest rates well below those in the international market, and grants. The regional banks also use donor contributions to make loans that are not financially viable in the market. By the 2020s, loans and credits made by these various institutions totaled in the hundreds of billions of dollars.

As in the case of the African and Islamic banks' association with ECOWAS, multilateral financial institutions work closely with the regional economic commissions established by the United Nations during the past seventy-five years. The Economic and Social Council (ECOSOC) created the first two of these commissions—the Economic Commission for Europe (ECE) and the Economic Commission for Asia and the Far East—in 1947. The latter was renamed, in 1974, the *Economic and Social Commission for Asia and the Pacific (ESCAP)*. These mechanisms encouraged regional cooperation in postwar reconstruction. Pressed by Latin American states to acknowledge that economic development was equally important in all parts of the world, the United Nations set up the Economic Commission for Latin America in 1948, redesignating it in 1984 as the *Economic Commission for Latin America and the Caribbean (ECLAC)*. ECOSOC inaugurated the Economic Commission for Africa (ECA) in 1958 and the Economic Commission for Western Asia (ECWA) in 1974, renamed the *Economic and Social Commission for Western Asia (ESCWA)* in 1985. The five regional commissions include countries within their respective regions and work with the regional multilateral banks, other regional organizations, the World Bank Group, and nongovernmental organizations (NGOs) in an effort to develop regional responses to economic and social challenges. The commissions are funded by the regular UN budget. They provide technical expertise, planning services, and sponsorship of regional development agencies.

Despite the new sense of cooperation among the various actors in the development effort, between 1990 and 1998 the GDP in the LDCs grew by only 3.2 percent, compared with 3.4 percent for the more fortunate developing countries. Much of the LDC growth by the turn of the century was explained by one state's progress—namely, Bangladesh. According to successive annual *Human Development Report* editions issued by UNDP, this growth rate was insufficient for LDCs to make any headway on ending crushing poverty and its attendant social problems. In this context, Secretary-General Kofi Annan opened the third UN Conference on Least Developed Countries on May 14, 2001, in Brussels. Charged with developing "measures for the sustainable development of the least developed countries and their progressive integration into the world economy," the conference set a goal of having rich countries provide development assistance equal to 0.15–0.20 percent of their gross national income (GNI); the United Nations later endorsed this goal as part of the Millennium Development Goals.[15] The conference set the following objectives: to halve the proportion of people living in extreme poverty and suffering from hunger by 2015, to increase LDCs' growth rates to 7 percent per annum (with a rate of investment to GDP of 25 percent), and to encourage public-private cooperation among North-South and South-South countries. Among the priority issues to be addressed, according to the conference report, were poverty eradication, gender equality, national governance, the environmental goals established in the Rio Declaration of the Earth Summit, and the reduction of HIV infection rates by 25 percent in the most affected countries. Finally, the conference called for the accession of the least developed states to the World Trade Organization, with the goal of achieving duty-free and quota-free access to the developed countries' markets.

This collection of recommendations reflected the merger of an evolving policy consensus on two fronts—economic development strategy and a global environmental policy that had been gestating for nearly thirty years. Secretary-General Annan highlighted the development strategy at the **Millennium Summit** in 2000. Noting that in the new century the United Nations must serve not only the states that are its members but the world's people as well, Annan called on the summit participants to end extreme poverty wherever it existed, calling such poverty "an affront to our common humanity."[16] He laid out an ambitious set of **Millennium Development Goals (MDGs)** and targets to be achieved by 2015.

MILLENNIUM DEVELOPMENT GOALS AND TARGETS

Goal 1	**Eradicate Extreme Poverty and Hunger** (by halving by 2015 the proportion of people who live on less than one dollar a day and suffer from hunger*)
Goal 2	**Achieve Universal Primary Education** (by ensuring by 2015 children everywhere, boys and girls alike, will be able to complete a full course of primary schooling)
Goal 3	**Promote Gender Equality and Empower Women** (by eliminating gender disparity in primary and secondary education, preferably by 2005, and to all levels of education no later than 2015)
Goal 4	**Reduce Child Mortality** (by reducing by two-thirds by 2015 the under-five mortality rate)
Goal 5	**Improve Maternal Health** (by reducing by three-quarters by 2015 the maternal mortality rate)
Goal 6	**Combat HIV/AIDS, Malaria, and Other Diseases** (by halting and reversing by 2015 the spread of HIV/AIDS and the incidence of malaria and other major diseases)
Goal 7	**Ensure Environmental Sustainability** (by integrating the principles of sustainable development into country policies and programs and reversing the loss of environmental resources; halving by 2015 the proportion of people without sustainable access to safe drinking water; and by 2020 achieving a significant improvement in the lives of at least one hundred million slum dwellers)
Goal 8	**Build a Global Partnership for Development** (by developing further an open, rule-based, predictable, nondiscriminatory trading and financial system; addressing the special needs of the least developed countries and the landlocked countries and small island developing states; dealing comprehensively with the debt problems of developing countries through national and international measures to make debts sustainable in the long term; developing and implementing strategies for decent and productive work for youth; and in cooperation with the private sector, provide access to affordable, essential drugs in developing countries and the benefits of new technologies, especially information and communications)

*Proportional targets for 2015 were in relation to 1990 base data.

Immediately following the summit, the General Assembly adopted the **Millennium Declaration** (see Resource 7 on the Routledge eResources webpage for Selected UN Resolutions), which enshrined these goals and eighteen specific development targets. The MDGs were a far cry from the NIEO and the South's persistent demands on a recalcitrant North that dominated a development debate in the 1960s and 1970s. The end of the Cold War, along with the economic realities of world debt and globalization, brought about a much more cooperative atmosphere in which a generally common strategy emerged with the United Nations—"as the most universal and most representative organization in the world"—playing "the central role." This situation did not mean, however, that policy differences no longer remained between developed and developing states. In fact, the latter continued to emphasize the structural impediments built into the Bretton Woods system, the need to overcome the economic inequalities between the two groups, and the elimination of debt as a precondition to economic development. Conversely, rich nations focused on the MDGs that called for better governance in LDCs, market liberalization, domestic responsibilities for education and health goals, and the impact of unbridled development on the global environment.

As we noted in Chapter 2, the United Nations was able to report in 2015 that adherence to the MDGs had helped "produce the most successful anti-poverty movement in history," and served as a stimulus for the new sustainable development agenda adopted in the fall of 2015. Extreme poverty declined by more than half, falling from 1.9 billion in 1990 to 836 million in 2015. More girls were in school, and women gained considerable ground in parliamentary representation around the world. The rate of child deaths before the fifth birthday declined by more than half, and the maternity mortality ratio fell 45 percent

Photo 8.1 Jeffrey Sachs, Director of the Earth Institute at Columbia University and the Secretary-General's special adviser on the Millennium Development Goals.

Source: UN Photo/Paulo Filgueiras. Reproduced by permission of the United Nations.

worldwide, with most of the progress recorded since 2000. At the same time, targeted investments in combating diseases such as HIV/AIDS and malaria and in improving sanitation—meeting MDG aspirations—brought unprecedented positive results. Still, the report pointed out, progress was uneven, serious inequalities persisted in parts of the world, and civil conflict remained the chief impediment to more substantial progress. (See discussion of "Eleanor's UN," Chapter 2.)

Partly because of budget constraints imposed on rich countries by the global economic downturn commencing in 2008, the focus of the fourth UN Conference on LDCs (held in Istanbul, 2011) reflected a growing awareness that aid alone could not solve all the fundamental problems facing LDCs. Business people and civil society representatives were among the most active of the nine thousand participants at the meeting. In the end, the Programme of Action renewed aid commitments, with donors again pledged to provide between 0.15 and 0.2 percent of their gross national incomes (GNIs) to aid the LDCs. Although civil society groups criticized that commitment as too little, the emphasis in Istanbul was on trade, investment, and productive capacities. The conference reaffirmed a decade-old commitment of tariff-free access to developed countries' markets for 97 percent of LDC's exports. At the same time, the conference adopted a set of measures to encourage developed nations' corporations to invest in LDCs. Rich nations' governments were expected to offer favorable fiscal incentives and special lines of credit. Delegates agreed to the need for investment in productive sectors, such as agriculture, industry, and infrastructure, areas described by the Programme of Action as "development multipliers."[17] (The Fifth UN Conference on LDCs, scheduled for Doha in January 2022, was postponed because of COVID-19 concerns.)

THE ENVIRONMENT AND SUSTAINABLE DEVELOPMENT

In his report to the Millennium Summit, Secretary-General Annan acknowledged the negative consequences that economic development practices were having on the global environment: "In rich countries, the by-products of industrial and agribusiness production poison soils and waterways. In the developing countries, massive deforestation, harmful farming practices and uncontrolled urbanization are major causes of environmental degradation."[18] He warned that without a strong global response, ecosystems and the ozone layer would continue to degrade, drinkable water would be difficult to find, biodiversity would diminish, and "the freedom of future generations to sustain their lives on this planet" would be in jeopardy. His message reflected a new object of UN concern, not contemplated by the institution's founders, and one with significant ramifications for UN development policy.

Nothing in the UN Charter specifically authorizes the organization to deal with environmental issues. In 1945, such issues were matters for national governments and for organizations outside the UN structure. Yet, beginning in the 1970s, the United Nations became the initiator and primary sponsor of global efforts to protect the environment from detrimental human activities and to ensure that its protection was compatible with social and economic development. The United Nations-sponsored world conferences, panels of experts, international conventions, and the creation of new environmental law and concepts, all came to define the international regime of environmental politics by the end of the century.

The UN-sponsored world conferences have often been defining events in fostering international legal regimes and policies. They are an innovation without specific authorization in the Charter. Article 1, however, commits the organization to serving as the "centre for harmonizing the actions of nations." Under this rubric, the world body has regularly convened delegates in ever-larger international meetings to address social, economic, environmental, and legal problems. The UN Conference on Trade and Development in 1964 was the first such meeting to garner broad international attention. In the actual formation of international policy, no area has seen a more adept use of the world conference approach by the United Nations than has the environment.

The 1972 UN Conference on the Human Environment (UNCHE), held in Stockholm, was the world body's first global conference on the topic. Earlier meetings sponsored by private groups and by some of the UN's specialized agencies—particularly the 1968 Biosphere Conference convened by the UN Educational, Scientific and Cultural Organization (UNESCO)—had put pressure on the General Assembly to convene a world conference focused on natural resource conservation. Also, at the 1968 U.S.-Soviet Summit meeting in Glassboro, NJ, the two superpowers called for international cooperation on environmental matters as a way to promote cooperation in East-West diplomacy. Finally, growing European concerns that unrestricted development in the Third World would damage the global commons and, consequently, the quality of life in the developed world led the United Nations to accept a Swedish invitation to host the Stockholm Conference.

UNCHE concentrated on conservation and pollution issues, seeing the natural environment as fundamentally under threat from economic development. The conference issued the "Stockholm Declaration," outlining the environmental obligations and duties of states, and a Plan of Action with 109 recommendations. The conference documents suggested that development and environmental protection were laudable movements that unfortunately required tradeoffs between the two. Environmental issues are inherently global concerns. National borders do not restrict the deleterious effects of bad environmental practices. Any efforts to limit these effects require the international community to direct its attention to the internal practices of nation-states. Consequently, sovereignty, the bedrock principle of the international system, must give way to some extent if the environment is to be protected. Methods to safeguard the environment sometimes seem to run contrary to development strategies put in place by developing states. These strategies, in turn, may cause environmental problems, or the effort to accommodate them to environmentally friendly techniques may be too costly. Thus, poorer nations at the conference viewed the demand that states alter their development programs to meet international environmental standards as an unwarranted and counterproductive intrusion into their internal affairs.

The apparent conflict between environmental conservation and development pitted the developed states with their concern for "quality-of-life" issues against developing states that wanted to protect their right to raise their people's standard of living through economic strategies unfettered by environmental regulation. Neither group of states wanted to undermine the fundamental principle of sovereignty. The Stockholm meeting attempted to balance the conflicting interests in the final declaration. **Principle 21** asserted:

> States have … a sovereign right to exploit their own resources pursuant to their own environmental policies … [but States also have] the responsibility to ensure that activities within their jurisdiction or control do not cause damage to the environment of other States, or of areas beyond the limits of national jurisdiction.

In addition, the conference established the "Polluter Pays Principle" (PPP) and the "Precautionary Approach" for all states. PPP obligated states to pay for pollution prevention. As a corollary, the conference asserted that a state was responsible for pollution emanating from it into areas beyond its borders. The precautionary approach required states, even when science had not yet fully proved the damaging environmental effects of various development activities, to take precautionary measures to avoid degrading the environment.

UN ENVIRONMENT PROGRAMME

The most important institutional outcome of the Stockholm meeting was the establishment of a new environmental agency. In December 1972, the General Assembly created the UN Environment Programme (UNEP). Its expenses were to be paid through a voluntary fund, and its headquarters was located in Nairobi to ease concerns in the developing world that UNEP might represent Northern nations' desires to limit development policies. During its first decade, UNEP became an effective and visible actor in promoting environmental awareness and in attracting major contributions from the industrialized states to international environmental projects.

On several occasions, UN conferences and meetings identified UNEP as the lead agency for international efforts to save the environment. However, unlike UNDP, which plays an equivalent role in the area of development, UNEP vies for leadership with other organizations and faces more limited funding in its endeavors to effect global environmental policy. Its success has been due in part to (a) the political talents of its successive directors—eight during its first half-century of existence: Maurice Strong (Canada), Mostapha Tolba (Egypt), Elizabeth Dowdeswell (Canada), Klaus Töpfer (Germany), Achim Steiner (dual citizenship—Germany and Brazil), Erik Solheim (Norway), Joyce Msuya (Tanzania), and Inger Anderson (Denmark); (b) the organization's mobilization of scientists, civil society organizations, and environmental NGOs on behalf of particular environmental initiatives; and (c) the scientific expertise it has developed in a number of monitoring and information-sharing programs. UNEP also serves as the secretariat for several of the international environmental conventions that member states have signed since its inception, including both the Basel Convention on the Movement of Hazardous Wastes and the Montreal Protocol on substances that deplete the ozone in our atmosphere. The latter agreement grew out of the 1985 Vienna Convention for the Protection of the Ozone Layer, itself the culmination of four years of negotiation initiated by UNEP.

On the tenth anniversary of the Stockholm Conference, seventy government representatives met at UNEP headquarters in Nairobi to assess progress on environmental matters. However, an impasse remained between poor nations' push for development on the one hand and efforts to conserve the environment on the other hand. Progress on either front seemed to undercut success on the other. The Nairobi meeting concluded that a reinvigorated international effort was needed. In 1983, the General Assembly established the World Commission on Environment and Development (WCED), with Norwegian prime minister Gro Harlem Brundtland as the commission's chairperson. Secretary-General Javier Pérez de Cuéllar charged the commission with establishing "a global agenda for change."

The twenty-one-member commission and its panel of experts held hearings and interviewed thousands of individuals and groups during a two-year period. The commission's final report, titled **Our Common Future**, proved to be one of the UN's most widely read and influential publications. It concluded that further progress could be made only if the legitimate claims of both camps were recognized. *Our Common Future* encouraged the world community to develop legally binding rights and obligations for states that recognized the direct links between development and the environment. It introduced the concept of **sustainable development**, defined as "development that meets the needs of the present without compromising the ability of future generations to meet their own needs." Sustainable development became the popular mantra for all future UN efforts to address global environmental challenges, culminating nearly thirty years later in a set of seventeen UN-approved Sustainable Development Goals (SDGs). While imprecisely defined, sustainable development appealed to political leaders in states with environmental concerns because it seemed to put a natural limit on economic development strategies. For developing countries, it officially recognized the legitimate claim to development.

The WCED called on the United Nations to convene another world conference, this one with the expressed purpose of drafting an international convention on the rights and duties of states in terms of sustainable development. The result was the UN Conference on Environment and Development (UNCED), also known as the *Earth Summit*, which convened in Rio de Janeiro in 1992. UNCED was the largest, most expensive, and most widely covered UN meeting to that time in history. One hundred seventy-eight national delegations and two-thirds of the world's heads of government attended. More than one hundred forty NGOs, with UN blessing, staged a Global Forum in tandem with the conference that attracted thirty thousand participants.

UNCED produced three important international agreements—the Rio Declaration, Agenda 21, and the Statement of Forest Principles—and served as the venue for the signing of the Framework Convention on Climate Change (UNFCCC) and the Convention on Biological Diversity (CBD). These documents attempted to balance the concerns of developed states for greater environmental protection—and their desire to avoid huge new financial responsibilities associated with the proposed global commitments—with the developing countries' desire to protect their sovereignty and pursue unrestrained national economic policies.

The *Rio Declaration* asserted twenty-seven "principles" that reflected the existing consensus on sustainable development. The first principle proclaimed, "human beings are at the centre of concerns for sustainable development," shifting the emphasis away from the prior (Stockholm's) emphasis on "nature" and environmental conservation. It elevated the right of development to equal status with environmental protection. It called on developed states to increase aid to poor nations to support the latter's efforts to meet the goals of the declaration, which, as operationalized in Agenda 21, were likely to impose huge new costs on involved governments. The declaration reasserted Stockholm's "Polluter Pays Principle" as well as Principle 21 of the Stockholm Declaration, which stated that governments, although free to develop their domestic resources as they wanted, were accountable for practices that injured the environment beyond their borders.

Agenda 21, an eight-hundred-page document, was filled with more than one thousand specific recommendations to achieve a "comprehensive plan for global action in all areas of sustainable development." It set international and national objectives and provided programmatic suggestions on how to fulfill the objectives.[19] The areas designated for remedial progress included world trade, poverty eradication, population, cities, atmospheric pollution, deforestation, drought, desertification, marine resource management, waste management, agriculture, biodiversity, and the transfer of technology. Agenda 21 identified many UN agencies, including UNEP, UNDP, the World Bank and its Global Environment Facility (GEF), the regional development banks, and UNCTAD, as actors with central responsibility for making sustainable development a reality. It encouraged broad participation by NGOs, individuals, subnational jurisdictions, business, labor, and the intellectual community. While reasserting sovereignty as an element of sustainable development, Agenda 21 sought to democratize diplomacy and remove it from the sole purview of national governments.

UNCED also issued the *Statement of Forest Principles*. This document fell far short of the world convention on forests that developed states and NGOs sought. Developing states that profited from the export of lumber products (such as Brazil and Indonesia) resisted international restrictions on the use of forests. With no possibility of an agreement between developing and developed states, the statement simply called for the protection of forests but recognized the right of states to use their forests as they wanted. After the Earth Summit, international negotiations continued within UN-sponsored bodies, culminating in the creation of the UN Forum on Forests (UNFF) by ECOSOC in October 2000. The new forum became a "subsidiary body" of ECOSOC, convening yearly after that, regularly recommending steps governments could take to protect their forests.

More than one hundred fifty nations and the European Union took the occasion of the Earth Summit to sign the UN Framework Convention on Climate Change and the Convention on Biological Diversity, which provided much of the perceived "success" of the Rio conference. Global media coverage, particularly of the climate change agreement, created an impetus for many national governments to establish domestic environmental programs and agencies. It also encouraged the General Assembly to endorse the negotiation of additional environmental conventions.

UNCED also established the Commission on Sustainable Development (CSD) as a functional body of the Economic and Social Council. With its membership of fifty-three states dominated by developing states, it was expected to pressure rich nations for the resources needed to cover extra costs in the Third World imposed by environmentally friendly development policies. Emphasizing the importance of the CSD, the General Assembly directed NGOs, other UN bodies, and intergovernmental economic organizations, on both global and regional levels, to participate in the commission's work. NGOs could submit written reports and address the commission, as well as conduct "consultations" with its members at the invitation of the chair or the UN Secretary-General. More than one thousand NGOs gained accreditation to CSD. In 1997, the Earth Summit +5 Special Session of the General Assembly directed CSD to begin work on identifying "indicators of sustainable development" that could be used to measure progress toward the goals established at Rio, a rubric that would become the measurement mechanism for the future MDGs and SDGs.

While sustainable development was enshrined at the 1992 Earth Summit as the overarching aspiration for all UN environmental activities and merged with all UN development efforts at the Millennium Summit in 2000, the Rio gathering additionally gave impetus to five areas of environmental policy that would then be pursued in the UN and other IGO settings. They were as follows:

- The atmosphere and climate change
- Water pollution and marine resources
- Biodiversity and natural resources
- Deforestation and desertification
- International financing of environmental initiatives

Atmosphere and Climate Change

Since the 1980s, the World Meteorological Organization (WMO) and UNEP have played the central roles in trying to halt the interrelated problems of ozone-layer depletion and global warming. Under their sponsorship, a number of countries agreed to the Vienna Convention for the Protection of the Ozone Layer in 1985. This convention made a general commitment to protect the ozone layer by reducing ozone-depleting chemical compounds in the atmosphere. At meetings following the inauguration of the convention, the signatories amended it several times. The most important elaboration was the Montreal

Protocol in 1987, which set specific production and consumption limits on refrigerant and industrial substances known as *chlorofluorocarbons*, or *CFCs*.

By the third decade of the twenty-first century, the 1992 Earth Summit-inspired approach to global warming had become of first importance to the United Nations. While greenhouse gases (GHGs) occur naturally and, indeed, are essential to life on earth—by keeping some of the sun's warmth from reflecting into space—the century and a half of industrialization with its accelerating use of non-renewable fossil fuels for energy production, along with deforestation and large-scale agriculture have resulted in spewing GHGs into the capped atmosphere to extremely high levels. The consequence is that the earth has been warming at an unprecedented and alarming rate. The UN, working with scientists via the Intergovernmental Panel on Climate Change (IPCC)—founded by UNEP and WMO in 1988— has studied the phenomenon of **climate change**, its causes, its rapidity, and its consequences. In 2007, the IPCC shared the Nobel Peace Prize with former U.S. Vice President Al Gore for contributing to the understanding of climate change. The IPCC comprises more than 1,000 scientists, policy makers, legal experts, and climate specialists from around the world. The work of the panel led to the UN Framework Convention on Climate Change (UNFCCC). This convention set an "ultimate objective" of stabilizing greenhouse gases at a level that would prevent dangerous human-induced interference with the climate system. These criteria proved difficult to define and elusive of agreement among the one hundred eighty-five ratifying nations. The UNFCCC, however, established a process for succeeding negotiation and the promulgation of amendments, or "protocols," that would establish specific targets that parties to the agreement would have to meet. The most important was the Kyoto Protocol. Adopted in 1997, the protocol set specific greenhouse gas emission targets for industrialized states to meet by 2012. The goal was to lower overall emissions of carbon dioxide (CO_2), nitrous oxide, methane, hydrofluorocarbons, perfluorocarbons, and sulfur hexafluoride.

The provisions of the Kyoto Protocol were directed at the industrialized states, which produced the overwhelming bulk of effluents responsible both for global warming and for ozone depletion. Annex I to the protocol specifically identified these nations. Annex I states committed themselves to emissions targets that were expected to reduce collective emissions of six key GHGs by at least 5 percent. The protocol required each country to achieve its target by 2012.

Photo 8.2 Two photos taken in the same location in Beijing in August 2005. The photograph on the left was taken after it had rained for two days. The right photograph shows smog covering Beijing in what would otherwise be a sunny day.

Source: Bobak via Creative Commons Attribution-Share Alike 2.5 Generic license.

CHRONOLOGY OF UN POLICY ON THE ENVIRONMENT

June 5–16, 1972	UN Conference on the Human Environment convenes (Stockholm)
October 2, 1973	United Nations Environment Programme begins its work
March 22, 1985	Vienna Convention for the Protection of the Ozone Layer opened for signature
October 19, 1987	*Our Common Future* submitted to the General Assembly
January 1, 1989	Montreal Protocol on the Depletion of the Ozone Layer enters into force
March 14, 1991	Global Environment Facility Trust Fund created
June 3–14, 1992	Earth Summit (Rio de Janeiro)
June 4, 1992	UN Framework Convention on Climate Change opened for signature
June 5, 1992	Convention on Biological Diversity opened for signature
February 12, 1993	Commission on Sustainable Development established
October 14, 1994	Convention to Combat Desertification opened for signature
June 23–27, 1997	Earth Summit +5 convenes (New York)
July 25, 1997	Intergovernmental Forum on Forests established
December 11, 1997	Kyoto Protocol adopted
April 1–3, 1998	First Assembly of the Global Environment Facility (GEF) convenes (New Delhi)
September 6–8, 2000	Millennium Summit (New York City)
August 7, 2002	Single largest replenishment in GEF history made to the Global Environment Facility ($2.92 billion)
September 11, 2003	Cartagena Protocol of the Convention on Biological Diversity enters into force
February 16, 2005	Kyoto Protocol enters into force
December 12, 2015	195 countries approve the Paris Agreement on Climate Change at COP21
October 31–November 13, 2021	*UN Climate Change Conference of the Parties (COP26) in Glasgow*

For the protocol to go into effect, it had to be ratified by fifty-five states that were parties to the UNFCCC and it had to be ratified by sufficient Annex I countries to account for 55 percent of carbon dioxide (CO_2) emissions in 1990. Without ratification of the agreement by the United States and European countries, including Russia (accounting for 17.4 percent of emissions at the time), the protocol would be stillborn. Developing states were not required to cut emissions in the first phase of the protocol's implementation. They were encouraged to report on their emissions and to take measures to cut them, contingent on the receipt of financial assistance and technology transfers.[20]

On May 31, 2002, the European Union presented its member nations' ratifications of the Kyoto Protocol to UN Secretary-General Annan in New York. He lauded the European states' decisions and expressed the hope that "others will follow suit."[21] His reference was directed at several major states that had not ratified, including chiefly the United States and Australia, whose governments had indicated that they did not support the agreement. With Canada's and Poland's ratification in December 2002, the second "trigger" was within reach, as industrialized countries accounting for 44 percent of carbon dioxide (CO_2) emissions had agreed to the provisions of the protocol. However, without either the United States or the Russian Federation signing on, it could not go into effect. The G. W. Bush administration expressed unaltered opposition to the arrangement, citing its "unfairness" by not including mandated cuts in emissions for developing states and its costs to U.S. producers in difficult economic times. In 2002, President Putin of Russia committed to submit the protocol to the Duma for ratification, but delayed submission once influential advisers urged him not to participate. They suggested that additional global warming might even be economically beneficial to Russia by warming areas that are now inhospitable for agricultural production.[22] Their objections were overcome when it became clear that Russia would actually profit from implementation of the protocol, given its weakened economy had already lowered pollution levels below the targets set by the accord. The Duma ratified the protocol and it went into force in February 2005. Still, the climate crisis persisted, the United States stayed outside the protocol's framework, and political and economic impediments seemed to make progress less likely.

Paris 2015

Despite the Kyoto Protocol failing to make appreciable progress on slowing global warming, signatories to the UNFCCC continued their negotiations through "conferences of the parties" (COP) and ongoing multilateral negotiations. In the opening pages of this volume, we described the successful 2015 COP meeting in LeBourget, France, that brought into being the Paris Agreement on climate change. Over 190 nations attended, and numerous NGOs surrounded the meeting. Delegates developed a strategy to reduce greenhouse emissions and combat climate change by requiring each signatory country to set a voluntary target for its GHG reduction and to report regularly on strategies and progress toward meeting their targets. The agreement called for zero net anthropogenic greenhouse gas emissions by the second half of the twenty-first century and for limiting temperature increases to 1.5 degrees Celsius. All parties to the conference agreed to adopt its provisions into their own legal systems. It was scheduled to become legally binding when ratified by at least fifty-five countries that together represent at least 55 percent of global greenhouse emissions.[23]

The progress made at Paris encountered a serious roadblock when U.S. President Donald Trump, on June 1, 2017, announced that the United States—one of the two largest greenhouse gas emitters, the other being China—was withdrawing from the agreement. The administration immediately set out to reverse pro-environment policies that the previous president had planned to meet Paris' requirements. The new president rescinded almost seventy environmental regulations, approved the controversial Keystone pipeline (to bring up to thirty-five million gallons of oil daily some 1,200 miles into the United States), and set out to auction oil and gas leases for drilling rights in the Alaska Arctic National Wildlife Refuge. Prospects for progress by way of UN-coordinated efforts appeared dim, given this volte-face by such an important country. But then, by 2020, odd and vexing events sounded heightened alarm about the problem of climate change: unprecedented temperature rises in the U.S. Pacific Northwest, freakish wildfires in California, Turkey, and Russia's southeastern Siberia; and rains, floods, and wild swings in weather patterns, not all easily attributable to global warming, but troubling enough to cause pause about the denial of any adverse impact from climate change.

In Washington, a change in presidential administrations by early 2021 resulted in the United States rejoining the Paris accord and agreeing to resume participation with the UN in addressing the climate crisis. The Paris settlement had required the participating parties to follow a process known as the "ratchet mechanism" in sequential five years to make enhanced commitments. The 2020 date for such a first of these meetings was postponed because of the coronavirus pandemic and was rescheduled for the fall of 2021. In the late summer before this gathering, the UN's Intergovernmental Panel on Climate Change issued its 2021 report, which carried an urgent tone. The report unequivocally concluded that the climate crisis was caused by human activities. It also pointed out that carbon dioxide levels in the atmosphere had reached their highest level in two million years. The scientists exhorted immediate and earnest measures by the international community.[24]

The Glasgow COP 26 summit met from October 31 to November 13, 2021. During the conference, there was a large protest march in Glasgow against inadequate action which was accompanied by other rallies worldwide, as critics saw insufficient resolution among the world's nations.[25] Nonetheless, the national delegations from virtually every country in the world made several pledges. (1) For the first time ever, they promised to "draw down" the use of coal. India argued for this language instead of "phase out." Still, this was the first explicit international commitment to reduce the use of coal. (2) They agreed to come back in one year (not the five originally prescribed at Paris) to report on their national commitments, indicating their sense of urgency. (3) They signed on to a separate initiative to reduce methane gases 30 percent by 2030 from 2020 levels. (4) They promised to halt the destruction of the world's forests which absorb roughly 30 percent of carbon dioxide emissions. And (5) they restated their commitment to the Paris requisites for controlling temperature levels. Over 140 countries, whose combined economies represented 90 percent of global GDP, pledged to reach net-zero emissions. Separately, the United States and China pledged to cooperate on measures to stop climate change, including lowering methane emissions, phasing out coal, and pursuing forest conservation.[26]

Water Pollution and Marine Resources

The 1972 Stockholm Declaration emphasized protecting the marine environment. In response, the UN Environment Programme developed a number of programs to improve marine fish stocks, ocean and freshwater bodies, and transboundary waterways. Under UNEP auspices, efforts to protect the world's oceans resulted in a number of regional seas agreements. Nine were signed in the 1970s, beginning with an agreement among countries bordering the Mediterranean Sea. Six more agreements were signed in the 1980s. In addition to UNEP, the Economic Commission for Europe played a critical role in developing the 1992 Convention on the Protection and Use of Transboundary Watercourses and International Lakes.

Central to the UN's activity to protect the world's oceans was the Law of the Sea Convention, adopted in 1982. Part XII of the convention dealt specifically with the protection of the marine environment. By the time of the convention, a serious concern had been expressed that the long-standing custom of "freedom of the seas" had contributed to overexploitation of oceanic fish stocks by expanded distant fishing fleets, had damaged the marine environment because of the uncontrolled acquisition of natural resources (especially oil and natural gas), and had caused further harm by tolerating increasing numbers of oil tanker spills. The agreement was augmented in 1995 with a global commitment to protect highly migratory fish stocks.

The Law of the Sea Convention created its own international tribunal to adjudicate cases that arose among parties to the agreement. These cases could involve matters related to the environmental clauses in the convention. In the fall of 2001, Ireland brought a case to the tribunal against the United Kingdom's operation of a nuclear reprocessing facility on its west coast. Fearful that waste dumping or a terrorist attack could pollute the Irish Sea between Dublin and the plant, Ireland sought an injunction until an arbitration panel could settle the matter.[27] Although the tribunal did not issue the injunction, it did note that

Part XII of the convention requires cooperation among the parties. The tribunal ordered Ireland and Great Britain to exchange information on the possible threat presented by the plant to the Irish Sea, to monitor the continuing risks, and to devise measures to prevent pollution of the marine environment.[28]

As critical as marine life and resources are to the world's population, sustainable development depends even more heavily on access to freshwater sources. In 2022, more than two billion people lacked sufficient safe drinking water, despite urgent efforts by national governments and UN agencies to meet SDG #6: to "ensure availability and sustainable management of water and sanitation for all by 2030." The United Nations declared its first "International Year of Fresh Water" in 2003, and that same year UNEP launched the World Water Assessment Programme (WWAP), which published the first *UN World Water Development Report*. The water assessment program provides freshwater data collection and dissemination for national governments, IGOs, and NGOs. Funded by a voluntary trust fund, WWAP, with its secretariat at UNESCO headquarters in Paris, serves as the "umbrella" for coordinating existing UN freshwater programs in other agencies and thus has created a global water information network.[29] It develops recommendations for capacity building in water-strapped states and seeks to find ways to improve the conservation of clean water from unnecessary pollution. WWAP's parent organization, UNESCO, along with 31 other UN bodies, is part of UN-Water, the world body's coordination mechanism for all freshwater-related issues.

UN clean water programs arose not only through the commitments of the various environmental gatherings that convened during the previous thirty years, but also through a separate conference process on this specific topic. In 1977, the United Nations convened a conference on water at Mar del Plata, Argentina, that led to the declaration of an International Drinking Water and Sanitation Decade beginning in 1981. In 1990, both the "global consultation" on safe water and sanitation held in New Delhi, India, and the World Summit on Children called for renewed international efforts. The momentum from these meetings culminated in the International Conference on Water and the Environment, meeting in Dublin, Ireland, during the same year as the Earth Summit. This conference issued the Dublin Statement on Water and Sustainable Development, establishing consensus principles on the protection and management of freshwater. The statement declared, among other principles, that water was an economic good and urged that its development and management be based on a participatory approach involving users, planners, and policy makers.

All the social and environmental UN conferences of the 1990s (UNCED, the UN Conference on Population and Development, the Fourth World Conference on Women, HABITAT II, and the World Food Summit) found room in their declarations and plans of action to include recommendations on the conservation and provision of freshwater. As a lead-up to the Millennium Summit, a World Water Forum convened in The Hague. It identified seven challenges (meeting basic needs, securing a food supply, protecting ecosystems, sharing water resources, managing risks, valuing water, and governing water wisely) that the world needed to address.[30] Thus, Kofi Annan's call at the millennium gathering for halving the number of people without water was not unexpected. However, a bonus of the focus on freshwater was the formation of a separate World Water Council. Created in 1997 with its headquarters in Marseilles, France, this council is a hybrid organization, including not only UN agencies such as UNDP, the World Bank, and UNESCO, but also private and public firms, foundations, national government agencies, NGOs, banks, and academic and research institutes. The council organized the March 2000 world forum, which fifty-seven hundred participants attended.

The UN remained active and concerned with water issues well into the twenty-first century. April 2015 witnessed the Seventh World Water Forum in Daegu, Korea, and later that year—in June—delegates gathered in Dushanbe, Tajikistan, for a High-Level International Conference on the implementation of the International Decade for Action, "Water for Life," 2005–2015. The High Level Meeting announced a new International Decade for Action under the motto "Water for Sustainable Development" as an important tool for promoting the implementation of SDGs related to water, particularly Goal 6, quoted above.[31] Brasilia, Brazil was the site of the Eighth World Water Forum; the ninth edition was postponed because of the **COVID-19** pandemic but then was held in 2022 for the first time in West Africa, when Dakar, Senegal hosted.

Biodiversity and Natural Resources

Pressed to do so by many environmental NGOs, UNEP sponsored negotiations on a convention to protect biological diversity. These negotiations resulted in the Convention on Biological Diversity (CBD), opened for signature at the Earth Summit in 1992. Under the terms of the convention, nations were required to take national inventories of biodiversity, develop national plans for the sustainable use of biodiversity, restore degraded ecosystems, provide fair and equitable sharing of genetic resources and technology, and regulate the release of genetically modified organisms. The convention established a Conference of the Parties (COP) to implement and enhance the pact through continuing negotiations. Within a decade of its signing, nearly all nation-states had ratified the agreement and joined the COP.

The most significant accomplishment of COP meetings was the promulgation of the Cartagena Protocol in January 2000, which created a regulatory system for the safe transfer, handling, and use of genetically modified organisms. At Cartagena, the parties made specific reference to Principle 15 of the Rio Declaration, which required all states to take a precautionary approach when dealing with highly sensitive, and possibly dangerous, genetic materials.[32] The protocol set standards primarily on genetically altered farm products for human consumption and animal feed. It set up a Biosafety Clearing-House to make scientific risk assessments. With Palau's ratification of the protocol in June 2003, enough states had agreed to it to bring the protocol into effect by the following fall.[33] The success of the protocol depended, however, on the financial ability of developing states to participate. To this end, UNEP, with the assistance of the Global Environment Facility, pumped more than $38 million into one hundred countries.

The Cartagena Protocol was critically needed to manage the burgeoning private trade in genetically modified living organisms. In 1996, UNCTAD had launched its Biotrade Initiative, which was meant to stimulate trade and investment in biological resources in the developing world. UNCTAD then established biotrade country programs to help governments identify opportunities for sustainable resource development. Based on the 1997 Memorandum of Understanding between the CBD secretariat and UNCTAD, the two organs identified partnerships that could be developed among governments, NGOs, and international agencies that had the potential to turn the protection of biodiversity into a development asset for LDCs. Their efforts contributed to the adoption of the Nagoya Protocol in 2014, which established legally binding rules for the fair and equitable sharing of benefits arising from the utilization of genetic resources.

Desertification and Deforestation

One area in which economic development and environmental protection are allies is in slowing land degradation. In Africa, the steady growth of the Sahara Desert has diminished arable land and, thus, undercut agricultural production and lowered the standard of living. The misuse of arid and semiarid land and the overgrazing of livestock have dramatically increased both deforestation and desertification. As multiple UN reports have concluded, desertification also lessens biodiversity, adds to global warming, increases water scarcity, forces human migration and promotes zoonoses—the transmission of diseases from animals to humans.[34] More than one hundred countries, mostly in the developing world, are affected by these phenomena. By 2020, 46 percent of Africa suffered from desertification and was at a high risk of devastating drought.[35] The Sahel region (between the Saharan Desert and Sudan's Savannah, encompassing ten countries) is especially vulnerable to drought and erosion. Estimates put 135 million people at risk from desertification directly, or from mass exodus and conflict in the dryland regions.

Pressed by Sahel nations, the Earth Summit recommended that the United Nations create a negotiating committee to draft a convention on the problem of desertification. The Convention to Combat Desertification (CCD) opened for signature in Paris in October 1994 and entered into force in December 1996. The CCD established its secretariat in Bonn, Germany.

The convention radically departed from the traditional approaches to desertification in its strong emphasis on a "bottom-up" approach with strong local participation in decision-making. The convention put local officials on an equal footing with other actors in the development process. Communities and their leaders, as well as NGOs, experts, and government personnel, were invited to make proposals for new programs and to participate actively in implementation efforts. By 2022, there were one hundred ninety-seven parties to the convention. To publicize its activities and aims, CCD declared 2006 to be the "International Year of Deserts and Desertification." Hundreds of NGOs are accredited

Photo 8.3 Cracked earth, from lack of water and baked from the heat of the sun, forms a pattern in the Nature Reserve of Popenguaine, Senegal.

Source: UN Photo/Evan Schneider. Reproduced by permission of the United Nations.

with an observer status for CCD meetings. Nongovernmental organizations have not only played a prominent role in the convention process, but also have raised public awareness of the convention and lobbied governments on behalf of desertification projects.

Activities recommended by the convention required extensive new funding. Unlike the biodiversity and climate change conventions that had funding mechanisms through the Global Environment Facility, the CCD had to set up its own funding structure. It did so through the International Fund for Agricultural Development (IFAD) in Rome. Its funds, never large under the IFAD arrangement, were directed at reducing poverty in arid and semiarid areas in the belief that poverty led to agricultural practices that exacerbated desertification. In August 2002, the convention's executive secretary asked the World Summit on Social Development (WSSD) to recommend GEF as the future funding mechanism for desertification projects. The conference did so, and the GEF council approved desertification and deforestation as a central area of its work. The convention's signatories could now apply directly to the facility for funding of national projects.

At the time of the Earth Summit, the positive connections between environmentally sound policies concerning forests and economic development in the underdeveloped world were not as clear as they were in the area of desertification. Industrialized states had become concerned by reports of significant damage to the rain forests and to tropical stands of timber as the result of land clearing, the sale of mahogany and other precious lumber, and development practices that threatened this part of the global commons. While deforestation produced land degradation, often in the form of erosion, LDCs argued that this practice was necessary if, first, land was to be made available for agricultural and industrial development and, second, forest products were going to be part of the nation's export production. As we commented previously in this chapter, this conflict limited the outcome of the Earth Summit to a vague Statement of Forest Principles.

The failure of the Rio meeting to reach agreement on proposals for preserving the world's forests was a harbinger of future negotiations. As one scholar on the subject said, compared with global efforts to address ozone problems, the attempt to create an international legal regime on forest management proved to be "a resounding failure."[36] The inability to demonstrate transborder dangers from forest degradation, the general perception that forests are a domestic resource beyond international control, and the belief that forest problems can usually be solved unilaterally by governments all diminished incentives toward reaching a binding treaty. In addition, no group of countries stepped forward with offers to finance international initiatives in this area.

The UN Commission on Sustainable Development (CSD) established an Intergovernmental Panel on Forests (1995–1997) and an Intergovernmental Forum on Forests (launched in 1997), which collectively put forward more than two hundred seventy proposals for action. These proposals "encouraged" countries to take a wide array of steps to protect their forests. Given the acknowledgment that states had the right to use their forest resources as they wanted for development purposes, the panels did not mandate international norms or action. However, the promulgation of the Kyoto Protocol in 1997 gave new impetus to international discussions about forest preservation. The incentives created by the protocol's "sinks" provisions rewarded states for planting and restoring forests. This opportunity demonstrated that progress in one area of environmental policy could open avenues for sound environmental progress in another. Nonetheless, the UN Forum on Forest's sixteenth session, held in New York in 2021, only emphasized hazy thematic priorities for the Forum to pursue into 2024. These priorities, corresponding to SDGs, included reversing the loss of forest cover, enhancing forest-based economic, social, and environmental benefits, and, importantly, mobilizing financial resources and strengthening scientific and technical cooperation for sustainable forest management.[37] The follow-up seventeenth annual session was held at UN headquarters in New York in May 2022.

Yet, real progress depended on a consensus among the negotiating states on the merits of a binding treaty. While many nations from both the developing and developed worlds supported an agreement, the antitreaty coalition included the United States, Brazil, Japan, Mexico, India, and Indonesia, among others.[38] Much like the impetus given by the Kyoto Protocol, new pressure was brought on these governments by the unanimous approval of the 2015 Paris Agreement on climate change. In order to keep the global temperatures from rising above the permitted level, the preservation of tropical forests took on increased importance, as they could provide the "sinks" necessary to capture greenhouse gases. In the wake of the agreement, several states launched diplomatic efforts to encourage a renewed look at the merits of a binding treaty on forests. France, for example, in summer 2020 launched the "Alliance for the preservation of tropical and humid forests" that rapidly garnered thirty-two government members.[39]

The public policy process concerning the world's forests, as well as the efforts to deal with drylands, freshwater, and biodiversity, reflects an arduous interconnected journey toward the creation of norms and policies. Many actors have played critical roles, none more important than the United Nations itself, in legislating reasonable protections for the global commons. For advocates on the forests and other elements of our global environment, they could take heart in the adoption of the 2015 Sustainable Development Goals (described in some detail below) that included Goal 15 committing the world to "sustainably manage forests, combat desertification, halt and reverse land degradation, (and) halt biodiversity loss."

International Financing

The inclusion of desertification as one of six focal areas for financing in the Global Environment Facility—the others being climate change, international waters, biodiversity, persistent organic pollutants, and the ozone layer—completed the emergence of GEF as the central financial institution for UN environmental initiatives. Created in 1991 as an experimental project of the World Bank to meet the Brundtland Commission's concerns about insufficient international financing of environmentally friendly development projects, GEF soon acquired significant donor assets for its projects. At the conclusion of UNCED, the conference secretariat estimated that $125 billion in foreign assistance to developing countries would be needed to implement all the Agenda 21 recommendations. This cost was nearly ten times the 1992 level of global aid. The facility became the central institution of international environmental financing. Its primary purpose has been to provide grants to developing countries for environment-related projects and to facilitate networking and cooperation among donors. From its inception to 2019, the GEF had allocated $18 billion—supplemented by more than $94 billion in co-financing—for more than 4,500 projects in 170 countries.[40]

The World Bank is the trustee of the GEF fund. It acts as one of the facility's three implementing agencies, along with UNDP and UNEP. In addition, the four regional development banks and several other UN specialized agencies can access GEF funds as "executing" bodies. GEF operations are directed by an assembly composed of its 183 member states, which meets every three years, and a council, which functions as a board of directors. Following the Paris Climate meeting in December 2015, eleven donors pledged about $250 million in new money to help the most vulnerable countries adapt to the demands of the climate agreement.[41] The facility is particularly welcoming of private and NGO participation. Nongovernmental organizations have managed more than one hundred fifty

GEF-financed projects. Much of the investment by GEF in the private sector has gone to power generation, but additional monies have been given to private companies to reduce greenhouse gas emissions, for renewable energy projects, and for biodiversity protection.

The regional development banks complement GEF financing. The Earth Summit encouraged the development banks to take a greater role in financing sustainable development. Each bank set up an environmental department to support methods of development that protect environmental interests. The decision to bring the banks within the restructured GEF organizational plan in 1994 made them key executing bodies for environmentally friendly development in their respective regions. Since then, the banks have worked within a cohesive and unified financing structure coordinated by the facility.

Sustainable *Human* Development

The Fight against HIV/AIDS

> HIV/AIDS pushes people deeper into poverty as households lose their breadwinners, livelihoods are compromised and savings are consumed by the cost of health care. The pandemic also adds to the strain on national institutions and resources, and undermines the social systems that help people to cope with adversity. In the most severely affected settings there is already evidence that HIV/AIDS is eroding human security and productivity, undermining economic development, and threatening social cohesion.
>
> —World Health Organization, Global Health Sector
> Strategy for HIV/AIDS: 2003–2007, p. 3

If human beings are at the center of the concern for sustainable development as the Rio Declaration asserted, then sustainable *human* development is the ultimate goal of UN efforts in the new millennium. In particular, poverty eradication has been identified by UN agencies as a critical step in providing healthier, safer, and more productive lives for the world's population. However, addressing poverty requires solving simultaneously the human afflictions that keep whole societies from economic progress. As the quotation from the World Health Organization's report suggests, widespread and rampant disease in poor parts of the globe not only undermines the prospects for improving standards of living, but also threatens international peace and security.

Disease is not the only social problem that stalemates development. Homelessness, refugee flows, human rights violations, narcotics, crime, and corruption all make sustainable development difficult. However, the presence of diseases such as measles and tuberculosis in the LDCs—long controlled in the richer nations of the world—and the quick spread of viruses in recent years due to globalization and human migration have focused the UN's attention on disease as a primary threat to development. At the beginning of the new millennium, the world community identified three diseases—HIV/AIDS, tuberculosis, and malaria—as the triple threat to poverty reduction and launched the Global Fund to fight them, with support from all UN agencies, the major economic world powers, and the nongovernmental community. In view of an estimated three hundred million cases of malaria worldwide each year, the United Nations undertook a global partnership—"Roll Back Malaria"—to halve that number by 2010. Tuberculosis cases increased 6 percent between 1997 and 1999.[42] The most significant increases occurred in African states affected by the HIV/AIDS crisis. "Stop TB" was launched as a global partnership to halt the incidence of the disease, particularly in twenty-two heavily affected states.

The pandemic of HIV (human immunodeficiency virus) and AIDS (acquired immunodeficiency syndrome), with an estimated eighty million people infected by 2021,[43] raises a particularly dire threat to all international efforts to achieve sustainable human development. The UN effort to mobilize world resources in the fight against HIV/AIDS has included the usual methods of world meetings; a General Assembly special session; and cooperative ventures with governments, NGOs, and the private sector.[44] The UN Security Council has also recognized the potentially destabilizing force of HIV/AIDS, particularly among communities ravaged by conflicts and warfare. Through a number of resolutions, and four sessions on the topic by January 2001, the council had identified the disease as the first health issue to be considered a threat to global peace and security. Particular attention focused on the links between regional conflicts in sub-Saharan Africa and the incidence of HIV/AIDS. The council expressed a particular concern about the epidemic's spread to peacekeepers participating in UN operations (Resolution 1308 (2000)).

Much of the UN campaign against HIV/AIDS has been made through its specialized agencies, particularly the World Health Organization. WHO set up its Special Programme on AIDS, renamed the *Global Programme on AIDS (GPA)* in 1987. From that point forward, WHO became the lead agency in the UN response to the crisis. The agency gave high priority to stopping the accelerated spread of the disease.

Despite interagency agreements under the leadership of the World Health Organization, coordinating policies, strategies, and support activities remained problematic. In response to rising difficulties and to the growing awareness that HIV/AIDS was not only a medical problem but also an epidemic with social, economic, and political complexities,

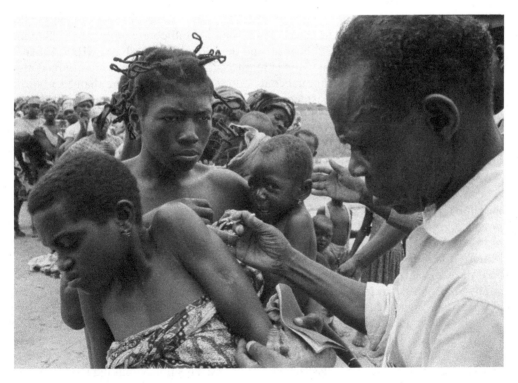

Photo 8.4 Vaccination in the Congo.
Source: UN/DPI Photo/B. Zarov. Reproduced by permission of the United Nations.

a new UN program, the **Joint UN Programme on HIV/AIDS (UNAIDS)**, was created in 1986. With eight agencies (the UN Children's Fund, UNDP, the UN Population Fund, WHO, UNESCO, the World Bank, the International Labour Organization, and the UN Drug Control Programme) operating under the leadership of a program secretariat, UNAIDS filled the need for greater coordination to combat the increasingly complex nature of this global scourge. An important element of the UNAIDS program design was cooperation with the numerous NGOs active in HIV prevention worldwide, as well as the active participation of national HIV/AIDS agencies, including the U.S. Centers for Disease Control. A "Country Response Monitoring Project" was just one of the UN's initiatives, in collaboration with national governments and NGOs, to provide the latest information on the epidemic in specific countries.

UNAIDS fosters expanded national responses to HIV/AIDS, particularly in developing countries, and identifies, develops, and advocates international "best practices" for HIV prevention. UNAIDS is governed by its Programme Coordinating Board, comprising government delegates, envoys from the participating UN agencies, and representatives from NGOs, which include associations of people living with AIDS. As such, UNAIDS was the first UN programme to include NGOs in its governing body. Its secretariat, based in Geneva, operates on behalf of the participating agencies to provide policy development and research, technical support, advocacy, and coordination. In the developing nations, where more than 95 percent of the world's infected population is found, UNAIDS works with national government agencies as well as NGOs to support the host governments' efforts to develop a comprehensive response to HIV/AIDS.

Despite the injection of significant international funds, most LDC government health programs are incapable of providing the necessary drugs and infrastructure to deal with AIDS. Secretary-General Annan met with and called on pharmaceutical companies to provide antiretroviral drugs at steeply reduced prices. He and the General Assembly called for a global AIDS fund to generate between $8 and $10 billion annually. The G-8 industrial countries promptly endorsed the idea, and the Global Fund to Fight AIDS, Tuberculosis and Malaria took form. Financial commitments of $2.6 billion flowed immediately into its coffers. By 2022, actual annual contributions had risen to more than $9.3 billion. During its first two decades of existence, the Global Fund was able to make grants worth more than $54 billion to more than one hundred fifty programs in ninety-two countries.[45] UNAIDS signed a Memorandum of Understanding with the fund, recognizing the latter as a "critical financing mechanism" in the fight against AIDS. The memorandum assigned UNAIDS the key tasks of strategic analysis, policy advice, and provision of technical expertise.

Within two years of its inception, the Global Fund took on much of the same role that the Global Environment Facility served in environmental matters. Like the GEF, the fund provided grants for public, private, and nongovernmental projects directed at prevention or treatment of the disease, or the care of AIDS patients. Its emergence marked a specialization of labor in the UN fight against HIV/AIDS that was the product of a maturing policy process at the international level.

The fund's governing board includes among its voting members an unusual combination of personages: government ministers, and NGO delegates, including groups representing individuals living with HIV/AIDS. Among the ex officio members are representatives of UNAIDS, WHO, UNESCO, UN Women, and the World Bank. In the United Nations of the twenty-first century, the fight against HIV/AIDS merged private and public in seamless ways, which produced a consensus global policy. This policy-making mode is significantly different from that contemplated by the UN founders or practiced in the field of development fifty years earlier.

Coronavirus Crisis and the WHO

On March 11, 2020, the UN's World Health Organization declared that the spread of the coronavirus across more than one hundred countries had qualified as a global pandemic.[46] By definition, a pandemic is a widespread *epidemic* that may affect entire continents, even the whole world. The most ominous recent historic example was the 1918 flu pandemic. However, from an epidemiologist's perspective, the Black Death in fourteenth-century Europe and AIDS in sub-Saharan Africa were pandemics.

WHO's World Health Assembly in 1969 adopted International Health Regulations (IHR) and revised them in 2005. The IHR is a legally binding instrument of international law empowering the WHO to act as the main global surveillance system. These regulations assume that there can be a health challenge that extends beyond disease in isolated nations and regions and thus should be designated as a Public Health Emergency of International Concern (PHEIC). In late December 2019, WHO invoked the IHR and requested information from China about the outbreak in Wuhan. China, on January 3, 2020, informed the organization of the outbreak—at the time alleged to have crossed from an animal (perhaps a bat) to humans. WHO publicized the news, convened international scientific consultations, and sought an invitation from China to conduct an on-ground investigation. China wavered on an invitation but shared the virus' genome with WHO.

In late January, WHO convened an Emergency Committee and its Director-General, Tedros Adhanom Ghebreyesus, flew to Beijing to meet with president Xi Jinping and appeal for more information. Again, China balked. On January 30, WHO declared a public health emergency. Warning governments to "act now," the WHO then declared the pandemic on March 11 (some thought too late). In spring 2020, WHO had created the COVID-19 Solidarity Response Fund to respond to the unprecedented show of support by individuals and companies to help WHO in the fight against COVID-19. During the first year and more of the pandemic, WHO shipped nearly 250 million items of personal protective equipment and vital medical supplies, including oxygen across more than 150 countries, strengthened hundreds of national and subnational laboratories with technical support, supplied more than 250 million COVID-19 tests; coordinated the deployment of more than 180 teams across the world; and supported more than 12,000 intensive care beds in health systems that might otherwise have been overwhelmed. According to Mara Pillinger of the O'Neill Institute, "WHO's response to Covid-19 is the most robust response to public health emergency that the agency has launched since SARS....But it also engendered much criticism."[47]

Indeed, WHO became enmeshed in a nasty international squabble between China and the United States. U.S. President Trump, who believed that WHO had been too submissive to China, determined in July 2020 to pull out of that UN organization and threatened to cut off one of WHO's most important sources of aid just as the global pandemic seemed to be accelerating. By law, the effective date for withdrawal could not be until July 6, 2021, and Democratic opponent Joe Biden swiftly assured that he would remain in the health organization if elected in November. President Trump promptly pressed home his "America First" posture, conspicuously declining to join a WHO-led 172-country multilateral effort to develop, manufacture, and equitably distribute a vaccine for COVID-19. (Administered by WHO and UNICEF, "COVAX" coordinates international resources to enable low- to middle-income countries to obtain equitable access to COVID-19 tests, therapies, and vaccines.) The Trump administration accused China of being solely responsible for the pandemic and of controlling the World Health Organization.

The president had a point. There was not an early transparent, independent investigation into the source of the virus. China had impeded such an on-site probe in Wuhan's outdoor market, which it reported as the originator of viral spread. The financially strapped WHO, privately frustrated, ceded control of any investigation to Chinese nationals and, hoping to keep Xi supportive, tended to praise China, as Trump fumed. While Xi seemed to want to constrain the WHO, and Trump seemed to want to destroy it, European allies scrambled to reform and empower it. In the meantime, the president continued to lash out at the WHO and thunderously campaign against the "China virus." Dr. Tedros, meanwhile, privately compared China and the United States to two playground bullies.[48]

A crisis that seemed befitting for bringing the world together, thus, instead seemed to exacerbate international tensions. And WHO was the unfortunate battering ram in the tussle, underscoring a datum we must acknowledge: the UN and its agencies are only so good as its membership. WHO, headquartered in Geneva, is an intergovernmental organization dependent upon the cooperation of its members, especially its most powerful members; it is highly decentralized, with six regional sub-organizations overseeing 150 country offices; and it is woefully underfunded. The crisis of 2020–2021 encouraged reform conversations for the organization, including, above all, finding a way to ensure sustainable long-term financing and, concomitantly, shifting to non-earmarked voluntary contributions (even from the likes of Bill and Melinda Gates). Coronavirus will not be the last fundamentally nonpolitical (and possibly existential) health crisis to confront the world, and the *global* UN, specifically the WHO, is the model organization to deal with that future. However, it requires money, cooperation, and support.

SUSTAINABLE DEVELOPMENT GOALS (SDGS)

Almost all of the issues discussed in this chapter touch upon, or culminate in, the **Sustainable Development Goals (SDGs),** perhaps the most ambitious UN project in the organization's history. The SDGs are found in a General Assembly Resolution (A/RES/70/1 of September 25, 2015).[49] The resolution is an intergovernmental agreement considered as a successor to the Millennium Development Goals. There are seventeen SDGs, with 169 targets encompassing a wide range of issues. The final document followed on several preliminary meetings and was adopted at the UN Sustainable Development Summit in September 2015 in New York—transpiring with the annual opening session of the United Nations. The title of the SDG program is *Transforming Our World: The 2030 Agenda for Sustainable Development.* The full list of goals, with explication, is contained in paragraph 54 of Resolution A/RES/70/1.

The origin of the SDGs dates to many of the UN conferences and initiatives we have already discussed in this chapter: the 1972 UN Environment Conference, the 1983 World Commission on Environment and Development, and the Rio Earth Summit on Environment and Development in 1992. Two decades later, and over a decade following the Millennium Summit, came the resolution known as "The Future We Want."[50] Therein, member states agreed (in 2012) on certain key themes, including poverty eradication, upgrading energy, water and sanitation, and achieving progress in human settlement. Three years later, the world community was ready to commit to a broad set of goals, representing an extension beyond the MDGs (2000–2015).

Specifically, the ambitious SDGs, to be achieved by 2030, were listed this way:

1 *Poverty*: end poverty in all its forms everywhere.
2 *Food*: end hunger, achieve food security, improve nutrition, and promote sustainable agriculture.
3 *Health*: cultivate healthy lives and nurture well-being for people of all ages.

4 *Education*: guarantee equitable, inclusive, and quality education, and advance life-long learning.
5 *Women*: secure gender equality and empowerment for women and girls.
6 *Water*: safeguard sustainable and available water and sanitation, and appropriate management of water resources for all people.
7 *Energy*: ensure access to affordable, reliable, sustainable, and modern energy for all people.
8 *Economy*: promote inclusive, sustainable and sustained economic growth, full employment, and decent and productive work for all people.
9 *Infrastructure*: construct sound and resilient infrastructure, certify inclusive and sustainable industrialization, and foster innovation.
10 *Inequality*: reduce inequality both within countries and among countries.
11 *Habitation*: render cities and human settlements inclusive, safe, and sustainable.
12 *Consumption*: ensure sustainable consumption and steady production patterns.
13 *Climate*: urgently combat climate change and its impacts.
14 *Marine ecosystems*: conserve the oceans, seas, and marine resources for sustainable development.
15 *Ecosystems*: restore, protect, and maintain terrestrial ecosystems, manage forests, combat desertification, stop land degradation, and arrest biodiversity loss.
16 *Institutions*: promote peaceful and inclusive societies with access to justice for all, with accountable and inclusive institutions at every level.
17 *Sustainability*: the overarching theme; effectively implement sustainable development and strengthen the global partnership for forwarding sustainable development.[51]

From the Millennium Summit onward, all UN agencies premised their activities on attaining, first, the MDGs, and, later, the SDGs. The World Bank's GEF, the WTO, and UNCTAD took on primary responsibility for enhancing financial and trade assistance to the Third World to help states reach self-sustaining development. As part of this effort, UNCTAD decided to make sustainable development the central theme of its work with LDCs. At the national and subnational levels, UNDP and UN-Habitat assisted with the capacity building and infrastructure necessary for a sustainable social and economic order. UNDP launched a *sustainable development network (SDN)* to foster dialogue among citizens and policy makers and to provide the latest technical information related to the topic.

Even relatively independent agencies such as the World Health Organization undertook their promotion. In fact, WHO underwent a structural reorganization to make "sustainable development and healthy environment" one of its primary "clusters" of activity after Gro Harlem Brundtland, the former chair of the World Commission on Environment and Development, took over as WHO's Director-General in July 1998. The WHO experience demonstrated that sustainable development had metamorphosed from solely a development and environmental construct. The UN had adapted it to other areas of concern. UNEP executive director Klaus Töpfer expanded the presumed universality of the concept by asserting that "the most toxic element in the environment is poverty."[52]

The Sustainable Development Goals Report 2020, concluded during the first full year of the COVID-19 pandemic, provided an update on progress, or the lack thereof, in implementing the goals. The report was prepared by the UN Department of Economic and Social Affairs with the input of over 200 experts from over 40 international agencies. The report noted that the COVID-19 pandemic had posed serious problems for SDG progress and in many cases was responsible for backsliding in several of the goals. At best, progress remained uneven, even before the onset of the pandemic. There had been visible gains: the share of children and youth out of school had fallen; communicable diseases were in decline; there had been improvements in access to safely managed drinking water; and women had continued to see an increase in leadership roles worldwide. Still, progress had stalled, particularly for the poorest and most marginalized of the world's people.[53]

SUMMARY

The UN efforts to meet the Charter's commitment to raise the standards of living and the social conditions of the world's poorest populations have been buffeted by both East-West and North-South struggles. These struggles have shaped development policy, using the architecture of the United Nations as the policy arena. However, the United Nations has also sought to make economic and social policies by mobilizing the world on behalf of particular agendas and strategies. Through many types of multilateral forums—world conferences, panels of experts, media events, General Assembly special sessions, and public campaigns—the United Nations has wedded environmental concerns to the search for economic progress in the developing world, producing with time a new conception of economic development as "sustainable" development. Through its worldwide system of programs, funds, specialized agencies, and offices, the United Nations has also addressed policy making in such personally human fields as health and individual rights and dignity, for sustainable development is possible only where sustainable *human* development is achieved. The United Nations has moved most dramatically toward a "people-centered" institution that sees its mission not only in terms of protecting the interests of the states that are its members. The whole UN System has gravitated to the center of global policy making, public and private, on human challenges previously thought peripheral to international politics.

KEY TERMS

Agenda 21 (299)

Climate Change (301)

COVID-19 (306)

Development Decades (287)

Group of 77 (G-77) (288)

Joint UN Programme on HIV/AIDS
    (UNAIDS) (312)

Millennium Declaration (295)

Millennium Development Goals
    (MDGs) (294)

Millennium Summit (294)

New International Economic Order (288)

Non-Aligned Movement (NAM) (287)

North-South Debate (286)

Our Common Future (298)

Point Four Program (285)

Principle 21 (297)

Sustainable Development (298)

Sustainable Development Goals (SDG) (314)

Theory of "Dependency" (288)

UN Conference on Environment and
    Development (289)

UN Conference on Trade and Develop-
    ment (UNCTAD) (287)

UN Development Programme (UNDP)
    (289)

DISCUSSION QUESTIONS

Are the sustainable development goals realistic and can they be achieved by 2030? What will be required of national governments, international organizations, and non-state actors to achieve them?

Given the United Nations is an organization of sovereign member states, should NGOs be included as active participants in the formulation and implementation of UN conventions and UN-administered public policies?

RESOURCES FOR FURTHER RESEARCH

Relevant Web Sites

Group of 77 (www.g77.org)
Millennium Development Goals (www.un.org/millenniumgoals)
Sustainable Development Goals (sdgs.un.org/goals)
UN Climate Change Conference 2015 (www.documentcloud.org/documents/2646001-Final-COP21-draft.html)
UN Conference on Trade and Development (www.unctad.org)
UN Development Programme (www.undp.org)
UN Division for Sustainable Development (www.un.org/esa/sustdev/index.html)
UN Environment Programme (www.unep.org)
UN Framework Convention on Climate Change (UNFCCC) and Kyoto Protocol (www.unfccc.int/2860.php)
UN Intergovernmental Panel on Climate Change (IPCC) (www.ipcc.ch)
World Health Organization (www.who.int)

Books, Articles, and Documents

Bastos, Cristiana. *Global Responses to AIDS: Science in Emergency*. Bloomington: Indiana University Press, 1999.
Bee, Ronald J. "The Renewed Climate Change Agenda." *Great Decisions 2022*. New York: Foreign Policy Association, 2022.
Chasek, Pamela S. *The Global Environment in the Twenty-First Century: Prospects for International Cooperation*. New York: United Nations University Press, 2000.
Collier, Paul. *The Bottom Billion: Why the Poorest Countries Are Failing and What Can Be Done about It*. New York: Oxford University Press, 2008.
Elliott, Lorraine. *The Global Politics of the Environment*. New York: New York University Press, 1998.
Pillinger, Mara, "The World Health Organization's Response to COVID-19." *Great Decisions 2021* New York: Foreign Policy Association, 2021.
Sachs, Jeffrey. *The Age of Sustainable Development*. New York: Columbia University Press, 2015.
Smith, Raymond. *Encyclopedia of AIDS: A Social, Political, Cultural, and Scientific Record of the HIV Epidemic*. Chicago: Fitzroy Dearborn, 2000.
UN Conference on Trade and Development. *The Least Developed Countries Report*. New York and Geneva: United Nations, issued annually.
Upton, Barbara. *The Multilateral Development Banks: Improving U.S. Leadership*. Washington, D.C.: Center for Strategic and International Studies, 2000.
World Commission on Environment and Development. *Our Common Future*. New York: Oxford University Press, 1987.

Notes

1 See John Allphin Moore, Jr., and Jerry Pubantz, *To Create a New World? American Presidents and the United Nations* (New York: Peter Lang, 1999), 46–53.
2 For a comprehensive discussion on the "idea" of economic and social development embodied in the United Nations and its work, see Louis Emmerij, Richard Jolly, and Thomas Weiss, *Ahead of the Curve? UN Ideas and Global Challenges* (Bloomington: Indiana University Press, 2001).
3 Office of the Federal Register, National Archives and Records Administration, *Public Papers of the Presidents of the United States, 1949* (Washington, DC: Office of the Federal Register, National Archives and Records Administration, 1949), 113.

4 *Public Papers of the Presidents of the United States, 1953* (Washington, D.C.: Office of the Federal Register, National Archives and Records Administration, 1953), 179.

5 *Public Papers of the Presidents of the United States, 1956* (Washington, D.C.: Office of the Federal Register, National Archives and Records Administration, 1956), 1072–1073. Also see Moore and Pubantz, *To Create a New World?* 93.

6 All sessions are listed on the UNCTAD Web site found at <unctad.org/meetings>.

7 Eco'Diagnostic, *International Geneva Yearbook 2000–2001* (Geneva, Switzerland: United Nations, 2000), 234–235.

8 Diana Ayton-Shenker and John Tessitore, eds., *A Global Agenda: Issues before the 56th General Assembly of the United Nations* (Lanham, MD: Rowman & Littlefield, 2002), 137.

9 Proposed programme budget for 2020, General Assembly, A/74/6 (Sect. 12), 11 April 2019, 4.

10 See <jobs.undp.org/cj_view_jobs.cfm?cur_categ_id=9>.

11 UN Conference on Trade and Development, "Gender & trade task force begins work," press release, UNCTAD/PRESS/IN/2003/59, July 22, 2003.

12 United Nations, *Trade and Gender: Opportunities, Challenges and the Policy Dimension*, UN document TD/392 (New York: United Nations, April 4, 2004).

13 General Assembly Resolution 128; see UN General Assembly, *Declaration on the Right to Development*, UN document A/RES/41/128, December 4, 1986, <www.un.org/documents/ga/res/41/a41r128.htm>.

14 The "G-8" was Germany, the United States, the Russian Federation, France, the United Kingdom, Italy, Japan, and Canada. In 2014, Russia was suspended from membership, partly due to disagreements over Ukraine.

15 For the program of action resulting from the third UN Conference on Least Developed Countries, held May 20, 2001, see UN General Assembly, *Programme of Action for the Least Developed Countries*, UN document A/CONF.191/11 (New York: United Nations, June 8, 2001), 51. See also UN Conference on Trade and Development (UNCTAD), *The Least Developed Countries Report 2004* (Geneva, Switzerland: UN Conference on Trade and Development, May 27, 2004), pt. I, Ch. 1, 20.

16 Kofi Annan, *We the Peoples: The Role of the United Nations in the 21st Century* (New York: United Nations, 2000), 19.

17 See André-Michel Essoungou, "Africa's Least Developed: Lands of Opportunity," *Africa Renewal*, August 2011, 24. Found at <www.un.org/africarenewal/magazine/august-2011/africas-least-developed-lands-opportunity>.

18 Annan, *We the Peoples*, 53.

19 See <sustainabledevelopment.un.org/content/documents/Agenda21.pdf>.

20 For a full discussion of the requirements imposed by the Kyoto Protocol and the structure and procedures created by the UN Framework Convention on Climate Change (UNFCCC), see Climate Change Secretariat, *A Guide to the Climate Change Convention Process*, preliminary 2nd Edition (Bonn, Germany: UNFCCC Secretariat, 2002).

21 UN Information Service, "Secretary-General Welcomes European Union Ratification of Kyoto Protocol," press release, SG/SM/ 8251, May 31, 2002.

22 Paul Brown, "Russia Urged to Rescue Kyoto Pact," *The Guardian*, February 26, 2003, at <www.guardian.co.uk/climatechange/story/0,12374,903094,00.html>.

23 The full text of the agreement can be found at <www.documentcloud.org/documents/2646001-Final-COP21-draft.html>.

24 IPCC 2021 report at <www.ipcc.ch/report/ar6/wg1/>.

25 See COP 26 News at <ukcop26.org/news/>.

26 COP26 Glasgow Climate Pact at <ukcop26.org/wp-content/uploads/2021/11/COP26-Presidency-Outcomes-The-Climate-Pact.pdf>.

27 International Tribunal for the Law of the Sea (ITLOS), "Order in the MOX Plant Case (*Ireland v. United Kingdom)*," press release 62, December 3, 2001, found at <www.itlos.org/cgi-bin/cases/case_detail.pl?id=10&lang=en>.

28 Ayton-Shenker and Tessitore, *Global Agenda: 56th General Assembly*, 272–273.

29 UN Educational, Scientific and Cultural Organization, *World Water Development Report: Water for People, Water for Life* (Paris: UN Educational, Scientific and Cultural Organization, March 2003), 3.

30 Ibid., 5.

31 See <www.un.org/waterforlifedecade/>.

32 Ayton-Shenker, *Global Agenda: 47th General Assembly*, 222.

33 UN Environment Programme, "Treaty on International Trade in GMOs to Become Law," press release, June 13, 2003.

34 UN News, "UN Chief: Desertification and Drought Destabilizing Well-being of 3.2 Billion People," June 16, 2021, <news.un.org/en/story/2021/06/1094122>.

35 <https://borgenproject.org/desertification-in-africa/>, April 22, 2020.

36 Radoslav S. Dimitrov, "Knowledge, Power, and Interests in Environmental Regime Formation," *International Studies Quarterly* 47 (March 2002): 134.

37 UNFF Report on Sixteenth Session, 2021, at <documents-dds-ny.un.org/doc/UNDOC/GEN/N21/120/62/PDF/N2112062.pdf?OpenElem>.

38 Dimitrov, "Knowledge, Power, and Interests," 136.

39 <www.oneplanetsummit.fr/les-coalitions-82/alliance-pour-la-preservation-des-forets-tropicales-et-humides-194>.

40 See <sgp.fas.org/crs/misc/IF10144.pdf>.

41 For details on GEF funding see <www.thegef.org/who-we-are/funding>.

42 Ayton-Shenker and Tessitore, *Global Agenda: 56th General Assembly*, 222.

43 UNAIDS, "Global HIV & AIDS statistics — Fact sheet," < www.unaids.org/en/resources/fact-sheet>.

44 In addition to engaging in their own activities, key UN agencies have served as cosponsors of the annual International AIDS Conference, along with national governments, NGOs, and pharmaceutical and other private corporations.

45 The Global Fund to Fight AIDS, Tuberculosis and Malaria, "Financials," <www.theglobalfund.org/en/financials/>.

46 <www.who.int/dg/speeches/detail/who-director-general-s-opening-remarks-at-the-media-briefing-on-covid-19---11-march-2020>.

47 Mara Pillinger, "The World Health Organization's Response to COVID-19," *Great Decisions 2021* (New York: Foreign Policy Association, 2021), 89.

48 Selam Gebrekidan, Matt Apuzzo, Amy Qin, and Havier C. Hernández, "In Hunt for Virus Source, W.H.O. Let China Take Charge," *New York Times*, November 2, 2020, at <www.nytimes.com/2020/11/02/world/world-health-organization-china-trump-coronavirus.html?action=click&module=Top%20Stories&pgtype=Homepage>.

49 For the full resolution, see <www.ipu.org/splz-e/unga16/2030-e.pdf>.

50 Outcome document of the United Nations Conference on Sustainable Development; Rio de Janeiro, Brazil, 20–22 June 2012; found at <sustainabledevelopment.un.org/content/documents/733FutureWeWant.pdf>.

51 For comprehensive coverage of the SDGs, see <sdgs.un.org/goals>.

52 UN Environment Programme, "Foreword," in *Global Environment Outlook 2000*, ed. Robin Clarke, 1–4 (New York: UN Environment Programme, 2000).

53 *The SDG Report 2020* is at <unstats.un.org/sdgs/report/2020/>.

Epilogue

Having now surveyed the United Nations (UN) from top to bottom and situated it in the political and theoretical traditions of modern international relations and organizations, we are obliged to conclude by addressing briefly the common query: "Is the UN worthwhile, given that it seems unable on many occasions to enforce its decisions or carry out its resolutions?" During the lead-up to the U.S. invasion of Iraq in 2003, Washington advanced the equally quotidian grumble that the United Nations had demonstrated its "irrelevancy" in modern world politics. Perhaps more ominously, in February 2022, Russia, like the United States two decades earlier, breached the UN Charter, which prohibits the "use of force against the territorial integrity or political independence of any state." Once again, and with added force, not only the relevancy but the very perseverance and efficacy of the UN in the face of a permanent member's egregious defiance was under scrutiny. Thus, by 2022, the UN confronted both a conventional complaint about its ineffectiveness plus a dangerous test causing alarm about its very permanence.[1] In these concluding remarks, we will take up both the complaint and the test.

Readers now know that the complex answer to the grumble rests within the pages preceding this epilogue. So, while a thorough response would hearken back to the full text, we recognize that these familiar comments require a reasonable summarizing parry.

To assess the UN's merits requires a preliminary recognition of its weaknesses. First, virtually all organizations that span geographic, population, and political realms—national and local governments, military alliances, universities, labor unions, chambers of commerce, and more—can at times seem irrelevant and incapable of effecting stated policies and goals. The UN is not immune, and may even be unusually susceptible to this caveat. Second, the United Nations, like the U.S. national and state governments, has developed a large bureaucracy and a confusing budget that sometimes appear to have lives of their own apart from the UN's advertised intentions; in Chapter 3, we detailed the UN's attempts to reform both of these. Third, as the Charter makes clear, the United Nations is unable to claim sovereign authority over its members as a nation-state can make such a claim over its citizens. The United Nations is an international intergovernmental organization, one we have characterized as more like a "confederacy" (made up of theoretically co-equal nations) than a "unitary" or "federal" government, which are the most familiar forms of sovereign nation-state polities. Consequently, the UN's ability to enforce its decisions is contingent on the actions of its members.

This is most obvious in the Security Council, the only organ of the organization that can claim an enforcement entitlement. For this reason, the Security Council is most often in the spotlight when complaints surface about the UN's inability to act. However, when a majority of the Council, along with all of the permanent veto-wielding members, *does* agree, then it has been able to act. To underscore the point, we recommend a comparison of our discussion in Chapter 6 of the genocide crisis in Rwanda in 1994, when the Security

DOI: 10.4324/9781003281535-10

Council certainly *did not act*, with the converse posture toward Iraq in 1991, in East Timor in the late 1990s, and in Liberia between 2003 and 2005. In East Timor and Liberia, the UN intervention eventually brought peace and a democratic election to poor, distraught nations. These cases demonstrate that the UN pursues its decisions and is effective when there is sufficient support by its members. There is no supra-national enforcement possibility above those nation-states. The UN's members—including, above all, the powerful permanent five—would not accede to such a reform. Nonetheless, as we have seen, the world's nations—including even the United States within a year of its invasion of Iraq in defiance of the Security Council—very often seek the legitimacy that only the UN, and particularly the Security Council, can bestow.

Yet, the Russian military invasion of Ukraine in late February 2022 caused heightened alarm about the UN's very durability, as well as its effectiveness. According to Richard Gowan, the UN director at International Crisis Group, "The Ukrainian conflict mark[ed] the most severe test for multilateralism since the end of the Cold War."[2] Goodwin saw the crisis as undermining any Security Council cooperation, rendering the maintenance of international peace and security—perhaps the primary function of the UN and its Security Council—nonviable. Moreover, tense great power hostilities seemed to suggest the improbability of Security Council cooperation on other international crises as they will undoubtedly surface.

We spoke to the recent decline of Security Council unanimity in Chapter 2. Did that decline become an existential crisis for the United Nations by 2022? Is the UN now faced with the same kind of escalating strain as was the League of Nations in the late 1930s when brazen authoritarians and spreading violence brought an end to Wilson's experiment and a collapse into world war? Or is the recent situation more akin to the equally ominous Cuban Missile Crisis of 1962? The League did not survive the late 1930s. The UN survived, and in some respects matured, after 1962.

We should keep in mind that the UN and UN-related organizations were at the center of the Ukrainian issue. In fact, the UN served as the epicenter of the international legal response to the war, partly because Ukrainian leaders, and their various supporters, decided to rely on the UN Charter, international legal institutions, and the major organs of the Security Council and the General Assembly as the crisis unfolded. From January 31, 2022, ongoing emergency sessions of the Security Council occurred well into the spring. These meetings featured, among many others, the U.S. Ambassador Linda Thomas-Greenfield, the U.S. Secretary of State Antony Blinken, and, incongruously, as the Security Council chair during February (based on a rotating formula), Russian Ambassador Vasily Alekseevich Nebenzya, who presided with proper decorum, while bearing the brunt of overwhelming, if usually diplomatic, criticism. On February 25, one day after the invasion, Russia was the sole vote against a Security Council resolution that deplored "in the strongest terms the aggression by the Russian Federation against Ukraine" and demanded that "the Russian Federation immediately cease its use of force against Ukraine" and "immediately, completely and unconditionally withdraw all of its military forces." The Security Council then, acting under the long-dormant Uniting for Peace Resolution (described in Chapter 5), referred the matter to the General Assembly, which on March 2 voted overwhelmingly (141–5; 35 abstentions) for the resolution. Four days after the invasion, Karim Khan, chief prosecutor of the International Criminal Court, announced that he was launching an investigation into possible Russian war crimes and crimes against humanity. By March 2, he had received 39 national referrals to proceed with the effort (not, however, from Ukraine, or even from the United States—neither a member of the Rome Statute!).

In the meantime, Ukraine submitted an application to the International Court of Justice to begin proceedings against Russia. Noting that Russia, like Ukraine, was a member of the Convention on the Prevention and Punishment of the Crime of Genocide, Ukraine shrewdly argued that the ICJ had jurisdiction to adjudicate the false Moscow claim of Ukrainian genocide of Russians. In a 13-2 ruling, the Court found that it did have jurisdiction over the allegations. The ICJ scheduled a hearing on March 7, but the Russians did not show up.[3] Then on March 15, the Court ordered Russia to stop all military actions in Ukraine tied to its February invasion of the country, and to revoke its claim that Ukrainian citizens requested Russia's military support.[4]

Even as the ultimate outcome of the crisis was unknown as of this writing, it is significant to note that the United Nations was in the thick of the Ukrainian predicament. Perhaps it is better that the organization is still present and is at work than if there was no UN. Moreover, we need to note that a complete breakdown of Security Council cooperation is not inevitable. In the aftermath of the Russian invasion of Crimea in 2014, the United States and Russia (as well as China), acting in their capacities as permanent Security Council members, cooperated in peacekeeping operations in Africa, in the Iran nuclear accord, and in the Paris Climate agreement. In late 2021, after the United States left Afghanistan and the Taliban returned to power, the Security Council renewed the mandate of the Assistance Mission in Afghanistan (UNAMA). At the very moment of the Russian incursion into Ukraine, Moscow and the United States were still working together in Vienna to revitalize the P5+1 Iranian nuclear agreement, which had been put on hold with the Trump administration's withdrawal. As conflict raged in central Europe in 2022, a Security Council renewal of the UN peacekeeping mission in Sudan was expected. Even in the Russian-Chinese Joint Statement of February 4, 2022, which was widely seen as a menacing challenge to the U.S.-inspired liberal international world order, Xi Jinping and Vladimir Putin voiced their intention (maybe sincerely?) "to protect the United Nations-driven international architecture and the international law-based world order, seek genuine multipolarity with the United Nations and its *Security Council* playing a central and coordinating role"[5] (italics added).

Other than the Security Council, we best understand most of the other organs of the United Nations as places where virtually all nations in the world can find a place to convene, defend their policies, try to persuade others to their point of view, insert crucial new issues into the global conversation, verbally assail adversaries, seek out friends, and attempt to craft common approaches to the planet's challenges. The United Nations provides a permanent site—actually a multitude of sites—to engage in what some see as irksome international *politics*, bearing in mind that one of the pre-UN options could be an international *conflict*.

Finally, we must say again, as we often do in this text, that there are both a traditional "old" and an emergent "new" United Nations, often intertwined, and comprehending within the full UN System the broadest spectrum of global activities. There are now important new structures created in the last quarter of a century that are meant to bolster the defense of long-recognized human rights principles—the Human Rights Council—and to promote stability in post-conflict societies—the Peacebuilding Commission. The old mechanism of peacekeeping itself has evolved in the same period into holistic democratic nation-building ventures.

To assess the continuing value of the United Nations in the face of the current crisis, let us consider a "theoretical" methodology occasionally used by professional historians: counterfactual history. Some scholars, by taking real world data, have asked, "what might have been" under altered, but imaginable, circumstances.[6] Students can easily understand how this is done. For example, we can ask the precise counterfactual, but reasonable, question: "Who would have been the victor in the 2000 US presidential election had Ralph Nader not been a third-party candidate in Florida?" Though counterfactual because Nader *did* run, the answer to the question seems undeniably that Al Gore would have won the election over George W. Bush. A more problematic, outsized, but suggestive question might be "What would have been the consequences had the South won the American Civil War?" Obviously, world history from that time onward would have been considerably different.

Falling somewhere between an explicit and a wide-ranging counterfactual inquiry is a question most germane to this text: "what if there had never been, or was not now, a United Nations?" Would the state of affairs be the same as it is today or quite different? And if different, can we speculate on the nature and quality of that difference? We should think hard about this question. Of course, there are serious problems that face us now just as they have in the past. But we can say some things with clarity. There was no world organization like the UN in the late nineteenth century; we had World War I. The League of Nations collapsed during the interwar period; we had World War II. The United Nations came into existence following World War II; we have not *yet* had World War III. Of course, there is no automatic one-to-one correspondence between these facts and possible outcomes. But in this stark way, we can raise the critical concern about potential alternative realities. The United Nations is almost eighty years old. Simply in terms of its longevity and its universal membership, it is the most successful international organization in history. Without it would the world be the same? Better? Worse?

Counterfactual history allows us to elevate human action (sometimes called human "agency") as important, even decisive in history, deflecting the notion that events happen inevitably and that history is "determined" apart from what humans actually do or don't do. The United Nations is a creature of human agency. In that sense, it is imperfect because all human-contrived institutions are imperfect. But that defect does not suggest that without it we would have a more peaceful and just world. Whether the United Nations works right or not may depend less on the UN as an abstraction and more on what the world's people do with it. Some of the answer to the query concerning the UN's value may be found in what people and governments have already done with it. They have decided *against* treating it as a static entity created in the 1940s to respond to the unique problems of that time. The United Nations has evolved *by choice*, not by a grand design or external undeterrable forces. The result is a different United Nations today than its founders or its Cold War participants imagined it would be. This kind of evolution—often imposed on the world body because of fresh crises, often because of frustration with its apparent ineffectiveness—is, in fact, evidence of its vitality and usefulness in the eyes of those with the final word on its survival. We trust that the foregoing pages supply key factual and analytical information to our readers, so that they can join the world's peoples in determining what indeed to do next with this *old* and *new* organization.

Notes

1 Richard Gowan, "The UN is Another Casualty of Russia's War: Why the Organization May Never Bounce Back," *Foreign Affairs*, March 10, 2022, at <www.foreignaffairs.com/articles/west-africa/2022-03-10/un-another-casualty-russias-war>.
2 Ibid.
3 See Dona A. Hathaway, "International Law Goes to War in Ukraine," *Foreign Affairs*, March 15, 2022, at <www.foreignaffairs.com/articles/ukraine/2022-03-15/international-law-goes-war-ukraine?utm_medium=newsletters&utm_source=fatoday&utm_campaign=How%20to%20Make%20Peace%20With%20Putin&utm_content=20220321&utm_term=FA%20Today%20-%20112017>.

4 <www.icj-cij.org/public/files/case-related/182/182-20220316-ORD-01-00-EN.pdf>.

5 "Joint Statement of the Russian Federation and the People's Republic of China," February 4, 2022, at <www.airuniversity.af.edu/Portals/10/CASI/documents/Translations/2022-02-04%20 China%20Russia%20joint%20statement%20International%20Relations%20Entering%20a%20 New%20Era.pdf>.

6 See Martin Bunzl, "Counterfactual History: A User's Guide," *American Historical Review*, June 2004, 845–858; and Robert Cowley, ed., *What If? 2: Eminent Historians Imagine What Might Have Been; Essays* (New York: Putnam, 2001). Cowley has edited four volumes of *What If* books; the others were published in 1999, 2002, and 2003. Also see Mark Grimsley, "Forays Into 'What If' History," and Yoav Tenmbaum, "Counterfactual History and the Outbreak of World War I," *Perspectives on History, The Newsmagazine of the American Historical Association*, 53, no. 5, May 2015, 42–45.

Resource 1

Charter of the United Nations

PREAMBLE

We the Peoples of the United Nations Determined

to save succeeding generations from the scourge of war, which twice in our lifetime has
    brought untold sorrow to mankind, and
to reaffirm faith in fundamental human rights, in the dignity and worth of the human
    person, in the equal rights of men and women and of nations large and small, and
to establish conditions under which justice and respect for the obligations arising from
    treaties and other sources of international law can be maintained, and
to promote social progress and better standards of life in larger freedom,

And for These Ends

to practice tolerance and live together in peace with one another as good neighbours, and
to unite our strength to maintain international peace and security, and
to ensure, by the acceptance of principles and the institution of methods, that armed force
    shall not be used, save in the common interest, and
to employ international machinery for the promotion of the economic and social advance-
    ment of all peoples,

Have Resolved to Combine our Efforts to Accomplish These Aims

Accordingly, our respective Governments, through representatives assembled in the city
    of San Francisco, who have exhibited their full powers found to be in good and due
    form, have agreed to the present Charter of the United Nations and do hereby estab-
    lish an international organization to be known as the United Nations.

CHAPTER 1: PURPOSES AND PRINCIPLES

Article 1

The Purposes of the United Nations are:

1 To maintain international peace and security, and to that end: to take effective col-
    lective measures for the prevention and removal of threats to the peace, and for the
    suppression of acts of aggression or other breaches of the peace, and to bring about
    by peaceful means, and in conformity with the principles of justice and international

law, adjustment or settlement of international disputes or situations which might lead to a breach of the peace;

2 To develop friendly relations among nations based on respect for the principle of equal rights and self-determination of peoples, and to take other appropriate measures to strengthen universal peace;

3 To achieve international co-operation in solving international problems of an economic, social, cultural, or humanitarian character, and in promoting and encouraging respect for human rights and for fundamental freedoms for all without distinction as to race, sex, language, or religion; and

4 To be a centre for harmonizing the actions of nations in the attainment of these common ends.

Article 2

The Organization and its Members, in pursuit of the Purposes stated in Article 1, shall act in accordance with the following Principles.

1 The Organization is based on the principle of the sovereign equality of all its Members.

2 All Members, in order to ensure to all of them the rights and benefits resulting from membership, shall fulfill in good faith the obligations assumed by them in accordance with the present Charter.

3 All Members shall settle their international disputes by peaceful means in such a manner that international peace and security, and justice, are not endangered.

4 All Members shall refrain in their international relations from the threat or use of force against the territorial integrity or political independence of any state, or in any other manner inconsistent with the Purposes of the United Nations.

5 All Members shall give the United Nations every assistance in any action it takes in accordance with the present Charter, and shall refrain from giving assistance to any state against which the United Nations is taking preventive or enforcement action.

6 The Organization shall ensure that states which are not Members of the United Nations act in accordance with these Principles so far as may be necessary for the maintenance of international peace and security.

7 Nothing contained in the present Charter shall authorize the United Nations to intervene in matters which are essentially within the domestic jurisdiction of any state or shall require the Members to submit such matters to settlement under the present Charter; but this principle shall not prejudice the application of enforcement measures under Chapter 7.

CHAPTER 2: MEMBERSHIP

Article 3

The original Members of the United Nations shall be the states which, having participated in the United Nations Conference on International Organization at San Francisco, or having previously signed the Declaration by United Nations of 1 January 1942, sign the present Charter and ratify it in accordance with Article 110.

Article 4

1 Membership in the United Nations is open to all other peace-loving states which accept the obligations contained in the present Charter and, in the judgment of the Organization, are able and willing to carry out these obligations.
2 The admission of any such state to membership in the United Nations will be effected by a decision of the General Assembly upon the recommendation of the Security Council.

Article 5

A Member of the United Nations against which preventive or enforcement action has been taken by the Security Council may be suspended from the exercise of the rights and privileges of membership by the General Assembly upon the recommendation of the Security Council. The exercise of these rights and privileges may be restored by the Security Council.

Article 6

A Member of the United Nations which has persistently violated the Principles contained in the present Charter may be expelled from the Organization by the General Assembly upon the recommendation of the Security Council.

CHAPTER 3: ORGANS

Article 7

1 There are established as the principal organs of the United Nations: a General Assembly, a Security Council, an Economic and Social Council, a Trusteeship Council, an International Court of Justice, and a Secretariat.
2 Such subsidiary organs as may be found necessary may be established in accordance with the present Charter.

Article 8

The United Nations shall place no restrictions on the eligibility of men and women to participate in any capacity and under conditions of equality in its principal and subsidiary organs.

CHAPTER 4: THE GENERAL ASSEMBLY COMPOSITION

Article 9

1 The General Assembly shall consist of all the Members of the United Nations.
2 Each Member shall have not more than five representatives in the General Assembly.

FUNCTIONS AND POWERS

Article 10

The General Assembly may discuss any questions or any matters within the scope of the present Charter or relating to the powers and functions of any organs provided for in the present Charter, and, except as provided in Article 12, may make recommendations to the Members of the United Nations or to the Security Council or to both on any such questions or matters.

Article 11

1   The General Assembly may consider the general principles of co-operation in the maintenance of international peace and security, including the principles governing disarmament and the regulation of armaments, and may make recommendations with regard to such principles to the Members or to the Security Council or to both.
2   The General Assembly may discuss any questions relating to the maintenance of international peace and security brought before it by any Member of the United Nations, or by the Security Council, or by a state which is not a Member of the United Nations in accordance with Article 35, paragraph 2, and, except as provided in Article 12, may make recommendations with regard to any such questions to the state or states concerned or to the Security Council or to both. Any such question on which action is necessary shall be referred to the Security Council by the General Assembly either before or after discussion.
3   The General Assembly may call the attention of the Security Council to situations which are likely to endanger international peace and security.
4   The powers of the General Assembly set forth in this Article shall not limit the general scope of Article 10.

Article 12

1   While the Security Council is exercising in respect of any dispute or situation the functions assigned to it in the present Charter, the General Assembly shall not make any recommendation with regard to that dispute or situation unless the Security Council so requests.
2   The Secretary-General, with the consent of the Security Council, shall notify the General Assembly at each session of any matters relative to the maintenance of international peace and security which are being dealt with by the Security Council and shall similarly notify the General Assembly, or the Members of the United Nations if the General Assembly is not in session, immediately the Security Council ceases to deal with such matters.

Article 13

1   The General Assembly shall initiate studies and make recommendations for the purpose of:

a   promoting international co-operation in the political field and encouraging the progressive development of international law and its codification;

   b   promoting international co-operation in the economic, social, cultural, educational, and health fields, and assisting in the realization of human rights and fundamental freedoms for all without distinction as to race, sex, language, or religion.

2 The further responsibilities, functions and powers of the General Assembly with respect to matters mentioned in paragraph 1 (b) above are set forth in Chapters IX and X.

Article 14

Subject to the provisions of Article 12, the General Assembly may recommend measures for the peaceful adjustment of any situation, regardless of origin, which it deems likely to impair the general welfare or friendly relations among nations, including situations resulting from a violation of the provisions of the present Charter setting forth the Purposes and Principles of the United Nations.

Article 15

1 The General Assembly shall receive and consider annual and special reports from the Security Council; these reports shall include an account of the measures that the Security Council has decided upon or taken to maintain international peace and security.
2 The General Assembly shall receive and consider reports from the other organs of the United Nations.

Article 16

The General Assembly shall perform such functions with respect to the international trusteeship system as are assigned to it under Chapters XII and XIII, including the approval of the trusteeship agreements for areas not designated as strategic.

Article 17

1 The General Assembly shall consider and approve the budget of the Organization.
2 The expenses of the Organization shall be borne by the Members as apportioned by the General Assembly.
3 The Assembly shall consider and approve any financial and budgetary arrangements with specialized agencies referred to in Article 57 and shall examine the administrative budgets of such specialized agencies with a view to making recommendations to the agencies concerned.

VOTING

Article 18

1 Each member of the General Assembly shall have one vote.
2 Decisions of the General Assembly on important questions shall be made by a two-thirds majority of the members present and voting. These questions shall include:

recommendations with respect to the maintenance of international peace and security, the election of the non-permanent members of the Security Council, the election of the members of the Economic and Social Council, the election of members of the Trusteeship Council in accordance with paragraph 1 of Article 86, the admission of new Members to the United Nations, the suspension of the rights and privileges of membership, the expulsion of Members, questions relating to the operation of the trusteeship system, and budgetary questions.

3 Decisions on other questions, including the determination of additional categories of questions to be decided by a two-thirds majority, shall be made by a majority of the members present and voting.

Article 19

A Member of the United Nations which is in arrears in the payment of its financial contributions to the Organization shall have no vote in the General Assembly if the amount of its arrears equals or exceeds the amount of the contributions due from it for the preceding two full years. The General Assembly may, nevertheless, permit such a Member to vote if it is satisfied that the failure to pay is due to conditions beyond the control of the Member.

PROCEDURE

Article 20

The General Assembly shall meet in regular annual sessions and in such special sessions as occasion may require. Special sessions shall be convoked by the Secretary-General at the request of the Security Council or of a majority of the Members of the United Nations.

Article 21

The General Assembly shall adopt its own rules of procedure. It shall elect its President for each session.

Article 22

The General Assembly may establish such subsidiary organs as it deems necessary for the performance of its functions.

CHAPTER 5: THE SECURITY COUNCIL COMPOSITION

Article 23

1 The Security Council shall consist of fifteen Members of the United Nations. The Republic of China, France, the Union of Soviet Socialist Republics, the United Kingdom of Great Britain and Northern Ireland, and the United States of America shall be permanent members of the Security Council. The General Assembly shall elect ten other Members of the United Nations to be non-permanent members of the Security Council, due regard being specially paid, in the first instance to the contribution of Members of the United Nations to the maintenance of international peace and

security and to the other purposes of the Organization, and also to equitable geographical distribution.

2 The non-permanent members of the Security Council shall be elected for a term of two years. In the first election of the non-permanent members after the increase of the membership of the Security Council from eleven to fifteen, two of the four additional members shall be chosen for a term of one year. A retiring member shall not be eligible for immediate re-election.

3 Each member of the Security Council shall have one representative.

FUNCTIONS AND POWERS

Article 24

1 In order to ensure prompt and effective action by the United Nations, its Members confer on the Security Council primary responsibility for the maintenance of international peace and security, and agree that in carrying out its duties under this responsibility the Security Council acts on their behalf.

2 In discharging these duties the Security Council shall act in accordance with the Purposes and Principles of the United Nations. The specific powers granted to the Security Council for the discharge of these duties are laid down in Chapters VI, VII, VIII, and XII.

3 The Security Council shall submit annual and, when necessary, special reports to the General Assembly for its consideration.

Article 25

The Members of the United Nations agree to accept and carry out the decisions of the Security Council in accordance with the present Charter.

Article 26

In order to promote the establishment and maintenance of international peace and security with the least diversion for armaments of the world's human and economic resources, the Security Council shall be responsible for formulating, with the assistance of the Military Staff Committee referred to in Article 47, plans to be submitted to the Members of the United Nations for the establishment of a system for the regulation of armaments.

VOTING

Article 27

1 Each member of the Security Council shall have one vote.

2 Decisions of the Security Council on procedural matters shall be made by an affirmative vote of nine members.

3 Decisions of the Security Council on all other matters shall be made by an affirmative vote of nine members including the concurring votes of the permanent members; provided that, in decisions under Chapter VI, and under paragraph 3 of Article 52, a party to a dispute shall abstain from voting.

PROCEDURE

Article 28

1 The Security Council shall be so organized as to be able to function continuously. Each member of the Security Council shall for this purpose be represented at all times at the seat of the Organization.
2 The Security Council shall hold meetings at which each of its members may, if it so desires, be represented by a member of the government or by some other specially designated representative.
3 The Security Council may hold meetings at such places other than the seat of the Organization as in its judgment will best facilitate its work.

Article 29

The Security Council may establish such subsidiary organs as it deems necessary for the performance of its functions.

Article 30

The Security Council shall adopt its own rules of procedure, including the method of selecting its President.

Article 31

Any Member of the United Nations which is not a member of the Security Council may participate, without vote, in the discussion of any question brought before the Security Council whenever the latter considers that the interests of that Member are specially affected.

Article 32

Any Member of the United Nations which is not a member of the Security Council or any state which is not a Member of the United Nations, if it is a party to a dispute under consideration by the Security Council, shall be invited to participate, without vote, in the discussion relating to the dispute. The Security Council shall lay down such conditions as it deems just for the participation of a state which is not a Member of the United Nations.

CHAPTER 6: PACIFIC SETTLEMENT OF DISPUTES

Article 33

1 The parties to any dispute, the continuance of which is likely to endanger the maintenance of international peace and security, shall, first of all, seek a solution by negotiation, enquiry, mediation, conciliation, arbitration, judicial settlement, resort to regional agencies or arrangements, or other peaceful means of their own choice.

2 The Security Council shall, when it deems necessary, call upon the parties to settle their dispute by such means.

Article 34

The Security Council may investigate any dispute, or any situation which might lead to international friction or give rise to a dispute, in order to determine whether the continuance of the dispute or situation is likely to endanger the maintenance of international peace and security.

Article 35

1 Any Member of the United Nations may bring any dispute, or any situation of the nature referred to in Article 34, to the attention of the Security Council or of the General Assembly.
2 A state which is not a Member of the United Nations may bring to the attention of the Security Council or of the General Assembly any dispute to which it is a party if it accepts in advance, for the purposes of the dispute, the obligations of pacific settlement provided in the present Charter.
3 The proceedings of the General Assembly in respect of matters brought to its attention under this Article will be subject to the provisions of Articles 11 and 12.

Article 36

1 The Security Council may, at any stage of a dispute of the nature referred to in Article 33 or of a situation of like nature, recommend appropriate procedures or methods of adjustment.
2 The Security Council should take into consideration any procedures for the settlement of the dispute which have already been adopted by the parties.
3 In making recommendations under this Article the Security Council should also take into consideration that legal disputes should as a general rule be referred by the parties to the International Court of Justice in accordance with the provisions of the Statute of the Court.

Article 37

1 Should the parties to a dispute of the nature referred to in Article 33 fail to settle it by the means indicated in that Article, they shall refer it to the Security Council.
2 If the Security Council deems that the continuance of the dispute is in fact likely to endanger the maintenance of international peace and security, it shall decide whether to take action under Article 36 or to recommend such terms of settlement as it may consider appropriate.

Article 38

Without prejudice to the provisions of Articles 33–37, the Security Council may, if all the parties to any dispute so request, make recommendations to the parties with a view to a pacific settlement of the dispute.

CHAPTER 7: ACTION WITH RESPECT TO THREATS TO THE PEACE, BREACHES OF THE PEACE, AND ACTS OF AGGRESSION

Article 39

The Security Council shall determine the existence of any threat to the peace, breach of the peace, or act of aggression and shall make recommendations, or decide what measures shall be taken in accordance with Articles 41 and 42, to maintain or restore international peace and security.

Article 40

In order to prevent an aggravation of the situation, the Security Council may, before making the recommendations or deciding upon the measures provided for in Article 39, call upon the parties concerned to comply with such provisional measures as it deems necessary or desirable. Such provisional measures shall be without prejudice to the rights, claims, or position of the parties concerned. The Security Council shall duly take account of failure to comply with such provisional measures.

Article 41

The Security Council may decide what measures not involving the use of armed force are to be employed to give effect to its decisions, and it may call upon the Members of the United Nations to apply such measures. These may include complete or partial interruption of economic relations and of rail, sea, air, postal, telegraphic, radio, and other means of communication, and the severance of diplomatic relations.

Article 42

Should the Security Council consider that measures provided for in Article 41 would be inadequate or have proved to be inadequate, it may take such action by air, sea, or land forces as may be necessary to maintain or restore international peace and security. Such action may include demonstrations, blockade, and other operations by air, sea, or land forces of Members of the United Nations.

Article 43

1 All Members of the United Nations, in order to contribute to the maintenance of international peace and security, undertake to make available to the Security Council, on its call and in accordance with a special agreement or agreements, armed forces, assistance, and facilities, including rights of passage, necessary for the purpose of maintaining international peace and security.
2 Such agreement or agreements shall govern the numbers and types of forces, their degree of readiness and general location, and the nature of the facilities and assistance to be provided.
3 The agreement or agreements shall be negotiated as soon as possible on the initiative of the Security Council. They shall be concluded between the Security Council and Members or between the Security Council and groups of Members and shall be

subject to ratification by the signatory states in accordance with their respective constitutional processes.

Article 44

When the Security Council has decided to use force it shall, before calling upon a Member not represented on it to provide armed forces in fulfilment of the obligations assumed under Article 43, invite that Member, if the Member so desires, to participate in the decisions of the Security Council concerning the employment of contingents of that Member's armed forces.

Article 45

In order to enable the United Nations to take urgent military measures, Members shall hold immediately available national air-force contingents for combined international enforcement action. The strength and degree of readiness of these contingents and plans for their combined action shall be determined, within the limits laid down in the special agreement or agreements referred to in Article 43, by the Security Council with the assistance of the Military Staff Committee.

Article 46

Plans for the application of armed force shall be made by the Security Council with the assistance of the Military Staff Committee.

Article 47

1 There shall be established a Military Staff Committee to advise and assist the Security Council on questions relating to the Security Council's military requirements for the maintenance of international peace and security, the employment and command of forces placed at its disposal, the regulation of armaments, and possible disarmament.
2 The Military Staff Committee shall consist of the Chiefs of Staff of the permanent members of the Security Council or their representatives. Any Member of the United Nations not permanently represented on the Committee shall be invited by the Committee to be associated with it when the efficient discharge of the Committee's responsibilities requires the participation of that Member in its work.
3 The Military Staff Committee shall be responsible under the Security Council for the strategic direction of any armed forces placed at the disposal of the Security Council. Questions relating to the command of such forces shall be worked out subsequently.
4 The Military Staff Committee, with the authorization of the Security Council after consultation with appropriate regional agencies, may establish regional sub-committees.

Article 48

1 The action required to carry out the decisions of the Security Council for the maintenance of international peace and security shall be taken by all the Members of the United Nations or by some of them, as the Security Council may determine.
2 Such decisions shall be carried out by the Members of the United Nations directly and through their action in the appropriate international agencies of which they are members.

Article 49

The Members of the United Nations shall join in affording mutual assistance in carrying out the measures decided upon by the Security Council.

Article 50

If preventive or enforcement measures against any state are taken by the Security Council, any other state, whether a Member of the United Nations or not, which finds itself confronted with special economic problems arising from the carrying out of those measures shall have the right to consult the Security Council with regard to a solution of those problems.

Article 51

Nothing in the present Charter shall impair the inherent right of individual or collective self-defence if an armed attack occurs against a Member of the United Nations, until the Security Council has taken measures necessary to maintain international peace and security. Measures taken by Members in the exercise of this right of self-defence shall be immediately reported to the Security Council and shall not in any way affect the authority and responsibility of the Security Council under the present Charter to take at any time such action as it deems necessary in order to maintain or restore international peace and security.

CHAPTER 8: REGIONAL ARRANGEMENTS

Article 52

1 Nothing in the present Charter precludes the existence of regional arrangements or agencies for dealing with such matters relating to the maintenance of international peace and security as are appropriate for regional action, provided that such arrangements or agencies and their activities are consistent with the Purposes and Principles of the United Nations.
2 The Members of the United Nations entering into such arrangements or constituting such agencies shall make every effort to achieve pacific settlement of local disputes through such regional arrangements or by such regional agencies before referring them to the Security Council.
3 The Security Council shall encourage the development of pacific settlement of local disputes through such regional arrangements or by such regional agencies either on the initiative of the states concerned or by reference from the Security Council.
4 This Article in no way impairs the application of Articles 34 and 35.

Article 53

1 The Security Council shall, where appropriate, utilize such regional arrangements or agencies for enforcement action under its authority. But no enforcement action shall be taken under regional arrangements or by regional agencies without the authorization of the Security Council, with the exception of measures against any enemy state, as defined in paragraph 2 of this Article, provided for pursuant to Article 107 or in regional arrangements directed against renewal of aggressive policy on the part of any such state, until such time as the Organization may, on request of the Governments concerned, be charged with the responsibility for preventing further aggression by such a state.

2 The term enemy state as used in paragraph 1 of this Article applies to any state which during the Second World War has been an enemy of any signatory of the present Charter.

Article 54

The Security Council shall at all times be kept fully informed of activities undertaken or in contemplation under regional arrangements or by regional agencies for the maintenance of international peace and security.

CHAPTER 9: INTERNATIONAL ECONOMIC AND SOCIAL CO-OPERATION

Article 55

With a view to the creation of conditions of stability and well-being which are necessary for peaceful and friendly relations among nations based on respect for the principle of equal rights and self-determination of peoples, the United Nations shall promote:

a   higher standards of living, full employment, and conditions of economic and social progress and development;
b   solutions of international economic, social, health, and related problems; and international cultural and educational co-operation; and
c   universal respect for, and observance of, human rights and fundamental freedoms for all without distinction as to race, sex, language, or religion.

Article 56

All Members pledge themselves to take joint and separate action in co-operation with the Organization for the achievement of the purposes set forth in Article 55.

Article 57

1   The various specialized agencies, established by intergovernmental agreement and having wide international responsibilities, as defined in their basic instruments, in economic, social, cultural, educational, health, and related fields, shall be brought into relationship with the United Nations in accordance with the provisions of Article 63.
2   Such agencies thus brought into relationship with the United Nations are hereinafter referred to as specialized agencies.

Article 58

The Organization shall make recommendations for the co-ordination of the policies and activities of the specialized agencies.

Article 59

The Organization shall, where appropriate, initiate negotiations among the states concerned for the creation of any new specialized agencies required for the accomplishment of the purposes set forth in Article 55.

Article 60

Responsibility for the discharge of the functions of the Organization set forth in this Chapter shall be vested in the General Assembly and, under the authority of the General Assembly, in the Economic and Social Council, which shall have for this purpose the powers set forth in Chapter X.

CHAPTER 10: THE ECONOMIC AND SOCIAL COUNCIL COMPOSITION

Article 61

1 The Economic and Social Council shall consist of fifty-four Members of the United Nations elected by the General Assembly.
2 Subject to the provisions of paragraph 3, eighteen members of the Economic and Social Council shall be elected each year for a term of three years. A retiring member shall be eligible for immediate re-election.
3 At the first election after the increase in the membership of the Economic and Social Council from twenty-seven to fifty-four members, in addition to the members elected in place of the nine members whose term of office expires at the end of that year, twenty-seven additional members shall be elected. Of these twenty-seven additional members, the term of office of nine members so elected shall expire at the end of one year, and of nine other members at the end of two years, in accordance with arrangements made by the General Assembly.
4 Each member of the Economic and Social Council shall have one representative.

FUNCTIONS AND POWERS

Article 62

1 The Economic and Social Council may make or initiate studies and reports with respect to international economic, social, cultural, educational, health, and related matters and may make recommendations with respect to any such matters to the General Assembly, to the Members of the United Nations, and to the specialized agencies concerned.
2 It may make recommendations for the purpose of promoting respect for, and observance of, human rights and fundamental freedoms for all.
3 It may prepare draft conventions for submission to the General Assembly, with respect to matters falling within its competence.
4 It may call, in accordance with the rules prescribed by the United Nations, international conferences on matters falling within its competence.

Article 63

1 The Economic and Social Council may enter into agreements with any of the agencies referred to in Article 57, defining the terms on which the agency concerned shall be brought into relationship with the United Nations. Such agreements shall be subject to approval by the General Assembly.
2 It may co-ordinate the activities of the specialized agencies through consultation with and recommendations to such agencies and through recommendations to the General Assembly and to the Members of the United Nations.

Article 64

1 The Economic and Social Council may take appropriate steps to obtain regular reports from the specialized agencies. It may make arrangements with the Members of the United Nations and with the specialized agencies to obtain reports on the steps taken to give effect to its own recommendations and to recommendations on matters falling within its competence made by the General Assembly.
2 It may communicate its observations on these reports to the General Assembly.

Article 65

The Economic and Social Council may furnish information to the Security Council and shall assist the Security Council upon its request.

Article 66

1 The Economic and Social Council shall perform such functions as fall within its competence in connexion with the carrying out of the recommendations of the General Assembly.
2 It may, with the approval of the General Assembly, perform services at the request of Members of the United Nations and at the request of specialized agencies.
3 It shall perform such other functions as are specified elsewhere in the present Charter or as may be assigned to it by the General Assembly.

VOTING

Article 67

1 Each member of the Economic and Social Council shall have one vote.
2 Decisions of the Economic and Social Council shall be made by a majority of the members present and voting.

PROCEDURE

Article 68

The Economic and Social Council shall set up commissions in economic and social fields and for the promotion of human rights, and such other commissions as may be required for the performance of its functions.

Article 69

The Economic and Social Council shall invite any Member of the United Nations to participate, without vote, in its deliberations on any matter of particular concern to that Member.

Article 70

The Economic and Social Council may make arrangements for representatives of the specialized agencies to participate, without vote, in its deliberations and in those of the commissions established by it, and for its representatives to participate in the deliberations of the specialized agencies.

Article 71

The Economic and Social Council may make suitable arrangements for consultation with nongovernmental organizations which are concerned with matters within its competence. Such arrangements may be made with international organizations and, where appropriate, with national organizations after consultation with the Member of the United Nations concerned.

Article 72

1 The Economic and Social Council shall adopt its own rules of procedure, including the method of selecting its President.
2 The Economic and Social Council shall meet as required in accordance with its rules, which shall include provision for the convening of meetings on the request of a majority of its members.

CHAPTER 11: DECLARATION REGARDING NON-SELF-GOVERNING TERRITORIES

Article 73

Members of the United Nations which have or assume responsibilities for the administration of territories whose peoples have not yet attained a full measure of self-government recognize the principle that the interests of the inhabitants of these territories are paramount, and accept as a sacred trust the obligation to promote to the utmost, within the system of international peace and security established by the present Charter, the well-being of the inhabitants of these territories, and, to this end:

to ensure, with due respect for the culture of the peoples concerned, their political, economic, social, and educational advancement, their just treatment, and their protection against abuses;

to develop self-government, to take due account of the political aspirations of the peoples, and to assist them in the progressive development of their free political institutions, according to the particular circumstances of each territory and its peoples and their varying stages of advancement;

to further international peace and security;

to promote constructive measures of development, to encourage research, and to cooperate with one another and, when and where appropriate, with specialized international bodies with a view to the practical achievement of the social, economic, and scientific purposes set forth in this Article; and

to transmit regularly to the Secretary-General for information purposes, subject to such limitation as security and constitutional considerations may require, statistical and other information of a technical nature relating to economic, social, and educational conditions in the territories for which they are respectively responsible other than those territories to which Chapters XII and XIII apply.

Article 74

Members of the United Nations also agree that their policy in respect of the territories to which this Chapter applies, no less than in respect of their metropolitan areas, must be based on the general principle of good-neighbourliness, due account being taken of the interests and well-being of the rest of the world, in social, economic, and commercial matters.

CHAPTER 12: INTERNATIONAL TRUSTEESHIP SYSTEM

Article 75

The United Nations shall establish under its authority an international trusteeship system for the administration and supervision of such territories as may be placed thereunder by subsequent individual agreements. These territories are hereinafter referred to as trust territories.

Article 76

The basic objectives of the trusteeship system, in accordance with the Purposes of the United Nations laid down in Article 1 of the present Charter, shall be:

a   to further international peace and security;

b   to promote the political, economic, social, and educational advancement of the inhabitants of the trust territories, and their progressive development towards self-government or independence as may be appropriate to the particular circumstances of each territory and its peoples and the freely expressed wishes of the peoples concerned, and as may be provided by the terms of each trusteeship agreement;

c   to encourage respect for human rights and for fundamental freedoms for all without distinction as to race, sex, language, or religion, and to encourage recognition of the interdependence of the peoples of the world; and

d   to ensure equal treatment in social, economic, and commercial matters for all Members of the United Nations and their nationals, and also equal treatment for the latter in the administration of justice, without prejudice to the attainment of the foregoing objectives and subject to the provisions of Article 80.

Article 77

1   The trusteeship system shall apply to such territories in the following categories as may be placed thereunder by means of trusteeship agreements:

    1   territories now held under mandate;

    2   territories which may be detached from enemy states as a result of the Second World War; and

    3   territories voluntarily placed under the system by states responsible for their administration.

2   It will be a matter for subsequent agreement as to which territories in the foregoing categories will be brought under the trusteeship system and upon what terms.

Article 78

The trusteeship system shall not apply to territories which have become Members of the United Nations, relationship among which shall be based on respect for the principle of sovereign equality.

Article 79

The terms of trusteeship for each territory to be placed under the trusteeship system, including any alteration or amendment, shall be agreed upon by the states directly concerned, including the mandatory power in the case of territories held under mandate by a Member of the United Nations, and shall be approved as provided for in Articles 83 and 85.

Article 80

1 Except as may be agreed upon in individual trusteeship agreements, made under Articles 77, 79, and 81, placing each territory under the trusteeship system, and until such agreements have been concluded, nothing in this Chapter shall be construed in or of itself to alter in any manner the rights whatsoever of any states or any peoples or the terms of existing international instruments to which Members of the United Nations may respectively be parties.
2 Paragraph 1 of this Article shall not be interpreted as giving grounds for delay or postponement of the negotiation and conclusion of agreements for placing mandated and other territories under the trusteeship system as provided for in Article 77.

Article 81

The trusteeship agreement shall in each case include the terms under which the trust territory will be administered and designate the authority which will exercise the administration of the trust territory. Such authority, hereinafter called the administering authority, may be one or more states or the Organization itself.

Article 82

There may be designated, in any trusteeship agreement, a strategic area or areas which may include part or all of the trust territory to which the agreement applies, without prejudice to any special agreement or agreements made under Article 43.

Article 83

1 All functions of the United Nations relating to strategic areas, including the approval of the terms of the trusteeship agreements and of their alteration or amendment, shall be exercised by the Security Council.
2 The basic objectives set forth in Article 76 shall be applicable to the people of each strategic area.
3 The Security Council shall, subject to the provisions of the trusteeship agreements and without prejudice to security considerations, avail itself of the assistance of the Trusteeship Council to perform those functions of the United Nations under the trusteeship system relating to political, economic, social, and educational matters in the strategic areas.

Article 84

It shall be the duty of the administering authority to ensure that the trust territory shall play its part in the maintenance of international peace and security. To this end the administering authority may make use of volunteer forces, facilities, and assistance from the trust territory in carrying out the obligations towards the Security Council undertaken in this regard by the administering authority, as well as for local defence and the maintenance of law and order within the trust territory.

Article 85

1 The functions of the United Nations with regard to trusteeship agreements for all areas not designated as strategic, including the approval of the terms of the trusteeship agreements and of their alteration or amendment, shall be exercised by the General Assembly.
2 The Trusteeship Council, operating under the authority of the General Assembly, shall assist the General Assembly in carrying out these functions.

CHAPTER 13: THE TRUSTEESHIP COUNCIL
COMPOSITION

Article 86

1 The Trusteeship Council shall consist of the following Members of the United Nations:

   a   those Members administering trust territories;
   b   such of those Members mentioned by name in Article 23 as are not administering trust territories; and
   c   as many other Members elected for three-year terms by the General Assembly as may be necessary to ensure that the total number of members of the Trusteeship Council is equally divided between those Members of the United Nations which administer trust territories and those which do not.

2 Each member of the Trusteeship Council shall designate one specially qualified person to represent it therein.

FUNCTIONS AND POWERS

Article 87

The General Assembly and, under its authority, the Trusteeship Council, in carrying out their functions, may:

a   consider reports submitted by the administering authority;
b   accept petitions and examine them in consultation with the administering authority;
c   provide for periodic visits to the respective trust territories at times agreed upon with the administering authority; and
d   take these and other actions in conformity with the terms of the trusteeship agreements.

Article 88

The Trusteeship Council shall formulate a questionnaire on the political, economic, social, and educational advancement of the inhabitants of each trust territory, and the administering authority for each trust territory within the competence of the General

Assembly shall make an annual report to the General Assembly upon the basis of such questionnaire.

VOTING

Article 89

1 Each member of the Trusteeship Council shall have one vote.
2 Decisions of the Trusteeship Council shall be made by a majority of the members present and voting.

PROCEDURE

Article 90

1 The Trusteeship Council shall adopt its own rules of procedure, including the method of selecting its President.
2 The Trusteeship Council shall meet as required in accordance with its rules, which shall include provision for the convening of meetings on the request of a majority of its members.

Article 91

The Trusteeship Council shall, when appropriate, avail itself of the assistance of the Economic and Social Council and of the specialized agencies in regard to matters with which they are respectively concerned.

CHAPTER 14: THE INTERNATIONAL COURT OF JUSTICE

Article 92

The International Court of Justice shall be the principal judicial organ of the United Nations. It shall function in accordance with the annexed Statute, which is based upon the Statute of the Permanent Court of International Justice and forms an integral part of the present Charter.

Article 93

1 All Members of the United Nations are ipso facto parties to the Statute of the International Court of Justice.
2 A state which is not a member of the United Nations may become a party to the Statute of the International Court of Justice on conditions to be determined in each case by the General Assembly upon the recommendation of the Security Council.

Article 94

1 Each Member of the United Nations undertakes to comply with the decision of the International Court of Justice in any case to which it is a party.

2 If any party to a case fails to perform the obligations incumbent upon it under a judgment rendered by the Court, the other party may have recourse to the Security Council, which may, if it deems necessary, make recommendations or decide upon measures to be taken to give effect to the judgment.

Article 95

Nothing in the present Charter shall prevent Members of the United Nations from entrusting the solution of their differences to other tribunals by virtue of agreements already in existence or which may be concluded in the future.

Article 96

1 The General Assembly or the Security Council may request the International Court of Justice to give an advisory opinion on any legal question.
2 Other organs of the United Nations and specialized agencies, which may at any time be so authorized by the General Assembly, may also request advisory opinions of the Court on legal questions arising within the scope of their activities.

CHAPTER 15: THE SECRETARIAT

Article 97

The Secretariat shall comprise a Secretary-General and such staff as the Organization may require. The Secretary-General shall be appointed by the General Assembly upon the recommendation of the Security Council. He shall be the chief administrative officer of the Organization.

Article 98

The Secretary-General shall act in that capacity in all meetings of the General Assembly, of the Security Council, of the Economic and Social Council, and of the Trusteeship Council, and shall perform such other functions as are entrusted to him by these organs. The Secretary-General shall make an annual report to the General Assembly on the work of the Organization.

Article 99

The Secretary-General may bring to the attention of the Security Council any matter which in his opinion may threaten the maintenance of international peace and security.

Article 100

1 In the performance of their duties the Secretary-General and the staff shall not seek or receive instructions from any government or from any other authority external to the Organization. They shall refrain from any action which might reflect on their position as international officials responsible only to the Organization.
2 Each Member of the United Nations undertakes to respect the exclusively international character of the responsibilities of the Secretary-General and the staff and not to seek to influence them in the discharge of their responsibilities.

Article 101

1 The staff shall be appointed by the Secretary-General under regulations established by the General Assembly.
2 Appropriate staffs shall be permanently assigned to the Economic and Social Council, the Trusteeship Council, and, as required, to other organs of the United Nations. These staffs shall form a part of the Secretariat.
3 The paramount consideration in the employment of the staff and in the determination of the conditions of service shall be the necessity of securing the highest standards of efficiency, competence, and integrity. Due regard shall be paid to the importance of recruiting the staff on as wide a geographical basis as possible.

CHAPTER 16: MISCELLANEOUS PROVISIONS

Article 102

1 Every treaty and every international agreement entered into by any Member of the United Nations after the present Charter comes into force shall as soon as possible be registered with the Secretariat and published by it.
2 No party to any such treaty or international agreement which has not been registered in accordance with the provisions of paragraph I of this Article may invoke that treaty or agreement before any organ of the United Nations.

Article 103

In the event of a conflict between the obligations of the Members of the United Nations under the present Charter and their obligations under any other international agreement, their obligations under the present Charter shall prevail.

Article 104

The Organization shall enjoy in the territory of each of its Members such legal capacity as may be necessary for the exercise of its functions and the fulfilment of its purposes.

Article 105

1 The Organization shall enjoy in the territory of each of its Members such privileges and immunities as are necessary for the fulfilment of its purposes.
2 Representatives of the Members of the United Nations and officials of the Organization shall similarly enjoy such privileges and immunities as are necessary for the independent exercise of their functions in connexion with the Organization.
3 The General Assembly may make recommendations with a view to determining the details of the application of paragraphs 1 and 2 of this Article or may propose conventions to the Members of the United Nations for this purpose.

CHAPTER 17: TRANSITIONAL SECURITY ARRANGEMENTS

Article 106

Pending the coming into force of such special agreements referred to in Article 43 as in the opinion of the Security Council enable it to begin the exercise of its responsibilities under Article 42, the parties to the Four-Nation Declaration, signed at Moscow, 30 October 1943, and France, shall, in accordance with the provisions of paragraph 5 of that Declaration, consult with one another and as occasion requires with other Members of the United Nations with a view to such joint action on behalf of the Organization as may be necessary for the purpose of maintaining international peace and security.

Article 107

Nothing in the present Charter shall invalidate or preclude action, in relation to any state which during the Second World War has been an enemy of any signatory to the present Charter, taken or authorized as a result of that war by the Governments having responsibility for such action.

CHAPTER 18: AMENDMENTS

Article 108

Amendments to the present Charter shall come into force for all Members of the United Nations when they have been adopted by a vote of two thirds of the members of the General Assembly and ratified in accordance with their respective constitutional processes by two thirds of the Members of the United Nations, including all the permanent members of the Security Council.

Article 109

1 A General Conference of the Members of the United Nations for the purpose of reviewing the present Charter may be held at a date and place to be fixed by a two-thirds vote of the members of the General Assembly and by a vote of any nine members of the Security Council. Each Member of the United Nations shall have one vote in the conference.
2 Any alteration of the present Charter recommended by a two-thirds vote of the conference shall take effect when ratified in accordance with their respective constitutional processes by two thirds of the Members of the United Nations including all the permanent members of the Security Council.
3 If such a conference has not been held before the tenth annual session of the General Assembly following the coming into force of the present Charter, the proposal to call such a conference shall be placed on the agenda of that session of the General Assembly, and the conference shall be held if so decided by a majority vote of the members of the General Assembly and by a vote of any seven members of the Security Council.

CHAPTER 19: RATIFICATION AND SIGNATURE

Article 110

1 The present Charter shall be ratified by the signatory states in accordance with their respective constitutional processes.
2 The ratifications shall be deposited with the Government of the United States of America, which shall notify all the signatory states of each deposit as well as the Secretary-General of the Organization when he has been appointed.
3 The present Charter shall come into force upon the deposit of ratifications by the Republic of China, France, the Union of Soviet Socialist Republics, the United Kingdom of Great Britain and Northern Ireland, and the United States of America, and by a majority of the other signatory states. A protocol of the ratifications deposited shall thereupon be drawn up by the Government of the United States of America which shall communicate copies thereof to all the signatory states.
4 The states signatory to the present Charter which ratify it after it has come into force will become original Members of the United Nations on the date of the deposit of their respective ratifications.

Article 111

The present Charter, of which the Chinese, French, Russian, English, and Spanish texts are equally authentic, shall remain deposited in the archives of the Government of the United States of America. Duly certified copies thereof shall be transmitted by that Government to the Governments of the other signatory states.

IN FAITH WHEREOF the representatives of the Governments of the United Nations have signed the present Charter.

DONE at the city of San Francisco the twenty-sixth day of June, one thousand nine hundred and forty-five.

Resource 2

Universal Declaration of Human Rights

PREAMBLE

Whereas recognition of the inherent dignity and of the equal and inalienable rights of all members of the human family is the foundation of freedom, justice and peace in the world,

Whereas disregard and contempt for human rights have resulted in barbarous acts which have outraged the conscience of mankind, and the advent of a world in which human beings shall enjoy freedom of speech and belief and freedom from fear and want has been proclaimed as the highest aspiration of the common people,

Whereas it is essential, if man is not to be compelled to have recourse, as a last resort, to rebellion against tyranny and oppression, that human rights should be protected by the rule of law,

Whereas it is essential to promote the development of friendly relations between nations,

Whereas the peoples of the United Nations have in the Charter reaffirmed their faith in fundamental human rights, in the dignity and worth of the human person and in the equal rights of men and women and have determined to promote social progress and better standards of life in larger freedom,

Whereas Member States have pledged themselves to achieve, in co-operation with the United Nations, the promotion of universal respect for and observance of human rights and fundamental freedoms,

Whereas a common understanding of these rights and freedoms is of the greatest importance for the full realization of this pledge,

Now, Therefore THE GENERAL ASSEMBLY proclaims THIS UNIVERSAL DECLARATION OF HUMAN RIGHTS as a common standard of achievement for all peoples and all nations, to the end that every individual and every organ of society, keeping this Declaration constantly in mind, shall strive by teaching and education to promote respect for these rights and freedoms and by progressive measures, national and international, to secure their universal and effective recognition and observance, both among the peoples of Member States themselves and among the peoples of territories under their jurisdiction.

ARTICLE 1

All human beings are born free and equal in dignity and rights. They are endowed with reason and conscience and should act towards one another in a spirit of brotherhood.

ARTICLE 2

Everyone is entitled to all the rights and freedoms set forth in this Declaration, without distinction of any kind, such as race, colour, sex, language, religion, political or other opinion, national or social origin, property, birth or other status. Furthermore, no distinction shall be made on the basis of the political, jurisdictional or international status of the country or territory to which a person belongs, whether it be independent, trust, non-self-governing or under any other limitation of sovereignty.

ARTICLE 3

Everyone has the right to life, liberty and security of person.

ARTICLE 4

No one shall be held in slavery or servitude; slavery and the slave trade shall be prohibited in all their forms.

ARTICLE 5

No one shall be subjected to torture or to cruel, inhuman or degrading treatment or punishment.

ARTICLE 6

Everyone has the right to recognition everywhere as a person before the law.

ARTICLE 7

All are equal before the law and are entitled without any discrimination to equal protection of the law. All are entitled to equal protection against any discrimination in violation of this Declaration and against any incitement to such discrimination.

ARTICLE 8

Everyone has the right to an effective remedy by the competent national tribunals for acts violating the fundamental rights granted him by the constitution or by law.

ARTICLE 9

No one shall be subjected to arbitrary arrest, detention or exile.

ARTICLE 10

Everyone is entitled in full equality to a fair and public hearing by an independent and impartial tribunal, in the determination of his rights and obligations and of any criminal charge against him.

ARTICLE 11

1 Everyone charged with a penal offence has the right to be presumed innocent until proved guilty according to law in a public trial at which he has had all the guarantees necessary for his defence.
2 No one shall be held guilty of any penal offence on account of any act or omission which did not constitute a penal offence, under national or international law, at the time when it was committed. Nor shall a heavier penalty be imposed than the one that was applicable at the time the penal offence was committed.

ARTICLE 12

No one shall be subjected to arbitrary interference with his privacy, family, home or correspondence, nor to attacks upon his honour and reputation. Everyone has the right to the protection of the law against such interference or attacks.

ARTICLE 13

1 Everyone has the right to freedom of movement and residence within the borders of each state.
2 Everyone has the right to leave any country, including his own, and to return to his country.

ARTICLE 14

1 Everyone has the right to seek and to enjoy in other countries asylum from persecution.
2 This right may not be invoked in the case of prosecutions genuinely arising from non-political crimes or from acts contrary to the purposes and principles of the United Nations.

ARTICLE 15

1 Everyone has the right to a nationality.
2 No one shall be arbitrarily deprived of his nationality nor denied the right to change his nationality.

ARTICLE 16

1 Men and women of full age, without any limitation due to race, nationality or religion, have the right to marry and to found a family. They are entitled to equal rights as to marriage, during marriage and at its dissolution.
2 Marriage shall be entered into only with the free and full consent of the intending spouses.
3 The family is the natural and fundamental group unit of society and is entitled to protection by society and the State.

ARTICLE 17

1 Everyone has the right to own property alone as well as in association with others.
2 No one shall be arbitrarily deprived of his property.

ARTICLE 18

Everyone has the right to freedom of thought, conscience and religion; this right includes freedom to change his religion or belief, and freedom, either alone or in community with others and in public or private, to manifest his religion or belief in teaching, practice, worship and observance.

ARTICLE 19

Everyone has the right to freedom of opinion and expression; this right includes freedom to hold opinions without interference and to seek, receive and impart information and ideas through any media and regardless of frontiers.

ARTICLE 20

1 Everyone has the right to freedom of peaceful assembly and association.
2 No one may be compelled to belong to an association.

ARTICLE 21

1 Everyone has the right to take part in the government of his country, directly or through freely chosen representatives.
2 Everyone has the right of equal access to public service in his country.
3 The will of the people shall be the basis of the authority of government; this will shall be expressed in periodic and genuine elections which shall be by universal and equal suffrage and shall be held by secret vote or by equivalent free voting procedures.

ARTICLE 22

Everyone, as a member of society, has the right to social security and is entitled to realization, through national effort and international co-operation and in accordance with the organization and resources of each State, of the economic, social and cultural rights indispensable for his dignity and the free development of his personality.

ARTICLE 23

1 Everyone has the right to work, to free choice of employment, to just and favourable conditions of work and to protection against unemployment.
2 Everyone, without any discrimination, has the right to equal pay for equal work.
3 Everyone who works has the right to just and favourable remuneration ensuring for himself and his family an existence worthy of human dignity, and supplemented, if necessary, by other means of social protection.
4 Everyone has the right to form and to join trade unions for the protection of his interests.

ARTICLE 24

Everyone has the right to rest and leisure, including reasonable limitation of working hours and periodic holidays with pay.

ARTICLE 25

1 Everyone has the right to a standard of living adequate for the health and well-being of himself and of his family, including food, clothing, housing and medical care and necessary social services, and the right to security in the event of unemployment, sickness, disability, widowhood, old age or other lack of livelihood in circumstances beyond his control.
2 Motherhood and childhood are entitled to special care and assistance. All children, whether born in or out of wedlock, shall enjoy the same social protection.

ARTICLE 26

1 Everyone has the right to education. Education shall be free, at least in the elementary and fundamental stages. Elementary education shall be compulsory. Technical and professional education shall be made generally available and higher education shall be equally accessible to all on the basis of merit.
2 Education shall be directed to the full development of the human personality and to the strengthening of respect for human rights and fundamental freedoms. It shall promote understanding, tolerance and friendship among all nations, racial or religious groups, and shall further the activities of the United Nations for the maintenance of peace.
3 Parents have a prior right to choose the kind of education that shall be given to their children.

ARTICLE 27

1 Everyone has the right freely to participate in the cultural life of the community, to enjoy the arts and to share in scientific advancement and its benefits.
2 Everyone has the right to the protection of the moral and material interests resulting from any scientific, literary or artistic production of which he is the author.

ARTICLE 28

Everyone is entitled to a social and international order in which the rights and freedoms set forth in this Declaration can be fully realized.

ARTICLE 29

1 Everyone has duties to the community in which alone the free and full development of his personality is possible.
2 In the exercise of his rights and freedoms, everyone shall be subject only to such limitations as are determined by law solely for the purpose of securing due recognition and respect for the rights and freedoms of others and of meeting the just requirements of morality, public order and the general welfare in a democratic society.

3 These rights and freedoms may in no case be exercised contrary to the purposes and principles of the United Nations.

ARTICLE 30

Nothing in this Declaration may be interpreted as implying for any State, group or person any right to engage in any activity or to perform any act aimed at the destruction of any of the rights and freedoms set forth herein.

Resource 3

Acronyms and Abbreviations

A4P	Action for Peacekeeping Initiative
ABM	Anti-ballistic missile
ACABQ	Advisory Committee on Administrative and Budgetary Questions
ACC	Administrative Committee on Coordination
ADA	Atomic Development Authority
ADFL	Alliance of Democratic Forces for the Liberation of Congo
AIDS	Acquired immunodeficiency syndrome
AIIB	Asia Infrastructure Investment Bank
AMIS	African Union Mission in Sudan
ANC	Armée Nationale Congolaise
ANCB	Afghan Nongovernmental Organizations Coordination Board
APEC	Asian Pacific Economic Cooperation Organization
ASEAN	Association of Southeast Asian Nations
ATT	Arms Trade Treaty
AU	African Union
BRI	Belt and Road Initiative
BRIC	Brazil, Russia, India, China
BWC	Convention on the Prohibition of the Development, Production and Stockpiling of Bacteriological (Biological) and Toxin Weapons and on Their Destruction (Biological Weapons Convention)
CAR	Central African Republic
CBD	Convention on Biological Diversity
CCD	Conference of the Committee on Disarmament; Convention to Combat Desertification
CD	Conference on Disarmament
CEB	(UN System) Chief Executives Board for Coordination
CEDAW	Convention on the Elimination of All Forms of Discrimination against Women
CFCs	Chlorofluorocarbons
CG	Contact Group
CIS	Commonwealth of Independent States
CMP	Meeting of the Parties
CO2	Carbon dioxide
CoNGO	Conference on Non-Governmental Organizations in Consultative Status with ECOSOC
COP	Conference of the Parties
CSD	Commission on Sustainable Development
CSOs	Civil Society Organizations

CSW	UN Commission on the Status of Women
CTBT	Comprehensive Nuclear-TestBan Treaty
CTBTO	Comprehensive Nuclear-TestBan Treaty Organization
CWC	Convention on the Prohibition of the Development, Production, Stockpiling and Use of Chemical Weapons and on Their Destruction (Chemical Weapons Convention)
DAW	Division for the Advancement of Women
DGC	Department of Global Communications
DPI	Department of Public Information
DPKO	Department of Peacekeeping Operations
DPO	Department of Peace Operations
DRC	Democratic Republic of the Congo
DSB	Dispute Settlement Body (WTO)
DSG	Deputy Secretary-General
ECA	Economic Commission for Africa
ECCC	Extraordinary Chambers in the Courts of Cambodia
ECE	Economic Commission for Europe
ECLAC	Economic Commission for Latin America and the Caribbean
ECMI	European Centre for Minority Issues
ECOFIN	Economic and Financial Committee (GA Second Committee)
ECOSOC	Economic and Social Council
ECOWAS	Economic Community of West African States
ECWA	Economic Commission for Western Africa
ENDC	Eighteen-Nation Disarmament Committee
EPTA	Expanded Program of Technical Assistance
ESCAP	Economic and Social Commission for Asia and the Pacific
ESCWA	Economic and Social Commission for Western Asia
EU	European Union
EULEX	EU Rule of Law Mission in Kosovo
FAO	Food and Agriculture Organization
FBI	Federal Bureau of Investigation
G-8	Group of 8
G-77	Group of 77
GA	General Assembly
GAO	General Accounting Office (U.S.)
GATT	General Agreement on Tariffs and Trade
GDP	Gross domestic product
GEF	Global Environment Facility
GHG	Greenhouse gas
GNI	Gross national income
GPA	Global Programme on AIDS
GSP	General System of Preferences
HABITAT II	Second World Conference on Human Settlements
HIPC	Heavily Indebted Poor Country
HIV	Human immunodeficiency virus
HIV/AIDS	Human immunodeficiency virus/Acquired immunodeficiency syndrome
HRC	Human Rights Council
IADA	International Atomic Development Authority
IAEA	International Atomic Energy Agency
IBRD	International Bank for Reconstruction and Development [World Bank]

ICAO	International Civil Aviation Organization
ICBL	International Campaign to Ban Landmines
ICC	International Criminal Court
ICCPR	International Covenant on Civil and Political Rights
ICESCR	International Covenant on Economic, Social and Cultural Rights
ICJ	International Court of Justice
ICPD	International Conference on Population and Development
ICSID	International Centre for the Settlement of Investment Disputes
ICTR	International Criminal Tribunal for Rwanda
ICTY	International Criminal Tribunal for the Former Yugoslavia
ICU	Islamic Courts Union
IDA	International Development Association
IFAD	International Fund for Agricultural Development
IFC	International Finance Corporation
IFOR	Implementation Force
IGOs	Intergovernmental organizations
IHR	International Health Regulations
ILO	International Labour Organization
IMF	International Monetary Fund
IMO	International Maritime Organization
INF	Intermediate Nuclear Forces Agreement
INGO	International nongovernmental organizations
INSTRAW	International Research and Training Institute for the Advancement of Women
IO	International Organization
IOM	International Organization for Migration
IPCC	Intergovernmental Panel on Climate Change
ISAF	International Security Assistance Force
ISIL	Islamic State in Iraq and the Levant
ISIS	Islamic State
ISIS-K	Islamic State Kurdistan
ITLOS	International Tribunal for the Law of the Sea
ITO	International Trade Organization
ITU	International Telecommunication Union
JCPOA	Joint Comprehensive Plan of Action (Iran Nuclear Agreement)
JIU	Joint Inspection Unit
KFOR	UN Kosovo Force
LAF	Lebanese Armed Forces
LDCs	Least developed countries
MDBs	Multilateral Development Bank
MDGs	Millennium Development Goals
MERS	Middle East Respiratory Syndrome
MFIs	Multilateral Financial Institutions
MICT	Mechanisms for International Criminal Tribunals
MIGA	Multilateral Investment Guarantee Agency
MINUSCA	UN Multidimensional Integrated Mission in the Central African Republic
MISCA	Integrated Support mission in the Central African Republic
MONUA	UN Observer Mission in Angola
MONUC	UN Organization Mission in the Democratic Republic of the Congo

MONUSCO	UN Organization Stabilization Mission in the Democratic Republic of the Congo
MPLA	Movimento Popular de Libertação de Angola
MSF	Médecins Sans Frontières
MUN	Model United Nations
NAFTA	North American Free Trade Association
NAM	Non-Aligned Movement
NATO	North Atlantic Treaty Organization
NDB	New Development Bank
NFZs	Nuclear weapons–free zones
NGLS	UN Non-Governmental Liaison Service
NGOs	Nongovernmental organizations
NIEO	New International Economic Order
NMUN	National Model United Nations
NPT	Treaty on the Non-Proliferation of Nuclear Weapons (Nuclear NonProliferation Treaty)
OAU	Organization of African Unity
OCHA	Office for the Coordination of Humanitarian Affairs
OHRLLS	Office of the High Representative for the Least Developed Countries, Landlocked Developing Countries and Small Island Developing States
OIOS	Office of Internal Oversight Services
ONUC	UN Operation in the Congo
OPCW	Organisation for the Prohibition of Chemical Weapons
OPEC	Organization of Petroleum Exporting Countries
OSCE	Organization for Security and Cooperation in Europe
P5	Five permanent members of the Security Council
P5 + 1	Five permanent members of the Security Council plus Germany
PBC	Peacebuilding Commission
PCIJ	Permanent Court of International Justice
PDD-25	Presidential Decision Directive 25
PDMs	Practical disarmament measures
PFA	Platform for Action (UN Fourth World Conference on Women)
PHEIC	Public Health Emergency of International Concern
PLA	Palestine Authority
PLO	Palestine Liberation Organization
PPP	Polluter pays principle
PRC	People's Republic of China
PRGF	Poverty Reduction and Growth Facility
R2P	Responsibility to Protect
RCEP	Regional Comprehensive Economic Partnership
ROK	Republic of Korea
RUF	Revolutionary United Front
SALT	Strategic Arms Limitation Talks
SALW	Small arms and light weapons
SC	Security Council
SDGs	Sustainable Development Goals
SDN	Sustainable development network
SDRs	Special drawing rights
SFOR	Stabilization Force
SG	Secretary-general
SMG	Senior Management Group

SNPA	Substantial New Programme of Action
SOCHUM	Social, Humanitarian and Cultural Committee (GA Third Committee)
SOFA	Status of Forces Agreement
SORT	Strategic Offensive Reductions Treaty
SRSG	Special representative of the secretary-general
SUNFED	Special UN Fund for Economic Development
SWAPO	South-West Africa People's Organization
TB	Tuberculosis
TPP	Trans-Pacific Partnership
TRIPS	Trade-Related Aspects of Intellectual Property Rights
UDHR	Universal Declaration of Human Rights
UN	United Nations
UNAEC	UN Atomic Energy Commission
UNAIDS	Joint UN Programme on HIV/AIDS
UNAMA	UN Assistance Mission in Afghanistan
UNAMID	UN Assistance Mission in Darfur
UNAMIR	UN Assistance Mission for Rwanda
UNAMSIL	UN Assistance Mission in Sierra Leone
UNC	UN Command in Korea
UNCDF	UN Capital Development Fund
UNCED	UN Conference on Environment and Development
UNCHE	UN Conference on the Human Environment
UNCIO	United Nations Conference on International Organization
UNCITRAL	UN Commission on International Trade Law
UNCLOS	UN Conference on the Law of the Sea
UNCTAD	UN Conference on Trade and Development
UNDOF	UN Disengagement Observer Force
UNDP	UN Development Programme
UNDP-DDC	UNDP Drylands Development Centre
UNEF	UN Emergency Force
UNEP	UN Environment Programme
UNESCO	UN Educational, Scientific and Cultural Organization
UNFCCC	UN Framework Convention on Climate Change
UNFF	UN Forum on Forests
UNFICYP	UN Peacekeeping Force in Cyprus
UNFIP	UN Fund for International Partnerships
UNFPA	UN Population Fund
UN-HABITAT	UN Human Settlements Programme
UNHCHR	UN High Commissioner for Human Rights
UNHCR	UN High Commissioner for Refugees
UNICEF	UN Children's Fund
UNICRI	UN Interregional Crime and Justice Research Institute
UNIDIR	UN Institute for Disarmament Research
UNIDO	UN Industrial Development Organization
UNIFEM	UN Development Fund for Women
UNIFIL	UN Interim Force in Lebanon
UNIPOM	UN India-Pakistan Observer Mission
UNISDR	UN Office for Disaster Reduction
UNITA	União Nacional para a Independência Total de Angola
UNITAF	Unified Task Force
UNITAMS	UN Integrated Transition Assistance Mission in Sudan

UNITAR	UN Institute for Training and Research
UNLDC	UN Conference on Least Developed Countries
UNMEER	UN Mission for Ebola Emergency Response
UNMIBH	UN Mission in Bosnia and Herzegovina
UNMIK	UN Interim Administration Mission in Kosovo
UNMIL	UN Mission in Liberia
UNMIT	UN Mission in Timor-Leste
UNMOGIP	UN Military Observer Group in India and Pakistan
UNMOVIC	UN Monitoring, Verification and Inspection Commission
UNODC	UN Office on Drugs and Crime
UNOG	UN Office at Geneva
UNOMIL	UN Observer Mission in Liberia
UNOMSIL	UN Observer Mission in Sierra Leone
UNON	UN Office in Nairobi
UNOPS	UN Office for Project Services
UNOSOM	UN Operation in Somalia
UNPOB	UN Political Office in Bougainville
UNPROFOR	UN Protection Force
UNRISD	UN Research Institute for Social Development
UNRPR	UN Relief for Palestine Refugees
UNRWA	UN Relief and Works Agency for Palestine Refugees in the Near East
UNSCO	Office of the UN Special Coordinator for the Middle East Peace Process and Personal Representative of the Secretary-General to the Palestine Liberation Organization and the Palestinian Authority
UNSCOM	UN Special Commission on Iraq
UNSCOP	UN Special Commission on Palestine
UNSOM	UN Assistance Mission in Somalia
UN-SWAP	UN System-Wide Action Plan on Gender Equality and the Empowerment of Women
UNTAC	UN Transitional Authority in Cambodia
UNTAET	UN Transitional Administration in East Timor
UNTAG	UN Transition Assistance Group
UNTCOK	UN Temporary Commission on Korea
UNTSO	UN Truce Supervision Organization
UNV	UN Volunteers
UN-Women	UN Entity for Gender Equality and the Empowerment of Women
UPU	Universal Postal Union
USAID	United States Agency for International Development
USG	Under-secretary-general
WBG	World Bank Group
WCED	World Commission on Environment and Development
WFP	World Food Programme
WHO	World Health Organization
WIPO	World Intellectual Property Organization
WMDs	Weapons of mass destruction
WMO	World Meteorological Organization
WSSD	World Summit on Social Development
WTO	World Trade Organization
WWAP	World Water Assessment Programme
WWF	World Wildlife Fund

Index

Note: *Italic* page numbers refer to figures and page numbers followed by "n" denote endnotes.

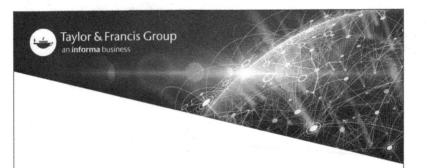